# THE TAO OF CRAFT

# THE
# TAO
# OF
# CRAFT

**FU TALISMANS and
CASTING SIGILS in
the EASTERN
ESOTERIC TRADITION**

## BENEBELL WEN

North Atlantic Books
Berkeley, California

Published by                          Cover art: *A Solitary Temple amid Clearing Peaks*
North Atlantic Books                  Cover and book design by Daniel Tesser
Berkeley, California                  Printed in the United States of America

*The Tao of Craft: Fu Talismans and Casting Sigils in the Eastern Esoteric Tradition* is sponsored and published by the Society for the Study of Native Arts and Sciences (dba North Atlantic Books), an educational nonprofit based in Berkeley, California, that collaborates with partners to develop cross-cultural perspectives, nurture holistic views of art, science, the humanities, and healing, and seed personal and global transformation by publishing work on the relationship of body, spirit, and nature.

North Atlantic Books' publications are available through most bookstores. For further information, visit our website at www.northatlanticbooks.com or call 800-733-3000.

Library of Congress Cataloging-in-Publication Data

Names: Wen, Benebell, 1981- author.

Title: The Tao of craft : fu talismans and casting sigils in the Eastern esoteric tradition / Benebell Wen.
Description: Berkeley, California : North Atlantic Books, 2016.
Identifiers: LCCN 2016003936 (print) | LCCN 2016007191 (ebook) | ISBN 9781623170660 (paperback) | ISBN 9781623170677 (ebook)
Subjects: LCSH: Taoism--Customs and practices. | Occultism--Religious aspects--Taoism. | BISAC: RELIGION / Taoism (see also PHILOSOPHY / Taoist). | BODY, MIND & SPIRIT / Reference.
Classification: LCC BL1923 .W45 2016 (print) | LCC BL1923 (ebook) | DDC 299.5/1432--dc23
LC record available at http://lccn.loc.gov/2016003936

2  3  4  5  6  7  8  9  UNITED  21  20  19  18  17

Printed on recycled paper

North Atlantic Books is committed to the protection of our environment.
We partner with FSC-certified printers using soy-based inks and
print on recycled paper whenever possible.

*To Mom, for nurturing my spirit;*

*To Dad, for nurturing my mind;*

*To both, for giving me this body.*

# Acknowledgments

Vanessa Ta, the ever gracious, tenacious, and talented editor, you are on point about everything. All my gratitude to you for your assiduous work. You have been the guiding hand that brought this book to life. It is a joy and privilege to work with you. Christopher Church, I am amazed at your surgical precision with words. I reckon you were pretty frustrated with the hot mess that my manuscript was. Thank you for your patience and diligence. Daniel Tesser, I am grateful for your artistic eye in putting together the cover and layout design. The heroes of that final hour: senior designer and creative manager Jasmine Hromjak and production coordinator Ondine Rangel, thank you, thank you. Bevin Donahue, thank you for helping me get the word out. I'm having a blast working with you. Tim McKee, thank you for encouraging me to publish this book.

While publication of the book would not have transpired without the magic that only North Atlantic Books knows, it could not have been written without my parents. Mom, I am glad I inherited your curiosity for the metaphysical and religious. I am trying to acquire some of the heightened sensitivities you have, but that is still a work in progress. Dad, thank you for your translations, interpretations, explanations, your wealth of knowledge on every topic, and your weakness for perfectionism. You've taught me how to reach higher. Cindy and Tansy, please read this. Please? Did you even touch my tarot book yet? My dear James, thank you for your unconditional love.

To my beloved Prince Marshall Rimbaud the Great, though you only ever answered to 乖乖, may you rest in peace.

# CONTENTS

# ILLUSTRATIONS

## FIGURES

**Page**

**Page**

**Page**

# TABLES

**Page**

# CHAPTER 1

# THE TAO OF CRAFT

| Shang Dynasty (1600–1050 BC) | Zhou Dynasty (1046–256 BC) | Qin Dynasty (221–206 BC) | Present Day |

Figure 1.1. Evolution of the character for Tao
(Courtesy of Richard Sears, Chinese Etymology.org)

## INTRODUCTION

**THIS IS NOT A BOOK ABOUT** Taoism. This book is about craft, and more specifically, one practice found in esoteric Taoism: Fu (符) talisman crafting. While the approach espoused herein takes into account the history and cultural practice of the Fu, it presents only one practitioner's interpretation of the craft, decoded in a way that will be intelligible to practitioners of Western esoteric traditions. It is a presentation that will encourage the blending of Taoist principles and practices with the Western practitioner's. Such syncretism makes sense, because Taoism itself has always been eclectic, integrating and harmonizing facets from other cultures and religions.[2] Also, this book is not intended to be all-encompassing of the craft or of esoteric Taoist thought, as I do not believe such a book is possible.

Esoteric Taoism is not a homogenous practice.[3] Between lineages and factions of esoteric Taoist practitioners, there are striking differences and disagreements. There were historic rivalries dating back to the Shang Dynasty (1600–1050 BC), with tensions pervading between imperial court-appointed magicians and unaffiliated folk shamans, one gaining the favor of the king and aristocracy while the other gained the popular favor of the people.[4] Records from the Song Dynasty (AD 960–1279) document rivalries between different Taoist magical lineages, which resulted in conflicts ranging from fisticuffs to magical battles. A classic example is the rivalry magic between the Zheng Yi and Lu Shan lineages, or the rivalries that both the Zheng Yi and Lu Shan lineages had with the Mao Shan.[5] Where there are tensions, each side makes a concerted effort to distinguish itself from the other, and so differing approaches to the same art emerge, while both sides continue to work under the umbrella of esoteric Taoism.

Within old lineages, there were interruptions in historic documentation of craft,[6] and so the new generation does its best to reconstruct and in many ways reinvent the ways of the old.[7] Outside of established and historic lineages, there is the eclectic practice of esoteric Taoism that is localized and conflated with Buddhism, Confucianism, Shintoism, and regional folk religions.[8] As diasporic Chinese communities developed far from the mainland, Taoist magical craft assimilated with the traditions of the new cultures, thereby changing the character and flavor of the craft.[9]

While certain elements of Taoism is religious, craft itself is not. You have your religion and you either choose to practice or not practice a form of craft. You can be areligious and still study metaphysics and train in the ways of working with energy, perhaps from a Taoist ontological perspective, even if you do not identify as a Taoist. The secular principles of Fu talisman crafting can be applied to deepen your knowledge and experience in metaphysics.

Religion does seem to get entangled with craft, as you will see throughout this book. Historically, orthodox Taoist practitioners of craft invoked deities and summoned spirits, which are the Taoist personifications of both physical and metaphysical energy in the universe. The myths of gods were often inspired by the observation of planets and constellations, of the awe that the sun and moon struck in our ancestors, and the formidable power that natural phenomena held over them. Today, we can continue to use the same religious vocabulary of Eastern traditions, subscribe to the same beliefs as our forebears, or we can understand the secular, metaphysical idea behind the vocabulary. I opt to use the religious vocabulary of Taoism and Buddhism, but in my mind, hold steadfast to the secular, metaphysical ideas that govern craft.

No one book can assert a definitive way of crafting Fu talismans. Thus, this book will try to expound on the theoretical basis, historic texts that reference Fu talisman crafting, and commonly found cultural practices of the craft so that the practitioner might be adequately prepared to craft Fu talismans.

The pedagogical approach of this book is to focus heavily on theory so that the practitioner might build a strong foundation in craft. Behavioral scientist and philosopher Abraham Kaplan proposed what he called the law of the instrument: "Give a small boy a hammer, and he will find that everything he encounters needs pounding."[10] As applied to the scientific community, Kaplan criticized individual scientists for their tendency to conceptualize their research only within the limited techniques of their training and educational background. They can only advance their research based on the limits of the instructions they were taught. In other words, there is a tendency among scientists to direct their scientific practice by the techniques they know best, rather than direct their practice by the critical appraisal of theory,[11] which might otherwise enable them to think more creatively. Kaplan's law of the instrument applies to metaphysical practitioners as well.

"The more we know how to do something, the harder it is to learn to do it differently."[12] When we can't think differently, we can't think creatively. When we aren't creative, we aren't intuitive. In metaphysical craft, your intuitive ability is essential. Any limitations on that will hinder the success of your craft. Hence, this book strives to offer theory and not specific methodologies because teaching specific methodologies will limit the practitioner. Theory, on the other hand, provides the fertile soil for the practitioner's creativity to take root and sprout.

While this book will still offer foundational instruction on how to craft Fu, such instruction is not to teach how to craft Fu, but rather to provide illustrated examples of one way that Fu might be crafted based on the theories

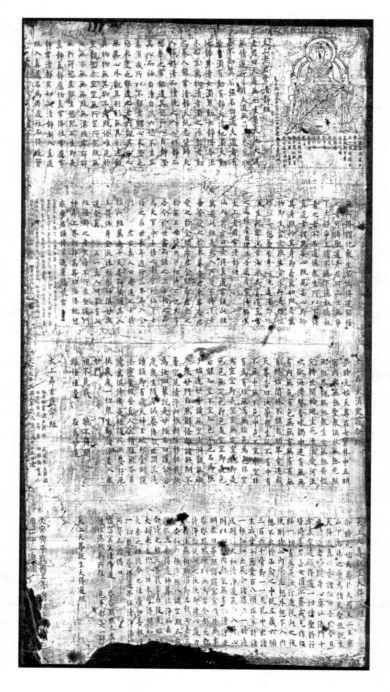

Figure 1.2. Lao Tzu's portrait and three Taoist scriptures; stele inscriptions, circa AD 980
(Courtesy of Special Collections, Fine Arts Library, Harvard University)

taught in the book. Thus, as you navigate your way through this book, do not try to pick up on the "how"; try to pick up on the "why." Once you understand why, your own creativity and intuition will be your instructors on the "how."

## EXOTERIC AND ESOTERIC TAOISM

When I refer to Taoism in the context of this book's subject matter, I am focusing on esoteric Taoism, which differs from the more canonical exoteric Taoism that is recognized as philosophy and religion.[13] Yet esoteric Taoism includes both philosophy and religion. The Taoism I refer to goes beyond philosophy because it presents occult ontological doctrines and mystical ritual. It also goes beyond the religious veneration of deities or otherworldly beings to address a more interactive relationship, and direct communion with spirit realms.

Exoteric Taoism, which is the Taoism that is more popularly conveyed to the public, is nature-based,[14] seeking a harmonious relationship with nature that conserves and strives to avoid excess; it is about curbing ambitions and seeking peace. Exoteric Taoism is rooted in a way of life that follows the principle of wu wei (無爲), a principle of nonaction. To understand what wu wei means, look to two seminal texts on Taoist philosophy, the Tao Te Ching (道德經), dating to around 600–501 BC, and the Zhuang Zi (莊子),[15] dating to around 300–201 BC.

According to the Tao Te Ching, wu wei is not literally nonaction, but rather it is balancing the affronts of yang with the softness and submissiveness of yin. The Tao Te Ching advises: "Blunt the sharpness.… Dim the glare." Nonaction is still action, though that action is to be like water.[16] Nonaction also means do no harm. "The sages also do not harm people."[17] In the Zhuang Zi, wu wei is "the stillness of the sages." It is "vacancy, stillness, placidity, tastelessness, quietude, silence, and nonaction."[18] Why these philosophical texts are mentioned when this is not a book about Taoism and purports to be one focused on craft should become apparent as the chapters progress.

Exoteric Taoism is the philosophical approach to Taoist principles that the West is more familiar with. It cultivates an individual who lives in harmony with nature, who does not act superfluously to interfere with its path or attempt to transform the course of fate.[19] Thus, Taoist philosophy teaches a profound way of cultivating inner peace and acceptance, to just let it be.

Taoism as a Chinese religion[20] tends to merge indistinguishably with folk religions,[21] venerating particular deities and integrating ancestor worship.[22] Exoteric Taoism as a religion is often about social kinship, or identifying oneself with a particular sect of religious Taoism, often one blended with Buddhism, Confucianism, Legalism,[23] and folk beliefs. That religious aspect of Taoism is also exoteric Taoism.[24]

Philosophical and religious principles of exoteric Taoism drive the practice of esoteric Taoism,[25] though the practice itself might be better aligned with Chinese shamanism,[26] which predates Taoism.[27] Relics of oracle bone divination from the Shang Dynasty (1600–1050 BC)[28] revealed a strikingly similar and shared ontology with Fu talismans and esoteric Taoism.[29] Shamans were integral to the culture and governance during the Zhou Dynasty (1046–256 BC).[30] The Zhou Dynasty also produced the philosopher Lao Tzu, credited with authoring the Tao Te Ching[31] and establishing Taoism as a philosophy.[32]

In contrast, esoteric Taoism is an active practice by Man, from the trinitarian principle of Heaven, Earth, and Man, which I will discuss in the subsequent section of this chapter, where Man raises energy or power from Heaven and Earth.[33] Heaven is representative of deities, immortals, or higher spirits, and Earth is representative of nature. In the practice of esoteric Taoism, Man, a practitioner of occult craft, seeks to direct and redirect forces from Heaven and Earth, a stark contrast from exoteric Taoism, where Man seeks to be like water,[34] moving with the ebb and flow of Heaven and Earth. Esoteric Taoism is a complement to exoteric Taoism, but the two are not the same. There is both concord and discord between esoteric and exoteric Taoism, much like yin and yang.

Esoteric Taoism is an engaged, occult practice, one that, unlike philosophical exoteric Taoism, would seek to transform the path of nature and the course of fate. Alchemy,[35] divination,[36] feng shui,[37] the quest for immortality,[38] shamanism, sorcery, and witchcraft are characteristic elements of esoteric Taoism.

Not every lineage of esoteric Taoism pursues all such occult practices, but all of them touch upon at least one. Historically, what I am referring to as esoteric Taoism would only be practiced by ordained priests and priestesses of orthodox Taoist magic.[39] Yet this is a book that seeks to impart practical knowledge on the craft of Fu that the practitioner, irrespective of cultural background, lineage, faith, or tradition, will be able to apply.

This text will assume an instructional function to reveal to the reader principles of Eastern esotericism, based primarily on Taoist cosmology. It assumes that the reader is an active practitioner of metaphysical arts, or one who seeks to attain insights into sacred mysteries beyond ordinary human knowledge.

## THE TAOIST ONTOLOGY FOR CRAFTING FU TALISMANS

Taoist theory is essential to understanding the principles and mechanics of craft. Craft is the skill and knowledge of exercising will over manifestations in the universe, a science that may resemble religion, but is one based on experimentation and observations recorded over thousands of years, though such records are often kept secret and passed on only to the few.

The Fu talisman is the crown of esoteric Taoist craft, one of the most potent manifestations there is of craft. To craft potent Fu talismans, all of the following ontological principles must be utilized. Thus, before a discussion can take place on what a Fu talisman even is, there must be a discussion of Qi, yin and yang, the Wu Xing, and the Ba Gua. Without an understanding of those principles, there can be no understanding of the Fu.

## THE VITAL FORCE OF QI

Fu talismans are ideograms and writings typically rendered on paper and empowered by means of invocations, ritual, and transferences of energy, or Qi as this book will refer to such energy.[40] Qi is life force, the breath that brings vitality. Qi is the unseen impetus behind all change, creative or destructive, whether it is initiation, continuation, transformation, or cessation. A theoretical principle presumed by the craft that will be presented in this book is the relationship between two characterizations of Qi that I'll refer to as personal Qi and cosmic Qi.

Personal Qi is the individual circuit of vital energy flowing through each one of us. Cosmic Qi is the principle that each one of our individual circuits is connected to every other, and a unifying connection of circuits emerges to form a collective energy force. The transactions and occurrences of cosmic Qi have a direct and relational impact on each individual circuit of personal Qi.

Figure 1.3. The taijitu, or
yin and yang symbol[42]

That concept can be likened to the Western occult maxim, "As above, so below,"[41] where events that happen at the macrocosm will also happen at the microcosm. Thus, a practitioner who understands his or her own personal Qi, who understands the self, can gain the wisdom of fully understanding the cosmic Qi, or understanding the universe. To know yourself is to know the universe. Study of the universe and the physical and metaphysical realities of the universe is thus a study of yourself. When the way of the macrocosm is veiled to you, look to the way of the microcosm, and then the mystery will be unveiled. That is the foundation from which you will build your knowledge of craft.

## THE BINARY OF YIN AND YANG

Within any given circuit of Qi, either personal or cosmic characterizations, the Qi life force subdivides into the dichotomy of yin and yang. Yin is represented by dark and yang represented by light. The two are opposites and they are complements. They are in concord and they are in discord. Yin is curved, while yang is straight. Yin is soft, yielding, while yang is hard, pushing. Yin is potential, and yang is kinetic. Qi is the current that runs through all components of the universe, and all components possess yin and yang.

Table 1.1 provides characteristic correspondences for yin and yang. Note that I've attributed the receiving hand with yin and the giving hand with yang, rather than note specifically left versus right. Texts will differ on the hand correspondences, some noting that yin is right and yang is left; others noting yin is left and yang is right; and still others noting that the palm of the hand is yin, but the fingers are yang. I attribute yin and yang with an individual practitioner's specific physiology. While in most cases the giving hand is the right hand because most people are right-handed, it makes more sense to me to characterize the hands by their function. For a more detailed explanation, see "The Giving Hand and the Receiving Hand" in "The 108 Recitations" section in chapter 8.

There are significant distinctions between the esoteric Taoist expression of yin and yang (for the purposes of craft) and exoteric Taoist philosophy. In exoteric

| Yin | Yang |
|---|---|
| Dark | Light |
| Night | Day |
| Moon | Sun |
| Contracting | Expanding |
| Yielding | Forceful |
| Passive | Active |
| Responsive | Assertive |
| Curved | Straight |
| Wet | Dry |
| Cold | Hot |
| Even Numbers | Odd Numbers |
| Proton | Electron |
| Estrogen | Androgen |
| Autumn | Spring |
| Winter | Summer |
| Spirit Realm | Sentient Realm |
| The Underworld | Celestial Kingdom |
| Occult | Canonical |
| Intuition | Logic |
| Diplomatic | Authoritarian |
| Mercy | Justice |
| Esoteric | Exoteric |
| Receiving Hand | Giving Hand |

Table 1.1. Yin and yang general correspondences

Taoist philosophy, yin is soft, yielding, and intuitive, and yang is hard, linear, and logical.[43] The Tao Te Ching explains the wisdom of yin—that to yield is to overcome.[44] Yin is a passive, internalizing contraction, whereas yang is an active, externalizing force.

In esoteric Taoist craft, yin is expressed as it would be in exoteric Taoist

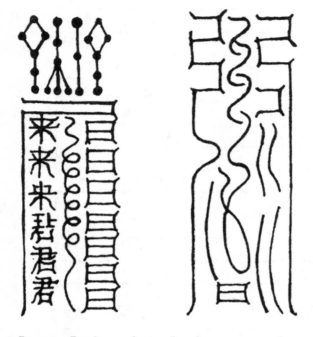

Figure 1.4. Fu talismans for expelling demonic poisons, from the Taoist Canons

philosophy, but in addition to those expressions, also embodies the energy that ghosts, hungry ghosts, and demons thrive upon. Yin relates to the spirit world and the underworld. To draw entities of these other realms toward you, you raise stronger yin energy to create an environment conducive to such spirits. Yin is also the realm of the occult.[45]

Yang relates to the celestial realm of deities, patron saints, and higher vibrational guardian spirits, or guardian angels. To exorcise, dispel, or banish ghosts, hungry ghosts, or demons, strong yang energy needs to be raised. Thus, in many historical documentations of Fu craft, such as the one pictured in figure 1.4 from the Taoist Canons,[46] symbols for yang energy, such as the Chinese character for "sun" (日) are used. Also, in the Fu talisman on the left, a guardian spirit or deity is being invoked, hence the character for "monarch" (君), in this context indicative of a celestial monarch, one reigning in the heavens.

## THE TRINITY OF HEAVEN, EARTH, AND MAN

The push and pull between yin and yang then give rise to a trinity, represented in Taoist cosmology by Heaven, Earth, and Man. The vesica piscis represents the trinitarian relationship of Heaven, Earth, and Man. Heaven and Earth together create Man. Thus, at least according to esoteric Taoist cosmology, were the origins of the universe and likewise, through the biological union of father and mother, creating child, the origins of every human life.

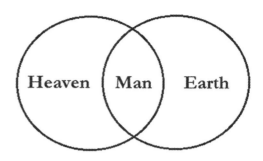

Figure 1.5. The vesica piscis: origins of life

Across many cultures, ancient civilizations have espoused a relational connection between Heaven and Earth, with the advent of astrology as the study of that connection. You will note later in chapter 3 that astrology is a core component to effective craft.

Science today proposes the same idea, albeit with different vocabulary. We now know that stars, when nearing the end of their lives, can synthesize complex organic compounds, which are then dispersed throughout the galaxy.[47] The chemical composition of stardust particles resembles the organic solids of meteorites, and meteorites are the remnants of primordial so-

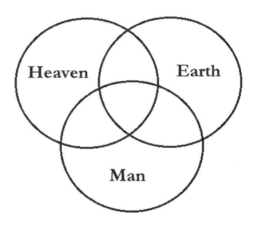

Figure 1.6. The triquetra: man's ascension

lar nebula.[48] In the early part of Earth's history, meteorites bombarded its surface, implanting the Earth with the seeds of primordial organic material from Heaven.[49] Thus the zygote for human life, for Man to arise, was formed. In that sense, Man is literally made up of Heaven (stardust) fertilizing the Earth (water), and on Earth (the womb) came life.

Heaven, Earth, and Man represent the trinity and source of all creation. Man's birth is sourced from Heaven, and Man's nourishment comes from Earth. Man then honors Heaven and Earth "through ritual and music."[50] While the vesica piscis in figure 1.5 is a diagram of the origins of Man, once Man advanced forward and matured, creating civilization and acquiring knowledge of Heaven and Earth, the vesica piscis became the triquetra. The triquetra be-

| 天 | 地 | 人 |
| --- | --- | --- |
| **Heaven** | **Earth** | **Man** |
| Sun<br>Moon<br>Stars | Mountain<br>Valley<br>Plain | Father<br>Mother<br>Offspring |
| Proliferation | Transformation | Choice |
| Celestial Kingdom | The Underworld | Humankind |
| Spirit | Resources | Manifesation |
| Pneuma | Soma | Psyche |

Table 1.2. The trinity of Heaven, Earth, and Man

comes a diagram of Man's ascension. Esoteric Taoism explains Man's origins through the vesica piscis, and then explains Man's (the practitioner's) craft through the triquetra. Craft is the knowledge and skill of becoming like Heaven, of Man becoming like the stars—capable of synthesizing and transmuting complex organic compounds. Craft is also the knowledge and skill of becoming like Earth, as receptive as Earth—capable of creation and, of course, destruction.

When calling upon the energies of Heaven in Taoist craft, Heaven is characterized as deity (or deities) and also as the sun, moon, and stars.[51] Earth is the physical, natural world, the four compass directions, and the five relative directions, which I will address later in this section. Man is the human, the sentient being occupying Earth, created from the union of Heaven and Earth.

Note, however, that the trinitarian principle of Taoist cosmology is applied in multiple ways. For instance, the metaphysical trinity is also expressed by the Three Pure Ones, who brought about the origins of all things, and who are typically personified as three deities.[52]

In the Taoist pantheon, the Three Pure Ones are the three highest deities. The Treasure of the Tao created Heaven and Earth from the yin and yang binary, though in the trinity, he represents Heaven. He later passed his authority to the celestial Jade Emperor. The "Pantheon of Deities" section in appendix B provides more information about the Three Pure Ones and the Jade Emperor. The second of the three, the Treasure of the Law, corresponding with Earth, is the keeper of all laws of physical nature. The Treasure of Knowledge is the master teacher and bringer of human civilization and culture. He corresponds with Man, though the highest evolved form of Man.

| Guardian | Celestial King | Season | Direction | Commission |
|----------|----------------|--------|-----------|------------|
|          |                | *Time* | *Element* |            |
| Black Tortoise | 多聞天王 Duō Wén Tiān Wáng | winter | North | Hears every sound, utterance, thought, and prayer |
|          |                | night | Water |            |
| Red Phoenix | 增長天王 Zēng Cháng Tiān Wáng | summer | South | Brings growth, advancement, and innovation. |
|          |                | noon | Fire |            |
| Azure Dragon | 持國天王 Chí Guó Tiān Wáng | spring | East | Supports, nurtures, develops, and brings nourishment. |
|          |                | morning | Wood |            |
| White Tiger | 廣目天王 Guang Mù Tiān Wáng | autumn | West | Sees every sight, act, deed, gesture, and movement. |
|          |                | evening | Metal |            |

Table 1.3. The Four Guardians of the four compass directions

The trinitarian principle is also found within each individual. We, as Man, are the byproduct of Heaven and Earth. We inherit from Heaven through our soul and Earth through our physical body. The synthesis of Heaven and Earth, soul and body, creates Man's consciousness, and our consciousness is what makes us unique. Consciousness is the manifestation of both Heaven and Earth, our divine father and divine mother, within us. Our sixth sense is how we connect to father and mother, connect with Heaven and Earth. What distinguishes a practitioner of craft from lay individuals is the heightened development of that sixth sense, that connection uniting Heaven, Earth, and Man within the practitioner. To be a practitioner is to hone that sixth sense. The purpose for honing that sixth sense is to establish a stronger connection and unity of Heaven, Earth, and Man within the practitioner.

## FOUR COMPASS AND FIVE RELATIVE DIRECTIONS

Taoist craft is also based on the four compass or cardinal directions and the five relative directions. The four compass directions are north, south, east,[53] and west, corresponding with the Black Tortoise, Red Phoenix, Azure Dragon (sometimes translated to Green or Blue), and White Tiger, respectively. The four directions have also been referred to as the Four Imperial Palaces (四御殿, Sì Yù Diàn) or the Treasured Ones of the Four Corners (四方寶人, Sì Fāng Baǒ Rén). These are the four quarters that are called upon at the start of ritual work.[54]

In craft, the four directions, or Four Guardians, also command four powers that a practitioner invokes, and by invoking the four powers during ritual,

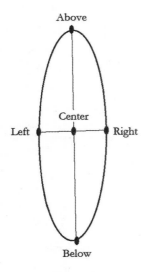

Figure 1.7. Five relative directions, above and below

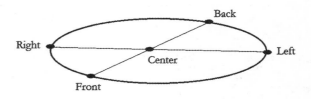

Figure 1.8. Five relative directions, front and back

assumes those qualities. The Black Tortoise can endow the practitioner with the power of clairaudience; the Red Phoenix with the power to create and bring growth; the Azure Dragon with the power of control over events; and the White Tiger with the power of clairvoyance. Thus, as will be discussed in chapter 8, on charging Fu sigils and ritual, the opening of a ritual typically includes calling upon the four directions, or Four Guardians, for the purpose of empowering the practitioner with the four powers.

Yet there are also the five relative directions (五方, Wǔ Fāng), which relate to and can be superimposed over the four cardinal directions. As an independent principle, the five relative directions are expressed as above, below, left, right, and center, and also as front, back, left, right, and center

The five relative directions are also expressed as north, south, east, west, and center. North is the house and residence of the Water phase from Wu Xing, to be discussed in the following section. Calling upon the guardians of the North will help raise either offensive or defensive energies of Water. South is the house and residence of Fire; East is the house and residence of Wood; West is the house and residence of Metal; and the center is the house and residence of Earth.

In the Zhou Dynasty, the five relative directions were expressed as five deities, referred to as the Five Emperors (五方上帝, Wǔ Fāng Shàng Dì) or the Five Lords (五君, Wǔ Jūn). In most traditions of Fu craft, the Five Emperors for the five relative directions had to be invoked, right along with the Four Guardians for the four compass directions.

The Five Emperors are typically called upon in unbinding spells, or to neutralize the spells of another witch or sorcerer. Such a practice is found across several Eastern esoteric traditions. For example, both the Taoist Scripture for

| Direction | Celestial Deity | Deity's Real Name (with honorific, 神尊) | Wu Xing |
|---|---|---|---|
| 北<br>North | 北路財神<br>Běi Lù Cái Shén | 姚少司神尊<br>Yáo Shǎo Shī Shén Zūn | 水<br>Water |
| 南<br>South | 南路財神<br>Nán Lù Cái Shén | 陳九公神尊<br>Chén Jiǔ Gōng Shén Zūn | 火<br>Fire |
| 中<br>Center | 中路財神<br>Zhōng Lù Cái Shén | 趙公明神尊<br>Zhào Gōng Míng Shén Zūn | 土<br>Earth |
| 東<br>East | 東路財神<br>Dōng Lù Cái Shén | 簫昇神尊<br>Xiāo Shēng Shén Zūn | 木<br>Wood |
| 西<br>West | 西路財神<br>Xī Lù Cái Shén | 曹寶神尊<br>Cáo Bǎo Shén Zūn | 金<br>Metal |

Table 1.4. The Five Celestials of Wealth

Unbinding Curses and the Buddhist Sutra for the Conjuration of Bewitchments explain the invoking of the Five Emperors to undo curses and hexes.[55] In esoteric Buddhism, Buddhas and bodhisattvas are invoked to exorcise demons, but for the more mundane craft of thwarting the malevolent acts of witches and sorcerers, the Five Emperors are called.[56] Thus, in the Eastern esoteric tradition, having a shared heritage in both Taoism and Buddhism, the Five Emperors serve as an antidote to malevolent magic.

The five relative directions have also been personified as the Five Celestials of Wealth (五路財神, Wǔ Lù Cái Shén), similar to the Five Emperors in mechanics, though the Five Celestials of Wealth are invoked for craft and cultivation that is specific to attaining prosperity.

Thus, Fu sigils crafted to generate greater financial stability and abundance often include invocations to the Five Celestials of Wealth (五路財神). The Center celestial deity (中路財神) is also known as Cai Shen, the God of Wealth. The legend of Cai Shen is provided later in chapter 8. Cai Shen and the Five Celestials of Wealth are part of both the Taoist and Tibetan Buddhist pantheons. Figure 1.9 is an example of a traditional Fu drawn for protection and prosperity. In the right column of Chinese characters, you will see an invocation for the Five Celestials of Wealth, or 五路財神.

How the five relative directions are characterized varies from lineage to lineage, and even changes according to the nature of the Fu to be crafted, for example, invoking the Five Celestials of Wealth for prosperity sigils.

Scriptures of antiquity from the Ling Bao lineage of Taoism anthropomorphize the five directions into five demons: the Demon Green Emperor, the De-

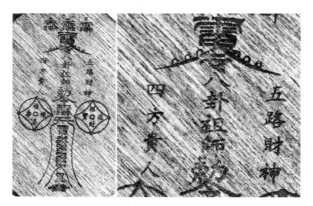

Figure 1.9. Traditional Fu for protection and prosperity

mon Red Emperor, the Demon Yellow Emperor, and the Demon Black Emperor.[57] Hexes and curses were thus the result of activity from the demons and countermeasures to undo the spells needed to address such demon activity directly. Thus, the demon for the corresponding direction related to the hex or spell would need to be summoned and ordered to stop its unruly activity.

A practitioner's ritual begins by calling upon the four compass and five relative directions.[58] Doing so forms a multidimensional sphere around the practitioner and his or her sacred space while the ritual takes place. More traditional or orthodox traditions personify the four compass and five relative directions into deities, spirits, or lords. How you choose to express the concept must resonate with you and your ontology. Yet the serious practitioner will not omit integration of these concepts into the opening of a ritual.

## The Wu Xing Five Phases

In turn, both the four cardinal directions and five relative directions relate to the five phases, or Wu Xing.[59] The Wu Xing refers to the basic Chinese cosmological concept of five phases that consist of dynamic moving elements.[60] The Wu Xing expresses the five basic transformations forming the physical concept of mass-energy equivalence, the scientific concept that mass is a measure of energy content, reliant on the speed of light. While $E = mc^2$ is the realm of physics, in the realm of metaphysics, at least according to Chinese esotericism, Wu Xing expresses the five phases of energy as it transforms into matter. Those five phases are expressed as Wood, Fire, Earth, Metal, and Water.

| Wu Xing | Physical Manifestations and Expressions |
|---------|------------------------------------------|
| 木<br><br>Wood<br><br>• Years ending with 4, 5<br>• Strong astrological aspects with Jupiter<br>• *Zodiac Signs:* Tiger, Rabbit | Idealism, optimism, and generosity. New beginnings. Generosity and altruism. Stoicism. Jingoism. Unyielding nations, resulting in greater global unrest. A strong influence of Wood will bring creativity, an artistic or academic nature, curiosity, inquisitiveness, and a greater attention to health care or holistic wellness. Arts and culture will thrive. Heightened sensitivity and erudition. |
| 火<br><br>Fire<br><br>• Years ending with 6, 7<br>• Strong astrological aspects with Mars (or the Sun)<br>• *Zodiac Signs:* Snake, Horse | Expansion, ambitions, a pioneering spirit. Upward mobility. Dynamic but restless nature. Aggressions, impulsiveness, but high vigor, vitality, and enthusiasm. Passion that warms but that can also burn. A strong influence of Fire will bring innovation, strong leadership, strong governments, social and political advancement, and the drive to bring fruition to endeavors. Heightened creativity and innovation. |
| 土<br><br>Earth<br><br>• Years ending with 8, 9<br>• Strong astrological aspects with Saturn<br>• *Zodiac Signs:* Dragon, Sheep, Dog, Ox | Grounding, centering, tempering opposites. Compromise. Inner reflection. Conservation. A more conservative nature. Greater empathy and patience. Diligence, hard work, and an industrious collective. Stability. A strong influence of Earth will bring stability in law, governments, business, real estate, and marriages or alliances. Heightened clarity and sagacity. |
| 金<br><br>Metal<br><br>• Years ending with 0, 1<br>• Strong astrological aspects with Venus<br>• *Zodiac Signs:* Monkey, Rooster | Willfulness, determination, and a controlling, ambitious nature. Courageous; dauntless. Independent and self-reliant. Progressive politics. Social reform. Business-oriented. Enjoyment of pleasure and material refinement. Loss, grief, social conflicts. A strong influence of Metal will bring clashes of egos, greater possibility of conflict, and a focus on military matters and conquest. Heightened instincts, perception, and ambitions. |
| 水<br><br>Water<br><br>• Years ending with 2, 3<br>• Strong astrological aspects with Mercury (or the Moon)<br>• *Zodiac Signs:* Boar, Rat | Wisdom, compassion, intelligence. Raised intuition and spirituality. Greater opportunities for wealth and prosperity, but Water energy can also bring instability, and thus what comes with ease will go with ease. Fluctuation. A strong influence of Water may bring floods, water issues to nations, but also greater likelihood for global diplomacy, positive international relations, and flourishing artistic advancement. There may be a greater focus on faith and religion. Heightened empathy, compassion, and clairaudience. |

Table 1.5. Wu Xing manifestations

Table 1.5 provides an overview of how the five phases are manifested and expressed. For an additional reference on Wu Xing correspondences, see table 8.5 in "The Timing of a Charging Ritual" section of chapter 8. Table K.8 in appendix K provides the physical body correspondences for the Wu Xing commonly used in

| Phase | Manifestations | Empowered by | Dominates over | Weakened by |
|---|---|---|---|---|
| WOOD | Water is essential to Wood.Wood sprouts. | Water | Earth | Metal |
| FIRE | Wood is essential to Fire.Fire blooms. | Wood | Metal | Water |
| EARTH | Fire is essential to Earth.Earth ripens. | Fire | Water | Wood |
| METAL | Earth is essential to Metal.Metal destroys. | Earth | Wood | Fire |
| WATER | Metal is essential to Water.Water is resting. | Metal | Fire | Earth |

Table 1.6. The interactive relations of Wu Xing

traditional Chinese medicine. Western practitioners who have studied Eastern esotericism often translate the Wu Xing as five elements, likened to the Western concept of four elements, Fire, Water, Air, and Earth. I also draw comparisons between the Wu Xing and the Western four elements because it's easier, but a more precise characterization of Wu Xing would be as phases, not elements.

In the Western concept of elements, Fire, Water, Air, and Earth are not dynamic per se. They are basic components, parts that will make up a greater whole. Fire and Air are assigned active qualities, and I equate that with innate yang. Water and Earth are assigned passive qualities, and I equate that with yin. Dynamic movement of the four elements in Western metaphysics comes from elemental dignities, the chemistry of the four elements as they interact with one another. The chemistry comes from how the two yang elements and the two yin elements interact.[61]

The Chinese have a different understanding for the Wu Xing. Wood, Fire, Earth, Metal, and Water are not parts of a whole. They are how Qi energy expressed as yin and yang move, change, shift, interact, and relate to each other as they form the Ba Gua trigrams and finally into a whole, whether that whole is a microcosm or macrocosm. Whereas Fire in Western cosmology is active yang, Fire in the Wu Xing can be either yin or yang and represents one of the five ways in which yin and yang interact with one another. Wu Xing would be better compared to the concept of elemental dignities,[62] the chemistry of how elements interact with one another, than the concept of elements.

The Western four elements represent parts or components. The Eastern Wu Xing represents how the parts or components move. Thus, while the Fire, Earth, Water terminology sounds the same, it is like trying to equate *wind* as a noun,

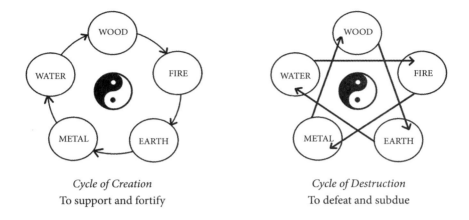

Cycle of Creation
To support and fortify

Cycle of Destruction
To defeat and subdue

Figure 1.10. Wu Xing: cycles of creation and destruction

"air in motion," with *wind* as a verb, "going in a circular or spiral direction," just because both are expressed with the same word and spelled the same way, or drawing an equivalence between *bear*, the animal, and *bear* as in "carrying a burden." Fire, Earth, and Water in the Western four elements just happen to be homographs of Fire, Earth, and Water from the Chinese Wu Xing.

In the annals of the philosopher Zhuang Zhi, also known as Zhuang Zhou, around the fifth century BC, Qi was described as giving "rise to the Five Tastes; display themselves as the Five Colors, and are evidenced by the Five Sounds."[63] He noted that Qi comes in six forms: yin, yang, wind, rain, dark, and light, and these six forms become the four seasons, which must be kept at homeostasis, or else they cause calamities and disease.[64]

In the third century BC, natural phenomena were described in fives, such as the Five Relative Directions. The concept of the Wu Xing dates back to the eighth century BC, though it wasn't until around 350–270 BC that the Wu Xing as it is systemized today became fully developed into the Five Powers of Wood, Fire, Earth, Metal, and Water.[65] Zou Yan (305–240 BC), a Chinese philosopher, alchemist, and magician, noted that these Five Powers caused, influenced, and could even predict the rise and fall of natural phenomena and of governments and civilizations.[66]

For instance, according to Wu Xing principles, Wood subdues Earth.

| WOOD | *is created by* | WATER | The rain produces plant life. Growth of Wood is dependent on the energy of Water. |
|------|----------------|-------|------------------------------------------------------------------------------------|
| FIRE | *is created by* | WOOD | The activated energy of Wood produces Fire. Fire is born from Wood energy. |
| EARTH | *is created by* | FIRE | Fire reduces all that it burns to ash, which creates Earth. Earth is dependent on the energy of Fire. |
| METAL | *is created by* | EARTH | Metal is produced deep within the Earth. Metal is born from Earth energy. |
| WATER | *is created by* | METAL | Water aggregates because of Metal. As Metal matures, it transmutes into Water. |

Table 1.7. Creation and transmutation of the Wu Xing

| WOOD | *yields to* | METAL | A metal blade will cut down a tree. |
|------|------------|-------|-------------------------------------|
| FIRE | *yields to* | WATER | Water extinguishes Fire. Water will weaken Fire. |
| EARTH | *yields to* | WOOD | Trees push into Earth and extract their nourishment from the Earth, depleting Earth. |
| METAL | *yields to* | FIRE | Fire melts and softens Metal, causing Metal to yield to Fire's control |
| WATER | *yields to* | EARTH | Earth forces the flow of Water. Earth absorbs nourishment from Water and depletes it. |

Table 1.8. Destruction and submission of the Wu Xing

| WOOD | *fortifies* | FIRE | Wood supports Fire. Fire empowers Wood. |
|------|------------|------|------------------------------------------|
| FIRE | *fortifies* | EARTH | Fire supports Earth. Earth empowers Fire. |
| EARTH | *fortifies* | METAL | Earth supports Metal. Metal empowers Earth. |
| METAL | *fortifies* | WATER | Metal supports Water. Water empowers Metal. |
| WATER | *fortifies* | WOOD | Water supports Wood. Wood empowers Water. |

Table 1.9. Wu Xing phases in concord

| WOOD | *subdues* | EARTH | Wood and Earth conflict. Wood dominates Earth. |
|---|---|---|---|
| EARTH | *subdues* | WATER | Earth and Water conflict. Earth dominates Water. |
| WATER | *subdues* | FIRE | Water and Fire conflict. Water dominates Fire. |
| FIRE | *subdues* | METAL | Fire and Metal conflict. Fire dominates Metal. |
| METAL | *subdues* | WOOD | Metal and Earth Wood. Metal dominates Wood. |

Table 1.10. Wu Xing phases in conflict

Therefore, a social or political order that is Earth-dominant can be conquered or overtaken by a force that is Wood, because Wood subdues Earth. Wood fortifies Fire. Therefore, a social or political order that is Fire-dominant can become even stronger by allying with a force that is Wood, because Wood fortifies Fire.

When it comes to craft, a practitioner must first identify the prevailing Wu Xing phase that the person or obstacle to be defeated is in. Is that person or obstacle best characterized by Wood, Fire, Earth, Metal, or Water? To use craft to defeat one who is Fire-dominant or in the Fire phase, raise the energies for Water through craft and direct it toward the one to be defeated.

Note table 1.10, with the reference of Water subduing Fire. Likewise, if an individual knows the self to be Fire-dominant, then he also knows that he is weakened by Water. So to seek protection and shielding from possible malevolence, craft a Fu to fortify the self with Wood to make the Fire even stronger, so that the Water energy sent is insufficient to overtake the stronger Fire. As shown in table 1.9, Wood fortifies Fire. Then add Earth so that the Earth can go on the offensive to defeat any Water directed toward the Fire-dominant individual, because, as shown in table 1.10, Earth can subdue Water.

Table 1.11 provides further correspondences for the Wu Xing five phases that can be used. According to the table, for example, to raise strong Wood energy, time any corresponding rituals for charging a Wood-dominant Fu with a strongly positioned Jupiter and call upon the guardian of the East for support. For a New Year protection Fu created for a year that ends in 6, such as 2016, raise the energetic support of Fire in the design of the Fu.

|  | 木<br>Wood | 火<br>Fire | 土<br>Earth | 金<br>Metal | 水<br>Water |
|---|---|---|---|---|---|
| Planet | Jupiter | Mars | Saturn | Venus | Mercury |
| Direction | East | South | Center | West | North |
| Season | spring | summer | Indian summer | autumn | winter |
| Color | Green | Red | Yellow | White | Blue |
| Last Digit of Year | 4, 5 | 6, 7 | 8, 9 | 0, 1 | 2, 3 |
| Timing | 11 p.m. to 3 a.m. | 11 a.m. to 3 p.m. / 7 p.m. to 11 p.m. | 7 to 11 a.m. | 3 to 7 a.m. | 3 to 7 p.m. |
| Sense | sight | speech | taste | smell | hearing |
| Mental | sensitivity | creativity | clarity | intuition | empathy |
| Finger | index | middle | thumb | ring | little |
| Life Phase | birth | youth | adult | mature | death |
| Heavenly Stem [Yang] | 甲<br>Jiǎ | 丙<br>Bǐng | 戊<br>Wù | 庚<br>Gēng | 壬<br>Rén |
| Heavenly Stem [Yin] | 乙<br>Yǐ | 丁<br>Dīng | 己<br>Jǐ | 辛<br>Xīn | 癸<br>Guǐ |

Table 1.11. Wu Xing correspondences[67]

Note that while the planetary correspondence for Water is Mercury, Water is also associated with the Moon. Here in table 1.11, for Earth's corresponding season, I have designated "Indian summer," or late summer, early autumn, when there is a harmonious balance between yin and yang, the equilibrium of what both summer and autumn have to offer. Earth is attributed with a balance of yin and yang and is considered neutral.

An understanding of yin and yang will result in a strong foundational knowledge of Eastern metaphysics and how Qi energy flows, but to master the art and science of craft requires a full understanding of Wu Xing. Utilizing Wu Xing is one of the most powerful techniques at a practitioner's disposal. It instructs the practitioner on how to defeat and protect against any affront. It

Figure 1.12. Earlier Heaven Ba Gua on a coin-shaped amulet

Figure 1.11. Earlier Heaven, Fu Xi Ba Gua

shows how to fortify and support any desired result. Wu Xing is the foundation of traditional Chinese medicine, inner body cultivation, alchemy, feng shui, Chinese fortune-telling and divination, the social and political cycles of human civilization, the cycles of the universe, the cycles of every individual life path, and, of course, the metaphysical art of craft. Appendix K will provide additional references and craft uses for the Wu Xing.

## EIGHT TRIGRAMS OF THE BA GUA

By way of the trinitarian principle, Taoist cosmogenesis holds that the trinity— Heaven, Earth, and Man—or the Three Pure Ones harnessed yin and yang in a way that brought about the eight trigrams. These eight trigrams express the eight permutations of trinary yin and yang lines that are the eight elements of the Ba Gua. The eight trigrams of the Ba Gua are a cornerstone of Taoist metaphysical theory. Taoist magic and Eastern esotericism cannot be fully understood without first mastering the Ba Gua.

The Ba Gua is the practitioner's periodic table for all work. It is a cornerstone of Taoist cosmological principles. The Ba Gua comprises yin and yang lines that form trigrams. Yin is represented by the broken line; yang is represented by the solid. When the two combine to form combinations of trinities, they produce a total of eight trigrams, which are the Ba Gua.[68] These eight trigrams are considered the fundamental building blocks of existence. They encompass both physical and metaphysical energy.

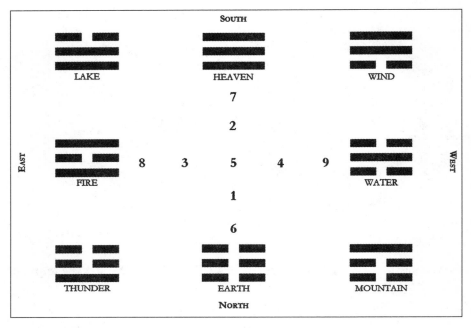

Figure 1.13. Earlier Heaven, Fu Xi Ba Gua

Figure 1.14. Later Heaven, King Wen Ba Gua

There are two sequences of the Ba Gua, known commonly as the Earlier Heaven, or Fu Xi Ba Gua, pictured in figure 1.11, and the Later Heaven, or King Wen Ba Gua, pictured in figure 1.14. Note that in figure 1.11 and figure 1.14, the "top" of the trigram is along the inner edge, closest to the Ba Gua, whereas the "bottom" of the trigram is along the outer edge of the Ba Gua.

The Earlier Heaven is based on a numerical sequence dating back to the reigns of the mythic demigod sovereigns who created human civilization, in particular, the legendary Fu Xi, father of humanity. That numerical sequence, called the He Tu (河圖, Hé Tú), or River Pattern, came before the Lo Shu nine sector magic square (discussed in the next section).

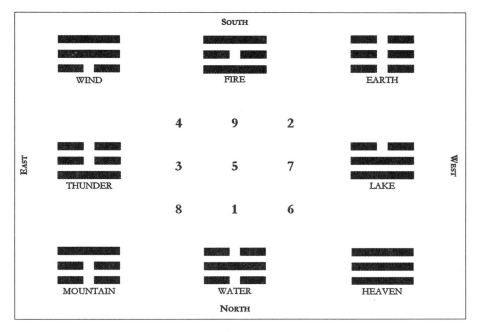

Figure 1.15. Later Heaven Ba Gua and the Lo Shu

The He Tu represents the spiral dance of creation, and when manifested as the Earlier Heaven Ba Gua, expresses the laws of physical nature, and the law of opposites; for example, the trigram Heaven is across from the trigram Earth to show that these forces are opposites. The He Tu will be covered in greater detail below in the section "The He Tu."

The Later Heaven Ba Gua, attributed to King Wen, expresses the laws of metaphysical nature. King Wen reigned during the latter part of the Shang Dynasty and established the subsequent Zhou Dynasty.[69] King Wen is credited with arranging the eight trigrams of the Ba Gua into the sixty-four hexagrams of the I Ching. The Later Heaven Ba Gua sequence, based on the Lo Shu magic square, is associated with divination, whereas the Earlier Heaven sequence is associated with Taoist cosmology. Thus, the Earlier Heaven sequence, based on the He Tu, became the expression of physical nature, and the Later Heaven sequence, based on the Lo Shu, became the expression of metaphysical nature.

Physical nature and metaphysical nature are by no means mutually exclusive, however. Rather, the Earlier Heaven sequence shows how physical nature

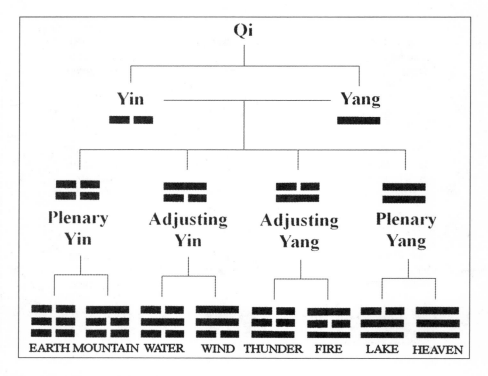

Figure 1.16. Origins of the eight trigrams

governs the metaphysical plane and that relationship of power between the two, while the Later Heaven sequence shows how metaphysical nature governs our physical earthly plane and that relationship of power. In Fu sigil crafting, the Later Heaven Ba Gua is typically the one consulted because sigil crafting seeks to tap into metaphysical energy.

Figure 1.16 depicts the formation of the eight trigrams. First, there is the one, or Qi, the Tao. The one becomes two, yin and yang. When combined in metaphysical chemistry, yin and yang form changing and unchanging lines, which I refer to as adjusting and plenary lines, respectively. Combined with the original yin and yang, trigrams are formed, for a total of eight. Each trigram is called a *gua*. There are eight of them, and the character in Chinese for eight is *ba*. Hence, the Ba Gua.

Whereas the Wu Xing five phases and the four elements of Western metaphysics are not equivalents, I feel comfortable drawing comparisons between the Ba Gua and the Western four elements.

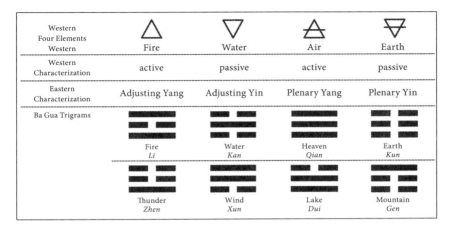

Table 1.12. Eight trigram correspondences with the Western four elements

These eight trigrams or Ba Gua represent the fundamental building blocks of all life and matter—that is, the metaphysical aspect of life and matter. Understanding the Ba Gua enables the practitioner to understand what to invoke and how to invoke it to manifest any will or intention in Taoist spell-crafting. A practitioner will work with both the Earlier Heaven and Later Heaven Ba Guas for different purposes.

The Earlier Heaven represents the philosophy that the practitioner operates with, the cosmological foundation of craft. It symbolizes the organization and ordered sequence of energies that the universe is composed of. In Eastern esoteric practices, such as feng shui, the Earlier Heaven Ba Gua is inscribed onto mirrors and used to neutralize atrophic or malignant Qi energy. The Earlier Heaven Ba Gua represents alignment, and in craft, is used to "align" natural Qi energy in an environment.

The Later Heaven sequence is the one used when a practitioner taps into the metaphysical dimension, applied in conjunction with the Lo Shu magic square. It represents the mechanics and application of craft. The Later Heaven Ba Gua symbolizes change, how Man can harness the energies of Heaven and Earth to manifest changes in the universe. That notion will be reiterated in the foundational principles of craft covered in chapter 3.

To explain the concept, think of figurines in a row on a cabinet shelf. The metaphysical energy represented by the Earlier Heaven Ba Gua when used in

| Trigram | Life Aspect | Binary | Wu Xing | Direction | Planet | Animal |
|---|---|---|---|---|---|---|
| Heaven | blessings, opportunities, allies and forging alliances, friends, fatherhood, government, national leadership | Yin | Metal | Northwest | Venus | Horse |
| Lake | fertility, creativity, nourishment, nurture, children, progency, success in gestation (both figurative for projects and physical pregnancy) | Yin | Metal | West | Venus | Sheep Tiger |
| Fire | ambitions, honor; fame; reputation; social status; innovation, initiations; achievement and gaining recognition for accomplishments | Yang | Fire | South | Mars | Phoenix |
| Thunder | family; familial relations; ancestry and heritage; family dynasty; safety, well-being, and harmony within the family, nuclear and extended | Yang | Wood | East | Jupiter | Dragon |
| Wind | wealth, finances, assets, material abundance; the conditions and circumstances in life that bring prosperity and financial riches | Yang | Wood | Southeast | Jupiter | Rooster |
| Water | career, profession, employment; professional path; life path; career development; work | Yin | Water | North | Mercury | Pig Tortoise |
| Mountain | knowledge, education; skills; wisdom; schooling, academics; arts and culture | Balanced | Earth | Northeast | Saturn | Wolf Dog |
| Earth | career, profession, employment; professional path; life path; career development; work | Balanced | Earth | Southwest | Saturn | Bull |

Table 1.13. Ba Gua eight trigrams and correspondences

craft might be likened to adjusting the current row of figurines ever so slightly so that they are aligned with each other, equidistant, and all facing in the same direction. One would not change the order that the figurines were found in, but the corrective adjustments result in greater balance and organization to the decor. In contrast, use of the Later Heaven Ba Gua could be likened to re-arranging the positions of the figurines entirely to conform to specific intent. Thus, the Later Heaven Ba Gua is the one typically used in the active practice of craft.

## THE LO SHU NINE-SECTOR MAGIC SQUARE

The Lo Shu (洛書, Luò Shū)[70] dates back to prehistoric China, during the Xia Dynasty (2100–1600 BC),[71] and was used by prehistoric shamans as far back as 2500 BC.[72] The Lo Shu comes with a fascinating mythology. It is said that a turtle emerged from a flooding river with the Lo Shu square imprinted on its shell. A shaman king, Yu the Great (大禹, Dà Yǔ or 夏禹, Xià Yǔ), saw the turtle shell and thus devised the Lo Shu.[73] Throughout history, the

Lo Shu square has been used in feng shui, fortune-telling, divination and other Eastern esoteric practices.

The Lo Shu is a magic square where the numbers 1 through 9 are positioned in a grid and equal the sum of 15 in every direction. In Chinese tradition, the number 15 represents the harmony of life and the order of the universe.[74] The number 15 is a product of 3, for the trinity of Heaven, Earth, and Man, multiplied by 5, for the Wu Xing five phases and the five directions of Chinese geomancy: north, south, east, west, and center. It is the number of the Tao, the Way.[75]

Figure 1.17 shows the original delineation of the Lo Shu. Note its similarity to the Later Heaven Ba Gua in Appendix E. The white dots represent yang, while the black dots represent yin.

The feng shui correspon-

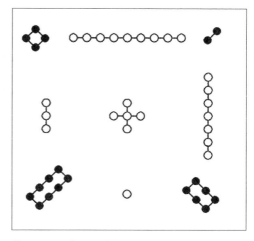

Figure 1.17. Original delineation of the Lo Shu

| 4 | 9 | 2 |
|---|---|---|
| 3 | 5 | 7 |
| 8 | 1 | 6 |

Figure 1.18. Lo Shu magic square, or the Nine Palaces (九宮八卦)

dences for the nine palaces depicted in figure 1.18 are used in craft in a way that might be likened to metaphysical acupuncture. For example, the ritual for empowering a Fu sigil crafted to generate prosperity, wealth, and financial security would have to trigger the fourth palace, invoke the energies or guardians of the southeast, arrange yin and yang energy in such a way as to create the trigram Wind in the essence of the Fu, and utilize Wood from the Wu Xing five phases.

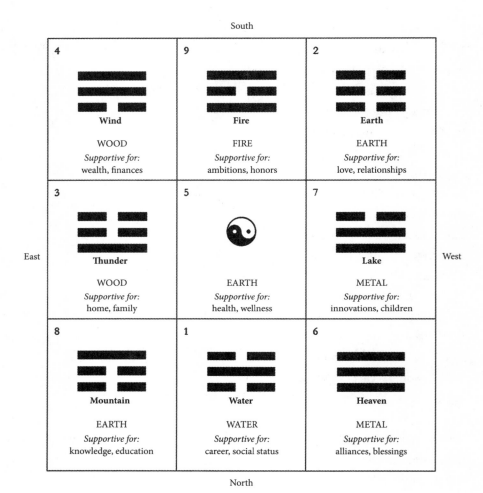

Figure 1.19. Lo Shu, the Ba Gua, and feng shui

## THE HE TU: A SPIRAL SEQUENCE FOR CREATION

According to mythos, the He Tu came from the Yellow River and the Lo Shu came from the Luo (or Lo), a tributary of the Yellow River.[76] Likewise, the He Tu was the first divine revelation of universal laws to govern humankind's creation. After the He Tu, an offshoot of the He Tu, and thus emerging from a tributary or offshoot of the Yellow River, came the Lo Shu, which revealed what is behind the veil. The Lo Shu became the second divine revelation, one of metaphysical laws that govern humankind's transformation, or transcendence.

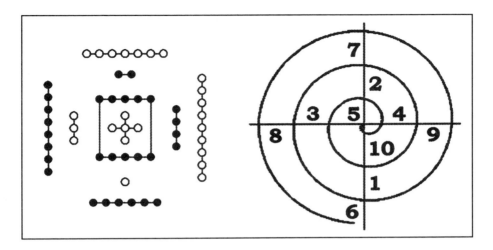

Figure 1.21. The spiral sequence of creation

The He Tu is attributed with the shaman king Fu Xi, also revered in the Taoist pantheon as a demigod. Along with his sister Nu Wa, Fu Xi created human civilization. The He Tu came to being when Fu Xi observed patterns on his horse's back as it emerged from the Yellow River. He documented the patterns with dark and light connected dots,[77] representing the nine numbers,[78] as shown in figure 1.20. The numbers are paired, yin and yang, lower number with higher number.

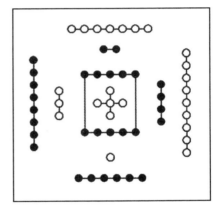

Figure 1.20. Original delineation of the He Tu

Each lower number represents a Creation Number (1, 2, 3, 4, and 5). Each higher number represents a Completion Number (6, 7, 8, 9, and 10).

Note that the sequence of Qi energy moves from lower digits to higher, inner to outer, in the form of a spiral (fig. 1.21). For instance, the Creation number 1 moves outward, changing into the Completion number 6, the transformation of yang to yin. Creation number 2 moves outward, changing into Completion number 7, yin to yang. The number 3 creates, transforms, and completes into number 8, yang to yin; 4 moves outward into 9, and 5 moves outward into 10.[79]

| | Number | | Binary | Wu Xing | He Tu<br>(Earlier Heaven)( | Lo shu<br>Later Heaven) |
|---|---|---|---|---|---|---|
| **Creation Number** | 1 | Yang | Heaven | Water | North | North |
| | 2 | Yin | Earth | Fire | South | Southwest |
| | 3 | Yang | Heaven | Wood | East | East |
| | 4 | Yin | Earth | Metal | West | Southeast |
| | 5 | Yang | Heaven | Earth | Center | Center |
| **Completion Number** | 6 | Yin | Earth | Water | North | Northwest |
| | 7 | Yang | Heaven | Fire | South | West |
| | 8 | Yin | Earth | Wood | East | Northeast |
| | 9 | Yang | Heaven | Metal | West | South |
| | 10 | Yin | Earth | Earth | Center | ————— |

Table 1.14. Correspondences for Creation and Completion numbers

The movement of these numbers from Creation to Completion in the Earlier Heaven or He Tu sequence forms the He Tu spiral, which is said to represent the creation of Heaven, the sequence of creation for Earth, and ultimately, the birth of Man. The origin of the yang odd numbers is Heaven, and the origin of the yin even numbers is Earth; in their He Tu spiral sequence, they produce Man.

Thus, creation pushes outward from a central point, though that point is not the beginning but rather a midpoint, the Creation number 5. Linear or nonlinear, 5 is always the present, the center, the fountainhead, the moment when potential becomes kinetic—the critical moment of shift. Creation numbers expand and shift outward to become the Completion numbers. In its essence, the spiral sequence of the He Tu characterizes an expanding, dynamic universe,[80] a revelation that a Chinese shamanic king discovered more than four thousand years before astronomer Edwin Hubble arrived at the same conclusion.[81]

The revelation of the Fu Xi is known as the He Tu (河圖, Hé Tú), or River Pattern. In Taoist cosmology, the He Tu is a map depicting the form and formation of the universe.[82] It represents the physical laws of nature, and subsequently manifested as the Earlier Heaven Ba Gua or the Fu Xi Ba Gua.

The He Tu tackles the question of the origins of life. The River Pattern is a spiral sequence that diagrams how we came to be. Meanwhile, twentieth- and twenty-first-century advancements in astrochemistry and astrobiology have only just begun to tackle that question of origins.[83]

While the He Tu represents the physical laws of nature, the Lo Shu represents metaphysical laws. More specifically, it reveals the hidden and the unseen. The Lo Shu is a map depicting the ebb and flow of energy through the metaphysical dimension that affects the physical.

## WHAT IS A FU TALISMAN?

A Fu talisman[84] is an ideograph that represents an intention. It consists of both drawings and writing, sometimes legible, but oftentimes not. The ideographs represent a systematic language or code that is used to facilitate communication between Heaven, Earth, and Man. Then, through craft, or ceremonial rituals, a practitioner accumulates Qi energy from sources in the environment and channels it in concentrated form into the Fu talisman, in effect using the practitioner's force to transmute the properties of that object, the Fu.

Metaphysical energy can be harnessed and transmuted to empower, amplify, strengthen, weaken, dispel, or block other metaphysical energy. In short, that is the purpose of a Fu—to tap into metaphysical energy in a way that can rectify perceived imbalances in the physical or material plane. Esoteric Taoist practitioners believe that is how luck can be changed—that is how the direction of physical manifestations can be altered. The Fu talisman works with the Qi in the practitioner's environment. Such energy is present everywhere, in everything that you see, be it a tree, thunder, a piece of crystal quartz, a bowl of rainwater, or emotions such as love and anger. That unseen energy increases in potency when two people fall in love or make love, when we hate or feel extreme jealousy, or when there is a large congregation of people gathered for a shared and unified purpose.

The crafting of a Fu talisman in effect redistributes the balances between the yin and yang of Qi energy, and in doing so, can better attract career, wealth, or romantic opportunities. Fu talismans can be used to strengthen or weaken certain personality characteristics. The craft of a Fu consists of pulling desirable metaphysical energy and channeling that energy into a concentrated space so that it might help to modify existing energies in that given space. Thus, a Fu for wealth is essentially a concentrated knot of Qi energy that is calibrated by a practitioner and keyed to rendering an environment more amenable to wealth-generating opportunities. If a Fu is crafted to ease emotional tensions in a domestic environment, such a talisman is a concentrated knot of energy that will weaken aggression and strengthen compassion, love, and gentility.

The craft of Fu is a form of alchemy that works with unseen metaphysical energy. It is the transmutation of that energy, of Qi. As the father of nuclear physics Ernest Rutherford discovered in 1919, channeling high-speed alpha particles through a vessel can transform one kind of atom into another.[85] That transmutation of elements was the core undertaking of medieval alchemists, which Rutherford proved centuries later. While to date there is no known scientific explanation for craft, I am convinced that in time, craft and the transmutation of unseen metaphysical energy can and will be understood through quantum mechanics. The unseen metaphysical Qi energy I speak of might be likened to the unseen neutrons that surround us every day, every moment, in our immediate vicinity. While we are all surrounded by them, scientists did not become aware of their existence until 1932.[86] I trust that likewise, in time, modern scientists will finally catch up to what practitioners of craft have known all along.

## A PRELIMINARY NOTE OF CAUTION

I once listened in on a lecture by the venerable Sheng-Yen, a Buddhist monk, teacher, and scholar, who spoke about magic and sorcery,[87] or as I refer to it, energetic workings beyond the physical realm.[88] He warned against reliance on energetic workings, such as magical practice, to help ourselves or even with the good intention of helping others. Those with the ability to work with such energies and who also possess divine wisdom will rarely use their abilities, and there is a reason for that. They understand that there is no enduring benefit.

He gave the example of a one-way romance. Say you want someone to marry you, but that person is not yet ready to consent to such a proposition. If you use energetic workings, like a magical spell, to get that person to marry you, then you have engaged in an act of deception. Aside from the matter of having acted deceptively, the greater problem is the debt you have incurred. In energetic workings such as magic, you are borrowing something that is not yours. At some point you will have to return it, with interest compounded, energetic interest on top of interest. You have to ask yourself: in the end, was it worth borrowing that little amount of energy?

The intent to use energetic workings beyond the physical realm to help others is commendable, but such good intentions can quickly run amok. The laws of cause and effect still apply. Figuratively, to use such workings to fill a hole for someone, you need to get the filler from elsewhere. In getting that filler, all you have done is create another hole somewhere else, a hole that perhaps you do not see, to patch the hole that you currently see. Where is the sense in that?

Also, there may be a greater karmic rationale at play for why that person incurred such a hole in the first place. You should not interfere with that karma, at least not without a complete understanding of that path, of your own path, and what could result from the interference. Using something like magic violates people's karmic paths. While trapped in the tempest of suffering, people forget the necessity of pain. Pain is part of the hero's journey to greatness, and both that pain and greatness could be part of someone's karmic path. Not allowing that person to suffer the necessary pain could be derailing him from the hero's journey. So always take care in how you proceed in energetic workings.

Yet there is a curious "stand your ground" principle among many esoteric Taoist practitioners.[89] Today, in the way craft is practiced, there seems to be a tacit agreement that energetic workings for the protection and defense of self is permissible, and retaliating against those who hurt us or threaten to hurt us, or assisting others with doing so, is part of the practitioner's work.[90]

That runs contrary to exoteric Taoist philosophy in a significant way. Exoteric Taoist philosophy teaches wu wei, to act in response to oppositional forces by not acting at all. Thus, while the venerable Sheng-Yen was speaking from a Chan Buddhist perspective, what the monk had to say about magic is aligned with the Taoist principle of wu wei. Taoist philosophy teaches to defend softly against another's hard offense. Wu wei is about cultivating the practitioner's mind and body to be like water, absorbing offenses without being harmed by offenses.

The highest echelons of defensive work is about attaining such power and indestructability of mind and body that any offensive attack is like an ant tickling the tip of your toe, and you do not retaliate against that ant because you show compassion and unconditional love for all. At the most advanced stage of cultivation, a practitioner of esoteric Taoism will reach the state of wu wei espoused in exoteric Taoism.

Crafting Fu sigils is a form of energetic working that should not be used lightly to help yourself or others. It is a curious practice to learn about and train in, but do not engage in it without wisdom. Teaching wisdom, regretfully, is beyond the scope of this book.

Figure 1.22. Investiture of a Taoist Deity, unidentified artist, circa 1641, ink and gold on silk handscroll (New York Metropolitan Museum of Art)

# CHAPTER 2

# A HISTORIC AND CULTURAL CONTEXT

**MAGICAL TRADITIONS** in the West are often hyperbolized in fiction and film, and likewise with Taoist magic in the East. The portrayal of Fu talisman crafting often gets a fantastical treatment. Sorcerers in long robes pull a slip of paper—the Fu—from their sleeves, point their fingers, mutter invocations for a summoning, and spirits from the underworld appear or disappear.

Historically, Fu talismans were cures for all conceivable ailments that the medieval Chinese might face, from alleviating illness, averting misfortune, magical attacks and curses, defending against assaults both physical and psychic, and avoiding poverty.[1] Religious and occult practitioners traveled frequently, venturing into the remote mountains in search of rare herbs for their alchemy. Thus, talismans safeguarding against the perils of travel, and "travel magic" became a common feature in the early third-century occult Taoist texts. These Fu talismans were intended to ward off ghosts and dangerous wildlife, and invoke the protection of deities.[2]

Contemporary real-life applications are only a little less fantastical. If a person is experiencing bad luck, then it must be because a malevolent spirit is haunting him, so a Fu talisman is crafted to vanquish the malevolent spirit or to protect an individual from the spirit's attacks. If a physical health condition can't be explained by modern science or medical doctors, it is probably because a malevolent spirit is causing the condition, so a shaman or Taoist priest is consulted, a paper Fu is crafted and burned, the ashes mixed with water and then imbibed as a method of curing the ailment.

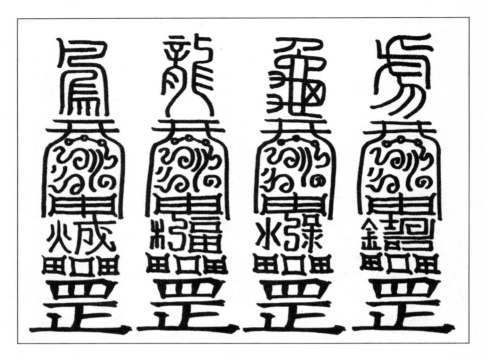

Figure 2.1. Four directions home-protection Fu

Fu are also used to protect a home from malevolent energies or to serve as feng shui cures. Typically a collection of four or eight Fu talismans are crafted and positioned around the house, forming a protective barrier. Figure 2.1 depicts a set of four Fu talismans that, left to right, are to be buried in the south, east, north, and west corners along the perimeter of a home to ensure protection, prosperity, and a peaceful family life. Note how each invokes the guardian spirit animal of the compass direction that the Fu is intended to safeguard. Left to right, the Fu for protection of the south (南, nán) invokes the Phoenix; the Fu for the east (東, dōng) invokes the Dragon); north (北, běi) invokes the Tortoise; and the Fu for protection of the west (西, xī), invoking the Tiger.

In this book, my explanation for the purpose of a Fu will take into account exoteric Taoist philosophy. The Fu is a concentrated battery of metaphysical energy charged by a practitioner, which helps to restore balance to imbalances of metaphysical energy. Physical ailments are caused by metaphysical imbalances of energy, and therefore the Fu's purpose is to rectify the metaphysical imbalance, which then corrects the corresponding physical ailment.

As noted in chapter 1, every given person or situation comprises yin and yang, and afflictions are the result of imbalances between yin and yang. Historically these imbalances have been anthropomorphized and expressed as good or evil, benevolent or malevolent spiritual entities. Thus, if a person is experiencing bad luck, one explanation is malevolent spirits, and therefore benevolent spirits are brought in to counteract the malevolent. Another explanation—and the one I subscribe to—is yin and yang. Irrespective of good or evil, an ailment that is plaguing someone might be due to excess yin, which, anthropomorphizing, might give the impression of a malevolent spirit. Raising yang energy and restoring yin and yang balance in that person's life by crafting a yang-dominant Fu talisman would be the metaphysical antidote to that person's bad luck. Thus, Fu talismans are rooted in Chinese or Taoist ontology of Qi, yin and yang, and the Ba Gua characterizations of how yin and yang manifest. Yet understanding spirit summoning and conjuring is part and parcel to understanding the history and culture of the craft.

Though the Fu are called talismans in most English translations, this book has opted to refer to the Fu as sigils rather than talismans. The actual practice of crafting the Fu is better likened to Western sigil crafting.[3] In Western traditions, sigils, or seals, are used by ceremonial magicians to summon supernatural entities. To do so, a combination of words, ideograms, and metaphysically symbolic line drawings is used, often designed through an alphanumeric magic square, which is then paired with set rituals to empower or activate the seals. These seals identify the name of a spirit, and by identifying the name, calls upon that spirit to manifest before the practitioner. Also, while the practitioner may have a clear understanding of what the sigil means, it often appears incomprehensible to the outsider looking in. The purpose of these sigils is multifaceted, ranging from conjuring the supernatural angelic or demonic realms to finding love, earning more money, and helping with weight loss.

In every way I have mentioned about Western sigils and seals, the Fu talisman is similar. In Western traditions, sigils can also be used as a form of spell, to will an intention to manifest, doing so by way of specific symbolism, rendering words or phrases into designs, and empowering the sigils through ritual. The Fu talisman is created for the same purposes and by essentially the same mechanics. It is a summons notice, a piece of paper charged with divine authority to call upon the entire spectrum of the supernatural, from deities, saints, and immortals to ghosts, hungry ghosts,[4] and demons from hell. Yet, the Fu is also used for finding love, earning more money, and even helping with weight loss. Thus, referring to the Fu as a sigil is more specific, whereas the term *talisman* can be overbroad, though both will be used interchangeably throughout this book.

## HISTORY OF FU CRAFT

Fu sigils have been around since the Warring States period in China, estimated to be about 475–221 BC[5] during the Eastern Zhou Dynasty. The earliest Chinese script was invented not so Man would communicate with Man, but so that Man could communicate with Heaven,[6] and thus craft itself and Eastern esoteric practices are based heavily on writing and the written form. The Fu sigil is the written correspondence by which Man can communicate with Heaven, and therefore nearly all forms of craft will rely on or incorporate the Fu. The Fu is not just one aspect of Chinese esoteric Taoist craft; it is an essential component to the way esoteric Taoist spell-crafting is practiced.

The very first writings, the predecessors of the Fu, were found on divinatory oracle bones cast by Neolithic shamans circa 10,000 to 2000 BC. The Chinese shamanic culture can be traced back through artifacts from northern and northeastern China that date to about 5000 BC.[7] The first leaders of civilization were shamans, like Fu Xi (伏羲), the mythical father of humanity, or Yu the Great (大禹), who conceived of the Lo Shu magic square. The Lo Shu was used in the magical practices of shamans in 2500 BC,[8] and the magic square is still used today by practitioners of Taoist craft. Artifacts of oracle bone divination from 2100 to 256 BC reveal divinations and prognostications performed by these shamanic kings.[9]

Shamans were viewed as messengers between worlds, granted authority from Shang Di (上帝),[10] a heavenly emperor, to issue sacred decrees (聖旨, Shèng Zhǐ) that ordered lesser deities and spirits to carry forth certain instructions,[11] such as vanquishing demons, summoning benevolent spirits to protect the king or malevolent spirits to curse the king's enemies, or calling upon nature gods to bring rain.[12] The shaman was in effect a messenger granted divine authority by a higher deity, typically Shang Di, to command instructions to a lower spiritual entity. The first Fu sigils represented that sacred decree and thus often resembled the verbiage of imperial decrees from the emperor to his subjects, bearing the characters 聖旨 (sheng zhǐ, meaning "a decree") or 令 (lìng, meaning "to order" or "to issue a command").

However, oracle bones dating back to the Shang Dynasty (1600–1050 BC) reveal a preexisting belief in a supervising deity, a Lord Di (帝) in the heavens or skies (上) who issued orders (令).[13] A shaman's responsibility was to divine messages from the nature gods and travel to the realms of these gods for communion. Given these findings, the Fu sigil is likely to predate the Zhou Dynasty and to have subsisted during the Shang. It was only during the Zhou Dynasty, with the rise of Taoism, that the talismanic practice of the shamans mixed with Taoism and was thus documented in Taoist texts.[14]

The first organized Taoist lineage credited with Fu sigil practice was the Tian Shi lineage,[15] established in AD 142 under Zhang Dao Ling,[16] the first celestial master of the lineage. The Tian Shi lineage was politically active, and is more commonly known for its rebellion against the Han Dynasty. Zhang Dao Ling is popularly credited for being a powerful magician.[17] He is also credited as the first to craft Fu sigils.[18] Later, Zhang Dao Ling's grandson, Zhang Lu,[19] would be popularly regarded as a practitioner of darker and more malevolent magical arts.[20]

The next great wave of Taoist magical practice is linked with the Mao Shan lineages (茅山派) named after its place of origin, Mount Mao. "Mao Shan" as referenced today can refer to any number of magical Taoist traditions from Mount Mao.[21] The best-known esoteric Taoist lineages from Mount Shan blended regional folk religions with Mahayana Buddhism,[22] with Amithaba (阿弥陀佛, Amítuófó), a celestial Buddha, often invoked and venerated.

Wei Huancun (魏華存), a Taoist priestess, founded one such lineage, the Shang Qing (上清), in the Jin Dynasty (AD 265–420), and the lineage was later continued by her sons.[23] In the pantheon of deities and spirits called upon by this sect, the primary deity venerated is the Jade Emperor, the "Treasure of the Tao" from The Three Pure Ones.

Figure 2.2 show three Fu sigils from the *Shang Qing Da Dong Zhen Jing* (上清大洞真經),[24] or *Perfect Scripture of Great Profundity*,[25] a medieval esoteric Taoist text from the Shang Qing lineage, also called the *Shang Qing Perfect*

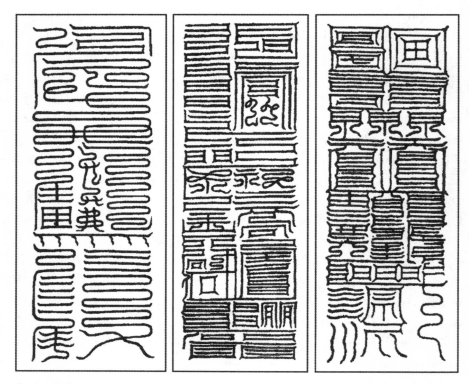

Figure 2.2. Inner cultivation Fu from the *Perfect Scripture of Great Profundity*

*Scriptures.* The text sets forth verses, much like mantras or invocations, intended for a practitioner to chant. Recitations of these invocations will cultivate purer Qi energy within a practitioner. It is believed that these invocations self-exorcise, or rid the body of toxins, impurities, and evils or malignant energies. The invocations also invite angelic beings into the body to help raise power and vitality.

The *Perfect Scripture of Great Profundity* explains invoking inner deities. The Shang Qing tradition espoused a pantheon of inner deities that dwelled within the practitioner's body. These inner deities, when healthy, can establish a stronger direct and divine connection with celestial deities.

Inner deities serve as administrators of various regions of the human body, each region referred to as a palace.[26] For instance, seven deities reside in palaces of the head, corresponding with the hair, brain, eyes, nose, ears, tongue, and teeth.[27] There were deities for the heart, lungs, kidney, liver, and spleen, and other luminous spirits, for a total of thirty-nine inner deities that a master practitioner would learn to invoke through Fu.[28] The three Fu pictured in figure 2.2 correspond with only three of such inner deities. Invocation of the inner deities was believed to assist with purification and cultivation of the physical body by cleansing it of metaphysical toxins, in effect ensuring a practitioner's physical longevity.[29] Doing so

Figure 2.3. Fu of Lao Tzu for psychics and mediums, worn to amplify their abilities and power[32]

also allowed for a stronger connection or rapport between the inner deities and celestial deities, which was the practitioner's pathway to immortality.[30]

To empower the Shang Qing sigils, a complex, multistep charging process was required. In the text, much of that instruction is coded in arcane language and not readily comprehensible to a lay reader. In broad terms, however, the ritual seems to involve Qi energy transfer through the practitioner's spittle and teeth clicking invocations.[31]

Around the same era that the Shang Qing arose, three Taoist masters, referred to as the Three Mao brothers, birthed several magical lineages from Mount Mao. These magical lineages placed strong emphasis on the practice of Fu sigils, among other arts, such as alchemy and mixing herbs to create elixirs for immortality.

Continuing in the Jin Dynasty, around AD 400, the Ling Bao lineage (靈寶派) was founded. It was one of the most enduring esoteric Taoist traditions, and much of Fu sigil crafting as it is practiced today can be traced back to the practices of the Ling Bao. The Ling Bao lineage blended Taoism with Mahayana Buddhism, reflecting core Buddhist concepts in fourth- and fifth-century Ling Bao Taoist scriptures.[33]

Figure 2.4. Ling Bao Fu
for feigning death

The Ling Bao believed in an underworld, a prison on earth where those with bankrupted karmic accounts were held captive. Many of their practitioners worked with hungry ghosts, or the spirits of deceased humans who, during their lives, had suffered so profoundly that in death, their spirits are not able to find the peace needed to transcend or move on.[34] The Ling Bao developed a great deal of magical practice to handle the underworld and hungry ghosts.[35]

The Ling Bao practiced ceremonial magic that often endeavored for the incredible. The Fu sigil depicted in figure 2.4 comes from the Ling Bao tradition, according to the lineage's scriptures, the *Ling Bao Order of the Five Talismans* (靈寶五符序, Líng Bǎo Wǔ Fú Xù).[36] The Fu's purpose is for feigning death. According to the scriptures, if the instructions are followed precisely, a practitioner's doppelgänger will appear dead to onlookers while the practitioner has absconded, alive and well, far from the premises. Yet when the doppelgänger corpse is being prepared for the funeral, the corpse will disappear, and no trace of the practitioner or the doppelgänger will remain.

While the Fu sigil in figure 2.4 must be drawn as illustrated, the charging ritual preceding it is what brings forth the power. Charging rituals will be discussed in chapter 7. The text gives instructions for making a total of eighty-one pills, which must be ingested by the practitioner in sets of three pills, three times per day, for a total of nine days. Ingredients must be harvested during certain seasons, even certain months, and at certain times of day. Timing corresponding with the Wu Xing Five Phases, as provided in the correspondence tables in chapter 8, must be followed.

Then the Fu sigil is prepared, held to the practitioner's stomach as the practitioner wills himself to a state of death. He then rises from the bed, leaves his clothes behind on the bed, and exits the vicinity. The instructions are very clear that he must change his name and never return. Meanwhile, others who enter his room will see his corpse where he had left his clothes. They will pronounce him dead, but in a short matter of time, his apparent corpse, too, will disappear.

The eighty-one pills are crafted through outer alchemy.[37] Procedure, methodology, and rituals are precise and detailed. One example is to slay a cow in mid-March and use its fat in the alchemical process. Other ingredients include mercury, tin, silver, and other metals that must be stored and

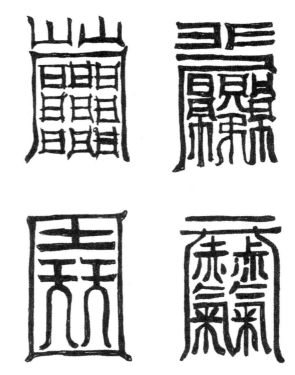

Figure 2.5. Four Fu sigils from the Ling Bao scriptures

processed on a remote mountaintop, using copper vessels and mixed with the cow fat under stringent, specific methodologies. An herb referred to in the West as Solomon's seal (黃精, huáng jīng) is also used.

The Ling Bao Fu pictured in figure 2.4 also illustrates a technique often utilized in craft: the repetition of significant Chinese characters. Note that along the left column of the Fu, there are two characters, each repeated three times. The top character is "illness" (病, bìng). The lower character is "die" or "death" (死, sǐ). Repetitions of characters for emphasis can also be seen in figure 2.5 and also in figure 4.26 below.

Figure 2.5 shows four more Fu sigils from the Ling Bao tradition, copied from third- and fourth-century Ling Bao scriptures.[38] They are medical Fu for the treatment of illnesses and health concerns, according to the principles of traditional Chinese medicine. The two Fu sigils at right, for instance, treat yang imbalances and are intended to control hot or dry ailments, meaning canker sores, nosebleeds, or constipation.

## Order of the Five Talismans from the Ling Bao

The five Fu talismans pictured in figures 2.6 to 2.10 are from the Ling Bao lineage (靈寶派), an esoteric Taoist faction traced back to the Jin Dynasty, around AD 400. The Ling Bao is covered earlier in this chapter. The talismans are sourced from scriptures of that lineage, the *Ling Bao Order of the Five Talismans* (靈寶五符序, Líng Bǎo Wǔ Fú Xù).[39] The date of the document is not known for certain, but it is believed to have been first discovered between AD 300 and 500.[40]

The *Order of the Five Talismans* describes five lords (帝, Dì)[41] who oversee the five relative directions, which are superimposed over the Wu Xing five phases. They are the Lords of the East, South, Center, West, and North and might be likened to the concept of the Five Emperors mentioned earlier in chapter 1. These talismans are used to guard against the dangers of external environmental elements, and are part of an occult practice known as outer alchemy.[42]

Figure 2.6 is the sigil for invoking protection from the Lord of the East, who commands Wood. Thus, the sigil and its corresponding charging method are utilized to protect a wearer from external environmental perils relating to Wood, such as the dangers and wild animals that might be lurking in a forest. Also, when traveling in the East, the Fu invoking the Lord of the East is used for safety and protection.

Figure 2.7 is the sigil for invoking protection from the Lord of the South, who commands Fire. Such a Fu might be used to protect against heat stroke or desert terrain. Also, when traveling in the South, the Fu invoking the Lord of the South is used for safety and protection.

Figure 2.8 is the sigil for invoking protection from the Lord of the Center, who commands Earth. It can be used to protect the wearer against the perils and wild animals that might be confronted on a mountain or environmental dangers relating to Earth. Also, when traveling across central China, the Fu invoking the Lord of the Center is used for safety and protection.

Figure 2.9 is the sigil for invoking protection from the Lord of the West, who commands Metal. Such a Fu might be used to render the wearer "blade-proof," a magical theory in Taoist craft.[43] Thus, the Fu for raising Metal is used to protect and defend against perils relating to Metal. Also, when traveling in the West, the Fu invoking the Lord of the West is used for safety and protection.

Figure 2.10 is the sigil for invoking protection from the Lord of the North, who commands Water. The Fu is used to protect the wearer against drowning or perils relating to Water. Also, when traveling in the North, the Fu invoking the Lord of the North is used for safety and protection.

Figure 2.6. Fu for Lord of the East, commanding Wood

Figure 2.7. Fu for Lord of the South, commanding Fire

Figure 2.8. Fu for Lord of the Center, commanding Earth

Figure 2.9. Fu for Lord of the West, commanding Metal

Figure 2.10. Fu for Lord of the North, commanding Water

Following the Jin Dynasty and into the Tang Dynasty (AD 618–906), the Zheng Yi lineage (正一道) arose.[44] Like the Ling Bao, the Zheng Yi was a lineage steeped in ritual and ceremonial arts. At this time, practitioners or priests from the Zheng Yi lineage also commercialized Fu sigils and began selling them as spells. To safeguard the practice, they instituted the Lu (錄), which became the recognized or orthodox registry of Taoist deities, spirits, and entities, as well as the methodologies for invoking or summoning them.[45] The Lu was in essence an agreed-upon roster of spirit profiles, a log book of all the spirit entities that can be invoked or summoned in orthodox Taoist tradition, typically consisting of demons, along with the precise methodology, the exact Fu design to craft, and descriptions of what these spirit entities looked like and their primary functions.[46] A practitioner's prestige was measured by how much of the Lu he or she had mastered.

From the Tang Dynasty onward, myriad lineages and magical traditions sourced from esoteric Taoism arose, some split from the historically established factions and new ones that blended regional folk religions, Buddhism, and Confucianism.[47] Some practiced the art of summoning, then imprisoning ghosts and other supernatural entities, which were then ordered to carry forth the practitioner's bidding. Others focused inward, on mental cultivation and seeking wisdom. Many were on the inner alchemical quest for immortality.[48]

During the Song Dynasty, the magical practice of Thunder Rites arose. The first traditions in Thunder Rites venerated Lei Gong, the God of Thunder.[49] Thunder magic, also called the Thunder Rites (雷法, Léi Fǎ), was considered one of the highest forms of magical cultivation, whereby a practitioner absorbs the energies of thunder into himself or herself to empower personal Qi with the Qi from thunder.[50] It was more commonly practiced in the southern regions of China.[51] Defining Thunder Rites as a unified tradition is impossible, however. As of AD 1216, there were records of over thirty-six different traditions and notable lineages in the Thunder Rites.[52] Rivalries among the different lineages gave rise to a competitive setting, with each lineage claiming to be the correct, or most authentic, or most powerful practitioners of thunder magic.[53]

The Taoist Canons provides ample references to Thunder Rites, instructing on crafting amulets, Fu talismans, and performing spells in the thunder magic tradition.[54] Shen Hsiao Tao (神宵道) and Tian Xing Zheng Fa (天心正法) are two lineages that specialized in thunder magic.[55] Taoist practitioners from any tradition or lineage will likely have studied thunder magic at some point. It is not limited to specific traditions, but rather has become a general form of magic within the broader category of esoteric Taoism.

Two general modes of thunder magic are practiced: one where the practitioner invokes a deity from the pantheon of deities, spirit generals and lords, angelic entities, or patron saints identified within thunder magic traditions; or by self-deification, where the practitioner deifies himself or herself, and through ritual alters the consciousness, entering a trancelike state and, in that moment, becomes the deity.[56] Within these two general modes are a plethora of specific methodologies that differ by lineage. In esoteric Taoism, thunder magic manifests as both a set tradition that certain orthodox lineages specialize in and also as an eclectic practice that individual practitioners will integrate into their craft.

Also in the Song Dynasty, the Tai Yi Tao lineage arose in AD 1138, founded by Hsiao Pao-Chen. Hsiao became known for crafting powerful Fu sigils. The Tai Yi Tao practiced healing magic, reconciled Taoist and Confucian philosophy, and incorporated Buddhism into their tradition.[57] Not much is documented or known about the Tai Yi Tao lineage, except that it was most likely merged with the Zheng Yi lineage since both shared similar beliefs.

Around 1142 came the Zhen Da Tao lineage, a tradition that adopted Buddhist principles of nonharm, compassion, and vegetarianism. Rather than practice magic or sorcery, the Zhen Da Tao lineage used prayer for healing and exorcisms.[58] The 1100s marked what some scholars refer to as a Chinese religious reformation, where emerging lineages diverged from the supernatural practices of prior lineages such as the Ling Bao or Zheng Yi traditions. Lineages such as the Zhen Da Tao, with other lineages such as the Quan Zhen (circa 1163), stressed moral and ethical cultivation.[59]

Today, many Taoist magical traditions thrive, especially in southern China, Taiwan, and Southeast Asia. Two of the more prominent are found in Taiwan: Black Hat (烏頭, Wū Tóu) and Red Hat (紅頭, Hóng Tóu) Taoists. The Black Hat lineage is an esoteric secret society that traces its traditions back to the Tang Dynasty (AD 618–907). Magical knowledge is passed down from father to son or master to disciple through the same liturgical rituals that have been used within the brotherhood since its founding.[60]

The Red Hat lineage is another esoteric secret society tracing its roots to the Song Dynasty (AD 960–1279), though since then it has been subdivided into smaller sects or schools.[61] Red Hat Taoists are typically mediums, not shamans, and there is a very clear distinction made between mediums and shamans. Mediums become possessed by spirit entities, and then such entities communicate to the human world or perform magic through the medium's body.[62] In other words, mediums don't "go" anywhere, and instead, spirit entities come to Earth through the medium. In contrast, shamans "leave" Earth and travel between worlds, entering the underworld, for instance, and communicate with entities residing in other realms to bring messages back to the human realm. Red Hat Taoist practitioners tend to be mediums.

Both Black Hat and Red Hat Taoist magical practitioners craft Fu sigils, though in the Red Hat lineage, sigils are often crafted through a form of Fu

Ji, or automatic writing, not through the Fu Wen or glyph crafting techniques taught in this book. Fu Ji (扶箕)[63] refers to spirit writing, and while spirit writing as a practice takes many forms, better known as a form of divination popularized during the Qing Dynasty,[64] as it is applied here for Fu sigil crafting, Fu Ji refers to the mode of spirit writing where a practitioner who is also a medium becomes possessed and through the medium's hand, a spirit renders the Fu sigil. Whereas Fu Wen is carefully designed and crafted by the practitioner, and then empowered through a charging ritual, Fu Ji flows out of the practitioner quickly and fluidly, often in one stroke or one full exhale. In Fu Wen the practitioner is the mastermind, an architect of destiny. In Fu Ji the handwriting is believed to come from the spirit entity, and the practitioner is not consciously involved in the writing.

## THE CULTURE OF FU SIGILS

Through the dynasties, the crafting of Fu sigils changed with the culture. The Fu descends from shamanic practices that predate Taoism, but in the first century AD it was merged into Taoism, and later, integrated Confucianism and Buddhism.[65] They are an important part of Chinese folk religions, which often integrate Taoism. These folk religions call upon a variety of deities, in the belief that each of the elements and forces of nature have a corresponding spirit, and each village or region may have its own supernatural guardians. All of these deities and spirits relate back to a singular god concept, which is often referred to as Heaven, the Heavenly Father (老天爺, Lǎo Tiān Yé), or the Emperor Up High (上帝, Shàng Dì).

Fu sigils are used to conjure spirits, banish spirits, invoke deities, or summon ghosts. They can perform mundane tasks, like attract fame, fortune, or love. If we define a spell as a combination of words, conduct, and objects that have been ritualized with the intent of manifesting a specific result, then a Taoist Fu sigil is a spell. For any purpose that a spell would be crafted, a Fu sigil can be rendered for that same purpose. It is used to protect, harm, cure, influence, create, destroy, and is used both offensively and defensively. The uninitiated mainstream would characterize Fu sigils as charms, either amulets or talismans.[66] The art of the Fu is in itself a complete world of spell-crafting.

According to legend, the mythic figure Cangjie (倉頡), who lived around

2650 BC, was the Yellow Emperor's imperial historian and the inventor of writing. Cangjie discovered writing by gazing at the footprints of birds. However, as soon as he invented writing, demons howled in fear. With the invention of writing, humans now wielded the power to control demons. The belief was that a practitioner could control a demon by knowing its name. Knowing the name was the same as knowing its true nature, and knowing its true nature meant knowing how to control the demon.[67] Thus, the early historic purpose of a Fu sigil was to control the unseen or supernatural world, and to control spirit entities, practitioners used writing. The Fu sigil was a written decree that allowed a practitioner to exert control over demons, spirits, and those from the underworld. On the more benevolent side, they also enabled practitioners to invoke or call upon deities and the Divine for help.

Covering the culture of Fu sigils requires, at minimum, a reference to exorcisms. Records from 316 BC note exorcisms of evil spirits by priests and priestesses on behalf of the imperial court,[68] a practice that was later absorbed into esoteric Taoist practices of the Han Dynasty, when Taoism thrived. Eleventh-century AD methods for exorcising demons included using written symbols or Fu for conjuring the dead, who would assist the Taoist practitioner with the exorcism. The ritual would include causing the demons to dispel and having them manifest as insects, which the practitioner would then trap inside a vase or container.[69] Even as craft is practiced today, references and symbols for insects are still found on Fu sigils crafted for exorcisms. Likewise, references to insects are used to implant a demon into a victim.

In Taoist practice, exorcisms were violent.[70] Fu sigils to such ends typically contained symbols for "murder" and "kill" (殺, shā), "slaughter" (宰, zǎi), or "destruction" (破, pò), to name only a few. Likewise, retaliatory craft or offensive Fu to infest one with demon possession would use characters such as "trample," "devastate," or "wreak havoc" (蹂, róu), as well as "kill" (殺, shā) and "slaughter" (宰, zǔi), "poison," or "infest with demon possession" (蠱, gǔ).[71] Note how that character (蠱) comprises three of the same radical, an etymological root for "insect" (虫, chóng). Figure 2.11 shows the Chinese ideogram for gu (蠱) during the Shang Dynasty (left), Zhou Dynasty (center), and as it is written today (right). Note how the medieval versions resemble insects within a vase or container.

Figure 2.11. Shang and Zhou Dynasty script for "poison" (courtesy of Richard Sears, ChineseEtymology.org)

Figure 2.12. Fu from the Tang Dynasty for dragon spirit conjuration

Under the folk religious beliefs of medieval China, and to a certain extent, even today, ills and suffering were characterized as demons possessing and thus poisoning an individual or space. To rid one of that poison, exorcise the demon. The professional in charge of such work was the Taoist priest or priestess. Viruses in the body causing illness or pains experienced in a physical body were also expressed as inner demons at work, and a Taoist practitioner, one skilled in the arts of healing, would be called in to exorcise the demon poison (蠱, gǔ) to heal the sickness.

Even today, in spite of scientific advancements, when a medical doctor is not able to diagnose a problem, a witch doctor is called in, typically one practiced in esoteric Taoist arts, and an exorcism is prescribed. The Fu and the rituals for empowering the Fu were and are still the ways of the practitioner to exorcise demons. Like pills that a medical doctor would prescribe, the witch doctor draws a Fu sigil, burns it to ashes, and has the patient swallow the Fu's ashes for healing.

Figure 2.12 is a Fu sigil from a Book of Methods dated around AD 800–900 during the Tang Dynasty.[72] While a few of the characters are recognizable, such as "fire," "sun," and "mountain," among others, much of it is illegible to the uninitiated. That seemingly illegible and coded writing style is used by Taoist practitioners to communicate with the supernatural world. It's a highly stylized form of Chinese calligraphy and intended to be indecipherable to lay readers. It was a special (magical) form of writing called Fu Wen (符文), integrated with Taoist symbols. In some lineages, the Fu Wen is referred to as Celestial Calligraphy, or Thunder Writing, which, like Fu Wen, is indecipherable scripts that are based loosely on actual Chinese characters.[73] In this book, Fu Wen will be referred to as "stylized glyphs" for corresponding Chinese characters.

Figure 2.13. Gu Dao Fu, for retaliatory magic[74]

Likewise, figure 2.13 shows some decipherable and some indecipherable Fu Wen. The characters for "swallow poison" (吞毒) are stylized near the top, and within the radical for "mouth" (口), there is a decipherable character for "magical poison" (蠱), a form of magic called Gu Dao, a craft that harnesses destructive energy to, in effect, poison others with malignant energies ("magical poison," 蠱). Fu Wen for "magical poison" (蠱) repeats throughout the Fu, along with the character for "multiply" (乘). At the base of the Fu is Fu Wen for "black" (黑), summoning yin energy, and a stylized glyph for "ghost" (鬼). Note also the inclusion of hexagram 18 from the I Ching, 蠱, to harness the energy of decay, rot, and deterioration.

Figure 2.14 is an example of designing Fu Wen for the Chinese character "thunder." Fu Wen for thunder is often found on sigils in reference to Taoist Thunder Rites (雷法, Léi Fǎ).[75] The illustration of the traditional Chinese character for "thunder" (雷) is on the left, and the other two images are two different stylized glyphs of "thunder." In Fu sigil crafting, the power of thunder is believed to be channeled into the sigil and thus the effect of the sigil emulates the power and swiftness of thunder.

Figure 2.14. Glyphs for "thunder" stylized into Fu Wen

Figure 2.15. Fu sigils etched on bronze, for prosperity and wealth[77]

Fu Wen is the synthesis of the magical power that the written word is believed to hold and the magical personal power of the practitioner who stylizes the writing. Fu Ji, in contrast, is a form of Taoist automatic writing that certain lineages of Taoist magic practitioners use in crafting Fu sigils. With automatic writing, the script is channeled through the practitioner and is generally illegible. This text will focus on Fu Wen.

The Fu paper sigil is most commonly found on paper that is rectangular and longer in length than width, though Fu sigils have also been found on metal amulets meant to be worn. Before the Han Dynasty, Fu were made out of bamboo or jade tablets.[76]

Variations of Fu sigils can be found across East Asia. In Japan, they are most frequently seen in the form of *ofuda* and *omamori*.[78] The ofuda is essentially a calling card in the form of a Fu sigil used to summon benevolent spirits into a household to protect that household. Ofuda are essentially the same as Fu sigils, but describe Fu sigils that are posted at a front entrance, gate, on a family altar, or placed around the home to safeguard its occupants. Omamori, popularly distributed by Buddhist temples and Shinto shrines, are also Fu sigils, typically made of paper or cloth, inscribed with a deity name or an invocation. An omamori is placed in a silk pouch or rolled into a scroll and placed inside a tube. The pouch or tube is then carried on the person to help manifest a particular intention. Ofuda and omamori are heavily influenced by traditional Taoist Fu sigil crafting. In Japanese culture, an ofuda is believed to be more powerful than an omamori, and usually costs more than an omamori.[79]

Like many magical traditions with no confirmed origin, the craft of Fu sigils is steeped in mystery. Knowledge of how to craft a Fu sigil is withheld from the public.[80] The common public opinion holds that only a Taoist priest, a Tao Shi (道士),[81] can craft Fu sigils,[82] and these Taoist priests must be claimed by a specific orthodox Taoist magical lineage, with each lineage having its own direct channel to the supernatural.

As noted earlier, the Lu (錄, Lù)[83] was a registry of Fu sigil crafting knowledge first established by the Zheng Yi lineage, which represented the only and orthodox summoning methodologies of Taoist spirits.[84] The Lu was a practitioner's credibility.[85] It was espoused that a Tao Shi's abilities were determined by the abilities he or she could demonstrate regarding the identification of deities or supernatural spirits from the Lu, the magical registry of spirits as known to the Taoist priest collective. Magic, sorcery, and summonings not established in the widely recognized Lu were not credited as authorized Taoist magic. Even today, that notion of exclusivity is disseminated to prevent individuals from dabbling with metaphysical energy in careless, negligent, possibly even dangerous ways. However, today there is no collectively accepted Lu. Priesthood, lineages, and Taoist craft such as Fu sigils are self-regulated.

Taoist practitioners and most of the Chinese folk religions that practice Fu sigil crafting believe in deities, a spirit world, and the supernatural. Every Fu traditionally called upon a spirit entity. Shen Fu (神符) is the act of invoking deities or summoning supernatural spirits by way of sigil crafting. Practitioners generally believed that spells were rendered effective only when accompanied by Shen Fu, where spirits were identified and invoked or summoned.

The ability to call upon spirits stems from either spiritual practice or training, or it can be bestowed from master to student, which is what most Taoist lineages

Figure 2.16. Fu sigil invoking
Celestial Master Zhang, the
deified Zhang Dao Ling
(eighteenth-century Book of
Methods)

believe. The celestial masters of a particular lineage will bestow their students with the gift of energetic workings in the traditions of that lineage. Figure 2.16 is an undated Fu believed to originate from an eighteenth-century Book of Methods called the *Talismans of the Celestial Master Zhang*.[86] It invokes Celestial Master Zhang, the deified version of Zhang Dao Ling after he transcended to immortality. When crafted by those who adhere to the Tian Shi traditions (the lineage founded by Zhang Dao Ling, its first celestial master), Celestial Master Zhang can be called upon to assist with a practitioner's magical craft.

The Fu pictured in figure 2.16 is crafted for exorcisms, or Shou Yao (收妖, shōu yāo), an occult practice by which a Taoist priest or practitioner extracts a demon that has possessed a human body. To empower the sigil, after the practitioner has drawn the Fu on paper, she must click her teeth three times,[87] swallow consecrated water, and spit the water eastward, then proceed with the repeated recitation of invocations as inscribed in the text.

Returning to Taoism as philosophy, a philosophy that explains cosmogenesis, a practitioner can retrace the origins, flow, and metaphysical laws of Qi energy. Rather than ingest the craft through lineages, the craft can be understood by understanding its source, and the theory of craft. When there is understanding of the theory of craft, the Fu sigil empowered by a Taoist priest from an orthodox lineage is no different from the Fu sigil crafted by you, so long as you have effectively empowered the sigil through understanding the theory and principles of craft.

Fu sigil crafting varies from Taoist tradition to tradition. Taoist magical practice consists of countless factions. These factions are religious sects that might agree on overarching general beliefs, but differ greatly on the details.

Yet there are a few commonalities these factions share about Fu sigil crafting. Fu sigils are most often crafted on strips of paper and written in ink, though they can also be carved into more permanent media like bronze coins or stone tablets. This book focuses on sigil crafting with paper.

Also, rituals are generally required to empower Fu sigils. These rituals include consecration, blessings, charging, and activation techniques. The precise method of ritual varies from tradition to tradition. A ritual can be a simple utterance of a few syllables or elaborate ceremonies that involve a large cast of magical tools. Most Fu sigils are a combination of Chinese characters, ideograms, and recognizable Taoist symbolism, though some Fu feature legible Chinese writing, while others are intended to be incoherent magical script that no one but the practitioner can read. Most also agree that for a Fu sigil to become empowered, it must be activated. Again, activation varies from tradition to tradition. It can be activated by being worn on the person, or it must be burned and the ashes imbibed with a goblet of liquor.

Like Western magical practices that invoke Latin for incantations but use Latin phrases in ways that may not make literal sense, so too do Taoist magical practices invoke Chinese characters for incantations. The phrases may not make literal sense to someone who is not schooled in the linguistic assignment of the phrases, but the magical practitioner will know the spiritual values assigned to the characters, and thus the phrases are coherent on a spiritual plane.[88] This book will offer historic examples of such magical incantations.

Contemporary scholars tend to view Fu talismans and the folk magic practiced by esoteric Taoists as "treating mental disturbance in a culturally appropriate way."[89] Depression, insomnia, pessimism, physical ailments, lethargy, apathy, ennui, and failures in life are explained as disturbances from the spirit world. This absolves the individual from feeling personal responsibility, and also encourages an optimistic outlook by sending that individual off with a talisman, a no-fuss antidote, one promised to cure all ailments. If nothing more, the placebo effect by itself cures the individual of the ailments.[90]

Esoteric Taoism and the practice of Fu sigil crafting has often been marginalized by both Eastern and Western scholars. Liang Qichao (AD 1873–1929), a renowned scholar, academic, and journalist of the Qing Dynasty (1644–1912), summarized the prevailing modern Chinese sentiment of esoteric Taoism:

"Taoism is the only religion indigenous to China … but to include it in a Chinese history of religion is indeed a great humiliation. Their activities have not benefited the nation at all. Moreover, down through the centuries, they have repeatedly misled the people by their pagan magic."[91]

Taoism declined in the Qing Dynasty. When the imperial library was constructed in the eighteenth century, Taoist books were intentionally excluded.[92] By the twentieth century, Taoism had become so shunned that only one complete copy of the Tao Zang remained.[93] Throughout the twentieth century, the heritage of Taoism sustained nationwide destruction. By the 1950s, science and modernity were celebrated, and Taoism was seen as the antithesis of rationalism and progress.[94] It was not until after 1979 that Taoism experienced a slight revival, though even today, esoteric Taoism is viewed negatively in the mainstream as superstition and witchcraft.

Moreover, fraud is a serious concern. Individuals purporting to be Taoist priests or priestesses manipulate innocent consumers into believing that they are possessed by demons or plagued by curses and prey on them. Small fortunes are swindled in exchange for Fu talismans that allege miraculous cures. Recent exposés on these fraudulent schemes have left the masses—and rightfully so—skeptical of Fu craft. Even ordainment into Taoist priesthood is up for sale these days. Organizations purporting to be Taoist lineages led by charismatic charlatans are selling priesthood. For an agreed-upon monetary exchange, anyone can become a powerful Taoist sorcerer. As a result, public stigma has been cast over the practice of esoteric Taoist craft. It would be remiss to discuss the culture of Fu talismans and not also mention the condescension that the practice has drawn.

## The Cultural Practice of Shou Jing

The Fu pictured in figure 2.17 highlights a traditional practice found in Taiwan and other parts of East Asia: Shou Jing (收驚, Shōu Jīng), a form of faith healing or exorcism performed on small children using a Fu. It was believed that when a child experienced a significant fright or shock, and then proceeded to behave erratically, a malignant spirit possession was taking place. To restore the child to his or her senses and remove the erratic behavior, the child was taken to a Taoist priest or priestess for a Shou Jing. Think of it as medieval child behavior control.

In the traditional practice of Shou Jing, a witch or witch doctor would craft a Fu sigil coded to exorcise the spirits or demons, like the one pictured in figure 2.17. The purpose of the Fu would be to draw out or "harvest" the shock from the child's body. The shock was believed to be a symptom of demon activity that had overtaken the child's senses. By drawing those demons out of the body, the child would be restored to normal, obedient behavior.

To perform the ritual, the crafted Fu sigil would be placed on the child's body while the priest or witch recited invocations. Specificities of the ritual for exorcising the demons vary from practitioner to practitioner of Shou Jing, but generally it will involve the laying of hands on the child and indecipherable utterances that sound like the practitioner is speaking in tongues. In my anecdotal observations, the laying of hands in Shou Jing is similar to the Judeo-Christian practice of hand laying.

The "laying on of hands" in the Judeo-Christian tradition is a practice of faith healing where the Holy Spirit is invoked and a practitioner lays his or her hands on the recipient for healing. In the Biblical practice of hand laying, citing Leviticus 16:21–22,[95] sin or guilt would be drawn out of one person by way of hand laying and transferred onto a goat, who would absorb that sin or guilt.[96] Then the goat would be set off into the wilderness, bearing the person's sin. Thus, by way of the ritual, the person's sin or guilt would be absolved.[97] In contemporary practices, a priest or practitioner would invoke the Holy Spirit and use the hands as the medium by which the Holy Spirit draws out the illness, pain, guilt, or problem from the subject.

In the practice of Shou Jing, instead of using a goat, the child's sins, miscon-

Figure 2.17. Fu sigil for Shou Jing

duct, and unruly behavior would be drawn out of the child by a Fu sigil. The child's behavior gets anthropomorphized as mischievous spirits or demons that have nestled inside the child's body. It is the mischief of spirits and demons causing the child's behavior, and therefore not the child's fault per se. If you watch the ritual of a Shou Jing, it looks uncannily similar to the modern day evangelical Christian practice of hand laying, with the addition of the Fu sigil. Although Shou Jing itself is a medieval practice, like Judeo-Christian hand laying, it is a form of faith healing that still takes place today, particularly in the rural regions of China and Chinese diasporas.

Figure 2.18. Taoist magician Lo Gongyuan arising from an inkstone. By Yashima Gakutei, circa 1827, woodblock print: ink and color on paper (New York Metropolitan Museum of Art)

# CHAPTER 3

# CLASSICS OF THE ESOTERIC TALISMAN

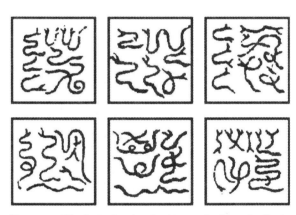

Figure 3.1. Glyphs in the cloud writing style, from the Taoist Canons

**TO CRAFT EFFECTIVE** Fu sigils, the practitioner must understand the guiding esoteric principles behind the craft. This chapter will provide a broad overview of the classical Taoist texts on Fu sigil crafting. However, the focus will be on the *Huang Di Yin Fu Ching* (黃帝陰符經, *Huáng Dì Yīn Fú Jīng*), *The Yellow Emperor's Classics of the Esoteric Talisman*.[1]

Around AD 302, a gravesite was erected just outside Luoyang, China, with a stone burial slab identifying Bo He, a legendary immortal and sage. According to myth, he was a human who transcended and attained great magical power. Bo He was believed to be the first to receive talismanic scriptures from the Divine, which brought the teachings of the Fu sigil craft.[2] Bo He was later referenced in the *Bao Puzi*.

The *Bao Puzi* (抱樸子, *Bào Pǔ Zi*),[3] *Book of the Master of Simplicity,* was written during the Jin Dynasty, circa AD 317–318. The text was authored by Ge Hong (283–343)[4], a well-known Taoist alchemist and metaphysician.[5] *Bao*

Figure 3.2. Ge Hong's Entrance through the Mountains Fu sigils[6]

Figure 3.3. Glyphs in the cloud writing style, from the *Three Caverns*

*Puzi* is subdivided between Outer and Inner Chapters. The Outer Chapters address social order, politics, and philosophy, or exoteric Taoism. The Inner Chapters address alchemy, demonology, and magic, or esoteric Taoism. Fu sigil crafting and images of sample Fu are in the Inner Chapters.

The five Entrance through the Mountains Fu sigils in figure 3.2 are attributed to Ge Hong. They are a form of travel protection magic. An alchemist traversing China's Five Sacred Mountains[7] would carry these five talismans for protection, one corresponding to each of the Five Sacred Mountains.

Likewise, a text titled *San Dong Shen Fu Ji* (三洞神符纪 , *Sān Dòng Shén Fú Jì*),[8] *Three Caverns of the Supernatural Fu Talismanic Records,* is dated about AD 400. The *Three Caverns* is part of the Tao Zang (道藏, *Dào Zàng*)[9] or Taoist Canons, a collection of arcane texts on Taoism. The *Three Caverns* includes a chapter titled "Shen Fu Lei" (神符類, Shén Fú Lèi), or "Types of Supernatural Fu Talismans."[10] The chapter explains a form of talismanic script called "cloud writing." The text notes that a practitioner's magical writing, or Fu Wen, should resemble the "condensation of clouds."

The *Three Caverns* further explains sigils as metaphors. By invoking a metaphor, a practitioner can cause an event to take place. For instance, according to the *Three Caverns* text, a spell might be, "Nine dragons launch a fire pearl. The dark tortoise is set on fire, and surrenders the golden lotus." A Fu sigil consists of a combination of glyphs like the ones pictured in figure 3.3. In the nine dragons spell, for instance, the number nine would hold numerological significance, calling upon Heaven's influence. The animals called upon are also symbolic. There are also references to the Wu Xing five phases being invoked. Appendix F provides a sampling of the talismans illustrated in *Three Caverns.*

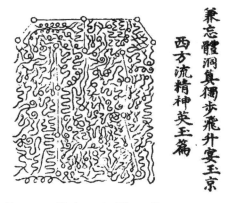

Figure 3.4. Fu from the *Three Caverns*

Altogether, the combination of glyphs creates a coded ideogram that expresses a spell. See figure 3.4 for what a resulting Fu would look like.[11] The Fu sigil in figure 3.4, in the cloud writing style, is made up of the glyphs seen earlier in figure 3.3.

Around AD 437, the *San Huang Wen,* the *Writ of the Three Sovereigns,* surfaced. The *Writ of the Three Sovereigns* discusses the craft of Fu sigils at length, instructing about it as a practice for invoking deities, summoning spirits, protection, and healing.[12] The *Writ of the Three Sovereigns* is believed to memorialize some of Bo He's oral teachings about Fu sigil crafting.[13]

While the *Three Caverns* and *Writ of the Three Sovereigns* offer instruction on crafting Fu sigils, the art of Fu sigil crafting itself is grounded in the metaphysical principles found in the *Huang Di Yin Fu Ching,* known in English as the *Yellow Emperor's Classics of the Esoteric Talisman.* This chapter is based on my interpretations of that text and how it applies to the approach a Western practitioner might take to crafting Fu sigils.

The *Classics of the Esoteric Talisman* is believed to date to the Zhou Dynasty (1046–256 BC), though to be clear, that remains a scholarly speculation. The first recorded documentation of the text surfaced around the Tang Dynasty (AD 618–907), whereas its Zhou Dynasty origin is apocryphal.

The principles found in the *Classics of the Esoteric Talisman* guide Fu sigil crafting. Thus, I contend that the practitioner need not be ordained into any given lineage or tradition. Instead, the practitioner needs to return to the source of the craft itself, such as the *Classics of the Esoteric Talisman*. There are two versions of the text, one shorter and one longer, and which is older and the sources of each are not known. This chapter will be based on my interpretations of the longer version.

It is dense reading material, but for a lay practitioner to craft powerful Fu sigils, he or she will want to understand the tenets of this text. I will try to summarize the salient points of the text as I have interpreted them, and attempt to do so in plain English. Keep in mind that these are my interpretations of the arcane text, and not every Taoist or scholar will agree with how I have expressed *Classics of the Esoteric Talisman*.

## 1. Align yourself with Heaven (or the Divine; Tao).

One interpretation of this point is alignment with a deity or deities that are representative of Heaven, or of the Divine. Most lineages of Taoist magical practice align with a particular deity to venerate and call upon in all energetic workings. That would be the alignment that such practitioners seek.

Another interpretation is alignment with the Tao, with a cosmic Qi energy that represents the whole of the universe. That Qi is further expressed as yin and yang, and so there are also lineages that affiliate with two deities, one female and one male, as the anthropomorphized representations of yin and yang.

Whether you characterize the alignment as one with deity or deities or the Tao, or simply an alignment with a higher consciousness, that sense of greater alignment is imperative to craft.

## 2. All manifestations in the universe can be generated by the practitioner's physical body, through the hand. The function is determined by the will of the practitioner. The mechanics are determined by the practitioner's mind.

I interpret the essence here to suggest that magic and magicians exist.[14]

The practitioner can harness or call upon any manifestation or energy in the universe around him or her through the channel of the physical body, and the most powerful channel is through the practitioner's hand. Thus, most Taoist rituals incorporate hand mudras, which will be covered in chapter 6.

How? The action, activities, ceremonies, and the purpose of craft is determined by the practitioner's will. The practitioner decides. As for the theoretical and practical application of magic to harness or call upon the manifestations and energies of the universe, the practitioner does so through the mind. Intent is everything.

## 3. Before every event, there are opportunities that Heaven presents to the practitioner to exercise triggering mechanisms that can then transform the path of nature or fate.

Basically, the text acknowledges free will, which is fascinating, given the fatalism that many Chinese seem to subscribe to.

Here, the text is saying that prior to the occurrence of any event, the practitioner has a window of opportunity to affect the outcome and transform that event. How? Through triggering mechanisms, of course. What are triggering mechanisms? I interpret it as meaning spells, Fu sigil crafting, or energetic workings.

Note that the concept referred to as "triggering mechanisms" throughout these points can also be understood as "spells," "craft," or "energetic workings."

## 4. Man can take from Heaven and Earth for personal enrichment and for exercising triggering mechanisms, but this taking is only permissible if the timing is proper and the triggering mechanisms are peaceful.

"Man" refers to the individual human; Heaven is the Divine or Tao, meaning Qi energy; Earth is the physical nature or environment around Man. The ontology is based on the Chinese cosmological principle of Heaven, Earth, and Man. Heaven is fate, but it is also that which the layperson cannot seem to control. Earth is the layperson's environmental surroundings and social setting. Man is the individual.

To me, this point is interesting because of the way it seems to suspend moral judgment. The point here is that Man, or the practitioner, can pull metaphysical energy from either Heaven or Earth for the practitioner's own ends. *Can,* yes, meaning it is doable, but is it permissible? According to the text, it is only permissible if the "timing is proper"[15] and the craft is "peaceful."[16] Those are the two conditions the practitioner must adhere to if he or she intends to take energy from Heaven or Earth.

## 5. Man takes from Heaven and Earth through the Wu Xing: Wood, Fire, Earth, Metal, and Water.

Assuming the practitioner takes energy from Heaven or Earth in a way where the "timing is proper" and the craft is "peaceful," as discussed above in point 4, the next foreseeable question is how. Here, the text notes that the practitioner does so by harnessing the chemistry of the five phases, or Wu Xing, as described in chapter 1. The practitioner must understand how Wu Xing works, which can be likened to understanding elemental dignities in Western esotericism.

## 6. Man's spirit is awake when Man is spiritual. Man's spirit is not awake when the spirit does not know itself to be spiritual.

To transcend beyond a layperson and thus be empowered to craft Fu sigils, a practitioner has to be spiritual. When the practitioner is spiritual, then the practitioner's spirit will be awake. Without that awakening, a practitioner won't be effectively positioned for energetic workings such as sigil crafting.

Per Eastern esotericism, Man becomes spiritual through four practices: (1) meditation, (2) cultivation of the body, (3) sacred rituals, and (4) the sacred arts. Meditation teaches the practitioner how to be aware of consciousness. It is a form of self-regulation for the mind. Cultivation is a form of self-regulation for the body. Practices such as qi gong, tai chi, and martial arts are a few examples of Taoist cultivation. Cultivation is about attentiveness to the body and learning to bring your mind and body into harmony. Sacred rituals raise the practitioner's awareness of other realms beyond the physical plane that his or her body occupies. Sacred rituals bring together meditation and cultivation and enable a practitioner to transcend both consciousness and body. The sacred arts include Fu sigil crafting, feng shui, divination, and the application of mystical knowledge.

## 7. The sun, moon, and stars relate to the numbers (numerology), and knowing this can transform the path of nature through triggering mechanisms.

For Chinese shamans, numerology has always been an integral expression of the universe, a practice that predates the invention of writing and language.[17]

Through numbers, a practitioner can understand the flow of Qi. That is why for most Eastern esoteric traditions, the Lo Shu square is fundamental to their form of craft. Likewise, a practitioner is proficient in astrology. For practitioners of Eastern traditions, that astrological study includes the Big Dipper, other constellations, the moon phases, and the Chinese zodiac.

The notion that a life path is influenced by the movements of celestial bodies and the spiral dance of the numbers touches upon a concept also found in Western occult traditions: "As above, so below."[18] Thus, to exercise triggering mechanisms, or practice effective craft, the practitioner must first understand astrology, numerology, how both relate to one another, and how both relate to any specific individual. Such knowledge will be crucial in the practitioner's craft of Fu sigils.

**8. When you don't use your eyes, you can hear what you couldn't hear before. When you don't use your ears, you can see what you couldn't see before. That is how your body masters your mind. Then your mind can learn to use your eyes and ears to affect triggering mechanisms.**

This point seems to be counsel on the logistics of ritual. To enable yourself to metaphysical sight, you must first learn how to shut out your physical sight. To hear what needs to be heard on the metaphysical plane of sound, shut your ears to physical sounds. One way to cultivate such mindfulness is through meditation. Thus, to follow this point, consider regular training by way of meditation.

**9. Heaven holds no special favors for any practitioner, and yet great favor from Heaven can be generated through the practitioner's mind (ego, self; personal will).[19]**

I have always maintained that the most powerful practitioners of craft must have large egos. This point seems to echo that sentiment. A large ego is the fuel that runs the engine of personal will. The stronger the self is here, the greater the practitioner's ability to take from Heaven and Earth and exercise triggering mechanisms, as noted in previous points.

No single practitioner is "chosen," is "The One," or is any more special than anyone else, objectively speaking. "Heaven holds no special favors for any practitioner." That being said, a practitioner can generate favor through the power of his or her mind. Intent is everything, a point that is emphasized again here. Beyond intent, the practitioner must be so fully convinced of his or her powers and abilities as a practitioner of craft that there is no shred of doubt in the practitioner's mind that the outcome of the craft will be exactly as the practitioner willed it to be.

**10. Magic is not sacred. Magic is philosophy. To understand magic, don't try to understand Heaven and Earth. Instead, try to understand the changing seasons and four directions.**[20]

The concept of magic, or triggering mechanisms, or craft is not supernatural. It is natural. It is tapping into the metaphysical dimension of the physical world. It is an understanding of how to best utilize that window of opportunity before any given event occurs. Since magic is natural, it operates by the same laws that physical nature abides by, and so to understand metaphysics, you have to understand physics. To raise energy for magic, do not look to the so-called supernatural. Instead, look to the natural world around you, the seasons, solstices and equinoxes, the four cardinal directions, and geomancy.[21] More than that, understand change. The successful practitioner understands the philosophy of change. Magic is neither Heaven nor Earth; it is change.

**11. Yin and yang push each other. Through the concord and discord between yin and yang, the practitioner can manifest transformations in the path of nature (or fate).**

"The Tao gave birth to one; one gave birth to two; two gave birth to three; three gave birth to the immeasurable."[22] That line from the Tao Te Ching is a cornerstone tenet of Taoism. The one arising from Tao is Qi.[23] From Qi comes the binary of yin and yang. The push and pull of yin with yang, how the two energies interact, will yield three, which is the cosmic trinity, the Three Pure Ones if expressed in deity form, or the trinity of Heaven, Earth, and Man. From that three, the rest of the universe arose. For effective Fu sigil crafting, the practitioner must first understand the relationship between yin and yang and use that in his or her triggering mechanisms, or craft.

**12. From the singularity that is Qi, eight phenomena are born, which are the eight trigrams of the Ba Gua.**

Now we get into the Ba Gua, the eight trigrams of the I Ching, which in Taoist cosmology represent the eight fundamental dynamic processes that form life. See appendix E for a nutshell summary of the Ba Gua.

## 13. The practitioner understands that spirits move through triggering mechanisms of yang, while ghosts move through triggering mechanisms of yin.

The final point I will cover is on summoning. Spirits, saints, immortals, angels, or metaphysical energies of the light, the more creative or constructive, are summoned by the practitioner through triggering mechanisms—or rituals and practices—that call upon yang energy, the light. Ghosts, hungry ghosts, the deceased, demons, energies of the dark, the more destructive, are summoned by the practitioner through rituals and practices that call upon yin energy, the dark.[24]

Figure 3.5. Defensive Fu sigil for neutralizing Gu Dao poison magic

My approach to Fu sigil crafting as set forth in this text is grounded on the foregoing principles from the *Classics of the Esoteric Talisman*. The serious Western practitioner of Fu sigil crafting will consider obtaining a translation

Figure 3.6. Inscription of the 10th-century Huang Di Yin Fu Jing (courtesy of Special Collections, Fine Arts Library, Harvard University)

of that text and read it for him- or herself to gain direct insights of the text's wisdom and instruction.[25] Nonetheless, I hope this chapter provides a few simple yet profound basics to work from.

# CHAPTER 4

# ANATOMY OF A FU SIGIL

**HISTORICALLY, DURING A** disciple's initiatory process into a magical lineage, the disciple would learn, copy, and memorize Fu sigils from a teacher or master within the lineage,[1] or it was transmitted from parent to child, where the meanings and explanations behind a sigil were kept secret within the lineage or family. During the Jin and Han dynasties, esoteric Taoism was practiced mainly by the aristocratic elite, and strong emphasis was placed on pedigree.[2]

However, this book teaches Fu sigil crafting outside any established tradition with the purpose of guiding a Western practitioner through creative and original conception of Fu sigils. While learning, copying, and memorizing set Fu makes sense when a practitioner is initiated into a lineage, it does not make sense when crafting Fu outside a lineage. It is also not my place to divulge the confidential and proprietary craft of the lineages.

Thus, this book will teach the practitioner how to craft his or her own Fu. There will be no copying of existing sigils, and therefore this text must begin with the structural anatomy of a Fu sigil, and from there, you, the practitioner, will be able to design your own secret language, codes, symbolism, and magical formulas.

This chapter is based on my examination and study of sigils crafted by dozens of magical lineages throughout the ages, from the Fu set forth in historic Taoist texts to the Fu crafted in modern times. From such study, I have concluded that you cannot reach a conclusion about what Fu sigils are like. They run the full gamut of styles. As soon as one generalization is made about what a Fu sigil is or is not, substantial Fu sigil designs negating that generalization can be found. There are too many exceptions to every purported rule to purport any rules.

Figure 4.1. Purification Fu from the Taoist Canons

Some include legible Chinese script; most are illegible. Some include hand-rendered drawings. Others feature diagrams of the constellations or I Ching hexagrams. Fu sigils can be a single stroke of a calligraphy brush, curving and meandering from the top all the way down to the bottom of a piece of paper. Or it can look like a series of ideograms that have been boxed into individual cells, which I will call cell sigils or house cells, explained later in this chapter.

One contemporary practitioner might insist that a Fu sigil must be drawn out in longhand with a consecrated calligraphy brush, while another contemporary practitioner will insist that digitally rendered computer printed Fu are perfectly fine. In the eighth century, Zhang Huaiguan, a calligraphy scholar, noted that the script on Fu sigils resembled seal scripts, which are the early forms of Chinese writing found on the oracle bones and bronze sculptures between 1600 and 206 BC.[3] Examples of seal script are provided in appendix B as reference for rendering your own Fu sigils based on that style. Yet many of the historic Fu pictured in this book do not resemble seal scripts at all. The classical text *Three Caverns of the Supernatural Fu Talismanic Records*,[4] part of the Taoist Canons, notes that Fu are rendered in a script likened to "cloud writing," that it should resemble "the condensation of clouds."[5] Nonetheless, countless examples of Fu Wen are nothing like cloud writing.

Figure 4.1 showcases two Fu from the Taoist Canons, or Tao Zang, a collection of scriptures dated between AD 400 and 1444. When empowered and charged according to the instructions in the scriptures, the Fu sigil on the left can exorcise demons from a home and cure house hauntings.[6] Its purpose is to purify areas or spaces with malevolent energy, demons, or hungry ghosts. The Fu sigil on the right purifies an individual's bad karma. When empowered and charged, which includes an extensive 120-day ritual, the sinner can find redemption. A primary use for the second sigil is to purify the karma of criminals.

In my examination, I found that the optimal way to teach the craft is to return to the basic ontological principles, and to adhere to the early medieval texts on craft, such as the *Classics of the Esoteric Talisman*. From there, I've opted to deconstruct a Fu into basic anatomy, which this chapter will cover. Even so, the Fu of many lineages do not follow this basic deconstructed anatomy. Ultimately, the Fu of a set magical lineage is intended to be indecipherable to those outside the lineage, so in theory, lay practitioners should not be able to decipher or deconstruct any Fu that is not their own.

The Fu sigils to be discussed in this book are paper sigils. Traditionally, thin rice paper was used, though in contemporary practice I have seen everything from construction paper and cardstock to copy paper pulled out of a printer tray. The paper used is most commonly yellow or white, but I have also seen blue, green, pink, orange—every color of the rainbow. The paper used is not quite as important as what will be drawn on it and, of course, consecrating the paper prior to use.

Fu paper sigils are generally rectangular in shape, about two and a half to three times longer than the width. However, Fu sigils can come in the form of medallions and thus can be circular. Octagonal Fu sigils are also popular, calling upon the Ba Gua. The circular and octagonal Fu sigils tend to be cast in metal, stone, or wood and will differ significantly from the anatomy described herein for paper sigils.

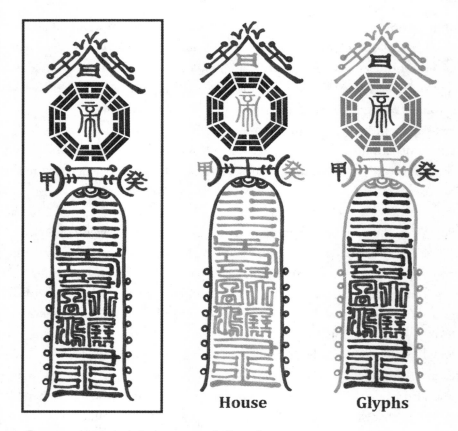

Figure 4.2. House and glyph anatomy of a Fu sigil

The sample Fu sigil pictured in figure 4.2 is a talisman crafted for those in the legal profession. To explain the anatomy of a Fu sigil, the example given in figure 4.2 will be used throughout the chapter. It is not very impressive to look at artistically, but the talisman works. So do not worry if you think your Fu sigils are lacking artistically. They are not intended to be masterpieces in visual art. Fu sigils are craft.

## THE HOUSE

First, not every Fu sigil will have a house, but many seem to. Enough sigil designs from the common practice of Fu include what I am calling a "house," so it warrants mentioning. A house is the framework for a Fu sigil. It can represent the subject matter of the sigil, or the lines of the house can delineate how energy should be channeled between the various powers of the glyphs in the sigil.

Figure 4.3. Fu talismans from the Zheng Yi lineage

Figure 4.3 depicts four Fu talismans from the Zheng Yi Dao tradition, from Mount Longhu in Jiangxi, China.[7] Note how each Fu seems to be organized within a stylized framework, in particular the bell shape at the bottom of three of the pictured sigils that encase additional symbols (much of which is not in a decipherable language, and is coded so only the practitioner, those of the same lineage, and the spirit entities called upon can comprehend the content).

Left to right, the first Fu invokes the Buddha (佛), as seen near the top of the talisman. Here, the Buddha is called upon to assist with the banishment of hungry ghosts or demons. The second Fu is intended to cure plagues and epidemics. Note how the third and fourth Fu are both framed as decrees (in-

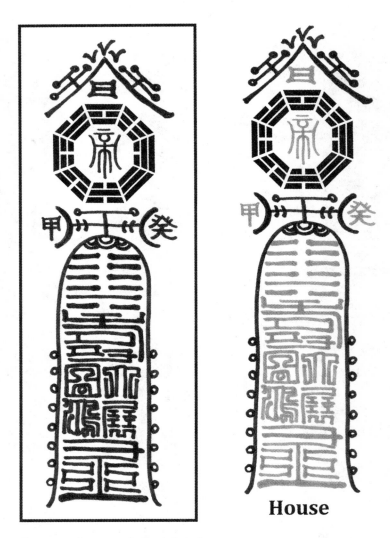

Figure 4.4. Anatomy of a Fu sigil: the house

corporating the character 聖, Shèng, meaning "holy," "sacred," indicative of a holy decree) issued to one spirit, assuming the practitioner's authorization to issue the decree at the behest of a higher spirit. The fourth Fu invokes the Taoist god Xuan Wu (玄武神, Xuán Wǎ Shén), the Enigmatic Warrior God, or as he is invoked in the Fu, the Enigmatic High Celestial God (玄天上帝, Xuán Tiān Shàng Dì).[8] Xuan Wu is the god of power and magic, and is often invoked for demon exorcisms.

Note also glyphs within the fourth sigil calling upon the spirit powers of the horse (馬, encased within the bottom bell, left side) and tiger (虎, encased within the bottom bell, right side). While these Fu are by nature coded in such a way that nonmembers of the lineage cannot decipher their true meanings, the fourth Fu seems to be one

*Mó*
Magic/
Sorcery

Figure 4.5. Magic and sorcery house

crafted to dispel or cure disease, or at least that would be my best guess.

Winding curved lines resembling spirals or lemniscates amplify Qi energy, and are seen here in these sigils. Effectively, they serve as energetic exclamation marks, amplifying potency. These lines are a common feature in Fu sigils, forming the houses or framework of the Fu. Houses composed of Fu Wen at the top with wording resembling an imperial decree or order are also common (like the two on the right in fig. 4.3), as are the bell shapes at the bottom of the sigils with glyphs encased within.

There is no clear or universal definition of what a house consists of, because they vary so much among traditions and even from practitioner to practitioner. Typically, the traditional Taoist sigils look like the ones pictured in figure 4.3: the roof of the house consists of Fu Wen and is usually a call-out to a particular deity or natural force (thunder, mountain, particular spirits, demons, and so on). The bottom half of the house often resemble a bell, encasing more glyphs.

Continuing from the previous example in figure 4.2, figure 4.4 shows the same Fu sigil, now with the house emphasized for study. The house consists of the top triangular peak, integrating the two stylized power crosses. The three strokes at the top that resemble checkmarks represent the trinitarian principle of Heaven, Earth, and Man, and the practitioner bringing the three planes to union. Traditional Fu sigils often display these three strokes. They not only

Earlier Heaven Ba Gua
(Fu Xi)

Later Heaven Ba Gua
(King Wen)

Figure 4.6. Earlier Heaven and Later Heaven
Ba Guas

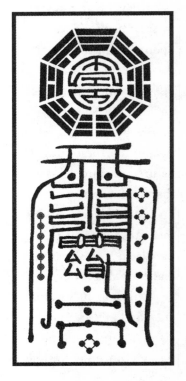

Figure 4.8. Fu for protection
from bodily harm during
competition

Figure 4.7. Fu Sigils for protection, good health,
and prosperity in the year of the sheep

call upon the Taoist trinity, but also represent the three strokes at the top of
the character "光" (guāng), for the White Light principle, or luminescence, in
a sense protecting the craft in a shield of divine White Light.

A stamp of the Ba Gua also makes up the structure of the house. What
is inscribed within the Ba Gua's center is the higher energy from the realm
of Heaven, or deity, to be invoked. Then the rest of the Fu sigil is framed by a
bell-shaped form. Along each side of the bell are eight energetic amplifiers. The
numerological indication for eight in Chinese is fortune and prosperity.

A house design can also be based on a character. For instance, the house
illustrated in figure 4.5 is based on the character for magic or sorcery. It is a

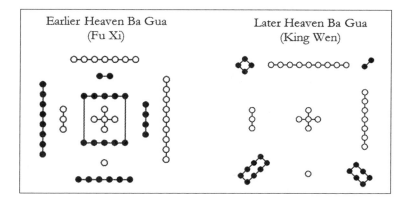

Figure 4.9. Earlier Heaven and Later Heaven numerical sequences

variation on a frequently used house in traditional Taoist sigil crafting.

The intent for designing a house based on the traditional Chinese character for magic or sorcery (魔) is to emphasize the occult or supernatural character of the work. It is commonly found on sigils for summoning specific entities or spirits, retaliatory craft, or generally more aggressive energetic workings.

The Ba Gua is another often used house, with the glyphs inscribed in the center of the Ba Gua. Either the Fu Xi Earlier Heaven version or King Wen Later Heaven can be used. The one selected often depends on tradition or lineage. However, in esoteric Taoism generally, the Earlier Heaven Ba Gua represents universal principles, and explains the laws of the natural or physical world. The Later Heaven Ba Gua represents esoteric principles and explains the laws of the supernatural or metaphysical world. Thus, given the esoteric nature of Fu sigil crafting, the Later Heaven Ba Gua is typically used.

While the Ba Guas depicting the eight trigrams are the ones more commonly recognized, the delineations in figure 4.9 are also used as Fu sigil houses. Glyphs would then be inscribed around the diagrams of yin and yang circles.

The Ba Guas are also frequently found as independent glyphs or integrated into the house design. It symbolizes the combined forces of nature working in support of the spell cast by the Fu sigil, and thus is often stamped to the top of a sigil or on the reverse side of the sigil paper.

Figure 4.10. General good luck amulet as a cell sigil

## House Cells

In lieu of traditional houses, cells can also be used. A Fu sigil can consist of many cells, each containing a symbol of power or protection, or glyphs, as explained in the previous section. I refer to such a Fu as a cell sigil. The Fu shown in figure 4.10 is an example of a cell sigil. Combined, the multiple symbols and glyphs act as a recipe. The cell sigil is the formula for the intended manifestation.

Figure 4.11 is a Buddhist-influenced cell sigil that invokes Amithaba. The

Figure 4.11. Buddhist-influenced prosperity and protection cell sigil

script in the left column reads "南无阿弥陀佛" (ná mó Amítuófó), meaning to pay homage to the Amithaba Buddha. Below an image of Amithaba in the right column is a lotus, one of the eight auspicious symbols in Buddhism. The lotus symbolizes liberation from suffering and prevailing against the odds. The twin

Figure 4.12. Nine-cell Fu sigil for protection from evil

fish is another one of the eight auspicious symbols, representing yin and yang. The twin fish represent courage and fortitude, the free movement through trials and tribulations. Below the fish are glyphs for Fu Lu Shou (福祿壽, "prosperity," "affluence," and "longevity").

In cell sigils, numerology is significant. The number of cells should bear numerological significance to the intention at hand. The size of each cell can also be significant. Symbols in larger cells are intended to lead and play a more dominant role in the charging. Symbols in smaller cells play a supporting, supplemental role.

Figure 4.12 is a protection amulet for dispelling malignant energies. The number nine corresponds with Fire, power, and strength. There are a total of thirty-six suns (日), which corresponds with the number nine (36: 3 + 6 = 9). The suns represent yang energy, which vanquishes yin, the energy of the dark and of rot. Note that the center cell features a glyph for the sun. The two characters left and right of the center cell are "保護" (bǎo hù, "to protect"). Above is "霆" (tíng), the divine thunderbolt of thunder magic for defeating evil and malevolent forces. Below is "殺" (shā), meaning to kill, exorcise, or vanquish evil. Altogether, the sigil design is an amulet for protection against the evildoings and ill will of others.

Cell sigils might not represent the orthodox traditional approach to Fu craft, yet they are talismans constructed by the same principles as orthodox traditional Fu. Typically a cell sigil Fu is folded and placed into a protective casing. Magical symbolism is also inscribed on the casing. Altogether, the casing and folded cell sigil Fu within it is the talisman or amulet. Earlier in this chapter, figure 4.7 includes a cell sigil crafted on a long strip of paper that is then folded and inserted into cardstock casing. The cardstock casing is then folded into a matchbook. Such matchbook sigils are explained further in chapter 10, and illustrated in figures 10.2 and 10.3.

## THE GLYPHS AND FU WEN

The more orthodox traditional Fu that are commonly seen are composed of glyphs. Glyphs can be actual drawings or illustrations, can be other sigils, or are made up of Fu Wen, a magical or stylized Chinese script. Once the house has been designed, the practitioner has to set about selecting (and even designing) the glyphs. The meat and bones of a Fu sigil are in the glyphs.

Each glyph of the Fu sigil is selected with care. Think of the glyphs as ingredients in a recipe. The right recipe of glyphs calls upon the right combination of spiritual energies needed to manifest the intent. That is the spell. Some glyphs in the Fu are larger and more prominent, suggesting a larger quantity of that particular energetic essence.

Most Fu sigils consist primarily if not entirely of Fu Wen, a magical script that mimics traditional Chinese script, but it is often stylized beyond ordinary recognition or is used in craft in a way that deviates slightly from its regular linguistic meaning. Fu Wen can be straight and legible Chinese script; oracle bone script,

Figure 4.13. Glyph for "ghost"

meaning ancient Chinese script; or heavily stylized and modified to the point of illegibility. One form of that heavily stylized and modified magical script is called cloud writing, discussed in chapter 3.

Figure 4.13 is a stylized version of the traditional Chinese character for "ghost" (鬼, guī). Since most Fu crafted out of the orthodox lineages involve summonings and control or command over ghosts, demons, and lesser spirits, a glyph for "ghost" is commonly found on historic Fu, and it continues to be utilized today in Fu craft. A glyph for "ghost" in Fu craft might be used in a manner that applies the dictionary definition of "ghost," such as for a spirit conjuration, or it can be used more figuratively, to indicate the exorcizing of one aspect of a person's shadow self, such as a Fu crafted to help kick a bad habit.

Figure 4.14. Glyph for the mantra "Na mo guanshiying pusa"

Glyphs are meant to be dynamic. Each glyph is in its own right a sacred symbol, one that emanates a specific spiritual, metaphysical, or supernatural power. Mantras for particular deities, for instance, are believed to vibrate at the same frequency as the vibration of that deity, and the utterance of these mantras calls out to that deity for assistance. Thus, a glyph can be a sigil or symbolic representation of a mantra phrase. Figure 4.14 shows a call-out to Kuan Yin, the goddess (or bodhisattva) of mercy and compassion.

In its essence, the mantra means "Honoring the venerable bodhisattva Kuan Yin." The phrase might be incorporated into a Fu sigil as a glyph. Figure 4.14 illustrates two different glyph versions of the mantra. The mantra is as follows:

南无觀世音菩薩

Ná mó guan shì yīn pú sà

In figure 4.14, the left column of characters is the mantra in legible traditional Chinese characters. The next two columns are two different glyphs for that mantra where the characters become heavily stylized and modified into a magical script.

Returning to the first Fu example from figure 4.2, which was a talisman to bring good luck, prosperity, and success for those in the legal profession, note the glyphs that the sigil comprises. The house for the Fu sigil was covered in figure 4.4. Here in figure 4.15, the glyphs are emphasized. Each glyph is selected specifically to empower the sigil with a particular energetic property. At the very top center is a stylized symbol for "sun" (日), representing success, radiance, and dominant yang energy. The legal profession is an extroverted profession, and so the focus on yang energy here will amplify the willpower, drive, and determination of the recipient of the sigil. Inscribed within the Ba Gua is the character for "god" (帝). In my application of the character, I use it generically to represent the Divine, the god principle, or the collective universal Qi that connects all of us. In its more ancient application, dating back to Bronze Age China as found on ancient oracle bones dating to that period, the character was used to denote a single god principle, the most powerful and almighty god in Heaven.[9] Here, the ancient seal script version of the character is used. Thus, how it is drawn on the Fu sigil looks slightly different from the character (帝) as it appears in this paragraph.

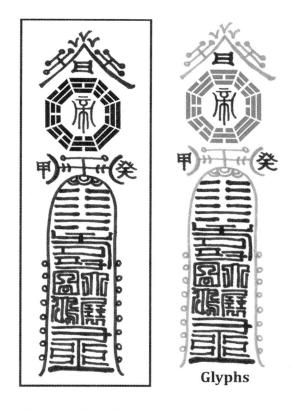

Figure 4.15. Glyphs for crafting a sigil to advance a legal career

Heavenly stems, a concept that will be covered in "The Timing of a Charging Ritual" in chapter 8 and in appendix K, are inscribed to the two sides of the Fu: Jia (甲) for Yang Wood and Gui (癸) for Yin Water. Note their energetic correspondences in tables K.2 and K.7 in appendix K at the back of this book. Together, the two heavenly stems work together to harness the attributes that empower a legal professional to be successful.

Leading the glyphs inside the bell-shaped form of the house is hexagram 7. The hexagram's meaning can be found in appendix E. Below the I Ching hexagram is a stylized glyph or Fu Wen for "longevity" (壽), which can be found ref-

| Chinese Characters | | Fu Wen |
| --- | --- | --- |
| 日 月 星 sun, moon, stars | *becomes* | |
| 靈 spirit | *becomes* | |
| 醫 healer | *becomes* | |
| 福 prosperity | *becomes* | |

Figure 4.16. Chinese characters and Fu Wen comparison

erenced earlier in table 4.1. Here, the character is rendered in a magical writing style, and thus may not be immediately legible as 壽. Next are four glyphs, 大展鴻圖, arranged into a square, appearing clockwise and again stylized so that they are not intrinsically legible as traditional Chinese characters. It is a phrase that means "great success and achievement of ambitions." The phrase can be used as a spell; this and others are found in appendix B.

Finally, making up the base of the glyphs is Fu Wen for Metal (金), from the Wu Xing. Metal is for ambition, conquest, and success in combative or litigious situations. The Fu Wen for Metal as it has been rendered here also resembles the traditional Chinese character for "book" (書), to symbolize knowledge, learning, and education. Note that the glyph also has the Fo and Fu, one of the twelve symbols of sovereignty, inscribed within it. The Fo and Fu, which represents divine justice, is depicted in figure B.34 in appendix B, along with the other symbols of sovereignty and their explanations.

This Fu sigil pictured in figures 4.2, 4.4, 4.15, and later in 4.30 can be used as an amulet by anyone seeking success in the legal profession. It raises the corresponding metaphysical energy to facilitate greater success in court proceedings, litigation, negotiations, and career advancement. The glyph inscribed within the Ba Gua can be replaced with another glyph to invoke the deity of the practitioner's choice.

In Fu sigil crafting, think of each glyph as an element of the final sigil. Crafting a sigil is thus a form of metaphysical chemistry, and the sigil that you are drawing itself represents the formula. Figure 4.16 provides examples of how traditional Chinese characters are transformed into Fu Wen glyphs. Fu Wen is considered magical writing, and therefore is often illegible to others. Only the practitioner who crafted the sigil can read its meaning. Each magical tradition has its own unique methodology for writing Fu Wen, and it is often guarded and kept secret.

Note the Fu Wen in figure 4.17, a Fu sigil crafted for safeguarding overseas travel. The sigil incorporates a house design with three main glyphs: an ancient seal script for "dragon" at the top, inspired by Shang Dynasty oracle bones; the seal script for "carriage," to symbolize travel, also from oracle bones; and personalized Fu Wen forv health and longevity (壽) at the base of the sigil.

Figure 4.17. A Fu Sigil for travel protection

You, the practitioner, will formulate your own approach to writing Fu Wen when crafting your Fu sigils. Appendix B will provide a selection of characters that are often used in sigil crafting and what the characters mean, plus typical uses in craft. You can then render your own Fu Wen based on those Chinese characters.

Approaches to Fu Wen are limitless. The three glyphs in table 4.1 represent three common Chinese characters found in modern day Fu sigils: Fu, Lu, and Shou. They represent the trinity of blessings. For more glyph variations of the character 福, "prosperity," see figure I.34 in appendix I.

Fu, Lu, and Shou represent the Three Blessings (福祿壽, Fú Lù Shòu) and are personified into the Three Stellar Gods (三星, Sān Xīng). The Three Stellar Gods, as noted in table 4.1, originate from regional Chinese folk religions, but are often integrated into esoteric Taoist practice, especially for contemporary Fu sigils crafted to manifest those blessings in one's life.

Trigrams from the Ba Gua and the sixty-four hexagrams of the I Ching are also commonly used as glyphs (and are also incorporated into the construction of houses). The eight trigrams of the Ba Gua are touched upon in appendix E.

| Fu Wen (Glyph) | Chinese Character | Meaning and Uses |
|---|---|---|
| 福 | 福<br>fú | **Prosperity.** Good fortune, prosperity, wealth, riches, and a blessing of material abundance<br><br>Personified in Chinese folk religions as [insert Chinese characters] (Fú Xīng), the Stellar God of Prosperity |
| 祿 | 祿<br>lù | **Status.** Achievement of high social status<br><br>Personified in Chinese folk religions as [insert characters] (Lù Xīng), the Stellar God of Status |
| 壽 | 壽<br>shòu | **Longevity.** Longevity and good health<br><br>Personified in Chinese folk religions as [insert characters] (Shòu Xīng), the Stellar God of Longevity |

Table 4.1. Three Blessings and the Three Stellar Gods

Figure 4.18. Fu Wen glyphs for "immortal." Left: the standard character xiān, "immortal" or "celestial being"; center and right: two different styles of Fu Wen for the same character

The Fu sigil appearing in figure 4.20 incorporates the trigrams for Water and Wind from the Ba Gua. The Water trigram appears at the very top, and the Wind trigram is inscribed within the bell form of the house. Note in table

Figure 4.20. Fu sigil with the trigrams Water and Wind as a glyph

Figure 4.19. The Stellar God of Longevity, Shou Xing (寿星) (courtesy of Special Collections, Fine Arts Library, Harvard University)

1.12 that both trigrams relate to the Western element of Water, corresponding with adjusting yin. Dark dots and curves throughout the sigil design amplify yin energy with numerology to invoke the spirit realm. The sigil in figure 4.20 is for invoking the metaphysical energy of Water, or adjusting yin, and can be empowered for several different purposes: for "rainmaking," or generating financial prosperity and improving business or career prospects, or to improve a practitioner's intuitive abilities and to heighten connection with the spirit world to facilitate conjuration. The specific effect of such a sigil design is programmed during the charging ritual, or through the manner of empowerment.

Consider the eight trigrams, or eight fundamental elements of Taoist cosmology, as building blocks that the practitioner can use as glyphs in sigil crafting. How the trigrams might be used in crafting Fu sigils is provided in appendix E, "Ba Gua and the I Ching."

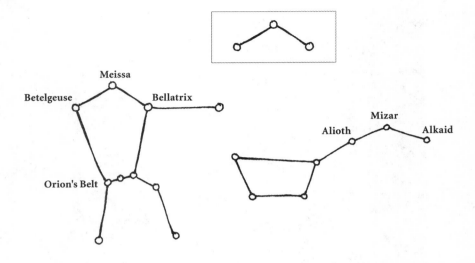

Figure 4.21. Three-star constellation in Orion and in the Big Dipper

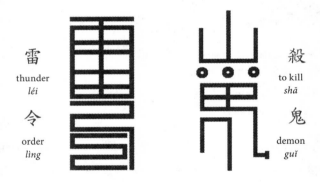

雷
thunder
*léi*

令
order
*lìng*

殺
to kill
*shā*

鬼
demon
*guǐ*

Figure 4.22. Glyphs for "thunder decree" and "kill the demon"

In imperial China, the royal garb of the emperor and empress was embroidered with the twelve symbols of sovereignty, one of which was the constellation of three stars, pictured in figure 4.21.[10] The symbol is often found atop traditional Fu sigils, calling upon the ontological trinity. Sources differ as to whether the three-star constellation was a reference to Betelgeuse, Meissa, and Bellatrix,[11] three stars in Orion pictured at left in figure 4.21, or Alioth, Mizar, and Alkaid, the three stars that make up the handle of the Big Dipper in Ursa Major, at right in figure 4.21. In contemporary practice and through my anecdotal experience, the three-star constellation symbol has now come to represent the Three Stellar Gods, as noted earlier in table 4.1: Fu Xing, the Stellar God of Prosperity; Lu Xing, the Stellar God of Status; and Shou Xing, the Stellar God of Longevity.

HOUSE:
魔
magic

力
strength
殺
vanquish

Figure 4.23. House and glyph assembly

One of the aspects of Fu sigil crafting that fascinates me the most is the signature of styles that emerge in craft. Individual practitioners, even practitioners of the same lineage, render Fu Wen, which are then used as glyphs, in ways that highlight that practitioner's unique art-

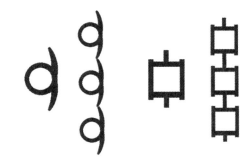

Figure 4.24. Stylistic yin and yang energetic amplifiers

istry. Figure 4.22 shows a more severe and austere hand at Fu Wen, stylizing the traditional Chinese characters in a boxy, nearly symmetrical manner.

Figure 4.23 offers an example of how Fu Wen might be incorporated into both the house and the glyphs. The house consists of Fu Wen, or magical script for the traditional character for "magic." The glyphs empowering the sigil are Fu Wen for "strength" and "vanquish," with the ideogram for "vanquish" much larger than the one for "strength," suggesting the primary purpose of the Fu sigil, which is most likely for the banishment or exorcism of a malignant spirit or energy.[12]

A stylistic adornment that I call "amplifiers" are also a common feature in the glyphs of a Fu sigil. Figure 4.24 show two common amplifiers in Fu sigils, historic and contemporary. The circular design invokes yin energy and the square design invokes yang. They are linked to create chains of strength, and

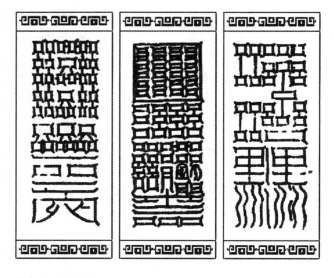

Figure 4.25. Fu for expelling demonic poisons, from the Shang Qing

often call upon numerology as well, with the number of circles or squares used being significant. A beginner's tutorial on how to design a Fu sigil is provided in appendix G and demonstrates how these stylistic amplifiers might be incorporated into a sigil design.

Note the use of the square amplifiers in figure 4.25, an example of a Fu crafted by the Shang Qing lineage for ex-pelling demonic poisons. The Shang Qing Fu use the chains of square amplifiers for harnessing yang.[13] Note also how certain squares in the sigil designs are linked or not linked, which I speculate has metaphysical significance, though that significance is not known to me.

The Fu on the left in figure 4.25 contains a total of thirty-nine squares (noting that odd numbers correspond with yang) linked or left unlinked in precise patterns. The middle Fu depicts a large square encasing smaller squares that, including the larger square, total twenty-five, another odd-number invocation for yang. The lower portion features twenty-seven smaller squares; note that two of the squares in the lower half are in fact part of other glyphs, and are thus not standalone squares. Finally, the Fu on the right contains a total of twenty-three squares, not including the two Fu Wen glyphs for black, 黑, that form the base of the Fu. Both yang-correspondent amplifiers and numerology associated with yang energy are used to harness yang, which is raised to dispel the yin energy otherwise conducive for demonic energies to thrive.

It should be noted, however, that the foregoing deduction on interpreting the chains of circular and square amplifiers are my own anecdotal observations of folk practice and is not adhered to by every practitioner. Take, for instance, the Fu pictured in figure 4.26. According to its corresponding instruction, this Fu, like the Shang Qing Fu pictured earlier, is for expelling demons. The chain of seven suns (日) forming a column on the right side creates a potent pillar of yang energy that the practitioner would use to dispel the yin. It might follow that a chain of squares would be used by the practitioner for adornment rather than a chain of circles.

Yet in the Fu in figure 4.26, a chain of six circles (or curled figures), denoting yin, in even numbers also denoting yin, is used. While we can speculate as to why the original practitioner may have designed this Fu in such a way (possibly symbolic representation of ensnaring or entrapping the yin), we cannot know for sure, other than that the Fu in figure 4.26 seems to run contrary to what I said earlier about the yin and yang expressions of circle and square chains. The takeaway point here is that for every point I make, there are clear and notable exceptions or counterpoints.

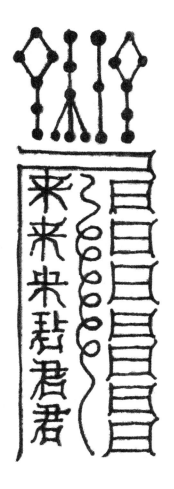

Figure 4.26. Fu for expelling demonic poisons, from the Taoist Canons

Astrological diagrams, or Hsing Tu (星圖), are also a common feature in Fu sigils. Diagrams of constellations are used as glyphs to align the sigil with corresponding powers that the stars were believed to hold. Chinese astrology is often incorporated into sigil crafting.

The Big Dipper is often used as a glyph in Fu sigil crafting because it is a cornerstone in Taoist magical practice. It is even incorporated into the charging ritual, as discussed in "Pacing the Big Dipper" in chapter 8. In Taoist magic, there

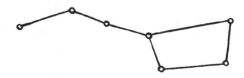

Figure 4.27. Seven-Star (Big Dipper) Hsing Tu glyph

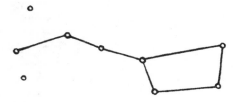

Figure 4.28. Nine-Star Big Dipper, according to esoteric Taoism

are two forms of the Big Dipper observed: the Seven Stars and the Nine Stars. The Seven-Star version is the one most Westerners are familiar with, as pictured in figure 4.27. The Nine-Star version is pictured in figure 4.28, showing two additional lesser stars:

The Nine-Star Big Dipper is said to relate to the Lo Shu magic square, covered briefly in appendix D, and is also utilized in a school of feng shui called the Flying Star sect, founded by Master Shen Zhu Ren during the Qing Dynasty. Hsing Tu diagrams that highlight these eighth and ninth stars can often be found on Fu sigils.

For the Western practitioner, you can consider incorporating a Hsing Tu for Taurus if a Fu sigil is being crafted for financial gain, career opportunities, or manifesting high ambitions. Consider utilizing the astrological symbol for Venus to manifest intentions for love and romance, Vesta for sexual healing, or Libra to amplify tender, loving, caring energy. To do so, for instance if a practitioner seeks to raise power, a practitioner would envision the astrological glyph for Aries, ∧, etched onto the ground, then during the ritual that the practitioner has designed for charging a sigil, pace through that envisioned symbol of Aries on the ground. Keep in mind to incorporate such pacing or Hsing Tu when the moon phase and astrology for the date and time of the ritual aligns with Aries.

Western astrological approaches work quite well with Taoist Fu sigil crafting, even if the craft hails from an Eastern heritage. Incorporating Western astrological glyphs into a Fu sigil could be used not only to raise certain energy corresponding with the planets or signs, but even used to indicate the timing and deadlines for the sigil.

From its inception, Fu sigils have been eclectic, commingling a variety of Eastern religions and iconography together. In contemporary Fu sigil crafting, that tradition of being eclectic is extended to Western religions and iconography as well.

## THE SEAL

Traditionally, Fu sigils are stamped with the practitioner's seal, typically in a contrasting ink color; if the sigil is crafted with black ink, then the practitioner's seal is in red, or vice versa. One of the last steps of crafting a Fu, after it has been designed, consecrated, charged, and divined to be effective, is for the practitioner who created it to then seal it. Sigils can be sealed anywhere on the front face of the paper where the Fu appears, or it can be stamped on the back. As seen in figure 4.30, a practitioner's seal is typically a stamp that is affixed to the sigil once it has been drawn. It marks the sigil as being sourced from that specific practitioner or a particular magical lineage.

Seals are a traditional form of signature used in many East Asian cultures. An individual's name is carved into a wood or stone block in either a positive or negative impression, which is then stamped on documents that require acknowledgement. The traditional practice of sealing a Fu sigil with the practitioner's authorship stamp served two purposes: the practical object of noting which Tao magical lineage the Fu sigil was coming from; and

Figure 4.29. Fu with "Sun in Leo" as a glyph

Figure 4.30. Fu sigil stamped with a practitioner's seal

Figure 4.31. Sample stamped Fu sigils. Left: a Fu sigil
with the practitioner's seal stamped on the front, at top
right. Right: a Fu sigil with the practitioner's seal stamped     Figure 4.32. Fu sigil
on the back, in the center                                        for exam success

the supernatural, invoking a channel between the physical and metaphysical
that the practitioner has invoked before, or in more basic terms, using a specific calling card to invoke spiritual or energetic intervention. There are several
perfectly workable alternatives to an ink stamp for sealing a Fu sigil, which are
covered in chapter 9, "Sealing the Fu Sigil."

The house, glyphs, and seal pretty much covers the basic anatomy of a Fu
sigil. A house frames a combination of glyphs that work much like a recipe,
with the chosen ingredients and the proportions of those ingredients working
together to call upon the energies needed for the intended effect. Sealing the Fu
sigil is a traditional practice included so that the spirits invoked can identify the
source of the sigil and the practitioner who has authored it.

Figure 4.32 shows a sample Fu sigil for examination success, integrating
both Eastern and Western esoteric ideograms. Appendix C outlines how Western sigil crafting techniques might be integrated with Eastern Fu. The sigil is

crafted in an eclectic style. The Western-style sigil is used to identify the examination that the beneficiary[14] of this Fu seeks to succeed in. Note that there is also a glyph crafted from the Lo Shu square, which identifies the beneficiary's seat number during the examination. Here, there is no discernible house used to frame the Fu, but the sigil itself is framed by a solid border. The practitioner's seal is shown in the top right corner. Note also the bottom left corner, which has been stamped with a banner, a Buddhist symbol for victory.

Yet the anatomy itself is not enough. Designing a Fu sigil is only the first of essentially eight steps, summarized as follows:

Figure 4.33. Fu sigil for prosperous love

1. Designing the Fu sigil
2. Consecrating the sigil
3. Setting the date for empowerment
4. Opening ritual
5. Charging the sigil: recitations
6. Postliminary divination
7. Sealing the Fu
9. Activating the Fu

## DESIGNING THE FU SIGIL

Traditional Fu are rendered by hand with a calligraphy brush. However, I use a regular ink pen or ultrafine-point marker. I have also found digitally designed Fu printed with modern technology, such as the one pictured in figure 4.33, to be effective. After all, block printing of Fu sigils has always been popular in East Asia. In block printing, the negative of a Fu sigil design is carved into wood blocks. Ink is applied to the block and the sigil stamped onto paper, and it is then empowered by a magical practitioner.

In figure 4.33, a Fu for prosperous love, the topmost glyph is "double happiness" (囍), a common Chinese glyph for marital bliss. Below it are the Earth and Heaven trigrams and glyphs for "dragon" (龍) and "phoenix" (鳳), which together symbolize the perfect civil union, an ideal romantic partnership. Below that are glyphs to represent abundance, happiness, material wealth, and prosperity for the couple. The foundation of the Fu shows "sun, moon, stars" (日月星), symbolizing destiny, the union (or reunion) with one's soul mate, twin flame, or one true love. The thought and intent behind how a Fu is designed is far more important than the precise manner in which it is produced. The Fu design in figure 4.33, whether rendered digitally or by hand, will be equally effective, so long as the principles from chapter 3 are complied with and the Fu itself is adequately charged.

As you craft your own Fu, rest assured that it is not the manner of rendering the Fu or materials used that are important. It is the process of empowering and charging Fu sigils that distinguish the effective from the noneffective. Whether you craft by hand with ink and paintbrush, print it from a computer, or heck, write in blood, the effect of the manner is the same, up until the point of empowerment. From there, how the practitioner imprints the Fu with the necessary Qi energy emanation is what matters.

All that being said, writers do have their preferences, and if they don't indulge in those preferences, they get flustered and cannot focus on the work at hand. If you must write poems in longhand in a sheepskin journal, then for heavens' sake, write poems in longhand in a sheepskin journal. There is no need to ask anyone for permission (except maybe the sheep you took the sheepskin from?). Likewise, if there is a preference in the way you craft Fu sigils, indulge in your preference. Preferences are not superficial. It is what resonates with you on an intuitive level.

Your Fu sigils can be as elaborate and colorful as works of art, or they can be quick, simple squiggles with a pen. Traditional Fu sigils, though, are not that colorful. They are most commonly done in black or red ink, or a combination of black and red ink.

Some Fu sigils are coherent prayers or mantras that anyone literate in the language can read. Other Fu sigils comprise Fu Wen that are so abstract that they resemble scribbles. Even lay Chinese people aren't able to decipher the characters those scribbles are based on.

Fu sigils can also be found in cell form, as discussed in the previous chapter. House cells contain an eclectic mix of symbology from Taoism, Confucianism, Buddhism, Hinduism, or Shintoism. Still others utilize the ancient forms of Chinese characters or more Fu Wen.

As a Western-based practitioner, feel free to integrate pagan symbolism or iconography from any of the Abrahamic faiths. The specific symbols used are up to the practitioner's traditions and must be sentimental to the practitioner for the Fu to work. Thus, do not force yourself to use Chinese characters and iconography or try to write in Fu Wen. Apply the process of crafting Fu sigils and integrate it with your personal traditions. By that same token, do not be afraid to try your hand at drawing your own Fu Wen. Study the traditional Chinese characters or even the seal scripts in appendix B. Then apply your creativity to render those ideograms into your own coded Fu Wen script.

While the appendices of this book provide a sampling of glyphs commonly used by Chinese practitioners, you are encouraged to consider what symbols are meaningful to you and to your magical tradition. Runes, for instance, are deeply meaningful to many Western practitioners, and so, in lieu of Chinese symbols, rune glyphs can be used. Symbols of religious significance to you and your heritage should be considered for glyphs, especially if you have already established a strong psychic resonance with those symbols. The blending of sacred cultures is not appropriation; it is synergy channeled into craft at its most potent. Craft transcends culture and religion. In fact, craft is a secular practice, and all this book does is address craft by using Taoist vocabulary.

Of most importance when designing Fu sigils is the practitioner's focused intent and how he or she is channeling energy while the ideograms are being rendered. The purpose for selecting symbols that bear certain meanings or significance to the practitioner is to help the practitioner concentrate on the craft at hand. It is much easier to channel energy toward manifesting wealth and prosperity when the practitioner is drawing the Chinese character for prosperity and devoting time to stylizing it.

# CHAPTER 5

# EMPOWERING A FU SIGIL

**THE MOST CRITICAL** aspect to an effective Fu sigil is the process by which it becomes empowered. Power is sourced from the intent that the practitioner forges into the sigil as it is being drawn through the practitioner's hand, and it is the charging ritual by which the practitioner harnesses Heaven and Earth. Charging rituals, specifically my approach, is covered in chapter 8. This chapter provides an overview of the concept so that the practitioner might better grasp the principles for empowering the Fu.

To empower a Fu sigil, it not only needs to be designed with particular symbolic representations through the Fu Wen and glyphs, which were deconstructed in chapter 4, but every step of the process of empowerment must be thought through with care and precision. Ink color matters. Paper color matters. Invocations used and the mechanics a practitioner observes must be planned out to the minutest detail. For example, the Fu in figure 5.1, a fourth-century Fu from the Shang Qing lineage of craft from the *Perfect Scripture of Great Profundity*,[1] delineates precise steps for empowering that Fu. Simply drawing or copying the sigil design is nowhere near enough.

While the text is arcane and not readily comprehensible by the lay reader, it can be gathered that as part of the ritual for empowering or using this Fu, the color red should be used, as red removes demonic possession and malignant energies. The name of the person who has been possessed should also be repeated during the ritual. Specific instruction for teeth clicking is given and is to be incorporated into the exorcism.[2]

In the Taoist tradition, a spell is an active engagement that requires the exhaustion of mental energy. Pacing, for instance will be discussed in chapter 8.

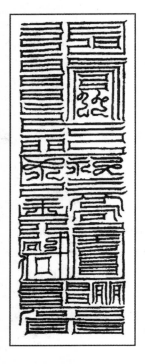

Figure 5.1. Fourth-century Fu sigil for exorcising inner demons, from the Shang Qing

The process of empowering a Fu sigil is, one could say, a holistic practice. It involves a variety of occult exercises (or what many Westerners might consider "occult") combined and integrated for the purpose of channeling concentrated energy. Medieval Fu craft could involve astral projection.[3] See, for instance, the empowerment techniques for the Fire Wheel Fu from the compilation of spells and rituals titled *Tao Fa Hui Yuan* (道法會元, Dào Fǎ Huì Yuán),[4] a fourteenth-century canonical Taoist text that teaches spell-crafting as it was commonly practiced throughout the twelfth, thirteenth, and fourteenth centuries.[5] The *Tao Fa Hui Yuan* was a practiced by celestial masters from various orthodox Taoist lineages. One such spell was the Fire Wheel Fu, as illustrated in figure 5.2.

The Fire Wheel Fu was a form of retaliatory craft or magic against a rival lineage. In other words, it was craft against other craft practitioners. The sigil's intent was to conjure a fire-breathing snake and other formidable beasts to destroy the temple of the rival lineage. The text states that if, and only if, another lineage of sorcerers has brought harm to the practitioner or the practitioner's lineage, the practitioner may retaliate with the Fire Wheel Fu.

The Fu sigil must be inscribed in red ink on pink paper. Here, note how the wheel invokes symbolism for the Ba Gua eight trigrams, the square for Earth, and the circle for Heaven. The glyphs below the larger top wheel are Fire (火).

An invocation for empowering the Fu sigil is also provided, which essentially reads phonetically as follows:

zu tsui ling guang sheng wei nei zhang shan yuan shi zhen gui bing tao
wang shen she tu wu xie jing hut sang ling tai shi ming chong hu wan
zang yu zhen wei er zuo shen jing tang shou hui zhi xia tou dais hen
guang zhi wei dong jing san shi jiu zhang zhong you chun xie long hu

Figure 5.2. Fourteenth-century Fire Wheel Fu

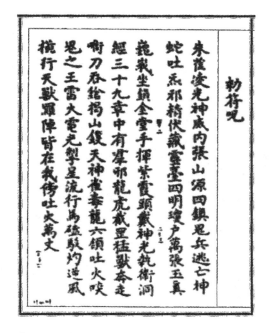

Figure 5.3. Invocation for empowering the Fire Wheel Fu

dai yi meng shou beng zou tsong li tun tsang jie san yi tian shen que du long liu he tu huo yen yi zhi wang lei da dian guang zhi xing liu xing ma ke buo zuo mi feng heng xing tian shou luo zhen jie zai wo pang tu huo wan zang

In general terms, the invocation is intended to conjure a snake deity, dragon demon, tiger demon, a bird deity, and a spirit horse (not characterized as either deity or demon) to help the practitioner in his or her magical endeavor.

Once the sigil has been crafted and empowered, the practitioner must astrally project to the temple's location, with the Fu in hand, enter the temple, and stand at the center. In the astral body, the practitioner then recites the invocation as instructed while envisioning the temple engulfed in flames and smoke. The invocation will in effect summon the referenced supernatural creatures to help destroy the temple. Once the temple is fully engulfed in flames, the practitioner turns and walks out the temple (in his astral body), leaving the Fu behind. The practitioner must exit the premises without a

Figure 5.4. Temple in Tainan, Taiwan

backward glance. Thus, the Fire Wheel Fu demonstrates how drawing out the Fu sigil design is nowhere close to being enough to activate a spell. The Fu sigil design is but one component of the Fu craft. The practitioner's ritual work is what empowers the Fu sigil.

There is an enduring and popular belief that only an ordained Taoist priest from a recognized lineage (or practicing faction of Taoist magic) can empower a Fu sigil. Without the priest, a sigil is just symbols on a strip of paper. Survey a sample of the East Asian population and you are likely to come up with a majority opinion that only priests and priestesses can empower Fu and practice Fu craft.

The opinion is based on the belief that the realm of spiritual beings is not accessible to just anyone.[6] Certain Taoist lineages have been granted access to particular regions of other worlds through specifically granted keys, or seals, passed down from master to student. Those who are not affiliated with a recognized Taoist lineage are purportedly not connected to Heaven.

I am reminded of a line I've interpreted from the *Classics of the Esoteric Talisman*: Heaven holds no special favors for any practitioner, and yet great favor from Heaven can be generated through the practitioner's mind (or self, or will, depending on the interpretation).[7]

Who is and is not an "ordained" Taoist priest is subject to human judgment, and I simply do not subscribe to any notion that would have Heaven delegate the authority of judgment into the hands of humans. Heaven—if you will believe the Taoist pantheon—delegates that authority to other celestial beings.

We are all connected individually to Heaven, our personal Qi connected directly into the cosmic Qi, and therefore each one of us has the potential of direct access to Heaven. "Heaven" itself is a metaphor for the concept of oneness, of metaphysical singularity. Every one of us, by nature of being human, of being Man in the Heaven-Earth-Man trinity, has direct access to that collective metaphysical energy. In that sense, access and the ability to negotiate components of Heaven and Earth are egalitarian. What might not be equal is each practitioner's level of ability.

Yet another belief is that craft ability is inherited. A magical family would keep its own Book of Methods (方書), covered later in chapter 6, and contain the family's Lu (錄), or roster of spirit entities that the family lineage is connected to. The family Book of Methods would contain reproductions of Fu sigils, each sigil's meanings and uses, and how to empower those sigils. These texts would remain a closely guarded secret within the families. Sigil crafting as practiced in that family's tradition would thus be passed on to family members only, and the secrets of the craft never revealed to outsiders. Also, typically these families believed themselves to be the descendants of renowned alchemists or Taoist magicians, and traced their abilities to empower Fu sigils back to such authorities.

I contend that the ability to craft and empower a Fu sigil transcends teachings, social constructs such as lineages, or family inheritance. When it comes to empowering Fu sigils, I believe in energy—physical energy that our sciences can explain and also metaphysical energy that our sciences are still working on. What this book refers to as "magic" is merely science that we don't quite understand yet. Once upon a time, fire was magical, and in many respects it still is, even if we now possess the scientific vocabulary to explain fire. I find my computer to be rather magical, mostly because I personally do not possess the scientific vocabulary to explain how it works. Advanced technology is, after all, indistinguishable from magic.

Each individual sentient being has self-contained metaphysical energy, which I refer to as personal Qi. Every contained personal Qi is connected to every other personal Qi, to form a universal cosmic Qi, that oneness and singularity I referred to. It is each practitioner's direct connection to that oneness and singularity that enables a practitioner to empower a Fu sigil, nothing more and nothing less.

Qi is the totality of cause and effect, and the totality of all synchronicity. It encompasses the laws of thermodynamics—concepts of equilibrium and energy transfer—and it assumes that the whole of the cosmos is one system. Cosmic Qi has been called many names: God, the Gaia principle, the Akashic Records, the collective unconscious.

The Taoist mythology is thus a metaphor for how one individual's personal Qi can connect to the cosmic Qi. When the personal Qi is connected to that cosmic Qi, that collective unconscious, when you are being one with the god concept, you can harness any part of that cosmic Qi, which comprises Heaven, Earth, and Man, to affect the personal Qi.[8] Deities and demons are how we personify, how we name, those metaphysical energies that we perceive, that we are intuitively able to sense as affecting us.

To empower a Fu sigil, the personal Qi must be connected to the cosmic Qi and be one with the greater collective unconscious. At the heart of it, that is how Fu sigils become empowered and effective. That is how point 1 of the *Classics of the Esoteric Talisman,* outlined in chapter 3, is satisfied: aligning yourself with the deity or deities you venerate in your tradition, and to the Tao, or that cosmic Qi. The authority to craft comes from your connection to that cosmic Qi, or how well aligned you are to Heaven. It is not a mysterious, mystical, secretive, and complicated art form reserved for ordained Taoist masters.

However, you cannot scrawl on a piece of paper and call it a Fu sigil. The intent must be present, along with an openness and receptivity to the greater unseen energies of the cosmos. While intent is the initial step toward empowering the Fu, it is not enough. The charging ritual and the precise metaphysical chemistry that has gone into crafting the sigil is what empowers it.

Objects must first be consecrated to rid them of any residual energy that might affect your craft. The idea is to work with a clean slate, to neutralize the energies present in the objects so that they are optimized for being imprinted with the energies you will be charging the objects with. Chapter 7 explains consecration techniques. Consecration of all items to be used in sigil crafting is almost always the first step to sanctifying the sigil in preparation of programming it to operate as a talisman or spell.

Rituals are important because they calm the consciousness and settle the everyday static of thought that blocks our spiritual receptivity. Rituals help us to open up to that oneness. That is why rituals are a requisite part of empowering Fu sigils. Through ritual, the practitioner is best able to raise energy from Heaven and Earth through the Wu Xing five phases and the Ba Gua, and, most importantly, to be spiritual.

The charging ritual is when the practitioner acts as a conduit for energy to be transferred into the Fu for the spell to take effect. Most lineages use hand mudras, explained in chapter 6, channeling manifestations of Heaven and Earth through the hand. Other lineages use breath, and during the charging ritual, blow on the Fu sigil to infuse it with the practitioner's own personal Qi energy, which is believed to be cultivated in such a way as to be more powerful and more connected to cosmic Qi. The Bai Yun Guan lineage in northern China teaches that Fu sigils are empowered by breath, whereby the practitioner's Qi is transferred onto the Fu. In that lineage, monks are taught to blow their own breath onto the Fu sigils to charge them.[9]

Crafting a Fu sigil begins with the understanding that personal Qi and cosmic Qi are connected, that one can affect the other, and that a Fu sigil, or the theory of magic, works because it is personal Qi redirecting and transforming cosmic Qi by reworking balances (or imbalances) of yin and yang. Of that yin and yang, we work with it in five phases, the Wu Xing. We work with the four directions and practice in harmony with nature, and thus we observe the four seasons. We understand the eight basic elements that make up the metaphysical dimension of the universe: the Ba Gua. The study of mathematics was born from our intuitive knowledge that numbers are an elucidation of how the universe functions. The esoteric facets are revealed to us through numerology. These natural phenomena are what empower Fu sigils, not priesthood or inheritance.

While the details of execution vary, the empowering of a Fu comes from the practitioner's mind working in collaboration with the practitioner's hand. With each stroke of every glyph in the sigil, the mind must be focused on a particular intent, either the specific invocation of a deity, a conjuration, the manifestation of an objective, or the occurrence of a transaction. The practitioner's mind is engaged in visualizations and is reciting invocations. Each line of the sigil is not simply drawn onto the paper; it is charged during the drawing process as the practitioner uses both mind and hand to press powerful energy into each stroke.

At the heart of craft, the objective of a Fu is to restore yin and yang balance to a situation. A situation causes grief to an individual because of a yin or yang imbalance. The purpose of the Fu is to inject yin energy to harmonize a situation that is in yang excess or lacking yin, and to inject yang where yin is in excess. When there is too much dark energy, the solution isn't more dark; it's light. That maxim has always held true. To quell hate, we use love, not more hate.

Finally, it should be noted that a critical component to effective empowerment of a Fu sigil is the practitioner's ego. In a sense, the practitioner must be egotistical. I have always maintained that ego is necessary for the highest forms of magic and metaphysical energetic work. The practitioner must hold a high degree of conceit for his or her personal power, abilities, and talent. The practitioner must, to the core, believe that he or she is special, chosen even, and that an authority has been conferred by the Divine, ordaining this practitioner with the gift of craft. And yet, paradoxically, according to the *Classics of the Es-*

*oteric Talisman,* Heaven holds no special favors for any one practitioner. There is no "chosen" or "The One," though a practitioner generates that favor from Heaven by channeling his or her power of mind. To do that, the requisite element is ego. To harness the forces of "Heaven and Earth for personal enrichment," in my opinion, takes swagger.

While that is often the one component not mentioned out loud, it is the most important aspect of effective craft. Without ego, a practitioner is, simply put, too receptive and not active enough to modify metaphysical energies and presences in the universe. The practitioner must adopt a point of view that emphasizes his or her own importance as a conduit for deities and the supernatural, and as a commander of metaphysical energy. That ego—or confidence, if you prefer—facilitates the mindset necessary for effective craft. Through unequivocal conviction in your abilities to craft effective Fu sigils,[10] you will be able to raise the requisite energy to do so.

## The Legend of Zhao Gong Ming (Cai Shen, God of Wealth) and a Traditional Spell for Attaining Wealth and Prosperity

Recall the reference to the Five Celestials of Wealth in "Four Compass and Five Relative Directions" in chapter 1. The Five Celestials of Wealth are invoked for the attainment of wealth and prosperity. The following is a traditional Chinese spell[11] invoking the Five Celestials that can be performed for you or on behalf of another; how that is distinguished is through the design of the Fu sigil that is being crafted. The methodology also provides an illustrative example of how a Fu sigil is empowered.

First, the practitioner should know the legend of Zhao Gong Ming (趙公明), the poorest of the poor who became the wealthiest of the wealthy and, eventually, was deified as an immortal god. Zhao Gong Ming was a humble beggar who had a black dog that could not bark and a hen that could not lay eggs. He subsisted on begging, and he fed the alms of food he received to his black dog and his hen. As a result, he never had enough to eat himself.

One night, Heaven's gates opened, and Zhao Gong Ming saw a rainbow sky and glistening white lights. Immortals appeared. It is said that Heaven's gates opens only

Figure 5.5. Zhao Gong Ming, the God of Wealth

once every three thousand years. The poor beggar dropped to his knees and prayed to Heaven that he might never be poor again, wishing for wealth and prosperity. Immediately thereafter, Heaven's gates closed. The beggar thought perhaps he had only been dreaming.

The next day, his black dog could now bark, and every time it barked, a silver ingot came rolling out of its mouth. The beggar's hen now laid eggs of gold ingots. He was now a wealthy man, and he used his wealth to help the poor. He was generous and benevolent with his abundance.

To thank Heaven for the blessing, Zhao Gong Ming commissioned eight priests to craft joss paper made from the silver and gold from his dog and his hen, and then burned the joss papers as offerings all day every day. The silver joss papers were burned for his ancestors and the gold burned for the gods.[12]

However, Zhao Gong Ming's prosperity attracted jealousy, and those who wished him ill tried to set the black dog, hen, and eight priests on fire to destroy his blessings. These men's malevolence was thwarted when the black dog transformed into a black tiger and mauled the men to death. The hen transformed into a phoenix and flew Zhao Gong Ming, the black tiger, and the eight priests upward into the sky toward Heaven. Heaven then transformed Zhao Gong Ming into an immortal. Once he was an immortal god, he selected four of his closest friends, men who were like brothers to him, to serve as lieutenant gods of the four directions while he occupied the center. Together they became known as the Five Celestials of Wealth.

Zhao Gong Ming is also venerated as Cai Shen, the God of Wealth.[13] It is said that when he is invoked by one of pure heart, humility, and generosity, one who embodies the traits that the beggar Zhao Gong Ming had demonstrated, Cai Shen and his Celestials of Wealth will descend to Earth to bless that person with abundance and prosperity.

Figure 5.6. The God of Wealth Fu

To cast the traditional Chinese spell invoking Cai Shen and the Five Celestials, render the Fu sigil pictured in figure 5.6, the God of Wealth Fu as I use it in my practice. The God of Wealth Fu begins with the three-star constellation at the top, from the imperial symbols of sovereignty. Inscribed within a power octagon, invoking the Ba Gua, is the traditional Chinese character for prosperity, money, or riches, 財 (Cái). A likeness of Zhao Gong Ming's tiger is rendered, with a Chinese coin in its mouth, to symbolize the delivery of wealth. Then below the tiger is the I Ching hexagram for increase, hexagram 42, 益 (Yi). Below it is the character for attracting wealth and prosperity toward you, 臨, which also evokes hexagram 19, for coming

Figure 5.7. Traditional Chinese coins

spring. The empty box at the base of the Fu should be filled in with the Fu recipient's name, either written out or rendered into a glyph. A practitioner crafting this Fu for him- or herself should stamp the practitioner's seal inside the box.

Then proceed with the ritual. The ritual will require an image or likeness of Cai Shen, who also represents the Five Celestials of Wealth. Cai Shen is also known as 趙公明神尊, "The Honorable Deity," which is simply "Zhao Gong Ming" (趙公明, Zhào Gōng Míng) with an honorific, "The Honorable Deity" (神尊, Shén Zūn).

The one likeness of Cai Shen embodies all five Celestials of Wealth. Zhao Gong Ming is the Celestial of Wealth ruling over the center of the five relative directions ( 中路財神, Zhōng Lù Cái Shén), and thus commands the deities, or lieutenant deities, of the other four directions. Zhao Gong Ming is more popularly referred to as simply Cai Shen ("God of Wealth").

For this specific spell invoking Zhao Gong Ming as Cai Shen, be sure to select an image or likeness that includes his black tiger. Cai Shen comes in many forms, varying from tradition to tradition. The folk tradition I grew up with happens to correlate Zhao Gong Ming with Cai Shen, the God of Wealth. Thus, following the instructions of this spell, the Zhao Gong Ming likeness of the God of Wealth should be used. To differentiate between the many incarnations and folk variations of Cai Shen, look for deity images of Zhao Gong Ming Shen Zun ("Shen Zun" being the honorific for his deified status), which are sure to include the black tiger.

An image of Cai Shen and his black tiger can be printed out or drawn on paper and used for this spell. However, since you are in effect inviting a god to enter the space, be sure to use the absolute best paper you can get your hands on, and the best and most carefully selected representation you can find. Better yet, especially if you're artistic, hand-draw the image of Cai Shen and the black tiger. Be sure to consecrate the image or likeness prior to commencement of the ritual.

Through a process called Kai Guang (開光), the Five Celestials of Wealth are invited into the image or likeness of Cai Shen that the practitioner has prepared. The purpose of Kai Guang is to empower that image or likeness with the deities' presence. To perform Kai Guang, the practitioner needs a calligraphy brush or pen with red cinnabar powder.

Begin by cleaning the work space for the charging ritual with consecrated water. Incense should be lit to send prayers upward to Heaven to facilitate communion between the practitioner and the deities. Next, set out offerings to the Five Celestials on the practitioner's altar. These offerings include the following:

- three traditional meats[14]
- tea
- wine
- fresh flowers
- fresh fruits

Then the Kai Guang may commence. With the practitioner's giving hand, hold the pen and dot the deity's likeness on the forehead with the red cinnabar powder. The practitioner's intent should be focused on inviting the Five Celestials into his or her sacred space, with a primary concentration on Cai Shen (or Zhao Gong Ming). Next, dot the deity's likeness on the left eye and then the right eye, then the left ear and the right ear, then the mouth, then the nose, then the left hand and the right hand, then the stomach, and then the left foot and right foot. If you are using an image of Cai Shen rendered on a piece of paper, using red ink from a consecrated pen in lieu of the cinnabar powder will suffice.

For statues, the cinnabar powder can be wiped off after the Kai Guang ritual. For a paper likeness, after the spell is complete and the practitioner no longer has a need for the paper, the best practice is to recite prayers while burning the paper to ashes along with incense, to send the energy back to Heaven. The paper can also be buried in the earth, again while reciting prayers. Tossing the paper likeness out with your trash might be considered irreverent.

The practitioner places a traditional Chinese coin, like the one pictured in figure 5.7, into the black tiger's mouth, or places it over the mouth area. The practitioner then proceeds to burn the Fu sigil to ash. Traditionally, the ashes are to be mixed with wine, and the one who seeks wealth and prosperity must drink the ash and wine mixture. However, in modern practice, I recommend transference of sigil energy into an object, such as a talisman, gemstone, or pendant. Transference of sigil energy is explained in chapter 10, "Activation Techniques."

Next, burn gold and silver joss papers to honor and thank the deities. Also, after the charging ritual, the offerings of meats, tea, wine, and fruits are considered blessed and auspicious to eat. Those who eat them will enjoy greater fortuity.

The foregoing spell invoking the Five Celestials of Wealth pays homage to the legend of Zhao Gong Ming and is believed to ensure prosperity and fortune to the beneficiary or recipient of the Fu energy. Like Zhao Gong Ming, if and when the spell works and the beneficiary reaps the results of the spell, the beneficiary must be generous and give to those less fortunate. One of the caveats to blessings from Zhao Gong Ming is that the recipient of his blessings must work hard and live a diligent, modest life. He does not endow blessings to the indolent.

# CHAPTER 6

# THE TOOLS OF CRAFT

**THIS CHAPTER WILL** offer an overview of the Taoist practitioner's tools. The listing provided here is by no means complete, nor is it suggesting that acquiring all of these tools is compulsory for craft. It is provided for the limited purpose of satiating a Western practitioner's curiosity for what goes into Eastern traditions of craft.

Figure 6.1. A Chinese seal or chop

## PRACTITIONER'S SEAL

A practitioner's seal, also called the Seal of the Law (法印, fǎ yìn), is an energetically charged signature used as a spiritual beacon to identify an individual practitioner. The seal is a stamp carved into a stone or block of wood

Figure 6.2. Positive and negative practitioner seals[1]

that represents and identifies a practitioner. Based on the symbolism, imagery, and delineations on the seal, the object comes to acquire a specific energetic frequency that represents the practitioner's work. That frequency is nurtured and strengthened over the course of a practitioner's lifetime. From frequent use, the practitioner can tune the seal, which is a mere object, to resonate with the same personal frequency as the practitioner. In effect, the seal becomes a call-out in the spiritual realm to identify the practitioner—hence, it is a signature.

The practitioner's seal serves as a key. The key is needed to "open" an altar so that it becomes connected to heaven. For a ritual to be effective, an altar must first be open and connected to heaven. Thus, a practitioner's seal is needed for empowering Fu sigils.

In the Taoist tradition, most practitioners have a magical name or craft name, which is then written in Fu Wen and inscribed onto a Chinese seal. That seal is used for opening an altar during rituals or energetic work, and it is affixed to all Fu sigils crafted by that practitioner to augment the sigil with the practitioner's personal power. The seals of renowned and powerful practitioners also come to possess metaphysical power and can be used as a glyph in Fu craft for invoking the power and abilities of that practitioner. That principle propels glyphs such as the Seal of Lao Tzu, pictured earlier in figure 2.3, now used as a talisman for protection. Whether the inscription was the actual seal of Lao Tzu is unknown (and is also not likely), but the stamped engraving is treated in principle as if it was Lao Tzu's seal.

Seals can be carved as either positive or negative. A positive seal is when the lettering is carved in such a way that when stamped, the characters are rendered with the ink and there is white space in the background. The left image in figure 6.2 shows a positive seal for a fictional practitioner with the craft name "White Swallow" (白燕巫師, Bái Yàn Wū Shī).[2] She has added the title "sorcerer" (巫師, Wū Shī) to her craft name, to identify the nature of craft she practices.[3]

Usually the positive seal features an inked border. A negative seal is when the lettering is carved in such a way that it is the background space behind the characters that is inked, and so the final stamped result appears darkened with the ink's color, while the actual lettering of the practitioner's name is the white space. The right image in figure 6.2 shows a negative seal.

A positive seal is considered to be yang-dominant, whereas a negative seal is considered to be yin-dominant. A practitioner will choose whichever form of seal best resonates with the nature of his or her craft. A practitioner could also possess both a positive and negative seal, and the one stamped onto a particular Fu sigil will depend on what work is being performed. When invoking higher spirits, deities, saints, the angelic realm, or immortals, the positive seal is used; when facilitating communication with all other spirit realms, summoning ghosts, hungry ghosts, those from the underworld, or demons, a negative yin seal is used.

Figure 6.3 is a mock sample of a Fu stamped with a positive seal. It shows the seal of a hypothetical practitioner, White Swallow, from the earlier figure 6.2. The Fu invokes He Xian Gu (何仙姑), one of the Eight Immortals, often invoked as a patron saint, who is said to assist fortune-tellers and diviners.[4] Glyphs along the top right column and in the bottom half of the Fu represent prosperity and the blessing of good business. Near the top right, there is a glyph rendered from the Lo Shu square, to trigger the feng shui sectors for wealth, ancestry (to also beseech White Swallow's ancestors for assistance), healing abilities, knowledge and skills, and profession. This Fu is crafted specifically for the prosperity and good business of a witch or sorceress who makes her living by telling fortunes, divining, and sharing her psychic abilities with others. Such a Fu would be crafted to pay homage to her patron saint, the female Immortal He

Figure 6.3. A Fu for stronger prophetic abilities

Figure 6.4. A retaliatory Fu for conjuring malevolent spirits

| Chinese Horoscope Sign by Birth Year | Essential Yin-Yang Dominance | Essential Fixed Element Dominance |
|---|---|---|
| Rat | Yang | Water |
| Ox | Yin | Water |
| Tiger | Yang | Wood |
| Rabbit | Yin | Wood |
| Dragon | Yang | Wood |
| Snake | Yin | Fire |
| Horse | Yang | Fire |
| Sheep | Yin | Fire |
| Monkey | Yang | Metal |
| Rooster | Yin | Metal |
| Dog | Yang | Metal |
| Boar | Yin | Water |

Table 6.1. Yin-yang and Wu Xing dominance in the Chinese zodiac

Xian Gu, who can endow White Swallow with the power to heal others and excel at divination. He Xian Gu is also a patron saint for women.

A negative seal might be used for yin-related craft. When I say yin-related craft, I mean energetic workings that involve lesser spirits. Figure 6.4 is an example of a Fu for retaliatory craft that is stamped with a negative seal so that the craft might be more yin-conducive. First, note that the Fu glyphs are crafted to indicate a summoning or conjuration. The name of the lesser spirit is encoded in the glyph stylized from the Lo Shu square (on the right side, right above the practitioner's negative seal stamp). A chain of squares is used to indicate yang energy, but is being transmuted by lemniscates into yin energy leading to the Chinese character for black (黑), to symbolize yin, or the yin-conducive setting for the lesser spirit to manifest in. Note further the use of demonic poison (蠱) in Fu sigils for retaliatory craft.

Yet be mindful that a positive seal is not associated with the "light" in a benevolent sense and a negative seal is not associated with the "dark" in a malevolent sense. There are no such subjective correspondences to the positive or negative seals (which are terms used here in a technical manner, and not to indicate a judgment of good or bad). One is just considered energetically to be more yang while the other is more yin. Yin and yang energies serve different purposes that any practitioner must be able to use with equal mastery.

Also, practitioners whose Chinese natal astrology reveals that they are yang-dominant may find a positive seal to resonate more strongly with them, and to be a better identifier for themselves. Those who are yin-dominant may find a negative seal to resonate more strongly. However, in direct contradiction to what I just said, an alternative thought on the matter would seek out yin and yang balance, and so those who are yin-dominant would opt for a positive seal with yang energy as a counterbalance to their own yin dominance, and an individual who is yang-dominant according to his or her natal astrology would opt for a negative seal and its yin energy for balance. The best way to sort through the confusion is to define your purpose, understand the reasoning behind your own craft, and then take the approach that is most aligned with your purpose and reasoning.

According to table 6.1, a practitioner born in the year of the Rat might find herself more yang-dominant. If that yang dominance has served her well in her craft, she may want to amplify it, and therefore commission a practitioner's seal that is positively carved (yang-dominant). However, if that practitioner has found her essential yang-dominant personality to be more troublesome and therefore seeks balance when proceeding with craft, she may opt for a negatively carved seal (yin-dominant).

My personal seal for everyday noncraft use (not that I have used it with any frequency; however, generally, most Chinese and Taiwanese people have a personal seal with their name commissioned on it) is a positive seal, and thus considered yang-dominant, though the practitioner's seal I use is a negative one that is yin-dominant.

But having a commissioned seal is not necessary for craft. It is the concept behind the practitioner's seal, not its actual form, that is important. If a practitioner does not have a Chinese seal stamp, other forms of seals may be used. A custom-designed seal as in the Western esoteric traditions can be conceived. The practitioner could also craft a personal mandala using only positive and negative space, likened to the carvings of a Chinese seal, and then commission to have the Western-style seal or mandala inscribed onto a rubber ink stamp. Customizing and ordering a professional-grade self-inking stamp would work well for a practitioner's seal.

In the Eastern tradition, a mandala is a pictorial representation of a part of the universe, and one can be designed by a practitioner to represent that practitioner's energetic frequency. The mandala is a circle enclosing a square. Generally the mandala begins with the Cartesian coordinate graph, with four equal circles connected at the (0,0) point. The four petals formed by the circles are the four points for a square while the outer points of the four circles connect to form a large circle.

Before a practitioner begins Fu sigil crafting, he or she will devise a personal seal that is the signature for the practitioner's craft, either opting to follow the traditional Chinese form of the seal with the practitioner's Chinese name rendered into Fu Wen, or following a Western tradition of a seal. The practitioner can also consider designing a personal mandala that represents the individual's magical practice or identity, though in terms of logistics, keep the design simple. A personal mandala that is too detailed will be difficult to customize into a rubber stamp.

The practitioner's seal is a signature. By Taoist magical theory, the seal also becomes an individual practitioner's key to channeling the supernatural planes. It is believed that the physical realm that human bodies and sentient beings occupy is one plane. All realms together make up the collective unconscious, which a practitioner can tap into through a bridge formed from his or her personal unconscious. Seals must be specifically crafted as a key for crossing that bridge into the collective unconscious and thus into the spiritual realms.

Yet another form the practitioner's seal can take is the atman candle. The atman candle is a candle that in every subjective way reflects the practitioner's self, or atman. The term *atman* refers to the essential self.[5] The candle is made of materials and of a color, scent, and style that resonate intensely with the individual practitioner. It can also be inscribed or carved with the practitioner's seal, a sigil that identifies the practitioner, or an inscribed craft name. The atman candle is thus a practitioner's signifier in rites and rituals. A 3-by-9-inch pillar candle with the practitioner's seal carved into the bottom and propped on a candle holder that best suits the practitioner's personal style would make an excellent atman candle.

Note that when an atman candle has been used down to its stub, it should be retired from further use and a new atman candle prepared. To retire the old atman candle, wait until a waning moon to bury it. One sample invocation to recite while burying the old atman candle is as follows: "I lay this atman candle to rest. I am the resurrection and the life. *Lazuli korah—Prajna paramita.*"

## THE ALTAR

The altar is the sacred space in a home for performing a charging ritual. It is the practitioner's work space, set up in the manner of the practitioner's tradition. The altar is likened to a portal or gateway, the point of contact between the physical world and the metaphysical world. It is the nexus that links Heaven, Earth, and Man during a ritual. In Taoist and Buddhist traditions, practitioners set up an altar in their homes to invoke holy spirits to descend and watch over the practitioner's work. Note that a Kai Guang ritual, covered in chapter 7, is often performed to consecrate any deity statues placed on an altar.

Chinese folk religions can be interpreted as both monotheistic and polytheistic, believing in a single unifying god concept, but under that god principle or "source energy," there are numerous deities and spirits that are venerated for more specific purposes. Most orthodox Taoist lineages and practitioners of craft venerate one deity as the main god (or two, a goddess and god concept to represent the yin and yang binary, though that yin and yang binary together still represents the unified "one god" principle, the Qi source energy) that the practitioners derive their power and authority from.

An altar that is set up permanently in the home will place a sizeable statue of that deity or deities at the front and center of the altar. However, practitioners also tend to accept a polytheistic religious view, and thus for a specific ritual, may focus on a deity other than the main deity or deities that the practitioner venerates. For instance, a practitioner might venerate Amithaba and Kuan Yin as the main deities and have a permanent altar set up in the home focused on Amithaba and Kuan Yin. Yet for a Fu crafting ritual intended to empower a sigil that will enhance one's divinatory or psychic abilities, a temporary altar focused on Bu Dai might be set up just for that ritual.[6] Thus, altar setups can be either permanent or temporary.

The positioning of an altar is highly personal and varies from lineage to lineage, even from practitioner to practitioner. For instance, Buddhist practitioners who venerate Amithaba might position the altar facing eastward (and therefore the practitioner, when facing the altar, would be facing westward). Taoist

Figure 6.5. Basic home altar setup

practitioners who base their rituals heavily around the Lo Shu square position an altar in the south, facing northward, so a practitioner who is facing the altar faces southward. For practitioners whose rituals are based heavily around the Big Dipper, the altar is likely to be oriented north. In general, you are likely to find more disagreements about altar placement than you will agreements. When in doubt, follow your intuition and be guided by what resonates with you. Figure 6.5 provides a very basic home altar setup, and the rest of this section offers instruction on commonly found elements of a practitioner's home altar.

**Image, statue, or likeness of deity.** Whether the altar is one to be set up permanently in the home or is set up temporarily for a ritual, the statue or likeness of the deity or deities must be at the highest elevation. If, for instance, you happen to have a small, humble statue, that's OK, but if your candles tower over that statue in height, then place the statue on a tall stand, so that the statue sits higher than the tips of the candles.

**Incense.** The traditional form of incense is joss sticks, which are placed into an incense pot positioned in a centralized location in front of the deity statue. Buddhist-based practitioners may opt for sandalwood spiral incense coils. Predating both joss sticks and incense coils was resin incense, and for many orthodox temples or orthodox practitioners, the preferred form of incense is resin. In modern applications, any form of incense that resonates with the practitioner may be used.

**Fresh flowers.** Typically two symmetrical vases of fresh flowers are placed on either side of the deity statue. As a contemporary alternative, silk flowers can be used, though my personal preference is to use fresh flowers when possible. For elaborate rituals, elaborate floral arrangements are used.

**Twin candles.** Two candles, one at each side of the altar, represent the sun and moon. Some traditions opt for identical twin candles, while others will use contrasting colors to call upon representations of yin and yang. The color of the candle wax may vary depending on the ritual at hand. Typically, the candles are red for prosperity and protection.

**Three staple offerings.** In front of the incense are three chalices of staple offerings: consecrated water to the left of the practitioner; tea in the center; and uncooked rice to the right. I remember the positioning by remembering that the moon and yin are to the left and the sun and yang are to the right. Water to the left for the moon and yin; rice (米, mī) to the right because the character for "rice" reminds me of the character for Light or luminescence (光, guāng), for yang.

**Bowls of fruit.** Most Chinese households with altars set out offerings of the fruits that they happen to have on hand, varying with the seasons. Oranges, mandarin oranges, or kumquats are typically set out, symbolizing the family's prayers for prosperity. Pomegranates, lychees, or longan are offered when a couple is praying for fertility, children, or healthy births. The pomelo or apple is set out as an offering for maintaining a harmonious, happy, and whole family unit. Note, however, that the traditional Taoist instruction is to set out five bowls of fruit that represent the Wu Xing: plum for Wood; apricot for Fire; jujube or dates for Earth; peach for Metal; and chestnut for Water.[7]

| | | |
|---|---|---|
| Southeast<br>**Wood** | South<br>**Fire** | Southwest<br>**Earth** |
| East<br>**Wood** | Center<br>**Earth** | West<br>**Metal** |
| Northeast<br>**Earth** | North<br>**Water** | Northwest<br>**Metal** |

Figure 6.6. Wu Xing and directionality for an altar

**Practitioner's seal and seal dish.** The practitioner's seal is put away when not in use, so an altar is not set up with the practitioner's seal in the foreground. However, when the altar is being used for a ritual, the seal is placed on the altar to open the altar, a technique further discussed in "Opening the Ritual" in chapter 8. The practitioner's seal can come in many forms, as discussed previously, and any sincere representation of the self can be used, such as the atman candle. Typically, a practitioner will also have a flat stone dish or mat on the altar for the seal to be placed on.

**Miscellaneous.** In the remaining space on the altar, a practitioner might place other tools of craft, such as the divination moon blocks, ceremonial bells, or wooden percussion blocks. One consideration for the miscellaneous items on the altar is to position them according to Ba Gua directionality and the Lo Shu magic square. See figure 6.6 for the Wu Xing and directionality correspondences on an altar top.

Assuming the altar setup illustrated in figure 6.5 has the deity positioned in the south sector of the altar top, facing north, the ceremonial bells are placed on the right side, corresponding with west for Metal, and the wooden percussion blocks are placed on the left, corresponding with east for Wood. Note that while divination moon blocks are typically made of wood, in figure 6.6 the divination blocks are placed toward the northwest corner, associated with the Heaven trigram. The purpose of divination moon blocks is to communicate directly with deity, or Heaven, and so, to me, it makes more sense to position them in a manner corresponding with Heaven rather than by Wood, the material the blocks are made of. Sweets, candies, or liquor can also be set out as offerings. Pursuant to folk religious beliefs, sweets are set out to "sweeten up" the deity or deities and liquor ensures that the deity or deities are in a good mood.[8]

Figure 6.7. A simple work space

You do not need to set up an altar for sigil crafting. A cleared tabletop to work on is more than sufficient. Figure 6.7 shows the ordinary manner in which I craft my Fu sigils. I light sandalwood or cedar wood incense, clear the work space physically and metaphysically with the opening techniques discussed in chapter 8, and then begin the charging invocations to empower the sigil. Although figure 6.7 shows the statue of Bu Dai present, the deity invoked for empowering that particular Fu, I often work without a deity image or likeness and opt for a few grounding stones instead.

## CONSECRATED INK

Traditionally, Fu sigils were painted with Chinese calligraphy in red ink.[9] Ge Hong (AD 283–343), an alchemist and writer from the Jin Dynasty, wrote about the crafting of Fu sigils. He noted that the calligraphy pen used by the

Figure 6.8. Chinese vermillion ink paste

practitioner should be made of peach wood, and the ink should be made from red cinnabar.[10] Cinnabar was believed by Taoist alchemists to be one of the key ingredients in an elixir for achieving immortality.[11] However, black ink is also common, and occult instructions for crafting sigil spells dating back as far as the tenth century AD indicate the use of black ink from an ink stone.[12]

Thus, the most common colors for ink are black and red. If the Fu sigil has been rendered in red ink, the practitioner's seal might be stamped in black. Likewise, Fu sigils in black ink might bear a practitioner's seal (or a temple's seal)[13] in red ink. There are, however, no immutable rules on ink requirements for craft, other than the rule that the color of ink you choose bears relevance to the craft at hand. Color correspondence is an important consideration. Red is used because it is believed to ward off evil, generate auspicious energy, and is the color of happiness and prosperity. Black is used for its strong protective properties.

In terms of the writing instrument, traditionally a bamboo or sandalwood brush was used with ink from an ink stick. Ink sticks are ink in solid form, made from soot, animal glue, and incense. The ink stick is ground against an ink stone, which is a mortar, and calligraphy ink is produced. For stamps, a red ink paste is used, also referred to as red seal paste.

Although the preference is still for Fu sigils to be painted by brush, a pen can certainly be used in its place. Whether a brush or a pen is to be used, it must first be consecrated like the Fu sigil paper. Personally, I use a pen, not a

Figure 6.9. Fu sigil paper

brush, but it has been consecrated and is reserved exclusively for sigil craft-ing—the pen is never used for any other purpose. I like to stock up on conse-crated ink. I buy boxes of ultrafine-point permanent markers, and when the moon phase and timing are right, I consecrate the boxes of pens all at once, and then store them away for later use.

## CONSECRATED PAPER

This book assumes that the Fu sigils being crafted will be on paper. Tradition-ally, the paper used is rice paper, but any type of paper will suffice, as long as it has been consecrated.

Today, throughout East Asia, Fu sigils are most commonly found on yel-low or white paper, though it is said that the "imperial yellow" paper color was the preferred paper for Taoist magicians.[14] A special type of edible rice paper should be used if the practitioner intends on ingesting the Fu. In certain prac-tices of craft, Fu sigils are eaten as a means of empowering the recipient. I do not subscribe to the practice of ingesting paper Fu sigils, and so I have never worried about whether my Fu paper is edible.

The practitioner might also consider selecting a color to match the intent of the sigil. Green is associated with wealth and luck, so for a Fu sigil intend-ed to manifest wealth or better fortune, the practitioner might want to use green paper for the sigil. Adding gold accents will further support intentions

Figure 6.10. Octagonal Ba Gua sigil for protection from psychic attacks

of wealth and status. For Fu sigils related to romance, consider pink paper. Factoring color symbolism in selecting paper can greatly enhance the efficacy of the Fu. Note, for instance, the specific paper-color instructions given for the Fire Wheel Fu referenced in chapter 5.

Traditionally Fu sigils are inscribed onto rectangular paper that is two and a half to three times longer than its width, like the paper sigil in figure 6.9. Such sigils can then either be posted, rolled into a scroll[15] and bound with red string, or folded and tucked away into a wallet. I like using standard bookmark-size paper, or 2 by 6 inches. Note that there is no set rule. Figure 6.10 shows a Fu sigil crafted into an octagonal shape to raise energies from the Ba Gua.

The practitioner can use any type, size, color, and shape of paper the practitioner chooses. What is important is that the selection process pulls the Fu sigils from the ordinary into the extraordinary for the practitioner. That is not for the sigils' benefit, but for the practitioner's. By ensuring a procedure that is out of the ordinary, when the practitioner engages in the procedure, his or her mindset will be elevated beyond the ordinary as well.

## BA GUA MIRROR

The Ba Gua mirror is a circular mirror affixed to the center of an octagonal Ba Gua, usually made of wood, painted in red, black, green, or gold. It is used in many different practices of esoteric Taoism, from feng shui to exorcisms, banishment spells, defensive or protective magic, to—at times—Fu sigil crafting.[16] A consecrated and empowered Ba Gua mirror is believed to deflect negative energies. Once a Ba Gua mirror is obtained by a practitioner, remember that at that point, it is a mere object. A Ba Gua mirror must be consecrated and empowered to serve in the practitioner's energetic workings.

Due to the innate metaphysical properties that practitioners believe Ba Gua mirrors wield, it should not be used as interior decor (with a few exceptions found in feng shui tenets) or kept out in the open (unless it is being hung outdoors).[17] It should be put away when not in use for a ritual. Ba Gua mirrors are believed to tamper with the flow of Qi in the environment, which is constructive when the practitioner is knowledgeable and intentionally using the mirror to control Qi. However, unchecked and uncontrolled, a Ba Gua can generate all sorts of energetic turbulence.

Figure 6.11. Ba Gua mirror

When I haven't had the chance to put away my Ba Gua mirror yet and it is out on my work desk, for instance, but not in active use, I keep it mirror-side down. If a Ba Gua mirror is purchased from a metaphysical proprietor, you might even notice a Fu sigil painted on the back. The purpose of the sigil is manifold: to generally empower the mirror (though the practitioner is still advised to consecrate and charge it upon acquiring a new one) and, when placed facing down, keep the energies around the mirror peaceful and controlled (although, of course, this depends on the nature of the sigil painted on the back side; I am speaking in broad generalizations here only).

Ba Gua mirrors can be found three ways: flat, with a smooth reflective surface; concave; or convex. The flat, smooth mirror is the most common and the one typically used in ritual. It contains a balance of yin and yang properties. If a practitioner opts to include a Ba Gua mirror in a charging ritual for his or her Fu sigils, the flat, smooth mirror is recommended.

Note that in some instances the concave or convex Ba Gua mirrors may be more appropriate. A concave Ba Gua mirror absorbs energy and can be used in rituals for a Fu sigil intended to take energy away from an object or entity, to extract, draw out, seize energy, or weaken the power of another so that it will be pulled into and absorbed by the mirror's concave surface. It can be used in offensive Fu sigil crafting to weaken or extract the powers of an adversary. In feng shui practice, a concave Ba Gua mirror is used to absorb atrophic or malignant Qi energies so that the mirror takes the hit and leaves the home environment free from the harmful effects of atrophic and malignant Qi. After each and every use of a concave Ba Gua mirror in ritual, it should be cleansed and consecrated. Basic instructions for consecration and purification are found in chapter 7.

A convex Ba Gua mirror deflects, reverses, and sends back energy that had been previously directed. Convex Ba Gua mirrors are used in defensive Fu sigil crafting. It can be used to deflect any curses believed to have been sent toward the practitioner or the recipient of a Fu sigil crafted to ward off the curse. A convex Ba Gua mirror is like a shield. It blocks and redirects energy. While convex Ba Gua mirrors should also be periodically consecrated and purified, it is not quite the imperative that it is for concave Ba Gua mirrors. That is because concave mirrors absorb the Qi, which remains within the mirror, while convex mirrors deflect the Qi back outward and don't keep that energy around.

Note that in feng shui, convex Ba Gua mirrors are not advised, because while it protects the one who has implemented the mirror, the atrophic or malignant Qi energy is refracted outward, bouncing off the surface of the mirror and redirected elsewhere. It can thus have an adverse impact on others, and the one who implemented the mirror will bear the karmic consequences of hurting others. Thus, any use of a convex Ba Gua mirror in feng shui would probably be with an offensive or malign intent.

In craft, however, the practitioner is controlling the redirection of energy, and so karmic consequences are mitigated through the specific techniques employed by the practitioner. Thus, for example, in using of a convex Ba Gua mirror to deflect a curse, the practitioner's intent is specific—to return the energy back toward the original sender. The practitioner's craft is what controls the direction of energy refracted from the Ba Gua mirror.

While either the Earlier Heaven or Later Heaven Ba Gua sequence can be used on such a mirror, the purpose and uses are different. The Earlier Heaven Ba Gua helps to restore energetic balance and bears a more neutralizing application. The Later Heaven Ba Gua transforms and facilitates transmutation of energy. The Earlier Heaven Ba Gua mirror is typically seen in feng shui practice, whereas in craft, or magic, the Later Heaven Ba Gua is used.

Note that Ba Gua mirrors are not a requirement for effective Fu sigil crafting. They are, however, a commonly found tool in the Eastern esoteric practices.

## CANDLES

Candles are an effective tool for focusing a practitioner's concentration. Lighting candles will set the tone and mood of the atmosphere in a way that is most conducive for a practitioner to elevate into the higher state of consciousness, which will facilitate the bridge into the unconscious.

Most Taoist altars feature two identical red candles, as the Chinese find red to be an auspicious color. Together the two candles represent the sun and moon, and the yin and yang dichotomy. Since I am not terribly fond of red candles and find them to be a bit garish, I prefer one light and one dark candle, generally white and black.

## DIVINATION MOON BLOCKS

Jiao Bei (筊杯)[18] divination moon blocks are crescent-shaped blocks, hence the namesake, typically made of peach wood or bamboo, though any material can be used, where one side is domed and the other is flat. The domed side is referred to as yin and the flat side is yang.

Divination moon blocks are used for yes-or-no queries. More specifically, they are used as a form of communication with deity or the spirit realm. The practitioner would invoke a deity or spirit by name, ask his or her question, usually phrased as a yes-or-no query, and then toss the moon blocks. The result is the deity or spirit's response.

It is important to note that the purported mechanics behind divination moon blocks are a means of communication with the spirit realm. The traditional explanation for why moon blocks work is not the "higher self" or synchronicity.[19] It is not a form of fortune-telling. Culturally and historically, it is a form of revelation. The presumption behind moon blocks is that a deity has been invoked, or a spirit or ghost summoned, and it is now present. Then the practitioner and the entity from the spirit realm communicate with one another through the moon blocks and by way of yes-or-no queries.

When one moon block is yin and the other is yang, as shown in figure 6.13, the deity or spirit's response is yes, in the positive. For Fu sigil crafting, the divination moon blocks are used as a form of postliminary divination to determine whether the Fu sigil has been successfully empowered for its intended effect. Postliminary divination is covered in chapter 8. When the result is one

Figure 6.12. Jiao Bei divination blocks

Figure 6.13. Affirmative answer from the Jiao Bei

Figure 6.14. Negative answer from the Jiao Bei

Figure 6.15. "Laughing Gods" response from the Jiao Bei

yin (curved side up) and one yang (flat side up), the Fu sigil is deemed successfully charged.

When both moon blocks fall as yin, with curved sides up, as shown in figure 6.14, then the answer is no, and in a postliminary divination with such a result, the practitioner has not succeeded at empowering the Fu sigil for its intended effect. The practitioner would then need to return to the conception phase and design a new Fu sigil for the intention. A double yin result from the moon blocks can also mean that the deity or spirit named is not present, and therefore the Fu sigil does not have that deity or spirit's blessing.

If both moon blocks fall as yang, with flat sides up, then it is suggested that the deity or spirit is laughing at the practitioner (see fig. 6.15). It is an indication that the spirit world is withholding its answer at this time and is not

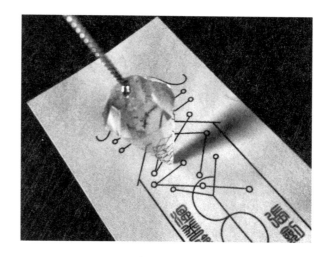

Figure 6.16. Using a pendulum for the postliminary divination

willing to reveal the outcome to you. The result is called "laughing gods," because the spirit world is, in a way, laughing at you. The double yang result generally indicates an answer of uncertainty, or "maybe." It does affirm deity or spirit presence, and therefore communion has been established, but the deity or spirit is refusing to provide a definitive answer to the practitioner.

While a practitioner is still free to proceed with the charging ritual if the practitioner is in a state of full confidence and conviction, most practitioners would probably set the matter aside for a day and rteturn to divine for an answer again at a later time. How a practitioner responds to a "laughing gods" response is personal.

An answer of uncertainty from the moon blocks could also indicate strong oppositional forces against the specific intent. A powerful and seasoned practitioner will note the uncertainty and harness stronger energy to overcome the oppositional forces. Thus, a practitioner would return to the drawing board and design a new Fu sigil, one crafted to raise even more power and energy than before, because now the practitioner is aware that there are strong oppositional forces that need to be dealt with. The inexperienced practitioner is advised to supplement the Fu sigil with other energetic workings that will amplify the power of the Fu sigil. He or she must also be conscious of taking assertive action in ordinary life to help along the specific intent.

Figure 6.17. My mother's incense burner

Divination moon blocks are commonplace in most Taoist temples. There is usually a bowl filled with red-painted divination moon blocks right by the altar. Visitors ask their questions to the deities and then consult the moon blocks to see how the deities answer. Taoist practitioners utilize these blocks in their private practice for yes-no divinations, communicating with deities and spirits, and, as this book will teach, for postliminary divinations to determine whether a Fu sigil has been properly charged.

**Divination Alternatives.** Moon blocks are not mandatory; any divination technique can be used. A pendulum works perfectly here. Using tarot cards or runes could also work, depending on the practitioner's personal skill level with tarot or runes. Chapter 11 demonstrates how all the techniques discussed independently in this book come together cohesively. In that demonstration, the hypothetical practitioner uses tarot cards for the postliminary divination, rather than the more traditional moon blocks.

## INCENSE

Crafting effective Fu sigils requires access to the collective unconscious so that greater energies may be harnessed for the practitioner's use. Some call that collective unconscious the spirit realm, and while the collective unconscious encompasses the spirit realm, it is more than that. It is the oneness of above and below.

| | |
|---|---|
| **Bergamot** | Empowerment; strength; work, career; wealth, prosperity; business, commerce; better fortunes, improved karma; protection, defense. |
| **Camphor** | Camphor is generally the preferred incense for mediums and shamans who traverse into the underworld. Camphor is used in energetic workings that involve communing with ghosts, the deceased, or ancestors. It is believed to have purification and protective properties that keep the practitioner safe during such energetic workings. |
| **Cedar Wood** | Purification, consecration; empowerment; strength; health, healing; work, career; wealth, prosperity; business, commerce; better fortunes, improved karma; raising intuition and wisdom, calming. Cedar wood has purification properties that keep the Qi energy in a space balance, healthy, and purified. |
| **Chamomile** | Health, healing; raising intuition and wisdom; calming depression or stress; inducing altered states for shamanic practices; communication with ancestors; psychic dreams. |
| **Cinnamon** | Grounding; career, business; professional success; health, healing; wealth, prosperity; money magic. |
| **Frankincense** | Protection, defense; banishing; grounding; health, healing; purification, consecration; empowerment; strength; better fortunes, improved karma. |
| **Ginger** | Intuition; calming; luck; prosperity; sensuality. When combined with orange, grapefruit, or lemongrass, will invigorate the physical senses and create a state of empowerment and vitality. Improves personal Qi energy and helps in health and wellness rituals. |
| **Jasmine** | Health, healing; work, career; wealth, prosperity; business, commerce. Jasmine incense is also used in love, romance, and relationship spells. Believed to help improve one's beauty or attractiveness. |
| **Lavender** | Purification, consecration; protection, defense; health, healing; love, reunions. Used in love, romance, and relationships. |
| **Lotus** | Health, healing; raising intuition and wisdom. For rituals to improve health, physical recovery, or reduce illness on the metaphysical plane, use lotus. |
| **Myrrh** | Purification, consecration; better fortunes, improved karma; protection, defense. |
| **Patchouli** | Beauty; love; attraction; work, career; wealth, prosperity; business, commerce. |
| **Sage** | Purification, consecration. |
| **Sandalwood** | Empowerment; strength; banishing; protection, defense; grounding; purification, consecration; better fortunes, improved karma; raising intuition and wisdom, calming. Sandalwood is generally the preferred incense for calling upon higher deities, the angelic realms, benevolent energies, and Heaven. Sandalwood is the traditional temple incense in Chinese Buddhist and Taoist culture. |

Table 6.3. Incense correspondences

| No. of Incense Sticks | Indication | Uses |
|---|---|---|
| 1 | mindfulness | Used by a practitioner during prayer, meditation, or cultivation. |
| 2 | yin and yang | Used for love-romance- or relationship-related Fu sigils. Calls to mind the Chinese phrase [insert characters] (hǎo shì chéng shuāng), which means "good things subsist in pairs." |
| 3 | heaven, earth, man | Used by practitioners to bring harmony and synthesis to the three planes, Heaven, Earth, and Man, for the ritual to follow. |
| 5 | wu xing | Used by practitioners to invoke the four compass directions and the fifth, according to geomancy, the center. Also used for its association with the Wu Xing phases. |
| 7 | netherworld | Used for summonings and connecting to entities from other realms of planes. |
| 8 | fortune, prosperity | Used in spell working for wealth and prosperity. |
| 9 | heaven | Used when the practitioner seeks to send a message directly to a deity or the heavenly plane. |
| 11 | angelic realm | Using the term "angelic realm" loosely here, eleven incense sticks can be used when contacting higher realms, those in Heaven, saints, immortals, or angels. |
| 12 | full year craft | Used for charging sigils that will be effective for a whole year; sigils to bring peace and prosperity for the upcoming year. |

Table 6.2. Incense sticks and ritual work

To access that collective unconscious, there must be a change of state in the practitioner, and to bring about a change in state, sights, sounds, and scents must be calibrated so that the desired change of state can occur.

In Eastern esoteric ritual work, incense is used to alter the practitioner's consciousness. In the shamanic cultures that predate Taoism, resin was the type of incense typically used in sacred rites. Most Taoist lineages today opt for joss sticks. Buddhist-dominant esoteric traditions often use incense coils.

The number of joss sticks that a practitioner opts to use for a ritual is symbolic. Generally, it is three, to represent the trinity of Heaven, Earth, and Man. Table 6.2 provides indications for the number of incense sticks selected in ritual work.

Figure 6.18. A japa mala with 108 prayer beads

Incense is also used to send prayers upward toward Heaven. It is believed that the energy and intentions raised by the practitioner during a ritual are transmitted to Heaven through the wafting incense smoke. For instance, traditionally, camphor incense is used by shamans when interacting with spirits from the underworld.[20] Sandalwood is the all-purpose incense used in Buddhism and Taoism for inner cultivation. Table 6.3 presents a general table of correspondences for the common incense found in Taoist craft.

Incense is an integral part of Eastern religious practice. Incense opens a portal, or line of communication, between the spirit world and the human.[21] It is through incense that Heaven, Earth, and Man can connect.

## PRAYER BEADS

Prayer beads are typically used by Taoist practitioners to keep count of their invocations during rituals. In most Eastern esoteric traditions, invocations, prayers, or spells are repeated not once, twice, or thrice, but hundreds of times. A *japa mala,* which contains 108 beads, is often used to help the practitioner keep count, especially since most rituals call for 108 recitations or a number that is a multiple of 108.[22]

Prayer beads made of Bodhi seeds are all-purpose, and thus great to have. Sandalwood works for empowerment, protection, and healing. Rattan seeds

Figure 6.19. Tingsha cymbals

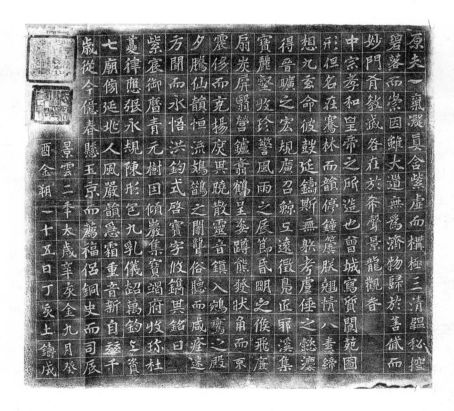

Figure 6.20. Bronze script on an eighth-century Taoist temple bell, Xi'an, China
(courtesy of Special Collections, Fine Arts Library, Harvard University)

Figure 6.21. Simple wood block

are also incredibly powerful for energetic work. To increase life span, longevity, knowledge, or merit, many practitioners opt for amber, gold, or copper. Amber beads are also believed to help with wealth and health. Rose quartz work best for emotional balance, love, and compassion. My personal favorite is one made with sodalite beads.

The practitioner is not required to have *mala* or prayer beads; they are entirely optional. They merely serve the functional purpose of keeping count.

## CEREMONIAL BELLS

Ceremonial bells are often part of a Taoist ritual because the sound is said to disperse negative and malignant energies or, in more direct magical terms, used to banish demons.[23] Taoist ceremonial bells are called the Bells of the Law (法鈴, fǎ líng), typically made of brass. The sound of bells catches the attention of benevolent spirits and is unappealing to negative spirits, and so will scatter malevolent or malignant spirit energies that may be present.[24]

In feng shui, bells or wind chimes[25] are believed to keep the Qi energy in an area benign. For rituals, bells are used as a form of purification of the air. They are rung at the commencement of a ritual to invite benevolent spirits and create an atmosphere of peace and harmony. At the close of a ritual, bells can be rung again to disperse the spiritual energies that had gathered for the ritual, returning the air and the vicinity back to the mundane.

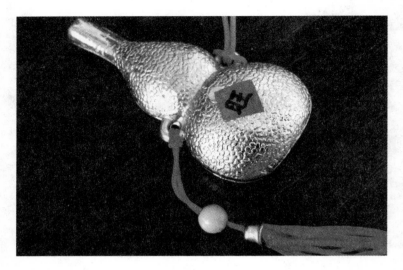

Figure 6.22. A metal gourd, an energy amplifier for health

I use *tingsha* cymbals, pictured in figure 6.19, though any bell will suffice. The ceremonial bells that a practitioner selects for ritual work should only be rung during ritual. After they are consecrated, most practitioners do not ring them arbitrarily outside of ritual, nor will they let others ring them arbitrarily when not in ritual.

## WOODEN PERCUSSION BLOCKS

Wooden percussion blocks, known as Chinese temple blocks or wood fish (木魚), are used in the same manner as the ceremonial bells, and are likely a practice borrowed from Mahayana Buddhism. In some lineages, the primary tool used is the ceremonial bell; for others, it's the wood fish. Still others use both. Generally, the sound of the bells is used when calling upon spirits or supernatural energy, or when scattering malevolent energy, such as banishing demons. Meanwhile, the sound of the wood blocks is used for meditation or strengthening the practitioner's receptivity to metaphysical energies. The rhythmic, repetitive sound of the wooden percussion blocks can put the practitioner into a trancelike state, which opens the practitioner up to greater connectivity to the practitioner's own unconscious or higher self, to the Divine, and allows the free flow of energy through the practitioner and into the sigil to be crafted.

To use the wood blocks, the practitioner must strike it at a consistent tempo. A suggested tempo is around one hundred beats per minute, or at an allegretto pace. However, the exact tempo that best facilitates the needed receptivity will vary from practitioner to practitioner.

## ENERGY AMPLIFIERS

Having energy amplifiers set up within the vicinity during a charging ritual can improve the charging's potency. Aesthetically a traditional Taoist ritual is ornate and vibrant with colors. All physical senses are stimulated, especially visual. Idols carved from stones with particular metaphysical energy correspondences are displayed around the altar with the intent of amplifying energy.

To harness wealth, for example, there might be gold ingots, statues of fish carved in cinnabar, marble horses, or jade turtles, all icons and materials that are associated with wealth energy. Icons of lions, tigers, and victory banners are believed to help with political ambition and to ensure conquest. Peaches are an essential part of any energetic working for long life and good health. A pagoda statue is not only relevant in feng shui but can be used as an energy amplifier for Fu sigil charging rituals related to academics, school, education, writing, literature, arts and culture, or any intellectual endeavor.

The bottle gourd, or *hu lu* (葫蘆) is also used as an energy amplifier for prosperity, longevity, health, wellness, healing, curing illnesses, and blessings. In strong defensive magic to ward off malevolent ener-

Figure 6.23. A pagoda statue, an energy amplifier for academic and literary success

gies or curses, a naturally dried gourd is used. Gourds carved out of jade are used as an energy amplifier for spells involving wealth and prosperity. Metal gourds are for health, healing, wellness, and longevity.

Fruits are not only offerings made to the deities that are part of the altar or practitioner's work space; they can also serve as energy amplifiers. They are typically found in groups of three or five—three for connecting Man to Heaven and Earth, and five to harness the power of the Wu Xing five phases and the four directions plus the fifth, the center. In elaborate ceremonies for charging rituals, such as charging Fu sigils for the upcoming New Year or for matters where the stakes are high, groupings of nine, eleven, or twelve are used. Nine is for sending prayers directly up to Heaven. Eleven is for communion with angelic or other spiritual beings. Twelve represents the twelve zodiac signs, and is used for charging New Year sigils.

Apples or bananas are used to harness added energies of wisdom and knowledge, or for crafting related to education or academics. Apricots, kumquats, or jujubes are used when crafting Fu sigils for wealth, prosperity, and business or commercial success. Oranges and tangerines are used for good fortune. Peaches are for health, wellness, and longevity and represent immortality. Peanuts also used for longevity, health, and riches. Pomegranates and pomelos are for fertility spells. I will also mention that fresh eggs, while not a fruit exactly, are also used as energy amplifiers for fertility.

The specifics of energy amplifiers used will differ from practitioner to practitioner. Tailor your energy amplifiers according to the thirteen points from the *Classics of the Esoteric Talisman,* summarized in chapter 3. For instance, energy amplifiers should be keyed to the Wu Xing, or five phases. As an alternative, the Western practitioner can rely on the four elements, Fire, Water, Air, and Earth. Energy amplifiers should also be positioned in such a way that they amplify the influence of the seasons and directions. Also consider yin and yang and how the energy amplifiers being used will bring harmony to the yin and yang elements of a ritual or craft.

For me, as a practitioner, I prefer crystals and gemstones, finding them to be great energy amplifiers, though that is certainly not "traditional." Likewise, it would serve the Western practitioner better not to worry too much about authenticity and think more about what best expresses their connection with nature, or Earth. If cultural appropriation is a concern, I address the topic in chapter 12.

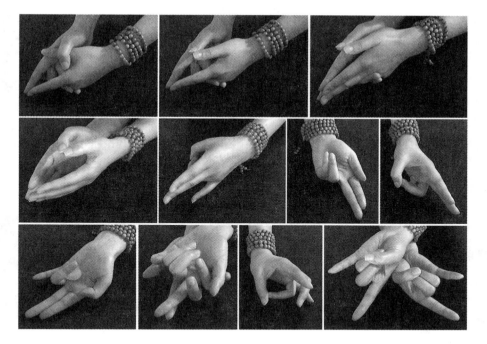

Figure 6.24. Hand mudras used in Taoist magic

## HAND MUDRAS

In Taoist practice, mudras are integral to channeling the practitioner's power or Qi into the Fu sigils. The tradition of using mudras is likely borrowed from Hinduism, which predates Taoism. The rationale for using hand mudras can also be interpreted from the *Classics of the Esoteric Talisman,* as set forth in point 2 in chapter 3: "All manifestations in the universe can be generated … through the [practitioner's] hand."

Mudras are hand gestures that are believed to help a practitioner send personal Qi into the Fu. The hand gesture helps to channel supernatural powers into the Fu through the practitioner's body. The mudra in Taoism is also a form of the practitioner's energetic seal, and each tradition or lineage of Taoist magical practice has its own mudras.

I do not consider mudras essential to sigil crafting rituals (though I do consider use of the hands a requirement). Yet those who practice within a traditional or orthodox Taoist lineage will probably assert that mudras are essential and a requisite to proper Fu activation. Whether mudras are to be incorporated into your practice depends on how you connect to energy. Mudras are said to help align, harness, and generally keep Qi energy controlled in the manner that you seek to control it.

As a general tip, any closed circuit, or physical gesture that connects the fingers to form a closed loop, contains energy and concentrates it; fingertips direct the movement and flow of Qi energy; and fists or fingers curled inward form knots that raise and collect energy. Most mudras combine hand gestures for concentrating energy with pointed fingertips to direct that concentrated energy toward the target. With those principles in mind, you can devise your own mudra to best serve your purposes.

Mudras consisting of fingers pointing at the Fu sigil are typically used during the sigil charging ritual, discussed in chapter 8. Mudras with open palms or closed circuits are used during grounding or shielding meditations, or for enabling a practitioner to raise energy. Both hands in mudras crossing each other in front of the practitioner's body help in defensive work or blocking.

## INVOCATIONS

First, note that I may be using the term *invocation* in a manner that differs from its application in Western traditions of magic. Generally, in Western traditions of magic (or magick), distinctions are made between invocation and evocation, with the difference being one of spirit hierarchies. In the greater hierarchy of the metaphysical realm, gods, demigods, archangels, and angels are above humans, while demons and archdemons are below.[26] Invocation is the interactive relationship between humans and the upper echelons in the hierarchy, whereas evocation is the interactive relationship between humans and the lower echelons.[27]

The practitioner's intent for an invocation is one of reverence, and the mechanics are a humbled request. In evocation, the intent is a command, and the mechanics are control, to exercise authority. Moreover, as I understand the Western tradition, invocations call a spirit into and within the practitioner's body, whereas evocation calls forth a spirit, but the spirit remains external to the practitioner's body.[28] Spirits are invoked into the practitioner's body for the practitioner to assume the powers of those entities. Spirit and practitioner become of one mind in an invocation.[29] Evocation is manifesting the spirit into a practitioner's work space, but as an entity, the spirit remains independent from the practitioner. In evocations, the practitioner has conjured the spirit and can issue orders to it.[30]

I use the term *invocation* in this book in a similar manner to the Western definition, except there is no presumption of unifying the practitioner with the spirit. When I say "invocation," the spirit called upon is still manifested externally and independent from the practitioner's mind and body. Spirit entities unified in mind and body with a practitioner are within the category of channeling and mediumship, as I use the terms here.

While I have not used the term *evocation,* any reference to the summoning of a lower entity—such as a ghost, hungry ghost, or demon—would be referring to mechanics that are similar to the Western definition of evocation. In the Taoist tradition, like the Western tradition, a summoning of a spirit entity below humans on the greater hierarchy—any ghost or hungry ghost occupying the earthly plane, or any ghost, hungry ghost, or demon from the underworld—is framed as an order, decree, or command.[31] The practitioner is not asking; he or she is telling.

When I refer to an invocation, I mean an incantation, the ceremonial utterance of words intended to yield a metaphysical effect. However, beyond a mere incantation, an invocation does have a specific intent—that of adjusting the vibrational frequency of a practitioner in such a way that he or she will become more aligned with the vibrational frequency of a higher spirit entity, such as a god, demigod, archangel, or angel. Invocation is about getting practitioner and spirit entity on the same, shared wavelength, but in no way does the practitioner become or assume any powers of the spirit entity, as the term implies in Western craft. When I invoke Kuan Yin, I in no way become Kuan Yin nor am I trying to empower myself with her abilities; rather, I am clearing the pathway of communication so that I might be heard by Kuan Yin.

In this book, I limit any instructional discussions of craft to invocations. Summonings are beyond the scope of this book and are only mentioned in the context of covering the history and culture of the Fu. To invoke is to seek guidance from that which by its nature endeavors for the greater good. To summon is an entirely different exercise, and before any practitioner proceeds with a summoning, he or she had better have a clear and defined purpose in mind, one that the practitioner is sure cannot be achieved without the summoning.

Invocations, or incantations that connect a practitioner to a deity, are essential to proper Fu sigil crafting, and without invocations, you cannot empower a sigil (assuming, of course, that summonings are out of the question). Samples and references for invocations are provided herein, but the efficacy of invocations is quite particular. Simply copying the wording of an invocation reference will not work. Invocations hold power only under certain circumstances: (1) it is passed directly from a master practitioner to a student, (2) it is inherited, (3) a significantly high level of inner cultivation has been achieved by the practitioner through routine repetition of that invocation, or (4) you craft your own invocation and it is one that resonates powerfully with your personal convictions.

East Asian practitioners of craft frequently use Buddhist or Taoist mantras as invocations. A priest or priestess ordained into a lineage will receive empowered invocations from a master through that lineage's proprietary craft. It can also be inherited from a parent who was a practitioner of craft. If neither of those paths resonate with the practitioner, a tried and true mantra can become empowered through inner cultivation. Inner cultivation means the practitioner recites the mantra or invocation outside of craft, such as during meditation, to cultivate a strong connection through that mantra. Then the mantra becomes an empowered invocation. Finally, a practitioner with an innately higher physiological ability for craft and energetic workings can draft personalized invocations that will be effective.

To be effective, the invocation must be profound to you. When you utter the words of your invocation, you must feel empowered and bigger than yourself. When an invocation is just right for you, you will feel the energy rising from in to out. You will feel a swelling, one that is warm, invigorating; a sensation that recalibrates your consciousness in a way that renders you a better person than you might normally be.

The optimal practice is to connect with a deity (or higher energy; higher self) and have a mantra or set invocation at a very young age, and to repeat that mantra or invocation throughout the course of the practitioner's life. Doing so strengthens the practitioner's signal and ability to connect into the frequencies for that deity or higher energy form. Then, when the practitioner calls upon it with the invocation, it is powerful, reliable, and always potent.

When I was just a little girl and scared of monsters in the closet, my mother taught me to recite a mantra, *Namo amitofuo guanshiying pusa* (南无阿弥陀佛观世音菩薩).[32] She would give me beads and tell me to count my recitations with the beads. "Recite that when you are scared. It will always protect you. No matter what the circumstance, use that recitation." In any situation where I might find myself in need of guidance or protection, my mother told me to recite that mantra. It became embedded into me to such a degree that for no apparent reason at all, I could start recitations of it. I had no idea what my mother was teaching me at the time, but it would turn out to be distinctly magical.

According to the esoteric sutras of Kuan Yin, if the bodhisattva's name is invoked through a *dharani* (or invocation)[33] every morning after bathing, at 108 recitations the invocation will help the practitioner avert physical suffering and disease, and raise the vibrations of the practitioner so that it is detected by higher deities and angelic beings, who will then come to the practitioner's aid any time he or she is in trouble, bring abundance and prosperity so he or she is never in need of resources, empower the practitioner to prevail over all enemies, guard and block the practitioner from evil charms or malevolent magic, and generally safeguard the practitioner from harm.[34]

A teacher my mother once studied under explained invocations to me, or more specifically, mantras. Mantras are phrases in sacred languages where the phonetic utterance is believed to raise certain power or amplify certain connections to deity or higher metaphysical energy. In both Buddhism and Taoism, mantras are used to reach certain states of mind. In magical practice, mantras are also used to reach certain states of mind, but more importantly, are used to connect the human practitioner with the higher energy form, or deity. Utterances in sacred languages are believed to hold the most power.

I doubt the following analogy is perfect, but it made sense to me when that teacher explained invocations in this way. Think about radio frequencies. Deities, or specific supernatural forces, are like the radio stations or towers broadcasting certain powerful energy. To tap into it, you have a radio. You are the personal radio. To hear your desired radio station clearly, meaning the deity you seek to invoke, you must turn your dial to the right position.

Likewise, invocations, or certain phonetic utterances, usually from sacred languages, have been established through centuries of use by powerful practitioners with strong connections to those deities, and thus can be used like a radio dial to tap into the energetic frequency of those higher energies. The more you have recited a mantra, the stronger your personal radio is to receiving those frequencies. Thus, during meditation and other training practices, practitioners will recite specific set mantras or sacred utterances over and over to strengthen their personal connections to those higher frequencies. Basically, you want to be as strong a radio as possible so that when you do engage in energetic practices such as sigil crafting, you connect to deity or divine forces right away. I would contend that none of the tools of craft mentioned in this chapter are required, except for the invocation. For effective craft, invocations are necessary.

So consider what sacred languages are closest to your soul and spirit, and then craft invocations that integrate those languages. Sacred languages raise power; spoken languages specify intentions. Common types of invocations used are mantras and dharanis,[35] which are generally recited in Sanskrit. Buddhist-dominant magical lineages and folk religions will likely invoke mantras. These mantras and dharanis are believed to emanate with protective powers that shield the practitioner from harm when performing craft.

Another reason to establish a personal invocation and thus a strong connection to a deity is for metaphysical protection. I was taught that as a practitioner develops his or her powers and abilities, that practitioner becomes more attractive to lower energies, such as ghosts and demons. A practitioner who does not know how to control these entities risks becoming controlled. A strong connection to a higher deity will ensure your protection and amplify your strength to dispel these lower entities.

An effective invocation has to come from your heart and your intuition. It must be meaningful to you. Words you copied that you do not feel an intuitive connection to will not be as meaningful or powerful as words you have crafted for yourself.[36]

To construct an effective invocation, the following elements are considered:

**Invoking a metaphor.** The practitioner's personal gnosis, mythology, or religious beliefs are invoked to strengthen the connection with the Divine.

**Acknowledging the greater purpose.** Each and every invocation serves a purpose. Acknowledge the purpose of the invocation that has been crafted.

**Call for the divine blessing.** Ask specifically for the blessing or empowerment that is sought.

**Affirmative language.** The invocation is generally constructed in affirmative language, or on the assumption that what has been willed by the practitioner shall for certain be manifested.

In chapter 8, under "Invocation References," I provide several invocations that I hold sacred. While you are encouraged to craft your own invocations, any of the mantras or dharanis provided would be a powerful addition to your craft. Note also that the reception invocations provided in chapter 7 can also be used for the 108 recitations of the charging ritual.

## PRACTITIONER'S SWORD

In many Western occult traditions, a wand is an essential tool for the practitioner. The wand is a rod wielded in the hand that is believed to assist a practitioner with the channeling of metaphysical energy. In Taoist traditions, the equivalent of the Western practitioner's wand is the practitioner's sword.[37]

Traditionally, the practitioner's sword is not an actual metal sword, but one carved out of peach wood. Peach wood is believed to possess innate powerful magic that will heighten a practitioner's abilities for harnessing from Heaven and Earth, and also protect the practitioner from malevolent attacks.

In Taoist craft, peach wood is believed to ward off evil.[38] Similar to the Western notion that a wooden stake will kill a vampire, there is a notion that peach wood can vanquish a demon. Sorcerers and exorcists during the Han Dynasty used wands made out of peach wood.[39] In medieval China, peach wood bows and arrows were weapons for fighting hungry ghosts and demonic forces.[40] Even today, peach wood continues to be a popular tool in exorcisms and most commonly manifests in the form of the peach wood sword.

Due to the difficulty in obtaining well-crafted peach wood swords, many modern Taoist practitioners have opted for metal swords and daggers that they consecrate. Note, though, that there are other forms of ceremonial swords used in Taoist craft. In lieu of a peach wood sword, there is a Big Dipper Sword, or Seven-Star Sword (七星劍, qī xīng jiàn), made of steel and engraved with the Big Dipper constellation.[41] Another ceremonial sword, also made of metal, is the Sword of the Law (法劍, fǎ jiàn), used by a practitioner to administer justice through spell-crafting. Also, rather than wield a sword, a practitioner can use his or her hands to form a sword mudra to channel energy.

## THE SNAKE WHIP

While the Taoist snake whip, or Cord of the Law (法繩, fǎ shéng), is an essential practitioner's tool for certain lineages, it is absent and not used at all in others. The Cord of the Law consists of a wooden handle carved into a snake's head, hence the name. The rest of the body is made of braided hemp. The snake whip is wielded by a Taoist priest or priestess to clear a sacred space of malignant energies or malicious spirits. It can be used during the opening of a ritual, discussed in chapter 8, to clear or consecrate the area of unwanted ghosts and spirits. It is also used in exorcisms to bind or dispel demons. To activate a snake whip, a mantra or invocation is used. The whip takes effect when the practitioner lashes the air with it while reciting an invocation, or coils the whip around one who is purported to be possessed by a demon to bind the demon from inflicting harm.

## BREATHING TECHNIQUES

An aspect of invocation philosophy in Eastern Taoist practice that does not seem to be as prominent in pagan practices and Western ceremonial magic is the importance of breath.[42] Taoists believe that there is a set amount of Vital Force, or personal Qi, in each of us, and control of that Vital Force through control of the breath is critical to a properly crafted invocation.[43] Thus, when a practitioner appears to be speaking in tongues, quickly and incoherently, the rhythm and tempo is meant to harness a large pool of Vital Force, more than what would be harnessed through ordinary breath, to infuse into the Fu sigils.

You can integrate basic Vital Force control into your practice by learning breathing techniques. Qi gong practice, discussed briefly in the subsequent section, and meditation are how most Eastern practitioners will master their breathing techniques for controlling their Vital Force.

A simple way to begin the practice is to set aside time daily to be attentive of your breath. Find a quiet, private, and secluded area where you will not be disturbed. Close your eyes and focus on your breathing. Focus on the counts for inhaling and exhaling, and work with different rhythms. When you need to swallow, consciously swallow after a full inhalation of breath. That is believed to help you "digest" external Qi energy and use it to enhance your personal Vital Force. As you practice, you will find a rhythm that resonates immediately with your body and will seem to give you a burst of energy and vitality. Different rhythms affect your personal Vital Force in difference ways. You'll need to be intuitive in discovering which rhythms are optimal for harnessing your Vital Force. Once you find that rhythm, remember it. Incorporate that rhythm of breath into the crafting of your invocations.

## QI GONG

Qi gong is a form of inner cultivation that seeks to strengthen physical health through the strengthening of Vital Force.[44] Qi gong is a physical practice that is integrated into other studies, such as esoteric Taoism. In its many forms, whether medical, philosophical, in martial arts, or even in occult practices, qi gong seeks to regulate the physical body and the mind by regulating breath and regulating thought, and in doing so, adjusts the Vital Force within.[45]

Historically, the practice of qi gong has also been associated with witchcraft.[46] It is associated with a method of metaphysical distance healing,[47] where a practitioner who is learned in qi gong is believed to possess the ability to tap into cosmic Qi through his or her personal Qi, reach out through that universal channel to tap into the personal Qi of another individual, who may be physically and geographically far away from the practitioner, and transfer some of the practitioner's own personal Qi to help balance out and strengthen that other individual's personal Qi, thereby healing that individual. Qi gong is also associated with the means for raising the energy needed to empower a Fu sigil, though chapter 8 will explain an effective way of doing so by applying the teachings of arcane Taoist texts and the tenets of the *Classics of the Esoteric Talisman.*

To put it in its simplest (perhaps oversimplified) terms, qi gong is the more organized and instructive approach to the breathing techniques for invocation discussed in the preceding section. Most magical lineages believe that qi gong is the means for raising the Vital Force or power that a practitioner needs for craft. Qi gong is how a practitioner manifests the universe, or cosmic Qi, by generating it through his or her physical body. Chinese shamans or witches (巫, Wū) use qi gong in their holistic healing practices, rituals, and Fu talisman crafting.[48]

The art and practice of qi gong is a lifelong study, and well beyond the scope of this book. A dedicated practitioner continues his or her study of qi gong to enhance the practitioner's craft. The following section offers an alternative for cultivating cosmic Qi—the accumulation of good deeds.

What is worth implementing right now, in terms of qi gong, are these simple practices espoused in a well-known Chinese precept called the Four Majesties: (1) walk like the wind, (2) stand like the pine, (3) sit like a bell, and (4) lie like a bow. Observe proper posture, follow the Four Majesties, and in every one of your movements, always be attentive to your body, your thoughts, and your breath.[49] Devote time each day to focusing the whole of your attention on breath, and control your breath in a slow and deliberate manner, breathing in deeply, and exhaling fully. Beyond that, qi gong is a study that the practitioner will have to learn from other texts.[50]

## ACCUMULATING GOOD DEEDS

I have added this section because in my personal practice, I have found it to be pertinent. While my views on morality should not have any bearing on your approach to craft, I have included this section for its historic relevance. Historically, many lineages, such as the Zhen Da Tao lineage[51] and Quan Zhen,[52] espoused moral accounting or moral cultivation as inextricable from the cultivation toward immortality. Immortality seems ambitious, but I will address my interpretation shortly. The rise in publication of morality books (善書, shàn shū), authored by practitioners of esoteric Taoism in the 1100s AD, also merged occult practice with doctrines of benevolence.[53]

Circa AD 316 to 317, the alchemist Ge Hong wrote the *Bao Pu Zi,* one of the classic Taoist texts on esoteric Taoist practices.[54] The text offers Ge Hong's instruction on achieving immortality. To become an "Earthly Immortal," a practitioner needs to accumulate 300 good deeds. To become a "Heavenly Immortal," the practitioner needs to accumulate 1,200 good deeds.[55] The practitioner's highest aspiration toward achieving immortality is to accumulate 1,199 good deeds. Ge Hong's instructions form the bedrock of how many Taoist magical lineages cultivate their practice.[56]

First, what constitutes a good deed? According to Ge Hong, to achieve transcendence, a practitioner must extend love to all life, "even those that creep and crawl, so that nothing breathing may come to harm."[57] The concept of good deeds is also informed by the Taoist philosophy of wu wei, the principle of nonaction. In chapter 2 (論仙), "On Immortality," of the Inner Chapters (內篇), the text reads: 仙法欲靜寂無為 (Xiān Fǎ Yù Jìng Jì Wú Wéi).[58] It is no easy task to translate that line, so forgive me if I err. As a practitioner, I interpret it, including some of the unspoken subtext of those characters, to mean, "The means or craft of achieving immortality is in forbearance, in the quietude and stillness of wu wei, to be voiceless and drifting."[59]

Therefore, I construe good deeds to be elucidated through the principle of wu wei (無為). A good deed is to be truly selfless, to demonstrate sincere altruism. A good deed cannot have any selfishness attached to it. Any deed, even one that benefits others, attached to self interest in any way whatsoever does not count as a good deed for the purpose of cultivating immortality.

Inherently, a good deed is a form of restraint, of sacrifice. When every last shred of yourself desires action in the name of self-preservation or self-interest, you then restrain yourself from action. To be voiceless is a most difficult request, as what many of us tend to desire most is to be heard. To be drifting suggests yielding to oppositional forces. Again, it is a difficult task. It runs against our fight-or-flight instinct. Drifting is neither fight nor flight. It is transcending beyond the fight-or-flight inclination.

Accumulating these good deeds is a form of cultivation that is difficult, and by its definition, more than just helping an elderly woman across the street or giving a dollar to a beggar, because subconsciously, there are still selfish interests attached to such acts. After all, doing so makes you feel good about yourself. Certainly continue your habit of helping elderly women across the street and giving alms to the poor; such habits are the initial phases of developing a path toward good deeds. But the good deeds that Ge Hong refers to are much more profound than that.

As for immortality, I interpret the concept in more practical terms. In every aspect of a practitioner's craft, he or she is extinguishing a piece of him- or herself, the practitioner's Vital Force or personal Qi. Our personal Qi is limited. The more energy we practitioners extinguish during craft, the less of our personal Qi is left.

That is metaphysical mortality. Immortality, then, is achieving never-ending Vital Force, to transcend limitations of personal Qi. The objective of immortality sought by inner cultivation could in theory be interpreted as an objective to achieve never-ending Vital Force for a practitioner to work with. Thus, a practitioner's power and abilities increase as he or she accrues good deeds, and so part of a practitioner's cultivation of craft is also the accumulation of good deeds.

The word 仙 (xiān), in addition to "immortality," also means "transcendence." Transcendence is to surpass present limitations, to be able to rise above or go beyond space and time. Transcendence is thus the ability of a practitioner to be more than just Man and be aligned with Heaven or the Tao, as in point 1 of the *Classics of the Esoteric Talisman,* summarized in chapter 3, or to deftly take from Heaven or Earth, as noted in point 4.

The means for achieving 仙, or transcendence, according to Ge Hong, is through good deeds, which—again referring to his texts—I interpret as deeds that apply the principle of wu wei. That, then, is the "secret" to transcendence, to 仙 or immortality: accumulating 1,199 good deeds.

The practitioner seeks transcendence—what the metaphor of immortality truly means—so that the practitioner may transcend space-time. To transcend space-time is to enable the practitioner's self to travel fluidly through time— past, present, and future—and fluidly through space—above, below, the four compass directions, and the five relative directions.[60] These are the abilities that empower a practitioner with effective craft.

Note that the foregoing is not the traditional or historic interpretation of immortality by Taoists. The traditional or historic interpretation is literal immortality, where one literally lives forever.[61] Only I have opted to reinterpret the concept and, based only on very limited anecdotal evidence, experienced the merits of such an interpretation. I do see the accumulation of good deeds as one way to cultivate the Vital Force a practitioner needs to craft powerful Fu sigils, though herein lies the rub: if you accumulate good deeds with the self-interested purpose of extending metaphysical mortality, of attaining power for craft, that deed is no longer "good," and does not serve the purpose you seek to achieve.

## THE BOOK OF METHODS

As early as the Tian Shi lineage in AD 142, there were records of esoteric Taoist practitioners' Fang Shu (方書, Fāng Shū), which I translate as Book of Methods.[62] Every Fang Shi (方士, Fāng Shì), which was what these esoteric practitioners were called,[63] would have had his or her personal Book of Methods. Fang Shi was the term used between 300 BC and about AD 500 to describe alchemists, diviners, astrologers, magicians, exorcists, shamans, and generally anyone who delved deeply into the esoteric realms. The term has been translated to "methods master,"[64] but the character Shi (士) is more akin to

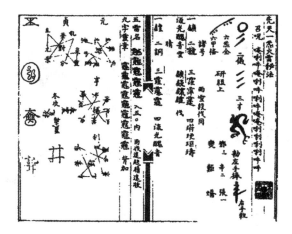

Figure 6.25. Excerpt from a Book of Methods from the Mao Shan lineage (from the private collection of Grand Master Lucas Huang and Kenny Wang)

"scholar" or "erudite." To qualify as a methods master, one would have to be learned in numerology, astrology, divination, and interpreting dreams, signs, and omens, as well as being a practitioner of magic (or craft) and being knowledgeable in exorcisms and healing.[65] The personal logs and journals that contained all of the Fang Shi's knowledge would be his or her Book of Methods. The Book of Methods, as described here, might be likened to a Western magical practitioner's book of shadows or grimoire.[66]

In orthodox Taoist lineages, an adept would copy the full Book of Methods from the master; that was the means of transmitting the magical records of the lineage down through the generations. The Book of Methods was a closely guarded secret text, and not all of a master's adepts would have access to it.[67] Only the most trusted adepts would earn the right to copy the master's book.

Presumably, a practitioner's Book of Methods contains exact drawings of Fu sigils that the practitioner uses, ritual script, charging methods, and explanations for how the sigils are crafted. A Book of Methods also contains the Lu, the registry of spirits and demons that the practitioner could summon, and the methods for summoning. In popular associations with the Fang Shu, it is an alchemist's lab book. It logs the experimentations of the alchemist or ceremonial magician as he works his way toward concocting the elixir of life, to attaining immortality.

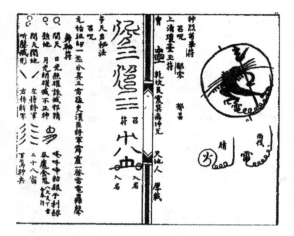

Figure 6.26. Excerpt from a Book of Methods from the Mao Shan lineage (from the private collection of Grand Master Lucas Huang and Kenny Wang)

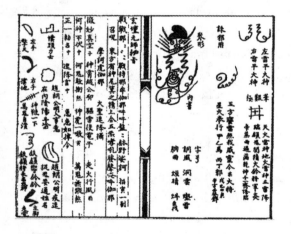

Figure 6.27. Excerpt from a Book of Methods from the Mao Shan lineage (from the private collection of Grand Master Lucas Huang and Kenny Wang)

Figure 6.25 is a page spread from an undated ancient Book of Methods from the Mao Shan lineage.[68] The pages read right to left. It makes reference to a "Xian Tian Yi Wu Huo Lei Mi Fa," or a form of Celestial Thunder Magic. An incantation is given, as follows, which might be likened to "abracadabra": *"An lee ong an lee ong lee ong an an lee lee lee lee ong ong."*

While the incantation is uttered, the left palm cups a Fu while the right hand grasps one. There are also references to the Ba Gua trigrams. Most of the wording on these pages is cryptic, but generally it gives directions for steps to a spell. Note the diagrams on the left half, which refer to pacing rituals based on the Lo Shu, covered in "Pacing the Lo Shu" in chapter 8.

In figure 6.26, instructions for a second spell are given, titled the "Xing Tian Jun Mi Fa." Again, a magical incantation is given: *"Yuan si tzu jieh yi wu fen zhen wu lei meng lee han chen jiang jun pi lee yi hua lei dian hongs hen."*

Like "abracadabra," an incantation that is believed to possess magical power when uttered but by itself does not make literal sense in any spoken language, these incantations do not make literal sense, but are believed to make sense on the metaphysical plane. It is the practitioner communing with the spirit world.

Another spell is featured on this page, for an exorcism. The practitioner begins by "opening the Heavens," though what that entails is not provided. It is presumed to be a particular ritual that the practitioner is readily familiar with, and that ritual would be the first step to the exorcism. Then, sunshine from the Heavens is used to exorcise devils, and moonlight from the Heavens is used to dispel malignant energy. Whether "sunshine" and "moonlight" are figurative or literal, the text is unclear. Finally, to complete

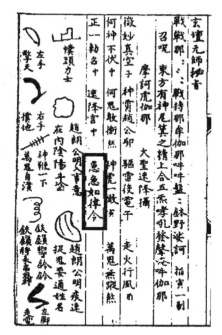

Figure 6.28. The incantation "ji ji ru lu ling" in a Book of Methods

the exorcism, the practitioner is to use the following incantation: *"An ong tee jieh ying yah lee rent un muo si gui. Ba da tian xia lei ling feng xing."*

The incantation will, according to the text, open Heaven's gates and release its massive army to launch an attack on the demonic forces. Note the Fu sigils drawn in the cloud writing style discussed in chapter 3, with glyphs rendered from Chinese radicals and the Ba Gua trigrams Fire (above) and Water (below).

The final sampling from the Mao Shan Book of Methods is figure 6.28; it provides instruction for a conjuration. With the authority of a higher deity, the practitioner is summoning a lower deity "on behalf of" the higher deity, ordering the lower deity to carry forth the practitioner's summons. The page consists mostly of incantations for the conjuration, along with references to the Ba Gua. On the last page, instructions for the practitioner's stance are given: the left hand is raised straight upward as if pushing up the Heavens, and the right hand points downward as if pushing down the Earth. Bells are also used toward the end to scatter any remnant energies.

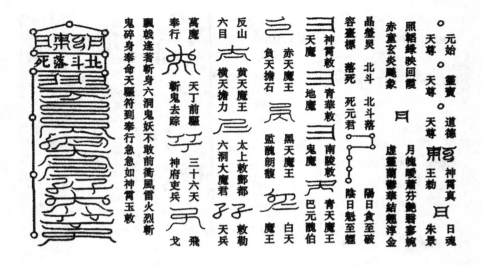

Figure 6.29. Divine curing Fu for a demon exorcism

In the closing of the incantation, highlighted in figure 6.28 with a square, note the last line, 急急如律令 (ji ji ru lu ling), which will be addressed in "By a Closing Invocation" in chapter 9. The utterance "ji ji ru lu ling" essentially means "it is so ordered," a typical closing to a Taoist magical incantation that might be likened to "amen" or "So mote it be."

Ge Xuan, a medieval Fang Shi, or magician and alchemist, during the Three Kingdoms Period (AD 220–265), wrote copious Fang Shu, or Books of Methods, that were later known as the Ling Bao (Numinous Treasure) Scriptures.[69] He was the grand uncle to the renowned Ge Hong.[70] Figure 6.29 is a reprinting of one page from such a Book of Methods that is now part of the Ling Bao Scriptures,[71] or more specifically, a text called *The Ling Bao Scripture of Spells for Infinite Human Transformation*.[72] It describes the anatomy of a Fu sigil design for exorcising demons and how to empower the sigil. The Fu is called the Divine Curing Fu for a Demon Exorcism (神霄治祟命魔殺鬼前驅符, Shén Xiāo Zhì Suì Mìng Mó Shā Guǐ Qián Qū Fú). While the page may not be readily comprehensible, the layout does offer insights to the practitioner on how pages of a Book of Methods can be structured. The invocations to be used are written out; timing instructions are provided; and note how the anatomy of the Fu sigil design is explained, glyph by glyph.

My personal Book of Methods is woefully disorganized. Fortunately, I have a good sense of where things are in it, but I cannot imagine someone else having to find anything in those pages. My Book of Methods is a discrete black perfect-bound art journal that I write in with a consecrated ink pen. It is not a scrapbook, and I don't cut and paste in printed text or images. All of it is done longhand, and all sketches are my own. Most of it is in black ink, though there are accents of red, blue, and green scattered throughout. Along the back cover I've glued in a folder pocket where I keep longer invocations that I've written onto individual cards. These can then be pulled out and used with ease during a ritual.

If given the chance to reorganize my book—and I say this so that the reader might take heed—I would organize it by sections. The sections would correspond with the categories of subjects that the practitioner studies. The adept studying to become a Fang Shi might keep the front-most section for more religious text, such as prayers, invocations, and general references relating to the deity or deities that the practitioner calls upon. There would also be a section for other invocations, such as ones for raising power, self-defense and protection, and the written-out scripts for rituals. Most orthodox Taoist priests and priestesses practice summoning and exorcism, and would therefore have a section in their Book of Methods containing their Lu, or detailed explanations, drawings, and summoning spells for manifesting various spirit or supernatural entities, how to deal with them, how to control them, or how to exorcise them.

Next might be the section on craft. It would include complete renderings of Fu sigils that have proven effective for the practitioner. Detailed explanations of each Fu's anatomy, uses, and corresponding charging rituals would be written out. The section on craft can be further subdivided into categories. Then there might be the references and correspondence tables for numerology, astrology, geomancy, feng shui, herbalism, and the forms of divination that the practitioner specializes in. I might also keep a section on symbolism to consult for interpreting signs and omens. Such a section develops over time, as a practitioner attunes his or her vibration to the vibrations of Heaven and Earth, and learns what signs and omens mean when presented to that practitioner. Finally, numbering the pages and creating an index in the back of my personal book would have been a good idea.

The term Fang Shu (方書) itself is antiquated and arcane, and not commonly used today. It is, however, found in the archives of esoteric Taoist history and adequately describes the journals I keep for myself about craft. Thus, I like using the term Book of Methods, to describe the habit of keeping notes. When it comes to Fu sigil crafting, the practitioner is strongly advised to keep notes. It is how you will devise your own portfolio of powerful Fu and will help you advance in your own journey with craft.

# CHAPTER 7

# CONSECRATION TECHNIQUES

**RAINWATER IS JUST** rainwater, a stone just a stone, and an ink pen just an ink pen if it is not consecrated. Consecration is the process through which an object's metaphysical energies are tuned toward a practitioner's intents. The materials and tools a practitioner acquires will come with residual energies. The residue needs to be cleared. In general, anything and everything used for craft or ritual needs to be consecrated. That is how the practitioner's tools become sacred.

## CONSECRATING WATER

I love crystals and gemstones. Every crystal and stone that passes my hand will get cleansed in consecrated water. I wipe down my sacred work space with consecrated water. The cloth wipes I use to wipe my tools are themselves cleansed in consecrated water. Any water used during a ritual must be consecrated water. Thus, a basic skill for a practitioner to learn is how to consecrate water.

Every lineage will have its own secret proprietary method for consecrating water, and for consecration in general. Some lineages do not consecrate water for use during rituals, but will consecrate and bless all objects to be used. The practitioner decides for him- or herself what approach works best. This section is provided only in the event that consecrating water is adopted into that approach. Even if you do not incorporate water into your rituals, keeping bottled consecrated water around is useful. Use it to wipe down your home to

Figure 7.1. Rainwater collected for consecration

cleanse it metaphysically. Doing so prevents Qi energy that has gone atrophic from becoming toxic or causing undue stress on the home's occupants.

I begin with either water purified through a carbon filter or boiled with sea salt and set out to cool. Collected rainwater also works very well, but this depends on the environment you live in. For urban dwellers, where polluted rainwater is a risk, stick with purified water. Your water doesn't have to be from the rain, although clean rainwater collected near the top of a mountain is ideal.

To start the consecration process, light incense, such as bergamot, frank-incense, or sandalwood. Every ritual in Taoist craft begins with the lighting of incense. The timing of consecration takes place either near the new moon or under the full moon, depending on the practitioner's intentions. Consecrate during the new moon, or the last moments of a waning crescent, for the simple sake of purifying and releasing metaphysical toxins so that the object in effect becomes a neutral or blank slate. Consecrate during a full moon to empower the object and to prepare it for sacred uses.

Candles can be lit. Then a Reception Invocation is recited until spirits are felt to be present. A Reception Invocation is a method of using words and thought to clear a channel from the collective unconscious through the personal unconscious and into the present personal consciousness so that the practitioner can be open and receptive. By being open and receptive, energies beyond oneself can come through and strengthen the practitioner's intentions. Reception Invocations are explained later in this chapter.

After the Reception Invocation, use moon blocks[1] or the practitioner's preferred mode of divination (a pendulum works well) to confirm the presence of divine energies. The primary purpose of using the moon blocks or a divinatory equivalent is to be assured that the spirits invoked are now present and ready to assist in the consecration. If the divination mode yields a negative response, continue your Reception Invocation and try again until it is affirmative. Other practitioners may take the negative response as a sign not to proceed at this time.

The Reception Invocation is an effective method of tuning your vibrations to the universe's collective frequency. Once tuned in, all subsequent ritual work can be done in a heightened state and thus improve its efficacy. The divination method is a way of checking to see whether the practitioner has tuned his or her frequency to that collective frequency. While not a perfect simile, it is a bit like using a tuning fork to tune a violin or to tune a guitar before one begins playing. Playing music with an out-of-tune instrument just seems silly.

Once tuned in, place the water to be consecrated into a stone bowl. I use a white alabaster bowl.[2] Waft incense smoke over the surface of the water in the bowl while reciting the Water Consecration Invocation. Your intentions must be concentrated and focused while reciting invocations. Your intention and focus will strengthen your reception to energetic signals.

For consecration, a line from a beloved sutra or psalm or verses from other sacred scriptures work well as an invocation. I like to write my own, but will incorporate lines from sutras or psalms that resonate strongly with me. Thus, I use a combination of original language and mantras I have taken from scriptures that I hold sacred. What's a good consecration invocation to use? One that you feel connected to. One that feels intense and authentic to your personal gnosis. If it feels silly to recite it, then that invocation is not right for you. It must be meaningful and personal.

---

## Consecration Invocation

---

### FOR WATER

With the full force of the one Divinity, I cast out all impurities and malignant energies from this water. With the power of the Holy Spirit, may this water be pure and consecrated, empowered to drive afar and banish all that threaten peace, benevolence, harmony, health, or healing, and may it pour down blessings and Light to those who come in touch with this water. Sanctified now, this water shall dispel malignancy, sickness, malevolence. It shall drive away darkness and uncleanliness from the faithful and the good of heart. Let no pestilent spirit, no corrupting atmosphere, remain where this water has touched. Let every trouble be put to flight by this consecrated water. May the Divinity itself flow through this water and make it holy, empower it to defend against all attacks, every ill will, and every evil. *Prajna paramita*: the spell to allay all suffering: *gaté gaté paragaté parasamgaté Bodhi svaha*, now here in this consecrated water is the heart of Perfect Wisdom. *Na mo amitofuo guan shi ying pu sa.*

Next, sprinkle sea salt into the water. Recite your Water Consecration Invocation a second time. Some practitioners will pour in a few drops of clear essential oil or alcohol; others omit this step. Recite the invocation a third and final time while stirring the water. Typically a ritual knife is used, or a branch of peach wood.

Then ring tingsha or ceremonial bells three times, allowing time for a full echo between each ring. The metal-on-metal sound is believed to scatter any residual malignant energies that are present. The music of bells and cymbals is also believed to vibrate at the frequencies of Heaven, deities, spirit, and spirits, and for communion with the spirit world. For some practitioners, ringing bells makes more sense preceding the Water Consecration Invocation. The order of events is up to you. Note that these bells, prior to ritual use, need to be consecrated.[3]

When complete, bottle away the consecrated water for later use. Rinsing any object in consecrated water is said to fully purify it. However, some of the tools for crafting Fu sigils may not fare well in water, so the general consecration technique is also used.

# GENERAL CONSECRATION TECHNIQUE

Any object may be purified of its residual metaphysical energies through a purification or consecration technique. In many lineages, this is substituted with a blessing, where the object is blessed. Whether speaking in terms of purification, consecration, or blessing, the objective is to rid an item of any trace energies or metaphysical toxins, and generally to prepare it for charging, further blessing, or ritual work. The idea is to use the practitioner's personal power to recalibrate the vibrations of the object.

When a material is to be used for craft, it should first be purified or consecrated so that the specific charge of the practitioner can be fully imprinted onto the material. An example of this is a gemstone to be used as part of a talisman or a lucky charm. In Fu sigil crafting, all tools of the practitioner must first be purified or consecrated (I use both terms interchangeably in this section). Observe the following consecration technique or your variation on it to consecrate all paper, ink, and items that you will be using for crafting Fu sigils.

Start by preparing a stone bowl filled with consecrated water. Light a new white candle or the atman candle, whichever is the practitioner's preference, and recite your Reception Invocation. The purpose here is to attune the practitioner to higher energy and to ensure the presence of a higher energy form. The next step is to use moon blocks to determine whether such a presence has been achieved.

Assuming all is proceeding in the affirmative, the practitioner then places his or her giving hand into the water and then sprinkles consecrated water in the four cardinal directions to cleanse the energies of the surrounding work area. If the object to be consecrated is waterproof, such as a gemstone or a piece of jewelry (in the event that the energies of a Fu sigil will be transferred; see "Transference of Sigil Energy into Another Object" in chapter 10), then also rub some of the consecrated water into it.

Prepare sandalwood, cedarwood, frankincense, or white sage for burning. In most Chinese traditions, sandalwood or cedarwood is used. I have also found white sage to work well. I place a few drops of sandalwood essential oil onto the dried white sage bundle to help start the flame.[4]

Pass the object to be consecrated through the smoke of the incense while reciting the Consecration Invocation. The sample Consecration Invocation provided in this section is a slight variation from the one provided in the previous section, modified to account for an object rather than the water.

---

## Consecration Invocation

---

### FOR AN OBJECT TO BE CONSECRATED

With the full force of the one Divinity, I cast out all impurities and malignant energies from this [*identify the object to be consecrated*]. With the power of the Holy Spirit, may this [*object to be consecrated*] be pure and consecrated, empowered to drive afar and banish all that threaten peace, benevolence, harmony, health, or healing, and may it pour down blessings and Light to those who come in touch with it. Sanctified now, this [*object to be consecrated*] shall dispel malignancy, sickness, malevolence. It shall drive away darkness and uncleanliness from the faithful and the good of heart. Let no pestilent spirit, no corrupting atmosphere remain within this [*object to be consecrated*]. Let every trouble be put to flight by this consecrated [*object to be consecrated*]. May the Divinity itself flow through and make this [*object to be consecrated*] holy, empower it to defend against all attacks, every ill will, and every evil. *Prajna paramita*: the spell to allay all suffering: *gaté gaté paragaté parasamgaté Bodhi svaha*, now here in this consecrated [*object to be consecrated*] is the heart of Perfect Wisdom. *Na mo amitofuo guan shi ying pu sa.*

---

After the first recitation of the Consecration Invocation, place the object on a shallow bed of sea salt. I like to go the extra step of surrounding it with protection stones. Examples of protection stones are onyx, obsidian, dark jaspers, moss agate, or pyrite, which form a protective metaphysical energy shield. Crystal quartz or amethyst can also be used to amplify the power of the purification, which will enable it to quell any malignant energies circulating around.

Next, the practitioner should place his or her giving hand over the object to be purified, which is resting on a bed of sea salt; position the hand as if transmitting his or her personal energy, or personal Qi, into the object; and recite the Consecration Invocation for a second time. Here, in most lineages, a hand mudra is used. A wand or practitioner's peach wood sword can also be used to facilitate the transfer of energy. Recite the Invocation a third and final time, again positioning the hand as if transmitting personal Qi into the object.

Then ring tingsha or ceremonial bells three times, allowing time for a full echo between each ring.

I do not think I can stress the following point enough: the practitioner is strongly encouraged to craft his or her own wording or, if the practitioner is already affiliated with a specific magical tradition or lineage, to utilize the invocations crafted by that tradition or lineage. The only purpose for providing any invocation texts in this book is to offer examples for reference. The examples reveal some of my personal practices, but if this book can stress only one point, it is this: like Western pagan and ceremonial magic practices, Taoist practices vary from tradition to tradition, lineage to lineage. Different practices are founded on different ideologies and principles. Your wording should be based on your belief systems. If it is not based on your own belief systems, there is insufficient conviction and intention behind the words to give those words any power.

To return to our home after a day of work, my husband and I take different routes. Both routes lead to the same destination, but I like mine better. If any road along my route happens to be blocked that day and I am forced to take the alternative, I run the risk of getting lost or taking a wrong turn, mostly because I am terrible with directions. I have a rapport with my route and have a thing for familiarity; that's all. There is no judgment as to the positivity or negativity of the alternative route that my husband takes. I know my path and my way like it is second nature, and likewise, you will have your preferred approaches, practices, phrasing, invocations, and rituals that take you to the same place I'm headed with mine. Each must take his or her own path. We will meet at the same destination and, I should note, there is no race to see who gets there first.

## RECEPTION INVOCATIONS

The concept behind a Reception Invocation is to attune you to the frequencies needed for connecting into metaphysical or spiritual planes. It is essentially to ensure that the practitioner is operating at the optimal pitch.

Craft assumes that the practitioner is an instrument for receiving, channeling, and transferring potent energy. At the commencement of a practitioner's communion or interaction with higher vibrational frequencies, or metaphysical energy—what we presently refer to as the supernatural—for that communion to work, the lower frequency must rise to meet the higher frequency. The Reception Invocation is one approach for the practitioner to achieve that.

Exactly like tuning a violin, when the string has been tuned to the perfect pitch and the tuning fork is struck, that string will vibrate all on its own. That's magic. Tuning an instrument involves experience and technique, but remarkably, also a great deal of intuition. And that too is magic. The purpose of a Reception Invocation is to raise the lower frequency of the practitioner's personal Qi to meet the higher frequency of cosmic Qi. A Reception Invocation is a form of tuning to harmonize and bring to concord the frequencies of the personal Qi and the cosmic Qi. When the two frequencies are harmonized, there is receptivity, and the metaphysical work of craft can commence.

## MY PERSONAL RECEPTION INVOCATION

*In Mandarin Chinese:*

Ná mó àmítuófó guānshìyīn púsà.

南无阿弥陀佛觀世音菩薩

"Na Mo Amitabha Buddha and Kuan Yin Bodhisattva."

The foregoing is an invocation to the celestial Buddha, Amitabha, in Mahayana Buddhism, and to the bodhisattva Kuan Yin. Na mo essentially means "I venerate" or "I honor."

Anthropomorphizing, we talk about deities and spirits. I view deities and the angelic guardians we attribute to Heaven as projections of higher consciousness, while demons are projections of our subconscious.[5] To reference a particular projection or energy, we use religious vocabulary. For me, an invocation that calls upon Amithaba and Kuan Yin brings me closer to a transcendental reality, and in plain speak, makes me happy. I like being happy.

In Taoist craft, invocations are believed to hold great power because words hold great power over Man, and the whole purpose here is to attune Man to Heaven and Earth. A practitioner's willpower manifests through the words spoken to him- or herself and to the gods. What are those words? Invocations. Words awaken spirit. Words build bridges, and here, build the metaphysical bridge between planes.

Your Reception Invocation is a short, concise phrase or mantra that holds extraordinary meaning for you. In a few deceptively simple words, it must express all that you believe in, all that gives reason for your spirit to be awake, and be both the sword and shield that arm you with extraordinary power. That is how you possess the capacity to consecrate water and charge Fu sigils, transforming matter into energy, and then, energy transforming again, manifesting into the matter you've willed. Under "Invocation References" in chapter 8, you will find mantras from Eastern religions that are often used as Reception Invocations.

## KAI GUANG: CONSECRATING DEITY STATUES

In Taoist and Buddhist traditions, the image or likeness of a deity, such as a statue, needs to be consecrated before the essence of that deity will enter the statue and empower a practitioner's craft. That consecration ritual is called Kai Guang (開光), addressed briefly in "The Legend of Zhao Gong Ming" in chapter 5.

Laypeople who are strong in these religious faiths might invite a priest, monk, or nun to perform a Kai Guang ritual on their deity statues before the statues are placed on the home altar. However, Kai Guang isn't necessary for laypeople, because the statue is there simply as a means to keep the devout mindful of the religious tenets that they have vowed to uphold.

For the practitioner of craft, I would say otherwise. For craft, Kai Guang is necessary, because it is integral to the process by which deity is invoked into the practitioner's sacred space. It is how essence from the deity is invited to reside in the statue and thus occupy the practitioner's altar.

*Kai* means "to open" and *Guang* means "the Light," as in the luminescence from source energy. Guang is also the word for "aura" (光環, guāng huán, literally "ring of Light"). The rationale for the ritual is to open a direct connection between Heaven, where deity resides, and Earth, where the practitioner resides, and through Man, who is the practitioner, Heaven and Earth can merge in the practitioner's sacred space to manifest the will of Man. Through the Kai Guang ritual, the statue, which was just an object, becomes divine, or filled with divine essence.

I propose that a practitioner performs the Kai Guang ritual him- or herself to consecrate deity statues for deities that will be invoked during craft.[6] For specific Fu charging rituals, such as the Traditional Spell for Attaining Wealth and Prosperity invoking Cai Shen, the Western practitioner might consider a paper reproduction of Cai Shen, in which case a Kai Guang ritual is definitely a requisite.[7] The Kai Guang ritual can be performed on any image or likeness of a deity, whether it is a statue or a drawing on a piece of paper. If and when using paper, however, try to source quality paper that has been consecrated prior to rendering the deity. That part is not necessary, but preferred, out of a general respect and reverence for deity.

The specifics of Kai Guang vary among the traditions. Every lineage is taught a set Kai Guang ritual that all members of the lineage observe. For your personal practice, think about the principles from the *Classics of the Esoteric Talisman,* your own religious beliefs, and your own philosophical and ontological beliefs, and then devise a Kai Guang ritual that aligns with your craft.

Generally, most Kai Guang rituals involve cinnabar powder (or red ink) and smudging the eyes of the deity's likeness with the cinnabar. Doing so is symbolic of opening the likeness's eyes so that the deity or deity essence can see through those eyes. Note that in the instructions provided for the Cai Shen Wealth and Prosperity spell, all major points of the body of the deity likeness are smudged with cinnabar. The purpose is to empower the whole likeness so that the essence of the deity that has descended to Earth can assist the practitioner in craft as fully as possible.

Another approach is to blindfold the statue or deity likeness with red cloth that stays on through the opening of the Kai Guang ritual and is only removed at the close of ritual, at which time the removal of the blindfold symbolizes the deity now being able to see through the eyes of the likeness. Blindfolding is a common practice in some orthodox Taoist traditions, but it has never resonated with me. I feel uncomfortable with the notion of putting blindfolds on a deity. I speculate that the blindfolding approach came about because practitioners did not want to risk staining their precious statues with the cinnabar. Thus, in the alternative, I use the consecrated calligraphy brush and cinnabar powder figuratively, never physically touching the statue with the brush or ink. When using a paper likeness of the deity, however, I actually smudge it with the cinnabar.

In my own anecdotal observations, Buddhist Kai Guang rituals appear more understated and conservative, whereas Taoist Kai Guang, especially in the southern regions, are elaborate, with drum beats, song and dance, and quite literally, bells and whistles (sometimes horns). In your personal practice, go with the style that best raises your consciousness. I tend toward the understated and conservative.

Some rituals include rendering a Fu sigil onto a mirror and using the mirror during the Kai Guang ritual to receive the Guang or Light from Heaven and reflect it into the deity likeness. Such a mirror is called the Mirror of the Law (法鏡, fǎ jìng). I subscribe to the mirror practice. The precise Fu sigil design to use, again, varies from practitioner to practitioner, but I have provided the one that I use (fig. 7.2).

Figure 7.2. Fu sigil for Kai Guang

Obtain a small hand mirror or Ba Gua mirror that you will use exclusively for Kai Guang rituals. Use red ink to paint the sigil in figure 7.2 (or a Kai Guang sigil you have designed yourself) onto the center of the mirror. A red permanent marker works well, but consecrate the marker first. Some practitioners draw the sigil on the back of the mirror, while others draw it on the front, right onto the reflective surface. Both are practiced. I paint the sigil on the back of the mirror (a Ba Gua mirror, to be precise) and leave the reflective surface clean. If you are purchasing a Ba Gua mirror, many come with a Fu sigil already on the back, but it is not usually one for Kai Guang. Thus, I paint over that pre-drawn Fu to create a blank slate, and then paint on the Kai Guang Fu.

To draw the sigil onto the mirror, start with the three dots at the top, symbolizing the trinity of Heaven, Earth, and Man. Move to the right top corner of the sigil and draw the character for "sun" (日). Then draw the character for "moon" (月). The house of the Fu sigil is based on the seal script for the character for "deity" from the Qin Dynasty.[8] Follow the order of strokes for draw-

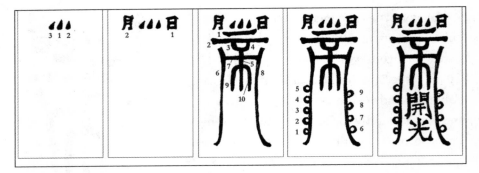

Figure 7.3. Order of strokes for rendering the Kai Guang Fu

ing the Fu sigil shown in figure 7.3.[9] Five spheres on the left represent the Wu Xing; the four spheres on the right represent the four directions. Inscribed within the sigil house are the words for Kai Guang (開光). This will become your Kai Guang mirror.

I don't find the timing of a Kai Guang ritual to be too critical, so I don't consult astrological references for the timing. Other practitioners do. For me, the ritual is performed as and when needed because the essence of deity is omnipresent and isn't stronger one day as compared to another; deity is strong every day.

To commence, set up the altar space with the statue or deity likeness as the focal point. Typically, offerings are placed on the altar. In Taoist rituals, you'll often find elegantly prepared meats. In Buddhist rituals, not so much; they tend to go vegetarian.[10] Fruits and fresh flowers are almost universally used. Chapter 6 walks you through the typical anatomy of an altar.

Start by opening the ritual, which is covered in chapter 8, although the discussion of Kai Guang made more sense here under consecration techniques. I light candles and incense, and set out delicate bowls of tea, rice, and fruit along with fresh flowers from my garden. Then I proceed with the opening of the ritual. Joss paper is burned as offerings. As the joss paper is burning, after the opening of the ritual, I recite the invocation for the deity: "Na mo Amitofuo," the Amitabha Sutra for invoking Amithaba, or "Na mo Guanshiyin Pusa," the Heart Sutra for invoking Kuan Yin. It is important that the practitioner know the invocation corresponding to the deity that the Kai Guang is for.

If I am using a one-time-use paper drawing of the deity for a specific purpose, next I outline the eyes, mouth, ears, hands, feet, and heart or chest area with cinnabar powder or red ink. If performing a Kai Guang ritual on a statue, I wield the calligraphy brush in a more figurative manner and either no ink is used or the brush never physically touches the statue. As I do so, I recite the invocation. Another popular method is to read sutras or scriptures.

I then move on to the Kai Guang mirror, holding it reverently with both hands, reflective side facing upward toward Heaven. In a meditative state, I continue recitations of the invocation, focusing on the base or core of my body, imagining potent, powerful energy collecting there, accumulating into a ball of white light. That ball of light then travels upward, through my arms and hands, and into the mirror, illuminating the mirror with the light.

Continuing with the invocation, I envision white light, far stronger than the white light I've provided, descend down directly from above, beginning in an unknown place in the skies, coming down through the ceiling and into the mirror, causing the mirror to grow brighter until the mirror itself isn't visible anymore, and all that can be seen through my mind's eye is a radiant, glowing ball of light wielded in both my hands. I then angle the mirror so the reflective side faces the deity statue or image, and envision all of the light, like a laser, directed into the statue or image.

I concentrate on the illumination of the points of the body I had outlined with the calligraphy brush. This continues, along with the recitations, until the white light is drained from the mirror and all of it has been directed into the statue or image. The mirror is restored to a mirror again, no longer illuminated, whereas the statue or image is now alight, fully illuminated. I envision the luminescent aura around the deity's head. I wind down the recitations and come to a close. The ritual ends with reverent ritualistic bows to the deity.

If the Kai Guang ritual is being performed for others to empower their statues, at this time, near the closing, all residents of the home that the statue will occupy bow and pay their homage to the deity. Incense will continue to be burned at the altar for the rest of the day and into the evening until midnight. The fruits and all offerings that had been left on the altar for the ritual are now considered blessed, and eating them brings peace and prosperity, or at the very least, is considered good luck.

# CHAPTER 8

# CHARGING FU SIGILS

HOW A FU SIGIL IS empowered differs from tradition to tradition, lineage to lineage. What one practitioner does for a charging ritual could very well be in contradiction to what another practitioner does. The instruction provided in this chapter is based on my readings of medieval Taoist texts, primary sources of practice, and secondary sources by observation of how various practitioners approach the charging ritual, and then synthesizing the salient points to formulate my personal approach to charging. Going forward, though, be mindful that it is hard to define or generalize the charging ritual. Every tradition has its own method for empowering Fu sigils, and there are far more differences between them than similarities.

As noted in chapter 2, Fu Ji is automatic writing, and in some traditions, the practitioner is a medium, and therefore does not design a sigil at all. Rather, the practitioner-medium enters a trance during a ritual. It is then believed that a spirit or deity enters the practitioner-medium's body. Wielding consecrated paper and ink, the practitioner-medium draws the sigil during the ritual, under the premise that the sigil is rendered through automatic writing, or Fu Ji, and a deity or spirit that has possessed the practitioner is the true author of the automatic writing.

This text takes a different approach and does not cover Fu Ji. It provides instruction to the practitioner who is not a medium and who is not going to be possessed by spirits. Through the practitioner's will and intent, crafting Fu sigils carefully with the consideration of principles from the *Classics of the Esoteric Talisman,* the practitioner will be equally successful at empowering sigils.

This text teaches how to design a Fu sigil using houses, glyphs, and the practitioner's own Fu Wen. After all, the mechanics of manifesting the universe are determined by the practitioner's mind, as indicated in point 2 of the *Classics of the Esoteric Talisman,* a seminal text on Fu sigil crafting, described in detail in chapter 3. A charging ritual is how a Fu sigil is empowered.

A charging ritual should be personally crafted by the practitioner, unless a particular Taoist lineage is being practiced. In a charging ritual, a deity or deities will be prayed to for assistance during the charging. The practitioner's hand remains his or her most important tool, as the manifestations of the universe are generated through the practitioner's hand.

In some way, the ritual will invoke the five phases of Wu Xing. The Western practitioner who is adopting sigil crafting into his or her tradition can invoke the four elements. "The Timing of a Charging Ritual" in this chapter discusses the application of astrology and numerology.

A very important aspect to the charging ritual is to adjust your physical eyes so they see beyond the physical plane, and your physical ears to hear beyond the physical plane. As noted in point 8 of the *Classics of the Esoteric Talisman,* the practitioner must consider how he or she will accomplish those conditions. It takes training and experience to identify exactly what an individual practitioner needs to reach the required state. In a way, like the approach with automatic writing, the practitioner enters a trancelike state during the ritual. Throughout the process, keep in mind point 9 from chapter 3. The practitioner must rise to the occasion and leave behind every insecurity and doubt. When the ritual commences, the practitioner is fully convinced, beyond insecurity and doubt, that he or she is empowered to charge the Fu sigil in the manner he or she has intended.

Consider the following points when preparing a ritual:

1. The five senses need to be heightened to a sensitivity level beyond their ordinary sensations, through the sixth sense of intuition. Think of how you can smell a freshly baked apple pie in the distance and immediately imagine the sweet and tart taste of it on your tongue, even if you aren't

actually eating apple pie; or how, when blindfolded, if you sink your fingers into the sand, you can see the sand in your mind's eye, despite being blindfolded. Likewise, what you sense through intuition must be as strong as what I've described. What comes to you by way of your sixth sense, through intuition, must trigger memory-experience in your vision, smell, hearing, taste, and touch.

2. Consider what aspects of ritual will help you to alter your state of mind so that the distinctions of physical reality, imagination, and a quasi-cataleptic trancelike mode are blurred.

3. Through your mind, you must will favors from Heaven. Recall point 9 in chapter 3. Be convinced of how powerful you are and have faith in your ability to manifest the universe through your body, and more specifically, through your hand. See point 2 in chapter 3.

How you can achieve those elements is precisely what every practitioner must discover for him- or herself. Over centuries of practice with energetic workings, master practitioners have shared collectively what seems to work well, and there are many points of agreement. Those points are worth considering by the beginner practitioner. Evening hours, candlelight, particular scents, particular visuals, particular sounds, and particular feelings that come from being near certain stones, crystals, or minerals have all been vouched for by master practitioners. This book will address a few of the main points of agreement.

## THEORETICAL PURPOSE FOR CHARGING

The charging ritual is the process by which concentrated, potent metaphysical energy is transferred into an object, in this case a paper Fu sigil. By altering the physical senses, a practitioner becomes more metaphysically sensitive. The purpose of ritual is to heighten sensitivity.

Thus, it isn't that charging rituals are necessary to empower a Fu sigil. It's that charging rituals are necessary for most practitioners to be in the right frame of mind to empower a Fu sigil. The ritual represents the process through which a practitioner concentrates and focuses Qi energy, in essence shifting prior balances or proportions of energy in order to channel it all into a sigil, thereby changing the balance and proportion of energies in the environment. It goes back to the point first discussed in chapter 1. Energetic workings, such as sigil crafting, involve the taking of energy or power from one source and transplanting it to another, the desired source. It is using the practitioner as the catalyst for the change sought.

Ceremony is an essential component to craft, and charging a Fu sigil is that ritualistic aspect. A ceremonial ritual must be performed in a particularized way to call upon Heaven and Earth. Established lineages in Taoism pass down ritual scripts from teacher to disciple,[1] with little or no change made to the script as it is passed from generation to generation within the lineage.

This text assume the practitioner is prepared to design his or her own rituals and ceremonies. Even when a ritual script is not passed down through a lineage and the practitioner must be the one to conceive of it, a ritual must be thought through carefully in advance, with every aspect, right down to the last detail, planned out and executed with precision.

Be mindful of the thirteen points from the *Classics of the Esoteric Talisman* outlined in chapter 3. When designing your charging ritual, consider those points to ensure effective craft.

## THE TIMING OF A CHARGING RITUAL

Recall point 7 from chapter 3: "The sun, moon, and stars relate to the numbers (numerology), and knowing this can transform the paths of nature through triggering mechanisms."[2] The triggering mechanism here is the charging ritual for the Fu sigil. While I believe that an effective charging ritual considers astrology and numerology, and I support that belief with medieval Taoist texts that espouse these practices, many contemporary Taoist practitioners craft Fu sigils on demand, without consideration of timing; such practitioners claim with equal conviction that their methods are effective. Thus, you must make a personal decision as to whether you will incorporate astrology and numerology into the timing of charging rituals. Also, if you do decide to consider timing, I contend that both Eastern and Western approaches to astrology and numerology will suffice.

The Western practitioner may feel more comfortable using Western electional astrology for timing charging rituals, in which case, feel free to skip this section. However, consistent with Eastern esoteric tradition, this section sets forth correspondences in Chinese astrology and numerology. Either Western or Eastern astrological and numerological systems may be used for the timing of rituals, and personally, I use a combination of both. Nonetheless, the orthodox approach is to adhere to the Chinese lunisolar calendar and numerological correspondences for dates. This section is provided for those whose interest is piqued by the more orthodox traditions. Be sure to consult the correspondence and reference tables in appendix K to assist with the timing of rituals.

## THE SOLAR TERM AND SEXAGENARY CALENDAR

Timing significant life events and charging rituals have to be in harmony with the Huang Tao, or Yellow Path (黃道).[3] The Yellow Path expresses the earth's orbit around the sun. The ancient Chinese subdivided the year that it takes for a complete revolution into twenty-four segments, or the twenty-four solar terms. Each point of those twenty-four solar terms places the earth in a specific position that renders the Qi energy of that point either auspicious or inauspicious for certain activities. Chinese astrology is the study of the social and personal significance of those points along the Yellow Path.

The twenty-four points make up the Chinese lunisolar calendar, a calendar system where days correspond with solar terms and moon phases. The twenty-four points of the solar term correspond with natural phenomena, such as rain, frost, or the habits of flora and fauna. These points represent the most relevant calendrical events for human society, with some theorizing that the twenty-four points were conceived based on agriculture, while others contend that they arose from the cycles of political affairs dealt with by the ruling classes.[4] I would guess that it was probably both.

These twenty-four points are timed to the four seasons and subdivided into increments of twelve, assigned to twelve earthly branches in increments of two, for a total of twenty-four points. Table 8.1 provides the solar term observed in the traditional Chinese calendar and the timing correspondences that are relevant to the practitioner.[5] The solar term calendar is still used today in traditional Chinese medicine, holistic practices that involve timing medical treatment to astrology, feng shui, and of course, metaphysical craft.

| Solar Term | Seasonal Term (Early Branch) | Western Calendar Dates | Western Zodiac Attribution |
|---|---|---|---|
| Start of Spring | Early Spring (寅, Yín) | February 3–5 | Aquarius |
| Spring Showers | | February 18–20 | Pisces |
| Insects Awaken | Mid-Spring (卯, Mǎo) | March 5–7 | Pisces |
| Vernal Equinox | | March 20–22 | Aries |
| Bright and Clear | Late Spring (辰, Chén) | April 4–6 | Aries |
| Gathering Rain | | April 19–21 | Taurus |
| Start of Summer | Early Summer (巳, Sì) | May 5–7 | Taurus |
| Green Buds Form | | May 20–22 | Gemini |
| Blossoms Form | MidSummer (午, Wǔ) | June 5–7 | Gemini |
| Summer Solstice | | June 21–22 | Cancer |
| Coming Head | Late Summer (未Wǔ) | July 6–8 | Cancer |
| Great Heat | | July 22–24 | Leo |
| Start of Autumn | Early Autumn (申, Shēn) | August 7–9 | Leo |
| Dissipating Heat | | August 22–24 | Virgo |
| White Dew | Mid-Autumn (酉, Yǒu) | September 7–9 | Virgo |
| Autumnal Equinox | | September 22–24 | Libra |
| Cold Dew | Late Autumn (戌, Xū) | October 8–9 | Libra |
| The First Frost | | October 23–24 | Scorpio |
| Start of Winter | Early Winter (亥, Hài) | November 7–8 | Scorpio |
| Light Snow | | November 22–23 | Sagittarius |
| Heaavy Snow | Mid-Winter (子, Zǐ) | December 6–8 | Sagittarius |
| Winter Solstice | | December 21–23 | Capricorn |
| Coming Cold | Late Winter (丑, Chǒu) | January 5–7 | Capricorn |
| Great Cold | | January 20–21 | Aquarius |

Table 8.1. Chinese solar term correspondences

Each of the twelve lunisolar months corresponds with twelve earthly branches and the twelve animals of the Chinese zodiac. Monthly correspondences are covered in the next section. Within those months, each week is

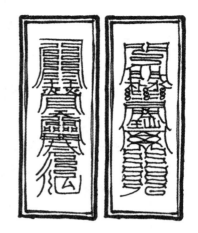

Figure 8.1. Fu sigils keyed to the solar term: spring and summer

Figure 8.2. Fu sigils keyed to the solar term: autumn and winter

subdivided into ten days, corresponding with ten heavenly stems. Such timing by heavenly stems and earthly branches is based on the traditional sexagenary calendar, which, if you believe the legends, has been used by the Chinese to track time since 2637 BC.[6]

The sexagenary calendar is based on a cycle of sixty years that was worked out by the imperial court of the Yellow Emperor.[7] The yearly calendar is expressed through the ten heavenly stems, which are the five phases of the Wu Xing—Wood, Fire, Earth, Metal, and Water—subdivided into yin and yang, with each yin and yang facet assigned one heavenly stem, as noted in table 8.2. The twelve earthly branches are then assigned the twelve animals of the zodiac. Multiplying the twelve zodiac signs with the five phases of Wu Xing, one per year, yields a total of sixty years for the sexagenary cycle. Table K.1 in appendix K provides all heavenly stem and earthly branch correspondences for the sixty-year sexagenary calendar. Additional references on the heavenly stems, earthly branches, and basic Chinese astrology are provided in appendix K.

The Fu pictured in figures 8.1 and 8.2 are from an early-twentieth-century wood-block-printed Book of Methods.[8] The text sets out Fu sigils corresponding with all points of the Chinese solar term for year-round protection and well-being.

Left to right, figure 8.1 shows three sigils from the Book of Methods corresponding to three different points of the solar term: Late Spring (represented

| Heavenly Stem | Binary | Direction | Wu Xing |
|---|---|---|---|
| 甲 (jiǎ) | yang | East | Wood |
| 乙 (yǐ) | yin | | |
| 丙 (bing) | yang | South | Fire |
| 丁 (ding) | yin | | |
| 戊 (wu) | yang | Center | Earth |
| 己 (jǐ) | yin | | |
| 庚 (gēng) | yang | West | Metal |
| 辛 (xin) | yin | | |
| 壬 (rén) | yang | North | Water |
| 癸 (guǐ) | yin | | |

Table 8.2. Heavenly stem correspondences

by the earthly branch 辰, Chén), Early Summer (巳, Sì), and Midsummer (午, Wǔ). The Late Spring Fu (left) is charged during the Dragon ascendant and empowered for use during the third lunar month, or April 4 to 21 in the Western calendar. The Early Spring Fu (center) is for the fourth lunar month, May 5 to 22, and charged during the Snake ascendant. The Midsummer Fu (right) is for the fifth lunar month, June 5 to 22, charged under the Horse ascendant. For ascendant hour correspondences, see tables 8.3 and 8.7. The two Fu in figure 8.2 correspond to Late Autumn (戌, Xū) and Early Winter (亥, Hài), the ninth and tenth lunar months, respectively.

## MONTHLY CORRESPONDENCES

In orthodox esoteric Taoism, and as I saw in many of the medieval Chinese alchemical texts, timing is keyed to heavenly stems and earthly branches. For example, in the *Ling Bao Order of the Five Talismans* (靈寶五符序), a text dating to the early fifth century AD, instructions for crafting a Fu and the accompanying rituals might read something like "甲子建天," with reference to the heavenly stem 甲 (jiǎ). Such a reference indicates that the instruction given must be carried out on the day (天) of the week corresponding with 甲.

| Season | Lunar Month | Zodiac Sign | Ascendant (Hour) | Earthly Branch |
|---|---|---|---|---|
| spring | month 1 | Tiger | 3 a.m. – 4:59 a.m. | 寅 (yín) |
| | month 2 | Rabbit | 5 a.m. – 6:59 a.m. | 卯 (mǎo) |
| | month 3 | Dragon | 7 a.m. – 8:59 a.m. | 辰 (chén) |
| summer | month 4 | Snake | 9 a.m. – 10:59 a.m. | 巳 (sì) |
| | month 5 | Horse | 11 a.m. – 12:59 p.m. | 午 (wǔ) |
| | month 6 | Sheep | 1 p.m. – 2:59 p.m. | 未 (wèi) |
| autumn | month 7 | Monkey | 3 p.m. – 4:59 p.m. | 申 (shēn) |
| | month 8 | Rooster | 5 p.m. – 6:59 p.m. | 酉 (yǒu) |
| | month 9 | Dog | 7 p.m. – 8:59 p.m. | 戌 (xū) |
| winter | month 10 | Boar | 9 p.m. – 10:59 p.m. | 亥 (hài) |
| | month 11 | Rat | 11 p.m. – 12:59 a.m. | 子 (zǐ) |
| | month 12 | Ox | 1 a.m. – 2:59 a.m. | 丑 (chǒu) |

Table 8.3. Timing correspondences by earthly branches

Heavenly stems are based on the ten days of the medieval Chinese week, dating back to the Shang Dynasty. In medieval China, shamans and Taoist practitioners of craft timed rituals, burials, and sacrifices to the heavenly stems, or the ten days of the week. Today, the medieval ten-day week is no longer observed by the Chinese, and so timing by heavenly stems is now an antiquated practice. Heavenly stems do remain relevant in Chinese astrology and feng shui, however. Table 8.2 provides a general reference for the heavenly stems. The yin and yang, Wu Xing, and five relative direction correspondences remain relevant today for raising energy, but are not relevant to the extent that timing is involved. Thus, admittedly, table 8.2 may be a bit out of place in this book. It is fascinating history, nonetheless. More practical instruction on timing by days of the week will be provided in the next section.

Earthly branches, which are still relevant today, are based on observations of Jupiter. The earthly branches represent twelve subdivided sections of

| Western Calendar Month and Day | | | Western Calendar Month and Day | | Wu Xing | Chinese Zodiac Sign |
|---|---|---|---|---|---|---|
| January | 6 | to | January | 19 | Earth | Ox |
| January | 20 | to | February | 3 | Earth | Ox |
| February | 4 | to | February | 18 | Wood | Tiger |
| February | 19 | to | March | 5 | Wood | Tiger |
| March | 6 | to | March | 20 | Wood | Rabbit |
| March | 21 | to | April | 4 | Wood | Rabbit |
| April | 5 | to | April | 19 | Earth | Dragon |
| April | 20 | to | May | 4 | Earth | Dragon |
| May | 5 | to | May | 20 | Fire | Snake |
| May | 21 | to | June | 5 | Fire | Snake |
| June | 6 | to | June | 20 | Fire | Horse |
| June | 21 | to | July | 6 | Fire | Horse |
| July | 7 | to | July | 22 | Earth | Goat |
| July | 23 | to | August | 6 | Earth | Goat |
| August | 7 | to | August | 22 | Metal | Monkey |
| August | 23 | to | September | 7 | Metal | Monkey |
| September | 8 | to | September | 22 | Metal | Rooster |
| September | 23 | to | October | 7 | Metal | Rooster |
| October | 8 | to | October | 22 | Earth | Dog |
| October | 23 | to | November | 6 | Water | Dog |
| November | 7 | to | November | 21 | Water | Pig |
| November | 22 | to | December | 6 | Water | Pig |
| December | 7 | to | December | 21 | Water | Rat |
| December | 22 | to | January | 5 | Water | Rat |

Table 8.4. Chinese zodiac and Wu Xing Western monthly correspondences

Jupiter's orbit and correspond with the twelve lunar months of the Chinese calendar. Each of the lunar months corresponds with a zodiac sign and an ascendant hour (in increments of two). Table 8.3 provides the monthly timing correspondences for the earthly branches.

| Wu Xing | Life Aspect Correspondences |
|---|---|
| **Wood**<br><br>*Coordinate with:*<br>Jupiter | Artistic endeavors; writing projects; publishing, teaching, social justice, health-care, health concerns; matters relating to books, academics, arts and culture, or more literally, trees, plants, flora, and the forest. Use to sprout or grow. Helps raise creative energy; initiations, nourishment, sowing and fertilizing. |
| **Fire**<br><br>*Coordinate with:*<br>Mars | Innovation, inventions; leadership; authority or government; politics; technology; performing arts; or more literally, for the practitioner to attain the power to control fire. Use to bring and endeavor to full fruition, to its full potential, or blossom. Helps raise creative energy; initiations, nourishment, sowing and fertilizing. |
| **Earth**<br><br>*Coordinate with:*<br>Saturn | Law, business, finance, real estate; seeking stability and security; fertility; marriage; or more literally, for the practitioner to attain the power to control earth. Can also be used to bring an endeavor to full fruition, to its full potential. Earth energy will fertilize the situation. |
| **Metal**<br><br>*Coordinate with:*<br>Venus | Law and policy; writing, rhetoric; academics; scholarship; military strategy, war, politics; or more literally, for a practitioner to control metals or weaponry. Use to reap. Helps raise destructive energy; banishment, release, cessation, severance, slaughter, abatement. |
| **Water**<br><br>*Coordinate with:*<br>Mercury | Spiritual endeavors; raising intuition or psychic development; wisdom and compassion; matters relating to diplomacy; international relations; global relations; public relations; artistic fields; creative entrepreneurship; or more literally, travel overseas, swimming, or matters relating to the bodies of water. Helps raise the power to subdue and can be used in binding spells against strong yang attacks or dominant Fire offenses. |

Table 8.5. Timing of rituals according to the Wu Xing

| Days of the Week | Planetary Correspondence | Energetic Correspondences for Spell Crafting |
|---|---|---|
| Sunday | Sun (日, Sun) | *Correspondence.* Yang. Personal goal setting; new ventures; exorcisms, dispelling malignant energy, destroying negativity. |
| Monday | Moon (月, Moon) | *Correspondence.* Yin. Moon magic, prophecy and divination, raising psychic power, conjuring, communion with the underworld, retaliatory magic; cloaking or concealment. |
| Tuesday | Mars (火星, Fire Star) | *Correspondence.* Fire. Creative projects, performing arts, ambitions, promotions, advancements; leadership, politics; war, military. |
| Wednesday | Mercury (水星, Water Star) | *Correspondence.* Water. Career, goal setting, intuitive work, diplomacy, social or community relations, family, home, the arts. |
| Thursday | Jupiter (木星, Wood Star) | *Correspondence.* Wood. Wealth, finances, money, finances; health, wellness, healthcare, medical; publishing, teaching, academics, education. |
| Friday | Venus (金星, Metal Star) | *Correspondence.* Metal. Law and policy, legal matters; music; writing, rhetoric, academics; fertility, innovation; business; combat, military. |
| Saturday | Saturn (土星, Earth Star) | *Correspondence.* Earth. Home, hearth, family, marriage; finance, real estate, estate planning, assets; seeking stability, sustainability, and financial security. |

Table 8.6. Days of the week correspondences

Thus, instructions in a practitioner's Book of Methods that say a particular ritual is to be performed on the 酉 month indicate month 8 of the lunar calendar, in autumn. Instructions for the ritual to be performed on the 酉 hour indicate a time between 5 p.m. and 6:59 p.m.

A more practical reference might be table 8.4, which provides Wu Xing and zodiac correspondences according to the Western calendar. Using that table as a reference, Fu sigil crafting keyed to or harnessing the energies of Wood, for example, which are matters relating to money, finances, academics, teaching, publishing, or health care, might best be performed during the Wood months, or in the Western calendar, February 4 to April 4. Fu sigil crafting keyed to or harnessing the energies of the zodiac sign Tiger or the Tiger as a guardian spirit, such as matters relating to war, the military, warriors or soldiers, justice, or social causes, are optimal during the Tiger months, February 4 to March 5.[9]

Use table 8.4 in conjunction with table 8.5. Note that there is some overlap; for example, writing projects can correspond with either Wood or Metal; matters relating to politics can correspond with either Fire or Metal, and so on. For an additional reference on Wu Xing correspondences, see table 1.5 from chapter 1.

## DAYS OF THE WEEK

Medieval China followed a ten-day week corresponding with the ten heavenly stems, and thus the heavenly stems were used for the timing of craft, or the magical and esoteric practices of the Taoist priests. Since that may be impracticable for the modern day practitioner, the following section will provide instruction on the timing of charging rituals by the seven-day week.

The seven-day week is based on the Qi Yao (七曜, Qī Yào), which might be likened to the seven sacred planets of Western astrology: the sun, moon, Mercury, Venus, Mars, Jupiter, and Saturn. To ancient astrologers, these were the seven visible "planets" in the heavens; for the purposes of astrology, we will refer to the sun and moon as "planets." It is not clear when the Chinese switched over to the seven-day-week system. Some scholars speculate that it did not take place until the sixteenth century with the coming of the Jesuits, although there are records referring to the Qi Yao, or seven luminaries system for tracking the week, that date back to AD 210.[10]

To charge a Fu sigil with more yang, a practitioner might opt for a Sunday to perform the ritual, and for one that is more yin, such as in summonings of ghosts or Fu related to the underworld, Monday might be better, when yin energy is dominant. See table 8.5 for the Tuesday through Saturday correspondences.

## HOURLY ASCENDANTS

In Chinese astrology, not only is each passing lunar year ruled by one of the twelve zodiac signs, but every two hours of the day, or ascendant, is also ruled by one of the twelve signs, as outlined in table 8.7. See also table K.3 in appendix K for supplemental zodiac correspondences. Ascendant zodiac signs express the aura, the nature of the innate Qi that governs a particular energetic field. In natal astrology, such as in Ba Zi or Four Pillars analysis, the ascendant sign indicates the attributes of the aura that a person emanates. In the timing of charging rituals, the ascendant sign corresponding to the hour of the ritual indi-

| Hour | Zodiac Sign | Correspondence per Commission of the Four Guardians |
|---|---|---|
| 1 a.m. – 2:59 a.m. | Ox | prayers and summonings; defensive work |
| 3 a.m. – 4:59 a.m. | Tiger | love, family, relationships, inner cultivation |
| 5 a.m. – 6:59 a.m. | Rabbit | love, family, relationships, inner cultivation |
| 7 a.m. – 8:59 a.m. | Dragon | love, family, relationships, inner cultivation |
| 9 a.m. – 10:59 a.m. | Snake | prosperity, wealth, advancement |
| 11 a.m. – 12:59 p.m. | Horse | prosperity, wealth, advancement |
| 1 p.m. – 2:59 p.m. | Sheep | prosperity, wealth, advancement |
| 3 p.m. – 4:59 p.m. | Monkey | ambitions, glory, career, social status |
| 5 p.m. – 6:59 p.m. | Rooster | ambitions, glory, career, social statu |
| 7 p.m. – 8:59 p.m. | Dog | ambitions, glory, career, social statu |
| 9 p.m. –10:59 p.m. | Boar | prayers and summonings; defensive work |
| 11 p.m. – 12:59 p.m. | Rat | prayers and summonings; defensive work |

Table 8.7. Ascendants, Chinese zodiac signs, and correspondences[1]

cates the energies most easily harnessed into a sacred space during that hour. It does not mean that only rituals relating to the governing energies can be performed at that hour—not at all. It simply means that if the practitioner seeks an easier time with a ritual, that particular corresponding hour will have a potent supply of metaphysical energy in the environment for the practitioner to tap into and raise into his or her sacred space.

While any type of craft may in principle be performed at any time, according to the Yellow Path, astronomical alignments at certain times will create a potent reserve of certain types of energies that a practitioner can harness to strengthen craft. Thus, by way of example, according to table 8.7, between 1 p.m. and 2:59 p.m., during the ascendant of the Sheep, the universe is aligned in such a way that craft for love and romance might be more conducive, and given the southwest correspondence, is best activated through the Ba Gua trigram Earth (see fig. 1.19) and Earth and Fire from the Wu Xing (see table 1.9, noting that Fire fortifies Earth). For an easier time, a practitioner might opt to perform the charging ritual for a love and romance Fu during the specified afternoon hour, but it is not in any way a requirement. Hourly ascendant correspondences are nothing more than another energetic variable that a practitioner might want to consider.

| Moon Phase | | Wu Xing | Binary | Ba Gua Trigrams | Zodiac Signs | Craft Timing Correspondences |
|---|---|---|---|---|---|---|
| new moon | | Wood | yang | Fire Thunder | Tiger Rabbit Dragon | sowing seeds initiation health, wellness |
| waxing | waxing crescent | Fire | yin | Water Wind | Snake Horse Sheep | innovation new romance conjurations |
| | first quarter | Fire | yin | Water Wind | Snake Horse Sheep | growth creativity development |
| | waxing gibbous | Fire | yin | Water Wind | Snake Horse Sheep | luck, wealth prosperity warrior spirit |
| full moon | | Metal | yang | Heaven Lake | Monkey Rooster Dog | power protection manifestation |
| waning | waning gibbous | Water | yin | Earth Mountain | Boar Rat Ox | release punishment vengeance |
| | last quarter | Water | yin | Earth Mountain | Boar Rat Ox | destruction severance retaliation |
| | waning crescent | Water | yin | Earth Mountain | Boar Rat Ox | slaughter bloodletting conjurations |

Table 8.8. Moon phases and correspondences

## Significance of Moon Phases

Lunar correspondences are also significant. The moon stabilizes the earth's axis of rotation,[12] affects the tides,[13] relates to how the night vision of many mammalian species evolved,[14] and is why there is a rich deposit of metals in the earth's mantle and minerals brought to shore by the young earth's tides, creating life.[15]

During a waxing moon, female estrogen levels seem to rise and then peak during the full moon,[16] just as eggs and sperm in many animal species build during the waxing moon and release upon the full moon. In waning crescent moons, hormone levels tend to be lowest. More babies are born during the full moon than any other phase, while birth rates are lowest during the three days of the new moon.[17]

When the moon is in an active, masculine sign such as Aries, Gemini, Leo, Libra, Sagittarius, or Aquarius, babies born will tend to demonstrate yang qualities and be ambitious, intellectual, and aggressive. Babies born when the moon is in a feminine sign, Taurus, Cancer, Virgo, Scorpio, Capricorn, or Pisces, will demonstrate yin qualities, such as sentimentality, diplomacy, and perceptiveness.

Likewise, coordinating rituals with moon phases can greatly enhance the efficacy of the rituals. Matters of growth and development are best as the moon waxes, while banishing and releasing are best as the moon wanes. Utilize a full moon to harvest power at its peak. For rituals that need active, masculine energies, utilize the dates that the moon is in an active sign; for the more subtle qualities of nurturing, utilize the dates that the moon is in a feminine sign. Table 8.8 provides a general reference for how charging rituals can be timed with the moon.

The new moon is a time for regeneration, rebirth, and new beginnings, and thus charging a Fu sigil for health and wellness during the new moon is optimal. Fu sigils crafted to ensure the auspices of a new venture or new phase in one's life are timed to the new moon. The new moon is a time for sowing, for creating new opportunities, and also a time for initiations.

A waxing moon is a time for growth, creativity, innovation, enhancement, and development. Luck, prosperity, and wealth matters can be heightened by a charging ritual timed with a waxing moon. A waxing moon is also an optimal time for home or business blessings. Fu sigils crafted to ensure the well-being, harmony, and success of a home or family are optimal during a waxing moon.

The full moon is the moon of power, empowerment, and manifestation. Sigils crafted for empowerment, virility, protection, fortification, strength, or domination are best charged during a full moon. Divination is believed to be more powerful when the moon is full. When power, force, transformation, or strong defensive or protective magic is needed, the full moon is optimal.

The waning moon is a time for releases, banishing, abatement, removal, severance, or to eradicate something that is undesirable. Matters of cessation or intents of vengeance work better during a waning moon. Bindings also work

| Direction | Season | Zodiac Sign | Binary | Wu Xing |
|-----------|--------|-------------|--------|---------|
| East | Spring | Tiger | yang | Wood |
| | | Rabbit | yin | Wood |
| | | Dragon | yang | Earth |
| South | Summer | Snake | yin | Fire |
| | | Horse | yang | Fire |
| | | Sheep | yin | Earth |
| West | Autumn | Monkey | yang | Metal |
| | | Rooster | yin | Metal |
| | | Dog | yang | Earth |
| North | Winter | Boar | yin | Water |
| | | Rat | yang | Water |
| | | Ox | yin | Earth |

Table 8.9. Directions, seasons, and the Chinese zodiac signs

during this phase. The waning moon was traditionally the time of sacrifices, slaughter, and bloodletting.

The crescent moons, both waxing and waning, prior to their respective quarters, are optimal times for communication with the spirit world. There is strong yin energy to crescent moons. The waxing crescent moon is more conducive for bringing through the Fire and yang-dominant (or alternatively, more masculine) spirit energies, whereas the waning crescent moon is more conducive for bringing through the Water and yin-dominant spirit (or more feminine) energies, though, of course, either masculine or feminine, yang or yin spirit energies can come through at any given time. The waxing crescent is merely an easier setting for the Fire and yang spirit essences, and the waning crescent merely an easier setting for the Water and yin.

## The Four Seasons

Refer again to points 5, 10, and 11 in the *Classics of the Esoteric Talismans,* as outlined in chapter 3, which recommend the consideration of the Wu Xing, seasons, and compass directions, and the yin-yang binary when designing a charging ritual. Table 8.9 provides the Chinese correspondences.

| Number | Wu Xing | Ba Gua Trigram | Reconciled Wu Xing and Ba Gua Trigram Correspondences |
|--------|---------|----------------|--------------------------------------------------------|
| 1 | primary influence Water ——— secondary influence Metal | Water | intuition; social relationships; creativity; arts and culture; career; social status; psychic abilities; protection, defense, evading danger |
| 2 | primary influence Earth ——— secondary influence Water | Earth | strong yin; motherhood; love; relationships, romance; business; legal matters, property issues; financial security |
| 3 | primary influence Wood ——— secondary influence Wood | Thunder | literature, writing; knowledge, education; social justice; change, revolution; inciting movement; family, ancestry, heritage |
| 4 | primary influence Wood ——— secondary influence Wood | Wind | literature, writing; knowledge, education; social justice; wealth, assets, finances; adapting to changes |
| 5 | primary influence Earth ——— secondary influence Wood | ☯ | business; legal matters; property issues; financial security; health, wellness; medical concerns; personal vitality; personal life force |
| 6 | primary influence Metal ——— secondary influence Fire | Heaven | strong yang; fatherhood; speech, communications; intellect; ambitions; independence; opportunities; alliances; seeking blessings; seeking harmony |
| 7 | primary influence Metal ——— secondary influence Fire | Lake | speech, communications; intellect; independence; ambitions; fertility, children; joy, happiness; receiving pleasure; fulfillment |
| 8 | primary influence Earth ——— secondary influence Earth | Mountain | business; legal matters; property issues; financial security; seeking stability in relationships; seeking knowledge, education, or wisdom |
| 9 | primary influence Fire ——— secondary influence Earth | Fire | leadership; power; courage, fortitude, strength; performing arts; creativity and intuition; insight, mental clarity; ambitions, honors, and fame; seeking glory |

Table 8.10. Reconciled Wu Xing and Lo Shu numerology

Irrespective of the Chinese metaphysical correspondences outlined in this section, charging rituals can generally be performed very early, before the sun has come up, or very late at night, well after the sun has set. These are the hours that unconscious attunement seems to be most heightened. Every practitioner is different, however. The primary concern is performing the ritual when the practitioner is most receptive and open to accessing the unconscious. If an individual practitioner's attunement to the collective unconscious is clear and present in the afternoon, then afternoon-timed rituals it is.

## NUMEROLOGY

Recall again the summarized principles from the *Classics of the Esoteric Talisman,* as outlined in chapter 3. Astrology and numerology are related to each other, so also consider the numerology of specific dates and times. For example, the sum of the six digits corresponding to a date can be considered, and if that sum is a double digit, the sum of the double digits, until a single digit is arrived at. That date is said to be optimal for matters corresponding with that single digit number.

For example, the date July 31, 2015 (7 + 3 + 1 + 2 + 0 + 1 + 5 = 19, 1 + 9 = 10, 1 + 0 = 1), according to Chinese (Lo Shu) numerology, is most potent for charging a Fu sigil designed to protect, defend against danger, heighten psychic abilities, or increase social status, career prospects, or matters relating to arts and culture. Interestingly, that date also corresponds with a full moon. In Western astrology, the moon is in Aquarius, and the sun is in Leo. Such a date would be quite auspicious and potent for magical work.

Table 8.10 is a reconciliation of Chinese numerology and the Wu Xing, according to the Lo Shu magic square:

## WHAT TO WEAR FOR THE RITUAL

In orthodox Taoism, the priest's robe that is worn today during ritual or ceremonies has changed little from the Taoist priest's robe that was worn during the Qing Dynasty (AD 1644–1912).[18] The color, detailing, and embellishments on the priest's robe depend on the lineage and traditions. However, they are generally black, gold, white, or red,[19] ornate, and made of fine silk. Mythical creatures such as dragons, Ba Gua trigrams, peach blossoms, and sacred Taoist

Figure 8.3. Qing DynastyTaoist priest's coat, made of silk and metallic threads, circa AD 1870 (courtesy Indianapolis Museum of Art, accession no. 2000.126v)

symbolism are embroidered onto the robe. The robe is based on a traditional style of Han Chinese clothing called *hanfu* (漢服).

The everyday attire, however, is simpler, discrete, and also in the traditional hanfu style, even today usually in black, navy, or white.

The traditional priest's robe is stunning and would be magnificent to wear, but it is by no means necessary. A generalized consensus for what to wear during ritual is something clean and comfortable that lets you forget about what you're wearing and instead facilitates your focus on the ritual work ahead.

However, a higher consciousness needs to be achieved during ritual, and for many, clothes matter. For many, clothes affect attitude, frame of mind, and, of course, consciousness. So wear what will convey to your own self that the work ahead is sacred work and that what you are doing transcends the normal, material plane.

Black tends to be protective and shielding, so if the ritual work ahead is defensive in nature, a bit on the riskier side, or there is summoning involved, black might be a prudent option as one extra layer of defensive energy to safeguard the practitioner.

White is for connecting with the supernal, for invoking divine assistance, or for those seeking transcendence. Paradoxically, white is also worn by shamans who travel through the underworld, and white is used to connect with the underworld, netherworld, or realms beyond the human plane of existence. White is considered more conducive for transformations.

| Guardian | Celestial King | Direction | Element | Season | Commission |
|----------|---------------|-----------|---------|--------|------------|
| Black Tortoise | 多聞天王<br>*Duō Wén*<br>*Tiān Wáng* | North | Water | Winter | Hears every sound, utterance, thought, and prayer. |
| Red Phoenix | 增長天王<br>*Zēng Cháng*<br>*Tiān Wáng* | South | Fire | Summer | Brings growth, advancement, and innovation. |
| Azure Dragon | 持國天王<br>*Chí Guó*<br>*Tiān Wáng* | East | Wood | Spring | Supports, nurtures, develops, and nourishes. |
| White Tiger | 廣目天王<br>*Guǎng Mù*<br>*Tiān Wáng* | West | Metal | Autumn | Sees every sight, act, deed, gesture, and movement. |

Table 8.11. Correspondences for the Four Guardians and Four Celestial Kings

Red raises power and helps to foster heightened awareness in the practitioner. Dark blue is the color of choice for knowledge-seeking erudite practitioners. Yellow or gold is the robe color of choice for celestial masters or those who hold a position of prominence in the metaphysical plane.

## OPENING THE RITUAL

In certain Western magical traditions, a circle is cast prior to a ritual. If that is your practice, commence with the casting of a circle. In lieu of circle casting, traditional Taoist practice consists of an opening prayer and the setting of the practitioner's seal on the altar to connect the trinity of Heaven, Earth, and Man. By setting the practitioner's seal on the altar with the opening prayer, the heavenly spirit plane, the earthly plane, and the practitioner become connected, and a clear channel opens for the ritual work to begin. Thus, think of the opening of a ritual as the process of connecting and synthesizing the three planes—Heaven, Earth, and Man ("Man" here being the practitioner, irrespective of gender).

Before commencing any ritual, the air is first cleared with wooden percussion blocks. The practitioner raps on the wood block while moving in a circle around the work area. Mantras are typically recited while this takes place. In some traditions, a peach wood sword is used to cut through evil in the air, in lieu of the wood block. Next, the practitioner moves around the same circle again, the second time sprinkling consecrated water. The rapping sound of the wood block combined with the mantra recitations are believed to scatter negative energy. As an extra measure, the water purifies. Next, ceremonial bells or tingsha cymbals are rung, again moving along the same circle. Thus begins the opening prayer. Also, note that the clearing does not necessarily need to be done in a full circle around the altar space. In many practices, only the area in front of the altar needs to be cleared.

The purpose of the opening prayer is to call upon the Four Guardians (四獸, Sì Shòu, or 四神風, Sì Shén Fēng) of Taoist cosmology. The four guardians represent the four cardinal directions and four seasons. Conceptually, the Four Celestial Kings (調雨順, Tiáo Yǔ Shùn) are the esoteric Buddhist equivalent. As noted in chapter 1, calling upon the Four Guardians brings forth four powers for the practitioner to use in his or her craft. The Black Tortoise is called upon to lend the power of clairaudience to the practitioner; the Red Phoenix with the power to create change and bring growth; the Azure Dragon with the power of control over events; and the White Tiger lends the power of clairvoyance.

To begin the opening prayer, the practitioner faces each direction in turn, forming hand mudras for receptivity and receipt of energy or power. Refer to "Hand Mudras" in chapter 6. Which hand mudra is used, which direction the practitioner faces first, and whether the practitioner moves clockwise or counterclockwise varies from lineage to lineage, tradition to tradition. How the four directions are called upon also varies. Pacing, covered in subsequent sections, is often involved, as well as dance-like movements. I opt for simplicity, and bow reverently in each of the directions.

Some begin by calling upon the guardian of the South and then move clockwise for magic involving creative forces, advancement, initiation, beginnings, or growth, and counterclockwise for magic involving destructive forces, protection, defense, vengeance, cessations, exorcisms, eradication, or banishments. Others follow the order of the Wu Xing elements and therefore begin East, move clockwise toward South, then West, then end on North.[20]

Magical lineages that are Buddhist-dominant will call upon the Four Celestial Kings by name, while those that are Taoist-dominant will call upon the Four Guardians. In essence, the concept remains the same, and even the directional, elemental, seasonal, and functional correspondences remain the same. The prayer or invocation used to call upon the four directions will generally include references to the directions, elements, and perhaps even seasons and functions.

Following is an example of a translated opening prayer:

## OPENING PRAYER, INVOKING THE FOUR DIRECTIONS

I am [*practitioner's name or magical name*] (*optional:* from the [*specify lineage or tradition*]), and I come forward now to call upon the Four Guardians.

Spirit of Red Phoenix commanding Fire in the South, I invoke you now and pay homage to you. Send me the power to create change and bring growth.

Spirit of Azure Dragon commanding Wood in the East, I invoke you now and pay homage to you. Send me the power of control over events.

Spirit of Black Tortoise commanding Water in the North, I invoke you now and pay homage to you. Send me the power of clairaudience.

Spirit of White Tiger commanding Metal in the West, I invoke you now and pay homage to you. Send me the power of clairvoyance.

I come in good faith, with pure heart, sincere intentions, and seek your guidance and blessings so that I might help those in need. In the name of [*deity or deities invoked for the ritual—the Jade Emperor, Lady of the Ninth Heaven, Kuan Yin, etc.*], lend me your powers so that I may command as mediator between Heaven and Earth, Earth and Man, Man and Heaven. [*Conclude with a closing—Ji ji ru lu ling, Na mo amitofuo, So mote it be, etc.*].

In general ritual work, calling upon the four quarters is sufficient. However, in deeper ritual work or rituals that involve summonings of entities from other worlds or planes (more specifically, I'm referring to demonology), work with ghosts, hungry ghosts, exorcisms, or in strong defensive magic to dispel evil or malignant energy, the five relative directions are called upon as well to form the strongest possible protective barrier around the practitioner and the practitioner's work space.

Not all practitioners subscribe to elaborate ritual for the crafting of every Fu. The first three strokes of the pen or ink brush can also serve as the opening of the ritual. As the practitioner renders the first lines, he or she invokes the deity, visualizes the connection of Heaven, Earth, and Man, and mentally empowers the surrounding space to become sacred space. Drawing the three-star constellation glyph at the top of the Fu pictured in figure 4.21, the three checkmarks at the top of the sigil (fig. 4.30), or the constellation as pictured at the top of the Wealth Sigil (fig. 5.6) can serve as the opening of the ritual.

## PRAYER, INVOCATION, SUMMONING

The semantics of prayer, invocation, and summoning are important if the practitioner wishes to be respectful of spiritual hierarchies. In general, the mechanics that a practitioner utilizes to connect or interact with spirit entities is through prayer, invocation, or summoning. I often say "call upon" simply for ease of reference. From an orthodox standpoint, for a practitioner to maintain his or her standing among the spirit realms, the practitioner must honor the hierarchies.

There are several variations on the cosmological theory of the universe's hierarchies, each differing in the number of heavens, how those heavens are characterized, the underworld, hell, and the number of courts in hell. However, generally speaking, there are several planes that make up Heaven, occupied by a pantheon of deities, guardian angels or guardian spirits,[21] bodhisattvas, immortals, devas, heavenly lords, or any other number of expressions for higher spiritual or celestial beings. The pantheon of celestial beings occupying Heaven is overseen by a ruling celestial emperor, the Jade Emperor, the god among gods. In some traditions, the Jade Emperor is referred to as Shang Di or Lao Tian Yie ("the heavenly father").

Then there is Earth, occupied by Man and animal. Animal spirits occupy Earth with Man. Ghosts oftentimes occupy Earth as well, along with hungry ghosts. However, ghosts and hungry ghosts can also be occupants of an underworld. The characterization of the underworld differs among the traditions. Some characterize it as distinct from the courts of hell, while others characterize all spirit realms beneath Man as the underworld. The courts of hell are realms where the souls of humans who have sinned greatly on Earth are cast to for the atonement of those sins. Which court of hell a human soul is cast into depends on the nature of the sins. Demons also occupy these courts of hell. All courts are overseen by a ruling underworld king.

Figure 8.4. The Northern Ladle

In orthodox Taoist craft, a practitioner is mindful of the foregoing hierarchy. Any celestial being above Man and Earth is prayed to or invoked. While animal spirits can be invoked, it is also acceptable to consider

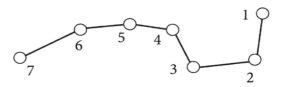

Figure 8.5. Pacing the Big Dipper

the calling upon of animal spirits as summoning. Ghosts and hungry ghosts occupying Earth are summoned; all beings beneath Earth, in the underworld or the courts of hell, are also summoned.

The mechanics of a summoning implies a certain level of control or command over the spirit that has been called upon, whereas in prayer or invocation, there isn't that same authority. It is at the celestial being's discretion whether to descend and assist the practitioner. Practitioners believe that the observation of respect, honorifics, and setting out proper offerings to the celestial beings substantially increases the chances of such celestial beings agreeing to help, though even then, it is at the whim of the deities. On the other hand, as long as the identity of a ghost, demon, or lesser spirit is known, naming the name during the summoning is enough to exert authority over that spirit.

When engaging with deities or angelic energies, it is best to refer to the practitioner's work as prayer or to characterize the calling upon of such energies as invocation. In all other incidences of supernatural interaction, the work may be referred to as summoning. Note, however, that whether a practitioner's work is prayer, invocation, or summoning depends less on the words uttered than it does on the true intent within the practitioner. Thus, it is not the words you should be mindful of; it is your intent. A sincere intent always produces the correct semantics.

## PACING THE BIG DIPPER

In traditional Taoist rituals, the practitioner recites invocations while forming hand gestures, such as mudras, or they form a sword (or a calligraphy pen; both references are used interchangeably) with the index and middle finger pointed outward to etch Fu sigils in the air during the invocations. A photograph demonstrating the sword mudra is provided in figure 11.13. Additionally, the practitioner is walking in a set formation around the altar space. The most common formation of this practice is referred to as Pacing the Big Dipper.[22]

First, there is no universally agreed upon approach to Pacing the Big Dipper. Rather, each lineage has its own procedure. Individual practitioners opt for what feels right to them. This book outlines a basic method that can be integrated into any practice, though the practitioner is encouraged to modify it until the method resonates personally with him or her.

The Big Dipper, or as it is known in Chinese, the Seven Stars of the Northern Ladle, is believed to emanate with extraordinarily strong energy that can be harnessed here on earth and channeled into particular intentions. One of the earliest Taoist deities worshipped, Tai Yi, also referred to as the Supreme Deity or Supreme Emperor of Heaven, was venerated for creating the universe.

According to myth, the Big Dipper, or Northern Ladle, was used by the god Tai Yi[23] to ladle out cosmic Qi energy or Vital Force to give life and breath to all living beings. The Northern Ladle was also described as Tai Yi's chariot, and through the Northern Ladle, the deity regulated the four corners of the universe, the yin and the yang, and the Wu Xing five phases. A delineation of the Northern Ladle depicted with lines and circles is often found in Taoist Fu sigils.

The objective of Pacing the Big Dipper is to ascend from earth up to the heavens to perform the energetic workings on a spiritual or supernatural plane between worlds. It is not unlike the concept of "As above, so below"[24] in Western esoteric traditions.

The practitioner begins at the point of number 7 in figure 8.5. Number 1 is before the altar. At each point, the practitioner takes two steps, left foot and right foot, while reciting invocations or prayers at each of the seven points, either using prayer beads to keep track of the recitation count or gesturing sigils in the air to consecrate the space around the Big Dipper. The precise methodology that is most effective varies from practitioner to practitioner. There are many paths to reach the same destination. Certain lineages offer roadmaps and directions for the tried-and-true paths, but you can also find your own way, guided by your intuition.

## PACING THE LO SHU

While the Big Dipper remains the best-known pacing practice, many lin-

| # | Direction | Letters | Corresponding Area of Human Life |
|---|-----------|---------|----------------------------------|
| 1 | North | A J S | social status, profession, career |
| 2 | Southwest | B K T | love, relationships, mother, family (nuclear), home, hearth |
| 3 | East | C L U | family (extended), ancestry, heritage, genetic foundations |
| 4 | Southeast | D M V | wealth, assets, resources, finanaces, growth potential |
| 5 | Center | E N W | health, wellness, verve, vitality, Qi energy levels |
| 6 | Northwest | F O X | allies, father, family (nonbiological; chosen; initiated into), friends, community |
| 7 | West | G P Y | innovation, children, fertility, beginnings and endings |
| 8 | Northeast | H Q Z | knowledge, education, arts and culture |
| 9 | South | I R | Ambitions, goals, accomplishments, glory, honors |

Table 8.12. Lo Shu, directionality, and alphabet correspondences

eages in Taoist magical practice also use the Lo Shu. The Lo Shu magic square corresponds with the eight trigrams of the Ba Gua (with the center section being the ninth, the fountainhead of Qi) and the Nine-Star Big Dipper. The Lo Shu is a principal basis for many Eastern esoteric and metaphysical practices. It is superimposed over the Ba Gua in Taoism and used for devising rituals. It is also used in feng shui, as mentioned in chapter 4. Appendix D, "Lo Shu–Designed Glyphs," also covers application of the Lo Shu to the craft.

For pacing with the Lo Shu, Taoist practitioners pace a formation in the Lo Shu square that corresponds with either a series of numbers of significance to the lineage, the specific spell or ritual at hand, or the nine sections corresponding with feng shui. The nine numbers correspond with nine areas of human life, as follows:

One method of using the Lo Shu square for pacing is to determine which numbers to invoke based on the subject matter of the sigil crafted. For example, a sigil created for career advancement and generating wealth should trigger sectors 1, 4, 9, and maybe also 6 and 8. Thus, a path might be devised as follows:

Note that the corresponding letters of the Latin alphabet were a recon-

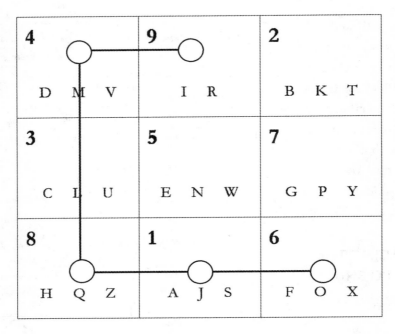

Figure 8.6. Pacing the Lo Shu for a wealth or career sigil-charging ritual

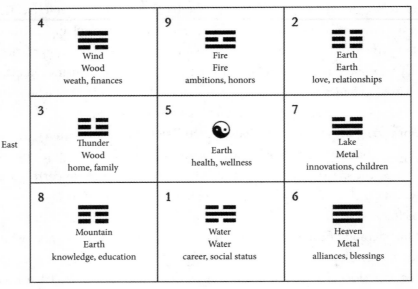

Figure 8.7. Lo Shu, Feng Shui, and the eight trigrams

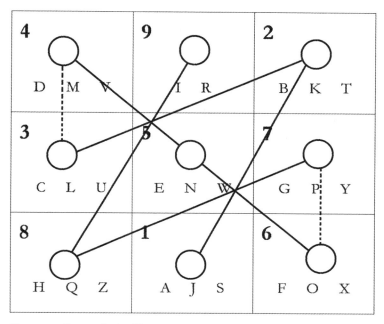

Figure 8.8. Pacing the Lo Shu

ciliation of Pythagorean numerology and the Lo Shu that I rendered. It is not aligned with any currently established Taoist or East Asian traditions to reconcile the Lo Shu with the modern Latin alphabet, but it is provided for Western practitioners who do follow Pythagorean numerology and seek to incorporate it into ritual practices for charging Fu sigils. To incorporate the Lo Shu pacing practice, a word can be spelled out into the Lo Shu by plotting the points into the square, and a path mapped out for that word.

To apply the Lo Shu to pacing, the practitioner envisions the nine-section magic square on the ground before the altar, corresponding with the four compass directions. A series of steps are taken within the nine sections to correspond with the nature or subject matter of the Fu sigil being crafted. Thus, in the instance of pacing the Lo Shu in a ritual for charging a wealth or career sigil, after plotting out the points on the Lo Shu, as shown in the figure 8.6, the practitioner then paces from sector 6 to 1 to 8, takes a giant step over to 4, and ends at sector 9.

Using figure 8.7 as reference for directionality, if the altar is positioned in the south (facing north) and the practitioner faces south, then pacing from 6 to 1 to 8 is moving from the right side of the altar to the left. Two steps, left and right, are placed first in sector 6, then a foot steps over to 1, the other foot is placed beside it in 1, and the same stepping pattern is repeated to pace over to 8. From 8, the practitioner takes a large step, skipping over sector 3, to land on sector 4, in front of the altar to its left, placing two steps in the sector, and then a final step over to sector 9, concluding with both feet in sector 9 at the center front of the altar.

Now, using the same pacing but with an east-facing altar (meaning it is positioned in the west corner), pacing from 6 to 1 to 8 is pacing backward from the front right corner of the altar, stepping leftward toward sector 4 along the left corner, then one step into sector 9, to the left of the altar's center. The practitioner ends at sector 9, to the left of the altar, and performs the 108 recitations charging ritual there in sector 9.

Figure 8.8 plots out the path for pacing the Lo Shu in order, 1 through 9. The practitioner starts at sector 1, paces to sector 2, then paces to sector 3. As the practitioner paces from 3 to 4, indicated in the figure 8.8 by a dotted line, the practitioner rings the ceremonial bells. Then he or she continues to sector 4, and paces in numerological order. From 6 to 7, the ceremonial bells are rung a second time. The practitioner concludes the pacing at sector 9, and upon reaching 9, rings the ceremonial bells for a third and final time. Sector 9 is most commonly positioned right in front of the center of the altar. Thus, altars for Taoist lineages that place emphasis on the Lo Shu are positioned in the south, and facing north. A practitioner performing rituals before his or her altar is thus facing south during the ritual.

Recall the pages from the Mao Shan Book of Methods in figure 6.25, showing a practitioner's handwritten notes and Lo Shu pacing diagrams.

## THE 108 RECITATIONS

Taoist rituals may seem exhausting to Western practitioners. An orthodox Taoist Fu charging ritual can consist of 1,080 invocation repetitions. However, I have found that 108 repetitions will work just fine. Thus, this book uses 108 repetitions.

Many Eastern metaphysical traditions hold the number 108 to be sacred and empowering. Mala, or prayer beads, typically have 108 beads to assist in the counting of 108 recitations. Vedic mathematicians theorize that the number 108 represents the wholeness of existence, or the collective unconscious.

Rituals commence with the ringing of bells. Here, I am instructing three rings of a ceremonial bell, which is symbolic of the three planes—Heaven, Earth, and Man. The Four Guardians are acknowledged, invoking the four directions, and finally, the practitioner lights any specific candles or incense to be used for the charging. Whether candles and incense are lit before or after the opening of a ritual varies.

The practitioner then meditates, visualizing white light, or enters a trance-like state. Then the practitioner commences the charging ritual with the 108 recitations. The recitations and the details of the ritual vary depending on the subject matter of the intention.

## Note on Repetitions

By some lineages, repetitions of 202, 220, or 222 are used for matters of wealth, career, employment, financial, and material prosperity.

Repetitions of 303, 330, or 333 are used for matters of health, healing, and fertility. These repetitions can also be used to manifest fruition in a creative project.

Repetitions of 616 are used for attaining greater power with energetic workings. Practitioners may use the 616 repetitions for ascension or for clearer channeling of the collective unconscious.

To charge the sigil, the giving hand forms a mudra that will channel Qi energy into the sigil, while the receiving hand thumbs the mala prayer beads to keep count of the 108 recitations.

It is permissible to have a copy of the recitation on the altar or work space in front of you while you charge the Fu sigil. Memorization is not mandatory, though it is strongly suggested. For me, playing music, when it comes from memory, I feel the music more intuitively, and likewise I feel the intention of the sigil charging more intimately when I don't have to focus my eyes on words written on a piece of paper. I find reading from a piece of paper during a ritual to be distracting. It can hinder the needed receptive state for an effective charging. However, what works and doesn't work is a determination that each practitioner must make for him- or herself through a process of trial and error. Most traditional magical lineages require memorization, however.

## THE GIVING HAND AND THE RECEIVING HAND

We tend to rely heavily on one hand over the other. Even most ambidextrous individuals have a preferred hand. If someone throws a ball straight at your face, you will prefer one hand over the other to try to catch or block the ball. That is your giving hand. Your giving hand is the more assertive hand. It is usually the hand you write with, but not always. For instance, even though I write with my right hand, in energetic workings, my giving hand is my left. (I also prefer to try to catch a ball with my left. I say "try to" because actually catching the ball is a rarity for me.)

The giving hand is the hand through which Qi energy is directed outward. It is the hand you use to influence energetic workings. The receiving hand is the passive hand, the one that receives Qi energy or supports the giving hand. Intuitively you will know exactly which hand is your dominant and which is your receiving.

## INVOCATION REFERENCES

Note that the following invocation references are provided as examples. You are by no means limited to these. Consider using these recitations for reference only, and craft your own recitations invoking deities or divine energies that you feel more connected to. Using a psalm, for instance, would make a fantastic recitation, as would calling upon patron saints. Tailor the concept of the 108 recitations to align with your personal faith and traditions.

## INVOCATION FOR RAISING THE PRACTITIONER'S ENERGIES FOR HEALING OR LIGHT WORK

USED TO RAISE the practitioner's energies and healing for craft that is for the healing of others or for the practitioner to raise his or her abilities to craft blessings for others. This invocation is framed as an affirmation toward one's own higher self.

*In Mandarin Chinese:*
Yuàn dé zhì huì zhēn míng liǎo.
願得智慧真明了
"May I gain wisdom and true understanding."

## POWERFUL ALL-PURPOSE INVOCATION

USED TO INVOKE Amithaba. The Buddha Amithaba will appear to all who invoke him by name, and will assist you in your journey of inner cultivation toward wisdom, irrespective of what religious path you've chosen. Use this invocation to raise your personal power for optimal spell-crafting.

*In Mandarin Chinese:*
Ná mó Amítuófó.

南无阿弥陀佛

"I invoke the venerable Amithaba [to endow me with all that I need to achieve]."

Note: The Amithaba Sutra is also used to invoke Amithaba.

## INVOCATION TO ALLEVIATE PAIN AND SUFFERING

USED TO INVOKE Kuan Yin. Kuan Yin appears to those who invoke the bodhisattva for mercy or help, irrespective of religious beliefs. The bodhisattva appears unconditionally for all those who are sincere. She bestows mercy and redemption on those who are guilty or have committed wrongs, and she alleviates the pain and suffering of all who invoke her, irrespective of their karma.

*In Mandarin Chinese:*
Ná mó Guānshìyīn Púsà.

南无觀世音菩薩

In Pali:
Namo Avalokiteshvaraya.

"I invoke the venerable Kuan Yin [to show mercy on me and save me from my own bad karma, and to alleviate my pain and suffering]."

Note: The Heart Sutra is also used to invoke Kuan Yin.

## INVOCATION TO ALLEVIATE PAIN AND SUFFERING

USED TO INVOKE the historical Buddha, or Shakyamuni Buddha (also called Gautama Buddha or Siddhārtha). Invoked when the prac-

Figure 8.9. The Bodhisattva Kuan Yin

Figure 8.10. Ganesha, a Hindu deity

titioner seeks guidance on a matter that he or she needs a solution for. Used to alleviate pain and suffering, and to gain perspective on a situation.

*In Pali:*
om muni muni maha muni sakyamuni svaha

"I invoke the venerable sage, Shakyamuni Buddha [to show me the way and illuminate my path]."

## INVOCATION FOR RAISING THE PRACTITIONER'S POWER

USED TO AMPLIFY the practitioner's power through Divine forces, shielded from the malignant, so that the energetic work to follow may be effective.

*In Sanskrit:*
Om mani pad me hom.
*Om:* Purify my ego to yield wisdom;
*Mani:* Purify my lust and desire to yield perfect speech, action, and thought;

*Pad:* Purify my ignorance so that I may be a benevolent protector of others;

*Me:* Ward off hungry ghosts,

*Hom:* Dispel all malignant forces.

## INVOCATION FOR REMOVING OBSTACLES

A MANTRA THAT INVOKES Ganesha (or Ganapati), a deity vener-ated by Eastern traditions of Hinduism, Buddhism, and Jainism, de-picted with an elephant head and by others as an inner deity residing within our bodies that, when activated, clarifies our karma. Ganesha helps to remove obstacles that stand between us and our highest goals.

*In Sanskrit:*
Om Gum Ganapatayei Namaha

"Invoking the venerable Ganesha [Ganapatayei]."

Note: Although I have not come across any orthodox Taoist lineages that venerate Ganesha, the elephant-faced Hindu god and patron of intellectuals, bankers, scribes, and writers,[25] I find Ganesha's man-tra to be grounding and centering. Invoke Ganesha to help remove obstacles and clear your life path toward success and achievement. He will use his ax to cut away ignorance and the bondages that cause suffering, and will destroy your hardships.

## INVOCATION FOR PROTECTION AND DEFENSE

FOR THE PRACTITIONER'S own defense and protection, the prac-titioner concentrates a shield of impenetrable energy around him- or herself while reciting the following invocation.

*In Pali:*
Nassantu paddava sabbe.
Dukkha vupa samentu me

"May all misfortune be destroyed.
May all my suffering cease."

Note: This invocation is based on the *Maha Jaya Mangala Gatha*,[26] or *Great Verses of Auspicious Victory*, a Buddhist invocation for divine protection and blessings.

## INVOCATION FOR PROTECTION AND DEFENSE

FOR THE PRACTITIONER'S own defense and protection, the practitioner concentrates a shield of impenetrable energy around him- or herself while reciting the following invocation.

*In Pali:*
Nakkhatta yakkha bhutanam
Papaggaha nivarana
Paritta sanu bhavena
Hantu mayham upaddave

"By the power of this protective recital
May my misfortunes due to stars,
Demons, harmful spirits, and ominous planets
Be prevented and destroyed."

Note: This invocation is based on the *Maha Jaya Mangala Gatha,* or *Great Verses of Auspicious Victory,* a Buddhist invocation for divine protection and blessings.

## INVOCATION FOR PROTECTION AND DEFENSE

IN THE DEFENSE and protection of another, the practitioner focuses energy and intent on the individual to be safeguarded, transferring defensive energy to that individual, while reciting the following invocation.

*In Pali:*
Bhavantu sabba mangalam.
Sada sotthi bhavantu te.

"May you be endowed with all blessings.
Ever in safety may you be."

# INVOCATION FOR HEALING, HEALTH, AND WELLNESS

USED TO INVOKE the Medicine Buddha to assist in craft for healing, health, and wellness.

*In Mandarin Chinese:*
Ná mó xiāo zāi yán shòu yào shī fó.
南無消災延壽藥師佛

*In Pali:*
om bhaishajye bhaishajye maha
bhaishajya samudgate svaha.

"I invoke the venerable Medicine Buddha to cure
All misfortune and to prolong health and wellness."

Note: The Sutra of the Medicine Buddha is also used to invoke the Medicine Buddha.

# THE INVINCIBLE INCANTATION[27]

USED TO INVOKE the great protectress, Sitatapatra. For the practitioner's own defense and protection, the practitioner visualizes a protective white light and a white parasol blooming above, larger and larger, covering and guarding what is to be protected.

*In Sanskrit:*
om sarva tathagata ushnisha
shitata patra hum phat
hom mama hom ni svaha

"I invoke the ushnisha Sitatapatra, the White Parasol,
Born from Buddha's crown, to protect and guard
Against wickedness, and to bring blessings."

Note: Mantra to Sitatapatra, Goddess of the White Parasol (also called Ushnisha Sitatapatra). "To cut asunder all malignant demons, the spells of others, enemies, dangers, and hatred": she protects against natural disasters (earthquakes, typhoon, storms, and so on) and the supernatural (necromancy, hungry ghosts, demons, and so on). Invoked for protection against malevolent or malignant energies. Often used by practitioners who seek to safeguard themselves from another's black magic. Sitatapatra's white parasol symbolizes protection from misfortune and harm, both natural and supernatural.

## INVOCATION FOR ACHIEVING SUCCESS

RECITED AS EITHER an invocation or for the activation of a sigil crafted to ensure victory, success, or prosperity.

*In Pali:*
Hotu me jaya mangalam
Bhavatu sabba mangalam
Sassa-sampatti hotu ca
Rakkhantu sabbadevata

"May joyous victory be mine.
May all good fortune come my way.
May there be a rich harvest.
May all the deities protect me."

Note: This invocation is based on the *Maha Jaya Mangala Gatha,* or *Great Verses of Auspicious Victory,* a Buddhist invocation for divine protection and blessings.

## INVOCATION FOR ACHIEVING SUCCESS

RECITED AS EITHER an invocation or for the activation of a sigil crafted to ensure victory, success, or prosperity. Used by practitioners from Buddhist-dominant traditions.

*In Pali:*
Sabbe Buddha balappatta
Paccekananca yam balam
Rakkham bandhami sabbaso

"By the power of all supreme Buddhas

By the power of all silent Buddhas
I secure protection in every way."

Note: This invocation is based on the *Maha Jaya Mangala Gatha,* or *Great Verses of Auspicious Victory,* a Buddhist invocation for divine protection and blessings.

## PROSPERITY INVOCATION I

USE TO INVOKE Lakshmi, Hindu goddess of wealth, fortune, and prosperity. Use for strengthening resonance with energies of material abundance, wealth, and prosperity.

*In Sanskrit:*
om shrim maha Lakshmi yei svaha

"I invoke Lakshmi for material wealth and abundance."

## PROSPERITY INVOCATION II

USE TO INVOKE Vasudhara, the Buddhist bodhisattva of wealth. Use for strengthening resonance with energies of material abundance, wealth, and prosperity.

*In Sanskrit:*
om Vasudhara svaha
*or*
na mo Vasudhara pusa

"I invoke Vasudhara, bodhisattva of wealth and prosperity."

Note: Vasudhara ("stream of gems" in Sanskrit) is the Buddhist bodhisattva or goddess of wealth and prosperity. She is the "wealth deity" in Tibetan Buddhism.

## INVOCATION FOR PURIFYING THE
## KARMA OF THE MOUTH

A DHARANI THAT is recited to purify the karma of the mouth.[28]

The Sanskrit phonetic transcription into Chinese dates to the eleventh century in the Dhārani Sūtra of Five Mudrās of the Great Compassionate White-Robed Kuan-yin.[29] Use after speech has perhaps hurt another or may have incurred negative karma onto the practitioner.

*Sanskrit transcription into Mandarin Chinese, written phonetically:*
An hsu li, shing li, muo huo hsu li,
hsu hsu li, suo puo huo svaha.

## INVOCATION FOR INNER CULTIVATION AND THE PURSUIT OF TRANSCENDENCE

THE FOLLOWING IS the last line of the Heart Sutra,[30] a holy scripture in the Mahayana Buddhist tradition, which is used as a dharani and recited as an invocation to assist with inner cultivation and the pursuit of transcendence. Used by practitioners to cultivate wisdom and to ensure the right practice of craft at all times, and to maintain alignment with Heaven and Earth.

*In Sanskrit:*
Gate, Gate, Paragate, Parasamgate; Bodhi Svaha.

"Gone, gone, gone beyond, gone altogether beyond; awakening."

*In Mandarin Chinese:*
Jiēdì, jiēdì, bōluó jiēdì, bōluósēng jiēdì, pútí suōpóhē
揭諦揭諦, 波羅揭諦, 波羅僧揭諦, 菩提薩婆訶

## CUSTOMIZED INVOCATION FOR WEALTH AND PROSPERITY SIGIL

CAI SHEN, GOD OF WEALTH: Grant [name of beneficiary or recipient of the Fu sigil] the power of abundance, riches, and success. Bring good fortune and prosperity to [*name of beneficiary or recipient of the Fu sigil*].

Note: Cai Shen (財神) is the God of Wealth and Prosperity venerated in Taoist and regional Chinese folk religions.

## CUSTOMIZED INVOCATION FOR
## CAREER ADVANCEMENT SIGIL

NAMO AMITOFUO: charge this sigil with the power [*name of beneficiary or recipient of the Fu sigil*] needs to advance in his/her career. Charge this sigil with the power of promotion and triumph.

Note: The foregoing recitation is a prayer to Amithaba, a venerated Buddha of the Mahayana sect. The typical honorific and mantra used to invoke Amithaba is "namo amitofuo." In film and Chinese popular culture, the go-to deity for magical invocations is Amithaba, and so in movies and stories that involve magic, you often hear the Taoist priest or magical practitioner recite "amitofuo."

## CUSTOMIZED INVOCATION FOR
## LOVE/ROMANCE SIGIL

(for a recipient identifying as female)

GRANT THE POWER of the White Peony to [name of beneficiary or recipient of the Fu sigil]. Bring love and romance into her life.

Note: White Peony (白牡丹) is a fascinating mythological character. She was a beautiful courtesan who seduced an immortal god to sleep with her. She later absorbed the god's essence and became a goddess. She is called upon in spells for attracting a man's attention (or an individual who is dominantly yang, as White Peony absorbed the yang essence of the god she slept with) or endowing a female recipient with a presence that will attract more men and lovers.

Also, of course, if the sigil is being crafted for you, then rephrase it so that you are saying "I" and "me," and not referring to yourself in the third person—although there is probably nothing wrong with referring to yourself in the third person.

## CUSTOMIZED INVOCATION FOR BETTER HEALTH AND WELLNESS SIGIL

NAMO GUANSHIYIN PUSA: Please lend your mercy and compassion. Strengthen the health and body of [*name of beneficiary or recipient of the Fu sigil*] and bring him/her wellness and longevity.

Note: The foregoing recitation is a prayer to Kuan Yin, the goddess of mercy and compassion. The typical honorific and mantra used to invoke her is "namo guanshiyin pusa."

## CUSTOMIZED INVOCATION FOR FERTILITY SIGIL

LONG MU, MOTHER of Dragons: Grant me the power of fertility and parenthood. With your graces, deliver an infant dragon to [*name of beneficiary or recipient of the Fu sigil*].

Note: Long Mu (龍母), also referred to as the Mother of Dragons, is a goddess who raised five infant dragons and is the venerated deity of parenthood, fertility, and filial piety.

## INVOCATION FOR TRANSFERENCE OF MERITS TO DEPARTED ONES

USED TO BLESS the recently departed, or those who have passed on, to ensure safe passage into the afterlife and provide additional positive karma for an auspicious rebirth. A Fu sigil can be crafted to be buried or cremated with the departed to ensure peaceful passage into the afterlife.

Idam vo nati nam hotu. Sukhita hontu natayo.

"Let this merit accrue to my departed
and may they be happy."

In some practices, a sigil is not per se charged with concentrated Qi energy for a recipient, but rather it is an order or decree that the practitioner has the authority to issue from his or her venerated deity, directed to a lesser spirit or

Figure 8.11. A Fu sigil scroll passed through incense

supernatural entity. The order or decree instructs that lesser spirit or supernatural entity to carry out a specific task. Such a practice is most commonly used for protection, defense, retribution, retaliation, or a more forceful power where a simple redirect of Qi energy won't suffice. In such instances, the invocation becomes a summoning, and is recited as a summons.

## SUMMONING AND ORDERING INVOCATION

USED TO AMPLIFY the practitioner's power through Divine forces, shielded from the malignant, so that the energetic work to follow may be effective.

I have summoned you, [Name of spirit or supernatural entity summoned to carry forth the practitioner's will], and with the power vested in me by [Name of deity or deities venerated by the practitioner or his/her magical lineage], I summon you to carry forth the directive of this sigil (optional: or Fu) to [state intended outcome for the Fu sigil].

## ENERGY TRANSFERENCE

Generally, hand mudras will be used during the 108 recitations. As the practitioner recites the invocation, a hand mudra is used and directed toward the Fu sigil to be charged. In accordance with the *Classics of the Esoteric Talisman,* that "All manifestations in the universe can be generated by the practitioner's physical body, through the hand," the hand mudra is used to transfer energy that is being raised through the practitioner's body and invocations into the Fu sigil to empower the Fu. For Western practitioners who are more accustomed to a wand for such purposes, a wand or crystal quartz point can certainly be used. Whether the practitioner opts for hand mudras or a wand, be sure to use your giving hand to transfer the energy into the Fu.

Particular traditions, such as the Bai Yun lineage from Northern China, referenced in chapter 5, use breath to transfer energy into a Fu. Likewise, you can envision an intense orb of energy or light accumulating in the stomach or torso region during the 108 recitations, and at the completion of the 108 recitations, at which time that envisioned orb of light is nearly solid, luminescent, and strong, envision the orb traveling up through the body and out of your mouth, just as you exhale a quick, hard breath and blow on the Fu sigil. As you do so, imagine the Fu sigil absorbing that luminescent orb of energy that grew stronger and brighter from your invocations. Doing so also transfers the energy accrued from the invocations and ritual into the Fu. In the method of transference by breath, hand mudras aren't necessary.

In lieu of the hand mudras, wands, or breath for transferring the energy into a Fu sigil, a practitioner can opt to charge a sigil by passing it through incense smoke. The common go-to incense for Chinese practitioners is sandalwood, for its purification and empowerment properties. The incense that is often wafting through Buddhist and Taoist temples is sandalwood. *Sakura,* or cherry blossom, is used for love spells. Figure 8.11 shows a Fu sigil that has been rolled into a scroll form and tied with red string, which is then beaded with black onyx. Note the black onyx energy amplifier utilized during the charging ritual.

A practitioner may prefer transferring energy by incense rather than channeling through hand mudras or wands, especially if the practitioner is uncomfortable with the prospect of being the physical medium for energy, whether that source of power is coming from supernatural forces or is the giving of the practitioner's personal Qi. Charging with incense smoke is a craft that calls upon environmental forces and powers in the vicinity of the ritual to channel through the incense and then into the sigil. The practitioner is then no longer the medium. Instead, divine energies and forces that have been invoked during the charging ritual are channeling the energies into the Fu through the incense smoke.

If energy transference by incense smoke is opted for, be sure the opening of the ritual is carefully crafted to ensure that the called-upon deities, divinity, or Spirit has been invoked and is now present. The Jiao Bei divination moon blocks are the ideal way to divine whether Spirit is present. Prior to the recitations, throw the moon blocks, asking whether the specifically named and identified deity or spirit you have invoked or summoned is present. Confirm through the moon blocks that the answer is yes before proceeding with the charging ritual by incense. Also, when divining with the moon blocks to determine presence, be sure to name and identify the spirit you seek to invoke with great particularity, detail, and specificity, using the exact invocation for invoking or summoning such a spirit. Otherwise, an answer "yes" might be given to denote any presence at all, and for safety's sake, you do want to ensure that the one named and identified is the only one present.

I can say that the one unanimously agreed upon point to how a Fu sigil becomes empowered is that it is done through energy transference. Metaphysical energy is transferred into a Fu sigil by a practitioner, empowering that sigil to become more than a mere object, giving that object a form of life, or purpose. How that is done is where opinions split. While my approach to charging a Fu sigil presents the practice as a rather time-consuming ritual, many other practitioners are far more expedient with their approaches. The drawing of the sigil and charging can be a two-in-one, with invocations recited at every step of the drawing. As each stroke of the pen or ink brush is made onto the paper, the practitioner recites an invocation or visualizes the image of a specific manifestation. When the last line of the sigil is drawn, so, too, has the charging ritual concluded, often with a closing invocation such as "急急如律令 (ji ji ru lu ling)," meaning "it is so ordered."

## THE BENEFICIARY'S VOW

When working with metaphysical energies, remember always that energies are transferred, and every action will be met with an equal and opposite reaction. As a practitioner, you transfer metaphysical energy. That is all you do. You raise concentrated, potent energy from one source and redirect it in a specific manner for manifesting your intentions. Thus, energy isn't really being created or destroyed, but transferred. If you keep that in mind in your practice of craft, you will be more thoughtful of measures to keep yourself safe energetically and karmically. An effective way to somewhat control the energy transfers, reaction, and exchange is to consider it as a barter.

A beneficiary, the person who desires the Fu sigil to be crafted for his or her direct benefit, can make a vow to perform an in-kind act when the intention of the sigil has manifested. By performing that in-kind act, the energetic exchange is completed in full faith and satisfaction. Note that the beneficiary must consent to upholding the vow. By consenting, the beneficiary unequivocally absolves the practitioner from the karmic energy transfer. The energy transfer becomes a matter strictly between the source of the energy and the beneficiary. The practitioner's karma is left intact because he or she becomes a mere conduit, a go-between (unless the practitioner is also the beneficiary, or for certain reasons the practitioner has agreed to assume the responsibility of fulfilling a vow; in those cases, it is the practitioner who must uphold the vow).

It is the practitioner's duty to fully inform the beneficiary of the importance of fulfilling the vow. It is the continuation of energy transfers in a way that will not harm the beneficiary or practitioner with any unanticipated consequences. The beneficiary's vow is one method of transferring energy in a controlled manner and to allow a practitioner of craft to work with metaphysical energy on behalf of others without ramifications to his or her own personal karmic account.

Some practitioners might say that the beneficiary's vow is only applicable for talismans, or Fu sigils charged with a specific intent where the beneficiary wants something particular to happen. Amulets, meaning sigils created for general well-being and good luck, therefore do not require a beneficiary's vow. Amulets are merely transmitters—the Fu sigil is using the beneficiary's own account of karma to help the beneficiary. For example, a sigil charged with the following invocation would not necessitate an exchange. Such a charge activates the sigil as a transmitter of the natural Light energy that is already around the individual, and the natural ebb and flow of karma should resolve the matter of energy transference and exchange on its own.

## SAMPLE SIGIL CHARGE THAT WOULD NOT NECESSITATE A BENEFICIARY'S VOW

IMPRINT THIS SIGIL with guiding Light for [beneficiary's name]. Protect and shelter him/her. Love him/her and give him/her warmth. May the sigil be the beacon that illuminates for him/her the path to peace, purpose, harmony, safety, health, and healing in his/her times of karmic need. May this sigil be a source of guiding Light that protects and shelters [beneficiary's name] so that he/she may always stay the course of his/her life path. Na mo amitofuo guanshiying pusa.

However, a Fu sigil crafted to meet a romantic partner within a set amount of time by particular parameters is best crafted with a beneficiary's vow. A Fu sigil for acquiring a certain job, getting a certain passing score on an examination, winning a particular battle, or for a specific purpose should also be accompanied with a vow. That is because a specific-purpose sigil isn't just a transmitter of energy; it is being tasked to channel concentrated energy borrowed from one source and then used in a very specific way that may go against the natural course of events. This defiance (or redirect; take your pick of wording) of the natural karmic course may open either the recipient of the sigil or even the practitioner to possibly unintended karmic consequences. The beneficiary's vow is a safeguard that can be implemented to safely channel the energy that has been taken and facilitate it in a more constructive direction. As a practitioner, be guided by your intuition in determining when to use the vow.

Practitioners who do not find the beneficiary's vow to be necessary have legitimate arguments.[31] The principles found in the *Classics of the Esoteric Talisman* could well be interpreted as not necessitating such a vow. There are certainly Taoist priests who do not subscribe to the practice at all. Historically, the beneficiary's vow isn't even a well-documented component to craft. The vast majority of Taoist texts make no mention of such an idea. You are sure to find Taoist practitioners who testify that they have practiced for decades without beneficiary vows and have not experienced any repercussions for omitting it.

However, I find that having a beneficiary's vow in place is a safer, more controlled method of energetic working. Without it, you are still taking energy from somewhere and summoning it to you to use for your benefit. The act of the energy transfer must have an "equal and opposite" reaction, a reaction that will be beyond your control. Such energy transfers under karmic laws are not necessarily one-to-one, and that's what makes it troublesome.

I am reminded of the Rule of Three,[32] a principle that some pagan faiths practice by. I suspect (and this is purely my own speculation) that the Rule of Three, which holds that the energy a practitioner sends out by way of a spell will be returned threefold, or three times stronger,[33] stems from the unpredictability of the reaction and consequences (positive or detrimental) of energetic workings when the transfer is not controlled.

Note, however, that there are differing and often disputing interpretations of the Rule of Three, and another perspective holds that minding the Rule of Three refers to approaching spell-crafting in a way that takes into consideration the totality of the Wiccan's ontological perspective, which includes the trinity of mind, body, and soul that is humanity and the trinity of the past, present, and future that make up one's fate.[34]

If you accept the Rule of Three as a matter of faith, then it shall be so; but an alternative understanding of the philosophy may reveal that the Rule of Three is a figurative expression of karmic energy flow. When you take energy from a source to benefit yourself, especially in a way that will be to the detriment of another, the energy you've taken bottlenecks if you do not channel it onward. The effects that manifest as a result of that bottleneck may be perceived as the Rule of Three. It may feel like interest compounded upon interest.

However, so long as the practitioner knows how to control that flow and guide it from source to source without detrimental impact to the practitioner or to the beneficiary, then energetic workings, no matter the intention, benevolent or malevolent, won't have the uninhibited impact that the Rule of Three seems to convey. That is why I subscribe to the beneficiary's vow. It is a bargained-for exchange that helps to keep your karmic account current.

## POSTLIMINARY DIVINATION

I follow a practice of performing a postliminary divination after a Fu sigil has been charged. Chapter 6 began the discussion of using divination moon blocks after a sigil has been prepared (but prior to charging) to determine whether it has been properly crafted. The postliminary divination is particularly critical if the Fu is crafted as an order or decree that the practitioner purports to be authorized to issue. In such an instance, a postliminary divination helps the practitioner confirm that authority has indeed been granted.

Moon block divination is used to determine whether yes, a sigil has been properly crafted for the practitioners' intended purpose, or no, the sigil has not been properly crafted and the practitioner must return to the drawing board. A response of uncertainty indicates strong oppositional forces, and the practitioner must be conscious that greater energy will be needed to manifest the intended purpose.

However, some Taoist traditions say that it is not about whether the sigil has been properly crafted; it is about whether spirits are present to assist in the matter. To these traditions, the postliminary moon block divination is performed at the altar before a ritual commences or during the opening of the ritual to determine whether spirits are present and favorable toward the practitioner's intentions. Thus, a negative response from the blocks indicates the lack of spirits present, not the incorrect crafting of the sigil. In my approach, however, it has been more effective simply to return to the sigil drafting stage if the moon blocks yield a negative response.

Either way, the purpose of a postliminary divination is to affirm that the channel between the personal and the universal is open and receptive, so that the energies needed to give the Fu sigil effect can come through and be channeled into the Fu. Moon blocks are one way to cover the postliminary divination step. However, any alternative, such as a pendulum, runes, the I Ching, or tarot cards, can be used if the practitioner is more adept with these divinatory methods.

The postliminary divination is not observed by every Taoist tradition. Many orthodox Taoist lineages do not. The approach I've delineated here may even come across as excessive. For me, in my own trials and experimentations with craft, I have found it to work, to be of value in my practice, and for that reason alone, I am including instruction on it herein.

# CHAPTER 9

# SEALING THE FU SIGIL

**AFTER A FU SIGIL** has been crafted and inscribed onto paper, it should be sealed. Sealing the Fu sigil can be likened to signing a contract or getting a document notarized. Sealing the Fu sigil is the conclusion of a ritual, at which time a Taoist priest will stamp the paper sigil with his or her practitioner's seal, often done in a loud, dramatic, and emphatic way, culminating in a booming sound.

My personal approach might seem a little less intense. I seal the sigil rather quietly, whispering a prayer or mantra under my breath, or a closing invocation, later explained in this chapter, while I stamp the sigil. And then it is done.

In addition to the practitioner's seal, a Fu sigil crafted at a temple will also be stamped with the temple seal.[1] Most lineages have their own proprietary seals as well, and each practitioner in that lineage also stamps the sigil with the lineage's seal.

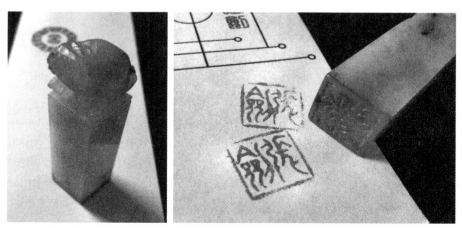

Figure 9.1. Stamp of a practitioner's seal

Figure 9.2. Practitioner's seal stamped
on the front

Figure 9.3. Practitioner's seal stamped
on the back

Figure 9.4. Practitioner's seal
stamped on the back, enclosed
by a Ba Gua stamp

## BY THE PRACTITIONER'S SEAL

In modern application, most Taoist magic practitioners have a personal seal, as discussed in chapter 6. Stamping the practitioner's seal onto the sigil paper, either on the front where the sigil is or on the back, seals the sigil. Typically it is done at the closing of the charging ritual and postliminary divination, after the sigil has been successfully charged.

Some lineages stamp the sigil immediately after drawing it. Others stamp it with the seal after the charging ritual has been completed. Still others perform a divination to ensure that the Fu sigil has been charged successfully before proceeding to stamp the sigil (as this book teaches, using the postliminary divination). The practitioner decides for him- or herself which order of events works best.

In some cases, Fu sigils are two-sided, and while the Fu itself is rendered on the front of the paper, a Ba Gua is printed or stamped onto the back. The center of the Ba Gua is blank. Then, after the charging ritual, the practitioner stamps the center of the Ba Gua with his or her seal.

## BY A CLOSING INVOCATION

Although both a closing invocation and a sealing of the Fu with a practitioner's seal might be used together, the two can be used separately as well, sealing the Fu with one or the other, at the practitioner's intuitive discretion.

To seal a Fu sigil with a closing invocation, recite the closing invocation after the 108th recitation of the selected invocation from the charging ritual, or after the postliminary divination yields a positive result. The order of events is at the practitioner's own intuitive discretion.

Culturally and historically, the most common closing invocation used in Taoist craft is as follows:

## TAOIST INVOCATION TO ACTIVATE A SPELL

急急如律令

Jí Jí Rú Lǜ Lìng

"It is so ordered."

Pronounce *jí* in a way that rhymes with "see?" with the question intonation at the end. *Rú* is pronounced "roo" using the same intonation as *jí*, rising like a question. As for pronouncing *lǜ*, note first how your mouth opens a bit when you say "lee." Instead, purse your lips as if you are whistling and then try to say "lee." It comes out almost sounding like "lu," with a trace hint of "ee." That's the pronunciation of *lǜ*, with your lips slightly pursed as you say "lee." Pronounce *lǜ* as a statement with an intonation of exclamation. The same goes for *lìng*, like an exclamation, and pronounced just as it looks, "ling."

Along the same lines as Western recitations of "amen" or "So mote it be"2 at the close of a prayer or spell, the concluding line of nearly every Taoist incantation is a closing invocation, typically "ji ji ru lu ling."3 Here, "ji ji ru lu ling" can be used to seal the Fu sigil. The phrase affirmatively concludes an incantation or ritual. Recall the Mao Shan Book of Methods from chapter 6, shown in figure 6.29, illustrating the use of "ji ji r ulu ling" at the close of an incantation or invocation.

"Ji ji ru lu ling" can be translated to "it is so ordered." As previously noted, original Fu talismans were crafted to resemble imperial decrees, and the spirit called upon to execute the intentions of the talisman had to obey the practitioner pursuant to the decree. Thus, it would follow that the closing invocation sounds like a court order.

Interestingly, in the U.S. legal system, unanimous or majority opinions or rulings passed by a court ends with the final line, "It is so ordered." The tradition originated from the English Parliament as early as 1641.4 How "ji ji ru lu ling" is used in the context of craft is very similar to the way "it is so ordered" is used in the context of court rulings.

## BUDDHIST/TAOIST INVOCATION

南无阿弥陀佛

Ná mó Amítuófó

"Honor to the venerable Buddha, Amithaba."

Although 南无阿弥陀佛 is considered a Buddhist mantra, it has been integrated into Taoist craft to such a degree that the mantra has become associated with Taoism as well.

The closing invocation that I use personally is "南无阿弥陀佛觀世音菩薩" (Námó Amítuó Fó Guānshìyīn Púsà), which references both a god and goddess, or more specifically, a Buddha and bodhisattva, which are definitely not direct equivalents of "god" and "goddess."

## BY THE PRACTITIONER'S SIGNATURE

The seal is the Chinese equivalent of a signature. Thus, in principle, signing the Fu with a practitioner's magical name works just as well as a stamp. In lieu of a Chinese seal, sign the sigil. When the crafting of a Fu sigil is complete, pick up a pen (a consecrated one) and sign it in an ink color different from the Fu sigil. It should be an ink color that resonates with you personally, though generally when there are two different ink colors on a sigil, the colors are red and black.

## WITH ANOTHER SIGIL

Craft a simple sigil that represents you, the practitioner. This can be an arrangement of stylized letters from your name (or magical practitioner name, if that is within your tradition to have one), Fu Wen you have created to represent your name, or your name in sigil form according to Western sigil crafting techniques. Integrating Western sigil crafting into Fu sigil crafting is explained in appendix C.

## BY A BLOOD PRINT

A traditional method of sealing a sigil is with a blood print. The thumb is pricked, and a thumbprint in the practitioner's blood can seal the sigil. As the practitioner places the blood print on the sigil paper, it is accompanied with a prayer or statement of intent. The prayer closes with a dedication to a particular deity.

Throughout Taiwan, southern China, and Southeast Asia, practitioners draw the blood from their tongues. The shard of a broken teacup or a nail is used to cut the tongue. Blood is drawn and imprinted onto the Fu sigil.[5] By doing so, the practitioner is in effect sealing the sigil. Please do not do this. It is mentioned here only to cover Fu history.

# CHAPTER 10

# ACTIVATION TECHNIQUES

**AFTER CHARGING A FU SIGIL,** it is imprinted with the specified intentions. The next step is activation. Activation techniques vary to such an extent that it is difficult to make generalizations. The traditional Taoist practice is to burn the sigil to ash and drink the ashes with consecrated water. I prefer not to activate a Fu in that manner and opt for alternatives, such as carrying the Fu in my wallet or transferring its energy into something wearable, like a necklace, or into an object I can carry around, like a pocket gemstone.

The purpose of activation is sourced back to intent. As long as the intent is there, any means of activation will, in principle, work. Activation is about enabling the recipient's personal energy field to be receptive and open to the frequency of energy that has been created in the Fu. Thus, any act that achieves this is an optimal activation technique. In modern New Age terms, the activation technique is a form of affirmation, to call upon the power of attraction.

If the beneficiary subscribes to a particular faith, a prayer aligned with that faith would work perfectly here, appealing to the deity or deities of choice to come to his or her aid. A secular affirmation works just as well. An affirmation is a positive statement asserted in the present tense and confirming the manifestation of the intention. For example, "I am the mother of a beautiful, healthy baby born this year" for a fertility sigil, or "I have multiple offers of well-paid, illustrious employment" for a career sigil.

The third method for concluding the activation is with a mantra. A mantra is similar to a prayer, as both are considered sacred. However, while the substance of a prayer is in the faith behind the prayer, in a mantra, it is the enunciation that gives it power. *Om* is a mantra in Sanskrit. The enunciation of om is believed to vibrate at the same frequency as the vibration of the collective unconscious, the universe, and the one united divinity. *Om mani padme hum* is a well-known Tibetan Buddhist mantra associated with the bodhisattva of compassion. *Namo amitofuo guanshiying pusa* is a mantra in Mandarin that I learned from my mother. It was one I uttered with great frequency as a child to keep the monsters under my bed at bay—that and Psalm 23. Like prayer, mantras are believed to give us strength. Mantras resonate with me, and so my approach to closing the activation of a sigil is by mantra. I speculate that in certain Western practices, "so mote it be" serves as a conclusion to the activation ritual.

Most importantly, the individual must visualize the intention coming true and manifesting while uttering the prayer, affirmation, or mantra. Activation need not be a literal act or physical gesture. Activation is a state of mind. It is about opening up the personal Qi of an individual so that a tempering process between the power of the Fu and the present state of that individual's Qi can commence. Activation can be a thought, though it must be an intense, focused, and genuine thought. The recitation of words is powerful—and magical—because speech holds power over thought and can push thought in the intended direction.

Sigils intended to act as talismans for good luck or protection are generally worn or carried on the person. Curses, acts of release, or banishment are generally burned and the ashes discarded in a purposeful way. To protect a home or particular living space, sigils are posted on the premises or buried along its perimeter. In certain incidences of cursing, the sigil is posted on the premises occupied by the one to be cursed or delivered to the one who is to be cursed.

Traditionally, Fu sigils for health or personal empowerment were dissolved in water, tea, or wine, and then the person would drink the dissolved sigil like medicine (where rice paper was used and the sigil was painted with ink made from organic, ingestible ingredients). I do not recommend ingesting Fu sigils unless you know without a doubt where your paper and ink for the sigil crafting is coming from. Another common method is to bathe in a dissolved sigil with the intent of having the sigil's energies be absorbed through the skin. This chapter will cover some of the more common means of activation in Taoist culture, but do not feel constrained to these methods. Seek out a method that aligns with the principle.

## PRAYER, MANTRA, AND AFFIRMATION

The efficacy of prayer has been well documented by scientists and psychologists.[1] Prayer is a form of mental exercise that improves our muscle of self-control.[2] It can also act as an antidote to offset the negative effects of stress, depression, and self-destructive thinking.[3] Here when I say "prayer," I also mean mantras and affirmations, though prayer from a Western religious perspective tends to seek outward, calling upon a deity in the beyond, whereas Eastern religious perspective tends to view prayer, or mantras and dharanis, as seeking inward, cultivating the inner mindset.[4] In Taoist craft, the activation of a Fu can be performed as a prayer, mantra, or affirmation. Depending on the particular tradition or lineage of Taoism, it can be either external, seeking outward to invoke a deity from beyond, or internal, seeking inward cultivation.

In one approach, a Taoist priest instructs the beneficiary to light three incense sticks, invoke the deity, and pray to the deity with the problem at hand, requesting the solution.[5] This is done while the beneficiary holds on to the Fu sigil that the practitioner had crafted, which acts like a metaphysical calling card to the deity. The sigil connects the beneficiary with the deity and allows that individual's prayer to be heard; that is what activates the sigil.

The prayer can be recited either by the practitioner or given to the beneficiary to recite. Both are seen in Taoist craft. Some practitioners conclude the sealing of a Fu sigil with a closing invocation, which also serves as the activation, the prayer that empowers the Fu. Others craft a prayer, mantra, or affirmation for the beneficiary to recite so that the beneficiary is the one activating the Fu. Again, to decide how you will approach activation techniques, look to the principle, and consider what technique will align with both the principles of craft and the personal practices that resonate with you.

## DRINKING A DISSOLVED PAPER FU SIGIL

One of the earliest recorded methods of activating a Fu sigil is to burn a paper Fu, dissolve its ashes into consecrated water, and drink the ashes. Drinking a dissolved paper Fu sigil was believed to heal the sick, cure illnesses, and ensure longevity. The practice dates back to the Zhou Dynasty and is documented among ancient Chinese shamans.[6]

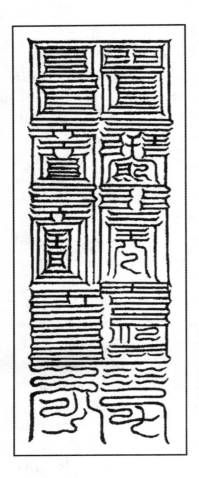

Figure 10.1. Fu sigil for evading
death, from the Shang Qing

The Fu pictured in figure 10.1 is from the *Perfect Scripture of Great Profundity*,[7] dating to the Jin Dynasty (around AD 265–420). The Fu's efficacy is based on the belief that a god or Lord of Death came to collect souls, and when he came to collect your soul, that was your time to die. One means of evading death was to conceal your soul from detection by the Lord of Death. If your soul was invisible to the Lord of Death, he would not come collecting. To achieve that invisibility, a Taoist practitioner would cast the Fu sigil seen in figure 10.1. Specific instructions on charging and empowering the Fu are given and, when complete, the one who was trying to evade death would have to drink the Fu to achieve invisibility and thus evade detection by the Lord of Death.

Personally, I do not subscribe to the method of dissolving paper Fu sigils for drinking. Yet it should be noted that it is an activation technique that many Taoist practitioners will prescribe, especially for Fu sigils intended to improve health and well-being.[8] After a Fu sigil is charged, it is given to the beneficiary, who activates it with a simple prayer or affirmation, and places the paper in water to dissolve. Another common practice is to burn the sigil and then dissolve the ashes in the water. Then the water with the dissolved sigil is drunk.[9] Instead of water, tea could be used, often a precise blend of herbs crafted by the practitioner to amplify the effects of the sigil. Wine or alcohol is another option.

If drinking a Fu sigil resonates with you, be sure you use paper and ink made from ingestible plant extracts and that, most importantly, does not contain lead or other toxic chemicals. Also keep in mind that sigil crafting for health concerns only addresses the spiritual and metaphysical imbalances of the health concern. The actual condition must still be treated by science and experienced medical professionals.

## WEARING OR CARRYING THE FU SIGIL

The *Writ of the Three Sovereigns*[10] says that Fu sigils invoking Lord Lao (老君, Lǔo Jūn) were to be worn on a practitioner's belt to help him or her control mountain spirits.[11] The ability to control mountain spirits meant safe journeys and protection while the practitioner traversed dangerous mountainous terrain. Likewise, Fu sigils are generally worn on the person, or in modern times, kept tucked inside a wallet or handbag for general protection.

To prepare a sigil for wearing or carrying, I craft the Fu sigil on thin paper that will easily fold and not get bulky. Then I prepare an envelope for the sigil using heavy cardstock. The Fu sigil is then inserted into the heavier cardstock envelope. It can now be carried in a pocket with ease, in a handbag, or stowed away in a motor vehicle. Typically, I consecrate and charge the envelope along with the sigil, and also inscribe either the Ba Gua or other meaningful symbols on the envelope.

I also like to create matchbook sigils. Using heavy cardstock, cut out a matchbook pattern, as depicted in figure 10.2.

The paper sigil, which is drawn or printed on long rectangular paper, is then folded and tucked into the folded matchbook. (Prior to assembly, all materials and tools should have been consecrated or purified.) The finished matchbooks are then charged in the charging ritual. Some practitioner may opt to charge only the long rectangular Fu sigil and then, once charged, activate it by securing it into the matchbook covering. I assemble the matchbook and charge the whole thing together, paper sigil and covering.

The matchbook charms are great for carrying Fu sigils around in a wallet. They fit snugly into the glove compartments of cars and motorcycles for travel protection or tucked discretely underneath doormats to attract the desired energies into a home or business. Personally, it is my preferred method of packaging a sigil.

A sigil can also be folded to fit into a locket. Since it is assumed by this stage that the sigil has already been fully empowered and charged, the locket

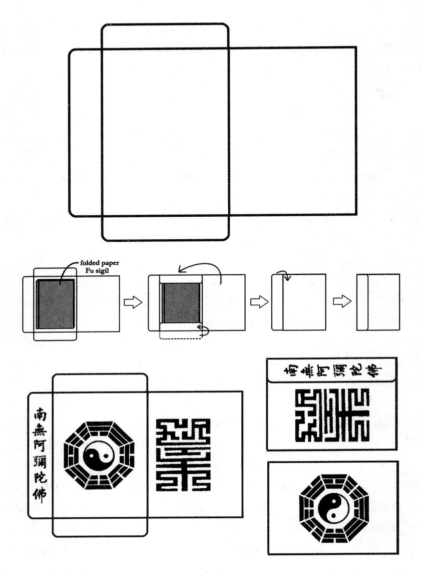

Figure 10.2. Pattern and folding instructions for matchbook sigils

does not need to be consecrated or charged for the sigil to be effective, though it certainly does not hurt should the practitioner feel better about consecrating and charging the locket as he or she would the envelope.

Omamori are Japanese amulets or talismans in the form of silk or cloth pouches containing slips of paper inscribed with prayers, blessings, or Fu sigils. They're often found for sale at temples in the form of amulets. Omamori

Figure 10.3. Fu sigils in the form of matchbook charms

can also be talismans when crafted in the manner described in this book for Fu sigils. They are a form of Taoist Fu sigil kept in a pouch for convenient transport and carried on the person.

To make your own, create the paper Fu sigil and sew a small pouch for the sigil. Fold the paper sigil, place it into the pouch, and sew the pouch shut. Such a pouch is then easy to carry in the back pocket of your pants or in the lining of your handbag.

For a more decorative version, sew to the outside of the pouch charms and gemstone beads that resonate with you and correspond to the intention at hand. Attach decorative string for hanging and displaying the talisman.

The following is a homemade example:

**1.** Start by crafting the paper Fu sigil. In this example, the style used is the cell sigil. At this point, the fully empowered sigil should have been charged in the charging ritual.

**2.** Cut a strip of fabric to make the pouch with. The pattern used is shown in figure 10.6.

Figure 10.4. General purpose hada omamori for protection (courtesy of the Tsubaki Grand Shrine of America)[12]

Figure 10.5. Kubosa omamori for business success (courtesy of the Tsubaki Grand Shrine of America)

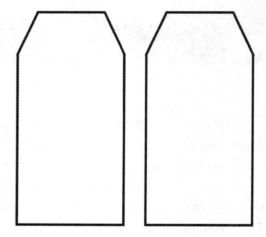

Figure 10.6. Pattern for omamori pouch

**3.** To add cord for a hanging pouch or to adorn the exterior with trinkets, consider sewing a buttonhole on one piece and either a button or the cord on the other. Trinkets can adorn the cord as desired.

**4.** By sewing the pouch inside out, the seams won't show when the pouch is complete. If you are not confident with your sewing skills, sewing the pouch inside out is the best option. Even if your seams are uneven or a bit of a mess, it won't be too noticeable on the final product.

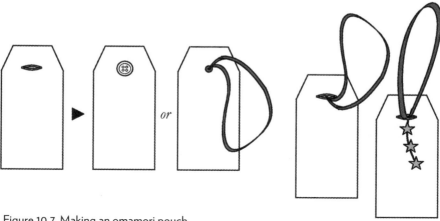

Figure 10.7. Making an omamori pouch

Figure 10.8. Michihiraki omamori for life path guidance (courtesy of the Tsubaki Grand Shrine of America)

**5.** Be sure to leave the top of the pouch open. Only sew the three rectangular sides.

**6.** Roll the Fu sigil into a scroll and place it into the pouch. The sigil can also be folded into a rectangle shape in conformity with the shape of the pouch. My personal preference is the scroll. Both approaches are fine.

**7.** You can then sew the pouch up, but I like to add a small gemstone to help amplify and supplement the sigil's energy.

**8.** I also add some corresponding dried herbs. Not only does it give the pouch a pleasant scent, but the herbs will also amplify and supplement the sigil's energy.

**9.** Then the opening is sealed shut.

**10.** While the pouch does not need to be consecrated or charged (the Fu sigil itself has already gone through both procedures), the beneficiary does need to activate the pouch with the beneficiary's vow and the prayer, affirmation, or mantra.

Simply rolling the paper sigil into a scroll and tying it with string is sufficient. The various techniques suggested in this section are for safekeeping a sigil only, so that wear and tear might not happen upon the sigil too quickly. The techniques are not necessary, however.

## POSTING A FU SIGIL

A popular method for activating a Fu sigil is to post it in the environment where the energy is needed. Protection sigils, such as ofuda, which are posted around the home or near a family altar, are most often activated by posting. A Fu sigil to ward off nightmares for children is often posted by the head or foot of the child's bed. In traditional Chinese homes, it would not be uncommon to see Fu sigils posted prominently around the house. However, for a more discrete way of activating Fu sigils for home protection, they can be buried. Typically, four Fu sigils are created, and one is buried at each of the four corners of the property. Paper Fu sigils can also be rolled up and posted discretely over the door of the front entrance, hidden along the top edge of the door frame.

Note that traditionally, it is believed that Fu sigils should not be posted at eye level or below eye level. They must be posted above eye level so that all who look upon it must look up to see the sigil.

## BURNING A FU SIGIL

For Fu sigils crafted with the intention of banishing, releasing, severing, voiding, or destroying, a common method for activating it is to burn it. The ashes are then discarded in a way that is significant and symbolic to the situation at hand. For example, to banish an unwanted personal habit, a Fu sigil can be crafted and burned, then the ashes flushed down a toilet or tossed out with the garbage. Traditionally, it would be scattered in a wind blowing away from the home or thrown into a stream or river. In certain cases, traditionally, the ashes of the burned Fu sigil are eaten by the intended beneficiary. For my own practice, I have steered away from ingesting sigils.

## BATHING IN FU SIGIL–CHARGED WATER

For empowerment sigils intended to enhance the personal power or energy of an individual, the beneficiary might consider bathing in sigil-charged water. Burn the sigil and mix the ashes with 1 cup Epsom or sea salt, 1 cup baking soda, and 5 drops of an essential oil that corresponds with the sigil's intentions, so that the essential oil might amplify the sigil's effects. Draw a bath and pour the mixture into the water. The beneficiary should be in a calm, open, receptive state during the bath and envision the energy of the sigil entering through the pores and empowering him or her, head to toe. Incense or candles can be burned around the bath to help set the mood.

## TRANSFERENCE OF SIGIL ENERGY INTO ANOTHER OBJECT

The energy and power of a paper Fu sigil can be transferred into an object and the object, once infused with the power of the Fu sigil, can be carried around as a good luck charm. Thus, rather than carry the paper sigil around, a palm stone or other charm can be carried on the person after the sigil's energy has been transferred into the object. Transference of sigil energy is by far my favorite method of activation.

To transfer a sigil's energy into an object, burn the sigil under a waxing crescent moon. Retain its ashes. Place the ashes in an airtight container, such as a glass jar, along with the object that the energy will be transferred into. In figure 10.9, the Fu sigil's energy is to be transferred into a palm-size piece of rose quartz. Set the sealed jar aside throughout the waxing phase of the moon until it is full. On the full moon, take out the object, which in the case of the photograph is a piece of rose quartz. The beneficiary should activate the object in the same manner as a paper sigil.

The object is then emanating with the energy and will have the efficacy

Figure 10.9. Stone infused with Fu sigil energy

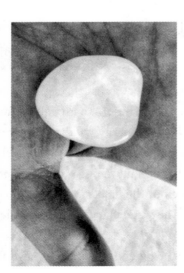

Figure 10.10. Stone charged by
Fu sigil transference

of the paper sigil. Where placement of a paper sigil might be inconvenient or too conspicuous, a nondescript object can be imprinted with the sigil's energy and used. A sigil's energy can be transferred into any object, so long as that object is first consecrated. For instance, to ease conflicts at the workplace, a sigil charged for that objective can be burned and its energy transferred into, say, a consecrated ballpoint pen or a paperclip, and that object can be placed inconspicuously at the office without raising attention.

## HOW LONG DOES AN ACTIVATED SIGIL LAST

A question often asked is how long an activated Fu sigil remains effective. There is no definitive answer. As I've interpreted point 2 in the *Classics of the Esoteric Talisman,* as outlined in chapter 3, "all manifestations in the universe … are determined by the will of the practitioner. The mechanics are determined by the practitioner's mind." Thus, it is the practitioner's will that determines how long an activated Fu sigil can last. How that will is accomplished is determined by the mechanics that the practitioner has set in place.

A well-trained practitioner of craft will be able to raise just the right dose of energy needed to channel into a Fu sigil for it to endure for the intended period of time. That period of time must be determined—and clearly defined—by the practitioner during the design of the sigil and during the charging ritual for the practitioner's will to be implemented. It follows that if a practitioner seeks for a Fu sigil to endure for an entire year or longer, then a great deal of energy and effort will be expended by that practitioner for both the design and the charging, because the mechanics must match the will. At every point of the craft, the practitioner must be focused on the intention for the sigil to endure for an entire year. More joss sticks than usual might be used, as noted in table 6.2, or more offerings presented on the altar, more gold and silver joss paper burned.

Think of the charged Fu sigil as a battery. The charging ritual channels concentrated metaphysical Qi energy into the sigil, or battery, and the practitioner's seal then seals the sigil into a closed circuit. Once that sigil is activated, Qi energy will be released to benefit the recipient of the charged sigil. That quantity of Qi energy is limited. When exhausted, that Fu is once again just a piece of paper.

When sigil energy is transferred into another object, such as jewelry, a charm, or a gemstone, the Qi channeled into that object by way of the Fu, also, will be released and exhausted. Thus, jewelry or a pocket stone being used as an amulet needs to be regularly recharged with transferences of sigil energy.

## The One-Hundred-Day Exorcistic Talisman

A reproduction of a One-Hundred-Day Exorcistic Talisman,[13] circa AD 1789, that was inscribed onto a stele on Mount Tai, in Tai'an, Shandong, China, is pictured in figure 10.11. Its purpose was to exorcise demons or malignant energies by invoking Bei Di (北帝, Běi Dì), the God of the North, also known as Xuan Wu, the Enigmatic Warrior God (玄武神, Xuán WǔShén). Bei Di is one of the most venerated deities in the Taoist pantheon, a sovereign administrator at the axis mundi of Taoist cosmology, with divine authority in both Heaven and Hell.[14] He is depicted as a great warrior, martial artist, and magician, with an unmatched power to control the elements of the four directions. The prominent glyph at the very top of the sigil is the call sign or invocation to Bei Di.

Below the Běi Dì invocation glyph are three dots that the practitioner renders while focusing mentally on the Taoist trinity. How that Taoist trinity is expressed varies, but it is essentially the invocation of Heaven, Earth, and Man. The center of the sigil, a stamp, features the practitioner's seal. Below the practitioner's seal is a series of seven glyphs combined to invoke the various metaphysical powers that will help manifest the practitioner's intent, i.e., the seven orders from the celestial or spirit realm to the Three Pure Ones, the Jade Emperor, and other deities from the Taoist pantheon.[15] You will also see a stylized glyph for "one hundred" (百, bǔi) and "undo" or "untying the knot" (解, jiě). The 百 glyph indicates the duration of the Fu: the beneficiary is to carry it on his or her person for one hundred days. By the end of the one hundred days, the malignant energy will have been exorcised completely from the beneficiary's body. The 解 glyph is a spell to nullify the adverse effects of the malignant energy, and finally, to undo the harm it has done and exorcise it from the beneficiary.

Figure 10.11. One-Hundred-
Day Exorcistic Talisman from
a stele on Mount Tai

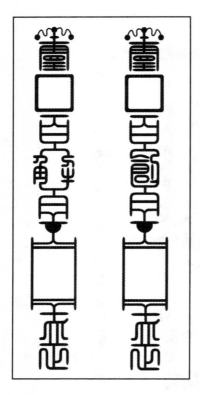

Figure 10.12. Designing a one-hundred-day talisman

A practitioner can design a one-hundred-day talisman based on the One-Hundred-Day Exorcistic Talisman from the stele. Figure 10.12 provides two templates for such a talisman. Both templates begin at the top with a stylized glyph for "Spirit" (靈, líng). It invokes the Divine in a general sense. If the practitioner seeks to invoke a specific deity or spirit by name, then a different glyph is used, one that represents the specific deity or spirit. Below the "Spirit" glyph in the first box, the practitioner inscribes his or her seal.

The sigil template on the left is to exorcise, excise, dispel, eradicate, or vanquish particular energy, and thus incorporates 解 (jiě), to undo, reverse, void, or nullify. Note how the left and right side of 解 are pulled apart, visually depicting a separation. The sigil template on the right is to establish or manifest additional energy into the beneficiary's life, and thus incorporates 創 (chuàng), "to establish" or "to create." The glyph for "one hundred" (百, bǎi) appears above these characters, 解 and 創, and in mirror form below. The second box is for specific glyphs crafted to identify the intent of the sigil. In a traditional Fu for exorcism, the glyphs identify the demon to be exorcised. In a more contemporary version of Fu craft, the second box for the left template with 解 identifies what the practitioner wants to remove from the beneficiary, such as a bad habit, bad karma, misfortune, or a tumor, whether "tumor" is used literally or figuratively. The second box for the right template with 創 notes what the practitioner wants to create for the beneficiary, such as good fortune, financial abundance, opportunities for new love, greater physical vitality, or achievement of success.

Below the second box is a stylized glyph representing the concluding glyph referenced in figure B.61 in appendix B, which signals the ending or close of the Fu sigil.

The intention for a Fu crafted in the style of figure 10.12 is for an unwanted energy to be removed within one hundred days or for the desired effect to manifest within one hundred days. The practitioner instructs a beneficiary to carry the activated Fu sigil on the beneficiary's person for the noted duration, one hundred days. A practitioner is by no means limited to the templates provided in figure 10.12. Rather, those templates represent a beginner's starting point only. Consider the principles discussed in this section on crafting a one-hundred-day talisman and apply those principles to design your own signature one-hundred-day sigils. For crafting such a Fu, I recommend a matchbook sigil, and folding the paper Fu and sealing it in heavier cardstock or a "matchbook" like the ones pictured in figure 10.3.

Figure 10.13. Bei Di, God of the North, the Great Warrior
God, with the "Bei Di Divides and Conquers All" Fu

# CHAPTER 11

# PUTTING IT ALL TOGETHER

**THE PRECEDING CHAPTERS** deconstructed the various components to preparing a Fu sigil. This chapter will demonstrate how the components come together into a complete process. Remember: the essential intent of each step in the process is necessary for successful craft, but how that step is accomplished varies from lineage to lineage, practitioner to practitioner. Read the following process with the clear understanding that you will most likely deviate from it. You have to make the process your own, tailored specifically to the way you connect with the metaphysical dimension of energy around you. If you follow a set spiritual path already, then Fu sigil crafting can be integrated into your practice, though to do so, you will need to adjust the process to align it with your path's traditions and customs.

The process of crafting a Fu sigil is illustrated by a hypothetical beneficiary, Cassia. Henceforth, the individual who will be receiving, using, or benefiting from the Fu is referred to as the beneficiary. The one designing and crafting the Fu is the practitioner.

Cassia, the beneficiary, requests the practitioner, in this case you, to prepare a Fu sigil or talisman for her. She currently feels like her career is on a plateau and she is seeking professional and business advancement. Cassia is also an entrepreneur on the side. She seeks financial success not only for her small business but from her work generally, whether it is coming from her nine-to-five career or the side business that she has started.

The practitioner starts by obtaining Cassia's date of birth, time of birth, and location of birth, assuming that the practitioner will be incorporating astrology into the selection of timing for the ritual. If not, the practitioner may skip this preliminary step and simply time the charging ritual to moon phases, as set forth in "The Timing of a Charging Ritual" in chapter 8.

The hypothetical will proceed assuming that the practitioner uses basic Western astrological concepts to select a charging date for Cassia. Cassia's date of birth is January 19, 1978, and she was born at 5:30 p.m. in San Francisco.

## THE BENEFICIARY'S VOW

If the practitioner observes beneficiary vows, at this time, prior to crafting the sigil, the practitioner should discuss the issue with Cassia. The principle of metaphysical energy transfer is explained to Cassia, and she is told that a beneficiary vow keeps the karmic scales in balance, so that energy taken will be adequately returned. Here in this hypothetical, Cassia vows that as soon as she feels or senses the sigil taking effect, she will donate ten percent of her earnings in the following fiscal quarter. The ten percent will go toward a charity that Cassia has decided upon.

The practitioner tells the beneficiary of the sigil that once the intent for the sigil has manifested, she must do as she has agreed. Again, note that the beneficiary's vow is an entirely optional process used only if it aligns with the practitioner's personal spiritual ideologies. It is not a step of the process that is observed across the board by all practitioners. The beneficiary's vow is not a requirement in effective sigil crafting. Many Taoist practitioners omit this step. However, I have found it to be an effective safety feature to mitigate unintended consequences.

## DESIGNING THE FU SIGIL

Devote thought and attention to designing a Fu sigil. A Fu sigil is like a recipe. You want to determine the ingredients or energetic elements to be added to the recipe, and their proportions. Such a determination will likely be based on your philosophy of life. Also keep in mind what the beneficiary's desired outcome is.

In Cassia's hypothetical, the practitioner decides on the following symbols to be incorporated into the Fu sigil:

**God (monotheistic).** Cassia wants to err on the side of the Divine, and while she cares for material prosperity, she will not earn it at the expense of straying from her faith. To limit the sigil's powers and keep it constrained under the supervision of the Divine, we use Cassia's monotheistic view of the Divine, or god principle, and the Chinese characters for God are used at the center position in a Ba Gua quadrant.

**Water.** Water amplifies the metaphysical energies corresponding with career. We will use the Chinese character for water as an element in the greater sigil to amplify energies specific to professional development.

**Wood.** Wood amplifies the metaphysical energies corresponding with wealth and finances. We will use the Chinese character for wood as an element in the greater sigil to amplify energies specific to wealth and generating income.

**Success.** These characters represent success and are used as an affirmation. They set the intent for the sigil.

Figure 11.1. "Attract wealth and summon treasures"

The sigil in figure 11.1 is a common Chinese indicator of blessings for wealth and prosperity, especially in business. It is not an actual Chinese character, but a synthesis of many characters often used by practitioners of magic to summon wealth and generate greater prospects of income.

Figure 11.2. "Every day, encounter riches"

The sigil in figure 11.2 is a common Chinese indicator of blessings for wealth and prosperity. Again, like the previous glyph in figure 11.1, it is a synthesis of many characters used in magical practices.

Figure 11.3. Glyphs for Fu Lu Shou

**Prosperity, Affluence, Longevity.** Incorporating traditional Chinese characters for Fu Lu Shou (福祿壽), as shown in figure 11.3, further ensures material gains and the longevity of those gains. "Fu" invokes fortune and financial abundance. "Lu" invokes gains in social status and a prosperous life. "Shou" invokes longevity and sustainability of success.

Figure 11.4. Auspicious symbol: wheel of life

**Wheel of Life.** Considered one of the eight auspicious symbols of Buddhism, but also incorporated into sigil crafting irrespective of religious faith, the dharma wheel, or wheel of life (fig. 11.4), is the wheel of a chariot, with eight spokes. In its essence, it is Wheel of Fortune, turned favorably for the beneficiary of the sigil. That Wheel of Fortune is a wheel on the chariot that we drive toward our life goals. The practitioner uses it to ensure that fortune turns favorably as a result of the Fu sigil.

Figure 11.5. Auspicious symbol: lotus blossom

**Lotus Blossom.** The lotus (fig. 11.5) is a powerful symbol for helping the beneficiary overcome adversity. It injects the beneficiary with strength so that all challenges may be overcome. It ensures the blossoming, or fruition, of the intent to be manifested by the Fu sigil. A lotus perseveres through the mud, reaching for the heavens, and at the end of its journey, blossoms beautifully. Its dew is believed to hold healing powers, and likewise, the beneficiary's successes will be productive and contribute in a humanitarian way to the world at large.

Figure 11.6. Auspicious symbol: twin fish

**Twin Fish.** The twin fish (fig. 11.6) symbolizes prosperity and abundance. Incidentally, for those with a strong Pisces presence in their natal charts, or if the timing of the sigil charging is keyed to the zodiac sign Pisces, practitioners will find use of this symbol highly effective in the sigil craft.

Figure 11.7. Auspicious symbol: the vase

**Vase.** The vase (fig. 11.7), rendered as full, not empty, symbolizes bounty, abundance, and the ability to retain savings. It is a symbol used to ensure that the

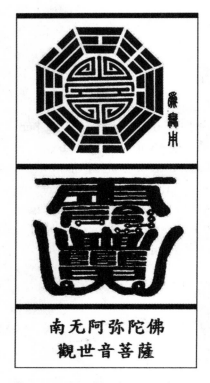

Figure 11.8. Matchbook exterior design

beneficiary will retain valuable resources, increase savings, and enjoy both stability and security. Vase symbolism is typically used for increasing one's assets, savings, or financial resources.

南无阿弥陀佛
觀世音菩薩

*Namo amitofuo guanshiying pusa*

A mantra used by the practitioner to call upon deity or the Divine. It includes both a god and goddess, Amitabha (from the Mahayana sect of Buddhism) and Kuan Yin. Note that the Fu crafted for Cassia bears a decided Buddhist leaning. In the actual practice of craft, Taoism and Buddhism are often conflated.

The Fu sigil is folded into a matchbook sigil. That way, Cassia can keep it in her wallet and take the Fu with her wherever she goes. See "Wearing or Carrying the Fu Sigil" in chapter 10 for more information on creating matchbook sigils. The outside covering for the sigil is pictured in figure 11.8. Note that part of the design pulls from another Fu sigil, invoking Zhang Dao Ling, as shown in figure 2.16.[1]

The final sigil design, in a cell sigil format, comes together in figure 11.9.

## CONSECRATION AND PURIFICATION

After the Fu sigil has been created, set it in a bed of sea salt on the night of a new moon. Place your giving hand over the sigil and repeat the following invocation:

With the full force of the one Divinity, I cast out all impurities and malignant

energies from this sigil. With the power of the Holy Spirit, may this sigil be pure and consecrated, empowered to drive afar all power of the enemy, to banish the enemy, and to emanate with blessings and Light to Cassia. Let no pestilent spirit, no corrupting atmosphere, remain where this sigil has touched. Let every trouble of the sigil's possessor be put to flight. May the Divinity itself flow through and empower this sigil to defend against all attacks of the body and of the mind, from an external source, or from within. *Prajna paramita:* the spell to allay all suffering: *gaté gaté paragaté parasamgaté Bodhi svaha,* now here in the heart of Perfect Wisdom. *Na mo amitofuo guan shi ying pu sa.*

Figure 11.9. The Fu talisman: a cell sigil design

If the optimal date of charging is a while later, the sigil can be stored away in an enclosed container covered in sea salt and consecrated ash and kept there until the time of charging. Figure 11.10 shows gemstones being used as energy amplifiers, specifically red and blue tiger-eye to help with Cassia's desired outcome.

## DETERMINING THE DATE OF CHARGING

Cassia's natal chart is consulted to determine an optimal date of charging. Her natal chart in whole signs Western astrology is provided in figure 11.11 for reference. The practitioner should use the form of astrology that most resonates with him or her.

Here, given that Cassia wants a sigil that is going to help her career, and specifically her business and entrepreneurial ambitions, which naturally involve money and wealth, a few points in her chart are examined:

Figure 11.10. Completed Sigil matchbook on sea salt and ash, surrounded by red tigereye and blue tigereye (photograph by the author)

- Her personal signs: the ascendant sign, sun sign, and moon sign. Note that she has the ascendant sign Leo, sun sign Capricorn, and moon sign Gemini.

- Her second house sign is relevant because energies relating to wealth, income, and resources need to be harnessed. Her second house is governed by Virgo, and the Earth sign. Amplifying Earth will be helpful in the sigil crafting process.

- The sigil is crafted for her career ambitions, after all, and so both the tenth house and the midheaven sign will be relevant. Here, the tenth house is governed by Taurus and, according to the practitioner's astrological approach, the midheaven sign is Aries situated in the ninth house. All these points bear relevance in the timing of the sigil charging.

The practitioner might note that Cassia's chart is dominated by Fire, and so a date and time for the sigil charging that is also Fire-dominant will connect more strongly with Cassia's personal energies. However, dominant or second-

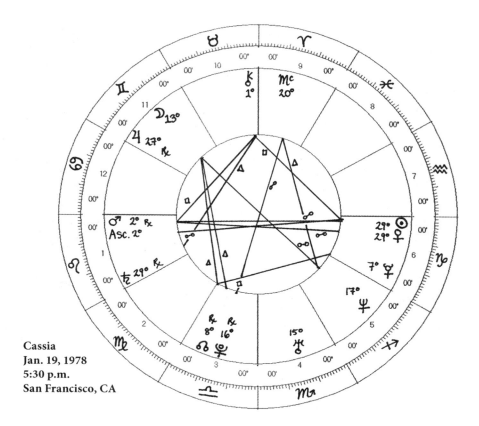

Cassia
Jan. 19, 1978
5:30 p.m.
San Francisco, CA

Figure 11.11. Natal chart for timing considerations

arily dominant Earth energies will be helpful, because wealth and income are main objectives, and also since Cassia's second house is governed by Earth.

Staying mindful of the personal signs, especially the ascendant sign and its ruling planet, and where that ruling planet is positioned during the date and time of charging, will help. Also look for positioning in the date and time of charging that will support Cassia's second house, tenth house, and midheaven sign. Teaching event astrology, also called electional astrology, is beyond the scope of this book, but it is a study that a practitioner should consider learning.

Figure 11.12. A practitioner's work space setup

## SETTING UP THE WORK SPACE

A clear space is set up with two candles and offerings of consecrated water, tea, and uncooked rice, as well as incense. Any other sacred relics aligned with the practitioner's lineage, tradition, or practice is also incorporated into the work space. The practitioner's own traditions and approaches should be integrated into the setup. The most important aspect of setting up the work space is for it to hold meaning to the practitioner. Thus, any aspect that does not hold meaning to the practitioner should be disregarded, and only the aspects that help to raise the practitioner's energy should be observed.

For the Cassia hypothetical, the practitioner sets up the work space as follows: to the left side are the ceremonial bells and prayer beads, and to the right, the wooden percussion block. Materials should be set out according to the directionality that makes the most sense to the practitioner, both logistically (objects used by certain hands are kept close to that hand) and religiously (per the practitioner's ideologies).

Figure 11.12 shows the Fu sigil placed at the center, still on the bed of sea salt and ash. Selected crystals or gemstones can be set up around the vicinity as energy amplifiers. In front of the Fu sigil (not pictured) will be a small slip of paper with the invocation written on it that is used for the 108 recitations. Note that in the photograph, the invoked deity is not pictured. It would stand on the crystal pedestal behind the Ba Gua mirror.

## OPENING THE RITUAL

In Western traditions of craft, a circle is cast. In Eastern traditions, practitioners pace the Big Dipper and then affix their seal to the altar, which I am referring to as a work space. Even in the practice of pacing, however, an enclosed sacred space is first cast. Thus, the first step to opening the ritual is to establish the practitioner's sacred space, which is to enclose the work space.

Here, the practitioner opts to light the candles and incense while reciting a Reception Invocation and setting the practitioner's seal on the work space, in front of the three offerings. A Reception Invocation such as the following might be used:

---

Terra Buhvana Aqua Jala, Bearer of Wealth and Prosperity: I call upon the immanence of the One Divinity. I am the conduit and through my intention I bless and empower this sigil for Cassia, imprinting it with Light that shall guide Cassia toward manifesting wealth, prosperity, and business success. May it channel to her good fortune, bounty, affluence, and abundance.

---

The ritual is now open and the charging may commence.

## THE 108 RECITATIONS TO CHARGE THE SIGIL

The practitioner holds the prayer beads in the left hand and the mallet for the wooden percussion block in the right. The right hand raps the block at a steady pace throughout the 108 recitations. The left hand uses the prayer beads to keep count. A full circle around the prayer beads means 108 recitations have been completed.

Wording for the recitation should be related to the Fu design. Here, the si-

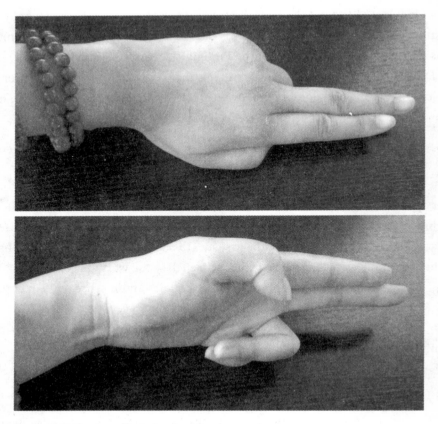

Figure 11.13. Common Taoist hand mudra: the sword

gil includes traditional Chinese text invoking Amithaba and Kuan Yin. Thus, it would make sense that the recitations also invoke Amithaba and Kuan Yin. For Cassia, the following recitation is crafted by the practitioner and recited 108 times during the charging:

---

*Namo amitofuo guanshiying pusa.* Raise abundance, wealth, and success. Bring good fortune to Cassia.

---

The practitioner's giving hand, which in this hypothetical I assume is the left, forms a hand mudra to channel Qi energy into the sigil. In this example,

Figure 11.14. Postliminary divination with tarot cards (Tarot of the Holy Light by Christine Payne-Towler and Michael Dowers)

let's say the practitioner uses the sword, a common Taoist hand mudra, which is pointed directly at the heart of the paper Fu sigil. All the while, the right hand thumbs through the mala prayer beads, which contain 108 beads, to count the 108 recitations. During the recitations, the practitioner must anchor his or her concentration on Cassia's personal energy and identity. Envision light energy bridging together the practitioner, Cassia, and the Fu sigil being empowered.

Every so often, during the recitations and at the practitioner's option, the practitioner uses the giving hand, still in the sword mudra formation, to inscribe a cross over the paper sigil. Other practitioners might inscribe a circle, for creative, amplifying, attracting, developing, and growth spells (to represent the creative cycle of the Wu Xing five phases in Chinese cosmology); or inscribe a pentagram, for destructive, defensive, protective, spirit-summoning, waning, or removal spells (to represent the destructive cycle of the Wu Xing). The power cross illustrated in figure B.64 in appendix B and its order of strokes, shown in figure B.65, can also be drawn with the sword mudra to amplify the energy being transferred into the sigil.

## POSTLIMINARY DIVINATION

After the sigil has gone through the consecration and charging rituals, a Taoist practitioner consults divination tools to determine whether the sigil has been properly charged for its intended purpose. Taoist practitioners might opt for

Figure 11.15. Stamping the sigil with the practitioner's magical seal

divination moon blocks as discussed in chapter 6. However, any divination tool that the practitioner is skilled with may be used here.

In the Cassia hypothetical, the practitioner uses tarot cards for the Postliminary Divination. The cards are shuffled while the practitioner inquires whether the sigil has been charged effectively for Cassia's objectives. Then a single card is drawn. The message on the card can be interpreted as validating or invalidating the sigil craft. Another method is to shuffle the deck, then slip the paper sigil anywhere into the deck of cards, and turn over the card that appears right behind the paper sigil,[2] as shown in figure 11.14. For the practitioner familiar with reading tarot, that upturned card is then read as either an affirmative or negative response.

Here, the Two of Wands can be interpreted as affirming that the sigil has been charged successfully for Cassia, who seeks business and professional advancement. The card assures Cassia that the friction and stress she has been experiencing on her career path were necessary milestones for the positive change that is up ahead.[3] This card correlates with the adage, "He who hesitates is lost,"[4] and so the divinatory message to the practitioner would be to go onward with the crafted sigil.

If, however, the divinatory result is negative, most practitioners consult another date and time for charging and do the ritual again with the same sigil. If the second time yields another negative result, the practitioner will discard the sigil entirely and start afresh, designing an entirely new Fu sigil. Repeated negative results are very significant. It may suggest that the sigil is not going to be a proper fit for the beneficiary, or that the practitioner must reconsider his or her entire process. A full divination might be consulted to get a sense of what is wrong.

## SEALING THE FU SIGIL

After the divination results in a validated sigil, t he practitioner seals the sigil. Here, the practitioner can either sign it, affix the practitioner's personal sigil or mandala, or stamp it with the practitioner's seal, as explained in chapter 9. It is typically affixed to the one of the corners of the sigil.

As the practitioner does so, the charging is closed with the following invocation:

---

*Prajna paramita*: the spell to allay all suffering: *gaté gate para gaté parasam gaté Bodhi svaha*, now here in the heart of Perfect Wisdom. *Namo amitofuo guanshiying pusa.* This sigil is hereby consecrated and charged, empowered for material wealth, abundance, and success to Cassia. *Namo amitofuo guanshiying pusa.*

---

## ACTIVATING THE FU SIGIL

Making sure the recipient is the first person to handle or hold the sigil is sufficient for activation. For the purpose of this hypothetical, we will assume that the practitioner has instructed Cassia to activate the sigil herself with a prayer.

Thus, to activate the Fu by prayer, the practitioner instructs Cassia that upon receipt of the sigil, she will reflect on her beneficiary's vow, which is to donate to charity ten percent of her earnings in the fiscal quarter after she first experiences positive results. The practitioner might write out a prayer and present it to Cassia to recite when she is home alone and in private. Such a prayer might be as follows: "By the power of this sigil, my career and business venture shall create such bounty in my life that I can pay off my mortgage. When that happens, in return, I shall give ten percent of all my earnings onward to charity."[5]

If a beneficiary vow is not observed, a closing invocation recited by the practitioner only can be used to both conclude the empowering of the sigil and to activate it. Thus, the activation is performed by the practitioner, not the Fu's recipient.

## PLACEMENT OF THE SIGIL

Cassia is then instructed to do any of the following that feel intuitively right to her:

- Keep the sigil in her wallet

- Store the sigil out of sight someplace in the southeast area of her office, home office, or work space, if her primary objective is wealth and finance related

- Store the sigil out of sight someplace in the north area of her office, home office, or work space if her primary objective is career advancement

- Keep the sigil in or by a cash register, if applicable to Cassia's business, or near a stash of money that she might keep at home

- Secure the sigil underneath a floor mat at the entrance of her home apartment to attract metaphysical energies that will generate wealth and financial prosperity

The only purpose of chapter 11 is to offer one example as a reference for how the many steps to Fu sigil crafting can be put together. By no means does it represent a compulsory approach. In fact, the power of a well-crafted sigil rests in the practitioner's unique and individual ability to connect with the Divine, with cosmic Qi, and with the metaphysical dimension of the universe. How a practitioner does that is a wholly subjective process. Your path and training, successes and failures at craft are how you figure out what ways you best connect to that metaphysical dimension. The ability to craft effective Fu sigils is not limited to a specific magical lineage, tradition, or even religious faith. The process can and should be adapted to what you personally practice.

CHAPTER 12

# A NOTE ON CULTURAL APPROPRIATION

**IT WOULD BE REMISS** of me to write this book for a Western readership and not mention cultural appropriation, though if you are reading this book because you are a serious practitioner of metaphysical craft, then this chapter doesn't apply. Cultural appropriation happens when a person takes an artifact from a culture that he or she does not belong to and uses that artifact outside of its cultural context, with no understanding of the significance of the artifact. By taking it out of context, the cultural meaning of that artifact effectively changes, which results in an adverse impact on the native culture.[1] Crafting Fu sigils within the context of any serious magical tradition is not cultural appropriation. Cultural appropriation happens if the Fu is treated as decorative ornamentation or if the practice is not regarded with the same veneration a practitioner would treat similar practices in his or her own tradition.

The swastika (卍) is a classic example of cultural appropriation by Westerners of sacred artifacts from the East. The word *swastika* comes from the Sanskrit root *su-asti,* which means good fortune and prosperity.[2] Archaeological records of the symbol from the Indus Valley date back to 2500 BC. For various indigenous cultures throughout human history, the swastika has been a symbol for the sun, the four directions, the four seasons, and almost universally across Asian culture, it is an auspicious symbol for well-being.

Buddhists associate the swastika with samsara, the cycle of birth and death, but also consider it a symbol of the infinite compassion of the Buddha. Taoists also associate the symbol with great fortune and luck. Hindus associate it with the god Vishnu.[3] For many cultures in the East, the swastika was a sacred, spiritual, and religious symbol that meant divine protection.

Then in the twentieth century, after Western colonization and imperialism had already left its stain on Asia, Nazi Germany appropriated the swastika symbol for its own use, taking the symbol outside the context it belonged in and, by using it in conjunction with anti-Semitism, effectively changed the cultural meaning of the Asian swastika.[4] That's cultural appropriation.

When I was a child, a Buddhist practitioner gifted me with a blessed and consecrated gold pendant that featured the swastika. Imagine the reactions I encountered when I wore that pendant to school in a small suburban all-white town in the United States. Western cultural appropriation of a sacred and religious Eastern symbol is why, to this day, so many from the marginalized Asian religious groups cannot wear a swastika without turning Western heads. That is the consequence of cultural appropriation.[5]

Another example is the hijacking of the deity name Shang Di (上帝), a deity found inscribed on oracle bones from as early as the Shang Dynasty.[6] Once, Shang Di referred to a Heavenly Emperor, a supreme deity in the skies who oversaw all other deities. But when Western Christian missionaries came to evangelize in China, they took the term Shang Di and decided it meant the Christian God. Now Shang Di refers to the monotheistic God of the Abrahamic faiths, and is no longer associated with its true heritage—the heavenly father of a polytheistic pantheon that predates Christianity by at least a thousand years.

When applied to Fu sigil crafting, the Western practitioner must take care that he or she values the Fu as sacred, and not as fanciful fun. Crafting a Fu sigil is not a Saturday afternoon art project. Do not reproduce a Chinese character simply because you like its aesthetic design. Do not carry around a Fu simply because it seems fashionable or different. Understand its meaning and symbolic associations. In appendix B, I have tried to provide a reference of commonly used characters found in Fu, but even so, do your due diligence. You should be able to articulate why exactly you have chosen to use a particular Chinese character or symbol in the crafting of your Fu sigil.

Understand the history and legacy of the Fu sigil so that if someone else sees the Fu you have crafted and asks about it, you're able to provide cultural context, and you are able to sound informed. Craft every aspect of your Fu sigil in compliance with how you have sincerely interpreted the principles from the *Classics of the Esoteric Talisman*. You might find much common ground between *Classics of the Esoteric Talisman* and Western esoteric doctrines. After all, Truth is universal.

The Chinese and indigenous practitioners of Eastern esotericism are sensitive—and rightfully so—to Western appropriation of Asian spiritual or religious thought. There is a feeling of taking without permission, and that can trigger a visceral reaction from native practitioners, even when it's just a miniature statue of Kuan Yin sitting on the desk of someone who knows nothing about the bodhisattva, or layers of mala prayer beads around someone's neck because she thinks it's costume jewelry. While each of these instances alone might not warrant a visceral response, it's the history of Western imperialism that witnessing such instances brings up, and that's why the visceral responses are triggered.

There is over a century's worth of history that accounts for the Opium Wars, Western occupation in China, putting up signs that read "No dogs and Chinese allowed" *in* China,[7] or the British appropriation of 23,000 priceless ancient Chinese artifacts that were looted from Beijing in the 1800s.[8] The traumatic humiliation and racism that the Chinese experienced in their own country throughout the nineteenth and early twentieth centuries has left an indelible mark on their psyche. Marginalized races around the world are all too used to their cultures and cultural artifacts being loved by Westerners while the people of that culture are discriminated against, tossed aside, and treated like second-class citizens.

Postcolonialism is the study of the aftermath of imperialism and colonization, and the social and psychological consequences shouldered by those who have inherited a legacy of imperialized or colonized experience.[9] Basically, postcolonialism is why a Chinese American might feel offended when he sees a white Midwestern housewife referring to herself as Celestial Master and teaching a course on feng shui. On its own, it shouldn't seem like such a big deal, but it is enough to trigger deeply embedded sentiments of humiliation and discrimination. So, justified or not, there is an unspoken feeling of, "You've taken so much already, and now you want feng shui, too?"

Yes, at the other end of the spectrum, minority groups often become hypersensitive to any use of their culture by a privileged or dominant group. I confess I've heard people cry "cultural appropriation" the way one might cry wolf. Not every Western practitioner's adoption of Eastern spiritual practice is cultural appropriation. Such hypersensitivity can lead to unnecessary tensions and conflict, when the very heart of Eastern spiritual practice is about harmony. Still, a rudimentary understanding of social history and Western imperialism in Asia will shed clear light on where that hypersensitivity comes from. Thus, even when the minority group is being hypersensitive, the privileged group should respond in a respectful and compassionate manner. Ultimately, you should respect cultural practices, but you do not need to obey the demands of individuals who are being unreasonable.

Also, what is cultural appropriation and what is globalization? Globalization is a process of interacting cultures and people who then integrate artifacts from the other culture into their own.[10] Such a process advances knowledge and technology, and in the matter of Fu sigils, advances the development of craft, a practice that transcends culture and religion because it strikes at a universal Truth. Cosmic energy does not belong to any one social group.

We live in a time when Western practitioners of craft can interact with Eastern practitioners of craft, and through that intellectual exchange and East-West syncretism, both sides mutually advance their wisdom.[11] Esoteric Taoism itself is a classic example of how a magical lineage can integrate artifacts from different religions (and often religions that are at odds with each other) to further that magical lineage.[12]

Authenticity is probably another concern that this book and its teaching of the Fu craft may raise. As an Asian American raised predominantly in the Western culture, not Eastern, I worry about authenticity. Am I "Asian enough" to be writing this book? Why is that a standard? What does being "Asian enough" mean? What exactly are the metrics for determining authenticity?

There were times I struggled with Chinese literacy in reading some of the texts I was researching and asked for help from native speakers. I found that in spite of someone being born ethnically Chinese in China with full fluency and literacy, esoteric texts are simply that—esoteric. Full literacy didn't help much if you weren't coming from a background rooted in craft. Non-Asian Western scholars with a background in ceremonial magic who also happen to read Chinese, to my great nationalistic chagrin, understood these same texts with insightful perspicacity. The issue that should be presented is not authenticity of culture, but authenticity of craft.

When it comes to culture, people tend to think that being authentic means mimicking the native ways as closely as possible. In the case of craft, that is the opposite of authentic. To be authentic is to not copy the Fu sigil design of another lineage or practitioner. Worry less about cultural authenticity and worry more about how you will apply metaphysical principles and laws to best manifest your intentions. Invest your mental energy in thinking about what truths you can uncover through your study of the Fu and how that study will advance your own craft.

My study of Western esotericism has deepened my understanding and appreciation for Eastern esotericism, and so I hope your study of Eastern esotericism can deepen your understanding and appreciation for what you practice now. Integrating Eastern metaphysics and Fu sigils into your craft isn't cultural appropriation. It's the advancement of craft. It's growth.

Taoist or not, unequivocally, a Western practitioner can craft Fu sigils, and I invite you to do so, freely and in an organic way that makes sense with your own culture and practices. Take the secular principles of craft and practice it in a way that remains aligned with your religion or spirituality. I have seen Fu sigil crafting blended with Christianity, with the use of psalms and invocations for God, the Holy Trinity, and Jesus, and it was lovely. The craft itself is a sacred process that will deepen your connection to deity, the Divine, and to a sense of higher purpose and design. There may be beliefs tied with how practitioners approach craft, but craft itself is not about beliefs; it is about connection.

The key to blending traditions is respect. Be respectful. No one will ever fault you for mispronouncing a Chinese word, but don't pronounce it with intentional affectation in an attempt to be funny. That is not respectful and will be construed as mocking. To be respectful, the Western practitioner must also be proactive about educating him- or herself on the cultural context of Fu sigil crafting. Know that esoteric Taoist practice is guided by Taoist philosophy, but deviates from it in significant ways. Know that your craft must answer to Heaven and Earth, however you define Heaven and Earth through your personal gnosis. There must be reverence for divinity and to the natural world around you. Your craft need not answer to social constructs. And yet, also know that there are social constructs that still hold on to the belief that only an ordained priest or priestess of a recognized Taoist lineage can craft a Fu sigil. Be respectful of those social constructs. Respect does not mean acquiescence.

I hope you will be using the basic principles found in this book to design your own Fu sigils in your own style and by your own methods. I hope you will be guided by your intuition, informed by a respect and reverence for a culture that is different from your own, and from there, craft sigils that blend East and West. Encouraging such blending and advancement of craft is the whole point of this book.

# CHAPTER 13

# FINAL THOUGHTS

**AFTER READING THROUGH** this book, reflect on what resonates with you and what does not, how the practices taught herein can be integrated into your own craft, and then proceed to make your first Fu sigils. In the end, no amount of reading can teach you craft. You must practice it, and that is why we call ourselves practitioners.[1] But you cannot practice before you know the principles. That is what I hope you get out of this book: the principles.

In high school, my father would tutor me for my science classes. My novice approach to passing these classes was memorization. I would make flash cards, copying physics formulas from a textbook onto these cards, and try to memorize them. I believed memorization was the way to getting such knowledge into my head. I would also memorize the solution to one problem and then attempt to apply that same solution to the new problem. "This is how I solved question 1, so I'm going to do the same exact thing for question 2."

One time I was struggling with my physics homework because question 2 was completely different from question 1, and I was at a loss. I asked my father for help. Although he isn't a physicist (but he is a scientist) and hadn't worked with high school physics equations for decades, he didn't need to consult my textbook for the formula as he tried to work through the problem himself. He deconstructed it to figure out the guiding principles behind it, and by doing so, created (or recreated) the formula to use. Basically, he reinvented the wheel—in that moment, he reinvented the physics formula needed for solving the problem. Therefore, no memorization of any formula was needed. My father scrawled out the formula he devised in his head and proceeded to solve the problem. Meanwhile I looked to my reference notes and stared at him in awe, as what he had scrawled out was exactly what was written in the textbook.

"Dad, you're able to recall that formula after all these years? You have a really good memory."

"No," he said. "I figured it out just now."

"How?" I asked.

"If you understand the basic principles of physics, you can use that understanding of the basics to solve any problem. Every formula you've been trying to memorize is based on those basic principles. It's very simple. Understand the principles, and you'll never have to memorize anything, because you'll understand."

While it might not be that simple for me when it comes to physics, I find it uncanny how applicable my father's approach is to craft. There is no need to memorize where "this" has to go, or where to put "that," what invocation to use, what to summon, or the exact order of steps to follow for a ritual.

Does "this" *have* to go "there" and is there requisite content that needs to go into an invocation, and precise orders of steps to a ritual? In one sense, yes, just as a set formula exists for solving that physics problem. But memorization isn't necessary if you understand the basic principles. That is why the bulk of this book has been devoted to imparting those basic principles.

Through understanding, and not memorization, you can work through the process needed to arrive at your objective, and just as it is in math and science, there are multiple approaches for arriving at the same objective. So when I said "this" *has* to go "there," I'm talking about metaphysical principles, not material logistics. That is why understanding theory is imperative for the practitioner of craft. Theory helps the practitioner advance farther in craft, whereas learning very specific methodologies limits the practitioner's craft. To find your own spiritual path, you need to know theory, not specific methodologies.

Be mindful that the approach to sigil crafting I have set out in this book is only one of many, and there is no need to try to embed it into your practice. Instead, try to understand the "why" behind my approach, apply that "why," and devise your own formula for reaching your objectives.

## YIN AND YANG IS NOT BLACK AND WHITE

I want to address the notion of white magic and black magic, from my perspective. Taoist magic is not identified by the dichotomy of white versus black,[2] or good versus evil,[3] or at least I do not identify energy in that way.[4] Rather, metaphysical energy (harnessed in a way that has been called "magic") is either creative or it is destructive.[5]

Energy is characterized as yin-dominant or yang-dominant. We work through the binary of yin and yang, and within the yin, there is yang, which can expand until yin dominance becomes yang dominance. Likewise, within yang there is yin, which can expand until yang dominance becomes yin. In other words, an intent to create through light and work within the subjective framework of "white magic" can quickly slip into destructive work that might otherwise be characterized as malevolent. Also, any time I have spoken of benevolent or malevolent energy in this book, I am addressing the intentions driving the force behind the energy, not the energy itself.

A Fu sigil harnesses energy to create—or more accurately, add to or amplify a life force—or it is used to destroy, to take away from or weaken a life force. An example of creative work might be enhancing a person with greater financial wealth prospects so that person may use that wealth to achieve his goals. But another example of creative work is triggering physical pain in a person's body or creating a torrent of misfortune and directing it toward someone, which few would call acts of "good" or "white magic."

Destructive work might be taking away from what a person has built, which is often the function of curses. Destructive work can also be the banishing of existing pain in an individual's life or removal of karmic merits that would otherwise lead to misfortune, which that person would hardly consider "evil." Destructive work can involve dismantling malignant and malicious forces that have been harming someone.

Note further that in Taoist cosmology (and in the law of conservation of energy), energy is in fact neither created nor destroyed; it is transferred. A practitioner summons energy from a particular source and transfers it to the beneficiary in question to manifest an intention, or the practitioner pulls energy away from the beneficiary and redirects it elsewhere, to another source. Thus, the practitioner must be aware at all times that energy does not appear from nowhere and does not simply vanish at your command. It comes from a source and was taken from that source and transferred to you by your summoning or invocation. When it seems to disappear, it has only disappeared momentarily from your line of sight; the energy has been redirected elsewhere and is having an impact elsewhere.

There are consequences to this. The impact elsewhere could very well be detrimental to your personal karma. Most consequences are tolerable, but others are not worth the gain that the energetic working has yielded. That is why the beneficiary's vow, which this book explains, is a recommended safeguard. It extends the manifestation after the effect of the sigil to include how energy will be redirected after the event.

Make no mistake: there are certainly such things as good and evil. Good and evil describe the practitioner's actions or the beneficiary's intent. These are not words to describe the actual energetic working itself. There is no good or evil gravity, black or white laws of physics. If someone uses gravity to push another over a ledge and harms that person, that is not the practice of black gravity, but I would contend that it is an example of someone acting evilly.

A practitioner can use either creative or destructive metaphysical energy to craft Fu sigils for evil intentions, and the more he or she does so, the more impact it will have on his or her karmic account. What that means, however, is not for me to say. Good deeds, on the other hand, as discussed briefly in chapter 6, are the means through which a practitioner transcends, and accrues, the Vital Force needed for powerful craft.

The irony is that once a practitioner transcends through the accumulation of good deeds, he or she finds the application of craft to be rather useless, much like the Venerable Sheng-Yen said.[6] Yet again, I must stress: my code of ethics and what I am for or against bears no relevance in your life. You must live by your own code and decide for yourself what you are for or against. After learning Fu sigil crafting, what you choose to do with your learned knowledge is on you.

## QUANTUM MECHANICS AND CRAFT

In the realm of quantum physics, Albert Einstein proved that energy and matter are interchangeable. In other words, $E = mc^2$.[7] Einstein asserted that all matter has within it untapped energy that by and large went unnoticed.[8] Thus, as Banesh Hoffman, a British mathematician and physicist and a former student of Einstein, noted, "Every clod of earth, every feather, every speck of dust [becomes] a prodigious reservoir of untapped energy."[9] Man, then, can take from Heaven and Earth "for personal enrichment and for exercising trigger-ing mechanisms,"[10] if the practitioner can access that prodigious reservoir of untapped energy, a concept from Taoist texts that predate Einstein by well over a thousand years.

For Man's spirit to be awake, to be spiritual,[11] is to realize a conscious, in-telligent matrix behind all that is in the universe, and how all that is, all matter, is connected and related to energy, as Einstein propounded. The practitioner can tap into that conscious, intelligent matrix—cosmic Qi—and thus tap into any matter through its energy by understanding vibrations.

All that goes into craft and ritual is about understanding vibrations. Theo-retical physicist Max Planck asserted that all physical matter consists of vibra-tions, and all matter subsists by a force that triggers a vibration. Thus, Planck deduced that a conscious, intelligent matrix is the force behind the vibrations,[12] and through craft, that is what the practitioner can come to appreciate.

Crafting Fu sigils is an experience that teaches the practitioner about how the universe works and how that which we perceive as not connected is, in cos-mic truth, connected. Craft teaches you how to see those connections. Craft is about understanding the mechanics of the binary code that instructs all life, all energy and matter, the yin and the yang. A Fu sigil, in its essence, is a bit-string that represents an instruction for how energy and matter is to be manifested.

An intelligent design is what causes the vibrations in matter, and those vi-brations result in energy, much of it unseen, undetected, and untapped. It is that energy that a practitioner has access to by way of craft, and to do so, the prac-titioner's approach is through matter and attaining dominion over that matter.

Whether it is by Eastern or Western traditions in craft, or by a union of both, the practitioner attains dominion over matter by understanding na-ture—the changing seasons and the four directions.[13] Eastern tradition under-stands the changing seasons and four directions through the trinitarian prin-ciple of Heaven, Earth, and Man, the Wu Xing five phases, and the Ba Gua, or eight trigrams. Western traditions have their own expressions, but both are unified in agreement as true expressions of nature—of the changing seasons and the four directions. Craft, therefore, is untouched by what any one lineage or school of esoteric thought has to say about it.

Taoism as a concept shirks from definition. Definitions are limitations, and the Tao is unlimited, an expression of that which is beyond the limited capability of humankind to grasp. Likewise, what is authentic Taoist craft is hard to say. Is Taoist craft that has been blended with Buddhism or Confucianism less pure, less Tao? Is a Western practitioner's interpretation of Taoist craft no longer authentic? To answer "yes" to any of these questions would be an attempt to define the Tao. To answer "yes" is an attempt at limiting the unlimited.

This book may be about Taoism after all. The Tao—or The Way, the practitioner's Path—cannot be spoken. It cannot be taught. It must be found. No lineage and no school of thought can articulate Tao, or articulate what craft is or is not. That which tries to articulate it is not the true Tao.[14] The Tao of craft is not about teaching a spiritual path; it is about finding your own, and a practitioner's spiritual path is the one that leads to concord of the trinity that is Heaven, Earth, and Man. Fu talisman crafting happens to be one well-established tried-and-true way to achieve that trinitarian concord.

Ultimately, exoteric Taoist philosophy is the highest aspiration of the esoteric Taoist practitioner. Fu sigils are not to be crafted for achievement. Achievement begets conflict. Nor should Fu sigils be crafted for prosperity and riches. Wealth begets greed and thievery. Desire confuses the heart. These are the teachings of the Tao.[15] The Tao of craft is to gain insight into the many theories of craft and then work with those theories to forge your own spiritual path.

True magic is cultivated for the pursuit of transcendence. The cultivation toward immortality that is the great work and pursuit of Taoist practitioners is transcendence, for Man to become like Heaven and Earth, which are everlasting because they do not exist for themselves.[16] To transcend, a practitioner learns, through craft, how not to exist for him- or herself.

The highest good, and the highest form of magic, is to be like water, and to be like water is the way of the Tao. Water nourishes and benefits without contention, and does not avoid what it dislikes.[17] Thus, do not use craft to avoid what you dislike. True mastery of craft is wu wei, or nonuse of craft.[18]

To develop proficiency in many areas of skill and knowledge enriches life. The more you can, the more you are; but just because you can, it does not mean you do. Spell-working for romance, career advancement, or wealth can be shortsighted, and a squander of a practitioner's gifts. The gift of craft is better exercised toward the highest form of magic, the way of the Tao. And yet craft is ironic in that way. To achieve that highest form, a practitioner must first bumble and stumble through the mechanics and the shortsightedness of craft. And, I contend, if there is one most fascinating way to bumble and stumble on the magical path, it is by way of the Fu sigil.

Figure 13.1. Circa AD 960–1127 stele carvings of the Buddhist/Taoist Canons of Marici [Marishiten] (courtesy of Special Collections, Fine Arts Library, Harvard University)

# APPENDIX A

# CONSIDERATIONS FOR THE HOUSE

**PROVIDED HERE ARE** a few house templates for reference and use. Be sure to review chapter 4 for more instructions on designing houses in Fu sigil crafting. A house is not a required component of a Fu, and as a reader might deduce from the historic Fu pictured in this book, it is often omitted. However, in my own practice, the house provides a structured framework from which to commence the design of a Fu. Thus, I prefer to start the conception process with a house, and one that is meaningful to the subject matter at hand.

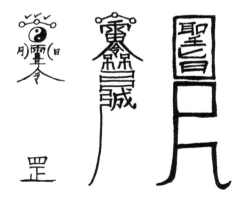

Figure A.1. Houses for summoning and conjuration

Figure A.1 shows three house styles that can be used for summoning or ordering a spirit or ghost to carry forth a practitioner's bidding. The top portion of the house identifies what the Fu is for. Left to right, the first two harness the three-star constellations and the Heaven, Earth, and Man trinity. They both use the word "order" (令) in the house design. The first two houses can also be used in Thunder Rites. The third, to the right, is framed as a holy decree that the practitioner is authorized and has been empowered to issue. Thus, there are the characters for "decree" (聖旨, Shèng Zhǐ). Through the Jiao Bei moon blocks or another form of divination is how the practitioner confirms whether he or she is authorized and empowered to issue such a holy decree. In a Fu sigil crafted to contain, restrict, or bind, use the house on the right. Place the subject to be bound inside the closed square.

Figure A.2. House for gateway

The house in figure A.2 is rendered from the Chinese radical for door, household, or gateway, 戶 (Hù). See the section "Chinese Radicals" in appendix B for more information about how to incorporate Chinese radicals into sigil design. Here, the radical has been stylized into a house. The house would thus be used to design a Fu sigil that will open or access a particular gateway. The radical also indicates a household, and this house would be optimal for home protection sigils as well.

Figure A.3 is a house that can be used for invoking a particular deity. The house is stylized from the traditional Chinese character for "deity," 帝 (Dì). Note that the character can also be translated as "emperor" or "imperial." Use it to denote the invocation of a higher spirit form that is being called upon by

Figure A.3. House for invoking deity

the practitioner for assistance. Glyphs are inscribed onto either side of the center vertical line.

Figure A.4. All-purpose bell house

The house in figure A.4 is all-purpose. It is versatile, easy to draw, easy to accessorize with energetic amplifiers, and can be used to denote the practitioner's control over the elements represented by the glyphs that will be inscribed inside the bell shape. To the right is an example of how the house can be used. Symbols for the sun and moon are added at the top of the house to call upon the god and the goddess energy. In this example, the heavenly stem for Yang Wood (甲) is doubled and combined with the character for "mountain" (山)

tripled. At the base of the sample Fu is hexagram 50, the Cauldron. In craft, this hexagram is often used by alchemists and magicians to amplify their energetic workings. Note also the double glyphs for "fire" (火) to the bottom left of the double glyphs for "ghost" (鬼).

Typically, although there are certainly exceptions to this general rule, when you see "ghost" in a Fu paired with a lot of yang energy, the sigil is for an exorcism or to dispel ghosts, to ward off the foul play of spirits. When you see "ghost" paired with a lot of yin energy, it is likely a sigil for conjuration, to summon a particular ghost. In such a sigil, there should also be glyphs that represent that particular ghost or spirit's identity. In figure A.4, that spirit's identity is marked near the top of the bell, with the heavenly stems (甲) doubled and the tripled mountain (山), along with the darkened Lo Shu glyphs, signifying yin. The five circles, as energetic amplifiers, added to the left of the bell, and the four to the right represent the four compass and five relative directions and are empowered with yang to defeat the yin. Inferring from the symbolism here, this Fu is for an exorcism or to ward off a specifically identified ghost.

Figure A.5. Cell sigil–style house

Figure A.5 is a house that can be used almost like a cell sigil. One way to use the house is to place subjects that need to be contained or controlled inside the enclosed cells, and glyphs relating to deity or sacred energetic concepts at the top. Place glyphs that drive, fuel, or power the success of the desired result at the bottom, like the stove fire beneath the cauldron.

The two houses pictured in figure A.6 are general or all-purpose house designs. Customized glyphs using the Lo Shu square or Western sigil crafting

Figure A.6. All-purpose houses

techniques can go inside the box for the house on the left. Note the three dots at the top of the house on the right. Rendering the three dots first as a practitioner crafts a sigil invokes a union of Heaven, Earth, and Man. The three dots represents the Taoist trinitarian principle and the practitioner's gift as a communicator between the three planes.

Figure A.7. House for bodily protection

The house style in figure A.7 works well in sigils for bodily protection. The top section, where a glyph for longevity (to ensure health and wellness) appears, can be replaced with any primary glyph. See how the house is used in the Fu sigil for travel protection shown in figure 4.17.

When crafting a Fu that calls for yang-dominant energy, consider designing a house stylized in a manner similar to figure A.8. Here, odd numbers, squares,

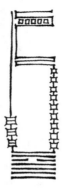

Figure A.8. Yang-dominant house with hexagram

and the Chinese character for "sun" (日) are used to call upon yang energy. In the square section near the top, inscribe a customized glyph, one rendered from the Lo Shu or Western sigil crafting techniques. The bottom portion of the Fu can be used to invoke the energy of an I Ching hexagram. Here, hexagram 14 is being used to form the foundation of the Fu.

Figure A.9. Yin-dominant house with two trigrams

Figure A.9 shows a yin dominant house that also invokes two trigrams, Heaven and Earth. Note also the character for "moon" (月) integrated into the house design and the ancient seal script for "moon" along the right column. The top of the house, where an invoking glyph would be inscribed, is shaped like a crescent. The dark constellations harness cosmic yin energy. There are eleven circles as energetic amplifiers to call upon the spirit world, as a yin dominant house would most likely be used for a summoning or conjuration. Note also the amplifier near the base of the Fu.

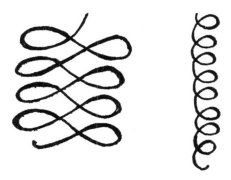

Figure A.10. Two details in house design

Figure A.10 show frequently used details in house designs. Both are energy amplifiers. The design on the left is often drawn near the bottom of the sigil, while the design on the right is drawn along the sides.

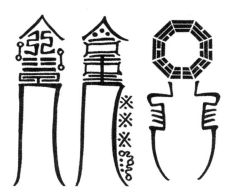

Figure A.11. Three house designs

In the three house examples shown in figure A.11, glyphs would be inscribed where there is blank space. The house on the left includes one of the twelve symbols of sovereignty, the Fo and Fu, for justice and divine power, along with the Ba Gua trigram for Thunder. Thunder raises the energy for advancement, movement, and progress. The center house is a sample multipurpose house, crafted to raise Qi energy and amplify it for spell purposes. Note the repetition of the rice grains symbol from the twelve symbols of sovereignty. Here, it is used to symbolize plenitude and prosperity, and to ensure success. The house on the right uses a Ba Gua stamp, and specifically, the Earlier Heaven Ba Gua. Forming the frame along the left and right are glyphs for "dragon." This house would be optimal in craft for Fu sigils intended to be feng shui cures.

Figure A.12. House for cloaking or shielding

The house in figure A.12 would be most suitable for a containment spell, cloaking, shielding, invisibility, or concealment. Generally, when crafting a Fu intended to bind another or restrict something from having an impact, the glyph that represents that thing to be contained should be illustrated as being contained.

Figure A.13 is a house crafted for a love spell. It is based on Fu Wen for happiness and marriage prosperity (囍, "double happiness"). The house incorporates the Heaven trigram for a blessed romance or relationship. The trigram is depicted as protected, or sheltered, which is symbolic of protection from external forces that might try to undermine the couple's love. The sun and moon bring in the god and goddess, but also represent the balance of yin and yang energy in a harmonious relationship. Note that yin and yang do not mean female and male; the genders are irrelevant here. No matter how the genders are paired in romantic love, for any relationship to prosper, it must

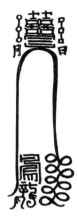

Figure A.13. Houses for love and romance

be a balance of yin (yielding, intuitive) and yang (leading, practical) energy. The base vscripts for "phoenix" (鳳) and "dragon" (龍). Pairing the two characters together is traditional Chinese symbolism for a blessed romantic union. The energetic amplifier, forming lemniscates along the bottom right, loops , symbolizing longevity.

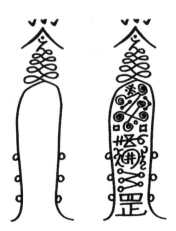

Figure A.14. Charge of the practitioner

Commonly found elements of traditional Fu sigils come together in figure A.14 for a house, pictured at left, used to represent a charge or order issued by the practitioner, commanding metaphysical energy to be directed in a manner as controlled by the practitioner. The three checkmark strokes at the top of the house invoke Heaven, Earth, and Man. Below it is a glyph for "order" (令), then lemniscate amplifiers that merge into a bell. Six yang energetic amplifiers further charge the sigil with power. Pictured at right is an example of how the house would be used, incorporating a number of glyphs for neutralizing a hex.

Figure A.15. Author's re-creation of the Ordination Scroll of Empress Zhang

For designing houses, look to historic Fu sigils for inspiration. Figure A.15 is a hand scroll from the Ming Dynasty, circa AD 1493. The original version is rendered with color ink and gold. Note the three sigils pictured on the scroll and how they feature the same house design with the three-star constellation at the top.

Figure A.16. House design inspired by the Ordination Scroll of Empress Zhang

Figure A.16 is a re-creation of the house style from the "Ordination Scroll of Empress Zhang." The scroll memorializes the ordination of Empress Zhang as a Taoist priestess and documents the pivotal role Taoism played during the Ming Dynasty.[1] For me, this is a great house style for a love and romance Fu. According to scholars, Empress Zhang was in one of the only monogamous marriages to an emperor in Chinese history;[2] he took no concubines out of a deep love for his wife. Since the historic Fu were crafted to commemorate an ordination, I might also use the house design for any Fu used to bless or bring prosperity to a new milestone in someone's life.

Figure A.17. Fu sigil invoking Ganesha

The Fu sigil pictured in figure A.17 is one crafted for invoking Ganesha. Note the oracle bone seal script for "elephant" at the top of the sigil. The Fu is used to remove impediments to success for an artistic project. Such a Fu, both invoking Ganesha and using the house design based on the Empress Zhang sigil house in figure A.16, would be optimal for assisting one about to embark on a new educational milestone in the liberal arts or humanities, such as starting university or graduate school, or one who is graduating from school and now seeking professional advancement.

The house framing the Fu in figure A.18 is based on the bell-shaped house from figure A.4, capped by the three-star constellation to call upon the union of Heaven, Earth, and Man. It is also part of a stylized glyph for "prosperity" (福). Below it is a stylized version of oracle bone script writing, for "affluence" (祿). It is fused with elements of the character for "multiply" (乘). Below that

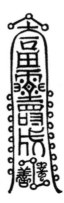

Figure A.18. Fu Sigil for success and prosperity

is stylized oracle bone script for "longevity" (壽). The three characters for Fu Lu Shou (福祿壽, "prosperity," "affluence," and "longevity") are found within. Next is the oracle bone script for "success and accomplishment" (成). Eight energetic amplifiers along the left side of the house call upon the energy of the Ba Gua, in an even number, for yin balance. Nine energetic amplifiers along the right call upon divine assistance and invoke longevity, in an odd number for yang balance. At the bottom base of the sigil is a Lo Shu–based glyph connecting the Lo Shu sectors for wealth, honor, career advancement, and heavenly blessings. Inscribed around the Lo Shu glyph are glyphs representing the individual or beneficiary for whom the Fu sigil is crafted.

Figure A.19. Success and prosperity Fu sigil template

These two glyphs, positioned along the left and right side of the Lo Shu glyph in figure A.18, are replaced by blank space in the subsequent figure A.19. Glyphs representing the beneficiary that the Fu is crafted for would be inscribed into that blank space. Figure A.19 can be used as a template for sigils crafted to bring success and prosperity. To cure atrophic Qi energy in a person and generate stronger vitality for accomplishment, craft a Fu using figure A.19 to help bring an individual off a professional or financial plateau. When crafting the Fu, be sure to include glyphs that represent the individual's name or identity and place them in the blank areas around the Lo Shu glyph at the bottom of the sigil.

Figure A.20. Versatile sigil house with concluding affirmation

# GLYPH DESIGN REFERENCES

**THIS APPENDIX IS** provided as a reference for designing a practitioner's own glyphs or to write in Fu Wen. It consists of frequently used Chinese characters in Fu sigil crafting. In your own craft, consider incorporating these characters into sigils by modifying them into your own personalized Fu Wen, or stylized glyphs. Study the original character as provided and think about how you might transform that character into your own magical script.

Below selected characters are the ancient seal scripts showing the historic evolution of the character, in the scripts found on oracle bones and bronze inscriptions from the Shang Dynasty (1600–1050 BC) and commonly found on bronze inscriptions and steles from the Zhou Dynasty (1046–256 BC) as well as the Qin Dynasty (221–206 BC).[1] A few Fu sigils are provided as examples for how the Chinese characters might be stylized into glyphs and applied to sigil crafting.

## TAOIST COSMOGENESIS

Glyphs for the following characters (or even stylized houses) are typically used to denote the source of energy (yang or yin) or used in a set pattern to represent a code that identifies the Taoist lineage that the sigil is from.

*Qi*

### Breath, Spirit, Vital Energy

Qi. Energy of life. Breath. Life force. Can be used as a glyph to amplify a spell with additional energy or life force. Most often found stylized into the house of a sigil.

| Shang Dynasty | Zhou Dynasty | Qin Dynasty |

Figure B.1. Seal script evolution of "Qi"

*Yin*

## Yin

Yin. Use for harnessing yin energy. Represents the source of reception, wisdom, the dark, feminine, mystical, or occult. The moon. Use to raise energies that are more nurturing. Peace and harmony in familial, social, or romantic relationships require yin. Yin is used for matters relating to the emotions, perceptions, wisdom, understanding, or mercy. Yin brings mercy and compassion. Cast a sigil with greater yin to influence others, for invisibility or invincibility, or occult matters relating to that which is unseen or hidden beneath the veil.

*Yáng*

## Yang

Yang. Use for harnessing yang energy. Represents the source of initiation, knowledge, the light, masculine, or canonical. The sun. Use to raise energies that are more forceful. Intellectual, scientific, or innovative pursuits require yang. Yang is used for matters relating to authority, government, civil matters, leadership, or justice. Cast a sigil with greater yang to achieve success in ambitious undertakings.

| 1. | Yin is the opposite of yang. Yang is the opposite of yin. |
|---|---|
| 2. | Yin cannot exist without yang. Yang cannot exist without yin. |
| 3. | Yin itself can be further subdivided to form Plenary yin (yin) and Adjusting yin (yang). Yang itself can be further subdivided into Plenary yang (yang) and Adjusting yang (yin). See also appendix E. |
| 4. | Yin holds the potential to become yang because within yin, there is yang. Yang holds the potential to become yin because within yang, there is yin. |
| 5. | All suffering and misfortune is caused by yin excess, yin deficiency, yang excess, or yang deficiency. Thus, a sigil crafted to correct yin excess or yang deficiency would require yang; a sigil crafted to correct yang excess or yin deficiency would require yin. |

Table B.1. Five basic principles of yin and yang

---

日

*Rì*

Sun

Sun. Use for harnessing or supporting yang energy. Success, victory. Glory. Fame. Recognition. In sigil crafting, can also be used to denote days. Thus, if the spell is to take effect within seven days (or expire within seven days), then seven 日 glyphs would be incorporated into the sigil. If a practitioner diagnoses a situation as being imbalanced with too much yin, and that yin excess is the cause of grief, the Fu sigil would raise stronger yang energy to balance that yin. One way to do so is through a sun glyph.

Shang Dynasty    Zhou Dynasty    Qin Dynasty    Western
                                               Astrological Glyph

Figure B.2. Seal script evolution of "sun"

*Yuè*

## Moon

Moon. Use for harnessing or supporting yin energy. Love, romance. Dreams coming true. Intuition. Psychic abilities. Mystical knowledge. In sigil crafting, the moon can also be used to denote months. Thus, if the spell is to take effect within three months (or expire within three months), then three 月 glyphs would be incorporated into the sigil. If a practitioner diagnoses a situation as being imbalanced with too much yang, and that yang excess is the cause of grief, then the Fu sigil would raise stronger yin energy to balance that yang. One way to do so is through a moon glyph.

Shang Dynasty    Zhou Dynasty    Qin Dynasty    Western
                                                Astrological Glyph

Figure B.3. Seal script evolution of "moon"

---

## 星

*Xīng*

## Stars

Stars. Use for achievement and accomplishment. When seeking attainment of a goal that might otherwise feel unattainable, use the stars glyph as energetic support. Optimal for use in crafting Fu sigils for attaining fame, recognition, or promotions at work.

| Shang Dynasty I | Shang Dynasty II | Zhou Dynasty I | Zhou Dynasty II | Qin Dynasty |

Figure B.4. Seal script evolution of "stars"

*Dào*

## The Tao

Tao. Primordial essence. Flow. Often used in the same way Fu Wen for Qi might be used. Optimal for use in crafting Fu sigils for gaining wisdom, insight, foresight, for attaining greater understanding or increasing peace of mind.

Also: Taoism (道教, Dào Jiào)

| Shang Dynasty | Zhou Dynasty | Qin Dynasty |

Figure B.5. Seal script evolution of "Tao"

## PANTHEON OF DEITIES

While the following list is by no means complete, it is intended to offer the reader a general idea of the deities that are most commonly invoked for sigil crafting due to their significance in Taoism, esoteric Buddhism, or regional Chinese folk religions.

Each Taoist lineage has its own deity or deities that the ordained practitioners invoke to carry forth their energetic workings and rituals. The practice can be traced from the *Classics of the Esoteric Talisman,* as summarized in point 1 in chapter 3. Folk religion practitioners tend to be more eclectic and call upon both Taoist-based and Buddhist-based deities.

I see deity as a human personification of natural or universal energies, forces, and phenomena. Through craft, these energies, forces, and phenomena possess a metaphysical dimension, which a practitioner can tap into and harness for energetic workings. The personification enables the practitioner to establish a closer personalized connection to that natural and universal energy, force, or phenomenon and pull upon its metaphysical source. Personification is part of the magic, an aspect of the energetic working. Through personification of these energies from Heaven, combined with the ritual that is harnessing energies from Earth, the practitioner, or Man, is best able to manifest his or her will. Thus, I believe that irrespective of faith or religion, invocations to specific deity names can be used by any practitioner from any lineage to draw forth the intended power or force. This section provides traditional Chinese characters for these names, from which the practitioner can stylize glyphs for Fu craft.

Please keep in mind that this listing is by no means anywhere near complete and merely represents the pantheon I have more familiarity with.

## Taoist Celestial Beings

There is a great deal of overlap between the Taoist and Buddhist pantheons, and both seem to have absorbed deities from regional Chinese folk religions. Thus, it is often difficult to define a deity as strictly Taoist or strictly Buddhist. For example, Cai Shen, the God of Wealth, is venerated in Taoism, Tibetan Buddhism, and also in folk religions; Guan Yu, a historic figure and national hero, became deified by folk religions and later venerated as a bodhisattva in Buddhism and a deity in Taoism. Shang Di, originally the highest god in Chinese folk religion, now denotes the Christian God.

*Shàng Dì*

### God

Dating to inscriptions on oracle bones from the Shang Dynasty (1600–1050 BC), "Shang Di" represented the concept of one supreme ruler in the heavens that oversaw all other deities, spirits, immortals, and human civilization.

However, over time, the name has become synonymous with the Christian God,[2] and today, references to Shang Di refer to the monotheistic God concept of Abrahamic faiths. The Chinese also refer to him as the Heavenly Father, or Lao Tian Ye.

Also: 老天爺 (Lǎo Tiān Yé, Heavenly Father)

---

*Di*

## Deity. A God. One Who Is Supreme. The Divine.

Di is the High God from the pantheon of deities venerated during the Shang Dynasty (1600–1050 BC). The High God was venerated as the most powerful of the gods, overseeing all other deities.3 Di controlled all human events. Di possessed the power to order the outcome of an event, and shamans would commune with Di, praying that Di would order certain outcomes.

Today, the term is an honorific that means "Supreme" or "Imperial." It is used generally to denote "god." Can indicate outer gods in the celestial kingdom or inner gods in inner alchemy. Often found on traditional Fu sigils, in various and diverse contexts. Used as an honorific for one of the invoked deities, along with an ideogram for the word "decree" or "order" (See the "Miscellaneous" section below) to indicate that the Fu sigil is a summons of a particular spirit at the authority of the invoked deity.

Shang Dynasty     Zhou Dynasty     Qin Dynasty

Figure B.6. Seal script evolution of "Deity"

*Yù Di*

## The Jade Emperor

Yu Di, also named the Heavenly Duke in Taoist mythology, is the emperor of the deities and very important to Taoist cosmology. The Jade Emperor oversees all natural phenomena on Earth. He is often called upon in sigils crafted for seeking justice. Compare the God of Thunder (entry on next page), the deity invoked for seeking vengeance or retaliation.

Figure B.7. Yu Di, the Jade Emperor

*Léi Gōng*

## God of Thunder

Both Lei Gong and Lei Shen are used to denote the God of Thunder, likened to Thor. Historically, Lei Gong is depicted as wielding a large dagger, which he used to punish those who have committed wrongs.[4] Glyphs referencing the God of Thunder are frequently found on Taoist Fu sigils because he is a punisher. While Lei Gong is invoked by those seeking justice, he is more commonly used by those who seek vengeance or to punish those who have done wrong.

Also: 雷神 (Léi Shén). Glyphs formed from these characters are pervasive because thunder magic is a substantial part of esoteric Taoism's history.[5]

---

*Cái Shén*

## God of Wealth (or Cai Shen)

Per Taoism, Tibetan Buddhism, and regional Chinese folk religions, Cai Shen is the God of Wealth and Prosperity. He is invoked in magical workings for increasing financial gains and material abundance. A section in chapter 8 tells the legend of Zhao Gong Ming, the man who became deified as Cai Shen, the God of Wealth, along with instructions on a traditional spell for attaining wealth and prosperity through invocation of Cai Shen and the Five Celestials of Wealth. However, note that Cai Shen simply means "wealth deity." The specific identity attributed to the title "wealth deity" varies regionally. That Zhao Gong Ming is the identity of Cai Shen, the God of Wealth, is but one of many possible manifestations of Cai Shen.

# 關公
## *Guān Gōng*

## Guān Gong (or Guan Yu)

The veneration of Guān Gong is as popular as the veneration of Kuan Yin. He is venerated as a bodhisattva in Buddhism and as a guardian deity in Taoism; also venerated regionally in many Chinese folk religions. He was a mythological figure from the *Romance of the Three Kingdoms,* a great warrior and military general who was later deified. There are, however, historical accounts that document the real life existence of such a figure. Guāng Gong or Guan Yu is invoked by fraternal organizations, as Guān Gong represents loyalty, fidelity, honor, and bravery. Signifies allegiance to brotherhood and strict adherence to a code of honor. In Taoism, often invoked for vanquishing spells against malignant forces. Used in both offensive and defensive magic. He brings strength, courage, bravery, audacity, and vigor.

Also: 關羽 (Guān Yǔ); 關帝 (Guān Dì), honorific, referring to him as Supreme or Lord Guan

---

# 文昌帝君
## *Wén Chāng Dì Jūn*

## God of Literature and Culture (or Wen Chang Di)

Wen Chang Di is the Taoist deity of literature and culture. Often invoked to aid in academia, schooling, examinations, writing, writing projects, artistic projects, or for crafting a Fu sigil relating to the arts and culture.

Also: 文昌王 (Wén Chāng Wáng)

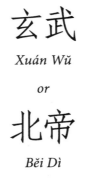

*Xuán Wǔ*

*or*

北帝

*Běi Dì*

## Enigmatic Warrior God or Bei Di, God of the North

The word "玄" (Xuán) isn't easy to translate. It's commonly translated to "mysterious," and so this deity is referred to as the Mysterious Warrior (or Military) God, or the Dark Warrior God. Also referred to as "dark" because as one of the visible constellations in the skies, the Warrior God is situated in the north (often depicted as a tortoise and a snake). "Xuan" is more in line with hidden, esoteric, what is behind the veil, or even occult. Thus, here I've opted to use the word "enigmatic."

There are many differing legends and myths for Xuan Wu, but here is the one I grew up with: He was born as a heavenly prince. After a heavenly queen, his mother, dreamt that she swallowed a sun, she woke up to discover she was pregnant. He is characterized as a powerful, courageous, and formidable warrior with the ability to vanquish demons.

Another version of the myth depicts Xuan Wu as a butcher who had slaughtered animals without remorse. One day he came across a woman by a river giving birth and in assisting her with labor, Xuan Wu had a vision of Kuan Yin, the bodhisattva of mercy. Thereafter, he repented for his killings and, seeking redemption, cut out his own stomach and intestines. Heaven bestowed mercy on Xuan Wu and instead of dying, he was transformed into an immortal. However, the organs he had carved out of himself, his stomach and intestines, were transformed into a demonic tortoise and snake. The tortoise and snake demons wreaked havoc on earth. Xuan Wu the immortal descended down to earth to neutralize the demons that he had inadvertently set upon the people. Xuan Wu was able to reign the demons in under his control and thereafter, the tortoise and snake became his generals. The myth is a story about repentance and facing one's personal demons and how facing those inner demons and learning how to control them can become our greatest strength.

Xuan Wu is invoked in craft seeking valiance, dominance, military success, litigation, or success in any confrontational or combative situations. He is also venerated as a powerful god of magic, and thus Taoist practitioners invoke him in craft that seeks to control natural phenomena or in exorcisms and the banishment of demon spirits.

Xuan Wu can also be invoked as Bei Di, the God of the North, though whether Xuan Wu and Bei Di are two different names for the same deity or two entirely different deities remains a point of contention.[6] Wrong or right, I conflate the two as referring to the same deity because the essential energy that Xuan Wu and Bei Di represent are, to me, similar if not the same. Bei Di, specifically, is given the title Chief of the Board of Exorcisms.[7] For many lineages, Bei Di is the go-to deity to invoke for exorcisms. Shang Qing (上清) lineage adepts, for instance, practice a form of exorcism that invokes Bei Di, called the Bei Di Method for Vanquishing Demons, 北帝殺鬼之法 (Běi Dì shā guǎ zhī fǎ).[8]

Also: 玄天上帝 (Xuán Tiān Shàng Dì); 真武大帝 (Zhēn Wǔ Dà Dì); 帝公 (Dì Gōng)

## 門神

*Mén Shén*

### Door Gods

Generally depicted as two deities on two separate panels, one on each side of a door or entranceway. Also, the two deities must be depicted or positioned facing each other, not facing away. Since peach wood was believed to hold spiritually protective properties, the Door Gods are carved into peach panels. (In modern times, often seen rendered on paper. Two Fu sigils can be created and placed on either side of an entranceway to call upon the protection of the Door Gods.) The Four Guardians or Four Celestial Kings are also used as Door Gods.

## *The Three Pure Ones*

三清

*Sān Qīng*

### The Three Pure Ones

Refers to the three highest deities in Taoist cosmogenesis. Generally only one of the three is invoked in a Fu sigil.

道寶

*Dào Bǎo*

### Primeval Lord of Heaven

"Treasure of the Tao." Also named Dao Bao. First of the Three Pure Ones. Created Heaven and Earth. First supreme administrator over earth, before turning the duty over to the Jade Emperor. He was born spontaneously from cosmic Qi and was the first to transform from "nonbeing" to "being." In traditional depictions, he holds the Pearl of Primordial Chaos (混元珠, Hùn Yuán Zhū), symbolizing the origins of life. In lieu of the pearl, other depictions show the yin and yang symbol. In depictions of the Three Pure Ones, Dao Bao is at the center.

Also: 元始天尊 (Yuán Shǐ Tiān Zūn), Primeval Lord of Heaven

# 經寶

*Jĭng Băo*

## Heavenly Lord of the Numinous Treasure

The numinous treasure is the Law. Also named Jing Bao. "Treasure of the Law." Second of the Three Pure Ones and second in rank after the Primeval Lord of Heaven. Keeper of the laws of nature. In depictions of the Three Pure Ones, Jing Bao is to the left of Dao Bao.

Also: 靈寶天尊 (Líng Băo Tiān Zūn), Heavenly Lord of the Numinous Treasure

---

# 師寶

*Shī Băo*

## Heavenly Lord of Virtuous Tao

Third of the Three Pure Ones. Also named Shi Bao. "Treasure of Knowledge (Wisdom)." Master teacher, teacher of teachers, the leader among sages. Bringer of culture and civilization. After Lao Tzu was deified, he was often associated with Shi Bao, and therefore many lineages of Taoism venerate Lao Tzu as Shi Bao. In depictions of the Three Pure Ones, Shi Bao is to the right of Dao Bao.

Also: 道德天尊 (Dào Dé Tiān Zūn), Heavenly Lord of Virtuous Tao; 太上老君 (Tài Shàng Lăo Jūn), Supreme Venerable Lord

## *Buddhist Influences on the Pantheon*

*Fó*

### A Buddha

Often stylized into houses or glyphs for sigils from Buddhist-based esoteric lineages. Use in sigils for calling upon the highest echelon of deities for assistance, especially in significant or momentous endeavors. Also used for protection sigils to block out malignant forces. Powerful when crafted into protection sigils to shield one with white light energy.

Zhou Dynasty          Qin Dynasty

Figure B.8. Seal script revolution of "Buddha"

*Ná mó*

### Na Mo

Not used by itself, and does not by itself denote a deity, but is as an honorific preceding the name of a Buddhist deity, such as Amithaba or Kuan Yin.

For example, 南无觀世音菩薩 (Na Mo Guanshiying Pusa), or, loosely translated, "Honoring the Venerable Bodhisattva, Kuan Yin."

Figure B.9. The Amithaba Buddha

# 阿彌陀佛

*Amítuófó*

## Amithaba

Celestial Buddha in the Mahayana sect of Buddhism. Called upon for invitation into his "Pure Land" realm of infinite, luminous Light. Vowed that those who call upon him during their lives will be ushered by him into the Pure Land, a form of paradise, in their afterlife. He is seen as a protector, and thus invoked in protection sigils. Also invoked to protect the practitioner in any work between different realms, especially when summoning spirits of unknown regions. Typically, to call upon Amithaba, the honorific Na Mo is used preceding his name, as in "ná mó Amítuófó," which is used as a mantra or dharani to raise a practitioner's connection to the Divine. Repetitive and routine recitations of "ná mó Amítuófó" are believed to help shield, protect, and safeguard a practitioner from evil, malevolence, and harm. Also, to invoke Amithaba, use the Amithaba Sutra.

---

*Guān Yīn*

## Kuan Yin

Full name: 觀世音菩薩, Guānshìyīn Púsà. Bodhisattva of mercy and compassion.

As venerated by the Chinese, Kuan Yin is depicted as female. However, she can assume any form when she descends to the earthly realm to aid those who call upon her. She demonstrates perfect, unconditional love. Kuan Yin vowed to go to the aid of those who call upon her in their darkest hours of need and desperation. She is invoked in sigils for healing, alleviating pain or depression, any form of suffering, and those seeking mercy or protection, and also for finding true love (not necessarily in a romantic sense, though certainly invoked in many love spells when the matter is getting desperate). Typically, to call upon Kuan

Yin, the honorific Na Mo is used preceding her name, as in "ná mó Guānshìyīn Púsà," which is used as a mantra or dharani to raise a practitioner's connection to the Divine. Repetitive and routine recitations of "ná mó Guānshìyīn Púsà" is believed to help shield, protect, and safeguard a practitioner from evil, malevolence, and harm. Alternatively (or additionally), to invoke Kuan Yin, use the Heart Sutra.

Also called Avalokiteśvara in Sanskrit and depicted as male in Indian, Tibetan, Sri Lankan, and Southeast Asian culture.[9] Repetitive and routine recitations of "Namo Avalokiteśvara" is believed to help shield, protect, and safeguard a practitioner from evil, malevolence, and harm, and help manage depression, grief, or loss.

Note: In Taoism, the bodhisattva Kuan Yin is commonly depicted as male.[10] The Lotus Sutra enumerates the thirty-three male and female forms that Kuan Yin can assume; Kuan Yin metamorphoses to accommodate whoever is calling for aid. In mythology, Kuan Yin is the Savior from Peril and is invoked to protect against fire, weapons, witchcraft, poison, demons, ferocious animals, venomous insects and snakes, and thunder magic.[11]

---

# 藥師佛

*Yào Shī Fó*

## The Medicine Buddha

A physician who cures illnesses and suffering. Invoked in sigils for healing. Also invoked by physicians to aid in their medical practice. Can be called upon to assist holistic health practitioners in their wellness work. Typically, to call upon the Medicine Buddha, the honorific Na Mo is used preceding his name, "ná mó Yào Shī Fó." Also known as the Medicine Master or Lord of Lapis Lazuli Light.

# 地藏王菩薩

*De Záng Wáng Púsà*

## Di Zhang Wang

A bodhisattva from Mahayana Buddhism, though he is also venerated in many Taoist traditions. He vowed to help end the suffering of hungry ghosts and release those trapped in hell from their torment. Di Zhang Wang is depicted as a monk holding a walking staff and a jewel empowered to fulfill wishes. According to myth, when called upon, he can send his dragons for protection, help to nullify bad karma, and assist with the recollection of past lives. Typically, to call upon the Di Zhang Wang, the honorific Na Mo is used preceding his name, "ná mó De Záng Wáng Púsà."

Note that in earlier Sanskrit texts, this bodhisattva was a young woman who tended to the karmic merits of those who were deceased or suffering. She then ascended to become a bodhisattva.

Also: Ksitigarbha (in Sanskrit)

---

# 文殊師利

*Wén Shū Shī Lì*

## Wen Shu

Full name: 文殊師利菩薩, Wén Shū Shī Lì Púsà.

Considered a bodhisattva in Mahayana Buddhism but a Buddha in esoteric Buddhism. He is the deity of meditation, inner cultivation, and wisdom. Often depicted with a lion, to symbolize the taming of the beast aspect of the self. When he is called upon, he can bestow the practitioner with prophetic visions.

Also: Manjusri (in Sanskrit)

*Bù Dài*

## The Laughing Buddha

The Laughing Buddha, also known as Bu Dai, is depicted as a laughing, rotund monk carrying mala prayer beads. Literally translated, his name means "cloth sack," to indicate his vow of poverty and his contentment with poverty. According to myth, prior to his Buddhahood, Bu Dai was jovial, eccentric, and deeply compassionate. It is believed that Bu Dai is based on a Chinese monk who lived in the ninth or tenth century.[12] According to regional Chinese folk religions, rubbing his belly will bring good luck (and dispel previously occurring bad luck). In folklore, Bu Dai is seen as the patron of psychics, diviners, and fortune-tellers, though he is also venerated as a god of happiness and a god of wisdom.[13] In the Japanese tradition, he is referred to as Hotei, and is seen as a god of fortune, wealth, and prosperity. After the monk attained enlightenment, the contents of his cloth sack were transformed into riches, which Hotei gives to those who invoke him through prayer.

摩利支天

*Mó Lì Zhī Tiān*

## Marishiten (or Dou Mu)

The goddess Marishiten is found across both Taoist and Buddhist traditions. Marishiten is a Chinese transformation of the Hindu god Marichi (also spelled Marici) and through that cultural transformation became a goddess. In Buddhism, Marishiten is a bodhisattva of the Light. In Taoism, Marishiten is synonymous with the Big Dipper Mother (斗母元君, Dòu Mǔ Yuán Jūn), or Dou Mu. Dou Mu is the Mother of the Great Chariot or Mother of the Big Dipper. The "Great Chariot" is the Big Dipper. According to Chinese mythology, Dou Mu, or Marishiten, is the mother of the seven visible stars of the Big Dipper and the two nonvisible ones. She is seen as the goddess to the god Shang Di. As the Big Dipper Mother—the Big Dipper commands all fates and fortune—she is called upon to alleviate ill fates and misfortune. She is called upon in craft for healing and medical treatment; safe pregnancies, fertility, and birth; and fighting inner demons or demon possession. In Taoism, she is referred to as the Heavenly Healer.

Figure B.10. The goddess Marici (Marishiten) or Dou Mu

# *The Eight Immortals*

*Bā Xiān*

## The Eight Immortals

Taoist equivalent of Roman Catholic saints. They were once human, but due to their greatness in character or acts, were immortalized and granted divine and supernatural abilities.[14] They are often invoked or called upon during Taoist magical rituals.

## 張果老

*Zhāng Guǒ Lǎo*

## Zhang Guo Lao

One of the Eight Immortals in the Taoist pantheon. He is arguably one of the most famous Fang Shi of Chinese history, a renowned magician, occultist, and alchemist, often depicted as eccentric and playful. Zhang Guo Lao is based on an actual historic figure, a hermit who lived in the remote mountains during the Tang Dynasty. His name is often invoked by necromancers. In craft, he is also invoked to amplify occult or magical powers. Canonized as one of the most powerful magicians and alchemists of all time, Zhang Guo Lao is invoked by magicians and alchemists for aid in magical or metaphysical work. Zhang Guo Lao was known to love wine and wine-making. According to mythology, the other immortals would drink his wine, as they believed it had healing properties. He is also invoked to help young families produce a male heir.[15]

# 鐘離權

*Zhōng Lí Quán*

## Zhong Li Quan

One of the Eight Immortals in the Taoist pantheon. He was a well-respected general in the imperial army during the Han Dynasty. He later became a famous alchemist. Legends of Zhong Li Quan involve him saving the lives of peasants and using magic and alchemy to help the indigent. He is a patron to men of the military, and also to alchemists, magicians, and practitioners of the sacred arts.[16]

---

# 呂洞賓

*Lü ˇDòng Bīn*

## Lu Dong Bin

One of the Eight Immortals in the Taoist pantheon. He is depicted as a scholar who imparts knowledge of the Tao. His sword is used to vanquish evil spirits and demons. From birth, Lu Dong Bin demonstrated high aptitude in poetry, the literary arts, philosophy, and metaphysical practices. Zhong Li Quan was his mentor. During Lu Dong Bin's apprenticeship, Zhong Li Quan asked the apprentice if he wanted to learn how to transform lead to gold, though the transformation would be temporary and eventually the gold would return to its original state of lead. The apprentice replied that he did not wish to learn an art that could potentially deceive people. After attaining his immortality, Lu Dong Bin continued to stay in the earthly realm to help those who invoke his name. He is often invoked for banishing spells, exorcisms, or to dispel evil or malignant energies. He is a patron for all healers, the literati, and practitioners of high ceremonial magic.[17]

# 何仙姑
*Hé Xiān Gū*

## He Xian Gu

One of the Eight Immortals in the Taoist pantheon. Her lotus flower is said to help heal the sick and cure illness. Thus, she is often invoked for health and wellness sigils. Before becoming an immortal, He Xiang Gu was believed to be able to tell people's fortunes and perform divination. Thus, she is often called upon by fortune-tellers and diviners. He Xian Gu is also a patron of women.[18]

---

# 李鐵拐
*Lǐ Tiě Guǎi*

## Li Tie Guai

One of the Eight Immortals in the Taoist pantheon. Legend has it that Lao Tzu descended to earth to become Li Tie Guai's mentor. Li attained great abilities in magic, alchemy, and the metaphysical arts. Li carries a gourd filled with a magical elixir that can help alleviate suffering and cure any illness. He is said to be benevolent to the poverty-stricken, the desperate, the indigent, and those most in need. He is often invoked in times of desperation and great suffering. Li Tie Guai is a patron of medical doctors and physicians, though he is often invoked by Taoist practitioners of craft to assist in magical work on behalf of the poor and downtrodden.[19]

---

# 曹國舅
*Cáo Guó Jiù*

## Cao Guo Jiu (or Royal Uncle Cao)

One of the Eight Immortals in the Taoist pantheon. He was an upright nobleman renowned for his integrity. After experiencing ennui and disappointment at the immorality of his own brother, Cao Guo Jiu ascended up the mountains where he met other Immortals. There, he learned Taoist magic and eventually cultivated himself into an Immortal. He is a patron of nobles and the nobility.[20]

韓湘子

*Hán Xiāng Zi*

## Han Xiang Zi

One of the Eight Immortals in the Taoist pantheon. He was a seeker and practitioner of various metaphysical arts. Han Xiang Zi was born into the aristocracy during the Tang Dynasty, and he sought a more reclusive lifestyle, often playing a flute to himself. The Immortal Lu Dong Bin became his mentor, and through cultivation, Han Xiang Zi achieved immortality. Due to his talents with the flute, Han Xiang Zi is a patron of musicians.[21]

藍采和

*Lán Cǎi Hé*

## Lan Cai He

One of the Eight Immortals in the Taoist pantheon. Lan Cai He's gender is ambiguous. Lan has been depicted as male, female, and at other times, as intersexual. Lan is an eccentric, peripatetic youth who would perform songs and dances in town squares, collect tips, and then donate the tips to the poor. Others view Lan as insane, lacking propriety, or uncouth, but the opinions of others never mattered to this Immortal. Lan lived at peace with no earthly concerns. Lan Cai He is a patron of beggars, actors, performing artists, and restless wanderers.[22]

## *Deities of Folk Religion*

*Jiŭ Tiān Xuán Nŭ*

### The Enigmatic Lady of the Ninth Heaven

The word 玄 (Xuán) isn't easy to translate. It's commonly rendered as "mysterious," and so this deity is referred to as the Mysterious Lady or sometimes the Dark Lady. However, better definitions are "deep," "profound," "difficult to understand," "occult."

According to myth, the Lady of the Ninth Heaven (Jiu Tian Xuan Nu) descended from the heavens to teach military strategy to the Yellow Emperor, who venerated her as his patron goddess.[23] While "goddess" is the common English translation, in the pantheon she is not characterized as a goddess. Perhaps a better Western equivalent would be "archangel." The Lady of the Ninth Heaven is also described as having feathered wings like a phoenix. She is generally depicted as beautiful, fierce, wielding a large sword in her right hand, and by her side, a gourd. The sword symbolizes victory in combat and battle, while the gourd symbolizes health, healing, vitality, and longevity. Through her sword, the Lady of the Ninth Heaven has the ability to destroy, and through her gourd, the power to heal. She is called upon for victory in any form of combat or where strategy will be crucial. Since the Lady of the Ninth Heaven also has the ability to cast spells, sorcerers and diviners call upon her as a patron goddess of their esoteric arts.

Figure B.11. Lady of the Ninth Heaven

# 無極母

*Wú Jí Mǔ*

## Wujimu (or the Unborn Mother)

Wujimu, also known as the Unborn Mother or Eternal Ancient Mother, is venerated in regional folk religions. She is the personification of Void and Truth. According to mythology, Wujimu conceived herself, and then proceeded to conceive yin and yang, personified as Fu Xi and Nu Wa, respectively. The sects of folk religion that venerate her believe in equality between men and women.

---

# 臨水夫人

*Lín Shuǐ Fū Rén*

## Lady Water Margin (or Triple Goddess)

Lady Water Margin, also named Lady Chen, is venerated in the southern Chinese provinces and Taiwan. She began as human, a woman named Chen Jing Gu (陈靖姑), born in the Hokkien region of China.[24] According to legend, Lady Chen and two other maidens vowed chastity and ascended to remote mountains for Taoist cultivation. The three maidens achieved transcendence and have since become deified under a single goddess, the Lady Water Margin, though she is also referred to as the Triple Goddess.

---

# 龍母

*Lóng Mǔ*

## Long Mu (or Mother of Dragons)

"Long Mu" means "Mother of Dragons." Long Mu was born human, as a woman named Wen Long Ji (溫龍姬), and became an orphan after her parents drowned in a great flood.[25] She then came to raise five orphaned baby dragons to adulthood, who were loyal to their human mother until her death. Long Mu was later deified for mothering the five dragons. She is venerated as the goddess of motherhood, parenthood, fertility, and filial piety.

*Yǔ shén*

## Rain God

Also named Yu Shi (雨師, Yǔ shī), Master of Rain. Venerated in the southwestern region of China. According to legend, he was a shaman named Chi Song Zi (赤松子, Chì Sōng Zǐ) who saved his people from a severe drought by performing a water rite. He was later deified as a celestial rainmaker and became known as the Rain God.

*Fēng Bó*

## Wind God (or Uncle Wind)

Also named Fei Lian (飛簾, Fēi Lián). A trickster figure who controls the weather, in particular the wind. Used in craft to control the weather, conjure wind, or use the natural elements to play pranks on others. In some depictions, the Wind God is female, referred to as Auntie Wind (風婆, Fēng Pó) or Madame Wind, depicted as an older crone. Male or female, the Wind God carries the wind in a bag, and opens it to release the wind at his or her will. Thus, Fu crafted to invoke the Wind God include glyphs or requests for the wind bag to be opened.

# 護法神

*Hù Fǎ Shén*

## Custodian Spirits (or Guardian Angels)

Custodian spirits, the Chinese equivalent concept of guardian angels (at least according to me), come from folk religion but are integrated into Taoist craft and cosmology. Custodian spirits are supernatural bodyguards. There are custodian spirits assigned to every person, every place, every phenomenon. The custodian spirits answer to the higher deities in the pantheon. Can be used in Fu craft to identify your guardian angel and to commune with that spirit or call upon that spirit for help. It is believed that guardian angels do not actually interfere with the course of one's fate, unless one has specifically invoked that guardian angel and asked specifically for assistance.

## The Three Stellar Gods (Chinese Folk Religion)

Although commonly attributed to regional folk religions in China, the three stellar gods are also invoked in Taoist craft.

# 福星

*Fú Xīng*

## Stellar God of Prosperity

The deification of Prosperity. Corresponds with the planet Jupiter. Invoked to bring good fortune, prosperity, wealth, riches, and material abundance.

Also: 福 (Fú); see the "Blessings" section below.

*Lù Xīng*

## Stellar God of Affluence

The deification of Affluence. Corresponds with Mizar and Alcor, twin stars in the Big Dipper. Invoked to raise one's social status, affluence, and reputation and to bring glory, fame, or honor. Invoked for support in achievements and accomplishments.

Also: 禄 (Lù); see the "Blessings" section below.

---

寿星

*Shòu Xing*

## Stellar God of Longevity

The deification of Longevity. Corresponds with Canopus, the second brightest star after Sirius. Invoked to bring good health, wellness, well-being, and longevity. Invoked for the blessing of a long, healthy, happy, and peaceful life.

Also: 壽 (Shòu); see the "Blessings" section below.

## *General Honorifics for Invoking Deity*

*Shén*

## God (or Spirit)

Since the etymology of the character is "altar" (礻) paired with "praying figure" (申), this character is often included as a glyph to demonstrate veneration toward Spirit, toward the divinity behind a Fu's efficacy. It is also used in deity names to indicate the status of the deity as a god.

*Líng*

## Spirit

Used to denote any spirit and can be used in either invocations or summonings. Relates to the unseen metaphysical counterpart to the physical. For example, an oak tree that you see has a Ling, a spirit, and to summon the spirit of that oak tree, or in other words, to harness the metaphysical energy of that oak tree, a Fu would summon its Ling. The character 靈 is used in conjunction with characters, ideograms, or glyphs that represent the oak tree.

Figure B.12. Stylized glyph for "spirit"

Note: Even when a sigil does not contain glyphs for a specifically named deity, either of these characters, 神 (Shén) or 靈 (Líng), are still included as glyphs in the final design.[26] Figure B.12 is an example of stylizing the character 靈 (Líng) into a house to be used in a Fu sigil for summoning spirits. Inside the house structure would be the practitioner's stylized glyphs to identify which spirit is being summoned and for what purpose.

*Shén Líng*

## Deity or Deities; Divinity

Can be stylized into a glyph with a traditional Chinese character for one of the Wu Xing elements, sacred planets, or natural phenomena to summon the corresponding deities or spirits. For example, instead of using a name or identity from a specific culture, such as Thor or Lei Gong for the corresponding deity of thunder, a practitioner could use the character for "thunder" and then the character for "deity," combine them, and form a glyph.

---

*Xiān*

## Celestial Being or Immortal

Used to summon spirits, especially in regional folk religions of China. Can be paired with other characters to identify the particular spirit. It invokes the metaphysical component to the physical manifestation and is often paired with a noun. When invoking particular immortals from the Taoist pantheon, the character 仙 is used. Can also be a literal reference to a practitioner's endeavor for immortality.

For example, a Fu sigil crafted with the objective of facilitating an auspicious move from New York to Paris might call upon the immortals watching over Paris to oversee the Fu recipient's safe and harmonious arrival there. While that may sound absurd to modern practitioners, the rationale behind it is to draw the metaphysical energy emitted from a specific location, in this case Paris, and channel it in such a way as to bring about the recipient's objective, which is tied to Paris. The characters 仙 (Xian), 神 (Shén), or 靈 (Líng) can be used for such purposes.

# *The Four Guardians*

The Four Guardians are four deities of Buddhist and Taoist mythology who govern the four cardinal directions. All four of them are protectors of the earthly world and defenders against evil. Under each one's command is a legion of divine creatures who can be summoned for protection and defense. Also referred to as the Four Celestial Kings or Four Heavenly Kings.

I have opted to separate the Four Guardians from the category "Pantheon of Deities" because these Four Guardians, in traditional practices of craft, should be called upon generally, to raise the energy of the four directions and four seasons, as noted in point 10 in chapter 3.

| Guardian | Celestial King | Direction | Element | Season |
|---|---|---|---|---|
| 龍<br>Dragon | 持國天王<br>Chí Guó<br>Tiān Wáng | 东<br>East | 木<br>Wood | 春<br>spring |
| 鳳<br>Phoenix | 增長天王<br>Zēng Cháng<br>Tiān Wáng | 南<br>South | 火<br>Fire | 夏<br>summer |
| 龜<br>Tortoise | 多聞天王<br>Duō Wén<br>Tiān Wáng | 北<br>North | 水<br>Water | 冬<br>winter |
| 虎<br>Tiger | 廣目天王<br>Guǎng Mù<br>Tiān Wáng | 西<br>West | 金<br>Metal | 秋<br>autumn |

Table B.2. The Four Guardians or Four Celestial Kings

*Lóng*

## Dragon

In Taoist mythos and Chinese esotericism, the Dragon is the Guardian of the East; element Wood; the spring equinox. Supports, nurtures, develops, and nourishes. Use as a glyph in a Fu sigil crafted for raising power, attaining power, or gaining authority.

The dragon is a supporter of power, and ideograms or Fu Wen representing the dragon are often found in Fu sigils because the power of the dragon is summoned to aid the practitioner.

Also: 持國天王 (Chí Guó Tiān Wáng) in Buddhist and Hindu mythos. The symbol of the lute summons his legion of celestial and immortal musicians. Protector and guardian of arts and culture, artists, musicians, and poets.

| Shang Dynasty | Zhou Dynast | Qin Dynasty |

Figure B.13. Seal script evolution of "dragon"

*Fèng*

## Phoenix

Per Taoist mythos and Chinese esotericism, the Phoenix is the Guardian of the South, the element Fire, and the summer solstice. Brings growth, advancement, and innovation. Use as a glyph in a Fu sigil crafted for education, academics, strategy, cunning, increasing intelligence and awareness, health, and longevity.

Using the dragon and phoenix ideograms together in a Fu sigil represents eternal love, soul mates, or marriage.

Also: 增長天王 (Zēng Cháng Tiān Wáng) in Buddhist and Hindu mythos. Symbol of the sword summons his legion of dwarflike spirits. Protector and guardian of soldiers and warriors. Facilitates greatness in combat, battles, and war. The sword is a symbol of martial prowess.

| Shang Dynasty | Zhou Dynast | Qin Dynasty |

Figure B.14. Seal script evolution of "phoenix"

*Guī*

## Tortoise

In Taoist mythos and Chinese esotericism, the Tortoise is the Guardian of the North, the element Water, and the winter solstice. Hears every sound, utterance, thought, and prayer. Use as a glyph in a Fu sigil crafted for defense, war, stability, resilience, protection, shielding.

Also: 多聞天王 (Duō Wén Tiān Wáng) in Buddhist and Hindu mythos. Symbol of the parasol summons his legion of nature and earth spirits. Protector and guardian of kings, nobility, and the aristocracy. The parasol is a symbol of nobility.

Shang Dynasty          Zhou Dynast

Figure B.15. Seal script evolution of "tortoise"

---

*Hǔ*

## Tiger

Per Taoist mythos and Chinese esotericism, the Tiger is the Guardian of the West, the element Metal, and the autumn equinox. Sees every sight, act, deed, gesture, and movement. Use as a glyph in a Fu sigil crafted for offense, war, strength, courage.

Also: 廣目天王 (Guǎng Mù Tiān Wáng) in Buddhist and Hindu mythos. Symbol of the snake summons his legion of powerful serpents. Protector and guardian against evildoing, demons, malicious acts, and temptation.

Shang Dynasty          Zhou Dynasty          Qin Dynasty

Figure B.16. Seal script evolution of "tiger"

## *The Four Directional Deities*

Expression of the four compass directions varies regionally. In ritual, the common custom is to identify the four directions by the Four Guardians or Four Celestial Kings. In folk religion, four particular often venerated deities are attributed to the four directions, which I refer to as the four directional deities. A practitioner may find that one of the four directional deities resonates most strongly and dedicate him- or herself to that deity. In turn, the practitioner's craft might become specialized in the craft correspondences of that deity.

For example, a practitioner dedicated to Xi Wang Mu, or Queen Mother of the West, a shamanic dark goddess of war, death, immortality, and creation and destruction, might set up a westward altar honoring the Queen Mother, celebrate the goddess during the autumnal equinox, and work primarily with the metaphysical energies that correspond with the dark goddess.

*Dōng Wáng Gōng*

### Grand Duke of the East

The Grand Duke of the East represents the principle of divine yang and is said to be married to the Queen Mother of the West, who is the divine yin. The Grand Duke of the East oversees the registry of immortals, the Taoist practitioners who have become ascended masters. He is also in charge of Man in the trinity of Heaven, Earth, and Man, and is thus connected to all human activity, in particular the rise of human civilizations. In craft, the Grand Duke of the East can be invoked for communion with other ascended masters, one's ancestors, and also for spell-crafting related to wealth, prosperity, and property. The Grand Duke of the East is at his most empowered state for invocations during the spring equinox.

Direction: East

Wu Xing: Wood

Season: Spring

Planet: Jupiter

# 祝融

*Zhù Róng*

## Zhurong, God of the Southern Fire

Zhurong is the god of fire and is thus connected with cooking, technology, and light. He began life as a man named Li (黎, Lí) who was born with a red face and a hot temper. Li was quick-witted, intelligent, ambitious, and possessed an unmatched skill at working with fire. According to myth, a great battle was fought between the god of fire, Zhurong, and the god of water, Gong Gong (共工, Gòng Gōng), ending with the god of fire defeating the god of water. Upset about his defeat, the water god committed suicide. His death resulted in the unleashing of a great flood upon the earth, causing great destruction.

The same name, Zhurong, and a deity or immortal of the south also corresponds with a female, traced back to Lady Zhurong from the fourteenth-century novel *Romance of the Three Kingdoms*. In the novel, Lady Zhurong was a warrior who led an army and fought battles alongside her husband, a chieftan of one of ancient China's southern tribes. Lady Zhurong was said to be a master at flying daggers. In some folk traditions, she became immortalized as the directional deity of the south, and thus there are practitioners who express the deity of the south as a goddess. In other tellings of the myth, Lady Zhurong is a descendant of the god Zhurong and it is because of that divine lineage that she possessed such great warrior skills.

In craft, Zhurong can be invoked for success in litigation, conquest, glory, success in battle, attaining honors and accolades, and for seeing through ambitious endeavors. The deity is at the most empowered state for invocations during the summer solstice.

Also: 重黎 (Zhòng Lí)

Direction: South

Wu Xing: Fire

Season: Summer

Planet: Mars

*Běi Dì*

## Bei Di, God of the North

Note the earlier entry for Xuan Wu, the Enigmatic Warrior God, under "Taoist Celestial Beings" in the "Pantheon of Deities." While the god of the north is Xuan Wu in some folk traditions, in others he is known as Bei Di, with similar mythological narratives and metaphysical correspondences as Xuan Wu. Bei Di oversees all matters of conquest. In craft, Bei Di can be invoked for career advancement or spell-crafting involving work, career, or professional matters. He is also invoked as the patron god of practitioners following certain magical or folk traditions from the north. Bei Di is at his most empowered state for invocations during the winter solstice.

Also: 玄武 (Xuán Wǔ), the Enigmatic Warrior God
Direction: North
Wu Xing: Water
Season: Winter
Planet: Mercury

---

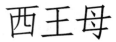

*Xī Wáng Mǔ*

## Queen Mother of the West

The earliest record of the Queen Mother dates to 1500 BC in folk religious traditions, with mythos predating Taoism, though she is often associated with Taoist magic. She represents the divine yin principle, while the Grand Duke of the West is the divine yang. The earliest depiction of the Queen Mother was of a dark, fearsome goddess who could bring havoc, chaos, and destruction to the world of Man when she was displeased. In the Taoist pantheon, however, she is given a milder depiction, a goddess of longevity, immortality, and magic, seated in her western celestial palace with many goddesses and female immortals attending to her. In one of her palace gardens grows a peach tree that not only bears the peaches of immortality but is also a gateway for shamans to travel between Heaven and Earth.

Female shamans and those who practice witchcraft often dedicate themselves to her as their patron goddess. Xi Wang Mu is a dark deity of the occult who endows her followers with the ability to see and travel beyond the veil. She is depicted as wielding formidable powers of both creation and destruction. The Queen Mother is associated with the animal spirit of the tiger, and in texts from the Zhou Dynasty, is herself depicted as having sharp teeth like a tiger's and an ornate headdress that conveys her high celestial status. Sui Dynasty depictions of the Queen Mother associate the Qing Niao (青鳥, qīng niǎo), a three-legged bird, with the goddess. The Queen Mother is at her most empowered state for invocations during the autumnal equinox.

Also: 瑤池金母 (Yáo Chí Jīn Mǔ)

Direction: West

Wu Xing: Metal

Season: Autumn

Planet: Venus

## *The Four Directions*

*Dōng*

### East

Directionality for summoning the Azure Dragon (Guardian) or Chi Guo Tian Wang (Celestial King). Repetitions of the character or a stylized glyph of "East" are used in sigil crafting to invoke the power of the Sun.[27]

*Nán*

## South

Directionality for summoning the Red Phoenix (Guardian) or Zeng Chang Tian Wang (Celestial King).

---

*Běi*

## North

Directionality for summoning the Black Tortoise (Guardian) or Duo Wen Tian Wang (Celestial King).

---

*Xī*

## West

Directionality for summoning the White Tiger (Guardian) or Guang Mu Tian Wang (Celestial King).

## *The Four Seasons*

*Chūn*

## Spring

When the Dragon Guardian is at its peak. In crafting glyphs for a Fu that indicate timing by season, stylize Spring into a glyph for the corresponding solar terms: Early Spring, Mid-Spring, and Late Spring. Can be used to indicate new beginnings, rejuvenation, renewal, the start of new projects or a new phase in life, fertility, or sowing seeds of growth.

*Xià*

## Summer

When the Phoenix Guardian is at its peak. In crafting glyphs for a Fu that indicate timing by season, stylize Summer into a glyph for the corresponding solar terms: Early Summer, Midsummer, and Late Summer. Can be used to indicate joy, happiness, love, harmony, peace and prosperity, abundance, plenitude, and celebration.

*Qiū*

## Autumn

When the Tiger Guardian is at its peak. In crafting glyphs for a Fu that indicate timing by season, stylize Autumn into a glyph for the corresponding solar terms: Early Autumn, Mid- Autumn, and Late Autumn. Can be used for reflection, maturity, maturation, understanding, wisdom, compassion, or for harvest.

*Dōng*

## Winter

When the Tortoise Guardian is at its peak. In crafting glyphs for a Fu that indicate timing by season, stylize Winter into a glyph for the corresponding solar terms: Early Winter, Mid-Winter, and Late Winter. Can be used in an offensive manner to cast a figurative winter onto another's life, to deplete, take away from, wither, or bring paucity to another. However, can also be used constructively for bringing clarity, insight, wisdom, compassion, and reflection through solitude.

## The Wu Xing Five Phases

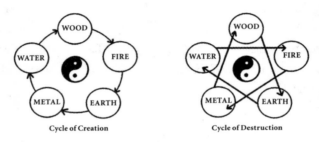

Figure B.17. The five phases of creation and destruction

The cycle of creation shows the interaction of phases that strengthen and support creation. It is represented by a circle; the concept of the circle for creation is often integrated into Taoist rituals. The cycle of destruction shows the interaction of phases that tend to weaken and attenuate toward destruction. Like the circle, the pentagram gets integrated into rituals for defense, protection, banishment, vanquishing malignant energies, dispelling negativity, exorcisms, and also in retaliatory craft.

Wood, Fire, Earth, Metal, and Water represent the five phases that all creation and destruction in the universe follow. Taoist craft is a form of metaphysical chemistry that utilizes the five phases to create or destroy as the practitioner intends. Understanding the correspondences of the five phases is to understand all aspects of that metaphysical chemistry. Tables 1.5 and 1.11 provides basic correspondences for the five phases; tables 1.6 through 1.10 explain how the five phases interact with one another, how they strengthen or attenuate one another's energies and potency.

*Mù*

## Wood

Artistic endeavors. Benevolence. Nobility. Pioneerism. Related professions: teaching, book publishing, writing, social justice, health care, policy making.

**Elemental chemistry:** Wood supports Fire. Fire empowers Wood. Wood and Earth are in conflict. Wood dominates Earth. In craft, aligning a Wood-based Fu conception or charging ritual with a strongly positioned Jupiter ("Wood Star") will strengthen the Wood energy.

| Shang Dynasty | Zhou Dynasty | Qin Dynasty |

Figure B.18. Seal script evolution of "wood"

---

*Huŏ*

## Fire

Passion. Power. Bravery. Courage. Useful in love spells. Also useful in spells for career or social status advancement. Related professions: corporate executives, government leaders, performing arts, design, technology, politics.

**Elemental chemistry:** Fire supports Earth. Earth empowers Fire. Fire and Metal are in conflict. Fire dominates Metal. In craft, aligning a Fire-based Fu conception or charging ritual with a strongly positioned Mars ("Fire Star") will strengthen the Fire energy.

Shang Dynasty                    Zhou Dynasty

Figure B.19. Seal script evolution of "fire"

---

*Tǔ*

## Earth

Loyalty, fidelity, marriage security, marriage commitment, lasting unions. Useful for seeking stability, reliance, or commitment. From a Western metaphysical perspective, useful in energetic workings related to business, commerce, money, finances, or attaining needed material resources. Related professions: law, finance, real estate, or highly technical and specialized fields.

**Elemental chemistry:** Earth supports Metal. Metal empowers Earth. Earth and Water are in conflict. Earth dominates Water. In craft, aligning an Earth-based Fu conception or charging ritual with a strongly positioned Saturn ("Earth Star") will strengthen the Earth energy.

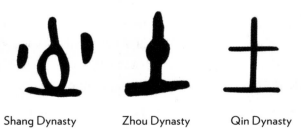

Shang Dynasty          Zhou Dynasty          Qin Dynasty

Figure B.20. Seal script evolution of "earth"

*Jīn*

## Metal

Justice. Righteousness. Musical endeavors. Legal matters. Court or government proceedings. Communications. Speeches. Public appearances. Related professions: law and policy, writing, rhetoric, academics, technology, music, art and design.

**Elemental chemistry:** Metal supports Water. Water empowers Metal. Metal and Wood are in conflict. Metal dominates Wood. In craft, aligning a Metal-based Fu conception or charging ritual with a strongly positioned Venus ("Metal Star") will strengthen the Metal energy.

Shang Dynasty       Zhou Dynasty       Qin Dynasty

Figure B.21. Seal script evolution of "metal"

---

*Shuǐ*

## Water

Wisdom, intuition. Compassion. Useful in spells relating to relationships, young romances, and friendships. Related professions: commerce in spiritual professions, international relations, public relations, diplomacy, any artistic field, entrepreneurs.

**Elemental chemistry:** Water supports Wood. Wood empowers Water. Water and Fire conflict. Water dominates Fire. In craft, aligning a Water-based Fu conception or charging ritual with a strongly positioned Mercury ("Water Star") will strengthen the Water energy.

Shang Dynasty          Zhou Dynasty          Qin Dynasty

Figure B.22. Seal script evolution of "water"

## *The Seven Sacred Planets*

In Western astrological tradition, as distinguished from astronomy, the seven sacred planets are the sun, moon, Mercury, Venus, Mars, Jupiter, and Saturn. Note how the Chinese refer to the five planets after the sun (日) and moon (月) according to the Wu Xing five phases.

*Mù Xīng*

### Jupiter

"Wood Star." Glyph can be used to harness Jupiter as an energy. In the alternative, the Western astrological glyph for Jupiter can be used. In sigil crafting, Jupiter is called upon for charity, benevolence, increasing opportunities, abundance, and physical health. Also used in sigils crafted for those in publishing, teaching, health care, or humanitarian professions.

*Shuǐ Xīng*

## Mercury

"Water Star." Although the Chinese associate Mercury with the Wu Xing element Water, the correspondences are similar to Western astrological attributions, with minor differences. In Chinese astrology, Mercury, and thus Water in the Wu Xing, represents wisdom, insight, knowledge, intelligence, and, of course, the communication and transmission of that wisdom, insight, and knowledge.

---

*Jīn Xīng*

## Venus

"Metal Star." Venus is called upon in sigil crafting for stronger willpower, confidence, greater discipline, and assertive force. It can also be used for those in the music profession. Also used in sigils crafted for justice, vengeance, retaliation, or sending out destructive forces.

---

*Huǒ Xīng*

## Mars

"Fire Star." Mars is called upon in sigil crafting for leadership, courage, bravery, and strength. Often used in sigils crafted for those in the military or corporate leadership positions.

# 土星
### *Tǔ Xīng*

## Saturn

"Earth Star." Saturn is called upon in sigil crafting for love, marriage, stability, loyalty, and fidelity. It brings stabilizing energy to craft. Often used in sigils crafted for those in the legal, financial, business, or real estate professions.

## *Twelve Symbols of Sovereignty*

The twelve symbols of imperial sovereignty (十二章紋, shí'èr zhāng wén) have been embroidered on the emperor's dragon robes since 2000 BC.[28] Historically, the twelve sovereign symbols could only be worn by the emperor.[29] Hereditary nobles could wear the sovereign symbols without the sun, moon, and stars. Second-tier nobles could wear the symbols without the sun, moon, stars, mountain, and dragon.[30] Thus, the number of sovereign symbols embroidered onto an aristocrat's robe indicated his rank.

In craft, the symbols of sovereignty are applied to represent the practitioner's sovereignty as a mediator between Heaven, Earth, and Man. As the emperor of medieval China was believed to be the mediator between Heaven, Earth, and Man (and thus the kings of the early dynasties were shamans), today the practitioner is that mediator.

Figure B.23. Symbol of sovereignty: the sun

## Sun

The sun represents the source of life, the source of sovereignty, enlightenment, and glory. Representations of the sun as a symbol of sovereignty often includes a three-legged crow (三足烏, sān zú wū), a mythical creature of Chinese lore that dates to 5000 BC in artifacts excavated near the Yangtze River.[31] The sun symbolizes the divine yang. It is often depicted in red.

Figure B.24. Symbol of sovereignty: the moon

## Moon

Representations of the moon as a symbol of sovereignty often includes a white rabbit busy concocting the elixir of life, or immortality. The moon symbolizes the divine yin. It is often depicted in a blue, green, or azure hue.

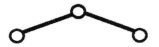

Figure B.25. Symbol of sovereignty: stars

## Three-Star Constellation

The three-star constellation symbolizes connection to the universe. It represents a practitioner's ability to manifest any intent and use his or her willpower to control the powers and energies of the universe. Represents the trinity of Heaven, Earth, and Man that is also representative of the collective cosmic Qi.

Figure B.26. Symbol of sovereignty: mountain

## Mountain

The mountain symbolizes the earth that the sovereign reigns over, denoting kingdom and domain. It represents the stability of reign and connection to nature. Use for grounding, stability, and protection. In Taoism, mountains are symbolic of the path toward immortality. Mountains are how Man communicates with Heaven, and are thus sacred locations. Corresponds with Earth from the Wu Xing.

Figure B.27. Symbol of sovereignty: imperial dragons

## Dragon

The five-clawed imperial dragon was sacred and could only be worn by the emperor. It was symbolic of the emperor's sovereignty. The dragon represents prosperity and transformation into higher consciousness, or the higher self. It represents the power and ability to defeat all opposition.

Figure B.28. Symbol of sovereignty: pheasant

## Fenghuang (Phoenix Pheasant)

The *fenghuang,* a mythical bird in Chinese lore that resembles a phoenix or pheasant, symbolizes beauty, elegance, dignity, arts and culture, and literary refinement. The fenghuang represents all the beauty that civilization and innovation have to offer. Also represents the animal kingdom.

Figure B.29. Symbol of sovereignty: twin bronze chalices

## Twin Chalices

A pair of twin bronze temple chalices represent piety, veneration of ancestors, and heritage. Symbolizes libations. In some renderings of the twin chalices, one will depict a lion (or tiger) for strength and courage, and the other will depict a monkey for intelligence and wit. Corresponds with Metal from the Wu Xing.

Figure B.30. Symbol of sovereignty: aquatic grass

## Aquatic Grass (Seaweed)

Seaweed represents wise rule, purity, and nourishment. It is symbolic of leadership, the way a wise ruler is pure at heart and nourish the people. Represents the aspiring traits of a leader. Corresponds with Water from the Wu Xing.

Figure B.31. Symbol of sovereignty: rice grains

## Rice Grains

Rice grains symbolize plenitude, harvest, prosperity, and fertility. It represents having the capacity to feed and sustain others. Corresponds with Wood from the Wu Xing. The symbol on the right is used as a glyph in Fu craft to represent rice grains, or more specifically, to manifest plenitude, abundance, a successful harvest, or fertility. The center house in figure A.11 in appendix A illustrates how the symbol might be used.

Figure B.32. Symbol of sovereignty: flame

## Flame

The flame symbolizes the zeal and love for life that one should have. It represents immanence, brilliance, and intelligence. Corresponds with Fire from the Wu Xing. Also corresponds with the summer solstice.

Figure B.33. Symbol of sovereignty: hatchet

## Hatchet

The hatchet symbolizes the ability to make the difficult and swift decisions that a wise ruler must make to punish those who have perpetrated wrongs. The hatchet is symbolic of justice and punishment. It also represents the military, the warrior class, and the might and power of the emperor's sovereignty.

Figure B.34. Symbol of sovereignty: Fo and Fu symbol

## Fo and Fu

The Fo and Fu symbol comprises twin stylized characters for the word "self" (己), back to back,[32] and implies the ability to distinguish the "good self" from the "evil self." It represents the discernment between right and wrong, moral and immoral, to know the difference between light and dark, when to create and when to destroy. Thus, the symbol has also come to represent divine justice, and the authority from Heaven for Man to take justice into his or her own hands. Corresponds with Fire from the Wu Xing.

## NATURAL PHENOMENA

The following represent some common natural phenomena called upon in Fu sigil crafting. In traditional folk religions, each phenomena is believed to be overseen by a spirit, and these spirits can be summoned to bring about the desired phenomenon. Summoning the spirit for rain in a magical working, for instance, was believed to help bring rain during a dry spell. Practitioners can summon these natural phenomena by invoking them through stylized houses. For literal summonings to bring rain during a drought, for example, the sigil is crafted specifically to bring it about. These natural phenomena can also be invoked as Fu Wen in glyphs for a figurative representation, for example, a stylized ideogram for "rain" can be devised by the practitioner and used as a glyph in a sigil to represent health and prosperity, and the bringing forth of abundance.

*Fēng*

## Wind

The character for Wind can be used in the context of its Ba Gua trigram, or used to call upon the natural phenomenon of wind and the spirits that govern it.

See also 風伯 (Wind God) in "Deities of Folk Religion" under "Pantheon of Deities," above.

Shang Dynasty          Zhou Dynasty          Qin Dynasty

Figure B.35. Seal script evolution of "wind"

*Wù*

## Fog

Can be stylized into either the top portion of a house or a glyph appearing near the top of a sigil to shroud the spell in "fog," or keep the spell invisible to would-be probing eyes. Used for shielding, protection, invisibility, and gen-

erally defensive or retaliatory craft. For such workings, is often paired with
glyphs for "spirit" (神), "magic" (魔), or "sorcery" (魔法).

*Yǔ*

## Rain

Used for sigils calling upon the natural phenomenon of rain and the spirits
that govern it. Can also be used as a metaphor for raining down abundance,
prosperity, health, and rejuvenation. Historically China was mostly an agricultural society, so many folk religion–based magical practitioners call upon
"rain" as symbolic of prosperity.

See also 雨神 (Rain God) in "Deities of Folk Religion" under "Pantheon of
Deities," above.

Shang Dynasty       Zhou Dynasty       Qin Dynasty

Figure B.36. Seal script evolution of "rain"

Léi

## Thunder

Used in Fu sigils enacted for punishing another, for those seeking vengeance,
or for implementing justice. Can also be used to call upon the God of Thunder (in "Taoist Celestial Beings" under "Pantheon of Deities," above). Typically
used in more forceful Fu sigils.

See also 霆 (Tíng, Lei Gong's Thunderbolt) in "Miscellaneous," below.

*Fēn Jiě*

## Decomposition

These characters indicate decomposition, dismantling, dissolving, or disintegrating. They are often used in destructive spells intended to break down or remove something.

*Cǎi Hóng*

## Rainbow

Symbolizes happiness, prosperity, love, strong familial and social bonds, peace, and harmony. It is often used in spells for ensuring peace, prosperity, and harmony.

## BLESSINGS

Characters for blessings or phrases that represent blessings are often stylized into Fu sigils to bring general luck, prosperity, and happiness.[33] They can be found in New Year's talismans, for bringing fortune and auspices to the coming year.

*Fú*

## Prosperity

Used as a blessing to raise prosperity, riches, abundance, wealth, and material plenitude.

See also 寿星 (Shòu Xing, Stellar God of Longevity), in "Deities of Folk Religion" under "Pantheon of Deities," above. Figure I.34 in appendix I provides ninety-nine variations of glyphs for "prosperity."

---

*Lù*

## Affluence

Used as a blessing to bring affluence, raise social status, achieve ambitions, ensure accomplishments, and gain fame, glory, or recognition for one's merits.

See also 禄星 (Lù Xīng, Stellar God of Affluence), in "Deities of Folk Religion" under "Pantheon of Deities," above.

---

*Shòu*

## Longevity

Used as a blessing to bring longevity. Can be used in Fu sigils for bringing health and wellness, to increase life span, or to increase the longevity and life span of a project or venture, such as the longevity of a business.

See also 福星 (Fú Xīng, Stellar God of Prosperity), in "Deities of Folk Religion" under "Pantheon of Deities," above.

---

*Xǐ*

## Happiness, Joy

Can be used as a supplemental glyph in a love spell or one for family protection. Brings joy, peace, and a calming sense of fulfillment.

*Xǐ*

## Double Happiness

This is not an actual character in the Chinese language but rather an ideogram often used during wedding celebrations. It represents a couple in happiness and joy together. Typically rendered in red ink. Used for love sigils, bringing good auspices to a newly married couple, for a wedding, or to encourage opportunities for marriage. The character is also referred to as Shuāng Xǐ, "double happiness."

---

*Chéng Gōng*

## Success

Used in Fu sigils for career advancement, professional success, to attain high marks on examinations, or to do well in school or work life. Can be used in any crafting where the objective is success and achievement.

---

*Fā Cái*

## Fortune and Prosperity

Used in crafting Fu sigils for wealth, financial gain, greater abundance, and more money. As a glyph, helps to activate the needed energies for income-generating opportunities and retaining wealth. The top part of the character Fa can be used as the top part of a house for a sigil to bring wealth, riches, and prosperity.

*Cháng Shòu*

## Long Life

Used as a blessing for a long, happy, and healthy life. Great in sigils crafted for the elderly.

---

身體健康

*Shēn Tǐ Jiàn Kāng*

## Physical Health and Vigor

Mantra for good health. Used as a blessing to bring good health and wellness. Incorporate into Fu sigils for healing.

---

永保壽考

*Yǒng Bǎo Shòu Kǎo*

## "Protect Perpetually; Ensure a Long, Peaceful Life"

Used as a blessing for an all-purpose, powerful Fu sigil that will protect and safeguard wellness and well-being.

---

健康

*Jiàn Kāng*

## Health; Healthiness

To be healthy. Used as an affirmation blessing in Fu sigils for health, wellness, and healing.

# 白蓮

*Bái Lián*

## White Lotus

Used as symbolism for rejuvenation, good health, spiritual wellness, calm, and peace. Use in Fu sigils for health, wellness, healing, and mental clarity.

---

# 治愈

*Zhì Yù*

## To Cure

Can be stylized into glyphs for Fu sigils to help alleviate suffering, cure a disease or illness, and generally bring relief from a specific ailment that is plaguing the recipient.

---

# 卻病

*Què Bìng*

## Cure a Disease

Cure an illness; prevent or treat an illness. Use stylized into a house or as a dominant glyph in a Fu sigil for healing, health, and wellness.

Also: 藥師佛 (The Medicine Buddha); see "Buddhist Influences on the Pantheon" in "Pantheon of Deities," above.

---

# 收成

*Shōu Chéng*

## Harvest

Blessing to bring about abundance and prosperity. Can be used in Fu sigils crafted for bringing about fruition in a particular endeavor or project. Can be used in agricultural sigils for a literal good harvest or for business ventures to encourage wealth, prosperity, and abundance. Used in any spell where the objective is to bring about harvest or fruition.

---

# 一路平安
*Yī Lù Píng An*

## Safe Journeys Ahead

Stylized into a glyph for a Fu sigil to protect its recipient during travel.

---

# 生意興隆
*Shēng Yì Qīng Lóng*

## Flourishing Business

Stylized into a glyph for a Fu sigil to bring wealth, abundance, and prosperity to a business or commercial venture.

---

# 恭贺新禧
*Gōng Hè Xīn Xǐ*

## "Good Fortunes and Luck in the Year Ahead"

Used for the start of a new year, often a sigil crafted during or before the New Year to bring good auspices for that coming year.

---

# 萬事如意
*Wàn Shì Rú Yì*

## "May All Go Well and Prosper"

Used for New Year sigils to bring protection and ensure good fortune in the coming year.

# 和氣生財

*Hé Qì Shēng Cái*

## "Harmony and Prosperity"

Typically used for New Year sigils, but can be used for any sigil to ensure happiness, peace, and wealth. Used for family Fu sigils to protect and safeguard an entire household.

Figure B.37. "A Bat Arrives from Heaven" talisman

# 蝠子天來

*Fú Zi Tiān Lái*

## "A Bat Arrives from Heaven"

Due to its homonymous sound with "fortune and happiness arrives from Heaven," the bat is used here as a metaphor for invoking fortune, prosperity, and happiness blessed upon the recipient from the Divine.

Figure B.37 shows seal script–inspired glyphs for the four characters, arranged in vertical order: top right, bottom right, top left, bottom left, in a descending motion the way a bat from Heaven would descend to bless one who is

here on earth. The four characters are then repeated to form a frame around the main glyph in the center. The frame of characters is arranged fifteen across in three rows, top and bottom, then three across in nine rows along the two vertical sides. Recall that fifteen is the magic number in the Lo Shu. Three calls upon the Taoist trinity. Nine is the number of Heaven. There are a total of 144 glyphs forming the frame, which numerologically emanate nine, the number of Heaven. Thus, a bat arrives from Heaven.

---

## 長命富貴
*Cháng Mìng Fù Guì*

### "Long Life; Wealth, Abundance, and Honors Bestowed"

These four characters appear together in stylized Fu Wen for a Fu sigil that will bring fortune, prosperity, and career advancement.

See figure B.38, where the four characters as glyphs are paired with a parasol, lotus, and lemniscate. The parasol symbolizes protection from inclement weather. The lotus represents health and well-being. The lemniscate amplifies the powers of the symbols in the sigil.

Figure B.38. " Long Life; Wealth, Abundance, and Honors Bestowed" talisman

# 大展鴻圖

*Dà Zhăn Hóng Tú*

## "Great Success and Achievement of Ambitions"

Used in Fu craft to bring success to an endeavor or project. Can be used in any manner and applied to any area of life where the success of ambitious undertakings is sought. Optimal in Fu sigils for academic achievement, examination success, and successful writing or literary projects.

Figure B.39 shows the four characters for "Great Success and Achievement of Ambitions" in clockwise order, starting at the top right. By itself, it can be used as a general good luck seal inscribed into a university student's school notebooks or textbooks to increase metaphysical energy toward academic success, or rendered into art that is framed and hung in a room as a form of "feng shui cure," to draw metaphysical energy into that room that will support the beneficiary's ambitions. In candle magic, the sigil as it appears in figure B.39 can be carved into the wax. Before a particular document, application, petition, or manuscript is submitted, one can perform a ritual during a waxing or full moon that includes tracing the sigil with your finger over that paper document. The sigil in figure B.39 is versatile and, when synthesized with a practitioner's strong intentions, can manifest power.

Figure B.39. "Great Success and Achievement of Ambitions" talisman

# TRAITS AND ATTRIBUTES

| Classic Fu Sigil | Chinese Meaning | Indication and Uses |
|---|---|---|
| | 孔孟好學<br><br>kǒng mèng hào xué<br><br>"Be as studious as Confucius and Mencius." | Optimal for students seeking to do well on examinations. Incorporate as a glyph into Fu sigils crafted for academic success. Typically used to assist students in their studies. Can also be sued by teachers, instructors, and professors for matters relating to academia, research, or innovation. |
| | 日日有見財<br><br>rì rì yǒu jiàn cái<br><br>"Every day, encounter riches." | Optimal for attracting greater wealth and material prosperity. Incorporate as a glyph into Fu sigils crafted for material abundance, wealth, financial prosperity, or business success. Typically used in Fu sigils for business and commercial success. |
| | 招財進寶<br><br>zhāo cái jìn bǎo<br><br>"Attract wealth and summon treasures." | Optimal for business dealings and commerce. Incorporate as a glyph into Fu sigils crafted for material abundance, wealth, financial prosperity, or business success. Typically used in Fu sigils for business and commercial success. |

Table B.3. Commonly found glyphs for blessings of success and prosperity

*Zhì*

## Ambition

This character is often stylized into Fu Wen to symbolize ambition, the manifestation of aspirations, and having dreams come true.

力

*Lì*

## Strength

Frequently found in Fu sigils, both to emphasize the strength and efficacy of the sigil and as a glyph to give the recipient physical or emotional strength.

強

*Qiáng*

## Power, Force

Used in Fu sigils to increase one's personal power or abilities. Used for raising energy, force, or power.

勁

*Jìn*

## Vigor

Used in Fu sigils to increase one's personal vitality and verve. Used for those suffering from fatigue, lethargy, or depression.

*Dǎn*

## Courage; Bravery

Used in Fu sigils for those going into combat, serving in the army or military, fighting a war, or who are about to enter a conflict situation or confrontation. Use in any energetic working to encourage bravery and fortitude in the recipient.

---

*Měi*

## Beauty

Used in houses and glyphs for Fu sigils crafted to beautify or render a recipient more attractive to others. Also useful in sigils for artists and poets.

---

*Yōu Yǎ*

## Grace, Elegance, Refinement

Used in houses and glyphs for Fu sigils crafted to render a recipient more attractive to potential lovers and mates. Often found in love spells for women seeking love and romance.

*Kāi Huā*

## Blooming Blossom

Can be used as a metaphor and invoked in sigils for development, puberty, encouraging one to grow into her own and shine, letting her inner beauty out so that others can see and be attracted to it.

---

*Huā*

## Blossom

Used in houses and glyphs for Fu sigils crafted to beautify or render a recipient more attractive to others. Used in beauty and attraction spells.

---

*Ài*

## Love

Render into a stylized house for a love and romance Fu sigil. Used to attract love, romance, and meaningful relationships into a recipient's life. Often seen as a glyph in love sigils. However, is not limited to romantic love. Can denote any nature or character of love.

*Qíng*

## Tenderness, Affection, Sentimentality

Can refer to love in general, whether between parent and child, between siblings, or between friends. Can be used in Fu sigils to nurture and maintain a current relationship or to reignite passion in a couple. Can also be used in Fu crafted for friendships, sisterhood, or to nurture positive affections between people in a social setting.

---

*Ài Qíng*

## Romantic Love

Used to denote lovers' love. This term would be reserved to indicate the sentimentality and affections between lovers.

---

*Xīn*

## Heart

Can be used in any Fu sigil that involves emotions, sentimentality, love, family, or relationships. Can encourage the recipient to be more heartfelt and sincere. Note also the history of heart symbolism: in Chinese lore, the heart is the palace of the inner deity who rules the entire body, the seat of spiritual intelligence. The heart was believed to be the seat of intellect.[34]

*Shàn*

## Benevolence

Often used in conjunction with sigils invoking Kuan Yin. Can be used in protection sigils that invoke Kuan Yin or any sigil that seeks to maintain the peace, light, and prosperity of a home. Can also be used in a sigil to encourage benevolence, charity, and kindness in someone.

Shang Dynasty       Zhou Dynasty I       Zhou Dynasty II       Qin Dynasty

Figure B.40. Seal script evolution of "benevolence"

*Jīng*

## Skill, Refinement

Used in Fu sigils cast for work promotions, career advancement, and raising one's professioval status. Can be used to improve business and commerce.

明

*Míng*

## Bright

Note that the character is the characters for "sun" and "moon" placed together. This character signifies brilliance and luminosity but also intelligence, wisdom, understanding, knowledge, and awareness. Used in sigils for strengthening mental clarity or mental abilities, or to excel in academics.

Shang Dynasty          Zhou Dynasty I          Qin Dynasty

Figure B.41. Seal script evolution of "bright"

*Zhi*

## Wisdom

Often used in conjunction with sigils invoking deities for protection and guidance. Can be used in any crafting that seeks to advance knowledge, especially knowledge of the craft, or spiritual attunement.

## MAGIC, CRAFT, AND SORCERY

*Mó*

## Magic; Craft

Often stylized into a house when crafting a sigil for summoning spirits or raising potent amounts of metaphysical energy for magical workings.

Figure B.42. Seal script for "magic" (Qin Dynasty)

---

*Mó Fǎ*

## Sorcery, Witchcraft

Often stylized into a house when crafting a sigil for summoning spirits or raising potent amounts of metaphysical energy for magical workings, especially when the practitioner identifies as a sorcerer or witch.

---

法術

*Fǎ Shù*

## A Spell

Can be stylized into an all-purpose house for sigil crafting that frames the sigil as casting a particular spell. In the context of esoteric Taoism, the term means the craft of Taoist magic.

---

*Wū*

## Witch, Shaman

Often used as a signature or identifying mark on a Fu sigil to denote that the author of that sigil identifies as a witch or shaman. Stylized into a house when crafting a sigil for raising potent amounts of metaphysical energy for magical workings. Note that there are distinctions made between a witch and a shaman. A witch is one who practices craft. A shaman is one who is able to change consciousness and, in effect, travel through the underworld or other planes beyond the physical human plane, to converse with spirits from these other worlds or planes.

Also: 觀落陰 (Guān Luò Yīn), a specific type of shaman who can enter a trance and descend into the underworld.[35]

| Shang Dynasty | Zhou Dynasty | Qin Dynasty |

Figure B.43. Seal script evolution of "witch," "shaman"

---

*Wū Shī*

### Sorcerer

Distinguishing this term from the preceding one for witch or shaman, Wu Shi implies a master at the craft, one practiced and well-versed in the art of magic, whereas Wu is more indicative generally of magic practitioners. Wu can be likened to witches, whereas Wu Shi indicates a high priest or high priestess. These two characters are often found in craft names, as a title that appears after the characters chosen for the practitioner's name.[36]

Also: 方士 (Fāng Shì), "Methods Master" or a scholar of alchemical and esoteric studies.[37]

---

*Wū Shù*

### Spirit Medium or Channel

While the term also means witchcraft generally, in the context of Taoist magical practice, Wu Shu is more specific, and refers to one who is a medium, who possesses the ability to channel spirits, ghosts, and otherworldly entities. The Wu Shu's craft involves deities or spirits entering or possessing the practitioner's body.

Also: 童乩 (Tóng Jī), a medium.[38] A Tong Ji is one who, during ritual or ceremony, has his or her body possessed by spirits or deities. These spirits or deities, through the Tong Ji's body, convey messages to the human world. A Tong Ji who crafts Fu sigils does so by means of automatic writing while in a trance state, which in theory is the writing of the spirit or deities possessing the Tong Ji's body.

*Gǔ*

## "Infestation of Malevolent Spirits"

Used offensively in crafting Fu to infest another's life with malevolent spirits, misfortune, hardships, or poison.

Also: 蠱道 (Gǎ Dào), the Chinese Taoist equivalent of "black magic,"[39] or "The Way of Malevolent Poisons" (note that 道 is the same as the 道 or in Taoism, or the Tao). Gu Dao the dark art of casting "poison spells," or crafting Fu sigils intended to poison another, be that physical harm or misfortune.

Shang Dynasty     Zhou Dynasty

Figure B.44. Seal script evolution of "poison magic" (Gu Dao)

蠱 毒 自 除

*Gǔ Dú Zì Chú*

## "Expulsion of Poisons"

Fu Wen rendered from this phrase[40] is used as an antidote to counteract any spells or curses attempting to infect one with Gu (蠱) or the "Infestation of

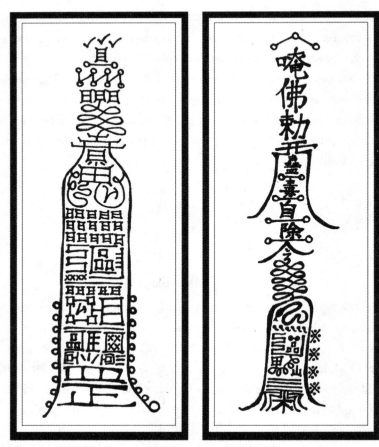

Figure B.45. Fu for the expulsion of poisons

Malevolent Spirits" and to counteract Gu Dao (蠱道).[41] Turn this phrase into Fu Wen for a Fu sigil to ward off evil intentions, the acts of enemies, malevolent attacks, and curses. In such a Fu, be sure to include glyphs for the Four Guardians (or equivalent), Five Emperors,[42] and the Ba Gua.

Figure B.45 shows two Fu sigils for the expulsion of poisons. In orthodox Taoist tradition, the specific poison that one has been infected with, the one who sent the poison, or the demon involved must be named and identified in the Fu design. In both Fu sigils in figure B.45, no specific poison has been named. Rather, in craft using such designs, the naming and identification is done during the charging ritual. Thus, the purpose of such Fu is to exert the force that a practitioner needs to expel the named poison or spirit. The sigil design on the left depicts yang energy with the "sun" glyph (日) overpowering glyphs for "ghost" (鬼) or the "ghost" glyph appearing trapped, held captive, or contained. The sigil design on the right invokes the Buddha. The top character, "唵," is Om, a sacred sound or mantra in Buddhist and Hindu traditions. In esoteric Taoism, Om is used as an incantation during spell-crafting to protect against evil spirits, dark or malevolent magic, and demonic activity.

Both designs would be considered a form of Talisman for Banishing Demons (see the entry below in this section), or 驅鬼符. Hence, you'll also see glyphs based on the characters 驅鬼. The Fu on the left in figure B.45 summons the collected powers of the practitioner, symbolized by the all-seeing eye (目) at the top of the Fu. Later, toward the bottom of the design, the all-seeing eye has entrapped a glyph (厶) reminiscent of the character for "ghost," or one of the root radicals in the "ghost" character. On the Fu at right in figure B.45, note the characters 蠱毒自除, which is the phrase "Expulsion of Poisons" inscribed directly into the Fu. The image of the snake shows the practitioner as a predator capable of overtaking the poison, or insects (蠱).

---

*Tūn Dú*

### Swallow Poison"

Used in offensive Fu crafted in the tradition of Gu Dao (蠱道). Often used in retaliatory craft to cause "poison," or harm and misfortune, to be "swallowed," or absorbed into the life of another.

---

*Shā Guǐ*

### "Vanquish Demons"

Stylized Fu Wen for these characters are commonly found on Fu sigils. Used to banish, exorcise, and dispel malignant energies, ghosts, or demons. Commonly found on Fu sigils crafted by exorcists. Can also be used to counteract malevolent craft where demons have been summoned and sent after another. Fu Wen stylized from these characters are used to neutralize (or rather, kill, as 殺 means "kill") such demons.

---

# 殺鬼降精
*Shā Guǐ Jiàng Jīng*

### "Vanquish the Demons and May Purity and the Beneficence of Spirit Descend upon Us."

Stylized Fu Wen for this phrase is used both to dispel malignant energies and bless the recipient with beneficent energies. Used in crafting powerful protective Fu sigils.

---

# 驅鬼符
*Qū Guǐ Fú*

### Talisman for Banishing Demons (or Hungry Ghosts)

The three characters used together indicate a Fu sigil that a practitioner has crafted for banishing or exorcising demons and hungry ghosts. In orthodox Taoist magical practice, a practitioner will have in his or her personal portfolio, or Book of Methods, at least one strong, well-crafted Fu sigil for banishing demons. That sigil is referred to as the practitioner's Qu Gui Fu.

---

# 入山符
*Rù Shān Fú*

### Entrance Through the Mountains Talisman

A type of Fu sigil described by the Taoist alchemist Ge Hong in the Inner Chapters of *Bao Puzi*.[43] Such a Fu sigil protects its wearer from all physical, mental, spiritual, or psychic malevolent harm. It is a protective Fu sigil and often considered one of the most powerful Fu sigils a practitioner can craft. A practitioner would design a version of such a Fu sigil for personal defense and protection. This book suggests that every practitioner devise his or her own signature Entrance through the Mountains Talisman.

## ANIMAL TOTEMS

Prior to 300 BC, a form of animal totemism was believed to exist in China,[44] though not in the same manner that animal totemism is often found in other cultures. Rather than worshipping an animal or claiming that a family line descends from a particular totem, animals were seen as signs and omens. Oftentimes family surnames were based on an animal,[45] with the hope that family members might manifest the same desirable traits and attributes of the animal. Also, lineages tended to claim to be descendants of a particular deity or supernatural entity, and that deity or supernatural entity was protected loyally by a particular animal.[46] That animal then becomes the one the family might honor, though it isn't per se the worship of the animal.

While I have not found significant documentation of animal totem references or symbolism in Fu sigil craft,[47] bringing totemism and the craft together would make sense, is aligned with the principles that Fu sigil crafting is founded upon, and conceivably, would strengthen the power of a Fu. Animals on Earth were assigned specific tasks from Heaven to assist Man. Thus, including Fu Wen for a selected animal would invoke the guardian spirit or essence of that animal to support the task at hand. For the more artistic, the actual animal can be drawn onto the Fu, in a cell sigil. Calling upon the power of an animal can also be done through stylized Fu Wen of the corresponding Chinese character. The following section offers a small sampling of possible animal powers to raise in a Fu. Animals from the Chinese zodiac are often summoned or integrated into the design of Fu sigils. The twelve animals of the Chinese zodiac are provided at the end of this section.

*Yàn*

## Swallow (Bird)

Messenger of good fortune, prosperity, happiness, peace, and springtime to come. Renewal and rejuvenation. For new beginnings, second chances, and budding opportunities. In Chinese superstition, if a swallow makes a nest on your home or business, great fortune and prosperity will come to you. (In other words, never disturb a swallow's nest if you come upon one on, near, or around your property.) A pair of swallows symbolizes enduring love and romance.

Figure B.46. Seal script for "swallow" (Zhou Dynasty)

---

*Yú*

## Fish

The fish symbolizes wealth, financial abundance, and having an abundance of resources. Depicting double fish is one of the eight auspicious symbols in Buddhism. It symbolizes riches and material plenitude. The fish is used to symbolize abundance, prosperity, and wealth. Use in Fu sigils crafted for generating money, income, riches, and financial security.

Figure B.47. Seal script evolution of "fish"

---

*Fú*

## Bat

The bat is a symbol of good luck and fortune. Emblematic of happiness, joy, and longevity. The Chinese believe that homonyms are auspicious omens, and the word for bat (Fú) is pronounced the same as the word for fortune and prosperity, 福 (Fú). Fu sigils that depict the character for bat five times represents the Five Blessings: (1) longevity, (2) wealth, (3) good health, (4) love, and (5) a natural, peaceful death.

---

*Māo*

## Cat

A cat is believed to disperse evil spirits. Since cats can see in the dark, a cat glyph in a Fu symbolizes gaining the ability to see or anticipate what your enemies are plotting. Can be invoked in Fu sigils for protection against malevolent energies, or defensive work; also used to "see through the dark," or gain greater perception and insight for a situation.

*Xióng*

## Bear

Animal totem for bravery, strength, and courage. A bear glyph symbolizes the ability to intimidate your enemies. Invoked in Fu for prevailing in combative situations.

---

*Chán*

## Cicada

The cicada represents immortality and is an auspicious omen for a good afterlife. Used in Fu for honoring the departed or the dead. Ensures safe travels through the underworld.

---

*Hè*

## Crane

The crane is an extremely auspicious symbol to the Chinese. The spirit of the crane can be summoned for blessings. When paired with Wood (木, Mù), the crane and Wood together symbolize wealth, riches, financial prosperity, and financial gains to come. When paired with another crane in a pair of cranes (鶴鶴), together they symbolize happiness, loyalty, and faithfulness in marriage, and bring love and romance. When paired with cloud (雲, Yún), the crane and cloud together symbolize wisdom, insight, foresight, and the ability to perform divinations. Used by practitioners to raise psychic abilities.

## CHINESE ZODIAC SIGNS

*Shǔ*

### Rat

Charming, innovative. The legend goes that before Buddha ascended, he wanted to summon all the animals, and he entrusted that task to the Rooster and Rat. The Rooster worked days, while the Rat worked nights. Instead of going on foot, though, the resourceful Rat asked for rides on the backs of other animals to get from place to place. The Rat totem is one for resourcefulness, intelligence, cleverness, and opportunities for making money. Rat personalities are believed to be incredibly talented at business, commerce, sales, and entrepreneurship.[48]

*Niú*

### Ox

Attainment of prosperity through hard work and dedication. The Ox totem is one for reliability, security, and stability. Positions of leadership and authority attained; a natural born leader; a self-made individual. Relied upon by all other animals, including humans. Dutiful, responsible, and full of honor and integrity. Traditionalists. Ox personalities tend to be well educated, faithful, reliable, and honest.[49]

*Hǔ*

### Tiger

Power, passion, and bravery. The Tiger is rebellious, unpredictable, and commands respect (even fear) from all. Tiger personalities are formidable offensive fighters. They possess incredible ability for strategy and war. The Tiger is a warrior who fights for social causes and justice. Possesses a vibrant personality. The Tiger totem is one for courage, strength, power, fight, and an indomitable spirit.[50]

---

*Tù*

## Rabbit

Graceful, beautiful, kind, sensitive, and diplomatic. Innately fortunate. The Rabbit is a totem symbolic of longevity and prosperity. The Rabbit derives its essence from the moon. Promise of a tranquil life. Scholarly. A great animal totem for those in fields of law, government, academics, or research. The Rabbit is also lucky in financial transactions. Can be diabolically cunning and uses the mind to outwit opponents rather than physical strength. Refined, comely, with impeccable manners.[51]

---

*Lóng*

## Dragon

Magnificence. Magnanimous. Enchanting. Equally eccentric and dogmatic. A proud aristocrat; noble, powerful, formidable. Great potential for accomplishment. The Dragon totem is used when seeking greatness or when in pursuit of high ambitions. The Dragon totem is the guardian of wealth and power, and calling upon the Dragon for support can bring great strength, a greater likelihood for success, and achievement of the purpose or mission.[52]

*Shé*

## Snake

Great wizard, master magician, philosopher, and theologian. Snake personalities wield tremendous inner power, psychic or intuitive abilities, and often leads a life that feels quite karmic. Snakes leave great first impressions; often the life of a party; beautiful in appearance; charismatic; and influential. The Snake totem has a strong supernatural essence and possesses great potential for magic and power. A pillar of strength.[53]

---

*Mǎ*

## Horse

Use as an animal totem for popularity and seeking to gain high social favors. The Horse is beloved by all, has few enemies, is naturally athletic with great prowess, and is full of high spirits. The Horse is performance-oriented and success-driven. Fiercely independent, willful, and confident. Also, the Horse is a quintessential multitasker.[54]

---

*Yáng*

## Sheep

The Sheep has a strong yin quality and is sincere, mild-mannered, gentle, and compassionate. The Sheep totem can be used for motherhood and patronage. The Sheep is often the beneficiary of fortunes and gifts from others. The Sheep is intelligent and uses soft skills to obtain what he or she wants.[55]

*Hóu*

## Monkey

The most intelligent of animals; quick-witted and clever. The Monkey is an inventor, an innovator, adaptable to changes, and quick on the feet. Often a jack of all trades, no, a master of all trades. The Monkey is highly skilled in many areas and is born with many talents. Use the Monkey totem to harness multiple talents and abilities at once or to harness cleverness and wit. A Monkey never ceases improvement and is constantly and consistently raising more and more power, further developing his or her talents and abilities.[56]

---

*Jī*

## Rooster

Dauntless, with a hero complex. The Rooster is physically attractive to all and gains the attention of many admirers. Acute, meticulous, organized, and alert. Use the Rooster totem for success in public performances, to gain influence over others, and for leadership or executive success. The Rooster totem can also be used to gain early success or to achieve more during the earlier stages of development, as the Rooster personality is incredibly precocious.[57]

---

*Gǒu*

## Dog

Considered the most likeable sign in the Chinese zodiac. The Dog represents honesty, loyalty, and integrity. Use the Dog totem for success and achievement in humanitarian endeavors. The Dog personality is a peacemaker and one who champions social justice. The Dog personality is a good judge of character and knows who to trust and who to avoid. Use the Dog totem for resilience, to never be without adequate resources, and to gain the admiration and trust of others.[58]

*Zhū*

## Boar

The Boar personality is gallant and stalwart, full of valiance and nobility. There are no pretenses about the Boar. Use the Boar totem for peace and harmony for the home and hearth, and for ensuring happiness. The Boar is a symbol of joy, well-being, and jubilation. The Boar also represents old-fashioned chivalry. The Boar personality is amiable and resilient, and while not a fighter, will put up an incredible fight and defeat opponents when pushed into the fight. The Boar can bring triumph and endurance to an undertaking.[59]

## CHINESE RADICALS

Traditional Chinese characters are based on radicals, which are graphical renderings with given meanings that indicate the subject matter or theme of the full character. For example, the Chinese radical 目 (Mù), meaning "eye," when integrated with a character, indicates that the subject matter or theme of the character relates to the eyes, sight, insight, or foresight. Thus, the character 見 (Jiàn) means "see," the character 看 (Kàn) means "look," and the characters 預 知 (Yù Zhī) mean "foresight" or possessing knowledge in advance. All these characters have the radical 目 (Mù), meaning "eye."

Likewise, Chinese radicals can be used in Fu sigil crafting, either rendered stylistically into the house or integrated into a glyph. In a Fu sigil, the radical becomes an indicator, just as it would be in the construction of Chinese characters.

Figure B.48 shows a Fu sigil that incorporates the radical 士 (Shì, "scholar") into the house design to indicate that the sigil is crafted for academic suc-

Figure B.48. Sigil with "scholar" and "eye" radicals

cess. The Fu consists of glyphs for the scholar radical, book (書), brilliance or intelligence (明), and the eye radical (目) to represent full sight, foresight, and insight. Note that as it appears here, the sigil is incomplete. The blank space underneath the bell shape at the base of the Fu must be filled with customized glyphs to indicate the specific academic or literary endeavor that the Fu is being crafted for.

Recall also the Fu sigil on the right in figure 1.4, showing a design that incorporates the radical 弓 (Gōng, "bow") for reverence to the invoked deity. Stylized glyphs of that radical are also seen in figure 2.2 as well. Stylized delineations of the radical are common in invocation sigils for high deity. Recall figures 4.2 and 4.4 which based the house design on the radical 金 (Jīn, "gold," though it also represents the element Metal from the Wu Xing). These are examples of how Chinese radicals can be incorporated into Fu sigil design.

*Hēi*

## Black

Used to draw in yin energy. Often found stylized as glyphs in traditional Fu for summoning ghosts or those from the underworld. Can also be used for cloaking or to keep one from seeing or discovering something you want to keep hidden.

---

*Chē*

## Carriage, Car

Used in travel protection sigils. Optimal for stylizing into a house or glyph for a sigil crafted to protect against car or motorcycle accidents. After the sigil is charged and activated, can be left in the glove compartment of a motor vehicle. Figure 4.17 is a travel protection sigil. Inscribed at the top inside the bell-shaped form of the house is the ancient seal script for 車. Figure B.59, below, provides the evolution of script for 車, "carriage" or "car."

---

*Dǎi*

## Death

Typically used in offensive or malevolent craft. Even though death itself does not bear a negative connotation, the way this radical is used in Fu craft often bears a negative connotation. Generally purports ill will or a wicked subtext when used in craft.

*Hù*

## Door, Household

Used in home protection sigils. Stylize into a house or glyph for a sigil empowered to protect a household. The completed and activated Fu can then be left by the family hearth or by the front door underneath a doormat; or four of the same Fu can be cast and buried at the four corners of the home's perimeter.

*Mù*

## Eye

Denotes the all-seeing eye. Used to see, whether with physical sight or psychic sight. Brings clarity and insight. Can be used in craft for psychics or fortunetellers to improve their foresight or maintain intuitive clarity.

Shang Dynasty        Zhou Dynasty        Qin Dynasty

Figure B.49. Seal script evolution of "all-seeing eye"

*Mén*

## Gate

Used in home protection sigils or to open portals or gateways to other planes. Stylized into a house or glyph for a sigil empowered to protect a household. The completed and activated Fu can then be left by every door or entranceway to the home. The character is used to protect entranceways and gateways. Note that it can also be used by shamans who traverse other planes. Stylized as a house, can serve as the foundation of a Fu for shamans who enter different metaphysical or supernatural worlds.

*Guǐ*

## Ghost

Frequently found on Fu sigils for summoning ghosts, exorcising or banishing ghosts, or any craft that involves lesser spirits or the deceased. Paired with dominant yang energy, for example, glyphs of the traditional Chinese character for "sun" (日), as seen in many traditional Fu craft, often indicates exorcism, banishment, or dispelling ghosts from an area. Paired with dominant yin energy, the Fu is one for inviting, conjuring, or communing with ghosts.

*Chóng*

## Insect

Note that the radical is found in the Chinese character for "poison." See the "Magic, Craft, and Sorcery" section above. Is often used in retaliatory craft or offensive magic to bring harm or infestation of misfortune onto another.

Figure B.50. Seal script evolution of "insect"

Shang Dynasty          Qin Dynasty

玉

*Yù*

## Jade

Used in several contexts. Can be a beacon for invoking the Jade Emperor through a Fu, or it can be a standalone symbol for prosperity or good health.

---

口

*Kǒu*

## Mouth

Used to denote intake. When paired with glyphs for poison or symbols of malevolent infestation of misfortune, the mouth glyph is used to essentially force the misfortune into the mouth of the victim. When paired with glyphs for healing, the mouth glyph is used to encourage the healing energy into the recipient and to encourage intake of the energy that is being generated and harnessed by the sigil.

---

*Bo*

## Mysticism; Prophecy

Used in Fu sigils to help facilitate prophecies or revelations. Use in Fu crafted for diviners or mystics to help with their work. Can also be used to indicate connection to the Divine.

*Shì*

## Scholar

Used in sigils crafted for academic or test-taking success. Can also be used by professors, teachers, or researchers to assist with their academic-related projects. Helps to generate greater intellectual clarity. Can be used in a sigil to support a writer or researcher with a literary project.

---

*Chè*

## Sprout

Used to grow, nourish, or encourage development. Often found in Fu with "Wood" from the Wu Xing. Helps a project, venture, or aspiration grow roots and grow shoots. Used to denote beginnings and initiations.

---

*Bāo*

## Wrap

Used to protect. Glyphs that are placed inside the stylized radical are protected by the symbolic defensive wall created by this radical.

## MISCELLANEOUS

*Tíng*

### Lei Gong's Thunderbolts

Used to vanquish demons and quell malignant energies. Also used in retaliatory craft or magic, to send vengeful thunderbolts of harm or misfortune toward one's adversaries. Most commonly found in Fu sigils crafted in thunder magic traditions.

Zhou Dynasty          Qin Dynasty

Figure B.51. Seal script evolution of "thunderbolts"

聖旨

*Shèng Zhǐ*

### Holy Decree

These two characters together are often found on Fu sigils to indicate the divine authority of the sigil's instructions. The word is translated as "holy decree" or "sacred decree," indicating that authority comes from the Divine. Practitioners may commission stamps with these characters (typically vertically) and then stamp their sigils with these characters, in red ink to contrast a sigil rendered in black. Note how one of the houses pictures in figure A.1 in appendix A utilizes these characters.

*Zhǐ*

## Imperial Decree

Frequently found at the top of a Fu sigil in a summons. Indicates that the practitioner hereby summons a particular spirit, ghost, or entity to do the practitioner's bidding, with the divine authority of the identified deity.

Shang Dynasty    Zhou Dynasty    Qin Dynasty

Figure B.52. Seal script evolution of "imperial decree"

*Ling*

## Order

Frequently found at the top of a Fu sigil in a summons. It is seen throughout many of the historic Fu sigils pictured in this book. The glyph indicates that the practitioner hereby summons a particular spirit, ghost, or entity to do the practitioner's bidding, with the divine authority of the identified deity. Typically found in Fu sigils for conjurations.

Shang Dynasty    Zhou Dynasty    Qin Dynasty

Figure B.53. Seal script evolution of "order"

*Zhào*

## Summon or Call Upon

Frequently found at the top of a Fu sigil in a summons. Indicates that the practitioner hereby summons a particular spirit, ghost, or entity to do the practitioner's bidding, with the divine authority of the identified deity.

---

*Jūn*

## Monarch, Lord, Ruler

Often found on traditional Fu sigils, in various and diverse contexts, especially in Taoist lineages that are heavily reliant on the I Ching hexagrams in their magical workings or Confucianism-based folk religions. The character is found throughout the I Ching, or Book of Changes, as in 君子. The word 君子 can represent the Higher Self, and rendered into a Fu sigil to call upon the Higher Self or to manifest the Higher Self. Used alone (君), the character calls upon the Master of your Self.

Also: 君子 (Jūn Zǐ)

Shang Dynasty     Zhou Dynasty     Qin Dynasty

Figure B.54. Seal script evolution of "lord"

*Jīng Shén*

## Spirit

There are several meanings to this word, each one distinct and yet related. "精神" means spirit, but it also means consciousness. It refers to the psyche, or one's fundamental essence, or one's personal vigor. It denotes both spirituality and psychology. The characters are stylized into glyphs for a sigil crafted to help modify or improve one's spirit.

The Fu in figure B.55, for example, is crafted to help ameliorate depression. Fu Wen for 精神 are near the top of the sigil to invoke the recipient's spirit guide for assistance. Both Fu Wen and the three-star glyph representing the word "star" (星) are added to trigger achievement, ambition, and motivate an inner drive. Twin characters for "moon" (月), which represents yin energy, relating to lethargy and depression, are contained. The center boxy glyph represents both the "sun" (日) and the Chinese radical for "eye" (目), or the all-seeing eye, to bring insight and foresight to the Fu's recipient.

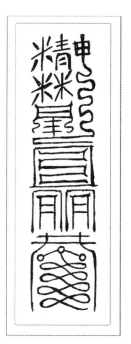

Figure B.55. Fu sigil for alleviating depression crafted with Fu Wen for "Spirit" (精神, Jīng Shén)

*Guāng*

## White Light

The character means "light" or "luster," but its usage in craft is the concept of white light. Used to cast a shield of white-light protection around a subject or invite in Divine light or higher-frequency energy. When crafting Fu outside religious beliefs, this character is an optimal one to include in your sigils for alignment with source energy, Spirit, or the Divine.

---

*Lián*

## Lotus

Used as a symbol to indicate the longevity and endurance of a sigil's magic. A lotus symbol is an amplifier. It will extend the life of a Fu sigil's efficacy.

---

*Shū*

## Book

A house can be designed based on the structure of this ideogram to denote a Fu sigil crafted for a matter relating to school, writing, publishing, literature, or academia. It can also be used as a glyph, one of the ingredients of the sigil.

Also: 文昌帝君 (Wén Chāng Dì Jūn), Taoist deity of literature and culture. See "Taoist Celestial Beings" in "Pantheon of Deities," above. Often invoked for sigils to pass exams, achieve high marks in school, or in any sigil for one who works in the writing and literature field.

Zhou Dynasty    Qin Dynasty

Figure B.56. Seal script evolution of "book"

*Kǎo Shì*

## "Taking an Exam"

For a sigil crafted to ensure high marks on an examination, these characters can be designed into glyphs to designate the subject matter of the sigil.

*Jiàn*

## Sword

Can be used as a supplemental glyph when invoking the Guardian of the South (see "The Four Guardians," above) to gain the authority to summon its legion of supernatural assistants. Can also be used in sigils seeking justice or vengeance.

刀

*Dāo*

## Dagger, Knife

Often used in Fu sigils relating to the martial arts, in reference to the Guan Dao (關刀), a classical weapon consisting of a pole and a blade. It is the weapon of Guan Yu, or Guan Gong (see "Taoist Celestial Beings" in "Pantheon of Deities," above), and so is often used as a glyph in any sigil invoking Guan Gong. Symbolizes strength in combat and mastery in the martial arts. Figure B.58 is an example of a stylized glyph that invokes the Guan Dao as the practitioner's metaphysical weapon.

Shang Dynasty        Zhou Dynasty        Qin Dynasty

Figure B.57. Seal script evolution of "dagger"

Figure B.58. Guan Dao
dagger glyph

*Qín*

## Musical Instrument

While the character itself does not mean "musical instrument," it is a character that appears in several words indicative of musical instruments, such as piano (鋼琴), violin (小提琴), or the *guqin*, a classical Chinese instrument (古琴), among others. Thus, in sigil crafting, irrespective of grammar, it is used to render Fu Wen that denote musicianship or musical talent.

車

*Chē*

## Carriage, Cart, Motor Vehicle

Used in Fu sigils for protection during travel, to protect those driving motor vehicles (cars, motorcycles, bicycles), and to safeguard against accidents or harm during travel.

Also: 輅 (Hé), Chariot

Shang Dynasty       Zhou Dynasty       Qin Dynasty

Figure B.59. Seal script evolution of "carriage" (car)

*Lù*

## Road, Pathway

Used in conjunction with Fu sigils crafted to safeguard travel by roadways, on land. Also used to indicate one's life path, and used in Fu sigil designs to ensure prosperity, happiness, and success along one's life path.

*Hǎi*

## Ocean, Sea

Used in conjunction with Fu sigils crafted to safeguard travel by water. For protection when traveling overseas.

*Cái*

## Money, Riches

Used to indicate money, riches, wealth, or valuable assets.

*Chéng*

## Multiply

Used in Fu sigils for increasing wealth and riches. Used to bring about greater fruition and gains. Often found as a supplemental glyph in conjunction with blessing glyphs for abundance and prosperity.

Note how the Fu in figure B.60 is simply a repetition of two characters: 財 (Cái) for riches, wealth, assets, and money, and 乘 (Chéng) for multiplying those riches eightfold.

Figure B.60. A basic "money multiply" Fu

Figure B.61. Energetic amplifier for conjurations and exorcisms

A stylized glyph for the Chinese character "ghost" (鬼) is incorporated into Fu sigils to indicate a conjuration or exorcism. While techniques vary from lineage to lineage and no all-encompassing rules can be taught, generally speaking, a dominance of yang energy accompanying the ghost glyph is indicative of an exorcism, whereas a dominance of yin energy is indicative of a conjuration or summoning. How the glyph is arranged can also be telling. When the glyph appears to be trapped, bound, or contained, the intent of the Fu is most likely for control over the spirit's will.

Figure B.62. Concluding glyph in
traditional Fu craft

The glyph pictured in figure B.62 is often found in traditional Fu craft, usually at the bottom base of the Fu as a form of concluding ideogram. For example, figures 2.1 and 4.3 illustrate application of the concluding glyph. The house on the left in figure A.1 and figure A.20 in appendix A make use of the glyph.

The glyph "罡" (gāng), an ideogram, is an astrological reference to the stars found in the Big Dipper, in particular the handle portion, the stars Alioth, Mizar, and Alkaid, as shown in figure 4.21. Thus, oftentimes a Fu sigil begins at the top with symbolism that calls upon the three-star constellation and closes with the 罡 glyph. See the left-most Fu house in figure A.1 for an example.

Beyond that, what 罡 means in the context of esoteric Taoist craft differs based on the lineage. The explanation provided herein merely represents the explanations I am aware of. The glyph consists of a root radical for "dish" (皿), inferred here as a reference to the magical tools of a Taoist priest. In the Song Dynasty, the Taoist priest would use the vessel for conjurations and exorcisms. Its incorporation here symbolizes the powers of the magus. Note that the radical is also seen in the word "poison" (蠱), from Gu Dao (蠱道), the traditional Taoist practice of poison magic that often utilized the alchemical vessel. Yet here, it is not a reference to poison magic. The radical 皿 is uplifted by the character indicating a positive, 正 (zhèng), which refers to integrity and moral rectitude.

Also, etymologically, 止 depicts a foot pressed up against a wall, indicating the end of a route or procedure, the conclusion. The character 正 is an affirmative or positive indication, and thus serves as a concluding affirmation of the spell's efficacy. It also takes five strokes to write the character 正, which represents the Wu Xing and the five fingers of the practitioner's hand, open, giving, and influencing. Recall the *Classics of the Esoteric Talisman*: "All manifestations in the universe can be generated by the practitioner's physical body, through the hand." Here, the character is illustrative of the practitioner's hand manifesting his or her intention. Thus, writing 正 at the bottom close of a Fu sigil is in effect a representation of "so mote it be." It is a concluding glyph that shows the end of the sigil.

Finally, the glyph is a reference to 剛風 (gāng fēng),[60] meaning a "swift, sudden, and firm gust of wind." The intent of that reference is for the order inscribed on the Fu sigil to be carried off with the wind, swiftly and with strength, to manifest the practitioner's will.

Figure B.63. Four directions protection glyph

In common use, the ※ is a punctuation mark, like a bullet point, indicating the start of a new line, or used as an asterisk. However, it takes on a different meaning in esoteric Taoist craft. In Fu sigil crafting, it is used as a symbol of divine protection. It represents the four directions and the four seasons, and is also a symbol used to represent rice grains, one of the twelve symbols of sovereignty. Thus, the glyph ※ is for protection and used in craft to manifest abundance or prosperity. It is also found in Fu sigils for exorcisms to ensure divine protection. The practitioner's intent is what empowers the glyph. As the X is drawn, the practitioner invokes Spirit, deity, or divine protection. The four dots are then drawn, and as each one is drawn, the directionality it represents is invoked. For instance, as the top dot is drawn, either the guardian of the north or south is invoked, depending on the practitioner's frame of reference. Assuming the top dot is south (Red Phoenix, and summer, the power to bring growth), then the bottom dot, as it is drawn, would invoke the guardian of the north (Black Tortoise, and winter, the power of clairaudience), the left dot would invoke the guardian of the east (Azure Dragon, and spring, the power of control), and the right dot the guardian of the west (White Tiger, and autumn, the power of clairvoyance).

Figure B.64. Thunder magic spirit summons glyph

Figure B.64 shows three variations on a thunder magic glyph that are typically inscribed at the top of a Fu sigil rendered in the Thunder Rites style of craft. Note the character 雷 (léi) for "thunder" stylized into each variation. Beneath "thunder" is the character for a summons or order, 令 (lìng). In figure A.1 in appendix A, see the left and center Fu houses for a sample application.

Figure B.65. Daoshi power cross

The Daoshi power cross pictured in figure B.65 is often found in traditional Fu sigil crafting as an energetic amplifier. It also happens to memorialize several of the Taoist principles from the *Classics of the Esoteric Talisman*. There is a specific order in which the lines of the power cross must be drawn by the practitioner, shown in figure B.66.

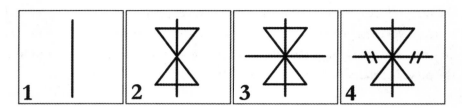

Figure B.66. Drawing the Daoshi power cross

Box 1 in figure B.66 shows the first step: a vertical line. It represents the practitioner's alignment with Heaven, the Divine, or Tao. It depicts universal or cosmic Qi descending as the practitioner draws the energy near to harness it for empowering the Fu. Next, as shown in box 2, the practitioner draws the two triangles. The two triangles symbolize Heaven and Earth meeting—Man taking from Heaven and Earth for triggering mechanisms, or to manifest the practitioner's intentions. The horizontal line drawn in box 3 represents the spirit world, and the practitioner's ability to now connect directly into that spirit or metaphysical world, after harnessing the powers of Heaven and Earth. Box 4 shows the two lines drawn on either side, representing the sun and the moon, or the god and the goddess energy—the divine binary.

Figure B.67. Ensnaring a psychic attack

Six spirals create a maze for ensnaring malevolent magic or energy, with Heaven, Earth, and Man symbolism to hold that malevolence at bay. Figure B.67 can be used as a glyph for a Fu crafted for defensive magic. If one suspects a psychic attack where hostile metaphysical energy, a hex, or a curse has been sent, a Fu sigil incorporating such a glyph ensnares and traps that hostile energy so that it cannot do harm to the otherwise intended recipient. Note the sample Fu sigil illustrated in figure A.14 in appendix A. It incorporates the glyph shown in figure B.67 into a Fu for warding off and neutralizing a hex.

Figure B.68. Xi Wang Mu, Queen Mother of the West

# APPENDIX C

# WESTERN SIGIL CRAFTING

**WESTERN SIGIL TECHNIQUES** can be integrated with Eastern Fu sigil crafting. Sigils rendered from Western traditions[1] can be made into powerful glyphs. A practitioner's seal can also be designed from a Western sigil. The following instruction[2] adopts the simple word method.[3] This appendix is a rudimentary explanation of Western sigils and is provided with the limited intent of offering ideas and inspiration for glyph conception in Eastern sigil craft.

### 1. Focus on your intention and envision the intended results manifesting.[4]

A well-defined purpose, will, and intent seem to be the first step of craft, whether you are talking about an Eastern or Western tradition. As you craft the sigil, keep that purpose anchored in your mind, and if you are visual, visualize it resting right at the point of your third eye, or that space between your two physical eyes, near the forehead. Maintain a vision of that purpose in that space, in your mind, as you proceed with the sigil design.

### 2. Write out an affirmation or phrase, worded positively, that will raise energy and command power.

A statement that represents the intent or outcome to be manifested is conceived and phrased affirmatively by the practitioner. Do not use negative terminology. In other words, instead of "I will not fail," phrase it as "I succeed" or "I prevail." The phrasing should also indicate absolute confidence that what is intended to happen will definitely happen. Phrasing in the present tense is suggested, though I see nothing wrong with future tense, so long as it is phrased in a way that demonstrates absolute confidence.

### 3. Cross out the repeating letters. Optional: all vowels can also be removed.

Here, I have found that texts on crafting Western sigils diverge. Some say to cross out the repeating letters only. Others note to cross out both repeating letters and vowels.[5] The practitioner is advised to use what feels most aligned with his or her purpose and practice. I tend to prefer removing all repeating letters and vowels so that only consonants are left.

### 4. Draw a box, and arrange the remaining letters into the box, in a design that resonates with you.

The remaining letters are then stylized in any artistic manner determined by the practitioner to create the sigil. For reference, a box can be drawn as the letters are arranged within the box to help the practitioner maintain a compact form. However, again, doing so is not necessary. It serves as a mere suggestion.

### 5. Remove the box and add amplifiers.

Like Fu sigil crafting, amplifiers are also added in the Western sigil crafting tradition. Stylized lines, triangles, and circles can adorn the sigil of letters that the practitioner has designed. Numerology also becomes relevant. For example, a set of three lines will call upon the numerological significance of three, for amplification and fruition. Spirals, as indicated in figure C.1, might be used to indicate a practitioner's path, meaning the right-hand path or the left-hand path.[6]

Figure C.1. Details in Western sigil craft

## 6. Sigil charging.

For sigils that will be used regularly as the practitioner's seal or as an empowered secret glyph that the practitioner will be using in craft with great frequency, the sigil itself should be charged and activated. If it is used as one glyph of many in a Fu sigil, then, at the practitioner's option, it can be charged following the ritual process of the Fu sigil and does not need to be separately charged.

Another approach to activating a sigil is to light it on fire, then set the burning sigil paper in sand. As you watch it burn to ash, visualize the intent and see it manifesting into life.[7]

# EXAMPLE 1: A PRACTITIONER'S SEAL

## 1. Focus on your intention and envision the intended results manifesting.

For this example, I will use the hypothetical practitioner's craft name, White Swallow (白燕).[8] The practitioner here seeks to design a sigil for that name, using the English lettering.

## 2. Write out an affirmation or phrase, worded positively, that will raise energy and command power.

In the instance of a craft name for a practitioner's seal, only the name is used, as follows:

WHITE SWALLOW

## 3. Cross out the repeating letters (optional: and vowels).

For this example, both repeating letters and vowels are crossed out.

W H T S L

## 4. Draw a box, and arrange the remaining letters into the box, in a design that resonates with you.

The five letters remaining in step 3 are arranged inside a box. The box is only used for reference.

Figure C.2. Sigil progress: inscribing
the letters into a box

### 5. Remove the box and add amplifiers.

Figure C.3 shows the resulting sigil, though no amplifiers have been added yet. Amplifiers are what stylize the sigil and also add energetic strength to it.

Figure C.3. Sigil progress: resulting sigil

In figure C.4, the practitioner has added the Western glyph for Air because the craft name White Swallow is Air-dominant. Additional amplifiers have been added, each one meaningful and symbolic to the practitioner and her intentions.

Figure C.4. Sigil progress: adding amplifiers

### 6. Sigil charging.

Here, since the sigil will become the practitioner's seal in all future Fu sigil crafting, the practitioner burns the sigil paper along with sandalwood incense to send the identification card up to Heaven, or the deity that the practitioner invokes.

## EXAMPLE 2: THE WORD METHOD

**1. Focus on your intention and envision the intended results manifesting.**
For this hypothetical, the practitioner will be designing a glyph for a Fu sigil that will benefit a recipient named John Doe. The glyph will be based on Western sigil crafting methods.

Here, the Fu sigil is to help John Doe manifest all of his New Year's resolutions. One of those New Year's resolutions is to be promoted to president of the company he currently works for. Assume the name of that company is Company. The practitioner will be designing a sigil according to the Western word method that will be used as one of the glyphs in John Doe's complete Fu sigil.

**2. Write out an affirmation or phrase, worded positively, that will raise energy and command power.**
The practitioner phrases the intention as follows:

JOHN DOE IS PROMOTED TO PRESIDENT OF THE COMPANY

**3. Cross out the repeating letters (optional: and vowels).**
In this example, the practitioner opts to cross out both repeating letters and vowels.

J H N D S P R M T F C Y

**4. Draw a box, and arrange the remaining letters into the box, in a design that resonates with you.**
Instead of using a box, the practitioner opts to stylize and arrange the letters into a circle, as follows:

Figure C.5. Circular stylized sigil

**5. Remove the box circle and add amplifiers.**
Once the reference circle is removed, amplifiers are added.

Figure C.6. Final sample sigil design

## 6. Sigil charging.

Since this sigil is going to be one glyph of many in a completed Fu sigil to be charged under the techniques outlined in chapter 9 and subsequently activated by the recipient, John Doe, through techniques outlined in chapter 10, the practitioner here opts not to perform any additional charging rituals specific to this sigil.

# LO SHU–DESIGNED GLYPHS

**IN ADDITION TO** using the Lo Shu for pacing rituals, as noted in chapter 8, the Lo Shu can also be used to design glyphs for a Fu sigil. Figure D.1 shows the Lo Shu square synthesized with Pythagorean numerology. With the Lo Shu, any word in the English language can be transformed into a glyph.

| 4<br><br>D  M  V | 9<br><br>I  R | 2<br><br>B  K  T |
|---|---|---|
| 3<br><br>C  L  U | 5<br><br>E  N  W | 7<br><br>G  P  Y |
| 8<br><br>H  Q  Z | 1<br><br>A  J  S | 6<br><br>F  O  X |

Figure D.1. Lo Shu square with alphabet correspondences

A word can then be spelled out and inscribed into the square, each letter representing the positioning of one dot in the final glyph. To illustrate, let's use the word *prosperity*.

| 4 | 9 | 2 |
|---|---|---|
| D M V | I R | B K T |
| **3** | **5** | **7**  ○ |
| C L U | E N W | G P Y |
| **8** | **1** | **6** |
| H Q Z | A J S | F O X |

Figure D.2. Glyph design
with the Lo Shu

First begins with a circle drawn in sector 7, corresponding to the letter *P,*
the first letter in the word *prosperity* (see fig. D.2).

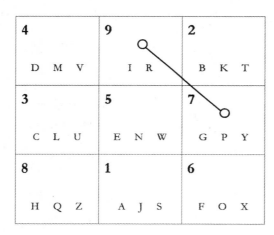

Figure D.3. Glyph design
progress: connecting the dots

Next, in figure D.3, the second letter, *R,* corresponds with 9. Draw a circle
in sector 9, then connect the one in 7 to the one in 9. That is the first line of the
crafted glyph for "Prosperity" using the Lo Shu.

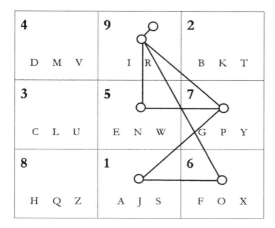

Figure D.4. Glyph design progress: recurring sectors

Continuing in figure D.4, O is 6, S is 1, then back to P in sector 7 again, then E is 5, and so on. Here, each letter is a new circle. Thus, a separate circle is formed for I even though a circle was already drawn in sector 9 for R. The Lo Shu square in figure D.5 shows the final sigil formed for "Prosperity."

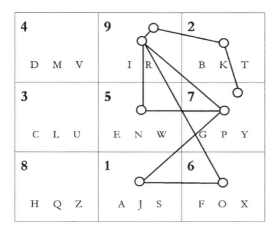

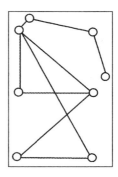

Figure D.6. Glyph for prosperity

Figure D.5. Glyph design progress: completed glyph

Figure D.6 is the glyph for "Prosperity" that can be incorporated into a Fu sigil, rendered from the Lo Shu square.

Your imagination is your only limit to designing glyphs. If you are artistic, you can draw animals to represent animal totems, if that is part of your belief system.

# APPENDIX E

# BA GUA AND THE I CHING

**THE I CHING**, or Book of Changes, is the heart of Chinese occult studies.[1] The text originates from the Zhou Yi, attributed to King Wen of Zhou,[2] and believed to have been authored by the shaman king sometime between 1600 and 1050 BC. As the story goes, King Wen combined the eight trigrams of the Ba Gua—the Later Heaven sequence—to form the sixty-four hexagrams of the I Ching, though today, the story is largely believed to be a myth, as there is no factual historical basis to confirm its veracity.[3] In the Han Dynasty, some time around 300 to 206 BC, the Zhou Yi was canonized in a collection of texts called the Ten Wings.[4] The I Ching as it is presented today is the compilation of the Zhou Yi and the Ten Wings. The eight trigrams and sixty-four hexagrams are integral to Eastern esoteric craft.

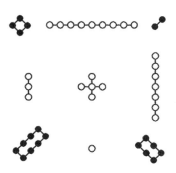 

Figure E.1. Lo Shu and the Ba Gua

The characterization for the eight trigrams to the extent they are referenced in Fu sigil crafting are provided as follows, according to the Later Heaven or King Wen sequence, to represent the metaphysical dimension of nature.

| Trigram | Characterization: Glyph Uses in Sigil Crafting; Supporting Element |
|---|---|

**Heaven**
*Qian*

The creative force. Divine yang. Strength in creation and initiation. Expansive energy, the sky. Leadership. New ventures.

*Element:* Metal

YIN
*Direction:* Northwest
*Life Aspect:* Fatherhood; blessings; allies; friends; opportunities
*Relationship:* Father, parenting yang
*Body Part:* Head
*Animal:* Horse
*Planet:* Venus

**Lake**
*Dui*

Nourishment, receiving pleasure, tranquility. Devotion. Joy, satisfaction, stagnation. A fertile womb; receptivity for further growth.

*Element:* Metal

YIN
*Direction:* West
*Life Aspect:* Children; fertility, nurturing
*Relationship:* Third offspring, daughter or nurturing yin
*Body Part:* Mouth
*Animal:* Sheep; also Tiger
*Planet:* Venus

**Fire**
*Li*

Radiance; eminence; innovation and cultivation. Giving light; illumination. Clarity. Rapid movement, radiance, the sun.

*Element:* Fire

YANG
*Direction:* South
*Life Aspect:* Ambition, honor, fame; reputation; social status
*Relationship:* Second offspring, daughter or nurturing yin
*Body Part:* Eyes
*Animal:* Phoenix; Pheasant
*Planet:* Mars

**Thunder**
*Zhen*

To shake or arouse. Inciting movement. Taking the initiative. Excitation, revolution, division. Change.

*Element:* Wood

YANG
*Direction:* East
*Life Aspect:* Family; ancestry; familial relations
*Relationship:* First offspring, son or creative yang
*Body Part:* Foot
*Animal:* Dragon
*Planet:* Jupiter

**Wind**
*Xun*

Gentle thoughts; entering gently, proceeding conscientiously. Flexibility. Adaptability.

*Element:* Wood

YANG
*Direction:* Southeast
*Life Aspect:* Wealth, finances; assets
*Relationship:* First offspring, daughter or nurturing yin
*Body Part:* Thigh/legs
*Animal:* Fowl
*Planet:* Jupiter

**Water**
*Kan*

Movement, momentum. Forging a path forward and up. Intuition. Harmony. Social status. Social gains.

*Element:* Water

YIN
*Direction:* North
*Life Aspect:* Career trajectory; life path
*Relationship:* Second offspring, son or creative yang
*Body Part:* Ear
*Animal:* Pig; also Tortoise
*Planet:* Mercury

Mountain
*Gen*

Stability. Conservation. Strength. Security. Resting. Respite. Completion.

*Element:* Earth

YIN-YANG BALANCE
*Direction:* Northeast
*Life Aspect:* Knowledge, education; skills; wisdom; schooling, academia, academics
*Relationship:* Third offspring, son or creative yang
*Body Part:* Hand
*Animal:* Wolf
*Planet:* Saturn

Earth
*Kun*

Nuturing force. Divine Yin. Receptive energy. Resoures. Fertile ground for growth. Receiving gifts and opportunities.

*Element:* Earth

YIN-YANG BALANCE
*Direction:* Southwest
*Life Aspect:* Love and relationships; motherhood
*Relationship:* Mother, parenting yin
*Body Part:* Stomach
*Animal:* Bull
*Planet:* Saturn

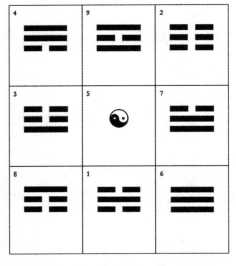

Figure E.2. Lo Shu, the Ba Gua, directionality, and feng shui

For the practitioner who is familiar with the I Ching, or Book of Changes, hexagrams can be incorporated as glyphs or part of a house design. I Ching divination and Fu sigil crafting can also be combined. For example, if I cast an I Ching divination that yielded both a primary and a secondary hexagram, and the secondary hexagram is a very desirable outcome to me, I might then craft a Fu sigil to assist me with manifesting

**1**

**Creative Power**

**Divine yang**

Man is aligned with Heaven. Use to raise yang energy and to foster creation, birth, or new beginnings. Use in communion with deities, angelic realm, saints, angels, or immortals. Helps to garner power and promote substantive, creative advancement.

**2**

**Supportive Power**

**Divine Yin**

Man is aligned with Earth. Use to raise yin energy and to foster nurture, fertility, or fertilization. Also used to summon those dwelling in the underworld.

**7**

**Military**

**The Army**

Use for combat situations to summon the warrior spirit. Brings order and discipline. Assists with mastery over the self. Use to help concentrate your personal energy, raise focus, and achieve ambitious goals. Helps to bring clarity, purpose, and motivation.

**泰**

Tai

## 11

### Harmony
### Balance

Use for seeking harmonious alliances, advantageous business partnerships, and fostering synergy between disparate or different energies. This hexagram's energy acts as temperance, and tempers hot with cold, light with dark, and brings all to the center for peace and prosperity. Also helps to create or attract new opportunities for either a successful business or a marital relationship.

**同人**

Tong Ren

## 13

### Fellowship
### Community

Great for those seeking to gain positions of leadership or to lead, persuade, inspire, or influence large social groups. Great for fostering solidarity within a collective. Use to bring good luck, fortune and harmony to a group, association, organization, or fellowship of practitioners.

**大有**

Da You

## 14

### Accolades
### Praise

Use to subdue evil or malicious intentions or attacks. Use to prevail over enemeies. Also used in Fu sigils crafted to bring professional success, public acclaim, public recognition, or meritorious gains. This hexagram bodes supreme success and blessings. Great harvest.

豫

Yu

**16**

**Enthusiasm**
**Motivation**

Use to combat lethargy, fatigue, or lack of motivation. Sure to generate greater energy, verve, ambition, and ambition, and motivation in someone. Also auspicious for Fu sigils crafted to win wars, ensure military success, and for boding well to military strategy. Great hexagram to be used by warriors, soldiers, and fighters.

隨

Sui

**17**

**Inspiring Followers**

Use to persuade, influence, or lead others. Use for one who seeks to lead others into victory and bring advancement to the collective. Sue for instilling social order, fostering solidarity, and uniting all under one common leadership or inspiration.

蠱

Gu

**18**

**Decay**

Note that "Gu" here is the same character as Gu Dao ([insert Chinese characters]) noted in the section "Magic, Craft, and Sorcery" of Appendix B. This hexagram can be used in offensive sigils for the purpose of overthrowing, destroying, defeating, and/or harming an enemy or adversary. Use to thwart or divert the success of another and bring harm. Use to destroy what another has built.

臨

Lin

# 19

# Spring Comes

Used to counteract Gu Dao (蠱道) or any craft that utilizes Hexagram 18. Use to overcome adversity and be the one who prevails. For new beginnings and achieving manifestation. Brings prosperity and gains in the face of hardships, adversity, and the malevolent intentions of others. Rebuilding after destruction. Healing after harms have been inflicted. Use as an antidote.

咸

Xian

# 31

# Attraction
# Chemistry

Used in love spells. Harnesses energies to influence another to return your affection. Use to amplify energies of romantic love, sexual chemistry, happiness, bliss, and mutual attraction. Use to bring fortune and prosperity to a romantic couple or union.

恆

Heng

# 32

# Endurance
# Perpetuation

Use to maintain the endurance, longevity, and prosperity of a married couple, a civil union, or those who have committed romantically to each other. Used for long-term commitments. Can also be used generally to foster strong bonds and enduring, mutually beneficial alliances. Used for the purpose of longevity.

**大壯**
Da Zhuang

**34**

**Great Power**
**Great Strength**

Use to summon the potent combination of both wisdom and strength. Ensures that your movements are aligned with Heaven and Earth for the greatest amount of power and strength to assist in the achievement of your goals. Raises great personal power and accumulates abundance, resources, and prosperity. Note that Fu sigils incorporating this hexagram are most powerful when charged during the spring equinox.

**蹇**
Jian

**39**

**Impasse**

Used to temporarily block someone from advancing. However, no malicious intent here, as the impasse that a sigil with this hexagram would create is temporary. In its own time, the blockage will be removed and no permanent harm shall be done to anyone. Used to temporarily thwart another, though without ill will, so that one can get ahead. Used to confuse someone, raise confusion, and create minor mishaps. In the end, however, the one for which the impasse was created for will regain clarity and success.

that secondary hexagram outcome. In that Fu sigil design, I would then incorporate that secondary hexagram. Each hexagram also holds power and can call upon specified energies. Following are selected hexagrams that I often like to use in crafting Fu sigils, along with a quick summary of correspondences.

益
Yi

# 42

# Increase, Ascent

To expedite increase, ascent, and gains. For a matter that is already in developmental phase, but needs an extra nudge or push. A Fu sigil crafted with this hexagram will give that needed surge forward. Brings advancement and progress. Facilitates movement forward. Facilitates better opportunities. Helps to open a window of opportunity for the beneficiary.

困
Kun

# 47

# Oppression,
# Iron Hand

Cause temporary confusion in another. Render one incapable of making decisions to advance forward. Cause regression. Hold someone back from making gains. Incur losses in another. However, no deep malice here; the situation created is temporary, and is intended only to open a window of opportunity for one to make gains and advance forward while the one being held back regresses just slightly and loses traction. Use to discredit another; use to take away another's credibility.

鼎
Ding

# 50

# The Cauldron
# Stability

This is the alchemical vessel symbolizing supreme success. Use for grounding and defense. For confidence and fortitude. Helps to maintain your center of gravity. Helps to nurture talent, virtue, and to initiate progress forward. Also used to help bring financial security or stability, and to ensure plentiful resources.

# GLYPH SAMPLES FROM THE SHEN FU LEI

**THE FOLLOWING IDEOGRAMS** are scans from the "Shen Fu Lei," a chapter in *San Dong Shen Fu Ji* (三洞神符纪, *Three Caverns of the Supernatural Fu Talismanic Records*), circa AD 400. I am referring to these ideograms as glyphs. They can serve as a reference guide to the types of glyphs that a practitioner might consider incorporating into a Fu sigil, based on stylized Fu Wen developed thousands of years ago. The reference is structured as follows:

Figure F.1. Key to Shen Fu Lei glyphs

Within each cell is a reproduction of the glyph, which is a stylized script, and its corresponding meaning in traditional Chinese. The content inside each cell is a reproduction from the *San Dong Shen Fu Ji*. Underneath the cell is the corresponding English translation of that glyph.

Figure F.2. Shen Fu Lei glyphs

# APPENDIX G

# BEGINNER SIGIL DESIGN TUTORIAL

**THE FOLLOWING TUTORIAL** is intended to assist a beginner with designing a Fu sigil. It is a severely limited approach to designing a Fu sigil and does not account for the best possible design a practitioner can craft to ameliorate a particular situation. Such a best possible design must come from the practitioner's creativity and must account for the practitioner's own personal gnosis. However, for one who has never designed a Fu sigil before, this is a good place to start triggering your mind to follow an organized process. Also consider the section "A First Sigil for the Novice" in appendix H for beginner crafting techniques.

## • Why are you crafting the Fu sigil? What is the intended outcome? State the intent with specificity.

Start by defining the goal for the sigil to be crafted. What is the intent to be manifested? What is the subject matter and nature of the intent? What is the problem that the Fu sigil will solve?

Be specific. For example, in a sigil crafted to facilitate high marks on an examination, render the date, time, location, and subject matter of the examination into glyphs. If you have been assigned a seat number ahead of time, render the seat number into a glyph. Be sure to invoke higher spirits and Heaven to assist in the matter, especially those who are known to be patrons of scholars and academics. If specific individuals are relevant, identify those individuals by rendering Western sigils or your own creative glyphs for such individuals. "Be careful what you wish for" is not just a cliché; it's good advice.

Once you have defined your intent with specificity and clarity, proceed with the following steps for designing the house and glyphs.

**Example.** To illustrate these steps, assume that a practitioner, Mary, will be crafting a Fu sigil to invoke divine and angelic protection over her second son, Abe, who is now a young adult and about to leave home to live out on his own. Mary will be crafting a Fu sigil that will be a beacon that calls out to angelic guardians, and serve as a prayer for them to watch over her son Abe. Also, sigils can be crafted for multiple purposes at once. Mary also intends the sigil to attract greater prosperity and career advancement for her son.

### • Will a specific deity or spirit entity be invoked? How will a house or glyph be designed to align with that deity's frequency?

Even when no specific deity is invoked, most Fu sigils will at the very least include a reference to Spirit, 神 (Shén), or High Lord, 帝 (Dì). Appendix B pro-

| 4     |       |   | 9   |     |   | 2   |     |   |
|-------|-------|---|-----|-----|---|-----|-----|---|
| D     | M     | V |     | I   | R | B   | K   | T |
| **3** |       |   | **5** |   |   | **7** |   |   |
| C     | L     | U | E   | N   | W | G   | P   | Y |
| **8** |       |   | **1** |   |   | **6** |   |   |
| H     | Q     | Z | A   | J   | S | F   | O   | X |

Figure G.1. Glyph for Spirit

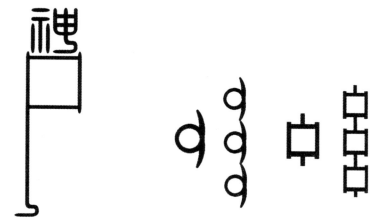

Figure G.2. House design
for Fu

Figure G.3. Yin and yang energy amplifiers

vides a selection of deity names commonly invoked by Taoist practitioners. A different deity may also be invoked. In that instance, a practitioner would design a seal or glyph that represents that deity's name or identity and incorporate it into the design of the sigil. Generally, glyphs or Fu Wen for venerated deities are placed at the top of the sigil, or at the very least, prominently positioned.

**Example, continued.** Mary decides to use a glyph for Spirit, 神 (Shén), to call upon Spirit as the divine protector. See figure G.1 for the glyph she renders for Spirit. Mary then proceeds to design a basic house for her sigil. Figure G.2 shows the house she starts with and the Spirit glyph positioned prominently at the top of the house.

- **To bring balance or to rectify the current situation, would the solution require more yin or more yang? Is the means of achieving your goal through stronger yin or stronger yang?**

Start by determining the yin and yang balance of the sigil you will be designing. Whether your sigil will be yin-dominant or yang-dominant depends on the intent. One way to call upon yin energy, as noted in "The Glyphs and Fu Wen" in chapter 4, is with a design that consists of curved lines, circles, and spirals, and to call upon yang energy, sharp, straight lines, distinct edges, angles, and points.

Figure G.3 shows an idea for how to incorporate yin and yang, along with

| Number | Indication | Wu Xing Element | Reconciled Wu Xing and Ba Gua Trigram Correspondences |
|--------|-----------|-----------------|--------------------------------------------------------|
| 2 | Yin and yang | Earth | Strong yin; motherhood; love, relationships, partnerships, romance; business; legal matters; property issues; financial security. |
| 3 | Heaven, Earth, Man | Wood | Literature, writing; knowledge, education; social justice; change, revolution; inciting movement; family, ancestry, heritage. Used by practitioners to bring harmony and synthesis to the three planes, Heaven, Earth, and Man, for the ritual to follow. |
| 5 | Wu Xing | Earth | Business; legal matters; property issues; financial security; health, wellness; medical concerns; personal vitality; personal life force. Used by practitioner to invoke the four compass direction and the fifth per geomancy, the center. Also used for its association with the Wu Xing five phases. |
| 7 | Netherworld | Metal | Speech, communications; intellect; independence; ambitions; fertility, children; joy, happiness; receiving pleasure; fulfillment. Also used for summonings and connecting to entities from other realms or planes. |
| 8 | Fortune, prosperity | Earth | Business; legal matters; property issues; financial security; seeking stability in relationships; seeking knowledge, education, or wisdom. Used in spell working for wealth and prosperity. |
| 9 | Heaven | Fire | Leadership; power; courage, fortitude, strength; performing arts; creativity and intuition; insight, mental clarity; ambitions, honors, and fame; seeking glory. Used when the practitioner seeks to send a message directly to Deity or the heavenly plane. |
| 11 | Angelic realm | ——— | Used when the practitioner seeks to connect or commune with higher realms, those in Heaven, saints, immortals, or angels. |
| 12 | Astrological zodiac | ——— | Used to call upon the power and assistance of the twelve zodiac animals. Used to invoke the power of the cosmos, the sun, moon, and stars to recalibrate one's fate or destiny. Used to, in effect, rewrite what had been written in the stars. |

Table G.1. Numerology, Wu Xing, and Ba Gua correspondences

numerology (noted in the next step). Adorn a sigil with circles to infuse the design with yin energy and squares to infuse it with yang energy.

## • Incorporate numerology into the sigil design.

Numerology is an essential aspect to sigil crafting. Consider which number might serve as an optimal amplifier for the intent at hand. Repetitions of three, five, or eight are common in sigils. Three invokes the trinity; five is for the Wu Xing; and eight is for the Ba Gua. While table G.1 offers numerological correspondences from an Eastern metaphysical perspective, the Western practitioner should feel free to observe Western numerological correspondences instead.

Incorporate the selected numerology into the sigil design through repeating circles or squares to infuse the sigil with yin or yang.

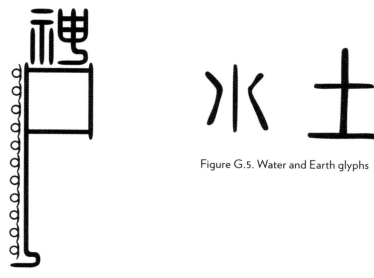

Figure G.5. Water and Earth glyphs

Figure G.4. Fu design with yin amplifiers

**Example, continued.** Mary intends this sigil to serve protective purposes, and hopes that it will call upon guardians of an angelic realm to watch over Abe. To call upon the angelic realm, according to the numerological correspondences in table G.1, the number 11 is used. Thus, figure G.4 shows how the number 11 and yin energy is incorporated into the design through repeating circles. In this example, Mary hopes to balance out Abe's innate and substantial yang energy with more yin, so she opts to delineate yin in her sigil. Furthermore, yin exemplifies the energies of nurture and care that she hopes the sigil will enrich Abe's life with.

- **Think of the five phases of the Wu Xing as possible ingredients for a recipe. What proportion of elements would best facilitate the intention?**

"The Wu Xing Five Phases" section in appendix B provides the general correspondences for the five phases. By understanding their properties, a practitioner can best assess which elements to incorporate into the Fu sigil and at what proportions. Using corresponding sacred planets, also provided in appendix B, can help strengthen the use of Wu Xing.

A Western practitioner might also consider using the four elements of Western thought, Fire, Water, Air, and Earth, in lieu of the Wu Xing. However, this book focuses primarily on the Wu Xing and does not delve into the correspondences for the four Western elements.

**Example, continued.** Figure G.5 illustrates the ancient seal scripts for the characters Water (left) and Earth (right), circa the Shang and Zhou Dynasties. Mary selects Water from the Wu Xing to support the Water trigram. The Wu Xing element Earth invokes physical health, wellness, and stability, which she hopes the sigil will endow Abe with. Earth also represents a mother's love.

- **Consider the eight trigrams of the Ba Gua and identify which trigram would best support the intent to be manifested.**

Review appendix E for an overview of the eight trigrams. Consider incorporating one of the eight trigrams as a glyph or stylized as part of the house. Note also that the boxed area of the sample house provided in figure G.4 would be ideal for featuring a hexagram. Thus, consider the selected hexagrams provided in appendix E.

Figure G.6. Water trigram

**Example, continued.** Mary decides to incorporate the trigram for Water into her sigil. Figure G.6 illustrates the trigram from appendix E. Note that, in the correspondences provided in appendix E, the trigram Water relates to the second offspring, specifically a son. Abe happens to be Mary's second child, and a son. Furthermore, she hopes the inclusion of the Water trigram will invoke greater career and professional support for Abe.

- **Review Appendices B, C, D, and F for glyphs that may resonate with you as suitable ingredients for your sigil recipe.**

The most common ways that glyphs are rendered for a Fu sigil are Fu Wen, a secret, stylized form of Chinese ideograms devised by a practitioner; or Fu Ji, a form of automatic writing that the practitioner channels by possession from a spirit. The Fu Wen is, in essence, a cohesive, comprehensible alphabet—comprehensible only to the practitioner or members of that lineage. Other forms of glyphs include legible Chinese characters, though often in a stylized, artistic script, or calling upon the Greater or Lesser Seal scripts for those characters. Selected Greater and Lesser Seal scripts, along with scripts from Shang Dynasty oracle bones, are provided in appendix B. Practitioners who craft Fu sigils with frequency will have devised their own confidential and proprietary Fu Wen glyphs. No one but the practitioner knows the meanings of the glyphs. A personal glossary of such glyphs is retained in the practitioner's magical records. If you see yourself crafting Fu sigils with some frequency in the future, I recommend that you start keeping a log of your own crafted glyphs and houses.

Assuming the beginner practitioner has not yet crafted a personal, proprietary Fu Wen alphabet and is not going to be observing Fu Ji practices, a combination of heavily stylized Fu Wen that the practitioner conceives of based on traditional Chinese lettering and actual legible characters can be used for glyphs.

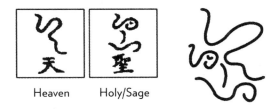

Heaven     Holy/Sage

Figure G.7. Glyphs in the cloud writing style

For the practitioner who is also an astrologer, consider the incorporation of planetary glyphs. The section on blessings might be helpful. Animal totems will call upon the corresponding attributes of the animal invoked in the sigil. A sigil that the practitioner has designed him- or herself according to Western sigil crafting techniques or through the Lo Shu square would be powerful.

**Example, continued.** Mary uses this book for reference in designing her glyphs, and she finds that the historic glyphs from the AD 400 text *San Dong Shen Fu Ji* (三洞神符纪, *Three Caverns of the Supernatural Fu Talismanic Records*), discussed in appendix F, resonates with her and her intentions for this Fu sigil. She chooses the glyphs for Heaven and Holy (or Sage) and combines both into a synthesized sigil. See figure G.7.

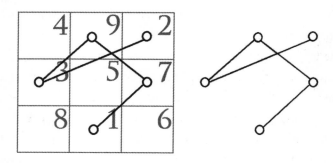

Figure G.8. Lo Shu rendered glyph

**Example, continued.** Mary also decides to incorporate birthday numerology through the Lo Shu square, according to the instructions in appendix D. Here, the relevant numbers for Mary are as follows: 1, 7, 9, 3, and 2. The birthday of Mary's late grandmother, Abe's great grandmother, was January 7. Mary's late mother, Abe's recently passed grandmother, was born on September 3. These two birthdays make up the first four numbers, 1, 7, 9, and 3. Since "good things subsist in pairs," according to a Chinese phrase (好事成雙, hǎo shì chéng shuāng), Mary uses the final number 2 to emphasize the auspices of the powerful maternal line, calling upon the spirits of both Mary's grandmother and mother to watch over her son Abe. Additionally, the numerology of $1 + 7 + 9 + 3 + 2 = 22$, a pair of 2s, while $1 + 7 + 9 + 3$ itself vibrates with the numerological frequency 2.

Figure G.9. Glyph for "Prosperity and Riches"

**Example, continued.** Mary continues to select glyphs for her sigil. On the left side of figure G.9 is the traditional Chinese character for prosperity, 發 (Fā, of 發財, Fā Cái), which she found in the "Blessings" section of appendix B. The right side shows Mary's Fu Wen glyph for the character.

Figure G.10. Symbol for shielding and protection

**Example, continued.** Mary selects a final glyph, an amplifier that represents protection and shielding energies, as discussed in appendix C.

### • Assemble the glyphs into the house to create the final Fu sigil design.

Arrange the selected glyphs into the house in a way that balances aesthetic design and emphasizes the proportionate significance of each glyph. What is most important or relevant should appear near the top of the glyph, or literally be one of the larger, more prominent glyphs.

**Example, continued.** Mary has designed a total of seven glyphs to fill the house. She decides that the glyph for prosperity in figure G.9 will be the most prominent (glyph 1) beneath Spirit; then comes the trigram for Water (glyph 2); then the characters for the Wu Xing elements Water and Earth (glyphs 3 and 4); the Lo Shu glyph she crafted for the maternal line birthdays (glyph 5); the synthesized glyph she created, inspired by the "Shen Fu Lei" in appendix F (glyph 6); and finally, the shielding and protection amplifier seen in figure G.10 (glyph 7). See figure G.11 for the completed Fu sigil that Mary crafted for her son Abe. Once

Figure G.11. Final sigil design for a protection Fu

the final design is complete, Mary uses a consecrated ink pen to draw it onto consecrated paper.

## • Decide whether the sigil will be drawn and charged at the same time or done on different days.

Most Taoist practitioners design and charge the Fu sigil all in one sitting. Generally, an ordained Taoist priest has committed to memory several Fu sigil designs for various purposes. For example, a priest might have one sigil design memorized for love and romance spells, one for wealth and prosperity, another for career advancement, one for weddings, one for accruing merits for a deceased person, and so on. Thus, on the date and time of crafting a sigil, the priest prepares the sacred space, open the ritual, then draw out the sigil onto consecrated paper and proceed right away with the charging or empowering.

However, I have found craft to be more effective when every step is carefully plotted out and timed. Thus, I design the sigils in advance, each one customized for the person and situation at hand. I don't use stock sigils for set categories of situations. Each one is unique and designed from scratch, though I do have a set of personally crafted glyphs that I will often use and incorporate into those unique, custom-designed sigils. My own crafted glyphs and their meanings, uses, and metaphysical correspondences are written into a personal reference notebook. I would recommend that serious practitioners consider doing the same, to keep his or her own Book of Methods, so that there is one go-to comprehensive text that the practitioner can consult when crafting Fu sigils.

**Example, continued.** Mary, the practitioner, opts to design the Fu sigil ahead of time. She does not concern herself with timing while she is designing the various parts of what will become her sigil for Abe. She draws out a rough sketch of what she wants on regular paper. Then, when she is ready, right before she begins the ritual, she sits down with the rough sketch and a consecrated pen and paper, and copies out the Fu sigil design onto the consecrated paper for the final Fu that will be given to Abe.

At this point, the Fu sigil, though now rendered onto consecrated paper, is still little more than a drawing. The practitioner must then charge the sigil for it to be empowered. See appendix H for beginner guidance on charging and activation.

# BEGINNER SIGIL CHARGING RITUAL

**THE FOLLOWING** instructions are intended to assist a beginner and will therefore be rather specific with the ritual procedure. A practitioner should use the following instructions as reference only. You will want to find a harmonious way to integrate the practices shown here with your personal traditions and customs. Blindly following another practitioner's method when you don't understand the rationale for the methodology will dilute the power and effect of the sigil you intend to craft. What gives a sigil its potency is you, and therefore every step of craft must be meaningful to you.

We will be continuing with the example begun in appendix G, with Mary, the practitioner, crafting a divine and maternal protection sigil for her son Abe. Note the beneficiary's vow in chapter 8 and referenced again in chapter 11. However, at Mary's discretion, she assesses the energetic nature of the Fu to be crafted and concludes that a beneficiary's vow won't be necessary.

## • The practitioner's seal.

First, these instructions assume the practitioner is a beginner, and thus it is also assumed that you do not have a personal seal yet. Please review the sections titled "Practitioner's Seal" in chapter 6, and chapter 9, "Sealing the Fu Sigil." A Chinese seal is essentially a signature, and therefore a Western practitioner may simply sign the sigil in lieu of using a practitioner's seal. If a Western practitioner prefers a Chinese seal, consider selecting a few nouns (as metaphors) or adjectives that represent how you identify yourself as a practi-

Figure H.1. Sample
practitioner's seal stamp

tioner of magic. Using a Chinese-English dictionary, note the characters for those words you have
chosen. Typically, one character is an adjective
and the second character is a noun, but the noun
is often in metaphor and is therefore symbolic of
particular attributes.

**Example.** Mary, the practitioner, opts for a
Chinese magical name. White is her favorite color
and she feels the symbolism for the color white
(白, bái) represents the attributes of her craft. According to the "Animal Totems" section in appendix B, Mary chooses the swallow (燕, yàn), a small
bird and messenger of good fortune and prosperity. Mary strives for her craft to facilitate good fortune and prosperity for others. Thus, she selects
the Chinese craft name Bai Yan for herself. Mary then finds a craftsman in
Chinatown and commissions a Chinese seal to be made with those characters,
carved in stone. See figure H.1.

Note that Mary has both the stone seal and the ink pad she will be using
consecrated using the instructions in chapter 7. Note that all tools to be used
during the charging ritual will have been consecrated prior to commencing
the ritual.

### • Consider the timing of your charging ritual. Also consider numero-
### logical associations with the date selected for the charging ritual.

For starters, the timing must be adequately in advance of the foreseeable or
projected timing of the event or outcome that the sigil is intended to manifest.
Review the section titled "The Timing of a Charging Ritual" in chapter 8. Consider the date, time, and numerology of the date or time that would best suit
your intention. Also consider the moon phase. In Chinese esoteric traditions,
moon phases are the most critical component to timing an event.

**Example, continued.** Mary consults chapter 8 of this book and decides
to time her charging ritual at 9 p.m., the hour ruled by the Boar. Note further
that the Boar corresponds with yin energy and Water. Mary also decides on a

date under the new moon, for the new beginnings and adventures that her son Abe is about to embark on. The precise date she chooses has the numerological vibration 2, which aligns with the design of her sigil.

## • Consider the deity or deities that will be invoked, or the spirit to be summoned.

The concept of deity and spirit here is an anthropomorphosis of an idea of a greater cosmic Qi. For a ritual to be effective, a practitioner must bridge Heaven, Earth, and Man—him- or herself. Earth is represented by the natural elements, whereas Heaven, that collective unconscious extending out into and connecting the universe, is often represented as deity or spirit. It is our concept of that which is Divine. It is also the Tao.

Historically, there were precise invocations and techniques for summoning spirits, and an ordained priest or priestess had to prove mastery of those techniques. Ordained Taoist priests would embed into their memories the names, identities, appearances, and methods of summoning for a portfolio of spirits that they would command to carry forth and manifest the instructions set forth on the Fu sigil.

**Example, continued.** Mary will be making references to Spirit or Divine, aligned with the Spirit she invokes in her sigil design. Thus, she will be making references to either Spirit or the Divine in the invocations she crafts.

## • Write out a prepared script for the charging ritual.

Prior to commencement of the charging ritual, write out a script for the ritual. Generally, this will include writing out a Reception Invocation, opening prayer, and the recitation to be used to charge the sigil. Prepare all tools in advance, making sure they are all consecrated. Be sure to review chapter 8. Also, consider what aspects of chapter 8's instructions you would like to discard and instead opt in with the methods of your own tradition.

Consider how "manifestations in the universe" will be generated through your hand, as discussed in the *Classics of the Esoteric Talisman*. Will you be using a wand or dagger in your tradition? Or will you be using a hand mudra? What materials will you need?

**Example, continued.** The following example provides Mary's personal approach, one she devised herself based on practices she has cultivated over the years, and incorporates some of the ritual considerations from this book.

Mary begins by listing out the items she will need:

candles (2)
consecrated water
wood block
ceremonial bells (tingsha cymbals)
practitioner's seal (and ink pad, if needed)
seal dish
mala prayer beads
pendulum (for the postliminary divination)
wand

Presumably, Mary has an altar set up. In this example, Mary's altar is set up against the south wall of a room, facing north. (Thus, when Mary is standing before her altar, facing the altar, she is facing south.) For more information about altars, see chapter 6. She will be using two candles, to call again upon the numerological frequency for the number 2.

Mary will begin the ritual by lighting the two candles at 9 p.m., the time she has set for the ritual. She will then proceed to sprinkle consecrated water in a circle around the altar space and where she will be charging the sigil. While she walks the circle sprinkling consecrated water, she will recite her Reception Invocation. The purpose of the Reception Invocation is like tuning, to ensure that she is tuned in to the metaphysical plane around her.

The Reception Invocation she chooses to use is "Om mani pad me hom," a mantra described in chapter 7. She will recite the Reception Invocation repeatedly while walking in a circle around her work space sprinkling first the consecrated water, and then making another round while rapping on the wood block and reciting her Reception Invocation. The third time will be with ceremonial bells, her tingsha cymbals, again while reciting her Reception Invocation.

Mary will then set her practitioner's seal on the seal dish upon her altar. The area where she will be positioned while charging the Fu sigil will be close

BEGINNER SIGIL CHARGING RITUAL

by the altar, within the circle she casts. Mary has written out her opening prayer onto a separate sheet of consecrated paper, which she will have with her during the ritual. The opening prayer she has drafted is as follows:

---

I come forward now to call upon the four guardians.

Red Phoenix commanding Fire in the South, I call upon you. [While she recites this, she faces south, with both palms outward and open, as if receiving, then proceeds to the east quarter within the circle.]

Azure Dragon commanding Wood in the East, I call upon you. [While she recites this, again with both palms outward and open, she faces east, then proceeds north.]

Black Tortoise commanding Water in the North, I call upon you. [While she recites this, palms open, she faces north, then proceeds west.]

White Tiger commanding Metal in the West, I call upon you. [While she recites this, palms open, she faces west, then proceeds back to the center to complete the prayer.]

In the name of the Divine, lend me your powers so that I might command as mediator between Heaven and Earth, Earth and Man, Man and Heaven.

Om mani pad me hom.

---

The opening prayer is based in part on one provided as an example in chapter 8. However, it is not complete yet. Mary has decided to incorporate pacing with the Lo Shu square. Since she used the Lo Shu square to design a glyph in her Fu sigil, she decides to use the same pattern for her pacing. See figure H.2. Review the section "Pacing the Lo Shu" in chapter 8.

After the opening prayer, Mary will approach the altar and pick up her wand, which she is accustomed to using, and with the wand pointing down at the ground within the circle, draw out the invisible lines of the Lo Shu square

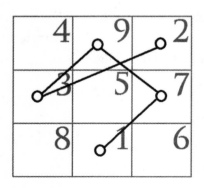

Figure H.2. Crafting the pacing according to the Lo Shu

before the altar. It is perfectly appropriate for Mary to have a diagram for reference during the ritual, though most intermediate and advanced practitioners likely will not need a reference.

Mary then paces through the Lo Shu in the order 1 (north), 7 (west), 9 (south), 3 (east), 2 (southwest), shown in figure H.2, all while reciting her invocation mantra, "Om mani pad me hom." As she paces into the final sector, at 2, she is standing before her altar, to the right. She then picks up the Fu sigil she has crafted for Abe and commences the charging ritual.

Mary has a meditation mat that is placed in front of her altar, in sector 2 of the Lo Shu square, where she ends her pacing. She charges the sigil from there, sector 2.

Mary has also written out the recitation she uses to charge Abe's sigil:

I call upon Spirit, the Great Divine, to safeguard my son Abe, bring him guidance by omens and signs. May the love of my mother and grandmother protect Abe and bring him peace. Divine Spirit, bring him abundance, riches, and success.

Although this book notes the more orthodox method of 108 recitations in "The 108 Recitations" in chapter 8, practitioners are not required to adopt such a practice. The practitioner can use his or her own discretion to determine what will work best. In the example of Mary, she does not feel that 108 recitations are needed in her practice. Thus, she opts for a total of 11 recitations, in line with the number 11 she incorporated into her sigil design.

## • Consider the charging method to be used.

"All manifestations in the universe can be generated by the practitioner's physical body, through the hand. The function is determined by the will of the practitioner. The mechanics are determined by the practitioner's mind."[1] It is important to understand the theory and principles behind craft so that the practitioner is best able to tailor his or her charging method.

Theoretically, the practitioner will be harvesting energy from matter in the universe beyond what is physically in front of the practitioner at the time, and through the practitioner's mind and willpower, transfer that energy from "the universe," pull it through his or her physical body, which becomes a conduit, and transfer that harvested energy into the Fu sigil, generally "through the hand."

Traditional Taoists will opt for a hand mudra. Others use a sword or small dagger made of peach wood in the same way Western practitioners of craft might use a wand. Still others, like Western practitioners, do use a wand. The practitioner must consider what method, through his or her hand, will work best for channeling energy into the sigil.

**Example, continued.** Mary is used to a wand, and so she incorporates a wand into her ritual. The paper Fu sigil is set out on a small table that she can place in front of her meditation mat while she performs the charging. Mary's giving hand is her right, and her receiving hand is her left. For more information about dominant and receiving hands, see the section titled "The 108 Recitations" in chapter 8.

Thus, Mary holds the wand with her right hand, directing it at the sigil, while her left hand holds the mala prayer beads to count out her recitations for the charging. As she performs the recitations, she concentrates the flow of energy through her hand, her wand, and into the Fu sigil for Abe.

### • Decide whether the postliminary divination will be incorporated into the practitioner's ritual.

Not all Taoist practitioners use a postliminary divination. In fact, most do not. However, in my interpretation of the classic texts on Fu sigil crafting, a postliminary divination better serves the principles of craft and ensures that all has been performed as it should be for the optimal effect.

However, I do understand why most Taoist practitioners opt out of the postliminary divination. Since most Fu sigils are sold, postliminary divinations are not economically efficient. I believe that the inefficiency and the burden of the postliminary divination is why, over the years, it has fallen out of favor. Person-

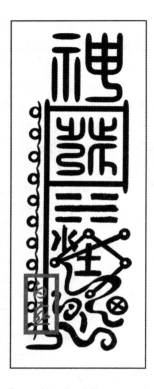

Figure H.3. Final Fu stamped with the practitioner's seal

ally, I like the insurance of the postliminary divination, which is why I observe it.

**Example, continued.** As a practitioner, Mary typically does not observe the postliminary divination and skips it. However, for this specific Fu sigil, which she is crafting for her son Abe, Mary decides to perform the postliminary divination just to make sure that it has been properly crafted for its intended purpose. After all, she wants to confirm that the sigil will indeed keep her son safe and protected. Thus, Mary performs the postliminary divination with her pendulum.

Mary does not use divination moon blocks, as she does not have any. Instead, she uses a divination method that she is more familiar with, and that is divining with her pendulum. For more information about the postliminary divination and also moon block alternatives, see the section "Divination Moon Blocks" in chapter 6, and the section "Postliminary Divination" in chapter 8.

### • Sealing the Fu sigil to complete the ritual.

Review chapter 9, "Sealing the Fu Sigil." At the conclusion of the sigil charging, after yielding a positive postliminary divination result, the practitioner then seals the sigil. Traditionally, a Taoist priest at a temple stamps the sigil with his personal seal and also one with the temple's seal. Those affiliated with a particular lineage will also stamp it with the lineage's seal. For the individual, stamping with the practitioner's seal will suffice.

**Example, continued.** When the postliminary divination is complete, and presuming Mary yielded a positive and affirmative result, Mary then stamps the sigil with her seal. She uses black ink to draw the Fu sigil, and red ink for her stamped seal. In figure H.3, you can see that Mary has stamped the sigil at the bottom left corner.

## • Consider activation techniques.

Perhaps the most traditional method of activating a Fu sigil in East Asian culture is to burn the sigil; mix the ashes with a liquid, either water or liquor; and drink it. Sigils intended to protect a home will be posted on a wall. Fu sigils are often used as a form of feng shui cure, placed in the home to help correct or alleviate a situation with the house that might otherwise prove to be "bad" feng shui. Review chapter 10 for various activation techniques.

**Example, continued.** In our Mary-Abe example, Mary, the practitioner, folds up the Fu sigil so that it might fit into Abe's wallet. As she does so, she recites prayers or blessings for Abe. Once complete, she gives the folded Fu sigil to Abe and instructs him to keep it in his wallet, and keep it with him at all times. The efficacy of the sigil will endure for as long as the piece of paper holds up in Abe's wallet.

## A FIRST SIGIL FOR THE NOVICE

Practice copying the Fu sigil design in figure H.4. It is a basic sigil for facilitating success and victory. No personal or event specifics are inscribed into this sigil; rather, it can be empowered for general good luck, to help clear roadblocks in one's life path and ensure a smoother journey toward an objective. While the sigil design is general, the charging ritual or means of empowering the sigil must be specific, and it is through the charging ritual that the design will function for a particular individual or situation.

Part of ensuring that the sigil works for you is to fully absorb its meaning. Study the anatomy of the sigil until you understand it, and anchor that understanding in your mind as you craft the sigil. The house design used is a basic bell form that can be found in historic sigils like the one pictured in figures 2.5 or 4.3. I often incorporate the house de-

Figure H.4. Fu sigil for ensuring success or victory

Figure H.5. Three-star constellation, sun, and moon

Figure H.6. Invoking the Divine Spirit

sign into my sigil designs, such as in figures 4.8 or 4.17. To me, the bell house represents protection.

Begin by drawing the three-star constellation, one of the twelve symbols of sovereignty. As you draw it, envision connection between you and the greater universe at large. As that connection strengthens with each stroke of your pen, feel your personal power increasing. Feel yourself absorbing power and abilities from the greater universe, the stardust within you, that you are made of, vibrating at the same frequency as the stardust above. Then draw the sun to the right (日, rì), symbolizing yang energy, and next, the moon to the left (月, yuè), symbolizing yin. Invoke the energy verbally by saying the word, either in English or Chinese (the pronunciation is provided in parentheses).

The next glyph invokes the Divine, or Heaven. It is the god principle, God, IHVH, or Spirit (帝, dì). Personally, I am not insistent on a stroke order, but if stroke order matters to you, review figure 7.3, which utilizes the same or similar glyph. To the Divine Spirit glyph, I've added energetic amplifiers in two triplet sets for a total of six, calling upon the numerological significance of six. See table 8.10 for my numerological correspondences. Six triggers the Ba Gua trigram Heaven, bringing blessings and opportunities.

Draw the body of the Fu sigil, which is the basic bell house form. Inside the bell, inscribe the four directions protection glyph from Appendix B, pictured in figure B.63. The four directions protection glyph invokes the four directions and four seasons, symbolizing protection from Earth in the Heaven, Earth, and Man trinity. It asks the natural forces and elements of Earth to support rather than hinder the objectives at hand.

| 勝 | 畗 | 財 | 火 | 強 |
|---|---|---|---|---|
| Metal | Earth | Wood | Fire | Water |
| 金 | 土 | 木 | 火 | 水 |

Figure H.8. Glyphs for victory, prosperity, money, glory, and fortitude

Within the bell house are five stylized glyphs of traditional Chinese characters. I've selected these characters to symbolize five desired blessings toward success and victory, representing five material manifestations that one would seek to measure success or victory. These five glyphs are also representative as facets of the Wu Xing five phases. My attributions may differ from or not resonate with how you would attribute these five blessings with the Wu Xing, in which case opt to use the correspondences that align with you. Here, in line with the prominence of Heaven, which is intensified by Metal, I've selected a glyph for "victory" (勝, shèng) and rendered it the most prominent glyph of the five.

Below "victory" are two glyphs (財富) that can be read as one word, right to left in the sigil design, meaning great wealth, prosperity, and riches. Separately, each character also bears symbolic meaning.

Figure H.7. The house and the four directions protection glyph

One of the characters, "money and riches" (財, cái) corresponds with Wood, and helps to generate income and material gains and increase assets; the other, "wealth and prosperity" (富, fù) corresponds with Earth, for stability and sustainability of that wealth and prosperity. In the bottom row, there is "fortitude and strength" (強, qiáng), manifesting from the force and power of Water, next to "glory" (榮, róng), manifesting from Fire. "Glory" (榮) is a character composed of twin flames (火) up top, and empowering the twin flames from below is the character for wood (木). In Wu Xing chemistry, Wood fortifies Fire.

Part and parcel to the charging ritual for this Fu sigil is understanding the symbolism and intent for every line of the design. Start by defining your specific intent. What is the objective for crafting this sigil? In what defined way should success or victory manifest? Be clear and unambiguous with what you want.

As you draw each glyph, think about what that glyph means as applied to your specific intent. Use the power of your mind to envision what that abstract concept would look like in your life, given your objective. What does the concept of "glory" look like as manifested pursuant to your goal? As you write "money and riches," what is the quantity you seek? Envision that quantity in a definitive way.

As you draw the sigil, copying it from figure H.4 onto consecrated paper, press your intentions into the design: with your mind, visualize and feel the energy of that idea traveling through your body into your hand and out through the ink of your pen. Take your time with the craft. Draw slowly and deliberately.

Once complete, light a candle or incense and perform the 108 recitations with an invocation of your choosing. An applicable invocation from chapter 8 can be used, or draft your own. Stamp the practitioner's seal onto the sigil when the invocation is complete and, for your own magical practice, document the sigil's efficacy. If it does not work the first time, rather than give up, adjust a few variables and try again. Through experimentation, you will find what works for you when it comes to craft.

# APPENDIX I

# EXERCISES FOR CRAFTING FU

**THE FOLLOWING** nine exercises are provided to help you craft a set of starter Fu sigils.

## EXERCISE 1: BASIC FU

You will craft a basic Fu sigil for yourself. Select one of the phrases from table I.1 and stylize the four characters into your own unique Fu Wen. For your sigil, stack the four characters vertically (note that in table I.1, the phrases are written horizontally, left to right). You can either use your stylized Fu Wen as glyphs and inscribe them within a house, selected from appendix A, or leave the glyphs as they are. With a consecrated pen, inscribe the sigil onto consecrated paper.

| 1 | 2 |
|---|---|
| 身體健康<br>Shēn Tǐ Jiàn Kāng<br><br>"Blessings of good health and physical vitality" | 永保寿考<br>Yǒng Bǎo Shòu Kǎo<br><br>"Protect perpetually, ensure peace and longevity" |
| 3 | 4 |
| 一路平安<br>Yi Lù Píng An<br><br>"Safe journeys in all travels" | 生意興隆<br>Shēng Yì Qing Lóng<br><br>"May business flourish" |
| 5 | 6 |
| 蝠子天來<br>Fú Zi Tiān Lái<br><br>"A bar arrives from heaven"<br>(Blessings of fortune and prosperity) | 大展鴻圖<br>Dà Zhǎn Hóng Tú<br><br>"Great success and achievement of ambitions" |

Table I.1. Selected phrases for a blessings Fu

| 1 | 2 |
|---|---|
| om mani pad me hom<br><br>"Endow me with wisdom. Ward off malevolence. Dispel all malignant forces." | nassantu paddava sabbe dukkha vupa samentu me<br><br>"May all misfortune be destroyed. May all my suffering cease." |
| **3** | **4** |
| bhavantu sabba mangalam sada sotthi bhavantu te<br><br>"Endowed with blessings; go in safety." | om Vasudhara svaha<br><br>"I invoke the goddess Vasudhara to bring wealth, fortune, and prosperity." |
| **5** | **6** |
| om shrim maha Lakshmi yei svaha<br><br>"I invoke Lakshmi for material wealth and abundance." | Na mo Amitofuo<br><br>"I invoke Amithaba to support me in my endeavor, and to bring me success." |

Table I.2. Selected invocations for a blessings Fu

For the phrase you have selected, find the corresponding invocation in table I.2. There is certainly no requirement that the practitioner use the invocation in box 1 for the phrase in box 1. The invocations in table I.2 are my recommendations only. What's more, a practitioner might consider crafting his or her own invocation for the charging.

If you have selected boxes 4, 5, or 6 and will be invoking the referenced deity, then consider a Kai Guang ritual prior to crafting your Basic Fu. Kai Guang was covered in chapter 7. Here, you can print out or draw an image or likeness of the deity to be invoked and perform a Kai Guang ritual on the illustration to prepare it for this exercise. Then, when following through with the charging ritual for this exercise, place the paper illustration (that has now been consecrated and empowered with the essence of the deity to be invoked) as the center focal point of your altar.

After rendering the Fu design onto consecrated paper, perform a charging ritual with the selected invocation or with one that you have crafted. Review chapter 8, "Charging Fu Sigils." Charge the paper Fu sigil accordingly. Afterward, seal the sigil as described in chapter 9, "Sealing the Fu Sigil."

Since the Fu is crafted for general support, no beneficiary's vow will be necessary. Once the charging is complete, recite the corresponding affirmation statement from table I.3 to seal the Fu, or you can craft your own. Think of this as the "So mote it be" or "amen" closing of a spell. When complete, fold up the Fu and tuck it into your wallet to carry with you at all times, or select one of the activation techniques from chapter 10.

| 1 | Shen Ti Jian Kahng "May I flourish with good health and wellness." | 2 | Yong Bao Shou Kao "I am protected and safeguarded. I live in peace and harmony" |
|---|---|---|---|
| 3 | Yi Lu Ping An "My journeys are safe and secure. All travels be merry and blessed" | 4 | Sheng Yi Ching Long "May my business flourish. May wealth come in abundance." |
| 5 | Fu Zi Tian Lai "Come now, blessings of fortune and prosperity." | 6 | Da Zhan Hong Tu "I am destined for success. I achieve what I set out to achieve." |

Table I.3. Selected affirmations for a blessings Fu

## EXERCISE 2: BA GUA-BASED FU FOR THE HOME OR OFFICE

You will craft a Fu sigil based on the Ba Gua eight trigrams. See table 1.13 and determine which life aspect you seek to improve through the Fu sigil. Note the corresponding trigram. That trigram will represent the perfection or completion of the intention to be manifested.

By way of example, say that I, the practitioner, am crafting a Fu sigil for someone named Kerry, a writer who seeks a little metaphysical help with the completion of her debut novel. The nature of Kerry's goal is related to creativity and is currently in its gestation phase. She wants to see this gestating creative endeavor come to term. Thus, I, the practitioner, might opt to use the Lake trigram to symbolize her intent.

In table 1.13, note the correspondences for the selected trigram: the binary (yin or yang), Wu Xing, direction, planet, and supporting animal totem. Continuing with my example for Kerry with the Lake trigram, the correspondences are as follows:

- binary: yin
- Wu Xing: Metal
- direction: West
- planet: Venus
- animal totem: Tiger

Note that either the Sheep or the Tiger are a corresponding animal totem for Lake. Here I have opted for the Tiger.

Next, consult appendix B to identify the Chinese characters for the binary, in the section titled "Taoist Cosmogenesis," and the Wu Xing, in "The Wu Xing Five Phases." For the direction, note "The Four Guardians" section in appendix B and use the characters corresponding with the direction. For the planet, see "The Seven Sacred Planets," also in appendix B. Note that the character is the same as the one for the Wu Xing, plus the addition of the character for "Star." Finally, note the animal totem, found in the section "Animal Totems" in appendix B.

In the example of the Lake trigram, the characters in figure I.1 are selected to be rendered into glyphs for Kerry's Fu sigil.

Note that for yin, the Chinese character for "moon" was selected to represent yin energy. In craft, the astrological glyph or Chinese character for "sun" can be used to denote yang, and the glyph or character for "moon" used to denote yin. Also note that the character for "tiger" is used to denote both the animal totem and the corresponding Guardian of the West, using the guardian animal, the tiger (虎). The Guardian's full name, Guang Mu Tian Wang, could also be used: 廣目天王. In more orthodox or traditional Taoist practice, the full name, Guang Mu Tian Wang, would be identified on the Fu. Personally, I have opted for the guardian animal.

Stylize the selected characters into Fu Wen glyphs, arrange them in an order that feels balanced and harmonious to you, and complete the design of your Fu sigil. A house may be used if you wish. The house may be selected from

| 月 | ䷹ | 金 |
| :---: | :---: | :---: |
| Moon (Yin) | Lake | Metal |
| 西 | 虎 | 金星 |
| West | Tiger | Venus |

Figure I.1. Selected glyphs for project completion

Figure I.2. Sample Fu design using the Lake trigram

appendix A or inspired by one of the Chinese radicals from appendix B. In the Lake trigram example, a house from appendix A is used and the selected glyphs rendered into the various compartments of the house, with the trigram holding the most prominent position (see fig. I.2).

After rendering the Fu design onto consecrated paper, perform a charging ritual that you have crafted. Review chapter 8, "Charging Fu Sigils." For the 108 recitations, use the following template:

---

## INVOCATION TEMPLATE FOR CHARGING THE BA GUA-BASED FU

---

The perfect [*insert selected trigram*], an endeavor balanced by [insert corresponding binary] and enforced by [insert corresponding Wu Xing]—that is [describe intent or goal to be manifested by the Fu]. I call upon the Guardian of the [insert corresponding direction], the sacred spirit of the [insert corresp*onding animal totem*], and hereby manifest the perfect [*insert selected trigram*].

---

References to the "perfect [*insert selected trigram*]" represent the perfect manifestation of the intent or goal, coming to term in exactly the way the practitioner seeks for it to manifest, which shall be as pure and divine as the trigram it is being represented by. In the example for Kerry, the template invocation would be completed as follows:

---

## INVOCATION FOR KERRY'S LAKE BA GUA-BASED FU

THE PERFECT LAKE, an endeavor balanced by yin and enforced by Metal—that is the successful completion of Kerry's debut novel. I call upon the guardian of the West, the sacred spirit of the Tiger, and hereby manifest the perfect Lake.

---

Then charge the paper Fu sigil according to the guidelines and principles in chapter 8. Afterward, seal the sigil as described in chapter 9, "Sealing the Fu Sigil."

Place the Fu in the area of the home or office corresponding with the direction correspondent of the Ba Gua trigram. Thus, in my example of the Lake trigram, the completed Fu would be placed in the west area of Kerry's home or office, depending on whether the specific intent to be manifested applies more to the home or the office. Say that Kerry writes at home on a particular study desk. She could be instructed to place the Fu in the corner of her desk facing west.

## EXERCISE 3: A CELL SIGIL

You will be crafting a Fu sigil for yourself using the cell sigil format described in chapter 4. Review the section "House Cells" in chapter 4 and the case study in chapter 11 before proceeding.

To begin, decide on the purpose for your cell sigil. Is it to bring in and support greater opportunities for love and romance in your near future? Is it to generate greater abundance, wealth, and prosperity? Are you seeking to pass an important examination for school? Do you want to improve your chances at a promotion for work?

After deciding on the purpose of the Fu, self-diagnose why there isn't as much success in that area of your life as you would like. Is it because you lack yin or because you lack yang? You lack yin if you need more wisdom, more nurturing, more creative or developmental energies, or seek the direct assistance of the Spirit world and haven't been able to make contact. You lack yang if you don't have the initiative, drive, or determination that would enable you to work harder toward achieving your goal. Yang is needed to "brighten," to make you more visible and noticeable to others.

Rì — Sun
Yuè — Moon

Figure I.3. Chinese characters for "sun" and "moon"

If you've decided that you're yin-dominant right now and thus lack yang, incorporate the Sun into your sigil design. The Sun will add more yang. If you are yang dominant and currently lack yin, then incorporate the Moon into your sigil design. The Moon will add more yin.

By way of example, say that I am crafting a cell sigil for a university student named Michael Bergeron, who seeks metaphysical energetic support to help in general academic success. According to the Ba Gua, as shown in table 1.13, the area of knowledge, education, and academics corresponds with the trigram

| East | South | North | West |
|---|---|---|---|
| 龍 | 鳳 | 龜 | 虎 |
| Lóng | Fèng | Guī | Hǔ |
| Dragon | Phoenix | Phoenix | Tiger |

Figure I.4. Chinese characters for the four animal guardians

Mountain, which is balanced between yin and yang. Thus, in my sigil design, I would include two glyphs, for both the sun and the moon. When both the sun and the moon are included, I might consider adding the glyph for the three-star constellation, as illustrated in figure 4.21. The three stars are positioned at the top of the Fu.

Next, review the Four Guardians and decide which of them will best be able to facilitate manifestation of what you want. Figure I.4 shows the characters for the guardian animals of the four directions.

For my Michael Bergeron example, according to the Ba Gua and table 1.13, the Mountain trigram corresponds with the northeast. Thus, here I would invoke both the animal guardian for the north, the Tortoise, and the animal

| 木 | 火 | 土 | 金 | 水 |
| --- | --- | --- | --- | --- |
| Mù | Huǒ | Tǔ | Jīn | Shuǐ |
| Wood | Fire | Earth | Metal | Water |

Figure I.5. Chinese characters for the Wu Xing five phases

guardian for the east, the Dragon, and seek out energetic support from both directions for the combined effect of the northeast.

Review the Wu Xing five phases and determine which of the five Wu Xing are to be used in the cell sigil. Also consider supporting Wu Xing for the selected Wu Xing.

| 木星 | 水星 |
| --- | --- |
| Mù Xīng | Shuǐ Xīng |
| Jupiter | Jupiter |

| 金星 | 火星 | 土星 |
| --- | --- | --- |
| Jīn Xīng | Huǒ Xīng | Tǔ Xīng |
| Venus | Venus | Venus |

Figure I.6. Chinese characters for the five traditional planets

For Michael's intentions, Earth is the correspondent for the trigram Mountain. However, the beneficiary of the Fu could also use more motivation to study hard, and so I've opted to include Fire as well. Note also that Fire supports Earth, so the inclusion of the Fire glyph will fortify the Earth energy. See tables 1.7, 1.8, 1.9, and 1.10 in the section "The Wu Xing Five Phases" in chapter 1.

Again noting the Ba Gua correspondences in table 1.13, identify the planet with the greatest influence and bearing over the life aspect that the Fu is intended to support. You may also want to time the charging ritual accordingly.

For Michael, a university student, Saturn is the strongest astrological influence because Saturn is the planetary correspondence for the trigram Mountain, and Mountain is the fundamental element that governs the life aspect of academics, education, and knowledge. For the charging ritual, I would also consult the charts to find a date and time with a leading Saturn or a strongly positioned Saturn.

Finally, include a character or glyph to call upon the active agents of the metaphysical dimension. Either a specifically identified deity or spirit may be invoked, or use one of the characters from figure I.7. In my example, I have selected the character 靈 for Divinity.

Figure I.7. Chinese characters for invoking spirit

Figure I.8. Sample stylized glyphs for Fu Lu Shou

Finally, choose a character to indicate the intended outcome. This will be the largest and most prominent glyph in the cell sigil. Consider Fu Wen stylized from characters for "success," "glory," "achievement," "marriage," "money," or what best represents the goal. The Chinese characters for these words can be found in appendix B. A sigil crafted in the Western tradition could also

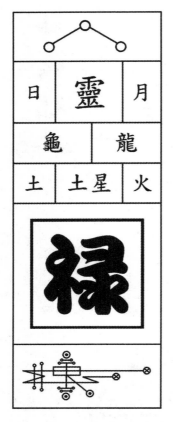

Figure I.9. General academic
success sigil for Michael Bergeron

be used as the most prominent glyph. See appendix C on Western sigil crafting.

Alternatively, one of the three symbols from Fu Lu Shou could be selected. See figure I.8, which offers sample glyphs of the characters for Fu, Lu, and Shou, stylized as medallions and as squares. Generally, one of the three symbols will cover the anticipated goal. As for medallion or square, select the one that best fits the general aesthetic of your cell sigil.

In my example, the symbol for Lu would best express Michael's desired outcome: achievement and success. I will make that glyph the most prominent one in the cell sigil.

Now consider the arrangement of the many glyphs or elements of the final cell sigil. Those glyphs invoking deity or the Divine should go at the top of the sigil. Note how in my example I left blank space at the bottom of the cell sigil. The recipient's name will be inscribed there to identify the Fu's beneficiary. In my example, that would be Michael Bergeron, which has been rendered into a Western-style sigil according to the instructions in appendix C.

At the practitioner's option, the recipient's name can be inscribed onto the sigil as is, spelled out fully in legible English (or Chinese), or it can be stylized into a glyph using any of the glyph-designing techniques found in this book. Here, I have opted to stylize Michael Bergeron's name into a sigil using Western techniques.

After rendering the cell sigil design onto consecrated paper, perform a charging ritual that you have crafted. Review chapter 8, "Charging Fu Sigils." Charge the paper Fu sigil accordingly. Afterward, seal the sigil as explained in chapter 9, "Sealing the Fu Sigil."

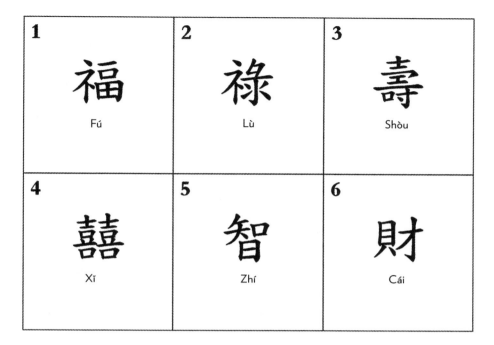

Table I.4. Selected characters for an aspirations Fu

In my example, after the charging, the sigil is delivered to the university student, Michael, and he is instructed either to keep the sigil tucked in his wallet or to keep it in a drawer of his study desk.

## EXERCISE 4: CLOUD WRITING AND A LUCKY GEMSTONE

Chapter 3 covered a style of Fu Wen dating back to AD 400 called cloud writing. That style renders Fu sigils in a manner where the design resembles the "condensation of clouds." You will craft glyphs based on the cloud writing style. Appendix F offers historic exam-

Figure I.10. Fu Lu Shou in cloud script

| 1 | 2 | 3 |
|---|---|---|
| Jade, Cinnabar<br>Aventurine<br>Green Moss Agate<br>Citrine Quartz | Tiger Eye<br>Amber, Garnet<br>Ruby, Sapphire<br>Red or Blue Goldstone | Bloodstone<br>Carnelian<br>Amber, Peridot<br>Sunstone |
| 4 | 5 | 6 |
| Rose Quartz<br>Hermatite<br>Kunzite, Opal<br>Mangano Calcite | Amethyst<br>Selenite, Moonstone<br>Lpais Lazuli<br>Malachite, Sodalite | Gold, Jade<br>Marble, Coral<br>Green Moss Agate<br>Red Goldstone |

Table I.5. Gemstone correspondences for aspirations Fu transference

ples of the cloud writing style. You can either copy those designs for this exercise or design your own.

To design your own, select the Chinese characters from appendix B that resonate most strongly with you, that truly exemplify what it is you most aspire to. Choose any character or characters you like, or for the sake of simplicity, choose one of the characters provided in table I.4.

Figure I.10 shows three personal examples of how the selected characters might be stylized into cloud writing. As it is in art, every hand will render the style of cloud writing in a different manner. Some practitioners' cloud writing is adorned with curls while others appear with sharper edges and are rendered in a boxy style.

After charging the Fu, you will transfer the energy into a gemstone. Thus, select a small pocket gemstone; a necklace or jewelry can also be used. Table I.5 offers a few suggestions for gemstones to use for corresponding Chinese characters. It cannot be stressed enough: you are not limited by or required to use the selections provided in table I.5. The selections are offered as beginner recommendations only.

After rendering the Fu design onto consecrated paper, perform a charging ritual that you have crafted. Review chapter 8, "Charging Fu Sigils." Charge the paper Fu sigil accordingly. Afterward, seal the sigil as described in chapter 9, "Sealing the Fu Sigil."

Next, burn the paper Fu to ashes in a fire safe container, with the intent of collecting all the ashes. Once the entire Fu has been burned to ash, mix the ash with consecrated salt and, optionally, add incense ash. I like to use sandalwood or cedar wood ash. Place the mixture of ash and salt in a closed container. Make sure there is enough so that the gemstone can be buried in the ash and salt mixture.

Close the lid of the container and set it aside for three, eight, or nine days, depending on which of those time frames most resonate with you and the purpose of your Fu. Once complete, the gemstone will have absorbed the energetic properties of the Fu and is now activated and ready to manifest the sought-after intention.

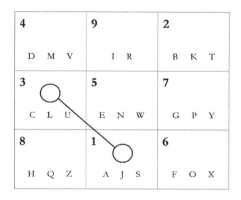

Figure I.11. Lo Shu reference square      Figure I.12. Lady Fortuna's glyph: L to A

## EXERCISE 5: LO SHU-DESIGNED FU

You will craft a Fu sigil using the Lo Shu. Review the section "The Lo Shu Nine-Sector Magic Square" in chapter 1 as well as appendix D, "Lo Shu–Designed Glyphs." Use the Lo Shu reference in figure I.11 to draw out a glyph that spells your name. If you use a craft name, spell out your craft name. The purpose of this sigil is to increase intuitive or psychic abilities and to enhance a practitioner's connection to Heaven and Earth.

I will illustrate with an example: a hypothetical practitioner with the craft name "Lady Fortuna." Using the Lo Shu square in figure I.11 as reference, she draws a circle in each sector corresponding with the letters of her craft name. Since her name begins with an *L* for Lady, she begins by drawing a circle in sector 3. Next, for *A,* she draws a second circle in sector 1. Then she connects the two circles with a solid line. The subsequent figure I.12 shows the first step of Lady Fortuna's process, L to A, or sector 3 to sector 1.

Continuing with Lady Fortuna's glyph, sector 1 for *A* is connected to sector 4 for *D,* then sector 7 for *Y,* for Lady.

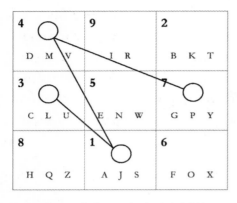

Figure I.13. Lady Fortuna's glyph: LADY

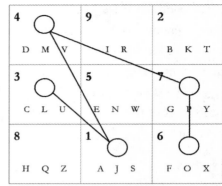

Figure I.14. Progress of Lady Fortuna's glyph: LADY FO

From sector 7, a circle is drawn in sector 6 for *F*. Note here that the next letter is *O*, which is also sector 6. Here, it is at the practitioner's discretion how to
render the glyph. Lady Fortuna decides to stay with only one circle in sector 6.
Thus, the one circle in sector 6 represents both the *F* and the *O* of her craft name.

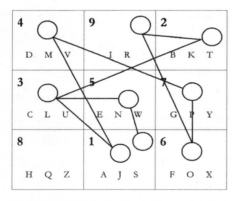

Figure I.15. Progress of Lady Fortuna's glyph: LADY FORTUNA

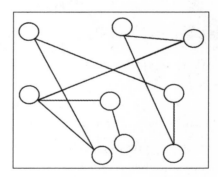

Figure I.16. Final glyph for Lady Fortuna

From sector 6 for both the *F* and the *O* of Fortuna, she continues into sector
9 for *R*, then sector 2 for *T*, and continues with the spelling of her craft name.

Note in figure I.15 that after the *N*, the *A* is in sector 1, where a circle has already been drawn for the *A* in Lady. Again, it is at the practitioner's discretion
how to proceed. Here, the practitioner decides to draw a second circle. Thus,

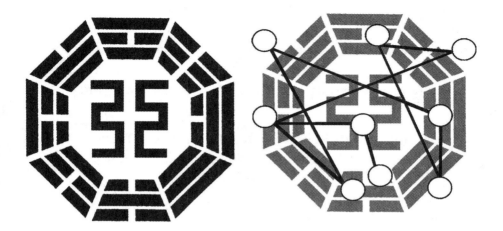

Figure I.17. Fo and Fu
empowerment glyph

Figure I.18. Progress of a customized
empowerment Fu

there are two circles in sector 1. Note also that in the rendering of the glyph, the circles can appear anywhere in the sector. It does not necessarily need to be drawn at the center of the sector. See, for example, the circles rendered in sectors 9 and 2.

The personalized glyph for the practitioner will be superimposed or layered on top of the glyph pictured in figure I.17 of the Ba Gua. The practitioner will do so by first drawing the glyph in figure I.17, and then atop that glyph, drawing out the Lo Shu glyph for the practitioner's craft name.

The empowerment glyph pictured in figure I.17 is the Ba Gua and the Fo and Fu symbol, representing divine justice. The Fo and Fu (not to be confused with the Fu character for Fu talismans) is one of the twelve symbols of sovereignty. In this context, it represents the responsible use of power, the ethical practice of craft. It is thus a vow to the Divine or spirit world that the power and abilities that the practitioner attains will be used responsibly and morally. The Fo and Fu is also symbolic of the practitioner's divine authority to wield power and craft.

Figure I.18 shows the final sigil design for Lady Fortuna. The empowerment glyph from the preceding figure I.16 is rendered in red ink and the Lo Shu glyph for Lady Fortuna's craft name is rendered in black ink.

For the charging, use one of the two invocations below for the 108 recitations. The invocation to be recited is in boldface. Again, at the practitioner's discretion, an alternative invocation may be used. These invocations, which appear in chapter 8 under "Invocation References," are provided for this exercise only, to guide a practitioner who might otherwise feel lost if an invocation isn't provided.

## INVOCATION FOR RAISING THE PRACTITIONER'S ENERGIES FOR HEALING OR LIGHT WORK

*In Mandarin Chinese:*

Yuàn dé zhì huì zhēn míng liǎo.

願得智慧真明了

"May I gain wisdom and true understanding."

## THE INVINCIBLE INVOCATION

*In Sanskrit:*

om sarva tathagata ushnisha

shitata patra hum phat

hom mama hom ni svaha

"I invoke the ushnisha Sitatapatra, the White Parasol,

born from Buddha's crown, to protect and guard

against wickedness, and to bring blessings."

After rendering the Fu design onto consecrated paper, perform a charging ritual that you have crafted, using either one of the two invocations provided above or one you have crafted yourself. Review chapter 8, "Charging Fu Sigils." Charge the paper Fu sigil accordingly. However, during the charging ritual, will cosmic or collective Qi energy to be accumulated and channeled into the sigil, rather than having your own personal Qi channeled. Imagine energy accruing into orbs of light expanding and growing more potent through the 108 recitations. As you recite the invocation, collect the envisioned orbs with your hand and direct it into the Fu sigil paper. Afterward, seal the sigil as instructed in chapter 9, "Sealing the Fu Sigil."

Choose a full moon night to activate your sigil. The purpose of this sigil is to enhance your intuitive abilities and your skills with craft, and to strengthen the bridge between your personal Qi and the cosmic or collective Qi. A beneficiary's vow is recommended. Vow to use the raised ability or power to serve and benefit others. Vow that what you have taken you will pass on and give to others in full.

## EXERCISE 6: SHIELDING AND PROTECTION SIGIL

You will craft a sigil for shielding and protection, to safeguard you from malevolent attacks. Every practitioner of craft must—and I dare say is required—to know how to craft energetic workings that will shield and protect him or her, blocking all possible malevolent energy that might potentially be directed toward the practitioner.

On a less severe note, oftentimes practitioners of craft are empathic, which means they are highly sensitive and susceptible to absorbing toxic or atrophic energies in the environment. They exhibit signs of fatigue and headaches more easily than others due to that high sensitivity and susceptibility. As a physical consequence, they often have weakened immune systems. An energetically crafted Fu sigil will help block out those toxic or atrophic energies in the environment, acting as a protective shield for the practitioner. In short, shielding and protective craft help keep a practitioner happy and healthy.

Start with the house that will form the protective energetic barrier. Note that the sigil to be crafted is square, so a square piece of consecrated paper should be used. Also, this particular Fu sigil is double-sided. Both sides of the paper will be drawn on.

Starting with the front side, eight characters are stylized into Fu Wen and inscribed into a circle, preferably in red ink, as red symbolizes protection. The characters in traditional form:

---

霆 殺 鬼 降 精 驅 鬼 保

Tíng; Shā Guǐ Jiàng Jīng; Qū Guī; Bǎo

---

While they do not make coherent grammatical sense when strung together, the magical meaning is as follows: "With a thunderbolt, I strike away, vanquish, defeat, and banish all demons. May purity and the beneficence of the

Figure I.19. Protection Fu, invocation

Figure I.20. Protection Fu, invocation and Later Heaven Ba Gua

Divine protect me. I am protected." In this case "demons" is used to denote any and all malignant forces that might be set against the practitioner or recipient of this Fu sigil. The eight characters are drawn into a protective circle, preferably in red ink. See figure I.19 for the configuration.

Figure I.21. Protection Fu with circle and square

Figure I.22. Protection Fu with the four seasons

The Later Heaven Ba Gua is then rendered in the center, within the circle of protective characters (fig. I.20).

Draw a circle around the Ba Gua and protective characters. Then enclose the circle with a solid square border. The square border should be at least twice

| | Top Left | Top Right | Bottom Left | Bottom Right |
|---|---|---|---|---|
| Season | 秋<br>Autumn | 春<br>Spring | 冬<br>Winter | 夏<br>Summer |
| Direction | 西<br>West | 东<br>East | 北<br>North | 南<br>South |
| Animal Guardian | 虎<br>Tiger | 龍<br>Dragon | 龜<br>Tortoise | 鳳<br>Phoenix |
| Wu Xing | 金<br>Metal | 木<br>Wood | 水<br>Water | 火<br>Fire |
| Celestial King<br>(天王) | 廣目<br>Guǎng Mù | 持國<br>Chí Guó | 多聞<br>Duō Wén | 增長<br>Zēng Cháng |

Table I.6. Sample glyphs for the four directions or the four seasons

as thick as the circle (fig. I.21).

In the four corners, render glyphs for the four guardians. These glyphs represent the four directions and four seasons. You can use glyphs for the four seasons or any of the traditional expressions for the four directions, for example, the Four Guardians.

For illustrative purposes, I will use the four seasons to occupy the four corners. Traditional characters for the four seasons are stylized and integrated into the sigil design in figure I.22.

Figure I.23. Sample completed protection Fu with a fictional seal

Stamp the center with your practitioner's seal. While the sigil is typically sealed at the conclusion of a charging ritual, for the purposes of this protection Fu, stamping with the practitioner's seal is part of the Fu design. Any variation on the practitioner's seal described in chapter 9 may be used. If, however, the Fu is being crafted for another, the practitioner would inscribe the name of the one to be protected into the center of the Ba Gua, and then stamp the practitioner's seal anywhere on the front or back of the Fu.

After rendering the Fu design onto consecrated paper, perform a charging ritual using the Invincible Incantation, below, to be recited 108 times. The invocation to be recited is shown in boldface. An explanation of the Invincible Incantation appears in chapter 8 under "Invocation References." If invoking Sitatapatra does not resonate with you, in place of the Invisible Incantation, use any protection invocation crafted in your practitioner's tradition.

## THE INVINCIBLE INCANTATION

*In Sanskrit:*
om sarva tathagata ushnisha
shitata patra hum phat
hom mama hom ni svaha

"I invoke the ushnisha Sitatapatra,
the White Parasol, born from
Buddha's crown, to protect
and guard against wickedness,
and to bring blessings."

To close the ritual, as a closing invocation, repeat the Invincible Incantation once more. You can transfer the sigil energy into another object, such as a pendant necklace or a gemstone, or simply carry the paper Fu with you in a wallet.

## EXERCISE 7: NEW YEAR GOOD LUCK FU

You will craft a sigil that will endure for an entire year, to bring good luck, abundance, and prosperity to the recipient, who can be either you or a loved one. Multiple copies of the same Fu can be charged simultaneously for this exercise,

| 鼠 | 牛 | 虎 | 兔 | 龍 | 蛇 |
|---|---|---|---|---|---|
| Rat | Ox | Tiger | Rabbit | Dragon | Snake |
| 馬 | 羊 | 猴 | 雞 | 狗 | 豬 |
| Horse | Sheep | Monkey | Rooster | Dog | Boar |

Table I.7. Chinese zodiac animals

each becoming an amulet for the recipient. As the term is used in this book, an amulet is a charm that is charged by a practitioner with general energy to benefit anyone that carries the charm. It is not crafted with a specific individual in mind. In other words, it is not customized. In contrast, a talisman is a customized charm, one crafted for a specific individual in mind. The New Year good luck Fu you will craft for this exercise can be either amulets or talismans. It is the intent during designing and charging that distinguishes a Fu as either an amulet or talisman.

Start by identifying the lunar year that the protection sigil is for. Then render a glyph for the corresponding zodiac animal, as shown in table I.7. For the artistically inclined, instead of using the traditional Chinese character, you can draw the animal. Alternatively, the practitioner of Western craft can simply follow the Western Gregorian calendar and use the year. Use the Lo Shu square to create a sigil or glyph to represent the year, omitting the digit 0; see appendix D.

Inscribe the zodiac animal for the corresponding lunar new year (or the Lo Shu–created glyph representing the Gregorian year) inside a Ba Gua. For practitioners who will be crafting Fu sigils with frequency, consider investing in a customized stamp with the Ba Gua. That way you do not need to hand-draw it every time you design a Fu. It can be stamped onto the Fu paper (after the stamp itself and the ink pad have been consecrated) to save you time.

After rendering the Ba Gua, draw the character and a circle around it as a protective shield. The theory behind the circle is to invite positive, constructive, and auspicious energy into that year only, and to block out the negative. The example provided in

Figure I.24. Seal script for "dragon" encircled by the Ba Gua

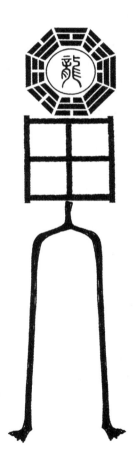

Figure I.25. House for the Year of the Dragon sigil

| 1 | 2 |
|---|---|
| 恭賀新禧<br><br>Gōng Hè Xin Xī<br><br>"Good fortunes and luck<br>in the year ahead." | 萬事如意<br><br>Wàn Shì Rú Yì<br><br>"May all go well."<br>(Blessing for peace and prosperity) |
| 3 | 4 |
| 和氣生財<br><br>Hè Qì Shēng Cái<br><br>"Harmony and prosperity"<br>(Blessings for happiness, peace, and wealth) | 大展鴻圖<br><br>Dà Zhǎn Hóng Tú<br><br>"May all go well."<br>(Blessing for peace and prosperity) |

Table I.8. Chinese New Year blessings

figure I.24 is for the Year of the Dragon, using the ancient seal script for the Chinese character "dragon." Seal scripts for selected characters are provided in appendix B.[1]

Select a house design from appendix A. Anticipate an area of the design that will be subdivided into quarters, to place four traditional Chinese characters. Figure I.25 is an example of how the house or framework for the sigil might be rendered.

With the quartered area, select one of the blessings from table I.8. The four phrases represent common blessings that are recited during the Chinese New Year. For my sample Fu, I will use number 3. See figure I.26 for the four characters, 和氣生財 (Hé Qì Shēng Cái), rendered into the quartered square. The phrase is intended to raise constructive energies for harmony and prosperity.

Then select a second blessing from the four in table I.8. The second one I've selected for my example is number 1, and in figure I.27 the characters, 恭賀新禧 (Gōng Hè Xīn Xī), are inscribed inside the bell. The phrase brings the auspices of good fortunes and good luck throughout the upcoming year. Finally, the frame for the Fu sigil—the solid rectangular border seen in figure I.27—can either be hand-drawn, or the consecrated Fu paper can be prepared that way.

Figure I.26. Continuation of
the Year of the Dragon Fu

Figure I.27. Completed
Year of the Dragon Fu

Render the Fu design onto consecrated paper. It would probably be best to use red ink, as red denotes good luck, fortune, protection, and prosperity for the coming year. Photocopies of the same Fu design can be made so that they can be produced en masse and given out as gifts during the New Year. After the photocopies are made, be sure to perform a consecration ritual on the stacks of photocopied Fu.

The charging ritual can be performed under a new moon, a waxing gibbous moon as close to the full moon as possible, or the full moon. For New Year sigils, I tend to prefer the new moon, but a waxing or full moon works just as well, given the increasing and developing power of those moons.

If practicable, select a time of day for the charging that corresponds with the lunar year, as shown in table I.9. Thus, for a Year of the Dragon Fu, the charging ritual would ideally take place between 7 a.m. and 9 a.m.

An alternative is to select a time that corresponds with that zodiac sign's guardian sign. Guardian sign correspondences are shown in table I.10. Guardian signs is discussed in more detail below in exercise 8. In the Year of the

| Hour | Zodiac Sign | Hour | Zodiac Sign |
|---|---|---|---|
| 1 a.m. – 2:59 a.m. | Ox | 1 p.m. – 2:59 p.m. | Sheep |
| 3 a.m. – 4:59 a.m. | Tiger | 3 p.m. – 4:59 p.m. | Monkey |
| 5 a.m. – 6:59 a.m. | Rabbit | 5 p.m. – 6:59 p.m. | Rooster |
| 7 a.m. – 8:59 a.m. | Dragon | 7 p.m. – 8:59 p.m. | Dog |
| 9 a.m. – 10:59 a.m. | Snake | 9 p.m. – 10:59 p.m. | Boar |
| 11 a.m. – 12:59 p.m. | Horse | 11 p.m. – 12:59 a.m. | Rat |

Table I.9. Ascendants and Chinese zodiac signs

Dragon example, if the hour of the Dragon is not feasible, the practitioner can consider the hour corresponding with the Dragon's guardian sign. The Dragon's guardian sign is the Rooster, which, as shown in table I.10, corresponds with 5 p.m. to 6:59 p.m.

| Your Zodiac Sign | Guardian Sign | Your Zodiac Sign | Guardian Sign |
|---|---|---|---|
| Rat | Ox | Horse | Sheep |
| Ox | Rat | Sheep | Horse |
| Tiger | Boar | Monkey | Snake |
| Rabbit | Dog | Rooster | Dragon |
| Dragon | Rooster | Dog | Rabbit |
| Snake | Monkey | Boar | Tiger |

Table I.10. Corresponding guardian signs for the zodiac signs

Once the timing is selected, either light twelve candles or twelve joss sticks (incense sticks). Proceed with the charging ritual as described in chapter 8. Use one of the following invocations for the 108 recitations, or craft your own. After the recitations, perform the postliminary divination. If the answer is negative, continue the ritual and recite the invocation 108 more times. Perform the postliminary divination again to determine success. Repeat until the postliminary divination yields an affirmative result.

Note that if the New Year Fu are being produced and charged en masse, each individual Fu sigil must still be stamped with the practitioner's seal. Thus, if a stack of twenty New Year Fu paper sigils are made for twenty loved ones, at the close of the charging ritual, the practitioner must individually stamp each and every one of those twenty paper sigils.

## EXERCISE 8: NATAL YEAR PROTECTION FU

You will craft a Fu for protection during your natal year, also known as the Ben Ming Nian (本命年, běn mìng nián) in Mandarin, the same lunar year as your lunar year of birth. Thus, if the current lunar year is the Year of the Monkey and you were born in the lunar Year of the Monkey, the present year is your Ben Ming Nian. The Ben Ming Nian takes place every twelve years (there are twelve zodiac signs, and so it takes twelve lunar years to cycle through the zodiac and return to your natal year).

The natal year is considered a year of unstable luck and greater risk of misfortune, but also the possibility for greater fortune. Your natal year is the year your Chinese zodiac sign is in opposition or clashing with Tai Sui (太歲, Tài Suì), which is a constellation of stars that is personified as Grand Duke Tai Sui, one of the chief administrators for the Jade Emperor in the Taoist pantheon. Tai Sui is believed to be a celestial body of energy that has an impact on world affairs. During your natal year, Tai Sui is positioned in such a way as to destabilize everyday life for those born under that zodiac sign.

The lack of stability causes significant changes during the natal year. While the popular characterization of the natal year is to construe it negatively, with fear of misfortune, the natal year is more about flux. It is a time of uncertainty and insecurity, which, yes, often leads to situations that feel unfortunate, but if the metaphysical energies are brought under control, then the natal year can bring abundance and great prosperity. This exercise will walk you through one way to craft a Fu sigil to ensure that the natal year leans toward fortune rather than misfortune, and to safeguard against instability.

For a Fu sigil crafted to dispel the negative energies that otherwise accrue during a Ben Ming Nian, be sure to use red ink. Red brings auspicious energy that will protect and also neutralize misfortune. For the consecrated paper, use yellow paper. Yellow, or gold, represents spiritual power and the ability to conquer evil spirits.

You might also consider transferring Fu sigil energy into a jade pendant on a red string or jewelry that can be worn throughout the natal year. After

| Your Zodiac Sign | Guardian Sign | Direction | Wu Xing |
|:---:|:---:|:---:|:---:|
| Rat | Ox | North | Water |
| Ox | Rat | Northeast | Earth |
| Tiger | Boar | Northeast | Wood |
| Rabbit | Dog | East | Wood |
| Dragon | Rooster | Southeast | Earth |
| Snake | Monkey | Southeast | Fire |
| Horse | Sheep | South | Fire |
| Sheep | Horse | Southwest | Metal |
| Monkey | Snake | Southwest | Metal |
| Rooster | Dragon | West | Metal |
| Dog | Rabbit | Northwest | Earth |
| Boar | Tiger | Northwest | Water |

Table I.11. Guardian sign correspondences

the start of my husband's natal year went awry, he asked that I "do something about it," in other words, turn to craft. I crafted a Fu sigil using instructions similar to this exercise and then transferred the sigil energy into a wristlet made with knotted and braided red string. According to him, all was smooth sailing for the rest of that lunar year. He had felt that the talisman brought him such great luck and abundance that year that at the end of it, he was hesitant to take it off. I finally convinced him to take it off by agreeing to make him another one, for the new, upcoming nonnatal year.

Start by identifying your guardian sign. Every zodiac sign has a supporting guardian sign. In some translations, the concept is referred to as a secret friend. The guardian sign is the best ally for your sign. In your darkest hour, invoking the guardian sign to support your zodiac sign will help to uplift you from dire straits. During your Ben Ming Nian, call upon the guardian sign through a Fu sigil to help alleviate misfortune, loss, and troubles. Guardian sign correspondences are provided in table I.11. Thus, if you were born in the year of the Rooster, then during any year of the Rooster thereafter, call upon your guardian sign, the Dragon, to pull you through the natal year.

Once you have identified your guardian sign, note the traditional Chinese

| | | | | | |
|---|---|---|---|---|---|
| 鼠 | 牛 | 虎 | 兔 | 龍 | 蛇 |
| Rat | Ox | Tiger | Rabbit | Dragon | Snake |
| 馬 | 羊 | 猴 | 雞 | 狗 | 豬 |
| Horse | Sheep | Monkey | Rooster | Dog | Boar |

Table I.12. Traditional characters for the zodiac signs

character for your zodiac sign and the one for your guardian sign. See table I.12 and table I.13 for either the traditional Chinese character or the ancient seal script. You will render Fu Wen based on your sign and your guardian sign.

The glyph for the guardian sign is the focal point of the Fu, close by the glyph for your zodiac sign and in a position that shows support and alliance for your sign. If the practitioner is a Rooster, the guardian sign is the Dragon. Figure I.28 shows sample glyphs of the two characters.

Table I.13. Ancient seal script for the zodiac signs (courtesy of Richard Sears, ChineseEtymology.org)

Next, stylize the two glyphs together. Figure I.29 is an example of how the Dragon and Rooster glyphs might be stylized. Note that the Rooster glyph has been inscribed inside a protective circle, and then surrounded by five guardian Dragons. The number five calls upon the Five Emperors of the five relative directions for protection, and also harnesses the power of the Wu Xing five phases.

The Later Heaven Ba Gua is considered highly protective, and so the practitioner might consider incorporating it into the Fu as part of its background to support the primary glyphs, as in figure I.30.

Figure I.28. Dragon and
Rooster glyphs

Figure I.29. Rooster surrounded by guardian dragons

Design and consecrate the sigil, preparing it for ritual on a new moon. Then proceed with the charging on the full moon before the commencement of the lunar new year. Also, noting the timing references in chapter 8, a charging time between 9 p.m. and midnight would support protection craft. These points on timing are certainly not required, but are suggested. Review chapter

Figure I.30. Completed protective
Fu design for natal year Rooster

Figure I.31. Fu stamped with the
practitioner's seal at bottom right

8 for charging ritual techniques.

Like exercise 7, since this is craft intended to last for an entire year, opt for twelve incense or joss sticks. The Fu sigil should then be sealed according to the instructions in chapter 9. My personal preference is to transfer the sigil energy into jewelry that can be worn throughout the year. Others will simply carry the sigil paper in their wallet or handbag.

| Hour of Birth | Ascendant Zodiac Sign | Supporting Wu Xing | Wu Xing Color |
|---|---|---|---|
| 1 a.m. – 2:59 a.m. | Ox | Earth | yellow |
| 3 a.m. – 4:59 a.m. | Tiger | Wood | green |
| 5 a.m. – 6:59 a.m. | Rabbit | Wood | green |
| 7 a.m. – 8:59 a.m. | Dragon | Earth | yellow |
| 9 a.m. – 10:59 a.m. | Snake | Fire | red |
| 11 a.m. – 12:59 p.m. | Horse | Fire | red |
| 1 p.m. – 2:59 p.m. | Sheep | Earth | yellow |
| 3 p.m. – 4:59 p.m. | Monkey | Metal | white |
| 5 p.m. – 6:59 p.m. | Rooster | Metal | white |
| 7 p.m. – 8:59 p.m. | Dog | Earth | yellow |
| 9 p.m. – 10:59 p.m. | Boar | Water | blue |
| 9 p.m. – 10:59 p.m. | Rat | Water | blue |

Table I.14. Hourly ascendants and color correspondences

Ideally you will want to use red ink for the sigil, and the Ba Gua in the background in an ink color that corresponds with the Wu Xing element corresponding to your hour of birth, or your ascendant sign according to the Chinese zodiac. This information can be gathered from the Wu Xing tables in the section "The Wu Xing Five Phases" in chapter 1, and table 8.7 in chapter 8. For quick reference, see table I.14.

For a person born at 4:20 p.m., or the ascendant hour 3 p.m. to 4:59 p.m., the ascendant zodiac sign in Chinese astrology is the Monkey, which has Metal as its supporting Wu Xing. Since the corresponding color is white and not entirely practicable for the purposes of crafting the Fu, the shape of the Ba Gua is traced over with an ultrafine black or gray ink pen, and the interior of the trigrams left blank. In effect, the Ba Gua trigrams are white, with thin black or gray borders. (If yellow paper is used for the Fu, consider painting in the Ba Gua in white.) If the time of birth is 9:30 a.m., for example, with an ascendant hour 9 a.m. to 10:59 a.m., corresponding with the Snake and Fire as the supporting Wu Xing, the color of the Ba Gua is rendered in red. In that particular case, I would use red ink for the Ba Gua, and then render the sigil glyphs in black ink.

## EXERCISE 9: THE PERENNIAL FU OF
## NINETY-NINE GLYPHS AMULET

The Fu of Ninety-Nine Glyphs, or Perennial Fu, is a grid of ninety-nine glyph variations on the same traditional Chinese character.[2] It is a potent cell sigil that challenges your intuitive creativity and channels your energy into the Fu through that creativity. Unlike typical Fu sigils that have a limited shelf life, the mechanics of how the Fu of Ninety-Nine Glyphs is crafted implies eternal power. Once crafted and charged, the Fu of Ninety-Nine Glyphs, in essence, lasts forever (or at least for as long as the medium it is crafted on lasts). Numerologically, the number ninety-nine emphasizes longevity and sustainability.

I refer to this Perennial Fu as an amulet because it is typically an original design that a practitioner conceives and then duplicates for every prospective recipient. While such amulets still need to be charged by ritual to be empowered, they are not charged specifically for an individual. They can be drawn onto a large plaque and framed in a home to invite blessings into that home or made into miniature size for pocket charms.

In this exercise, you will design your own proprietary ninety-nine-glyph amulet that you can then create for your loved ones. Once the design for your ninety-nine-glyph amulet is set, it can be copied or duplicated for as many recipients as you like. Your Perennial Fu design is unique to you, and is an original work of craft. It becomes one of your signature sigils.

Typically, a significant batch of them can be made all at once, though I would not make more than nine during any one charging ritual. The multiple copies of the Fu are then empowered all together by a charging ritual. For the artistic, consider drawing one on large canvas to hang in a home as both art and as a feng shui cure.

The modern practitioner might consider rendering the ninety-nine-glyph amulet digitally on a computer and then printing them out. Just note that since your hand did not inscribe each glyph manually (an exercise that by itself infuses the amulet with a great deal of Qi power, see point 2 from the *Classics of the Esoteric Talisman,* summarized in chapter 3), you will need to focus even more intently during the charging ritual.

Start by using a template such as figure I.32, or a grid of ten by ten square sectors. Choose any Chinese character that represents the blessing you seek.

| 福<br>Fú<br><br>Wealth, abundance,<br>prosperity | 囍<br>Xǐ<br><br>Double Happiness<br>(Love and marriage) |
|---|---|
| 祿<br>Lù<br><br>Affluence, social status,<br>advancement | 財<br>Cái<br><br>Monkey, riches;<br>assets and resources |
| 壽<br>Shòu<br><br>Longevity,<br>health and wellness | 安<br>An<br><br>Peace, harmony;<br>safety and security |

Table I.15. Selected characters for the ninety-nine-glyph amulet

Table I.15 outlines a few common characters used for the ninety-nine-glyph (or the one hundred–glyph)[3] amulet. You are by no means limited to these characters and are encouraged to be as unique and as original as you can. Peruse the single-character entries in appendix B for more ideas. Consult an English-Chinese dictionary. Use the corresponding character for your animal totem or the name of a deity you venerate. Use a character that represents your greatest aspiration. If, however, you feel overwhelmed and do not know where to start, use one of the characters in table I.15.

Next comes the tedious part of the exercise. Using a template such as the one shown in figure I.32, or any ten-by-ten grid you've created, draw that same character in ninety-nine different variations. These will be ninety-nine different renderings of Fu Wen unique to your personal craft.

For one of the glyphs, I like to use the traditional Chinese character. Note in the example given in figure I.33 how I've started the first sector of the grid (the top left corner) with the original character. I've also left the last sector (the bottom right corner) empty for my practitioner's seal. The seal is stamped onto the Fu only after the charging ritual has concluded. Each duplicate of the amulet, even if it is a photocopy or print, has an original seal on it. You can opt to keep the grid lines as part of the aesthetic for the Fu, or erase them. Figure I.34 shows the same Fu, the Perennial Prosperity Fu, as in figure I.33, without the grid lines and with a practitioner's seal stamp in that last bottom right corner sector.

In my practice, I design the Fu of Ninety-Nine Glyphs by hand, using a consecrated piece of paper, consecrated pencil, and pen. I prepare my sacred space first, and follow a ritualistic process as described in the section "Opening the Ritual" in chapter 8. This is done during a full moon. Once the space is prepared, I draw the ninety-nine glyphs by hand, leaving the last sector in the bottom right corner blank. While drawing, I burn incense and listen to sutras playing in the background. I keep the meaning of the word in mind as I render the glyphs, stylizing the glyphs in a way to convey the meaning.

For example, in the Perennial Prosperity Fu, many of the glyphs feature a stylized rendering of the character for "Wood" (木), the supportive energetic phase for generating wealth and financial prosperity. See figure 1.19 back in chapter 1 for reference. I also prominently feature the character for "field" or "land" (田) in many of the glyphs, symbolic of assets, property, resources, and, of course, the potential for yielding harvest and abundance. The Lo Shu is another great source of inspiration for the glyphs. I think about what "prosperity" means to me, express that in other words, and use the Lo Shu to design a corresponding glyph.

A second Perennial Fu is provided in figure I.35, one for healing and curing ailments. The character used for the glyphs is 醫[4] (yī), meaning the study and science of medicine (醫學, yī xué), medical doctor (醫生, yīs hēng), or medical treatment (醫療, yī liáo), but also for traditional Chinese medicine (中醫, zhōng yī). The amulet is for medical doctors and holistic healers to assist in their professional work. It can also be used as a metaphysical aid to medical treatment, to assist with someone's medical care and healing.[5] Again, note the last empty sector in the bottom right corner of figure I.35. The individual practitioner who uses the Fu will stamp that sector with his or her seal after the Fu has completed charging. Figure I.34 illustrates how the Perennial Fu looks after it has been stamped by the practitioner's seal.

When the Perennial Fu is completed, I use a divinatory method to determine whether the Fu has been properly crafted for its intended purposes. I proceed only if the divination yields an affirmative result. If negative, I start over. That may seem daunting and excessive, and if it does, you are urged to decide for yourself what resonates with the way you practice your own craft.

The postliminary divination is simply my own way of expressing my faith.

I then scan in the original version of the Perennial Fu so that it is a high-resolution digital file. As needed, copies of the Perennial Fu design are printed out on regular paper with regular printer ink. I then follow general consecration techniques outlined in chapter 7 to consecrate the stack of printed Fu. For me, no more than nine copies of the Fu are made at any one time. Next comes the charging ritual, following techniques discussed in chapter 8. Here, I do skip the postliminary divination, since it was performed already during the conception phase of the Fu. I proceed to seal each copy of the Perennial Fu with my practitioner's seal, in the bottom right corner. Alternatively, if the size of my seal is too small compared to the size of the ninety-nine glyphs, I will inscribe my seal by hand, with consecrated ink.

Poster-size versions can be framed and hung on the walls of a home. Printer paper–size copies can be folded and tucked into a matchbook amulet to be kept in a wallet or handbag. See figure 10.2 for folding instructions for matchbook sigils.

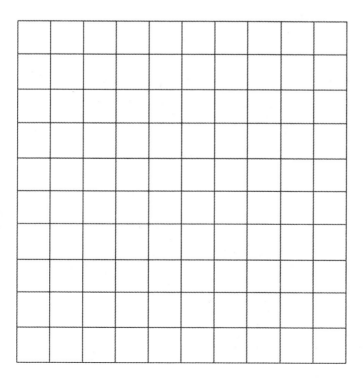

Figure I.32. Template for the Fu of Ninety-Nine Glyphs

Figure I.33.
The Perennial
Prosperity Fu,
with grid

Figure I.34.
The Perennial
Prosperity Fu,
without grid

Figure I.35.
The Perennial
Healer's Fu

# TIMELINE OF TAOIST HISTORY THROUGH THE CHINESE DYNASTIES

**THE FOLLOWING** timeline of the Chinese dynasties provides a general chronology of events referenced in this book. This appendix summarizes the key events of Chinese Taoist history as it pertains to craft and as covered in the preceding chapters. Here, "history" is used loosely to include mythology. Much of China's early history is a blend of documented history and hearsay legend. Other than references to the extraordinary, it is often difficult to know where history ends and mythology begins.

## NEOLITHIC PERIOD
(新石器時代, Xīn Shí Qì Shí Dài)
10,000–2100 BC

- The He Tu comes out of the Neolithic period of China. Fu Xi, a mythical shamanic king, was the founder of human civilization, and formulated the He Tu sequence after seeing patterns on his horse's back.

- The Earlier Heaven Ba Gua is attributed to Fu Xi, conceived when he formulated the He Tu sequence.

- The Yellow Emperor, or Huang Di, is recognized as the first emperor of China. It is unclear whether he is a mythical or historical figure, or perhaps a combination of both. The Yellow Emperor was a shamanic king later deified and venerated in certain Taoist traditions. According to legend, he gained supernatural or occult knowledge that he learned from a supernatural mentor, the Enigmatic Lady of the Ninth Heaven. In Taoist craft, the Yellow Emperor is considered a god of the esoteric arts.

• The mythical Cangjie, imperial historian for the Yellow Emperor, is credited as the inventor of writing. His inspiration for script came from gazing at the footprints of birds. Writing was an important milestone in human civilization, though according to Taoist practitioners of craft, not for the usual reasons cited, but because it is through writing that humans can wield the power to control demons. Thus, Taoist craft relies heavily on writing, and most significantly, on the Fu sigil.

• Invention of the sexagenary calendar, which is still used today in esoteric Taoist craft, is attributed to the Yellow Emperor.

• The earliest Chinese writing found on divinatory oracle bones is dated to this era.

• Artifacts of Neolithic shamanic culture are found in northern and northeastern China.

## XIA DYNASTY
### (夏朝, Xià Cháo)
### 2100–1600 BC

• The Lo Shu magic square is formulated. Legend holds that Yu the Great, a shamanic king, was visited by a tortoise with the Lo Shu sequence embedded on its shell. Following the sequence of the Lo Shu, Yu the Great was able to save China from a great flood.

• Yu the Great is believed to have established the Xia Dynasty, though the Xia is considered by some scholars to be a mythical dynasty, not one that is historically documented.

• The Xia is considered a golden age where the people lived in harmony with the gods and nature, credited to the practices of the shamans.

# SHANG DYNASTY

(商朝, Shāng Cháo)

1600–1050 BC

- Oracle bones dating to the Shang Dynasty refer to a supreme deity residing in Heaven, Lord Di or Shang Di.

- Nature gods are venerated. Mountains, rivers, and other natural landforms and natural phenomena such as rain and thunder are believed to be the physical manifestation of gods.

- Records from this era show an ontological belief in five natural forces that created all life. The five natural forces, whether or not they are related to the Wu Xing, at the very least created the foundation for the Wu Xing.

- Records of magical practice included the calling upon of the four directions at the commencement of a ritual. Also, prior to an oracle bone divination, the four cardinal directions had to be invoked.

- The predecessors of Fu sigils were inscribed decrees or orders that invoke a supreme deity as authorizing a shaman to issue that decree or order to a lesser spirit to do as the shaman commands.

- Shamans and imperial court–appointed magicians held great power in society. Every imperial and aristocratic family would retain a shaman to serve as an adviser, diviner, and healer for the family.

- All kings were also believed to possess shamanic gifts, born with the ability to commune with Heaven and manifest the connected powers of Heaven, Earth, and Man. The Chinese character for "king" (王) comes from this belief, with the three horizontal lines symbolizing the trinity and the vertical line symbolizing the king's ability to connect all three realms.

- While imprisoned by the ruling Shang king, King Wen arranges the eight trigrams of the Ba Gua into the Later Heaven sequence and formulates the sixty-four hexagrams of the I Ching. King Wen divined with the I Ching to predict the fall of the Shang Dynasty and the rise of the Zhou.

# ZHOU DYNASTY
(周朝, Zhōu Cháo)
1046–256 BC

- Conception of the Tai Yi creation myth date to the Zhou Dynasty. According to the Tai Yi creation myth, Tai Yi, or "The Most Venerable One," created Water. With Water, Tai Yi created Heaven (the universe beyond earth). With Heaven, Tai Yi created Earth (the planet earth was created from elements in the universe). Heaven and Earth, together, expanded into all that is above, and all that is below (stellar matter from the universe fertilized the earth to form human life), creating primordial yin and primordial yang, which in turn created the four seasons and four directions.

- Records from this era document court magicians performing exorcisms on behalf of the imperial family.

- The Tao Te Ching, dated around 600–501 BC, is considered one of the most important texts for both exoteric and esoteric Taoism. The text is attributed to Lao Tzu, a sage and scholar in the imperial court, though authorship is disputed.

- Lao Tzu is recognized as the founder of Taoist philosophy. He is immortalized as a deity in Taoist religion. In esoteric Taoist craft, Lao Tzu is invoked by some lineages to assist with magical spells and to empower psychics, diviners, and intuitives.

- Feng shui and geomancy flourish during the Zhou Dynasty, in particular the period 770–475 BC.

- First documented Fu sigils during the Warring States period (475–221 BC) of the Zhou, though the practice of sigil crafting at this time predates Taoism.

- The Shakyamuni Buddha, or Siddhārtha Gautama, is enlightened and teaches Buddhism around 500 BC. Buddhism as a religion is established.

- Confucius (551–479 BC) advances a philosophy and school of thought for morality, setting forth ethical principles for the individual and for social order.

- Magical records from the Zhou Dynasty show that to activate a Fu sigil, the paper talisman was burned or dissolved into consecrated water, and then ingested.

- Fang Shi, or alchemists, diviners, astrologers, magicians, exorcists, and sha-mans, gain in prestige among the imperial families and the aristocracy.

- The Zhuang Zi, dated around 300–201 BC, is given the same level of im-portance in Taoist philosophy as the Tao Te Ching. Authorship is credited to Zhuang Zi, also known as Zhuang Zhou, a philosopher and court official during the Warring States period. The Zhuang Zi is considered both one of the greatest works of Chinese philosophy and also of Chinese literature, as many scholars consider it a literary masterpiece.

- Zhuang Zhou's descriptions of Qi, yin and yang, and the Wu Xing form the enduring ontological principles of Taoist philosophy and also of esoteric Tao-ist craft. He expresses these principles as manifesting through the six fun-damental forms: yin, yang, darkness, light, wind, and rain, which together become the four seasons and four directions. These six forms must be kept at homeostasis. Imbalances of these six forms are what cause calamity and disease, the rise and fall of natural phenomena, and the rise and fall of social systems. These philosophical principles are incorporated into esoteric Taoist craft in a sense to curb or compel calamity and disease, and to control natural phenomena and social order.

- *The Classics of the Esoteric Talisman,* a text on metaphysical principles that guide magical practices and craft, is speculated to have been written around the time of the Zhou Dynasty. (However, note that the earliest copy of the text dates to the Tang Dynasty.)

## QIN DYNASTY

(秦朝, Qín Cháo)

221–206 BC

- The Emperor Qin Shi Huang, unifies China after the Warring States period of the Shang and Zhou. He is obsessed with Taoist alchemy and the quest for an elixir of immortality, employing a sizable legion of Fang Shi, or Taoist alchemists in pursuit of that quest. Qin Shi Huang is credited with building the Great Wall of China and the terra-cotta army.

- The Mao Shan lineage thrived during the Qin Dynasty, as did Taoist ceremonial magic.

- The prevalent political philosophy during this era was Legalism, emphasizing the autocratic power of the emperor, rewarding obedience and severely punishing disobedience. Legalist concepts are often integrated subconsciously into orthodox Taoist craft: obedience to the gods (or to the practitioner, who arrives at authority through his or her raised occult powers) is rewarded in abundance and disobedience is punished without mercy.

- Rise of Neo-Taoism, which focused on the metaphysical or esoteric aspects of Taoist thought. Neo-Taoism emphasized Mystical Learning through a Taoist philosophical framework.

## HAN DYNASTY

(漢朝, Hàn Cháo)

206 BC–AD 220

- Zhong Li Quan, one of the Eight Immortals, was believed to have lived during the Han Dynasty.

- Shamanic practices and magical traditions, including Fu sigil crafting, are merged with Taoist thought.

- Confucianism and esoteric Taoist craft are blended together. It became common for aristocrats and government officials to identify publicly as Confucian, but in personal religious practice, they were Taoist.

- First magical Taoist lineage, the Tian Shi, established under the powerful magician and alchemist Zhang Dao Ling, who was later immortalized.

- Around 100 BC, Mahayana Buddhism, a distinct sect of the Buddhist faith, is established. In Chinese cultural practice, Mahayana Buddhism and Taoism are often syncretized.

- Emperor Wu expended substantial court resources to hire alchemists and magicians to create the elixir of immortality.

- Taoist magical practitioners achieved their greatest heights of power. Taoist practice during this era focused heavily on divination.

- A well-accepted ethical code was followed by practitioners of Taoist craft: if a practitioner harms another or brings harm to either Heaven or Earth, then a celestial administration would adjudicate on these deeds and return a punishment of great suffering to that practitioner or the practitioner's descendants. Fear of such repercussions greatly informed the ethical code adhered to by magical practitioners.

- There was a widely circulated prophecy of a Taoist messiah, the reincarnation of Lao Tzu. Such messianic beliefs played a significant role in medieval Taoism.

- Pacing the Big Dipper is a ceremonial practice descending from a practice started during the Han Dynasty called Flying to the Stars. The mystical pacing method was incorporated into rituals and magical craft.

## THREE KINGDOMS
(三國, Sān Guó)

AD 220–265

- Before the Three Kingdoms era, around AD 184, the Tian Shi lineage of Taoist magicians led the Yellow Turban Rebellion against the Han Emperor. The Tian Shi priests were able to gain wide public favor because they performed healing magic for the people without charge. However, around AD 211, Zhang Lu, a descendent of Zhang Dao Ling and a leading priest in the Tian Shi lineage, surrendered to Cao Cao, a warlord during the Han Dynasty. Doing so, however, gained great favors and political power for the Tian Shi lineage during the Three Kingdoms era.

- Wei Huancun, a Taoist high priestess, established the Shang Qing lineage, which focused on inner alchemy.

- Ge Xuan, a Fang Shi, or magician and alchemist, receives occult knowledge on Fu sigil crafting from deities and transcribes that knowledge into what will later be known as the Ling Bao (Numinous Treasure) Scriptures.

- The Three Mao Brothers establish what would become the legacy of some of the most powerful Taoist magical lineages in Mao Shan.

## JIN DYNASTY
### (晉朝, Jìn Cháo)
### AD 265–420

- One of the most enduring Taoist magical lineages, the Ling Bao, was established, blending Taoist magic with Mahayana Buddhism. The Ling Bao were known to be powerful practitioners of ceremonial magic.

- Bo He, a legendary immortal and sage, receives talismanic scriptures from Heaven, which he uses to craft powerful Fu sigils. Instructions for crafting Bo He's Fu sigils were later memorialized in the *Bao Puzi,* authored by the alchemist and metaphysician Ge Hong.

- Ge Hong, an alchemist and aristocrat, writes extensively about esoteric Taoism. Ge Hong stressed nonharm and to forebear from retaliatory craft or magic. In terms of Fu sigil crafting, he noted that the writing instrument used by the practitioner had to be made out of peach wood and the ink from red cinnabar.

- Cloud writing script for Fu craft is popularized, most notably found in the text titled *Three Caverns of the Supernatural Fu Talismanic Records.*

- The *Writ of the Three Sovereigns,* a seminal text on traditional Fu sigil crafting, outlines summonings, invocations, and exorcisms and is believed also to include Bo He's talismanic teachings.

## SUI DYNASTY
### (隋朝, Suí Cháo)
### AD 581–618

- Magic mirrors were an integral part of exorcisms and Taoist magic, and were used as metaphysical weapons against demons and forces from hell.

- National Taoist institutions were established.

- Relations between Taoists and Buddhists were complicated. There was a great deal of syncretism between Taoism and Buddhism, with Taoist practice integrating Buddhist thought. However, there was also tension between the two as both struggled against each other for social and political power.

# TANG DYNASTY
(唐朝, Táng Cháo)
AD 618–906

- Three of the Eight Immortals, Zhang Guo Lao, Lu Dong Bin, and Han Xiang Zi, were believed to have lived during the Tang Dynasty.

- Taoism flourished during this era and gained great favor with the imperial family, due to the imperial family's claim of lineage tracing back to Lao Tzu.

- The rise of Taoism came at the expense of Buddhism. Buddhists were persecuted during the ninth century.

- Zhang Guo Lao, one of the Eight Immortals, was a historic figure from the Tang Dynasty. He was a hermit living in the remote mountains who practiced necromancy, alchemy, and other magical arts. He is credited as the most powerful magician ever to have lived, and was thus later immortalized.

- Han Xiang Zi was documented as an aristocrat who later cultivated himself to achieve immortality. Memorialized as one of the Eight Immortals and a patron of musicians.

- The earliest copies of the *Classics of the Esoteric Talisman,* a text on metaphysical principles that guide magical practices and craft, are dated to the Tang Dynasty, though it has been speculated that it was written around the Zhou Dynasty.

- The Zheng Yi lineage, comprising practitioners of ceremonial magic, commercialized Fu talismans and began selling them as spells.

- The Lu, a formalized roster of craft, was established, and only certified Taoist priests or practitioners familiar with the contents of the Lu were authorized to craft Fu sigils.

- Most contemporary Taoist lineages claim a magical heritage that dates back to one of the lineages established during the Tang Dynasty.

- Substantial syncretism of Taoism with Buddhism and Confucianism.

## SONG DYNASTY
(宋朝, Sòng Cháo)
AD 960–1279

- Cao Guo Jiu, one of the Eight Immortals, was believed to have lived during the Song Dynasty.

- A branch of magic called Thunder Rites, or thunder magic, arose. Thunder magic could be found in both orthodox traditional lineages of Taoist craft and as an eclectic practice adopted by individual practitioners.

- Hsiao Pao-Chen established the Tai Yi Tao lineage, a tradition that practiced healing magic and reconciled Confucianism and Buddhism with Taoist craft.

- The Quan Zhen lineage, a tradition that emphasized morality, ethical cultivation, and the accumulation of good deeds to achieve immortality, was established.

- The Red Hat lineage was established as a tradition of trained mediums, distinguished from shamans, who became possessed by spirits and allowed the spirit world to communicate through them, rather than the more popular shamanic approach of traveling to the underworld to commune with spirits.

- The Shen Hsiao lineage flourished during this era and was notable for its veneration of Lei Gong and the practice of Thunder Rites, or thunder magic.

- The Chinese Religious Reformation resulted in Taoist lineages diverging from sorcery, ceremonial magic, and outer alchemy toward inner cultivation, meditation, and inner alchemy.

- Records of exorcisms note processes that involve drawing out evil spirits from the body that the spirit is possessing (or the space that the spirit is haunting) and transferring them into insects that are then trapped into a vase. To draw out and transfer the evil spirits, the practitioner used Fu sigils to command the evil spirits.

- Outer alchemy and aspects of ceremonial magic in esoteric Taoism begin to decline.

## YUAN DYNASTY
(元朝, Yuán Cháo)
AD 1279–1368

- Li Tie Guai, one of the Eight Immortals, is believed to have lived around the time of the Yuan Dynasty.

- The Zhen Da Tao lineage, a magical tradition that practiced Buddhist principles of nonharm, compassion, and vegetarianism, was established. Practitioners used prayer and mantras for healing and exorcisms, rather than the ceremonial magic practices of preceding traditions.

- Kublai Khan and the Mongols rule China. (China also becomes more open to Western influences.) The Yuan emperor institutes Buddhism as the official state religion, at the expense of Taoism.

- Taoism is suppressed. A purge of Taoist texts results in the burning of many Fang Shu, or Books of Methods.

## MING DYNASTY
(明朝, Míng Cháo)
AD 1368–1644

- An orphaned peasant boy turned Buddhist monk turned leader of a rebellion against the Yuan Dynasty becomes the first emperor of the Ming.

- Taoism regained favor during the Ming Dynasty, and Taoist magicians and alchemists were appointed to the imperial court.

- Fu sigil crafting, sorcery, and exorcism grow in popularity.

# QING DYNASTY
(清朝, Qīng Cháo)

AD 1644–1912

- As part of the overthrow of the Ming Dynasty and rise of the Qing, the Qing court denounced Taoist magic and sorcery.

- Taoism declines dramatically during the Qing. Taoist texts on craft were intentionally excluded from the imperial library.

- There is a public shift away from esoteric Taoist craft, condemning the metaphysical practices of Taoism as superstitious and an antithesis of modern science.

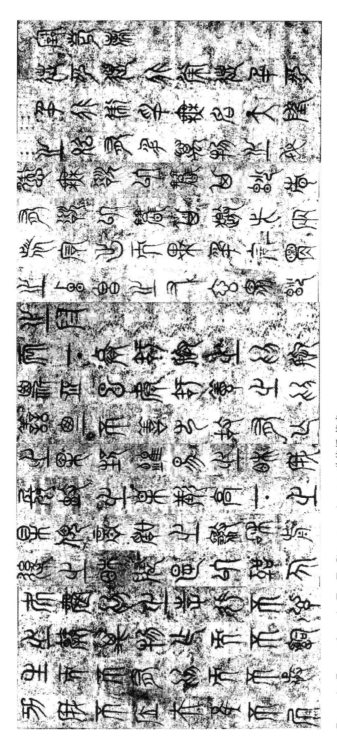

Figure J.1. Excerpt from the Tao Te Ching in seal script, 道德經篆書

# APPENDIX K

# CHINESE ASTROLOGICAL CORRESPONDENCES

**AS NOTED IN** chapter 8, in the section "The Timing of a Charging Ritual," determining when a ritual is performed is a critical component in craft. Since the conception of the Chinese sexagenary calendar, with its heavenly stem and earthly branch correspondences, and the Chinese zodiac, and for as long as practitioners have been observing the moon phases, craft has been timed to astrology, one of the foundational theoretical principles of metaphysical practice. In my personal work, I have found Western and Eastern astrological correspondences equally effective for timing craft. However, this appendix will focus on Eastern approaches.

Eastern esoteric craft, from feng shui and Ba Zi (Four Pillars of Destiny) natal fortune-telling to ceremonial magic, begins with the sexagenary calendar. To engage with Taoist craft, a rudimentary understanding of the Chinese calendar system is necessary. The following steps outline converting Western Gregorian calendar years to determine the corresponding Chinese sexagenary year. Each year, according to its heavenly stem and earthly branch, is predominantly governed by certain energies that can influence social and personal events for that year.

Used in conjunction with the reference tables in chapter 8, this appendix will enable the practitioner to time his or her craft according to traditional tried-and-true Taoist metaphysical principles. These tables are also informative in basic Ba Zi determinations. Ba Zi, also known in the West as the Four Pillars of Destiny,[1] is a form of Asian fortune-telling (I say "Asian" because it is practiced by numerous Eastern cultures) that considers astrological phenomena and their correspondences according to the sexagenary system, but also analyzes

| 1 | 2 | 3 | 4 | 5 | 6 | 7 | 8 | 9 | 10 |
|---|---|---|---|---|---|---|---|---|---|
| 甲 (jiǎ) 子 (zǐ) | 乙 (yǐ) 丑 (chǒu) | 丙 (bǐng) 寅 (yín) | 丁 (dīng) 卯 (mǎo) | 戊 (wù) 辰 (chén) | 己 (jǐ) 巳 (sì) | 庚 (gēng) 午 (wǔ) | 辛 (xīn) 未 (wèi) | 壬 (rén) 申 (shēn) | 癸 (guǐ) 酉 (yǒu) |
| 11 | 12 | 13 | 14 | 15 | 16 | 17 | 18 | 19 | 20 |
| 甲 (jiǎ) 戌 (xū) | 乙 (yǐ) 亥 (hài) | 丙 (bǐng) 子 (zǐ) | 丁 (dīng) 丑 (chǒu) | 戊 (wù) 寅 (yín) | 己 (jǐ) 卯 (mǎo) | 庚 (gēng) 辰 (chén) | 辛 (xīn) 巳 (sì) | 壬 (rén) 午 (wǔ) | 癸 (guǐ) 未 (wèi) |
| 21 | 22 | 23 | 24 | 25 | 26 | 27 | 28 | 29 | 30 |
| 甲 (jiǎ) 申 (shēn) | 乙 (yǐ) 酉 (yǒu) | 丙 (bǐng) 戌 (xū) | 丁 (dīng) 亥 (hài) | 戊 (wù) 子 (zǐ) | 己 (jǐ) 丑 (chǒu) | 庚 (gēng) 寅 (yín) | 辛 (xīn) 卯 (mǎo) | 壬 (rén) 辰 (chén) | 癸 (guǐ) 巳 (sì) |
| 31 | 32 | 33 | 34 | 35 | 36 | 37 | 38 | 39 | 40 |
| 甲 (jiǎ) 午 (wǔ) | 乙 (yǐ) 未 (wèi) | 丙 (bǐng) 申 (shēn) | 丁 (dīng) 酉 (yǒu) | 戊 (wù) 戌 (xū) | 己 (jǐ) 亥 (hài) | 庚 (gēng) 子 (zǐ) | 辛 (xīn) 丑 (chǒu) | 壬 (rén) 寅 (yín) | 癸 (guǐ) 卯 (mǎo) |
| 41 | 42 | 43 | 44 | 45 | 46 | 47 | 48 | 49 | 50 |
| 甲 (jiǎ) 辰 (chén) | 乙 (yǐ) 巳 (sì) | 丙 (bǐng) 午 (wǔ) | 丁 (dīng) 未 (wèi) | 戊 (wù) 申 (shēn) | 己 (jǐ) 酉 (yǒu) | 庚 (gēng) 戌 (xū) | 辛 (xīn) 亥 (hài) | 壬 (rén) 子 (zǐ) | 癸 (guǐ) 丑 (chǒu) |
| 51 | 52 | 53 | 54 | 55 | 56 | 57 | 58 | 59 | 60 |
| 甲 (jiǎ) 寅 (yín) | 乙 (yǐ) 卯 (mǎo) | 丙 (bǐng) 辰 (chén) | 丁 (dīng) 巳 (sì) | 戊 (wù) 午 (wǔ) | 己 (jǐ) 未 (wèi) | 庚 (gēng) 申 (shēn) | 辛 (xīn) 酉 (yǒu) | 壬 (rén) 戌 (xū) | 癸 (guǐ) 亥 (hài) |

Table K.1. Sexagenary year: heavenly stem and earthly branch correspondences

a person's fate based on patterns in events and human behavior observed for thousands of years.[2]

A Fu sigil or basic amulet can be crafted for general good luck and protection in a given year to guard against certain general negative Qi energy that could be generated by astronomical positions during that year, and also to amplify certain general positive Qi energy. The following steps can also be used to design a personal good luck and protection talisman by year of birth. Determine the correspondences for the recipient's year of birth to craft the Fu. Such a Fu sigil can then be used as a general talisman for those born in that year.

## Step 1. Subtract 3 from the Western Gregorian calendar year.

To convert a Western Gregorian calendar year to the Chinese sexagenary year, begin by subtracting 3 from the year. Three examples will be used to illustrate each of the steps for conversion. For example 1, to convert the year 1978 to the sexagenary year, subtract 3 from 1978 to get 1975.

| Example 1 | The Fu to be crafted relates to the year 1978. | 1978 - 3 = 1975 |
| Example 2 | The Fu to be crafted relates to the year 1981. | 1981 - 3 = 1978 |
| Example 3 | The Fu to be crafted relates to the year 2017. | 2017 - 3 = 2014 |

Figure K.1. Step 1 in converting a Western Gregorian calendar year to the Chinese sexagenary year

## Step 2. Divide the resulting number by 60. If there is a remainder, ignore the remainder. Focus on the whole number.

Take the resulting number from step 1 and divide by 60. There will likely be a remainder. Ignore the remainder.

| Example 1 | The resulting number was 1975. $1975 \div 60 = 32.9166...$ Only consider the whole number. | Whole number: 32. Step 2 result is 32. |
| Example 2 | The resulting number was 1978. $1978 \div 60 = 32.9666...$ Only consider the whole number. | Whole number: 32. Step 2 result is 32. |
| Example 3 | The resulting number was 2014. $1975 \div 60 = 33.5666...$ Only consider the whole number. | Whole number: 33. Step 2 result is 33. |

Figure K.2. Step 2 in converting a Western Gregorian calendar year to the Chinese sexagenary year

## Step 3. Take the number resulting from step 1 minus 60 multiplied by the number resulting from step 2.

The formula is: [step 1 result] – (60 × [step 2 result]).

| | | |
|---|---|---|
| Example 1 | Step 1 result: 1975. Step 2 result: 32. | 1975 – (60 x 32) = 55 |
| Example 2 | Step 1 result: 1978. Step 2 result: 32. | 1978 – (60 x 32) = 58 |
| Example 3 | Step 1 result: 2014. Step 2 result: 33. | 2014 – (60 x 33) = 34 |

Figure K.3. Step 3 in converting a Western Gregorian calendar year to the Chinese sexagenary year

## Step 4. Locate the resulting number from step 3 in table K.1.

For each of the sixty sexagenary years, table K.1 shows the corresponding heavenly stem and earthly branch. Figure K.4 is the key for table K.1. The number for each cell indicates the year in the sexagenary cycle. Below the sexagenary year, on the left is the heavenly stem, and on the right is the earthly branch. Thus, for example 1, the result from step 3 was 55: the Western calendar year 1978 converts to the 55th year of the Chinese sexagenary calendar. Table K.1 provides the heavenly stem and earthly branch correspondence for the 55th year.

| Sexagenary Year | |
|---|---|
| Heavenly Stem | Earthly Branch |

Figure K.4. Key to table K.1

## Step 5. Assess the heavenly stem correspondence for the year.

Locate the corresponding heavenly stem (left cell) in table K.2. The heavenly stem informs the practitioner whether that year is yin-dominant or yang-dominant. It also provides insight into the Wu Xing phase that the given year is governed by. The correspondences offer metaphysical influences borne by the heavenly stem.

In Chinese astrological determinations, such as calculations of Ba Zi, or the Four Pillars of Destiny, these correspondences can be used to consider character attributes by heavenly stem and the prevailing Wu Xing phase. Thus,

| Example 1 | Step 3 result: 55.<br><br>Thus, the Western calendar year 1978 corresponds with the 55th sexagenary year in the medieval Chinese calendar. | Table correspondence:<br><br>**55**<br>戊 (wù) \| 午 (wǔ) |
| Example 2 | Step 3 result: 8.<br><br>Thus, the Western calendar year 1981 corresponds with the 58th sexagenary year in the medieval Chinese calendar. | Table correspondence:<br><br>**58**<br>辛 (xīn) \| 酉 (yǒu) |
| Example 3 | Step 3 result: 8.<br><br>Thus the Western calendar year 2017 corresponds with the 34th sexagenary year in the medieval Chinese calendar. | Table correspondence:<br><br>**34**<br>丁 (ding) \| 酉 (yǒu) |

Figure K.5. Finding the heavenly stem and earthly branch

the table need not be limited to craft timing considerations. The heavenly stems also relate to personality traits. One whose natal chart is Water dominant, for instance, may find many of the traits attributed to Water, as shown in table K.2, resonant. If the Ren heavenly stem dominates, that Water is more yang; if the Gui stem dominates, Water traits manifest more as yin.

## Step 6. Determine the earthly branch correspondence for the year.

Locate the corresponding earthly branch (right cell) in table K.1. The earthly branch informs the practitioner of the zodiac sign that the year will be governed by. The earthly branch and corresponding zodiac sign relate to certain metaphysical energies and timing. Table K.3 can serve as a reference for optimal harnessing of the energies relating to the earthly branches and Chinese zodiac signs. Note additional zodiac sign attributions in the section "Animal Totems" in appendix B.

To continue with the three examples for determining heavenly stems and earthly branches by sexagenary year, once the earthly branch is identified in table K.1, the corresponding zodiac sign for the given earthly branch can provide greater insight into the dominant energies for that year.

| Heavenly Stem | Binary | Wu Xing | Correspondences |
|---|---|---|---|
| Jiǎ 甲 | yang | Wood 木 | Leader of new beginnings; strong abilities in business ventures; great potential for generating grown, in self and in others. A pioneer. Often a voracious reader and seeker of knowledge. Idealistic and visionary. Strong sense of ethics and goodwill. Optimistic. Possesses a great deal of vitality and verve. An evergreen character. Seeks to lead the collective through vision, aspiration, creativity, and social justice. Innately a teacher-scholar personality. Dominates or overpowers Yin Earth. |
| Yǐ 乙 | yin | | Deeply knowledgeable, intelligent, insightful, and full of good advice. Seeks harmony with the collective. Nurtures development of the self and of others. Strong emphasis on utility and contributing to society or having a purposeful social cause. Tendency to be inflexible and often too stubborn to change course, even when going in the wrong direction. Empowerment with Yang Water yields greater success and accomplishment. |
| Bing 丙 | yang | Fire 火 | Ambitious growth upward. Motivation for ascent. Spontaneous. Passionate. Intense. Hard to control. Can be prone to extremes. Anti-authority often anti-establishment. Seeks to create. Superior leadership abilities; charismatic. Decisive. Innovative and creative. Dynamic. Dominates or overpowers Yin Metal. |
| Ding 丁 | yin | | Steady growth. Generates many great ideas, but lacks execution and starts more endeavors than finishes. Dedicated to humanitarian services. Seeks to be a fire that illuminates the pathway for others. Spiritual leadership. Inspires and motivates that collective. Empowerment with Yang Wood brings even greater success and accomplishment. |
| Wù 戊 | yang | Earth 土 | Flourishing in resources. Can be stubborn, willful, embodying the mountain. Seeks great heights of achievement and acquisition, but that same aspiration can be a persona obstacle. First to experience the sunlight, but first to sustain the wind and rain. Enterprising; methodical and intelligent in business startups, raising capital, and spotting fruitful investments. Can be too cynical of others' intentions or motivations. Dominates or overpowers Yin Water. |

Table K.2. Heavenly stems and Wu Xing correspondences

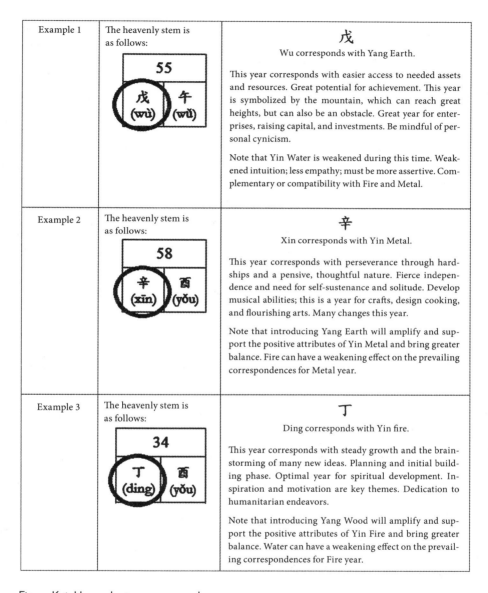

| Example 1 | The heavenly stem is as follows: | 戊 |
|---|---|---|

Example 1 — The heavenly stem is as follows: **55** 戊 (wù) 午 (wǔ)

戊
Wu corresponds with Yang Earth.

This year corresponds with easier access to needed assets and resources. Great potential for achievement. This year is symbolized by the mountain, which can reach great heights, but can also be an obstacle. Great year for enterprises, raising capital, and investments. Be mindful of personal cynicism.

Note that Yin Water is weakened during this time. Weakened intuition; less empathy; must be more assertive. Complementary or compatibility with Fire and Metal.

Example 2 — The heavenly stem is as follows: **58** 辛 (xīn) 酉 (yǒu)

辛
Xin corresponds with Yin Metal.

This year corresponds with perseverance through hardships and a pensive, thoughtful nature. Fierce independence and need for self-sustenance and solitude. Develop musical abilities; this is a year for crafts, design cooking, and flourishing arts. Many changes this year.

Note that introducing Yang Earth will amplify and support the positive attributes of Yin Metal and bring greater balance. Fire can have a weakening effect on the prevailing correspondences for Metal year.

Example 3 — The heavenly stem is as follows: **34** 丁 (ding) 酉 (yǒu)

丁
Ding corresponds with Yin fire.

This year corresponds with steady growth and the brainstorming of many new ideas. Planning and initial building phase. Optimal year for spiritual development. Inspiration and motivation are key themes. Dedication to humanitarian endeavors.

Note that introducing Yang Wood will amplify and support the positive attributes of Yin Fire and bring greater balance. Water can have a weakening effect on the prevailing correspondences for Fire year.

Figure K.6. Heavenly stem correspondences

| Earthly Branch | Zodiac Sign | Energetic Correspondence | Timing Correspondence |
|---|---|---|---|
| 寅 Yìn | 虎 Tiger | Facilitates favorable metaphysical energy for proactive action, competition, combat; increasing courage, bravery, and willpower. | Auspicious for acquisitions, games, and advancing action during the ninth lunar month. |
| | | Optimal for craft related to love, romance, home, family, the domestic sphere, social relationships, or to facilitate harmonious social or civil engagements. (Based on the powers and authorities of the ruling Guardian of the East, who nurtures and protects the realms.) | Early spring: February 3–20 (Aquarius and Pisces) |
| 卯 Mǎo | 兔 Rabbit | Facilitates favorable metaphysical energy for fertility, compassion, sincere relationships, luxury and comfort, domestic bliss, sentimentality, and increases patience and understanding. | Auspicious for acquisitions, games, and advancing action during the eleventh lunar month. |
| | | Optimal for craft related to love, romance, home, family, and the domestic sphere, social relationships, or to facilitate harmonious social or civil engagements. (Based on the powers and the authorities of the ruling Guardian of the East, who nurtures and protects the realms.) | Mid-spring: March 5–22 (Pisces and Aries) |
| 辰 Chén | 龍 Dragon | Facilitates favorable metaphysical energy for achievement, manifesting ambitions; innovation; supportive of the free spirit; raises power; strengthens the abilities and craft of the magician. | Auspicious for acquisitions, games, and advancing action during the second lunar month. |
| | | Optimal for craft related to love, romance, home, family, the domestic sphere, social relationships, or to facilitate harmonious social or civil engagements. (Based on the powers and authorities of the ruling Guardian of the East, who nurtures and protects the realms.) | Late spring: April 4–21 (Aries and Taurus) |
| 巳 Sì | 蛇 Snake | Facilitates favorable metaphysical energy for analytical scientific, innovative, or scholarly endeavors; raises intuition and psychic powers; brings balance to good and evil, dark and light; protective or defensive magic; can be wielded powerfully in defensive or retaliatory craft. | Auspicious for acquisitions, games, and advancing action during the fourth lunar month. |
| | | Strengthens or supports energies for asset acquisition, business, finances, wealth, and advancement in social status. (Based on the powers and authorities of the ruling Guardian of the South, who brings growth, innovation, creativity, and initiations.) | Early summer: May 5–22 (Taurus and Gemini) |

Table K.3. Earthly branches and zodiacal correspondences

| Earthly Branch | Zodiac Sign | Energetic Correspondence | Timing Correspondence |
|---|---|---|---|
| 午<br>Wǔ | 馬<br>Horse | Facilitates favorable metaphysical energy for successful social engagements, ensuring safe travel and adventures, business prosperity, comfort, luxury, and material abundance, and advancement in social status.<br><br>Strengthens or supports energies for asset acquisition, business, finances, wealth, and advancement in social status. [Based on the powers and authorities of the ruling Guardian of the South, who brings growth, innovation, creativity, and initiations.] | Auspicious for acquisitions, games, and advancing action during the sixth lunar month.<br><br>Midsummer: June 5–22 (Gemini and Cancer) |
| 未<br>Wèi | 羊<br>Sheep | Facilitates favorable metaphysical energy for diplomacy, peace between disputing factions, harmony and prosperity for all, humanitarian endeavors, increasing the resources of the indigent, and social advancement.<br><br>Strengthens or supports energies for asset acquisition, business, finances, wealth, and advancement in social status. [Based on the powers and authorities of the ruling Guardian of the South, who brings growth, innovation, creativity, and initiations.] | Auspicious for acquisitions, games, and advancing action during the eighth lunar month.<br><br>Late summer: July 6–24 (Cancer and Leo) |
| 申<br>Shēn | 猴<br>Monkey | Facilitates favorable metaphysical energy for the jack of all trades. Raises energy for greater intelligence, quicker wit, and expresses the gifts of the multitalented and well-rounded. This earthly branch and corresponding zodiac sign is versatile and multifunctional.<br><br>Strengthens or supports energies for education, scholarship, ambitions and aspirations, professional or career development, and advancement in social status. Also conducive for improving health or personal vitality. (Based on the powers and authorities of the ruling Guardian of the West, who sees all, brings sight and insight, perception, and clairvoyance.) | Auspicious for acquisitions, games, and advancing action during the tenth lunar month.<br><br>Early autumn: August 7–24 (Leo and Virgo) |
| 酉<br>Yǒu | 雞<br>Rooster | Facilitates favorable metaphysical energy for advancement in social status, manifesting ambitions, the teaching profession, the entertainment profession, and endeavors related to arts and culture.<br><br>Strengthens or supports energies for education, scholarship, ambitions and aspirations, professional or career development, and advancement in social status. Also conducive for improving health or personal vitality. (Based on the powers and authorities of the ruling Guardian of the West, who sees all, brings sight and insight, perception, and clairvoyance.) | Auspicious for acquisitions, games, and advancing action during the twelfth lunar month.<br><br>Mid-autumn: September 7–24 (Virgo and Libra) |

Table K.3. Earthly branches and zodiacal correspondences (continued)

| Earthly Branch | Zodiac Sign | Energetic Correspondence | Timing Correspondence |
|---|---|---|---|
| 戌 Xū | 狗 Dog | Facilitates favorable metaphysical energy for legal matters, health and vitality, or for ensuring loyalty or resourcefulness. Helps to win political favor. Improves one's popularity or social prominence.<br><br>Strengthens or supports energies for education, scholarship, ambitions and aspirations, professional or career development, and advancement in social status. Also conducive for improving health or personal vitality. [Based on the powers and authorities of the ruling Guardian of the West, who sees all, brings sight and insight, perception, and clairvoyance.] | Auspicious for acquisitions, games, and advancing action during the first lunar month.<br><br>Late autumn: October 8–24 (Libra and Scorpio) |
| 亥 Hài | 豬 Boar | Facilitates favorable metaphysical energy for ensuring tranquility, peace, and harmony in the domestic sphere; likewise, can be used to raise energy that will disrupt another's tranquility, peace, or harmony in the domestic sphere. Highly creative power. Also conducive for improving health or personal vitality.<br><br>Prayers and conjurations; defensive or retaliatory work where a practitioner seeks to cause another to be blindsided. TO do so, Hai and Boar must be "turned on its head" through craft, or transformed into ill-dignified energy. [Based on the powers and authorities of the ruling Guardian of the North, who hears all, brings heightened sensitivity, and clairaudience.] | Auspicious for acquisitions, games, and advancing action during the third lunar month.<br><br>Early winter: November 7–23 (Scorpio and Sagittarius) |
| 子 Zǐ | 鼠 Rat | Facilitates favorable metaphysical energy for money magic, advancement in social status, business success, financial investments, and real property. Likewise, can be used to raise energy that will disrupt another's business success, financial status or bring detriment to another's property matters.<br><br>Prayers and conjurations; defensive or retaliatory work where the practitioner seeks to cause another to be blindsided. To do so, Zi and Rat must be "turned on its head" through craft, or transformed into ill-dignified energy. [Based on the powers and authorities of the ruling Guardian of the North, who hears all, brings heightened sensitivity, and clairaudience.] | Auspicious for acquisitions, games, and advancing action during the fifth lunar month.<br><br>Mid-winter: December 6–23 (Sagittarius and Capricorn) |
| 丑 Chǒu | 牛 Ox | Facilitates favorable metaphysical energy for stability, security, peace of mind, and general, year-round prosperity. Likewise, can be used to raise energy that will disrupt another's sense of personal or professional stability and security. Also conducive for improving health or personal vitality.<br><br>Prayers and conjurations; defensive or retaliatory work where a practitioner seeks to cause another to be blindsided. To do so, Chou and Ox must be "turned on its head" through craft, or transformed into ill-dignified energy. [Based on the powers and authorities of the ruling Guardian of the North, who hears all, brings heightened sensitivity, and clairaudience.] | Auspicious for acquisitions, games, and advancing action during the seventh lunar month.<br><br>Late winter: January 5–21 (Capricorn and Aquarius) |

Table K.3. Earthly branches and zodiacal correspondences (continued)

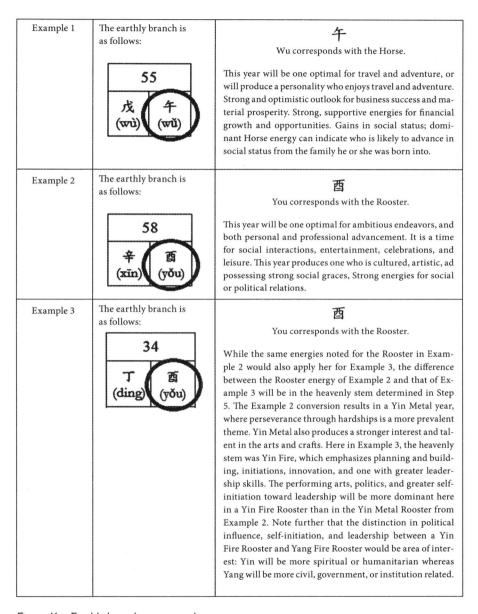

| Example 1 | The earthly branch is as follows: | 午<br>Wu corresponds with the Horse.<br><br>This year will be one optimal for travel and adventure, or will produce a personality who enjoys travel and adventure. Strong and optimistic outlook for business success and material prosperity. Strong, supportive energies for financial growth and opportunities. Gains in social status; dominant Horse energy can indicate who is likely to advance in social status from the family he or she was born into. |
|---|---|---|
| | 55<br>戊 (wù)　午 (wǔ) | |
| Example 2 | The earthly branch is as follows: | 酉<br>You corresponds with the Rooster.<br><br>This year will be one optimal for ambitious endeavors, and both personal and professional advancement. It is a time for social interactions, entertainment, celebrations, and leisure. This year produces one who is cultured, artistic, ad possessing strong social graces, Strong energies for social or political relations. |
| | 58<br>辛 (xīn)　酉 (yǒu) | |
| Example 3 | The earthly branch is as follows: | 酉<br>You corresponds with the Rooster.<br><br>While the same energies noted for the Rooster in Example 2 would also apply her for Example 3, the difference between the Rooster energy of Example 2 and that of Example 3 will be in the heavenly stem determined in Step 5. The Example 2 conversion results in a Yin Metal year, where perseverance through hardships is a more prevalent theme. Yin Metal also produces a stronger interest and talent in the arts and crafts. Here in Example 3, the heavenly stem was Yin Fire, which emphasizes planning and building, initiations, innovation, and one with greater leadership skills. The performing arts, politics, and greater self-initiation toward leadership will be more dominant here in a Yin Fire Rooster than in the Yin Metal Rooster from Example 2. Note further that the distinction in political influence, self-initiation, and leadership between a Yin Fire Rooster and Yang Fire Rooster would be area of interest: Yin will be more spiritual or humanitarian whereas Yang will be more civil, government, or institution related. |
| | 34<br>丁 (ding)　酉 (yǒu) | |

Figure K.7. Earthly branch correspondences

## LUNAR MONTH CONVERSIONS

Converting a date from the Western Gregorian calendar to a lunar month is more complicated than the simple formula for converting years. Typically, a practitioner would consult an almanac or use a conversion tool.[3] In the three examples provided here, a conversion tool is used to determine the corresponding lunar months for the three given Gregorian calendar dates.[4]

| Example 1 | An Individual's date of birth is December 26, 1978. | Using a conversion tool, the date falls within: 11th lunar month. |
|---|---|---|
| Example 2 | An individual's date of birth is September 24, 1981. | Using a conversion tool, the date falls within: 8th lunar month. |
| Example 3 | What are the timing correspondences for a Fu sigil to be charged on August 8, 2017? | Using a conversion tool, the date falls within: 6th lunar month. |

Figure K.8. Converting Western dates to lunar months

Like each sexagenary year, each lunar month is assigned a heavenly stem and an earthly branch. Table K.4 shows the lunar month correspondences. To use table K.4, locate the heavenly stem for the given Gregorian year after converting it to the sexagenary year. Then find the converted lunar month, and the two will provide the heavenly stem and earthly branch for the given date. In table K.4, the lunar month correspondences for the three examples are shown in Figure K.9.

Refer back to tables K.2 and K.3. The attributions provided, as applied to the given lunar month, express the most prevailing energies for that month. Although the method of determination is quite different from the sun signs in Western astrology (Aries, Taurus, Gemini, and so on), in terms of what it expresses, it can be likened to the sun signs. The heavenly stem and earthly branch corresponding to the lunar month offers insight into the external or outward appearance of a person or situation, the persona, and the primary indicator of the most prevailing metaphysical energies at play. It is the nature of the engine that drives the trajectory first determined by the sexagenary year correspondences.

| Example 1 | December 26, 1978:<br>11th lunar month<br><br>Heavenly stem for 1978:<br><br>戊 | Lunar Month Correspondence: | |
|-----------|---------------------------------|---------------------------------|---|
| | | Heavenly Stem | Earthly Branch |
| | | 甲<br>(jiǎ) | 子<br>(zi) |

| Example 2 | September 24, 1981:<br>8th lunar month<br><br>Heavenly stem for 1981:<br><br>辛 | Lunar Month Correspondence: | |
|-----------|---------------------------------|---------------------------------|---|
| | | Heavenly Stem | Earthly Branch |
| | | 丁<br>(ding) | 酉<br>(yǒu) |

| Example 3 | August 8, 2017:<br>6th lunar month<br><br>Heavenly stem for 2017:<br><br>丁 | Lunar Month Correspondence: | |
|-----------|---------------------------------|---------------------------------|---|
| | | Heavenly Stem | Earthly Branch |
| | | 丁<br>(ding) | 未<br>(wèi) |

Figure K.9. Finding lunar month correspondences

The purpose of appendix K is to provide supplementary references for the timing of Fu sigils, and also to introduce the sexagenary calendar system to the Western practitioner. Most branches of study in esoteric Taoism are based on the sexagenary system and correspondences for the heavenly stems, earthly branches, Wu Xing, and Chinese zodiac.

| Wu Xing | Heavenly Stem | | Earthly Branch | | | |
|---------|---------------|---------------|----------------|---------------|---------------|---------------|
| Wood | 甲<br>(jiǎ) | 乙<br>(yǐ) | 寅<br>(yín) | 卯<br>(mǎo) | 辰<br>(chén) | |
| Fire | 丙<br>(bing) | 丁<br>(ding) | 巳<br>(sì) | 午<br>(wǔ) | 未<br>(wèi) | |
| Earth | 戊<br>(wù) | 己<br>(jǐ) | 辰<br>(chén) | 戌<br>(xū) | 丑<br>(chǒu) | |
| Metal | 庚<br>(gēng) | 辛<br>(xīn) | 申<br>(shēn) | 酉<br>(yǒu) | 戌<br>(xū) | 卯<br>(mǎo) |
| Water | 壬<br>(rén) | 癸<br>(guǐ) | 亥<br>(hài) | 子<br>(zī) | 丑<br>(chǒu) | |

Table K.5. Wu Xing heavenly stem and earthly branch assignments

The heavenly stems and earthly branches relate to the Wu Xing five phases. The heavenly stems and earthly branches represent the points along the Yellow

| Year Heavenly Stem ▽ | Month — Heavenly Stem and Earthly Branch ▽ | | | | | |
|---|---|---|---|---|---|---|
| | **1** | **2** | **3** | **4** | **5** | **6** |
| 甲 (jiǎ) / 己 (jǐ) | 丙 (bing) 寅 (yín) | 丁 (ding) 卯 (mǎo) | 戊 (wù) 辰 (chén) | 己 (jǐ) 巳 (sì) | 庚 (gēng) 午 (wǔ) | 辛 (xin) 未 (wèi) |
| 乙 (yǐ) / 庚 (gēng) | 戊 (wù) 寅 (yín) | 己 (jǐ) 卯 (mǎo) | 庚 (gēng) 辰 (chén) | 辛 (xin) 巳 (sì) | 壬 (rén) 午 (wǔ) | 癸 (guǐ) 未 (wèi) |
| 丙 (bing) / 辛 (xin) | 庚 (gēng) 寅 (yín) | 辛 (xin) 卯 (mǎo) | 壬 (rén) 辰 (chén) | 癸 (guǐ) 巳 (sì) | 甲 (jiǎ) 午 (wǔ) | 乙 (yǐ) 未 (wèi) |
| 丁 (ding) / 壬 (rén) | 壬 (rén) 寅 (yín) | 癸 (guǐ) 卯 (mǎo) | 甲 (jiǎ) 辰 (chén) | 乙 (yǐ) 巳 (sì) | 丙 (bing) 午 (wǔ) | 丁 (ding) 未 (wèi) |
| 戊 (wù) / 癸 (guǐ) | 甲 (jiǎ) 寅 (yín) | 乙 (yǐ) 卯 (mǎo) | 丙 (bing) 辰 (chén) | 丁 (ding) 巳 (sì) | 戊 (wù) 午 (wǔ) | 己 (jǐ) 未 (wèi) |

Table K.4. Lunar months: heavenly stem and earthly branch correspondences

| Year Heavenly Stem ▽ | Month Heavenly Stem and Earthly Branch ▽ | | | | | | | | | | | |
|---|---|---|---|---|---|---|---|---|---|---|---|---|
| | 7 | | 8 | | 9 | | 10 | | 11 | | 12 | |
| 甲 (jiǎ) | 壬 (rén) | 申 (shēn) | 癸 (guǐ) | 酉 (yǒu) | 甲 (jiǎ) | 戌 (xū) | 乙 (yǐ) | 亥 (hài) | 丙 (bǐng) | 子 (zǐ) | 丁 (dīng) | 丑 (chǒu) |
| 乙 (yǐ) | 甲 (jiǎ) | 申 (shēn) | 乙 (yǐ) | 酉 (yǒu) | 丙 (bǐng) | 戌 (xū) | 丁 (dīng) | 亥 (hài) | 戊 (wù) | 子 (zǐ) | 己 (jǐ) | 丑 (chǒu) |
| 丙 (bǐng) | 丙 (bǐng) | 申 (shēn) | 丁 (dīng) | 酉 (yǒu) | 戊 (wù) | 戌 (xū) | 己 (jǐ) | 亥 (hài) | 庚 (gēng) | 子 (zǐ) | 辛 (xīn) | 丑 (chǒu) |
| 丁 (dīng) | 戊 (wù) | 申 (shēn) | 己 (jǐ) | 酉 (yǒu) | 庚 (gēng) | 戌 (xū) | 辛 (xīn) | 亥 (hài) | 壬 (rén) | 子 (zǐ) | 癸 (guǐ) | 丑 (chǒu) |
| 戊 (wù) | 庚 (gēng) | 申 (shēn) | 辛 (xīn) | 酉 (yǒu) | 壬 (rén) | 戌 (xū) | 癸 (guǐ) | 亥 (hài) | 甲 (jiǎ) | 子 (zǐ) | 乙 (yǐ) | 丑 (chǒu) |

Table K.4. Lunar months: heavenly stem and earthly branch correspondences (continued)

| Example 1 | December 26, 1978. | Year | | Month | |
|---|---|---|---|---|---|
| | | **Yang Earth** | | **Yang Wood** | |
| | | **Horse** | | **Rat** | |
| | | *In addition to the Yang Earth Horse attributions:* Yang Wood Rat will indicate one who enjoys travel, with strong business acumen. There will be gains in financial and social status in this lifetime. Here is one governed by a strong sense of ethics, a seeker of knowledge, and one full of personal vitality. | | | |

Year / Month table for Example 1:

| Year | | Month | |
|---|---|---|---|
| 戊 (wù) | 午 (wǔ) | 甲 (jiǎ) | 子 (zǐ) |

| Example 2 | September 24, 1981 | Year | | Month | |
|---|---|---|---|---|---|
| | | **Yin Metal** | | **Yin Fire** | |
| | | **Rooster** | | **Rooster** | |
| | | *In addition to the Yin Metal Rooster attributions:* Yin Fire Rooster will indicate one who thrives on arts and culture, scholarship, and would do well in teaching, entertainment, or any of the creative fields. Strong interest in the liberal arts and humanities. The Yin Fire can mean a lack of focus, but one who is a luminary. Possesses a highly creative mind. | | | |

Year / Month table for Example 2:

| Year | | Month | |
|---|---|---|---|
| 辛 (xīn) | 酉 (yǒu) | 丁 (dǐng) | 酉 (yǒu) |

| Example 3 | August 8, 2017 | Year | | Month | |
|---|---|---|---|---|---|
| | | **Yin Fire** | | **Yin Fire** | |
| | | **Rooster** | | **Sheep** | |
| | | *In addition to the Yin Fire Rooster attributions:* Yin Fire Sheep, echoing the Yin Fire energy from example 2, will likewise tend to lack focus but demonstrate strong potential for being a luminary. This is a month that is filled with highly creative energy. Additionally, given the ruling Sheep, energies of diplomacy and altruism are strong, as is a need to bring harmony and peace. The collective energies for this date means one optimal for launching a business in a creative field and ensuring prosperity and success in creative, artistic, or humanitarian endeavors. | | | |

Year / Month table for Example 3:

| Year | | Month | |
|---|---|---|---|
| 丁 (dǐng) | 酉 (yǒu) | 丁 (dǐng) | 未 (wèi) |

Figure K.10. Interpreting sample dates

Path, or twenty-four solar terms, and each stage of the sixty-year cycle, on the principle that the course of human events runs on a sixty-year cycle, and each year of that cycle is subdivided into the twenty-four solar terms that mark the changing seasons. Multiplying 60 by 24, there are 1,440 unique dignities to every cycle. These 1,440 unique dignities can be categorized into 288 manifes-

|  | Compatibility |  |  |  |  | Tension |  |  |  |  |
|---|---|---|---|---|---|---|---|---|---|---|
| **Heavenly Stem** | 甲 (jiǎ) | + | 己 (jǐ) | = | Earth | 甲 (jiǎ) | 㔯 | 戊 (wù) | 己 (jǐ) 㔯 | 癸 (guī) |
|  | 乙 (yǐ) | + | 庚 (gēng) | = | Metal | 乙 (yǐ) | 㔯 | 己 (jǐ) | 庚 (gēng) 㔯 | 甲 (jiǎ) |
|  | 丙 (bing) | + | 辛 (xīn) | = | Water | 丙 (bing) | 㔯 | 庚 (gēng) | 辛 (xīn) 㔯 | 乙 (yǐ) |
|  | 丁 (ding) | + | 壬 (rén) | = | Wood | 丁 (ding) | 㔯 | 辛 (xīn) | 壬 (ding) 㔯 | 丙 (xīn) |
|  | 戊 (wù) | + | 癸 (guǐ) | = | Fire | 戊 (wù) | 㔯 | 壬 (rén) | 癸 (wù) 㔯 | 丁 (rén) |
| **Earthly Branch** | 子 (zǐ) | + | 丑 (chǒu) | = | Earth | 子 (zǐ) | 㔯 | 午 (wù) |  |  |
|  | 寅 (yín) | + | 亥 (hài) | = | Wood | 卯 (mǎo) | 㔯 | 酉 (yǒu) |  |  |
|  | 卯 (mǎo) | + | 戌 (xū) | = | Fire | 寅 (yín) | 㔯 | 申 (shēn) |  |  |
|  | 辰 (chén) | + | 酉 (yǒu) | = | Metal | 巳 (sì) | 㔯 | 亥 (hài) |  |  |
|  | 巳 (sì) | + | 申 (shēn) | = | Water | 辰 (chén) | 㔯 | 戌 (xū) |  |  |
|  | 午 (wǔ) | + | 未 (wèi) | = | Sun & Moon | 丑 (chǒu) | 㔯 | 未 (wèi) |  |  |
|  | 申 (shēn) | 子 (zǐ) | 辰 (chén) | = | Water |  |  |  |  |  |
|  | 亥 (hài) | 卯 (mǎo) | 未 (wèi) | = | Wood |  |  |  |  |  |
|  | 寅 (yín) | 午 (wǔ) | 戌 (xū) | = | Fire |  |  |  |  |  |
|  | 巳 (sì) | 酉 (yǒu) | 丑 (chǒu) | = | Metal |  |  |  |  |  |
|  | 辰 (chén) | 戌 (xū) | 丑 (chǒu) | = | Earth |  |  |  |  |  |

Table K.6. Compatibility and tensions for the heavenly stems and earthly branches

tations expressed by the five phases of the Wu Xing (1,440 divided by 5 is 288), based on the pairings of ten heavenly stems and twelve earthly branches that manifest both numerological (the numbers 1 through 10) and astrological (the 12 Chinese zodiac signs and, resonating with Western astrology, the 12 houses and 12 signs) principles. Taken altogether, the sexagenary calendar is a perfect esoteric system that tempers science and mathematics with religion and metaphysics. It is the perfect expression of Taoist craft.

| Heavenly Stem | Wu Xing | Image / Essential nature | Craft Uses |
|---|---|---|---|
| 甲 (jiǎ) | Yang Wood | The trunk of a tree | • Rectifies injustice<br>• Facilitates success in artistic or literary endeavors<br>• Raising generative or regenerative power<br>• Ensuring upright growth toward success<br>• Use to subdue Earth energy |
| 乙 (yǐ) | Yin Wood | Bamboo shoot | • Absolves past transgressions<br>• Ensures successful development of new business or new ventures<br>• Facilitates transition to a new life stage<br>• Bring about new beginnings<br>• Use as supplement to Fire energy |
| 丙 (bing) | Yang Firie | The sun | • Facailitates career success<br>• Success in the performing arts<br>• For attaining promotions, advancements, gains in social status, glory, or frame<br>• Seeking public recognition for merits<br>• Use to subdue Metal energy |
| 丁 (ding) | Yin Fire | Stove; cauldron | • The magician's secret metaphysical weapon: nurtures power for craft<br>• Increases robust, vital Qi energy<br>• Amplifies transmutations<br>• Facilities inner spiritual cultivation<br>• Use as supplement to Earth energy |
| 戊 (wù) | Yang Earth | Mountain | • Supportive metaphysical properties to ensure longevity, stability, and security<br>• Can also be used in retaliatory magic to create obstacles and impediments to thwart or delay another's success<br>• Use to subdue Water energy |
| 己 (jǐ) | Yin Earth | Soil | • Promotes creativity and fertility<br>• Facilitates the needed environment or setting to foster creative growth<br>• Ensures safe and healthy childbirth<br>• Fosters creative, artistic energies<br>• Use a supplement to Metal energy |
| 庚 (gēng) | Yang Metal | Iron ore, the sword | • Assures victory in combat or litigation<br>• Facilitates greatness, achievement, and social, political, or military success<br>• Fox retaliatory magic, to strike back; optimal for defeating others<br>• Use to subdue Wood energy |
| 辛 (xīn) | Yin Metal | Gold jewelry, bronze vase | • Enhances beauty or romantic attraction<br>• Enhances wit, social graces, and charisma<br>• Increases social standing<br>• Offensive magic to cause misery, hardship, or suffering for another<br>• Use as supplement to Water energy |
| 壬 (rén) | Yang Water | Rivers, waterfalls | • Forges a clear path toward success or to manifest the desired outcome<br>• Generates Qi energy to improve physical health, personal vitality, or mitigate illness<br>• Artistic, cultural, or civil advancement<br>• Use to subdue Fire energy |
| 癸 (guǐ) | Yin Water | Snowfall, morning dew | • Divine knowledge gained through hardship<br>• Communication or transmission from Heaven; use to manifest Heaven on Earth<br>• Facilitates prophetic and intuitive abilities<br>• Fosters empathy, sensitivity, and wisdom<br>• Use as supplement to Wood energy |

Table K.7. Harnessing heavenly stems in Fu craft

Figure K.11 is an example of a Fu crafted with stem and branch glyphs. The top center medallion features the ancient seal script for the heavenly stem Ding (丁), which corresponds with Yin Fire. As outlined in table K.7, Yin Fire raises power and energy for the magician. Thus, the heavenly stem indicates what the Fu is for: inner cultivation. To its left and right, the medallions feature the seal script for Wood (木) on the left, for creative, initiatory energy; and Earth (土) on the right, for the fertility and resources needed to harness the magician's magical manifestations. Both Wu Xing phases are energetically supportive of Yin Fire, the heavenly stem. Outside the Fu house are two earthly stems: Chen (辰), corresponding with Dragon, and Si (巳), corresponding with Snake. The Dragon correspondence is used here to raise power and strengthen the abilities of the magician, to establish the magician's sovereignty and authority in the spirit world. The Snake raises intuition and psychic powers. Its energies help the practitioner to use a balance of dark and light energy.

Figure K.11. Empowering the Magus Fu: a Fu sigil with stem and branch glyphs

All glyphs within the house in figure K.11 are crafted to assist a practitioner with connection to the spirit realm, the underworld, and to harness metaphysical energy. Note the stylized glyph for "ghost" (鬼), which is delineated in the sigil in a way that renders it detained, captive, or suppressed, and thus compelled to do the practitioner's bidding. Note further the overpowering yang energy throughout the Fu: the nine (an odd number) light circles and the suns (日). The Fu design in figure K.11 can be used by a practitioner seeking to develop stronger abilities in connecting to the spirit world, but seeking development that is safeguarded by divine light energy, or Heaven. At least in principle, when the Fu sigil is wielded by the practitioner during his or her craft, it can strengthen the practitioner's intuitive and connective abilities and do so under the constraints and supervision of Heaven, or the Light. Be sure to craft a ritual that includes shielding the practitioner with Light (光, Guāng).

| | Physical Body Correspondences |
|---|---|
| 木<br><br>Wood | Wood governs the eyes, liver, gall bladder, and abdominal area. Imbalances of Wood yin and yang can cause imbalances in the corresponding areas of the physical body.<br><br>Wood imbalances will have an impact on the tendons, and the emotions of anger, goodwill, sense of charity or benevolence, and generosity. Wood correspondences can be assessed in the thumb, and is most influenced by the astrological positions of Jupiter.<br><br>*Wood is related to Fire*<br>In Wood related health concerns, also consider Fire related body correspondences: the heart, blood, circulatory system, or small intestine.<br><br>*Weakened by Metal*<br>Thus, when there is a strong Yang Earth or in sexagenary years that are Yang Metal, be more attentive of health concerns related to the respiratory system, lungs, or large intestine. |

Table K.8. The Wu Xing and physical body correspondences

| | Physical Body Correspondences |
|---|---|
| 火<br><br>Fire | Fire governs the heart, blood, circulatory system, and small intestine. It also governs the physical sense of touch. Imbalances of Fire yin and yang can cause imbalances in the corresponding areas of the physical body.<br><br>Fire imbalances will have an impact on the heart, pulse, or sweat glands, and the emotions of passion, sensuality, sexuality, joy. Fire correspondences can be assessed in the index finger, and is most influenced by the astrological position of Mars.<br><br>*Fire is related to Earth*<br>In Fire related health concerns, also consider Earth related body correspondences: the digestive system, spleen, or immune system.<br><br>*Weakened by Water*<br>Thus, when there is strong Yang Earth or in sexagenary years that are Yang Water, be more attentive of health concerns related to bones, the urinary tract, or kidneys. |

Table K.8. The Wu Xing and physical body correspondences (continued)

| | Physical Body Correspondences |
|---|---|
| 土<br><br>Earth | Earth governs the digestive system, spleen, and immune system. It also governs the physical sense of taste. Imbalances of Earth yin and yang can cause imbalances in the corresponding areas of the physical body.<br><br>Earth imbalances will have an impact on the muscles, and the emotions of personal security, love, nervousness, and depression. Earth correspondences can be assessed in the middle finger, and is most influenced by the astrological position of Saturn.<br><br>*Earth is related to Metal*<br>In Earth related health concerns, also consider Metal related body correspondences: the respiratory system, lungs, or large intestine.<br><br>*Weakened by Wood*<br>Thus, when there is strong Yang Earth or in sexagenary years that are Yang Wood, be more attentive of health concerns related to the liver, gall bladder, or abdominal issues. |

Table K.8. The Wu Xing and physical body correspondences (continued)

| | Physical Body Correspondences |
|---|---|
| 金<br><br>Metal | Metal governs the nose, respiratory system, lungs, large intestine, and skin conditions. It also governs the physical sense of scent. Imbalances of Metal yin and yang can cause imbalances in the corresponding areas of the physical body.<br><br>Metal imbalances will have an impact on the skin, in skin conditions, flow of mucus, and the emotions of courage, conviction, or empathy. Metal correspondences can be assessed in the ring finger, and is most influenced by the astrological position of Venus.<br><br>*Metal is related to Water*<br>In Metal related health concerns, also consider Water related body correspondences: the bones and skeletal system, the urinary tract, or kidneys.<br><br>*Weakened by Fire*<br>Thus, when there is a strong Yang Earth or in sexagenary years that are Yang Fire, be more attentive of health concerns related to the heart, blood, circulatory system, or small intestine. |

Table K.8. The Wu Xing and physical body correspondences (continued)

| | Physical Body Correspondences |
|---|---|
| 水<br><br>Water | Water governs the bones and skeletal system, the urinary tract, and kidneys. It also governs the ears and the physical sense of hearing. Imbalances of Water yin and yang can cause imbalances in the corresponding areas of the physical body.<br><br>Water imbalances will have an impact on the bones, urine, and the emotions of fear, intuitive abilities, and peacefulness. Water correspondences can be assessed in the little finger, and is most influenced by the astrological position of Mercury.<br><br>*Water is related to Wood*<br>In Water related health concerns, also consider Wood related body correspondences: the liver, gall bladder, and abdominal area.<br><br>*Weakened by Earth*<br>Thus, when there is a strong Yang Earth or in sexagenary years that are Yang Earth, be more attentive of health concerns related to the digestive system, spleen, or immune system. |

Table K.8. The Wu Xing and physical body correspondences (continued)

# NOTES

## 1. THE TAO OF CRAFT

1. Oracle bone script, greater seal script, and lesser seal script from Richard Sears [Uncle Hanzi (汉字叔叔)], "Chinese Etymology," 2013, http://www.chineseetymology.org. Reprinted with permission.

2. "The attitude of Taoism in general, I think, is extremely eclectic. It's a 'whatever works' kind of tradition." Ming Liu, "Ming Liu on Chinese Daoism," presentation given at the ACS Colloquium, California Institute of Integral Studies, San Francisco, March 2014, https://youtu.be/xEphouqTF9M.

3. "The heterogeneous nature of Taoism is well known." Isabelle Robinet, *Taoist Meditation: The Mao-shan Tradition of Great Purity,* trans. Julian F. Pas and Norman J. Girardot (Albany, NY: State University of New York Press, 1993), 1. For instance, the Tao Zang, or the Taoist Canons, compiled circa AD 1442, comprise over one thousand treatises, some on traditional Chinese medicine, others on philosophy, geomancy, liturgical texts, meditation techniques, ethics, alchemy, as well as Fu talisman crafting and other forms of mysticism and magic. It varies from exoteric to esoteric, philosophy to religion, scientific or medical to occult. From that diverse assembly of treatises, countless traditions and lineages, all citing Taoism as their foundation, have risen over the centuries. Foreseeably, a Taoist tradition that espouses Fu talisman crafting and sorcery will have many disagreements with a Taoist tradition that espouses philosophy and ethics. Given the scope of the Taoist Canons, it is incredibly difficult to define or characterize Taoism.

4. Not only did established magical lineages struggle against each other, vying for favor from the imperial court, but there was also hostility between established lineages and unaffiliated folk practitioners. As early as the Shang Dynasty, there were official court-appointed magicians versus freelancing magicians who achieved power from their popularity. Sayed Idries Shah, *Oriental Magic* (1956; repr. London: Octagon Press, 1992), 149.

5. Michael Saso, "Taiwan: Old Gods and Modern Society," in *Religions and Societies, Asia and the Middle East,* ed. Carlo Caldarola (Berlin: Walter de Gruyter/Mouton, 1982), 598.

6. During the Cultural Revolution, between 1966 and 1976, Taoist temples and sacred sites across China were destroyed. Monks and priests were sent to labor camps, and any practice

of their religion, let alone Taoist magic, was suppressed. It was not until after 1979 that Taoism experienced a revival. Robyn E. Lebron, *Searching for Spiritual Unity: Can There Be Common Ground?* (Nashville: Cross Books, 2012), 431.

7. During the Cultural Revolution, the Red Guard army ransacked homes, temples, and churches across China to confiscate and destroy all relics of dynastic China, including calligraphy, art, ancient books, and religious and occult texts. Jiehong Jiang, *Burden or Legacy: From the Chinese Cultural Revolution to Contemporary Art* (Hong Kong: Hong Kong University Press, 2007), 4. As a result, most Taoist magical lineages lost all of their sacred texts, magical journals, and knowledge.

8. Due to the open cultural and social interactions among Buddhism, Confucianism, and Taoism, along with regional folk religious and shamanic beliefs, Taoist practice is most often found in hybrid form, eclectic and merged with other religions and philosophies. Hsiao-Lan Hu and William Cully Allen, *Taoism (Religions of the World)* (New York: Chelsea House, 2007), 60. That eclectic mixing, or ontological syncretism, is as old as esoteric Taoism itself. Records of it taking place between Taoism and shamanic folk religions date back to the Han Dynasty (206 BC–AD 220), where the lore of the folk religions was integrated into Taoist philosophical thought. Thus, the cosmological principles of yin and yang, Heaven, Earth, and Man, the Wu Xing five phases, and the Ba Gua eight trigrams melded with the quest for immortality, alchemy, and astrology. Fabrizio Pregadio, ed., *Encyclopedia of Taoism* (New York: Routledge, 2008), 20. Thus formed the beginnings of esoteric Taoism.

9. See Jan Dodd and Mark Lewis, *The Rough Guide to Vietnam* (New York: Penguin, 2009), 487: between the eleventh and fourteenth centuries, Chinese immigrants to Vietnam brought Taoist philosophy and religion, introducing Taoist magical practice, to Vietnam; and Justin Thomas McDaniel, *The Lovelorn Ghost and the Magical Monk: Practicing Buddhism in Modern Thailand* (New York: Columbia University Press, 2013), 265, noting the establishment of Chinese Taoist communities in Thailand.

10. Abraham Kaplan, *The Conduct of Inquiry: Methodology for Behavioral Science* (San Francisco: Chandler, 1964), 28.

11. Howard E. A. Tinsley and Steven D. Brown, *Handbook of Applied Multivariate Statistics and Mathematical Modeling* (Waltham, MA: Academic Press, 2000), 40.

12. Ibid.

13. To the best of my knowledge, there is no widely recognized distinction made between exoteric and esoteric Taoism; that distinction is my own. There are, however, distinctions between Taoism as a philosophy and Taoism as a religion, and oftentimes the mystical aspects of Taoism that I refer to as esoteric Taoism gets lumped in with Taoism as a religion. Jennifer Oldstone-Moore, *Understanding Taoism: Origins, Beliefs, Practices, Holy Texts, Sacred Places* (London: Watkins Publishing, 2011), 13. See also Igor M. Diakonoff, *The Paths of History* (Cambridge, UK: Cambridge University Press, 1999), 52, making a distinction between philosophical Taoism and religious Taoism, with what I refer to as esoteric Taoism tucked under the religious Taoism category; Julian F. Pas, *Historical Dictionary of Taoism* (Lanham, MD: Scarecrow Press, 1998), 1, noting that Western scholar-

ship makes a distinction between Taoism as a philosophy and Taoism as a religion; and Ray Billington, *Understanding Eastern Philosophy* (New York: Routledge, 1997), 88.

14. Ulrich Libbrecht, *Within the Four Seas: Introduction to Comparative Philosophy* (Leuven, Belgium: Peeters, 2007), 546.

15. The Zhuang Zi (莊子) text is named after the author attributed to the book, Zhuang Zi (or Zhuang Zhou, 莊週) (369–286 BC). Thorsten Botz-Bornstein, *Inception and Philosophy: Ideas to Die For* (Chicago: Open Court, 2013). The text contains thirty-three chapters, subdivided into three parts. The famous "butterfly dream" is attributed to Zhuang Zi, who wrote that he dreamed he was a butterfly, fluttering about. He was conscious of his existence as a butterfly, and unaware of himself as Zhuang Zi. Yet when he awoke, he was himself, Zhuang Zi, again, and unaware of existence as a butterfly. He thus had to confront the question: who is he? Is Zhuang Zi a man dreaming that he was a butterfly, or is he a butterfly now dreaming that he is a man?

16. Pas, *Historical Dictionary,* 11–12. Tao, or "The Way," is to be like water, giving life to others, being generous, and yet never demanding. Water is fluid, appearing weak and soft, but it is water that can wear away a mountain.

17. Eva Wong, *Taoism: An Essential Guide* (Boston: Shambhala, 2011), 24–25. In the Tao Te Ching, the principle of wu wei is expressed as follows: "When the world knows beauty as beauty, ugliness arises. / When it knows good as good, evil arises" (chap. 2); "The highest goodness resembles water. / Water greatly benefits myriad things without contention" (chap. 6); "Close the mouth. / Shut the doors. / Blunt the sharpness. / Unravel the knots. / Dim the glare. / Mix the dust." (chap. 52); and "The sages also do not harm people" (chap. 60). In Derek Lin, trans., *Tao Te Ching: Annotated and Explained* (Woodstock, VT: Sky-Light Paths, 2006), http://www.taoism.net/ttc/complete.htm.

18. Wong, *Taoism,* 24–25. In the chapter "The Way of Heaven" from the Zhuang Zi, there are expressions of wu wei as the "stillness of the sages" and the line "Vacancy, stillness, placidity, tastelessness, quietude, silence, and nonaction—this is the level of Heaven and Earth, and the perfection of the [Tao] and its characteristics." *See* 中國哲學書電子化計劃 [The Chinese Texts Project], 天道 [*The Way of Heaven from Zhuang Zi*], n.d., http://ctext.org/zhuangzi/tian-dao.

19. Oldstone-Moore, *Understanding Taoism,* 6–7.

20. Since the Han Dynasty (206 BC–AD 220), despite a diversity of religions scattered throughout China, the belief in Tao, which formed Taoism; the belief in the yin and yang subdivision; and the Wu Xing five phases unified these different groups. Saso, "Taiwan," 581.

21. Folk religions in China and Taiwan tended to be territorial and regional, by village. Each village would, as a community, venerate particular deities. P. Sangren, *History and Magical Power in a Chinese Community* (Stanford, CA: Stanford University Press, 1987), 73. Tu Di Gong (土地公), the Earth God, is one example. In some villages, Tu Di Gong is paired with a female counterpart, for a god and goddess, the female being Tu Di Po (土地婆), considered his wife. Tu Di Gong and Tu Di Po were believed to oversee the affairs and welfare of a particular village or locale.

22. A point about Chinese ancestor worship should be clarified here. The Chinese do not "worship" their ancestors in the same way one might worship deities. Rather, ancestors are honored and remembered, and their spirits are sought in times of need and desperation to bring guidance to the family. It is believed that the spirits of ancestors live on to ensure the protection of their posterity. Thus, the spirits of ancestors are sought for counsel, but not worshipped exactly. The means of communing with ancestors is through burning incense, sending up prayers, and other ritual practices that might remind Westerners of worship. Wong, *Taoism*, 34. Joss papers, representing spiritual money or goods that the ancestors or departed would be able to use in the afterlife, are viewed more like gifts to your relatives who happen to be dead, not a form of worship.

23. Legalism was a political philosophy that arose around the Zhou Dynasty, along with Confucianism and Taoism. The school of thought focused on government and the military, the enforcement of law. While there is no single recognized founder for the political philosophy, Han Feizi (280–233 BC) was one of the most prominent writers on Legalist thought. Han held that under Legalism, a leader maintains sovereignty by issuing punishment and favor: heavily punish those who strike against you, and heavily favor those who support you. See Eileen Tamura, *China: Understanding Its Past*, vol. 1 (Honolulu: University of Hawaii Press, 1997), 54. During the Warring States period of China, Legalism rose to prominence, and most noblemen and aristocrats identified publicly as Legalists but then privately practiced Taoism.

24. Taoism as a philosophy is said to have emerged around 1046–256 BC, whereas Taoism as a religion, incorporating shamanism and magical traditions, came about during AD 1–200 in China. Wong, *Taoism*, 3.

25. Even while Lao Tzu is better associated with exoteric Taoism, his frequent references to the "power of the Tao" and "the secrets within it" are just one of many facets of his teachings that led to esoteric Taoist and occult practices. Shah, *Oriental Magic*, 150.

26. Chinese shamanism and esoteric Taoism have similar stripes, and it is because they are the same entity as both evolved through time. When Confucianism dominated, the Confucian tradition labeled Chinese shamanism as Taoism, conflating the two, and thus over time, the two practices became interchangeable. Chinese shamanism was absorbed into esoteric Taoism. See Liu, "Ming Liu on Chinese Daoism."

27. Prior to the Zhou Dynasty (1046–256 BC), shamans were part of the imperial court and retained by the aristocracy as advisers, diviners, and healers. These early shamans invoked spirits, communed with Heaven, interpreted dreams, read omens, performed divinations, and healed. Shamanism fell a bit out of favor during the Zhou Dynasty, as philosophy came to flourish at this time, though pockets of it remained in the outer regions of China. Fu talismans from this time have been found bearing talismanic scripts. The practice was later integrated into Taoist magic traditions. Wong, *Taoism*, 16–17.

28. Dynasty dates in this book are sourced from Asia for Educators, "Timeline of Chinese History and Dynasties," Columbia University, 2009, http://afe.easia.columbia.edu/timelines /china_timeline.htm.

29. During the Shang Dynasty (1600–1050 BC), nature gods were venerated. Mountains, riv-

ers, and other natural landforms as well as natural phenomena such as rain and thunder were believed to be the physical manifestation of gods. To ensure the protection of the natural landform or to remain free from the harms a natural phenomenon might cause, sacrifices had to be made to these gods. In fact, the Shang calendar was based around the cycle of these sacrifices. There was also a sense of a supervising deity, a Lord (帝) that issued orders or decrees (令). John Lagerwey and Marc Kalinowski, eds., introduction to *Early Chinese Religion, Part One: Shang through Han (1250 BC–AD 220)* (Boston: Brill, 2011), 4–5. See also Saso, "Taiwan," 581. Pre-Taoist shamans would commune with these nature gods, perform oracle bone divinations to counsel the Shang king, and perform the sacrificial rites, which included burning for communion with heaven, burying for communion with earth, or throwing into bodies of water for water spirits. Lagerwey and Kalinowski, *Early Chinese Religion,* 5. Note that when Fu sigils bear Fu Wen for those two characters (帝令) near the top of a sigil or stylized into the house, the sigil is designed in an early Shang Dynastic style.

30. Wong, *Taoism,* 11.

31. Regarding both the Chinese characters used in this text and the spelling or Romanization of Chinese words: first, when I say "Chinese," I mean Mandarin Chinese. The characters printed herein are in Traditional Chinese (as opposed to Simplified Chinese), which is the written form of Chinese that the Taiwanese use. I am of Taiwanese heritage, and so I grew up learning Traditional Chinese. The mainland Chinese, in contrast, read using Simplified Chinese. As for romanization, the Taiwanese use the Wade-Giles system, whereas the mainland Chinese use pinyin. My approach to romanization is an informal and admittedly muddled hybrid of Wade-Giles and pinyin. I grew up learning Wade-Giles romanization, so that is the foundation I build upon, but in my university years and after marrying a mainland Chinese man, I picked up on pinyin. Thus, "Tao" and "Taoism" (Wade-Giles) resonate with me more than "Dao" and "Daoism" (pinyin). However, in this text I opt for Zhang and Qi (pinyin) instead of Chang and Ch'i (Wade-Giles). Those are a few examples of how I've shuffled around between the two systems. I apologize for any confusion this approach causes.

32. Wong, *Taoism,* 22–23.

33. What I refer to as esoteric Taoism has also been referred to as magical Taoism, which I consider to be within the umbrella of esoteric Taoism. Whereas philosophical Taoism teaches the Tao, or "The Way," magical Taoism teaches "The Way of Power." Through the Way of Power, a practitioner raises energy from the natural elements and invokes the assistance of deities, immortals, and spirits toward the Way of Power, a very different approach from philosophical Taoism. Wong, *Taoism,* 5. Other historical branches of Taoism include divinatory Taoism (such as astrology, feng shui, and I Ching divination), ceremonial Taoism (liturgy and ritual), and alchemical Taoism (the quest for immortality), all of which I consider under esoteric Taoism.

34. Pas, *Historical Dictionary,* 11–12. Tao, or "The Way," is to be like water, giving life to others, being generous, and yet never demanding. Water is fluid, appearing weak and soft, but it is water that can wear away a mountain.

35. In Taoist esoteric tradition, alchemy is subdivided into two practices, outer alchemy and inner alchemy, though both involve the quest for immortality. Outer alchemy seeks herbs and

elements from nature to chemically create an elixir for immortality, whereas inner alchemy seeks inner cultivation of Qi, on the belief that all that a human needs to achieve immortality can be found within his or her own body. Pas, *Historical Dictionary*, 19. Outer alchemy is a form of craft that seeks protection and defense from external, environmental elements. Higher energy forms or the characterizations of deity in outer alchemy are depicted as Lords that guard specific geographic areas, natural phenomena, elements, directions, seasons, and so on. Inner alchemy is a form of craft that seeks cultivation of a person's internal personal Qi. Higher energy forms or the characterizations of deity in inner alchemy are depicted as Lords that are internal, within the body, that guard specific organs. The First Emperor of China, in the Qin Dynasty (221–206 BC), was believed to be obsessed with outer alchemy and the quest for immortality. He sought out the craft of Fang Shi, or alchemists, diviners, astrologers, magicians, exorcists, and shamans, to aid in his quest for immortality. Jeaneane D. Fowler, *An Introduction to the Philosophy and Religion of Taoism: Pathways to Immortality* (East Sussex, UK: Sussex Academic Press, 2005), 132. Emperor Wu of Han, in the Han Dynasty (206 BC–AD 220), also expended substantial imperial resources, hiring Taoist alchemists. In the Song Dynasty (AD 960–1279), greater focus was placed on inner alchemy. Pas, *Historical Dictionary*, 20. See also Wong, *Taoism*, 4–5. Esoteric Taoism flourished during the Han Dynasty, where divinatory arts were practiced, from reading omens to the art of magic and sorcery. Robinet, *Taoist Meditation*, 10. In the Han Dynasty, Taoist magical practitioners achieved their greatest heights of power. They were often court-appointed, both priests and priestesses, and wielded much influence over the sitting emperors. Shah, *Oriental Magic*, 149.

36. "Divination was among the traditions that influenced the formation of Taoism in the Han dynasty. The earliest documented instance of such prediction may be dated to the Shang court (circa 1600–1045 BC)." Pregadio, *Encyclopedia of Taoism*, 113–14.

37. While feng shui and geomancy are practices independent from and predating Taoism, feng shui became a more organized study because of Taoism. The legend goes that King Wen from the Zhou was imprisoned by the Shang, who were then in power (the Shang Dynasty). During his captivity, he studied the eight trigrams of the Ba Gua and combined them to form the sixty-four hexagrams. Through these sixty-four hexagrams, which were later memorialized in a book called the I Ching, or Book of Changes, King Wen predicted the fall of the Shang Dynasty and the rise of the Zhou. Then, during the Zhou Dynasty, the compass was invented, and Taoist practitioners synthesized use of the compass with their study of the I Ching. Feng shui flourished during the Zhou Dynasty, around 770 to 475 BC. That formed the technical foundations of the feng shui that is practiced today, though various schools of feng shui outside esoteric Taoism were formed from the Han Dynasty onward. See Rameshwar Prasad, *The Magic of Feng Shui: Golden Tips of Feng Shui with Causes and Cures of Problems* (New Delhi: Diamond Pocket Books, 2004), 6–7; Susan Levitt, *Taoist Feng Shui: The Ancient Roots of the Chinese Art of Placement* (Rochester, VT: Inner Traditions, 1999), 4.

38. See generally John Eaton Calthorpe Blofeld, *Taoism: The Road to Immortality* (New York: Random House, 1979).

39. An "ordained" priest or priestess was one who had received the secret teachings of a rec-

ognized magical lineage, passed down from parent to child or master to disciple. As for an "orthodox" Taoist lineage, I borrow the idea from Michael Saso, a professor and scholar on Taoism and an ordained Taoist priest from the Zheng Yi lineage. See generally Michael Saso, "Asian Art and Religion," http://www.michaelsaso.org. Orthodox Taoist magic is a magical tradition that is widely recognized and based on the Lu established by the Zheng Yi lineage. Michael Saso, "Orthodoxy and Heterodoxy in Taoist Ritual," in *Religion and Ritual in Chinese Society,* eds. Arthur P. Wolf and Robert J. Smith (Stanford, CA: Stanford University Press, 1974), 326. Meanwhile, heterodox Taoist magic bears a negative connotation of one that is not recognized widely among the Taoist magical community or one that cannot claim lineage (ibid., 328).

40. Hu and Allen, *Taoism,* 54. The Fu talisman is believed to contain invoked energies from the cosmos to affect the future outcome of an individual fate.

41. "As above, so below" is a Western esoteric principle sourced from the eleventh or twelfth centuries in the Hermetic tradition. It is believed to be derived from the first lines of the Emerald Tablet: "That which is above is from that which is below, and that which is below is from that which is above, to accomplish the miracles of one." The Emerald Tablet is credited to an author who went by the name Hermes Trismegistus and refers to the "three parts of the wisdom of the whole universe." Mark Rogers, *The Esoteric Codex: Hermeticism I* (self-published, 2011), 7.

42. The yin and yang symbol, or taijitu, as we are familiar with it today only became popularized during the Qing Dynasty (AD 1644–1911), though versions of it existed centuries before. Micah L. Issitt and Carlyn Main, *Hidden Religion: The Greatest Mysteries and Symbols of the World's Religious Beliefs* (Goleta, CA: ABC-CLIO, 2014), 251.

43. Helen Mitchell, *Roots of Wisdom: A Tapestry of Philosophical Traditions* (San Francisco: Cengage Learning, 2014), 74.

44. Ibid., 75.

45. Those who are yin-dominant in their personal Qi or essence also tend to have a stronger connection to the spirit world and stronger intuitive or psychic abilities. Although yin does not correspond directly with feminine and yang does not per se indicate masculine, whether biological or socially nurtured, women in society tend to be more yin than men, and so women also tend toward having a stronger intuitive or psychic connection to the spirit world. Yin-dominant men will also demonstrate stronger intuition and psychic connection.

46. Original author not known, n.d. Taoist talismans to expel *gu* poison. In Christine Mollier, *Buddhism and Taoism Face to Face: Scripture, Ritual, and Iconographic Exchange in Medieval China* (Honolulu: University of Hawaii Press, 2009), 87.

47. Sun Kwok, *Stardust: The Cosmic Seeds of Life* (New York: Springer Science & Business Media, 2013), xvii.

48. Ibid.

49. Ibid.

50. Patricia Buckley Ebrey, *Chinese Civilization: A Sourcebook,* 2nd ed. (New York: Simon and Schuster, 2009), 57.

51. There are three main cosmological theories for Heaven: (1) the Veil Theory (i.e., 蓋天說), (2) the Ellipsoid Theory (i.e., 渾天說), and (3) the Infinity Theory (i.e., 宣夜說). In a text that I will refer to as *The Classics of the Mathematical Paths of Heaven* (周髀算經, Zhōu Bì Suàn Jīng), a book on astronomy and mathematics dated to the Zhou Dynasty (1046–256 BC), Heaven was expressed as a veil that canopies Earth, a realm above us in the skies, among the sun, moon, and stars. A second theory emerged during the Han Dynasty, by Zhang Heng (張衡) (AD 78–139), a polymath who advanced the study of astronomy and mathematics in medieval China. Zhang Heng expressed Heaven as an ellipsoid that encased Earth and rotated around us. The third theory is from the *Book of Jin* (晉書, Jìn Shū), from the Jin Dynasty (AD 265–420), which expressed Heaven as infinity, a boundless continuum beyond Earth, and an expanse of perpetuity.

52. In some lineages, such as the Shang Qing tradition of esoteric Taoism, an offshoot of the Mao Shan lineages, the Three Pure Ones are personified as three spirit guardians within the human body. The Three Pure Ones represent spiritual energy, vital energy, and generative energy. Spiritual energy might be likened to the deity personification Dao Bao, the "Treasure of the Tao," residing between the eyes, where the third eye or crown chakra would be, relating to intuition, connection to the Divine, potential for nirvana or enlightenment, and governing over the mind. It is the connection point between cosmic Qi and personal Qi. Vital energy resides in the central region of the human body, the heart and chest area, and might be likened to Jing Bao, the "Treasure of the Law." Vital energy governs over the physical body. It is the personal Qi. Generative energy resides near the reproductive organs and might be likened to Shi Bao, "Treasure of Knowledge." Vital energy is sensory experience. It is the sexuality of sentient beings. Thus, an important aspect of inner alchemy is endeavoring to keep the Three Pure Ones residing within the body strong, vibrant, and unclouded. See generally Wong, *Taoism*, 55. The source of the principle that the Three Pure Ones reside as guardians within the human body comes from the *Upper Scriptures of Purple Texts Inscribed by the Spirits*, where the Three Pure Ones—Dao Bao, Jing Bao, and Shi Bao—reside in the upper region, central region, and lower region of the body, respectively. Ming Wang, "The Apocryphal *Jia* Section in *Taipingjing Chao*," in *Taoism*, ed. Zhongjian Mou, trans. Pan Junliang and Simone Normand (Leiden, Netherlands: Brill, 2012), 69.

53. In both Taoist and Confucian cosmology, yang energy grows from the East, where the Azure Dragon reigns, and thus both the Ba Gua trigrams and the five phases begin in the East. Youlan Feng and Derk Bodde, *A History of Chinese Philosophy*, vol. 2 (Princeton, NJ: Princeton University Press, 1952), 104.

54. For more information, see table 8.11, and "The Four Guardians" section in appendix B.

55. Mollier, *Buddhism and Taoism*, 79–80.

56. Ibid., 80.

57. Zongyu Wang, "The Taoist Concept of the 'Six Heavens,'" in Mou, *Taoism*, 131, note 27.

58. Note that some practitioners only call upon the four compass directions and reserve the five relative directions for defensive, protective ritual work; exorcisms; or summoning ghosts, demons, or lesser spirits, where greater metaphysical protection might be necessary.

59. During the Shang Dynasty (1600–1050 BC), which predates the Zhou Dynasty and Taoism, records show an ontological belief in five natural forces (方士) that created all life. While there is no certain connection between the Shang belief of five natural forces and the Zhou and Taoist cosmological principle of Wu Xing or five phases, the parallels are still worth noting. Robert Eno, "Shang State Religion and the Pantheon of the Oracle Texts," in Lagerwey and Kalinowski, *Early Chinese Religion,* 46.

60. In Confucian thought, the five phases manifest in Man as five virtues (五德): love, righteousness, propriety, wisdom, and faith. Feng and Bodde, *History of Chinese Philosophy,* 104.

61. For an overview of the four elements and the Western theory of elemental dignities, see Benebell Wen, *Holistic Tarot: An Integrative Approach to Using Tarot for Personal Growth* (Berkeley, CA: North Atlantic Books, 2015), 436–50, 522.

62. In the Western esoteric tradition of elemental dignities, the four elements, Fire, Water, Air, and Earth, are held to possess complementary, conflicting, or neutral relationships with each other. "Dignity" indicates the external manifestation of an element's innate properties when it comes into contact with another element. Each element is characterized as active (i.e., yang) or passive (i.e., yin). Fire and Air, which are active, empower one another when they interact; Water and Earth, both passive, also empower upon interaction. Fire and Water, however, attenuate, similar to the Fire-Water opposition theory found in Chinese feng shui. Air and Earth also attenuate, due to the active-passive clash. The interactions not mentioned are considered neutral. Wen, *Holistic Tarot,* 437–38.

63. Ang Tian Se, "Five Phases (Wuxing)," in *Encyclopaedia of the History of Science, Technology, and Medicine in Non-Western Cultures,* ed. Helaine Selin (New York: Springer Science & Business Media, 2008), 939.

64. Ibid.

65. Ibid., 939–40.

66. Ibid., 940.

67. Note that in the Wu Xing correspondences in table 1.11, each Chinese zodiac sign is subdivided into five expressions of persona, according to the dominant Wu Xing. Thus, for example, there are five personas for the Rooster: a Wood Rooster, Fire Rooster, Earth Rooster, Metal Rooster, and Water Rooster. To identify the persona for the zodiac sign that a particular year or an individual falls under, look to the last digit of that year or year of birth. For example, for the year 1981, the last digit of the year is 1, which corresponds with Metal. Say that an individual was born in the lunar year of the Rooster, in 1981. That individual would thus be a Metal Rooster. Metal corresponding character traits modify that individual's fundamental Rooster personality. Astrologically, the planet Venus has a more influential bearing on that individual's life path. Also, in terms of forecasting global events for 1981, the Metal Rooster persona would be relevant.

68. The craft of a Fu sigil, its conception and design, might be likened to the conception and design of life. One life is all life just as all life is one. In Taoist ontology, the universe was born in the same way a human is born, and so the human birth is similar to the birth of the universe. The exchange between Heaven and Earth, yin and yang is what creates life (and

through the medium that is Man, you, the practitioner, that exchange represents the same method by which you create and design your Fu). Thus, at the moment of exchange, or at the moment of conception, a human life is created. Taoist ontology would therefore hold that a baby is "alive" and has its own life essence (精, jīng) upon conception or fertilization of the egg. However, the physiological elements of that human life are formed progressively, and it is the Qi within the mother's body, as well as spirits and the Divine within the mother's body, that will determine the fate and fortune of that human life. "Mortal knots," or the challenges that one will be presented with in their lifetime, are believed to be formed in the embryo. See Pregadio, *Encyclopedia of Taoism,* 85. At the moment the practitioner has conceived of the Fu sigil, there has been an exchange of Heaven and Earth, and that sigil is designed from yin and yang. However, true life or the potency of the sigil has not been formed yet. That is a progression that will be influenced by the practitioner's actions and conduct of empowerment. After the Fu has been given its life essence from yin and yang, after it has been conceived by the practitioner, it is alive. However, it is the harnessing of the Wu Xing five phases and the Ba Gua by the practitioner, along with how the practitioner empowers the Fu sigil during the sigil's gestation period, that will determine the results of that Fu. In other words, every minute detail in the stages leading from conception of a Fu to the charting ritual is critical, because any misstep, in theory, can create "mortal knots" that will hinder the efficacy of the Fu.

69. From a Western perspective, the names of historic figures can render the history a bit confusing. King Zhou was the king of the Shang Dynasty, the first formal dynasty of China, later followed by the Zhou Dynasty. King Wen, prior to becoming king, was a vassal in the court of King Zhou. However, King Wen himself was said to have been such a virtuous noble that he attracted the loyalty of many powerful feudal lords. King Wen was the ruler of a tribe called Zhou (but with the surname Ji) just outside the central regions of the Shang Dynasty. At the time, the Shang Dynasty was made up of a centralized region under the direct rulership of King Zhou (the king of Shang) and an outer region that was still considered part of the Shang Dynasty, but had a great deal of autonomy, with local lords achieving independent power over their states. In one such state rose the Zhou tribe within the Shang Dynasty, ruled by King Wen. Tensions arose between the outer-region Zhou tribe and the central Shang Dynasty under King Zhou. While King Wen is credited as the founder of the Zhou Dynasty, following the fall of Shang, it was his son, King Wu, who led the revolt against the Shang and ascended to be king in 1100 BC, formally establishing the reign of the Zhou Dynasty under the Zhou tribe. The Zhou Dynasty was not formally established until near the death of King Wen. The final victory for the Zhou tribe was when King Zhou of Shang's own imperial army turned on the Shang king to fight in support of King Wen and King Wu. King Zhou fled and committed suicide by setting himself on fire. Legend holds that when King Wen, a shaman king, divined with the I Ching, the I Ching prophesied the fall of Shang and the rise of the Zhou Dynasty, a kingdom that went on to rule for over two hundred years and eleven generations. The foregoing history should be significant to practitioners of craft because many lines in the I Ching, the Book of Changes, reference the history of the Shang and Zhou. See generally Editorial Committee of Chinese Civilization, *China: Five Thousand Years of History and Civilization*

(Hong Kong: City University of Hong Kong Press, 2007), 29–32; Stephen H. West and Wilt L. Idema, *Monks, Bandits, Lovers, and Immortals* (Indianapolis: Hackett, 2010), 173, note 18.

70. If written correctly, Lo Shu should be spelled Luo Shu (Luò Shū), according to pinyin, but it has been written incorrectly in the West as Lo Shu for so long now that I fear if I use Luo Shu, it would cause more confusion than clarity. Therefore I have opted to continue in error and refer to the Luo Shu as Lo Shu.

71. Zhongxian Wu, *Seeking the Spirit of the Book of Change: 8 Days to Mastering a Shamanic Yijing (I Ching) Prediction System* (Philadelphia: Singing Dragon, 2009), 223.

72. Ibid., 83, 85.

73. Yu the Great built waterways modeled after the Lo Shu pattern, which saved China from the great floods that overtook the lands during the Xia Dynasty (2100–1600 BC). Ibid., 82.

74. Ibid., 82–83.

75. Ibid., 83.

76. Ibid., 79.

77. Ibid., 79–80.

78. Ibid., 80.

79. Ibid., 86–87.

80. See Robert W. Smith, *The Expanding Universe: Astronomy's "Great Debate"* (Cambridge, UK: Cambridge University Press, 1982), v, noting that American astronomer Edwin Hubble discovered that "the Universe is not static" and "it is indeed expanding."

81. In 1929, while observing photographs of spiral nebulae, or galaxies, American astronomer Edwin Hubble discovered that the universe is expanding. Moreover, he concluded that the age of the universe could be determined by measuring that rate of spiral expansion. See Observatories of the Carnegie Institution for Science, "1929: Edwin Hubble Discovers the Universe is Expanding," https://cosmology.carnegiescience.edu/timeline/1929.

82. Wu, *Seeking the Spirit,* 81.

83. Kwok, *Stardust,* 1.

84. Fu (符) is a noun. The Fu *is* the talisman or sigil in question. Therefore, to say "Fu talisman" or "Fu sigil" is to state the same noun redundantly. However, for the benefit of Western practitioners, I have done just that, stating the noun twice, once in its Chinese terminology and again in English, to assist the understanding of the Western practitioner.

85. Victor Guillemin, *The Story of Quantum Mechanics* (Mineola, NY: Courier, 1968), 120–21.

86. Ibid., 123.

87. A recording of the complete lecture is available online: Great Dharma Drum, *Supernatural Power and Its Impact on Society (GDD-7, Master Sheng Yen),* video file, May 7, 2012, https://youtu.be/KKqmPSToWUU.

88. "Magic is a field where intensive and creative study may show that many so-called supernatural powers are in fact reflections of hitherto little-understood forces, which may very well possibly be harnessed to individual and collective advantage." Shah, *Oriental Magic,* xvii.

89. The contemporary practice of craft in East Asia, especially among Taoist practitioners, often involves retaliatory craft or magic. See, for example, Min Tzu, *Chinese Taoist Sorcery:*

*The Art of Getting Even* (San Francisco: Vision Press Films, 2000).

90. However, generalizations cannot be made about what Taoist practitioners believe or do not believe. Fourth- and fifth-century texts on esoteric Taoism suggests that true transcendental magic cannot be used to kill others, even if it is to save one's own life; steal from others, even if it is to provide for oneself; act in a prideful manner; engage in material and superficial excesses; or indulge in vanity. See, for example, 三洞珠囊 [Sān Dòng Zhū Náng, *Three Caverns of the Pearl Theca*], http://baike.baidu.com/view/343215.htm. These scriptures have also been translated into English as "A Bag of Pearls from the Three Caverns" or "Pearl Satchel of the Three Caverns." The text is believed to have been written around the time of the Tang Dynasty (AD 618–907). The concept of nonharm and forbearance from retaliation in magic or Taoist craft predates the Tang Dynasty, however, and can be found in the works of Ge Hong. In the *Writ of the Three Sovereigns,* written around AD 437, over a century after Ge Hong's *Bao Puzi,* acts such as self-defense, or killing to save one's own life, stealing in an attempt to provide for oneself, falsely advertising one's own abilities, no matter the intent, or indulging in materialism will bar a practitioner from achieving immortality. See Dominic Emanuel Steavu-Balint, "The Three Sovereigns Tradition: Talismans, Elixirs, and Meditation in Early Medieval China" (doctoral dissertation, Stanford University, 2010), 26, http://searchworks .stanford.edu/view/8572529/.

## 2. A HISTORIC AND CULTURAL CONTEXT

1. Steavu-Balint, "Three Sovereigns Tradition," 11, noting the practical applications of Fu talismans in medieval southern China.

2. Ibid., 11.

3. "A Sigil is a magical symbol created to represent the desire of the witch, and is used to condense your intent into direct symbolism. They are made up of letters, which are rearranged into a design and reworked until a pleasing design is created, which ends up as a symbol and has no direct resemblance to the original power phrase. Although primarily made up of letters, other relevant symbols can also be added to the Sigil." Vikki Bramshaw, *Craft of the Wise: A Practical Guide to Paganism and Witchcraft* (Hampshire, UK: John Hunt, 2009), 133.

4. Generally, East Asian occultists make a distinction between ghosts and hungry ghosts. Ghosts are rather benign. A ghost is a person who has died and passed on, though for the time being, the spirit essence of that person remains. However, a hungry ghost is a person who died a violent, unexpected, or unnatural death that the living world has left unresolved, a spirit who feels neglected or forgotten by his or her descendants, or who was in some way deeply deprived of a good life while he or she was living. Clifton D. Bryant, *Handbook of Death and Dying* (Thousand Oaks, CA: SAGE Publishing, 2003), 84. A practitioner might summon a hungry ghost to carry forth certain orders, generally ones bearing ill will for another from the living world, under the rationale that hungry ghosts are more desperate and easier to control or command. To do so, a practitioner uses divining methods to obtain the name of the hungry ghost, then uses that name to craft a Fu sigil. The Fu sigil is crafted in such a way as to act as a summons notice, ordering the hungry ghost to carry out the practitioner's will. There are

profound, often unforeseeable consequences to summoning hungry ghosts, however, and is not a practice for the novice to perform.

5. Wong, *Taoism*, 16–17.

6. Steavu-Balint, "Three Sovereigns Tradition," 135.

7. Wu, *Seeking the Spirit*, 23.

8. Ibid., 83–85.

9. Ibid., 23.

10. See chapter 12 on the later cultural appropriation of the name and identity Shang Di.

11. Wong, *Taoism*, 16–17.

12. Lagerwey and Kalinowski, *Early Chinese Religion*, 4–5, and Saso, "Taiwan," 581. See also note 29 in chapter 1.

13. Ibid.

14. Wong, *Taoism*, 16–18.

15. The Tian Shi lineage under Zhang Dao Ling was believed to be the first organized Taoist religion and the beginnings of Taoist mysticism, or what this book refers to as esoteric Taoism. See Wong, *Taoism*, 3, citing the Tian Shi lineage's transformation of Taoism as a philosophy into Taoism as a religion, combining magic and devotional work, and 31.

16. The name is spelled here according to pinyin. The Wade-Giles spelling is Chang Tao-Ling. Oldstone-Moore, *Understanding Taoism*, 16.

17. Pas, *Historical Dictionary*, 17. Zhang Dao Ling claimed divine insights bestowed upon him by the spirit of Lao Tzu, the founder of Taoism, and it was the spirit of Lao Tzu who endowed him with magical powers and the ability to exorcise demons. See also Wong, *Taoism*, 34.

18. Pas, *Historical Dictionary*, 17.

19. Zhang Lu, a descendent of Zhang Dao Ling and a leading priest in the Tian Shi lineage, is most remembered for his surrender to Cao Cao, a warlord during the Han Dynasty. In AD 184, peasants revolted against the Han emperor in the Yellow Turban Rebellion, which was said to be led by Taoist sorcerers from the Tian Shi lineage. These practitioners were healers and did not charge fees for their healing of the sick and poverty-stricken. However, in AD 211, after the death of his brother, Zhang Lu surrendered to Cao Cao, but he impressed the warlord to such an extent that Zhang Lu and the Taoist Tian Shi lineage won favors from the court. Cao Cao's sentiments toward Zhang Lu must have been mixed, as he both reviled Zhang Lu as "a demonic sorcerer" (and former leader of the rebellion) and yet married his daughter to Zhang Lu's son, the next in line to lead the Tian Shi lineage. The alliance between Cao Cao and Zhang Lu was mutually beneficial. It gave rise to the prominence of Taoist magic and esoteric Taoism, while Cao Cao sought to control these magical lineages under his authority and governance. Cao Cao coordinated conventions of Taoist magicians to meet at his court in effect to keep his eye on them, hoping that as long as he appeased the Taoist magicians, he could suppress the Yellow Turban Rebellion. Gang Li, "Cao Cao and Taoism," in Mou, *Taoism*, 104–5.

20. "Zhang Lu ruled people with demonic Taoism." Ibid., 104.

21. Oldstone-Moore, *Understanding Taoism*, 16–17.

22. Ibid., 17.

23. The Qin Dynasty and the Mao Shan lineage, and the subsequent new lineages that formed from it, represent the golden age of mystical or esoteric Taoism. Esoteric Taoist practitioners were believed to possess the power to fly and interact with guardian spirits that dwelled both within the human body and in Heaven. In contrast to earlier shamanic-influenced esoteric Taoism, where Man interacted with a Heaven or with deities beyond himself, the Mao Shan descended lineages sought interaction with a Heaven within, likened to the modern age's "Higher Self" concept. Heaven, or Divinity, resided within each human, and a Taoist mystic sought to manifest that inner divinity toward ends such as immortality or acquiring metaphysical power. See generally Wong, *Taoism,* 44–46. The Qin Dynasty also gave rise to Neo-Taoism, a revival of Taoist philosophy through an esoteric or metaphysical lens. Neo-Taoism focused on esoteric Taoism, or "Mystical Learning." Fowler, *Philosophy and Religion of Taoism,* 146–47.

24. 上清大洞真经 [Shàng Qīng Dà Dòng Zhēn Jīng, *Perfect Scripture of Great Profundity*], 10–11, 13, http://vdisk.weibo.com/s/dEhRrv4RfUF2U.

25. The *Perfect Scripture of Great Profundity* was the fundamental scripture of the Shang Qing lineage. Isabelle Robinet, "Shang Qing—Highest Clarity," in *Taoism Handbook,* ed. Livia Kohn (Boston: Brill, 2000), 201.

26. Fabrizio Pregadio, "Early Daoist Meditation," in *Daoism in History: Essays in Honour of Liu Ts'un-yan,* ed. Benjamin Penny (London: Routledge, 2006), 135.

27. Ibid., 134.

28. Ibid., 134–35. See generally the *Perfect Scripture of Great Profundity.*

29. 上清大洞真经 [*Perfect Scripture of Great Profundity*], 13.

30. In Taoist inner alchemical theory, longevity, even immortality, is achieved through the removal of inner demons and replacing them with inner gods. Taoist practitioners of inner alchemy express the human body as composed of inner gods (or angelic beings) and inner demons, perhaps an anthropomorphizing of benevolent and malignant energy, or yin and yang balance.

31. 上清大洞真经 [*Perfect Scripture of Great Profundity*], 13.

32. Authorship not known, n.d. The "all-powerful" seal of Lao-Tze (Lao Tzu), used in Taoist magic—"bringer of good fortune." Worn by psychic mediums. In Shah, *Oriental Magic,* 155.

33. 謝世維 [Hsieh, Shu-Wei],古靈寶經中的大乘之道: 論中古時期道教經典型態之轉變 ["The Way of Great Vehicle in Early Lingbao Scriptures: The Transformation of Daoist Scriptures in Medieval China"], 成大中文學報 *[The Chinese Journal of the National Cheng Kung University]* 第三十六期 [vol. 36, March 2012], 1–36, http://bec001.web.ncku.edu.tw/ezfiles/335/1335/img/1450/3601.pdf.

34. One often sought-after purpose for Fu sigils is to keep ghosts at bay. Fu sigils are crafted to control spirit entities and to safeguard against their antics. See Jean Elizabeth DeBernardi, *The Way That Lives in the Heart: Chinese Popular Religion and Spirit Mediums in Penang, Malaysia* (Stanford, CA: Stanford University Press, 2006), 89.

35. See generally Stephen R. Bokenkamp and Peter Nickerson, *Early Daoist Scriptures* (Daoist

Classics, No. 1) (Berkeley, CA: University of California Press, 1999); See also Wong, *Taoism,* 35.

36. See also note 39 below.

37. See note 35 in chapter 1 for an explanation of inner alchemy and outer alchemy.

38. The Ling Bao scriptures, circa AD 397, offer incredible insights into historic Fu sigil crafting. Many of the texts in the scriptures describe Fu talismans and provide illustrated examples. Of note are the chapters titled "Text of the Self-Generating Five Talismans of Correspondence" (ziran wucheng wen) and "Preface to the Five Talismans of Ling Bao" (lingbao wufu xu), considered the most important sacred text for the Ling Bao lineage.

39. See 清微藏書閣 [Qīng Wēi Cáng Shū Gé], 太上靈寶五符序 [Tài Shàng Líng Bǎo Wǔ Fú Xù, *The Ling Bao Order of the Five Talismans*], in 洞玄部神符類 [Dòng Xuán Bù Shén Fú Lèi], 1997, http://www.ctcwri.idv.tw/godking.htm. The text's title has also been translated into English as *Preface to the Five Most High Numinous Treasure Talismans.* Shawn Arthur, "Eating Your Way to Immortality: Early Daoist Self-Cultivation Diets," *The Journal of Daoist Studies* 2:33 (2009).

40. Frederick Shih-Chung Chen, "Who Are the Eight Kings in the *Samādhi Sūtra of Liberation through Purification*? Otherworld Bureaucrats in India and China," paper presented at the North American Graduate Student Conference in Buddhist Studies, University of California, Berkeley, April 2009, 66, note 38, http://www2.ihp.sinica.edu.tw/file/1103rKHQApp.pdf.

41. Arguably, 帝 (Dì) could also be translated to "emperor," "deity," or "god." For the purposes of describing the five talismans of the *Order of the Five Talismans,* the character will be translated as "Lord."

42. See note 35 in chapter 1 for an explanation of inner alchemy and outer alchemy.

43. The "blade-proof" theory holds that, through cultivation and training in the craft, a practitioner can become effectively invincible to knives, blades, daggers, and swords.

44. Taoism as a religion flourished during the Tang Dynasty. There had always been power struggles among Taoism, Confucianism, and Buddhism as each vied to gain political favor. The imperial family of the Tang Dynasty believed they traced their lineage back to Lao Tzu, the founder of Taoism, and so Taoism found great favor during this era. Oldstone-Moore, *Understanding Taoism,* 16. The imperial court of the Tang Dynasty strived to harmonize Taoism with the more popular Confucianism and Buddhism. Pregadio, *Encyclopedia of Taoism,* 21.

45. Saso, "Orthodoxy and Heterodoxy," 326.

46. The Lu (錄) might be likened to the *Goetia* in *The Lesser Keys of Solomon* in Western demonology. The *Goetia* is a seventeenth-century roster of seventy-two demons, featuring the sigils with which to summon them.

47. The number of individuals who identify as Taoist are few. Instead, tenets of Taoism are blended into Buddhism, Confucianism, or regional folk religions. When Confucianism rose to prominence, many of the elite Confucianist scholars, despite being publicly at odds with Taoism, were themselves quiet practitioners of mystical Taoist arts, such as alchemy. Oldstone-Moore, *Understanding Taoism,* 8–10.

48. See, for example, Richard Shek, "Daoism and Orthodoxy," in *Heterodoxy in Late Imperial*

*China,* eds. Kwang-Ching Liu and Richard Hon-Chun Shek (Honolulu: University of Hawaii Press, 2004), 159–60, referring to the Taoist goal of attaining immortality and its relation to moral cultivation.

49. One prominent lineage that venerated Lei Gong, the God of Thunder, and practiced thunder magic was the Shen Hsiao lineage during the Song Dynasty (AD 960–1279). Pas, *Historical Dictionary,* 29. See also Shah, *Oriental Magic,* 154.

50. The term *thunder magic* refers to a form of magical practice adopted by several lineages, and thus it varies from lineage to lineage. Shifu Lin, *"Thunder Magic" Taoist Traditions of the Tao Jiao Lei Fa and Their Relationship to Nei Kung Meditation* (Lung Hu Shan Publications, 2013), Amazon e-book (ASIN B00CNFX85O). See also Pregadio, *Encyclopedia of Taoism,* 117.

51. Judity Magee Boltz, "Not by the Seal of Office Alone," in *Religion and Society in T'ang and Sung China,* ed. Patricia Buckley Ebrey (Honolulu: University of Hawaii Press, 1993), 272.

52. Ibid., 273.

53. Ibid.

54. Florian C. Reiter, *Basic Conditions of Taoist Thunder Magic* [道教雷法] (Wiesbaden, Germany: Otto Harrassowitz Verlag, 2007), vii.

55. Ibid., 2.

56. Ibid., 31.

57. Pas, *Historical Dictionary,* 30.

58. Ibid.

59. Shek, "Daoism and Orthodoxy," 149.

60. See Saso, "Taiwan," 598, which refers to the lineage as Blackhead instead of Black Hat.

61. Ibid., which refers to the lineage as Redhead instead of Red Hat.

62. A medium is someone whose body can become possessed by spirits, who then performs magic, crafts Fu sigils, or gives prophecies while possessed. A shaman is someone who does not become possessed, but rather is able to travel to other realms, such as the underworld, and facilitate communication between worlds.

63. Fu Ji, or spirit writing, in its original and more popular manifestation is a form of divination. A medium enters a trance and the seeker asks a question. The spirit that is possessing the medium's body then answers the seeker's question, often in riddle, arcane poetry, or obscure verse that the medium writes down. Ivette M. Vargas-O'Bryan and Zhou Xun, *Disease, Religion and Healing in Asia: Collaborations and Collisions* (London: Routledge, 2014), 59. Traditionally, ink and paper is not used; rather, the medium uses a special divining stick and writes into a shallow tray of sand or ash. The practice of Fu Ji was historically steeped in ritual, beginning with offerings to the gods, incense burning, bows in veneration to the spirits invoked, and invocations. Fu Ji was popularized during the Qing Dynasty, though it remained practice exclusive to men, specifically scholars. Women did not typically engage in spirit writing or consult spirit writing divination. Richard J. Smith, *Mapping China and Managing the World: Culture, Cartography and Cosmology in Late Imperial Times* (London: Routledge, 2013), 144–45.

64. Smith, *Mapping China,* 144.

65. Historically, there were rivalries between Taoism and Buddhism as both establishments struggled to win favor from the imperial courts, which would have meant power and resources for their establishments. Taoism often allied with Confucianism. Together, the two saw Buddhism as an outsider, an alien religion, whereas at least both Taoism and Confucianism were native and indigenous to China. Among the three establishments, tensions were strongest between Taoism and Buddhism. See Thomas F. Cleary, *The Taoist Classics* (Boston: Shambhala, 2003), 215, noting the tensions between the Taoist and Buddhist institutions during the Sui Dynasty. Meanwhile Buddhism made a clear distinction between Taoism as a philosophy and Taoism as a religion, or more specifically, what I refer to as esoteric Taoism. Buddhists tended toward holding a belittling and negative view of esoteric Taoism, given the Taoist reliance on the supernatural, alchemy, spell-crafting, and quest for immortality that seemed to subsist in Taoism as a religion (esoteric Taoism), whereas Taoism as a philosophy shared many points of similarity with Buddhism. To distinguish Buddhism from Taoism as religions, Buddhism developed itself into a more elitist and erudite practice, focusing on cultivating the mind rather than engaging in sorcery and shamanism. Interesting enough, esoteric Taoist practitioners often integrated Buddhist deities, mantras, and doctrines into their supernatural invocations, alchemy, and spell-crafting. See Xiuping Hong, "Lao-Tzu, the Tao of Lao-Tzu, and the Evolution of Taoism," in Mou, *Taoism,* 95–96. See also Pregadio, *Encyclopedia of Taoism,* 21. Just as Buddhists held a negative view of Taoism, Taoists held a negative, condescending view of Buddhism. Robert Patterson Steed, "To Extend Love to All Creeping Things: Ethics in Ge Hong's 'Baopuzi'" (doctoral dissertation, University of Iowa, 2008), 31–32, noting the Taoist alchemist Ge Hong's negative attitude toward Buddhism during the Jin Dynasty, describing Buddhist temples as encouraging moral transgressions.

66. In this book, a charm with a general, universal property of protection will be referred to as an amulet, while a charm that has been specifically charged with a purpose or intention for a specific individual is referred to as a talisman. Fu sigils are typically talismans and crafted on a case-by-case basis, though it can also be an amulet when multiple versions are collectively charged with general protection or good luck energies and disseminated out to a number of individuals. Many practitioners will charge Fu sigils en masse as protection amulets. When a Fu is charged with energy and intended to benefit anyone who activates it, it is an amulet. When the Fu is crafted in a customized way for one specific individual, it is a talisman.

67. Steavu-Balint, "Three Sovereigns Tradition," 136–38.

68. Lagerwey and Kalinowski, *Early Chinese Religion,* 12–13.

69. Edward L. Davis, *Society and the Supernatural in Song China* (Honolulu: University of Hawaii Press, 2001), 197–98.

70. Boltz, "Not by the Seal," 274.

71. I adhere to certain ethical rules when considering retaliatory craft. First, it is never to be used on the defenseless: if you are aware that you are in a privileged position over the other, are stronger, more capable, or more powerful than the other, then no matter what that other does to you, do not engage in retaliatory craft against that person. Second, the objective must always be about restoring balance: the purpose is not to hurt, even if it means hurting may be

involved; the purpose is to restore balance. Hurting is incidental, never the specific objective that the practitioner bears in mind while performing craft. If the perpetrator is hurt in the process of restoring balance, then so be it, though the wise practitioner will be mindful of minimizing the hurt. Finally, there must be bright-line moral boundaries that the practitioner agrees, in advance of any craft, that he or she will never cross, without exception. As for when retaliatory craft may be acceptable, there are only two guidelines. First, it must be in self-defense or to stand against unjust, unreasonable interference with an innocent's personal liberties or pursuit of happiness. Second, all other means of putting an end to the interference must have been attempted by the practitioner before resorting to retaliatory craft.

72. From a Tang Dynasty Book of Methods, *Highest Purity Jade Girdle and Golden Crown, Golden Script Book of the Great Ultimate* (Pelliot Chinois 2409), in the archives at the Bibliothèque Nationale de France, Paris.

73. Shah, *Oriental Magic,* 153.

74. See note 2 in chapter 13.

75. Pregadio, *Encyclopedia of Taoism,* 117. The practice came about during the Song Dynasty and is often associated with inner alchemy.

76. Steavu-Balint, "Three Sovereigns Tradition," 140.

77. These bronze Fu talismans were from my late maternal grandmother in Tainan, Taiwan, and date to the 1920s. These talismans are shaped to resemble Zhou Dynasty spade coins, the form of currency used between 1045 and 256 BC. Etched onto the coin replicas, however, are Fu sigils for wealth and prosperity.

78. See generally Daniel Sosnoski, *Introduction to Japanese Culture* (North Clarendon, VT: Tuttle/Periplus, 2013).

79. Ian Reader and George J. Tanabe Jr., *Practically Religious: Worldly Benefits and the Common Religion of Japan* (Honolulu: University of Hawaii Press, 2004), 184.

80. Magical secrets are transmitted from master teacher to disciple and carefully guarded with secrecy. Oaths are sworn to maintain vows of confidentiality. Saso, "Taiwan," 598.

81. Traditionally it was believed that only an ordained Taoist priest with orthodox knowledge of Taoist magic could craft effective Fu sigils. Saso, "Orthodoxy and Heterodoxy," 326. Also, what "only a Taoist priest" or priestess means does need to be clarified here. Unlike Buddhism and other religions, most Taoist priests do not renounce the material world or live reclusively in monasteries. They live among the people, with families, and set up an altar room in their homes where they take consultations from the community. People from the community then visit the home of the Taoist priest or priestess for magical Fu talismans. Khoo Boo Eng, *A Simple Approach to Taoism* (Singapore: PartridgeSingapore, 2013), 39. The origin of esoteric Taoist practice was not accompanied by monasticism, where monks and nuns (or priests and priestesses) renounced the mundane world to live a secluded life in a monastery. Ordained Celestial Masters, or Taoists priests and priestesses, married, had children, and passed their magical teachings down to their children. That being said, around the fourth and fifth centuries, especially among lineages that absorbed Buddhist influence, esoteric Taoist practitioners did espouse monastic life and renounced marriage, though renunciation and celibacy were

not conditions of ordained priesthood (i.e., the grant of authority to craft Fu sigils). Then, around the Song Dynasty (AD 960–1279), celibacy was more formally required of Taoist priests. Pregadio, *Encyclopedia of Taoism,* 102–3, 105. Even after monastic life was formalized in some lineages, it was not renunciation that authorized a Taoist priest or priestess to craft Fu sigils; it was the practitioner's Lu, or mastery of spirit names and summoning methodologies, according to orthodox instructions first provided by the Zheng Yi lineage. The vast majority of those who practice Taoist magic live among society, have mortgages, bills to pay, children, pets, and are, in every other way, normal.

82. The mainstream belief is that a practitioner is qualified to craft Fu sigils only if that practitioner has received, directly from a Taoist master, a Lu, also referred to as a register or magical book, instructing on Fu sigil crafting techniques. Fu crafted outside or not in accordance with these registers, or magical books, are not empowered. "Talismans," in *The Daoist Encyclopedia,* FYSK Daoist Culture Centre, http://en.daoinfo.org/wiki/Talismans. However, an understanding of the ontological and metaphysical principles behind the craft would suggest that the ability to craft Fu sigils is not limited by registers, lineages, or social rules. The ability comes from inner cultivation and compliance with the natural laws behind craft. These principles are set forth in the *Classics of the Esoteric Talisman,* as interpreted through the lens of this book.

83. Paul R. Katz, *Demon Hordes and Burning Boats: The Cult of Marshal Wen in Late Imperial Chekiang* (Albany, NY: State University of New York Press, 1995), 107.

84. Saso, "Taiwan," 598. Also, ordained priests and priestesses of orthodox Taoist magic, according to the Lu, were assigned a ranking and title in accordance with the spirits or deities they were able to describe or summon. Saso, "Taiwan," 598.

85. Saso, "Orthodoxy and Heterodoxy," 326.

86. The Fu sigil pictured in figure 2.16 is from an undated, uncredited Book of Methods with unknown origins, titled 張天師符 [*Talismans of the Celestial Master Zhang*], author unknown, found by the author in approximately 2006 at Tainan, Taiwan, among the belongings of her late grandmother.

87. See note 42 in chapter 6 on teeth clicking, a common practitioner's technique integrated into Taoist exorcisms.

88. In other words, it's OK if you're illiterate in Chinese and use the various Chinese characters for your Fu sigils in a way that may be laughable to the literates. It just has to make sense to you on your spiritual-psychic plane. The language should come intuitively. Not knowing Chinese works to your advantage in many ways. It means you cannot rely on learned knowledge but instead must rely on your intuition. In essence, by crafting sigils in Chinese without knowing the Chinese language, you have to rely on your intuitive rather than cognitive abilities as you conceive your own Fu Wen.

89. DeBernardi, *Way That Lives,* 100.

90. Ibid.

91. Ching Kun Yang, *Religion in Chinese Society: A Study of Contemporary Social Functions of Religion and Some of Their Historical Factors* (Long Grove, IL: Waveland Press, 1991), 5.

92. Lebron, *Searching for Spiritual Unity,* 431.

93. Ibid.

94. Ibid.

95. "And Aaron shall lay both his hands on the head of the live goat, and confess over it all the iniquities of the people of Israel, and all their transgressions, all their sins. And he shall put them on the head of the goat and send it away into the wilderness by the hand of a man who is in readiness. The goat shall bear all their iniquities on itself to a remote area, and he shall let the goat go free in the wilderness." Leviticus 16:21–22, English Standard Version.

96. Clayton D. Robinson, "The Laying on of Hands, with Special Reference to the Reception of the Holy Spirit in the New Testament" (doctoral dissertation, Fuller Theological Seminary, Pasadena, CA, 2008), 21.

97. Ibid.

## 3. CLASSICS OF THE ESOTERIC TALISMAN

1. 中國哲學書電子化計劃 [The Chinese Texts Project], 黃帝陰符經 [*Yellow Emperor's Classics of the Esoteric Talisman*], n.d., 35–36, http://ctext.org/yinfujing/zh.

2. Steavu-Balint, "Three Sovereigns Tradition," 35–36.

3. 中國哲學書電子化計劃 [The Chinese Texts Project], 抱朴子 [*Bao Puzi, Book of the Master of Simplicity*], n.d., http://ctext.org/baopuzi/zh.

4. Steed, "To Extend Love," 14–15, noting the dates of birth and death for Ge Hong.

5. Keith Knapp, "Ge Hong (Ko Hung, 283–343 CE)," *Internet Encyclopedia of Philosophy: A Peer-Reviewed Academic Resource,* http://www.iep.utm.edu/gehong.

6. See "Magic, Craft, and Sorcery" in appendix B.

7. The Five Sacred Mountains are positioned in the north, south, east, west, and central regions of China and in Chinese geomancy are believed to form a power grid. The Five Sacred Mountains were recognized as early as 400 BC and have strong Taoist, Buddhist, and Confucianist presence.

8. 中國哲學書電子化計劃 [The Chinese Texts Project], 三洞神符纪 [*Three Caverns of the Supernatural Fu Talismanic Records*], n.d., http://ctext.org/library.pl?if=gb&file=98630&page=1&remap=gb.

9. Here, my spelling blends pinyin and Wade-Giles to form the unofficial spelling Tao Zang. In pinyin, it should be Dao Zang, and in Wade-Giles, Tao Tsang. Some texts include a hyphen, Tao-Tsang. See Robinet, *Taoist Meditation,* 32.

10. 中國哲學書電子化計劃 [The Chinese Texts Project], 神符類 [Shen Fu Lei, "Types of Supernatural Talismans"], n.d., http://ctext.org/wiki.pl?if=gb&chapter=465546#口神符類.

11. 三洞神符纪 [*Three Caverns*], 37.

12. Steavu-Balint, "Three Sovereigns Tradition," 134.

13. Ibid., 135.

14. "For centuries, perhaps thousands of years, magic flowed slowly but powerfully through the human race. In its most ritualistic form, the flow was distinctly from east to west." Shah, *Oriental Magic,* xvi.

15. Divinatory tools are generally used to determine whether the timing for a "triggering mechanism" is proper. While this book explains a postliminary divination in chapter 8, practitioners will differ on whether they opt for a preliminary or postliminary divination. A postliminary divination takes place after all rituals and chargings of a Fu sigil. Doing so is to determine whether the process, in its totality, including the timing of the craft, has been blessed by the gods and is therefore effective. A preliminary divination takes place prior to conception of a Fu sigil, and the purpose is to divine from the gods whether timing for such an intended craft is proper.

16. Taoist ethical thought governs how a practitioner interprets "peaceful." Ancient shamanic views that endured through the Zhou Dynasty and into the Han Dynasty influence the ethical code that Taoist practitioners of magic abide by. Supernatural or energetic workings, or "exercising triggering mechanisms" by taking from Heaven and Earth, are governed by a reciprocity principle. If a practitioner harmed another or brought harm to either Heaven or Earth, a celestial administration would adjudicate on these deeds and return a punishment of great suffering. See generally Pregadio, *Encyclopedia of Taoism,* 99.

17. Wu, *Seeking the Spirit,* 81.

18. See note 41 in chapter 1.

19. Note that there are conflicting views here. While the text seems to suggest that "Heaven holds no special favors" to any one Man, in other words that there is no messiah, messianic beliefs did play a significant role in medieval Taoism. Pregadio, *Encyclopedia of Taoism,* 94. Prophecies of a Taoist messiah were popular in the Han Dynasty and onward, suggesting a reincarnation of Lao Tzu, the founding father of Taoism; or Shi Bao, also known as Dao De Tian Zun, one of the Three Pure Ones, the Master Teacher.

20. References to calling upon the four directions during a ritual have been inscribed onto divinatory oracle bones from the Shang Dynasty. Eno, "Shang State Religion," 67. Thus the ritual of calling upon the four directions to invoke deity or supernatural presence has been used by shamanic and magical practitioners since 1600–1046 BC. Archeological discoveries of oracle bones from the Shang Dynasty reveal the invocation process prior to a divination. First, the main deity is called. During the Shang Dynasty, it was typically an ancestor of a governing lord or king, or a nature god, such as the corresponding deity for a mountain or river. After the main deity was invoked, the four cardinal directions were named and then sacrifices made toward each direction. Eno, "Shang State Religion," 67–68.

21. Geomancy is believed to be the predecessor of feng shui. In the earliest shamanic times, the positioning of mountains, hills, valleys, and bodies of water were believed to play a crucial role in the fates and fortunes of men. Geomancy was practiced by shamans to connect the shapes and locations of natural land forms with artificial land forms, even graves and burial sites, to ensure blessings and mitigate misfortunes. Saso, "Taiwan," 581.

22. "Tao produces one / One produces two / Two produce three / Three produce myriad things / Myriad things, backed by yin and embracing yang / Achieve harmony by integrating their energy." Lin, *Tao Te Ching,* chap. 42.

23. A distinction is made between the one as Tao and the one as Qi. Qi is considered a life force

and is neutral, like any form of natural element, gas, or property. Qi is simply energy. On the other hand, the Tao is characterized as benevolent. The Tao, although unlike monotheistic religions that might express the same concept as one singular god principle or deity, in Taoism the Tao is not personified, and yet is characterized as benevolent, seeking to "benefit others and not to cause harm." Thus, while Qi is a neutral and natural energy force, the Tao is not considered neutral, and is considered divine. See Wong, *Taoism,* 24.

24. A cultural note: according to Chinese beliefs, some humans are able to see ghosts, but such individuals tend to have low luck. The ability to see ghosts and communicate with the deceased comes with it misfortune, a life of sadness, and tragedy. Those with great luck are not able to see ghosts and tend to go through life without any incident or encounter with ghosts. DeBernardi, *Way That Lives,* 89.

25. The Chinese Texts Project maintains an incredible wealth of literature for the curious. The *Classics of the Esoteric Talisman* text comes with decent Chinese-to-English translations. The side-by-side comparison of the traditional Chinese text and the English translation can be found at http://ctext.org/yinfujing/zh.

# 4. ANATOMY OF A FU SIGIL

1. For most of esoteric Taoist history, knowledge of craft, such as Fu sigils, was passed down by initiation from master teacher to disciple. Pregadio, *Encyclopedia of Taoism,* 16.

2. Steavu-Balint, "Three Sovereigns Tradition," 26.

3. Ibid., 136.

4. 中國哲學書電子化計劃 [The Chinese Texts Project], 三洞神符纪 [*Three Caverns of the Supernatural Fu Talismanic Records*], n.d., http://ctext.org/library.pl?if=gb&file=98630&page=1&remap=gb.

5. As introduced in chapter 3.

6. Note the repetitive use of 日, the character for "sun," symbolic of yang energy for dispelling yin. Demons and hungry ghosts are considered yin. Thus, a large dosage of yang—using the character "sun"—inscribed into the Fu will overtake the residing yin.

7. *Fu Talismans from Zheng Yi Dao,* n.d., from the Shang Qing Temple, Jiangxi, China.

8. See the entry for the Enigmatic Warrior God under "Taoist Celestial Beings" in appendix B.

9. See Eno, "Shang State Religion," 67–68.

10. Powerhouse Museum, "Chinese Dress in the Qing Dynasty," https://www.powerhouse museum.com/hsc/evrev/chinese_dress.htm, noting the twelve symbols of sovereignty, which were the sun, moon, three-star constellation, mountain, dragon, pheasant, pair of bronze goblets, waterweed, rice, fire, an ax, and the Fo and Fu, a symbol of justice. See also "Twelve Symbols of Sovereignty" in appendix B.

11. The three stars correspond with Betelgeuse (Alpha Orionis), Meissa (Lambda Orionis), and Bellatrix (Gamma Orionis, or the Amazon Star). See the image of the Orion constellation in Chris Sasaki, *The Constellations: Stars and Stories* (Edison, NJ: Sterling, 2003, 86–87.

12. To me, the religious expression of exorcisms is symbolic. While I don't have proof one way or the other, I don't believe that a possession means there is a literal demon residing in some-

one's body. Rather, I do find it credible to assert that there is a metaphysical counterpart of unseen energy to the physical form we can sense—perhaps, in the case of demon possession, Qi energy that is excessively yin—and that there is a means for accessing that metaphysical energy to influence the physical form. Thus, what we perceive as a possession is an excessive imbalance of Qi energy that is causing certain symptoms to manifest in the physical form. A practitioner who is skilled in the craft of harnessing Qi energy, or that metaphysical counterpart, taps into that Qi to restore balance. When balance is restored, as when excessive yin is neutralized with a potent dose of yang in an exorcism, symptoms of imbalance go away and the physical form is brought to equilibrium.

13. 上清大洞真经 [*Perfect Scripture of Great Profundity*].

14. Throughout this book, "beneficiary" refers to the person receiving a Fu sigil and who is the one intended to benefit from the sigil craft. I use "beneficiary" and "recipient" interchangeably.

## 5. EMPOWERING A FU SIGIL

1. 上清大洞真经 [*Perfect Scripture of Great Profundity*], 11.

2. Ibid. See note 42 in chapter 6 for more historic context on the practice of teeth clicking in Taoist rituals.

3. Astral projection is the process by which a practitioner transforms his or her personal Qi into *shen* (神) energy and manifests personal consciousness into that energy. The practitioner's consciousness, now manifested as an astral body, leaves the physical body. Through that astral body as shen (神), the practitioner can then travel at will around the physical plane of the earth or beyond, to other realms. It is, in effect, an out-of-body experience. The mechanics for astral projection differ from practitioner to practitioner, but it generally begins with grounding or centering to fix the physical body before astral travel commences. Personal Qi energy is then gathered into a concentrated form, typically envisioned as a spinning wheel of light near the stomach or core of the body. Once all personal Qi has been gathered, it is pulled upward toward the crown of the head, where the personal Qi connects to the cosmic Qi, and from the crown of the head, the astral body, that concentrated form of personal Qi, now manifesting as shen (神), leaves the physical body along with the practitioner's consciousness. Astral projection is not an exercise for the lay individual to try. According to esoteric Taoist principles, it requires inner cultivation through processes such as qi gong. Qi gong is discussed very briefly in chapter 6. Typically, a practitioner becomes connected to a particular deity, white light energy, or higher vibrational force by way of an invocation, for example, 南无阿弥陀佛觀世音菩薩 [ná mó Amítuófó Guānshìyīn Púsà, "Honor to the venerable Amithaba Buddha and Kuan Yin bodhisattva"], and that invocation is recited to ensure safe astral travels.

4. 中國哲學書電子化計劃 [The Chinese Texts Project], 道法會元 [*Tao Fa Hui Yuan*], http://ctext.org/wiki.pl?if=gb&res=54910.

5. William H. Nienhauser, *The Indiana Companion to Traditional Chinese Literature* (Bloomington, IN: Indiana University Press, 1986), 155–56.

6. Perhaps a more practical rationale for the exclusivity is an ancient form of intellectual property protection. Powerful lineages sold Fu talismans to the public. If anyone could craft

these charms, the lineages' revenue stream would be diluted and the market flooded with competitors. By requiring affiliation with a recognized lineage, the number of competitors was limited and the commercial venture of selling Fu could remain protected. The exclusivity requirement also helped with consumer protection. The public knew that an effective Fu has to come from a temple, where the practitioners undergo training, are supervised by masters, and abide by codes of ethics. Members of the public were less likely to get swindled from buying talismans at a temple than from peddlers on the streets, who might not be as committed to a code of ethics. All that is to say that the exclusivity requirement was a social construct and not necessarily one that is part of craft itself.

7. See point 9 in chapter 3.

8. Another equally compelling theory is that Fu sigils do not need to be empowered or charged at all. Instead, it isn't the Fu sigil that wields power; it is our own power of mind that manifests results. The Fu sigil, then, is in effect an unnecessary prop. Yet the human mind is such that it is easier to accept an inanimate object as possessing power over us than it is to accept ourselves as possessing the power from within. As an intermediate step in the greater journey toward understanding life, that's fine. So we craft Fu sigils.

9. Pregadio, *Encyclopedia of Taoism*, 117.

10. "If the practitioner does not believe the rituals will work, they will not work." Lin, "*Thunder Magic*," noting one of the requisites for effective craft is an absolute, unequivocal confidence in the efficacy and power of craft.

11. The traditional Chinese spell as taught in this text is based on 漳和國中 [Zhāng Hé Guó Zhōng], 五路財神 [Wŭ Lù Cái Shén, The Five Celestials of Wealth], 2010, http://mail.chjh .ntpc.edu.tw/chjh99/e06.htm.

12. Traditional basic joss paper (金紙, jīn zhǐ) comes as square sheets of paper, some with a gold leaf square in the center and some with a silver leaf square in the center. The gold leaf sheets are burned for venerating deities and for sending prayers to Heaven. The silver leaf sheets are burned for honoring ancestors and for sending prayers of protection. Typically these square sheets are folded origami-style into ingots, and the ingots are burned as the offerings. The gold and silver joss paper practice is said to come from the legend of Zhao Gong Ming.

13. The name Cai Shen means simply "Wealth God." Throughout China's diverse religious history and culture, there have been many male deities associated with bestowing wealth and prosperity, and these deities can all be referred to as Cai Shen, as in a god of wealth. Here, and generally throughout this book, my reference to Cai Shen is to Zhao Gong Ming, as he is one of the more popular and better known manifestations of a Chinese god of wealth. Zhao Gong Ming in reference to a Cai Shen, or Wealth God, also happens to be the version of the mythology that I am familiar with.

14. In formal ceremonial offerings to deities or ancestors, three traditional meats are left on the altar. What these three meats are varies by region in China, depending on the diet common to that area. In the south, fish is almost always used as one of the three; in the north, duck is more common. Pork and poultry are typical. In many agricultural communities, beef was not eaten out of

respect for cows and oxen, who were often of immense value to their families, helping till the lands.

# 6. THE TOOLS OF CRAFT

1. Chinese Seal Generator, Chinese-Tools.com, http://www.chinese-tools.com/tools/seal.html.

2. See note 36 in appendix B.

3. Compare the practitioner identifying as a witch to one who identifies as a medium, a 童乩 (Tóng Jī). See note 38 in appendix B.

4. See the section "Pantheon of Deities" and the subsection "The Eight Immortals" in appendix B.

5. According to Hindu principles, the atman (Sanskrit for "self" or "breath") is the eternal core of a personality, or self. The atman migrates from life to life, body to body through reincarnation. *Encyclopedia Britannica,* s.v. "atman," http://www.britannica.com/topic/atman.

6. Bu Dai, also known as the Laughing Buddha or Hotei, is believed to be based on a Buddhist monk who lived in the ninth or tenth centuries AD and carried a large sackcloth with him as he wandered from village to village; he was often seen playing with children. Richard A. Gardner, "The Laughing Buddha," in *Encyclopedia of Humor Studies,* ed. Salvatore Attardo (Thousand Oaks, CA: SAGE Publications, 2014), 93. Bu Dai is attributed to many specialties, and his primary service will vary depending on who you ask. He is a god of fortune, and is thus invoked for Taoist craft that seeks to raise energies for fortune and prosperity. It is believed that his sackcloth contains endless riches that he distributes to those who pray to him. He is also a god of happiness, and is invoked for attaining inner wisdom and bringing harmony and happiness to a home. Bu Dai is also the patron god of psychics, diviners, and fortune-tellers, and is often invoked by such practitioners to enhance their metaphysical practices. See Gardner, "Laughing Buddha," 94.

7. For a reference table of Wu Xing or Five Phases correspondences, including the fruit correspondences, see Donald E. Reynolds, "Chinese Five Elements," Northern Shaolin Academy, 2005, http://www.northernshaolinacademy.com/new/docs/FiveElementsChart.xls.

8. The custom could have come from the tradition of leaving liquor and sweets out for the Kitchen God (灶君), Zào Jūn, God of Home and Hearth. In both regional folk religions and Taoism, it was believed that the Kitchen God resided in the kitchen hearth, and before every lunar new year, he ascended back up to Heaven to report to the Jade Emperor whether a family deserved to be rewarded or punished in the forthcoming year. The liquor and sweets were left out as offerings for the Kitchen God right before his ascent to Heaven, in the hopes that doing so would result in him reporting good things about the family.

9. Shah, *Oriental Magic,* 153.

10. Ibid.

11. DeBernardi, *Way That Lives,* 112.

12. Mollier, *Buddhism and Taoism,* 88.

13. See chapter 9 regarding the temple seal.

14. Shah, *Oriental Magic,* 156.

15. Figure 8.11, in the "Energy Transference" section in chapter 8, is a photograph of a Fu sigil scroll.

16. In Chinese occult tradition, magic mirrors are considered essential for battling with de-

mons and demonic energy. Seminal treatises on the magic mirror's importance were written about in the Sui Dynasty (AD 581–618). Shah, *Oriental Magic,* 151–52.

17. Magic mirrors should only be used for their magical purposes, and kept covered or put away when not in use. These tenets were espoused by the Taoist magicians of old. Shah, *Oriental Magic,* 153.

18. A pair of divining crescents is often found in Chinese and Taiwanese temples. *See* DeBernardi, *Way That Lives,* 71.

19. I tend to subscribe to "higher self" rationales and the power of synchronicity, especially when it comes to the divination forms I practice. Synchronicity, apophenia, patternicity, the Barnum effect, and projective psychology were topics I addressed in my first book. See Wen, *Holistic Tarot,* 16–25. However, for inexplicable reasons, with moon blocks, I eschew the "higher self" and synchronicity logic to indulge in the more superstitious.

20. DeBernardi, *Way That Lives,* 4, noting that spirit mediums tend to burn camphor incense when communing with *datuk* spirits and sandalwood for saints.

21. Incense is also symbolic of mortality. As a joss stick burns, it is reduced, shorter and shorter, like a human life as we live, our essence returning back to the ether, back to source energy. DeBernardi, *Way That Lives,* 91.

22. It is likely, though wholly my own speculation, that Taoist practitioners adopted the 108 recitation practice from Buddhism. In Buddhism, sutras are cited in multiples of 108, and ceremonies, liturgy, and other rituals incorporate the number 108. An example of this is the funeral procession of the Xianfeng Emperor of the Qing Dynasty, where 108 Tibetan Buddhist and 108 Chan Buddhist monks performed the rites in nine-day segments. Evelyn S. Rawski, *The Last Emperors: A Social History of Qing Imperial Institutions* (Oakland, CA: University of California Press, 1998), 280. See also Robert E. Buswell and Donald S. Lopez Jr., *The Princeton Dictionary of Buddhism* (Princeton, NJ: Princeton University Press, 2013), 380, noting that recitations of mantras or sutras with the japa mala prayer beads were often in multiples of 108, with 1,080 being a typical maximum. The 108 tradition originated from the Hindu practice of reciting mantras in 108 repetitions. Doing so empowered a practitioner and opened the gateways to other worlds and a higher consciousness. Audrey A. Irvine, *Infinite Possibility: Frameworks for Understanding Extraordinary Human Experience* (Bloomington, IN: AuthorHouse, 2008), 145.

23. Shah, *Oriental Magic,* 154. The Taoist practitioner's use of ceremonial bells is speculated to come from India.

24. Haruji Asano, "Fa Qi: Ritual Tools," in Pregadio, *Encyclopedia of Taoism,* 414.

25. However, according to superstition, if wind chimes seem to ring suddenly when there is no wind or provocation, it is an indication that ghosts or spirits are present.

26. Steve Savedow, *The Magician's Workbook: A Modern Grimoire* (Newbury Port, MA: Weiser Books, 1996), 1.

27. Ibid., 3.

28. Frater W.I.T., *Advanced Enochian Magick: A Manual of Theory, Training, and Practice for the Novice and the Adept* (Denver: Outskirts Press, 2008), 14.

29. Ibid.

30. Ibid.

31. Summonings used by most Chinese Taoist practitioners sound like legal judgments, or imperial decrees. Fu sigils for summoning are characterized as judgments, orders, or decrees from the higher, supernatural court. For example, a phrase often heard in Taoist summonings is "in accordance with the statutes and ordinances," mimicking the language of old Han imperial decrees.

32. A bit more personal detail is provided on this point in chapter 7, under "Reception Invocations."

33. The Buddhist and Taoist syncretism results in many Taoist practitioners engaging in the practice of using dharanis and mantras for invocations. It is a form of inner cultivation believed to strengthen the practitioner's power and abilities at craft, and to protect the practitioner in the event he or she is threatened.

34. Yü, Chün-fang, *Kuan-yin: The Chinese Transformation of Avalokiteśvara* (New York: Columbia University Press, 2001), 54–55.

35. *Encyclopedia Britannica,* s.v. "dharani," http://www.britannica.com/topic/dharani-Buddhism-and-Hinduism and Mantra; *Encyclopedia Britannica,* s.v. "mantra," http://www.britannica.com/topic/mantra.

36. Fu sigil crafting hails from Eastern esoteric culture, and so often the invocations used are in languages sacred to the East. However, the practice of craft itself is not culture-specific, or even lineage-specific. It taps into a universal concept of metaphysical energy that any practitioner can work with. Yet craft and energetic workings rely on the strengths of connections. That is why uttering invocations that sound like nonsense to you will not work. You have to craft your own invocations that are deeply meaningful to you. Use sacred languages that are you are connected to. That is how you in turn connect with higher divine power sources. Then use your spoken language to craft the specificities of your intentions.

37. When a wand is used by a practitioner, like the sword, it is made of peach wood. Even more specific, wands should be made of branches harvested from a peach tree personally by the practitioner, and the branch itself should be one that faces east. As the branch is being cut, an invocation or blessing is recited. The peach wood wand should also be harvested in the daytime, before nightfall. Wands tend to be the tool for mediums, a specific type of magical practitioner. Mediums also tend to use automatic writing for crafting Fu sigils in lieu of Fu Wen.

38. Frederick J. Simoons, *Food in China: A Cultural and Historical Inquiry* (Boca Raton, FL: CRC Press, 1990), 218, noting the supernatural significance of peach wood as protection against evil.

39. Ibid.

40. Ibid.

41. Asano, "Fa Qi," 411.

42. A common technique seen in esoteric Taoist texts is teeth clicking, which was believed to be a means of raising energy for "shen," or light, celestial spirits. Texts that document the practice of teeth clicking date back to the Han Dynasty (206 BC–AD 220). Taoist ceremonial

magicians of the time would press the tips of their tongues against the roof of the mouth, and by doing so, create a clicking sound. Here in this particular example, the process involves rinsing the mouth with consecrated water, then clicking the teeth three hundred times. Doing so was believed to cure physical ailments and also to strengthen the resident Three Pure Ones within the body and keep a practitioner's spiritual, vital, and generative energies. Wang, "The Apocryphal *Jia*," 70. See also note 52 in chapter 1.

43. Sufficient personal Qi or Vital Force is required to perform craft. See Lin, "*Thunder Magic*."

44. Zixin Lin, Yu Li, Guo Zhengyi, Shen Zhenyu, Zhang Honglin, and Zhang Tongling, *Qigong: Chinese Medicine or Pseudoscience?* (Amherst, NY: Prometheus, 1998), 13.

45. Ibid.

46. Ibid., 11. Note, however, that the authors of the cited text seem to imply the use of qi gong in witchcraft is "depraved."

47. Robert S. Bobrow, *The Witch in the Waiting Room: A Physician Examines Paranormal Phenomena in Medicine* (Boston: Da Capo Press, 2006), 41.

48. Zhongxian Wu, *Chinese Shamanic Cosmic Orbit Qigong: Esoteric Talismans, Mantras, and Mudras in Healing and Inner Cultivation* (London: Singing Dragon, 2011).

49. Lin, *Qigong*, 21.

50. The following books are informative texts on learning qi gong: Tina Chunna Zhang, *Earth Qi Gong for Women: Awaken Your Inner Healing Power* (Berkeley, CA: Blue Snake Books, 2008); Jun Wang, *Cultivating Qi: An Introduction to Chinese Body-Mind Energetics* (Berkeley, CA: North Atlantic Books, 2011); Elise Dirlam Ching, Kaleo Ching, and Gilles Marin, *Healing Buddha Palms Chi Kung* (Oakland, CA: Chi Nei Tsang Institute, 2011).

51. See chapter 2 and Pas, *Historical Dictionary*, 30.

52. See chapter 2 and Shek, "Daoism and Orthodoxy," 149. The Quan Zhen lineage focuses on inner cultivation, incorporating the practice of qi gong, and sets aside many of the practices more commonly found in esoteric Taoism, such as summoning and invocations, astrology, or spell casting. Lin, *Qigong*, 18.

53. See generally Shek, "Daoism and Orthodoxy," 149.

54. As noted in chapter 3, the esoteric Taoist practices that I refer to—alchemy, Fu talisman crafting, demonology, and so on—are found in the Inner Chapters of the text.

55. See the translation of the quoted section from the *Bao Pu Zi* in Shek, "Daoism and Orthodoxy," 161.

56. The *San Huang Wen*, or *Writ of the Three Sovereigns*, written around AD 437, over a century after Ge Hong's *Bao Pu Zi*, addresses the concept of purification as the inner cultivation needed to achieve immortality. It is instructive on the concept of good deeds as discussed in this section. According to the *Writ of the Three Sovereigns*, acts such as self-defense, or killing to save one's own life, stealing in an attempt to provide for oneself, falsely advertising one's own abilities, no matter the intent, or indulging in materialism will bar a practitioner from achieving immortality. See Steavu-Balint, "Three Sovereigns Tradition," 102–3.

57. Steed, "To Extend Love," 32, citing James R. Ware, *Alchemy, Medicine and Religion in the China of AD 320: The Nei Pien of Ko Hung* (Mineola, NY: Dover, 1981), 43.

58. 中國哲學書電子化計劃 [The Chinese Texts Project], 抱朴子 [*Bao Pu Zi, Book of the Master of Simplicity*], chap. 2, 論仙, in 內篇 [Inner Chapters], n.d., http://ctext.org/baopuzi/lunxian/zh.

59. This translation and interpretation is a synthesis of my father's viewpoint and mine. He and I had disagreed on exactly how to interpret it. Because he is a scholar and possesses one of the most intelligent minds I have ever come across in my life, his interpretation should be given more weight. He does not read an implication of craft when reading the word 法 (Fǎ), whereas I did, in 魔法 (Mó Fǎ), or witchcraft, and 法術 (Fǎ Shù), spell-crafting. He also interpreted wu wei to include purposelessness, whereas I did not. My compromise was to use the term *drifting* instead of *purposelessness*. "Drifting" suggests not taking an action against the current or tides.

60. See generally Wu, *Chinese Shamanic Cosmic Orbit Qigong*.

61. Taoists hold that, through cultivation, a practitioner can achieve immortality, or "become gods and return to heaven, escaping the cycle of death and rebirth." DeBernardi, *Way That Lives*, 84.

62. The character 方 can mean "method," "direction," "prescription," or "recipe," and is also the radical for "square." 書 means "book."

63. Robert Ford Campany, *Making Transcendents: Ascetics and Social Memory in Early Medieval China* (Honolulu: University of Hawaii Press, 2009), 33–34, 89, 248, 295, referring to Fang Shi as "masters of esoterica."

64. Fabrizio Pregadio, *Great Clarity: Daoism and Alchemy in Early Medieval China* (Stanford, CA: Stanford University Press, 2005), 29, translating fang shi as "master of methods." The term has also been translated as "Master of Esoterica" by Arthur, "Eating Your Way to Immortality," 33.

65. Pregadio, *Great Clarity*, 29.

66. See, for example, *The Gardnerian Book of Shadows,* compiled by Aidan A. Kelly, 1949–1961, http://www.sacred-texts.com/pag/gbos. A grimoire is a book containing the descriptions of magical symbols, their uses, and the methodologies of traditional European ritual magic. Internet Sacred Text Archive, s.v. "grimoires," http://www.sacred-texts.com/grim.

67. Steed, "To Extend Love," 23, commenting on Ge Hong's biography; even he did not gain full access to his master's Book of Methods.

68. Lucas Huang and Kenny Wang, "Old Maoshan Grimoire," *Malaysia: Taoist Texts,* 2011, http://taoist-texts.blogspot.com/2011/06/old-maoshan-grimoire.html.

69. See generally Pregadio, *Encyclopedia of Taoism,* 444.

70. Robert F. Campany, *To Live as Long as Heaven and Earth: A Translation and Study of Ge Hong's Traditions of Divine Transcendents* (Berkeley, CA: University of California Press, 2002), 401–5.

71. 正統道藏電子文字資料庫 [Electronic Database of Traditional Taoist Texts], 靈寶無量度人上經大法卷之三十六 [*The Ling Bao Scripture of Spells for Infinite Human Transformation,* vol. 36], n.d., CH010801-36, http://www.ctcwri.idv.tw/.

72. Regarding the translation of the title of the text, I've opted for *Ling Bao Scripture of Spells*

*for Infinite Human Transformation,* translating 法 to "spells." That translation, or interpretation, is debatable. Generally, the word 法 means "method" or "approach." It can also mean "law." In my interpretation, the 法 (fǎ) reference in this context is to 法術 (fǎ shù), or "spell-crafting." Thus, given that context, I translated 法 in the title to "spells." Note also that "magic" is often translated to 魔術 (mó shù). In colloquial usage, 魔術 bears negative connotations, suggestive of malevolent magic or dark arts. 魔術 is typically the term for magic, spells, or spell-crafting. In contrast, 法術 has more positive connotations, and is also not typically translated to mean "magic" or "spells" per se, since magic and spells bear negative connotations. Nonetheless, here I have translated 法術 to "spells," bearing the positive connotation. Initially I had wanted to translate 度人 (dùo rén) to "healing" in the title, but my father insisted on "human transformation," so that is what I went with. Finally, there may be contention over 無量 (wú liàng), which means "no limit on the amount," and in terms of adjectives, means "great," "ultimate," "immeasurable," or "infinite." I opted for "infinite."

## 7. CONSECRATION TECHNIQUES

1. See chapter 6 for an explanation of divination moon blocks, or Jiao Bei, and also divinatory substitutes if the practitioner does not have moon blocks.

2. I like using alabaster dishware in ritual work, especially for holding water to be consecrated, or for holding any item that is to be consecrated, because I believe the metaphysical properties of alabaster help to draw out the impurities. Chinese amulets are often carved out of alabaster with the belief that when it is worn against the body, it will draw out impurities from the body. There is certainly no requirement that a practitioner must use alabaster for anything at all. This is merely a personal preference, and a practitioner will, through experience, discover what his or her own personal preferences are.

3. If all this is new to you and you have neither consecrated water nor a consecrated ceremonial bell, it could be a chicken-or-egg situation. Just apply reasonable judgment.

4. A general note of caution: observe all proper fire safety protocols. If there is alcohol in the consecrated water because that is part of your practice, and you have rubbed that water into an object, be exceedingly careful when you pass the object over a flame. In general, exercise caution, prudence, and sound judgment.

5. Frater W.I.T., *Advanced Enochian Magick,* 17, noting that angels are projections of superconsciousness and demons are projections of the subconscious, both pieces of the personal psyche.

6. The traditional Kai Guang ritual is for consecrating relics that represent deities, so that the deity energy will enter the relic and be present during the practitioner's rituals. However, a technique similar to Kai Guang can be used to summon the dead. Follow the given instructions for Kai Guang, using a photograph of the deceased or a personal effect belonging to the deceased that was of intense sentimental value to him or her. I said earlier that in traditional Kai Guang, timing is a nonissue, but in this kind of spirit summoning, seek out a time during a waning crescent moon (note the section "Significance of Moon Phases" in chapter 8). The fifteenth day of the seventh lunar month is also considered a day when the veil between

the living and the dead is thinnest, facilitating stronger communications between the two worlds. The seventh lunar month is considered the ghost month (鬼月, GuXYuè), when those in the underworld can visit the living. In the Western calendar, the seventh lunar month often coincides with either late July, August, or early September, varying year to year. Conversion applications are easily accessible to help a practitioner convert between Chinese lunar months and the Western calendar for date and time selection. Start as usual by opening the ritual, then proceed with the consecrated brush or writing instrument. Use red ink or cinnabar powder. If using a personal effect rather than a photograph or paper likeness, wield the calligraphy brush figuratively and dot the five relative direction points around the object. In summoning the dead, a Kai Guang mirror is not used. Instead, a summoning invocation is recited as joss paper is burned as offerings. The wording of the invocation calls upon the deceased person by name. Once the presence is felt, a mode of communication is used, such as Jiao Bei blocks. In the West, it could be a spirit board. To close, according to the Eastern tradition, the practitioner bows in respect, thanks the spirit, and bids the spirit away with a sendoff invocation. Consecrated water is used to figuratively cleanse the personal item used during the summoning. If using a photograph, presumably a copy of an original and thus not one that holds direct sentimental value, it would then be folded and burned. Blessings, mantras, dharanis, or invocations for karmic merit or Transference of Merits to Departed Ones (See "Invocation References" in chapter 8) is recited during the burning. Mix the ashes with the ash from a purifying or protective incense, such as sandalwood, and consecrated sea salt. The ash mixture is then either spread over the deceased's grave site, if practicable, or buried in a private, quiet, remote area.

7. Of course, what I mean is a "requisite" according to me. I would not be surprised if you could find Taoist practitioners who disagree, and I always encourage individuals to exercise their own discretion and think critically about everything they read. For me, at least, I contend that the Kai Guang ritual is a requirement.

8. See the entry for 帝 (Dì) under "Pantheon of Deities" in appendix B.

9. Note also that in Chinese calligraphy, there is a set order of strokes for writing any character, and thus writing the characters 日, 月, and 開光 each have their own order, though that may be getting too technical for the purposes of craft.

10. I mention Buddhism here because in people's actual practice, Buddhism and Taoism are blended together.

# 8. CHARGING FU SIGILS

1. Magical secrets are transmitted from master teacher to disciple and are highly guarded with secrecy. Oaths are sworn to maintain vows of confidentiality. Saso, "Taiwan," 598.

2. In medieval China, all significant events in life had to be timed according to the auspiciousness of dates. The solar term and sexagenary calendar, with the heavenly stem and earthly branch correspondences, had to be consulted for the arrangement of marriages, wedding dates, funerals, and business—hunters would even select specific dates for their hunts. Beasts could only be killed intentionally on certain dates: the 戌 (xū) of the first lunar month, 辰

(chén) of the second lunar month, 亥 (hài) of the third, 巳 (sì) of the fourth, 子 (zǐ) of the fifth, 午 (wǔ) of the sixth, 丑 (chǒu) of the seventh, 未 (wèi) of the eighth, 寅 (yín) of the ninth, 申 (shēn) of the tenth, 卯 (mǎo) of the eleventh, and 酉 (yǒu) of the twelfth. Beijing Foreign Language Press, *Chinese Auspicious Culture* (Singapore: Asiapac Books, 2012), 199. 戌 (xū), 辰 (chén), 亥 (hài), and so on refer to earthly branches that correspond with certain days during each lunar month.

3. Beijing Foreign Language Press, *Chinese Auspicious Culture*, 2.

4. Yongxiang Lu, *A History of Chinese Science and Technology*, vol. 1 (New York: Springer, 2014), 87–89.

5. Hong Kong Observatory, "The 24 Solar Terms," 2012, http://www.hko.gov.hk/gts /time/24solarterms.htm.

6. Paula R. Hartz, *Daoism* (New York: Chelsea House, 2009), 95.

7. Ibid.

8. *New Edition of the Yin and Yang Si Ji Yuan Book of Methods*, 民國三年夏上海. 鏡童圖書局 印行 [Shanghai: Jìng Tóng Tú Shū Jú Yìn Xíng], 1914.

9. Rat, Dragon, and Monkey months are optimal months for craft intended to advance intellectual, scholarly, artistic, or cultural endeavors. Ox, Snake, and Rooster months are industrious and are optimal for employment and career matters and endeavors relating to science, technology, or math. These are good months to raise abilities at detail-oriented work. Tiger, Horse, and Dog months are optimal for craft intended to bring love, romance, or domestic harmony. Humanitarian endeavors are also best during these months. The Rabbit, Goat, and Pig months, like the Rat, Dragon, and Monkey months, are great for arts and culture, though the Rabbit, Goat, and Pig months are more about the apprentice working hard, seeking a breakthrough or golden opportunities. Rat, Dragon, and Monkey months are more about one who is already established and seeking advancement from an already established position. Timing in Chinese astrology is beyond the scope of this book, and this represents broad generalities only.

10. Brian Gregory Baumann, *Divine Knowledge: Buddhist Mathematics According to the Anonymous Manual of Mongolian Astrology and Divination* (Leiden, Netherlands: Brill, 2008), 67.

11. Theodora Lau and Laura Lau, *The Handbook of Chinese Horoscopes*, 7th ed. (New York: Harper-Collins, 2007), xxv.

12. Neil F. Comins and William J. Kaufmann, *Discovering the Universe* (London: Macmillan, 2011), 191.

13. Ibid.

14. Bernard Foing, "If We Had No Moon," *Astrobio*, October 29, 2007, http://www.astrobio .net/topic/exploration/moon-to-mars/if-we-had-no-moon, noting that the eyesight of mammals is sensitive to moonlight; also, the night vision of many species has evolved to work with lunar illumination.

15. Comins and Kaufmann, *Discovering the Universe*, 191.

16. Sandy Fritz, *Mosby's Essential Sciences for Therapeutic Massage: Anatomy, Physiology, Biomechanics, and Pathology* (Atlanta: Elsevier Health Sciences, 2013), 179, noting that women's

menstrual cycles were often in sync with the phases of the moon, with menstruation taking place around the full moon. See also Molly Hall, *Knack Astrology: A Complete Illustrated Guide to the Zodiac* (Blue Ridge Summit, PA: Rowman & Littlefield, 2010), 50.

17. Hall, *Knack Astrology,* 50.

18. Steven Little and Shawn Eichman, *Taoism and the Arts of China* (Oakland, CA: University of California Press, 2000), 193–99.

19. Gary Marvin Davison and Barbara E. Reed, *Culture and Customs of Taiwan* (Westport, CT: Greenwood, 1998), 160.

20. If I give any specific instructions here on the order of directions, I will get into trouble, because truly, it varies so much from tradition to tradition.

21. The Chinese religious concept of custodian spirits (護法神, Hù Fǎ Shén) are in effect guardian spirits who protect those who yield their faiths to these spirits. These spirits are likened to celestial security guards or bodyguards who protect certain locations or certain individuals, or even accompany other celestial beings as their protectors. It is believed that a guardian spirit looks after each and every one of us, but to invoke your guardian spirit to act proactively on your behalf, you must have faith in that guardian spirit and call upon the spirit directly. The idea of custodian spirits is found across Buddhism, Taoism, and regional Chinese folk religions. I am taking the liberty of syncretizing guardian angels from Western cosmology with these custodian spirits of Eastern cosmology.

22. During the Han Dynasty, Chinese shamans used a mystical pacing method intended to "fly to the stars" through the pacing of constellation patterns. Pacing the Big Dipper is a ritual descending from that ancient shamanic tradition, specifically, a pacing method called "The Pace of Yu." Wong, *Taoism,* 17. The Pace of Yu is named after Yu the Great (大禹) (2200–2100 BC). D. E. Mungello, *The Great Encounter of China and the West, 1500–1800,* 4th ed. (Summit, PA: Rowman & Littlefield, 2012).

23. According to Taoist creation myth, Tai Yi (太一), whose name simply means "Most Venerable One," created Water (yin). With Water, Tai Yi created Heaven (yang). With Heaven, Tai Yi created Earth (yin). Heaven and Earth, together, expanded into all that is above, and all that is below, creating primordial yin and primordial yang, which in turn created the four seasons and four directions. Thus, to know Tai Yi, the Most Venerable One, is to know Water. We were all created from Water. To know where the Most Venerable One moves, know the movements of the four seasons and four directions. The Tai Yi creation myth originates from a circa 300 BC Zhou Dynasty text, 太一生水 (Tài Yī Shēng Shuǐ), *The Most Venerable One Gives Birth to Water.*

24. See note 41 in chapter 1.

25. Wendy Doniger, *Encyclopaedia Britannica,* s.v. "Ganesha: Hindu Deity," http://www.britannica.com/topic/Ganesha.

26. Jaibheem.com, "Maha Jaya Mangala Gatha: Recital for Blessings and Protection," http://www.jaibheem.com/bv-page-20.htm.

27. Miranda Eberle Shaw, *Buddhist Goddesses of India* (Princeton, NJ: Princeton University Press, 2006), 277. The "Invincible Incantation" or "Incantation of the Unconquerable Goddess" *(aparajita dharani)* is used to cultivate inner strength to such a degree that one who

invokes Sitatapatra through repeated recitations "cannot be defeated by anyone." Sitatapatra is the "Queen of Magical Spells." Shaw, *Buddhist Goddesses*, 277. According to religious mythology, the Shakyamuni Buddha manifested Sitatapatra from the crown of his head and appointed her a protector goddess "to cut asunder completely all malignant demons, to cut asunder all the spells of others ... to turn aside all enemies and dangers and hatred." When activated to protect the practitioner, she will appear to the enemy as a "fierce, terrifying goddess, garlanded by flames, a pulverizer of enemies and demons, who manifests in the form of a graceful, beauteous maiden." Shaw, *Buddhist Goddesses*, 277.

28. Yü, *Kuan-yin*, 126.

29. Ibid., 126–27.

30. Read the full text of the Heart Sutra translated into English by Thich Nhat Hanh, "New Heart Sutra Translation by Thich Nhat Hanh," Plum Village, 2014, http://plumvillage.org /news/thich-nhat-hanh-new-heart-sutra-translation.

31. While the beneficiary's vow is not necessary, there are consequences for the audacity of seizing energy from one place and transplanting it to someplace else. Think of every energetic working that you do as a bargained-for exchange. Do not always ask for gifts. What you take, you must return in kind. That is how you control the transfer of energy. Otherwise, the void you caused will try to restore itself, and will often do so at your karmic expense, in ways beyond your control that will make you feel helpless. Be proactive and protective with your energetic workings.

32. A. J. Drew, *A Wiccan Bible: Exploring the Mysteries of the Craft from Birth to Summerland* (Pompton Plains, NJ: New Page, 2003), 53–54, reprinting one version of the Wiccan Rede, where the Rule of Three appears. In line 23 of the twenty-six-line poem that is the Wiccan Rede, "Less in thy own defense it be, always mind the Rule of Three." Note also the last line, line 26: "These eight words the Wiccan Rede fulfill: An ye harm none, do as ye will." Drew, *Wiccan Bible*, 54.

33. Gary Cantrell, *Wiccan Beliefs & Practices: With Rituals for Solitaries & Covens* (St. Paul, MN: Llewellyn Publications, 2001), 45, interpreting the Rule of Three to mean that the energy sent out by a spell, good or bad, will be returned threefold, or three times stronger.

34. Drew, *Wiccan Bible*, 53–64, dispelling the more commonly held notion that the Rule of Three suggests what is put out will return threefold.

## 9. SEALING THE FU SIGIL

1. DeBernardi, *Way That Lives*, 112.

2. "So mote it be" is a phrase from the Freemasonry tradition. It is spoken at the commencement and conclusion of every Masonic lodge meeting. The phrase comes from the Anglo-Saxon word *motan* (meaning "to be allowed" or "so may it be") used in prayer and in deference to God, "the will of God be done." The phrase was also found in the works of poet Geoffrey Chaucer. John K. Young and Barb Karg, *The Everything Freemasons Book: Unlock the Secrets of This Ancient and Mysterious Society* (Avon, MA: Adams Media, 2006), 179. "So mote it be" are also the final words of the Regius poem, also known as the Halliwell Manu-

script, a cornerstone text in Freemasonry. See "The Regius Poem: The Halliwell Manuscript," Pietre-Stones Review of Freemasonry, http://www.freemasons-freemasonry.com/regius.html: "Amen! Amen! So mote it be! So say we all for charity."

3. Again, it is imprudent to make generalizations about what Taoist practitioners do. Some may recite the closing invocation, for example "ji ji ru lu ling," at the close of an incantation, but well before the conclusion of a ritual. Alternately, a practitioner might wait until the very end, or might recite "ji ji ru lu ling" a few times throughout a charging ritual. Consider the contexts in which "amen" or "so mote it be" might be used, and in those same contexts, "ji ji ru lu ling" works as well.

4. American Bar Association, s.v. "It is so ordered," http://www.americanbar.org/groups /public_education/publications/insights/teaching_legal_docs/reading_a_supremecourt-brief/it_is_so_ordered.html.

5. DeBernardi, *Way That Lives*, 113.

## 10. ACTIVATION TECHNIQUES

1. Bernard Spilka and Kevin L. Ladd, *The Psychology of Prayer: A Scientific Approach* (New York: Guilford Press, 2012), vii, noting that psychologists have written on and researched prayer for well over a century, with systematic objective research documented from the 1980s onward. Spilka and Ladd review the scientific and psychological research on the power and efficacy of prayer. Spilka and Ladd, *Psychology of Prayer*, 1–2.

2. Clay Routledge, "5 Scientifically-Supported Benefits of Prayer," *Psychology Today*, June 23, 2014, https://www.psychologytoday.com/blog/more-mortal/201406/5-scientifically-supported -benefits-prayer.

3. Ibid.

4. Michael J. Formica, "The Science, Psychology, and Metaphysics of Prayer," *Psychology Today*, July 28, 2010, https://www.psychologytoday.com/blog/enlightened-living/201007/the -science-psychology-and-metaphysics-prayer.

5. DeBernardi, *Way That Lives*, 113.

6. During the Han Dynasty, Zhang Dao Ling of the Tian Shi lineage used talismanic water, which was consecrated water with the ashes of a Fu sigil, to heal the sick, and it is through his talismanic water that he first gained notoriety as a powerful magician or shaman. Wong, *Taoism*, 35.

7. 上清大洞真经 [*Perfect Scripture of Great Profundity*], 12.

8. Traditionally, Fu talismans were burned, the ashes dissolved in water, and the water drunk as a mystical cure for ailments. Hu, *Taoism*, 54.

9. One account cites a Taoist adept who prepares a paper Fu sigil, stands facing east during sunrise, recites an invocation, and then swallows the paper Fu sigil, chasing it down with a glass of water. The intent was to summon six spiritual entities (likened to fairies). Stephen Eskildsen, *Asceticism in Early Taoist Religion* (Albany, NY: State University of New York Press, 1998), 58.

10. See chapter 3 for an introduction to the *Writ of the Three Sovereigns* text.

11. Steavu-Balint, "Three Sovereigns Tradition," 13.

12. Tsubaki Grand Shrine of America, "Omamori," http://www.tsubakishrine.org/omamori/omamori.html.

13. Patrice Fava and Tianyu Chi, *The One-Hundred-Day Exorcistic Talisman* (Ann Arbor, MI: University of Michigan, 2008), film. The film was produced for the "Spirit into Script" exhibition (February 19, 2008), sponsored by the Institute for the Humanities at the University of Michigan.

14. Christine Mollier, "Beidi," in Pregadio, *Encyclopedia of Taoism*, 222–23. Note that Mollier distinguishes Bei Di from Xuan Wu, the Enigmatic Warrior God, and contends that the two deities are not related. However, in other sources, Bei Di and Xuan Wu are conflated into the same deity or deity representation. In the Yuan Dynasty, the deity Xuan Wu was characterized with traits associated with Bei Di, the God of the North. Pierre-Henry De Bruyn, "Daoism in the Ming (1369–1644)," in *Daoism Handbook (Handbook of Oriental Studies/Handbuch der Orientalisk—Part 4: China, 14)*, ed. Livia Kohn (Leiden, Netherlands: Brill, 2000), 598–99.

15. Fava and Chi, *One-Hundred-Day Exorcistic Talisman*.

## 11. PUTTING IT ALL TOGETHER

1. The Fu sigil pictured in figure 2.16 is from an undated, uncredited Book of Methods with unknown origins, titled 張天師符 [*Talismans of the Celestial Master Zhang*], author unknown, found by the author in approximately 2006 at Tainan, Taiwan, among the belongings of her late grandmother.

2. I am not original enough to have conceived this brilliant idea for divining with the tarot. Carrie Paris, creator of divination tools and oracle decks, presented a method of using a tarot deck for psychometry, where a photograph could be placed into a shuffled deck and used to divine the photograph's origins. Carrie Paris, "Tarot and Psychometry," presentation San Francisco Bay Area Tarot Symposium, San Jose, CA, August 15, 2015. See also Carrie Paris, http://carrieparis.com. Charlie Harrington, tarot reader and host of *Tarot Visions* and *The Amethyst Oracle* podcasts, is the person who brought up the idea of integrating tarot divination with Fu sigil crafting. Without Paris and Harrington, I would not have thought of such a clever divination method.

3. Christine Payne-Towler and Michael Dowers, *Tarot of the Holy Light: A Continental Esoteric Tarot* (San Bernardino, CA: Noreah/Brownfield Press, 2015), 141–42.

4. Ibid., 144.

5. While some practitioners avoid using future tenses in crafting affirmations, I don't mind it as much, and find that use of "shall" (compared to "will") is quite effective in manifesting results.

## 12. A NOTE ON CULTURAL APPROPRIATION

1. Cultural appropriation is often defined as "the taking—from a culture that is not one's own—of intellectual property, cultural expressions or artifacts, history, and ways of knowledge and profiting at the expense of the people of that culture." Christian Huck and Stefan

Bauernschmidt, "Trans-Cultural Appropriation," in *Travelling Goods, Travelling Moods: Varieties of Cultural Appropriation (1850–1950)* (Frankfurt: Campus Verlag, 2013), 232. See generally Susan Scafidi, *Who Owns Culture?: Appropriation and Authenticity in American Law* (New Brunswick, NJ: Rutgers University Press, 2005).

2. Charles M. Townsend, "Swastika," in *Encyclopedia of Asian American Folklore and Folklife,* ed. Jonathan H. X. Lee and Kathleen M. Nadeau (Goleta, CA: ABC-CLIO, 2010), 86.

3. Ibid., 87.

4. Ibid.

5. If we are to believe all things have energy, that our conduct and actions create, destroy, or modify energy, then cultural appropriation is a powerful and very harmful form of magic, an energetic working by one who is already more powerful taking even more power away from one with less power.

6. Eno, "Shang State Religion," 67–68.

7. During the British occupation of China in the 1800s, the British would post "No dogs or Chinese allowed" signs in their areas of residence and their favorite parks, such as the beautiful Huangpu Park in Shanghai. John M. Hobson, "Racism and Anglo-Saxon Imperialism," in *Global Standards of Market Civilization,* eds. Brett Bowden and Leonard Seabrooke (New York: Routledge, 2006), 68. The British also entitled themselves to live as independent states within a state, immune to Chinese laws and only subject to their own British laws. They abolished by force the traditional Chinese custom of having foreigners kowtow to the Chinese dignitaries; that way the British and other Westerners wouldn't have to show respect to the Chinese. Hobson, "Racism," 68. These are only a few points from China's history of Western imperialism.

8. "'Give us back our treasure': Chinese Demand Cameron Returns Priceless Artifacts Looted during 19th-Century Boxer Rebellion," *Daily Mail,* December 4, 2013, http://www.dailymail.co.uk/news/article-2518111/China-demand-David-Cameron-return-Boxer-Rebellion-artefacts.html.

9. See generally John McLeod, *Beginning Postcolonialism* (Manchester, UK: Manchester University Press, 2010); and Robert J. C. Young, *Postcolonialism: A Very Short Introduction* (Oxford, UK: Oxford University Press, 2003).

10. "What is Globalization?" in Globalization 101, SUNY Levin Institute, New York, http://www.globalization101.org/what-is-globalization.

11. "Remarkable in the study of magical practices, there is no disguising the fact that many of the operations found in European 'Black Books,' and known to be undertaken by Western sorcerers, are paralleled in Chinese [Taoist] magic." Shah, *Oriental Magic,* 150.

12. See, for example, note 8 in chapter 1 and note 65 in chapter 2.

## 13. FINAL THOUGHTS

1. We are all connected to source energy, and therefore anyone can be a practitioner of craft. Each one of us is fully equipped to connect our personal Qi with that collective cosmic Qi. However, some among us might seem innately more talented for doing so while others seem to be quite terrible at it. Like any talent, craft can be a gift. Some are predisposed to musical

ability and can pick up a violin with no training and then play beautifully, to the great frustration of those who have been practicing for decades yet who cannot seem to command that same musicality. Nonetheless, decades of earnest violin practice will absolutely, assuredly enable you to become a rather decent violinist. Likewise, the ability to work with metaphysical energy is a talent, a gift, and without a doubt, incontestably also a skill. If you don't have the gift, put in more effort than everybody else and acquire it as a skill.

2. Note, however, that in the culture of Taoist magic, there is such a practice that would be referred to as black magic: 降头 (jiàng tóu), the dark art of using Fu sigils to summon demons or malevolent spirits. As part of the rituals for charging such Fu sigils, practitioners use menstrual blood, the burned skin of corpses, or poisons collected from venomous snakes and insects. See generally Jean Elizabeth DeBernardi, "Historical Allusion and the Defense of Identity," in *Asian Visions of Authority: Religion and the Modern States of East and Southeast Asia,* ed. Charles F. Keyes, Laurel Kendall, and Helen Hardacre (Honolulu: University of Hawaii Press, 1994), 132–33, noting the black magic culture of Southeast Asia known as *gong tau* (Hokkien for 降头, jiàng tóu). Gu Dao (蠱道), another form of malevolent use of magic, traps a number of poisonous insects into a vessel, such as centipedes or scorpions, until they fight each other to the death. In the end, only one insect is left, believed to be the insect that contains the potency of all the poison from the other insects it devoured. Ritual magic, typically combined with Fu sigil crafting, charges or empowers the poison of that one insect. An example would be crafting a Fu sigil, burning it, and mixing the ashes with the insect poison. That poison is then administered to the victim. See H. Y. Feng and J. K. Shryock, "The Black Magic in China Known as Ku," *Journal of the American Oriental Society* 55:1 (2011), 1. The cure or antidote to such poisonous or black magic is to invoke a higher deity or an immortal to subdue the demon. DeBernardi, "Historical Allusion," 132. In my practice, fearlessness, kindness, and recitations from holy books will defeat such malevolent craft; that and an artfully constructed Fu sigil.

3. Generalizations of "what Taoist practitioners believe" cannot be made here. Unsurprisingly, there are differences in opinion. For example: There is a "belief pervading the minds of many Singapore Chinese that it is possible for a person to use black magic to cast a spell on a victim.... black magic is known by the Singapore Chinese as *kongtow*." Wen-Shing Tseng and David Y. H. Wu, *Chinese Culture and Mental Health* (Waltham, MA: Academic Press, 1985), 238. It is believed that kongtow spells are cast onto objects that the victim is anticipated to touch, and when he or she does, the black magic takes effect; or food or drink contains kongtow that the victim unwittingly ingests; or kongtow is performed on the victim's photograph. Tseng and Wu, *Chinese Culture,* 238.

4. Human intentions are an entirely different matter. Human intentions certainly can be characterized as either good or evil. The intent behind craft can be characterized as good or evil, benevolent or malevolent, although that characterization does not extend to the energy involved. The energy involved is still either yin or yang, creative or destructive.

5. You do not create or destroy metaphysical energy during the Fu sigil crafting process, or any energetic working, for that matter. You simply draw upon it from one source and redirect

it elsewhere, the energy modified and empowered by your intentions. Bear this metaphysical law in mind during your craft and you will surely tailor more effective workings.

6. See the section titled "A Preliminary Note of Caution" in chapter 1.

7. Michio Kaku, *Einstein's Cosmos: How Albert Einstein's Vision Transformed Our Understanding of Space and Time* (New York: W. W. Norton, 2005), 66.

8. Ibid., 67.

9. Ibid., 67.

10. See point 4 in chapter 3, as interpreted from the *Classics of the Esoteric Talisman,* circa AD 600.

11. See point 6 in chapter 3, as interpreted from the *Classics of the Esoteric Talisman.*

12. Clifford Pickover, *Archimedes to Hawking: Laws of Science and the Great Minds behind Them* (New York: Oxford University Press, 2008), 417.

13. See point 10 in chapter 3, as interpreted from the *Classics of the Esoteric Talisman.*

14. A reference to the Tao Te Ching: "The Tao that can be spoken is not the eternal Tao. / The name that can be named is not the eternal name. / The nameless is the origin of Heaven and Earth." Lin, *Tao Te Ching,* chap. 1.

15. Tao Te Ching, chap. 3.

16. Ibid., chap. 7.

17. Ibid., chap. 8.

18. "The Tao is empty. When in use, it is not filled up." Lin, *Tao Te Ching,* chap. 4.

## APPENDIX A

1. The Art Institute of Chicago, "Ordination Scroll of Empress Zhang," 2000, http://www.artic.edu/taoism/church/e66.php.

2. Lily Xiao Hong Lee and Sue Wiles, *Biographical Dictionary of Chinese Women, Volume II: Tang through Ming, 618–1644* (Hoboken, NJ: Taylor and Francis, 2015), 582.

## APPENDIX B

1. Oracle bone script, greater seal script, and lesser seal script from Richard Sears [Uncle Hanzi (汉字叔叔)], "Chinese Etymology," 2013, http://www.chineseetymology.org. Reprinted with permission.

2. See also chapter 12 on the cultural appropriation of the name and identity of, Shang Di.

3. Eno, "Shang State Religion," 70–71.

4. Boltz, "Not by the Seal," 273.

5. For example, The Five Thunder Method (Wu Lei Fa). Many Taoist magical practitioners in Taiwan claim mastery and knowledge of this method of exorcism. The practice involves possession of the practitioner's body by a thunder spirit, and through the practitioner's body, the thunder spirit's performs exorcisms or other forms of magical cures. Saso, "Taiwan," 598.

6. See note 14 in chapter 10. See also DivineHere.com, s.v. "北帝" [Bei Di], http://www.divine-here.com/gods/0301005.html, referring to 北帝 (Bei Di) and Xuan Wu, specifically 玄天上帝

(Xuán Tiān Shàng Dì), as the same deity.

7. Fava and Chi, *One-Hundred-Day Exorcistic Talisman.*

8. Mollier, "Beidi," 223.

9. Yü, *Kuan-yin,* 2.

10. Mollier, *Buddhism and Taoism,* 174–93.

11. Ibid., 186.

12. Gardner, "Laughing Buddha," 93.

13. Ibid., 94.

14. Jiang Qing Pu, "八仙考" [Ba Xian Kao, Studies of the Eight Immortals], *Tsing Hua Journal of Chinese Studies* 11:1 (1936).

15. New World Encyclopedia, s.v. "Zhang Guo Lao," 2008, http://www.newworldencyclopedia .org/entry/Zhang_Guo_Lao.

16. New World Encyclopedia, s.v. "Zhongli Quan," 2008, http://www.newworldencyclopedia .org/entry/Zhongli_Quan.

17. New World Encyclopedia, s.v. "Lu Dong Bin," 2008, http://www.newworldencyclopedia .org/entry/L%C3%BC_Dongbin.

18. New World Encyclopedia, s.v. "He Xiangu," 2008, http://www.newworldencyclopedia.org /entry/He_Xiangu.

19. New World Encyclopedia, s.v. "Li Tieguai," 2008, http://www.newworldencyclopedia.org /entry/Li_Tieguai.

20. New World Encyclopedia, s.v. "Cao Guojiu," 2008, http://www.newworldencyclopedia .org/entry/Cao_Guojiu.

21. New World Encyclopedia, s.v. "Han Xiang Zi," 2008, http://www.newworldencyclopedia .org/entry/Han_Xiang_Zi.

22. New World Encyclopedia, s.v. "Lan Caihe," 2008, http://www.newworldencyclopedia.org /entry/Lan_Caihe.

23. In Taoist tradition and lore, male rulers venerated and worshipped as their master a female deity, as the Yellow Emperor venerated and worshipped the Lady of the Ninth Heaven as his master. Xiaogan Liu, "A Taoist Perspective: Appreciating and Applying the Principle of Femininity," in *What Men Owe to Women: Men's Voices from World Religions,* eds. John C. Raines and Daniel C. Maguire (Albany, NY: State University of New York Press, 2001), 247–48. In turn, she bestowed him with esoteric secrets and military strategy that enabled him to rule as one of the greatest emperors of Chinese civilization.

24. Ngoc Tho Nguyen, "Goddess Beliefs in the Chinese Ling-Nan Area," Harvard-Yenching Institute Working Paper Series (Ho Chi Minh: Vietnam National University, 2009), 7, http:// www.harvard-yenching.org/working-paper-series.

25. Ibid., 8.

26. Shah, *Oriental Magic,* 156.

27. Ibid., 155.

28. Charles Alfred Speed Williams, *Chinese Symbolism and Art Motifs: An Alphabetical Compendium of Antique Legends and Beliefs, as Reflected in the Manners and Customs of the Chi-*

*nese* (North Clarendon, VT: Tuttle, 1941), 409–10.

29. Ibid., 410.

30. Ibid.

31. Archeologists have "excavated articles bearing the bird-sun totem, a heritage observed in the later Yangshao Culture and Longshan Culture" dating to 5000 BC and "colored potteries depicting a bird totem with the sun in the wing" dating to 4000–3000 BC. Ah Xiang, "Chinese Pre-History," ImperialChina.org, http://www.imperialchina.org/Pre-history.html.

32. Williams, *Chinese Symbolism,* 410.

33. Shah, *Oriental Magic,* 156.

34. Williams, *Chinese Symbolism,* 221.

35. A shaman is someone who is able to travel to other realms, such as the underworld, and facilitate communication between worlds. Shamans are not mediums and their bodies do not become possessed with spirits. Compare to a medium, who is someone whose body can become possessed by spirits, who then performs magic, crafts Fu sigils, or gives prophecies while possessed. A medium does not necessarily travel to other realms, but rather, spirits from other realms travel to earth and enter the medium's body.

36. In the same manner that a craft name in Western traditions might begin with the title "Lord" or "Lady," or how a practitioner might take on the title "psychic," "intuitive," or "empath," craft names in Chinese can appear with the title 巫師 (Wū Shī). For example, if a practitioner has selected the craft name White Swallow (白燕, Bái Yàn) and identifies as a witch, wizard, sorcerer, sorceress, or shaman, the characters 巫師 might appear after the chosen name: 白燕巫師 (translated directly, "White Swallow Shaman"). Culturally, it is permissible and not presumptuous to use the Wu Shi title in a craft name, assuming, that is, that you do sincerely identify as a witch, wizard, sorcerer, sorceress, or shaman.

37. See the section on "The Book of Methods" in chapter 6 for more on the Fang Shi.

38. A medium is someone whose body can become possessed by spirits, who then performs magic, crafts Fu sigils, or gives prophecies while possessed. Compare to a shaman, someone who does not become possessed, but rather, is able to travel to other realms, such as the underworld, and facilitate communication between worlds.

39. See also the section "Yin and Yang is Not Black and White" in chapter 13.

40. The phrase is found in a tenth-century Buddhist manual on defending against witchcraft. The phrase 蠱毒自除 (Gǔ Dú Zì Chú) is stylized into Fu Wen and has to be rendered into a Fu sigil before sunrise on the fifth day of the fifth lunar month in black ink from an ink stone. The afflicted individual using this Fu sigil to ward off the evil curse must then eat seven to eight apricots and three jujubes. Mollier, *Buddhism and Taoism,* 88.

41. An interesting historic note: in medieval Chinese alchemical texts, the antidote to Gu Dao poison spells was "jade flower." What jade flower is, however, is a point of contention. It was believed to be an ingredient in the elixir for immortality that Taoist alchemists sought. A Taoist text from the Han Dynasty seemed to suggest that "jade flower" was jade powder. However, a meditation technique for cultivating longevity was also referred to as "jade flower." See Timothy Wai-Keung Chan, "'Jade Flower' and the Motif of Mystic Excursion," in *Interpretation*

*and Literature in Early Medieval China,* ed. Alan K. L. Chan (Albany, NY: State University of New York Press, 2010), 175–77.

42. See "Four Compass and Five Relative Directions" in chapter 1.

43. See chapter 3 for more information about Ge Hong, his *Bao Puzi* text, and the "Entrance through the Mountains" talisman.

44. See generally Michael Loewe and Edward L. Shaughness, *The Cambridge History of Ancient China: From the Origins of Civilization to 221 BC* (Cambridge, UK: Cambridge University Press, 1999), indicating animal totemism among the Bronze Age cultures in archaic China.

45. James George Frazer, *Totemism and Exogamy,* vol. II (New York: Cosimo, 2013), 338, noting the history of surnames with animal references and animal totemism in southern China.

46. See generally Anne Birrell, *Chinese Mythology: An Introduction* (Baltimore: JHU Press, 1999), 59, citing implications of animal totemism practice in China.

47. However, many ethnic groups in China do practice animal totemism. For these cultures, the venerated animal totem can never be harmed, and if such an animal is killed, rites are performed to honor the dead animal. See Beijing Foreign Language Press, *Chinese Auspicious Culture,* 199.

48. Lau and Lau, *Handbook of Chinese Horoscopes,* 2–3.

49. Ibid., 28–32.

50. Ibid., 56–58.

51. Ibid., 83–85.

52. Ibid., 110–12.

53. Ibid., 138–42.

54. Ibid., 166–70.

55. Ibid., 194–99.

56. Ibid., 222–25.

57. Ibid., 252–58.

58. Ibid., 284–88.

59. Ibid., 314–19.

60. Republic of China Ministry of Education, Dictionary of Chinese Character Variants, s.v. "疋," entry B03508, 2000, http://dict.variants.moe.edu.tw/yitib/frb/frb03508.htm.

## APPENDIX C

1. For additional literature on Western sigil crafting, see generally Mark B. Jackson, *Sigils, Ciphers and Scripts* (Somerset, UK: Green Magic Publishing, 2013); Frater U. D., *Practical Sigil Magic: Creating Personal Symbols for Success* (Saint Paul, MN: Llewellyn, 2012); and Phillip Cooper, *Basic Sigil Magic* (San Francisco: Weiser, 2001).

2. The approach to Western sigil crafting taught herein is based on Bramshaw, *Craft of the Wise,* 133–35.

3. The term *word method* is borrowed from Frater U. D., *Practical Sigil Magic,* 2.

4. "Occidental magic is known to rest on two main pillars, namely on *will* and on *imagination.* Connected with these are analogous thinking and symbolic images." U. D. Frater, *Practical*

*Sigil Magic,* 9.

5. In Bramshaw's instructions on sigil crafting, only repeating letters are removed, not vowels; Bramshaw, *Craft of the Wise,* 133–34. Other texts show the removal of both repeating letters and vowels; see Nick Margerrison, "A Beginner's Guide to Sigil Craft," *Disinformation,* December 4, 2012, http://disinfo.com/2012/12/a-beginners-guide-to-sigil-craft.

6. The right-hand path is often associated with acting for the greater good, for harnessing the powers of creation—building, expanding, and bringing forth the light. There is a strong belief in a higher authority when a practitioner walks the right-hand path, and in upholding moral obligation. The left-hand path is the individual quest of self-fulfillment and personal honor. It can also be about harnessing the powers of destruction, though that is not necessarily "evil" or negative. Destruction means rebirth and transformation, progress, revolution, change, uprisings. Destruction is also the vanquishing of evil and overthrowing the status quo. The left-hand path is about breaking taboo, personal anarchism, and a focus on self-power. See Wen, *Holistic Tarot,* 69. A leftward spiral invokes the left-hand path, indicating the inner realm of intuition, the unconscious mind, and the astral body, whereas a rightward spiral invokes the right-hand path, indicating the external realm of rational thought, the consciousness, and the physical body. The leftward spiral relates to the moon, invoking yin energy and that which is considered heterodox. The rightward spiral relates to the sun, invoking yang energy, and that which is considered orthodox. A leftward spiral is used for summoning, necromancy, communing with the underworld, or delving deep into the shadow self or unconscious. A rightward spiral is used for communing with higher realms, such as deities, angels, saints, or immortals. It can also be used to invoke faith, work with consciousness, or seek union with the Divine. Wen, *Holistic Tarot,* 276.

7. Bramshaw, *Craft of the Wise,* 133–34, noting that a sigil is charged when it is passed through a flame while the practitioner visualizes the intentions coming true; also notes to place the burning sigil in sand.

8. See the examples given in the "Practitioner's Seal" section in chapter 6. In the hypothetical example, the practitioner's craft name is White Swallow, 白燕, but note that in Chinese, the full craft name might be written out as 白燕巫師. The added 巫師, which means "sorcerer" or "sorceress," signifies that it is a craft name.

# APPENDIX E

1. Michel Strickmann, *Chinese Poetry and Prophecy: The Written Oracle in East Asia,* ed. Bernard Faure (Stanford, CA: Stanford University Press, 2005), 2.

2. S. J. Marshall, *The Mandate of Heaven: Hidden History in the I Ching* (New York: Columbia University Press, 2001), ix, 3.

3. Ibid., xi.

4. Ibid., 3.

# APPENDIX H

1. See point 2 from the *Classics of the Esoteric Talisman,* outlined in chapter 3.

# APPENDIX I

1. Seal scripts have been graciously provided by Richard Sears [Uncle Hanzi (汉字叔叔)], "Chinese Etymology," 2013, http://www.chineseetymology.org. Reprinted with permission.

2. Shah, *Oriental Magic,* 151, noting a charm with one hundred variations of the traditional Chinese character for "felicity"). See also DeBernardi, *Way That Lives,* 61, noting two charms of one hundred variations on the same character, Fu (福) and Shou (壽), from Fu Lu Shou. However, anecdotally and from personal observations, I am more familiar with the ninety-nine variations charm, with the hundredth sector of the quadrant reserved for the practitioner's seal stamp. Also, numerologically, in terms of numbers that are considered auspicious, ninety-nine makes more sense than one hundred. Thus exercise 8 explains the ninety-nine glyphs amulet rather than the one hundred.

3. Ibid.

4. Throughout medieval China, disease and illness was believed to be caused by demon possession, so to cure the physical ailment, a practitioner needed to exorcise or dispel the demon from the body. That work was first done by witch doctors, shamans, or spirit mediums (巫). Eventually the ideogram 巫 evolved into 毉 (note the radical 巫 still at the base of the character) and then to 醫, which is now the word for medicine.

5. Never use a Fu sigil to replace professional medical treatment. The original intent for the Perennial Healer's Fu was an amulet for medical students and young medical doctors to help them with their profession, to amplify the metaphysical energy around them so they could be more effective in both their studies of medicine and their healing work. It then extended to use for healers, witch doctors, and holistic health practitioners as well. (Note how several of the glyph variations contain the character for "shaman" or "witch," 巫, which is part of the etymological origin of the word 醫, as discussed in the previous note.) The energy that this amulet can in principle manifest, however, also makes the Fu suitable for those who are undergoing medical treatment and who could use additional good luck to ensure the success of such treatments.

# APPENDIX K

1. During the Han Dynasty, scholars and metaphysicians observed correlations between shifts in human civilization and the patterns of the sexagenary calendar. By the Tang Dynasty, those observations were organized into the Ba Zi natal divination system, also known as the Four Pillars of Destiny. Lily Chung, *The Truth of Ups and Downs: Cosmic Inequality* (Durham, CT: Eloquent Books, 2009), 8.

2. The legend of the history of the *Chinese Almanac* (通勝, Tōng Shèng), also referred to as the 黃曆 (Huáng Lì), or simply *Almanac,* holds that it was first penned by the imperial court of the Yellow Emperor, between 2698 and 2598 BC. Purportedly, every year thereafter, a new

edition of the Almanac was published, up to the present day. See, for example, 二〇一五(乙未)年通书编委会 [The Editorial Board of the 2015 (Yi Wei) Annual Almanac], 二〇一五(乙未)年通书 平装 [*The 2015 Yi Wei Almanac*], 第1版 [1st Edition] (广西人民出版社 [The Guangxi People's Publishing House], 2014 (in Simplified Chinese). The Almanac is based on the lunisolar calendar and is used in feng shui, Ba Zi or Four Pillars of Destiny natal fortune-telling, and for selecting auspicious dates for weddings, funerals, business grand openings, and all other major social events.

3. The author's recommendation for online Western Gregorian to Chinese lunar calendar conversions is from the Government of the Hong Kong Special Administrative Region, The Hong Kong Observatory, "Gregorian-Lunar Calendar Conversion Table," http://www.hko .gov.hk/gts/time/conversion.htm.

4. The Hong Kong Observatory, "Gregorian-Lunar Calendar Conversion Table of 1978 (Wu-Wu—Year of the Horse)," http://www.hko.gov.hk/gts/time/calendar/pdf/1978e.pdf; "Gregorian-Lunar Calendar Conversion Table of 1981 (Xin-You—Year of the Rooster)," http://www.hko.gov.hk/gts/time/calendar/pdf/1981e.pdf; "Gregorian-Lunar Calendar Conversion Table of 2017 (Ding-You—Year of the Rooster)," http://www.hko.gov.hk/gts/time/calendar /pdf/2017e.pdf.

# BIBLIOGRAPHY

American Bar Association. "It is so ordered." http://www.americanbar.org/groups
/public_education/publications/insights/teaching_legal_docs/reading_a_suprem-
ecourtbrief/it_is_so_ordered.html.

Arthur, Shawn. "Eating Your Way to Immortality: Early Daoist Self Cultivation Diets."
*The Journal of Daoist Studies* 2:33 (2009).

The Art Institute of Chicago. "Ordination Scroll of Empress Zhang." 2000. http://www
.artic.edu/taoism/church/e66.php.

Asia for Educators. "Timeline of Chinese History and Dynasties." Columbia University,
2009. http://afe.easia.columbia.edu/timelines/china_timeline.htm.

Baumann, Brian Gregory. *Divine Knowledge: Buddhist Mathematics According to the
Anonymous Manual of Mongolian Astrology and Divination.* Leiden, Netherlands:
Brill, 2008.

Beijing Foreign Language Press. *Chinese Auspicious Culture.* Translated by Evy Wong,
Loh Li Cheng, Chuah Siew Boon, Wong Su Ee, and Julie Chong. Singapore: Asiapac Books, 2012.

Billington, Ray. *Understanding Eastern Philosophy.* New York: Routledge, 1997.

Birrell, Anne. *Chinese Mythology: An Introduction.* Baltimore: JHU Press, 1999.

Blofeld, John Eaton Calthorpe. *Taoism: The Road to Immortality.* New York: Random
House, 1979.

Bobrow, Robert S. *The Witch in the Waiting Room: A Physician Examines Paranormal
Phenomena in Medicine.* Boston: Da Capo Press, 2006.

Bokenkamp, Stephen R., and Peter Nickerson. *Early Daoist Scriptures* (Daoist Classics,
No. 1). Berkeley, CA: University of California Press, 1999.

Boltz, Judity Magee. "Not by the Seal of Office Alone." In *Religion and Society in T'ang
and Sung China,* edited by Patricia Buckley Ebrey Honolulu: University of Hawaii
Press, 1993.

Botz-Bornstein, Thorsten. *Inception and Philosophy: Ideas to Die For.* Chicago: Open Court, 2013.

Bramshaw, Vikki. *Craft of the Wise: A Practical Guide to Paganism and Witchcraft.* Hampshire, UK: John Hunt, 2009.

Bryant, Clifton D. *Handbook of Death and Dying.* Thousand Oaks, CA: SAGE Publishing, 2003.

Buswell, Robert E., and Donald S. Lopez Jr. *The Princeton Dictionary of Buddhism.* Princeton, NJ: Princeton University Press, 2013.

Campany, Robert Ford. *Making Transcendents: Ascetics and Social Memory in Early Medieval China.* Honolulu: University of Hawaii Press, 2009.

———. *To Live as Long as Heaven and Earth: A Translation and Study of Ge Hong's Traditions of Divine Transcendents.* Berkeley, CA: University of California Press, 2002.

Cantrell, Gary. *Wiccan Beliefs & Practices: With Rituals for Solitaries & Covens.* St. Paul, MN: Llewellyn, 2001.

Chan, Timothy Wai-Keung. "'Jade Flower' and the Motif of Mystic Excursion." In *Interpretation and Literature in Early Medieval China,* edited by Alan K. L. Chan. Albany, NY: State University of New York Press, 2010.

Chen, Frederick Shih-Chung. "Who Are the Eight Kings in the *Samadhi Sutra of Liberation through Purification*? Otherworld Bureaucrats in India and China." Paper presented at the North American Graduate Student Conference in Buddhist Studies, University of California, Berkeley. April 2009. http://www2.ihp.sinica.edu.tw /file/1103rKHQApp.pdf.

Ching, Elise Dirlam, Kaleo Ching, and Gilles Marin. *Healing Buddha Palms Chi Kung.* Oakland, CA: Chi Nei Tsang Institute, 2011.

Chung, Lily. *The Truth of Ups and Downs: Cosmic Inequality.* Durham, CT: Eloquent Books, 2009.

Cleary, Thomas F. *The Taoist Classics.* Boston: Shambhala, 2003.

Comins, Neil F., and William J. Kaufmann. *Discovering the Universe.* London: Macmillan, 2011.

Cooper, Phillip. *Basic Sigil Magic.* San Francisco: Weiser, 2001.

Davis, Edward L. *Society and the Supernatural in Song China.* Honolulu: University of Hawaii Press, 2001.

Davison, Gary Marvin, and Barbara E. Reed. *Culture and Customs of Taiwan.* Westport, CT: Greenwood, 1998.

DeBernardi, Jean Elizabeth. "Historical Allusion and the Defense of Identity." In *Asian Visions of Authority: Religion and the Modern States of East and Southeast Asia,* edited by Charles F. Keyes, Laurel Kendall, and Helen Hardacre. Honolulu: University of Hawaii Press, 1994.

———. *The Way that Lives in the Heart: Chinese Popular Religion and Spirit Mediums in Penang, Malaysia.* Stanford, CA: Stanford University Press, 2006.

De Bruyn, Pierre-Henry. "Daoism in the Ming (1369–1644)." In *Daoism Handbook (Handbook of Oriental Studies / Handbuch der Orientalisk—Part 4: China, 14),* edited by Livia Kohn. Leiden, Netherlands: Brill, 2000.

Diakonoff, Igor M. *The Paths of History.* Cambridge, UK: Cambridge University Press, 1999.

Dodd, Jan, and Mark Lewis. *The Rough Guide to Vietnam.* New York: Penguin, 2009.

Drew, A. J. *A Wiccan Bible: Exploring the Mysteries of the Craft from Birth to Summerland.* Pompton Plains, NJ: New Page, 2003.

Ebrey, Patricia Buckley. *Chinese Civilization: A Sourcebook,* 2nd ed. New York: Simon and Schuster, 2009.

Editorial Committee of Chinese Civilization. *China: Five Thousand Years of History and Civilization.* Hong Kong: City University of Hong Kong Press, 2007.

Eng, Khoo Boo. *A Simple Approach to Taoism.* Singapore: PartridgeSingapore, 2013.

Eno, Robert. "Shang State Religion and the Pantheon of the Oracle Texts." In *Early Chinese Religion: Part One: Shang through Han (1250 BC–AD 220),* edited by Marc Kalinowski and John Lagerwey. Boston: Brill, 2011.

Eskildsen, Stephen. *Asceticism in Early Taoist Religion.* Albany, NY: State University of New York Press, 1998.

Fava, Patrice, and Tianyu Chi. *The One-Hundred-Day Exorcistic Talisman.* Film. Ann Arbor, MI: University of Michigan, 2008.

Feng, H. Y., and J. K. Shryock. "The Black Magic in China Known as Ku." *Journal of the American Oriental Society* 55:1 (2011).

Feng, Youlan, and Derk Bodde. *A History of Chinese Philosophy,* Volume 2. Princeton, NJ: Princeton University Press, 1952.

Foing, Bernard. "If We Had No Moon." *Astrobio.* October 29, 2007. http://www.astrobio.net/topic/exploration/moon-to-mars/if-we-had-no-moon.

Formica, Michael J. "The Science, Psychology, and Metaphysics of Prayer." *Psychology Today.* July 28, 2010. https://www.psychologytoday.com/blog/enlightened-living/201007/the-science-psychology-and-metaphysics-prayer.

Fowler, Jeaneane D. *An Introduction to the Philosophy and Religion of Taoism: Pathways to Immortality.* East Sussex, UK: Sussex Academic Press, 2005.

Frater U. D. *Practical Sigil Magic: Creating Personal Symbols for Success.* Saint Paul, MN: Llewellyn Worldwide, 2012.

Frater W.I.T. *Advanced Enochian Magick: A Manual of Theory, Training, and Practice for the Novice and the Adept.* Denver: Outskirts Press, 2008.

Frazer, James George. *Totemism and Exogamy,* volume II. New York: Cosimo, 2013.

Fritz, Sandy. *Mosby's Essential Sciences for Therapeutic Massage: Anatomy, Physiology, Biomechanics, and Pathology.* Atlanta: Elsevier Health Sciences, 2013.

*Fu Talismans from Zheng Yi Dao.* Undated. From the Shang Qing Temple, Jiangxi, China.

Gardner, Richard A. "The Laughing Buddha." In *Encyclopedia of Humor Studies,* edited by Salvatore Attardo. Thousand Oaks, CA: SAGE Publications, 2014.

Great Dharma Drum. *Supernatural Power and Its Impact on Society (GDD-7, Master Sheng Yen).* Video file. May 7, 2012. https://youtu.be/KKqmPSToWUU.

Guillemin, Victor. *The Story of Quantum Mechanics.* Mineola, NY: Courier, 1968.

Hall, Molly. *Knack Astrology: A Complete Illustrated Guide to the Zodiac.* Blue Ridge Summit, PA: Rowman & Littlefield, 2010.

Hartz, Paula R. *Daoism.* New York: Chelsea House, 2009.

*Highest Purity Jade Girdle and Golden Crown, Golden Script Book of the Great Ultimate.* Pelliot Chinois 2409. In the archives at the Bibliothèque Nationale de France, Paris.

Hobson, John M. "Racism and Anglo-Saxon Imperialism." In *Global Standards of Market Civilization,* edited by Brett Bowden and Leonard Seabrooke. New York: Routledge, 2006.

Hong Kong Observatory. "The 24 Solar Terms." 2012. http://www.hko.gov.hk/gts /time/24solarterms.htm.

Hong, Xiuping. "Lao-Tzu, the Tao of Lao-Tzu, and the Evolution of Taoism." In *Taoism,* edited by Zhongjian Mou, translated by Pan Junliang and Simone Normand. Leiden, Netherlands: Brill, 2012.

Hu, Hsiao-Lan, and William Cully Allen. *Taoism (Religions of the World).* New York: Chelsea House, 2004.

Huang, Lucas, and Kenny Wang. "Old Maoshan Grimoire." *Malaysia: Taoist Texts.* 2011. http://taoist-texts.blogspot.com/2011/06/old-maoshan-grimoire.html.

Huck, Christian, and Stefan Bauernschmidt. *Travelling Goods, Travelling Moods: Varieties of Cultural Appropriation (1850–1950)*. Frankfurt: Campus Verlag, 2013.

Internet Sacred Text Archive. *The Gardnerian Book of Shadows*, compiled by Aidan A. Kelly. http://www.sacred-texts.com/pag/gbos/.

Irvine, Audrey A. *Infinite Possibility: Frameworks for Understanding Extraordinary Human Experience*. Bloomington, IN: AuthorHouse, 2008.

Issitt, Micah L., and Carlyn Main. *Hidden Religion: The Greatest Mysteries and Symbols of the World's Religious Beliefs*. Goleta, CA: ABC-CLIO, 2014.

Jackson, Mark B. *Sigils, Ciphers and Scripts*. Somerset, UK: Green Magic, 2013.

Jaibheem.com. "Maha Jaya Mangala Gatha: Recital for Blessings and Protection." http://www.jaibheem.com/bv-page-20.htm.

Jiang, Jiehong. *Burden or Legacy: From the Chinese Cultural Revolution to Contemporary Art*. Hong Kong: Hong Kong University Press, 2007.

Kaku, Michio. *Einstein's Cosmos: How Albert Einstein's Vision Transformed Our Understanding of Space and Time*. New York: W. W. Norton, 2005.

Kaplan, Abraham. *The Conduct of Inquiry: Methodology for Behavioral Science*. San Francisco: Chandler, 1964.

Katz, Paul R. *Demon Hordes and Burning Boats: The Cult of Marshal Wen in Late Imperial Chekiang*. Albany, NY: State University of New York Press, 1995.

Knapp, Keith. "Ge Hong (Ko Hung, 283–343 CE)." *Internet Encyclopedia of Philosophy: A Peer-Reviewed Academic Resource*. http://www.iep.utm.edu/gehong.

Kwok, Sun. *Stardust: The Cosmic Seeds of Life*. New York: Springer Science & Business Media, 2013.

Lagerwey, John, and Marc Kalinowski. *Early Chinese Religion: Part One: Shang through Han (1250 BC–AD 220)*. Boston: Brill, 2011.

Lau, Theodora, and Laura Lau. *The Handbook of Chinese Horoscopes*. 7th edition. New York: Harper-Collins, 2007.

Lebron, Robyn E. *Searching for Spiritual Unity: Can There be Common Ground?* Nashville: Cross Books, 2012.

Lee, Lily Xiao Hong and Sue Wiles. *Biographical Dictionary of Chinese Women, Volume II: Tang through Ming, 618–1644*. Hoboken, NJ: Taylor and Francis, 2015.

Levitt, Susan. *Taoist Feng Shui: The Ancient Roots of the Chinese Art of Placement*. Rochester, VT: Inner Traditions, 1999.

Li, Gang. "Cao Cao and Taoism." In *Taoism,* edited by Zhongjian Mou, translated by Pan Junliang and Simone Normand. Leiden, Netherlands: Brill, 2012.

Libbrecht, Ulrich. *Within the Four Seas: Introduction to Comparative Philosophy.* Leuven, Belgium: Peeters, 2007.

Lin, Derek, translator. *Tao Te Ching: Annotated and Explained.* Woodstock, VT: SkyLight Paths, 2006. http://www.taoism.net/ttc/complete.htm.

Lin, Shifu. *"Thunder Magic" Taoist Traditions of the Tao Jiao Lei Fa and Their Relationship to Nei Kung Meditation.* Lung Hu Shan Publications, 2013. Amazon e-book ASIN B00CNFX85O.

Lin, Zixin, Yu Li, Guo Zhengyi, Shen Zhenyu, Zhang Honglin, and Zhang Tongling. *Qigong: Chinese Medicine or Pseudoscience?* Amherst, NY: Prometheus, 1998.

Little, Steven, and Shawn Eichman. *Taoism and the Arts of China.* Oakland, CA: University of California Press, 2000.

Liu, Ming. "Ming Liu on Chinese Daoism," presentation given at the ACS Colloquium, California Institute of Integral Studies, San Francisco. March 2014. https://www.youtube.com/watch?v=xEphouqTF9M.

Liu, Xiaogan. "A Taoist Perspective: Appreciating and Applying the Principle of Femininity." In *What Men Owe to Women: Men's Voices from World Religions,* edited by John C. Raines and Daniel C. Maguire. Albany, NY: State University of New York Press, 2001.

Loewe, Michael, and Edward L. Shaughness. *The Cambridge History of Ancient China: From the Origins of Civilization to 221 BC.* Cambridge, UK: Cambridge University Press, 1999.

Lu, Yongxiang. *A History of Chinese Science and Technology,* Volume 1. New York: Springer, 2014.

Margerrison, Nick. "A Beginner's Guide to Sigil Craft." *Disinformation.* December 4, 2012. http://disinfo.com/2012/12/a-beginners-guide-to-sigil-craft.

Marshall, S. J. *The Mandate of Heaven: Hidden History in the I Ching.* New York: Columbia University Press, 2001.

McDaniel, Justin Thomas. *The Lovelorn Ghost and the Magical Monk: Practicing Buddhism in Modern Thailand.* New York: Columbia University Press, 2013.

McLeod, John. *Beginning Postcolonialism.* Manchester, UK: Manchester University Press, 2010.

Mitchell, Helen. *Roots of Wisdom: A Tapestry of Philosophical Traditions.* San Francisco: Cengage Learning, 2014.

Mollier, Christine. "Beidi." In *Encyclopedia of Taoism,* edited by Fabrizio Pregadio. New York: Routledge, 2008.

———. *Buddhism and Taoism Face to Face: Scripture, Ritual, and Iconographic Exchange in Medieval China.* Honolulu: University of Hawaii Press, 2009.

Mungello, D. E. *The Great Encounter of China and the West, 1500–1800.* 4th edition. Summit, PA: Rowman & Littlefield, 2012.

*New Edition of the Yin and Yang Si Ji Yuan Book of Methods* (民國三年夏上海. 鏡童圖書局印行). Author unknown. [Shanghai, China: Jìng Tóng Tú Shū Jú Yìn Xíng], 1914.

Nguyen, Ngoc Tho. "Goddess Beliefs in the Chinese Ling-Nan Area." Harvard-Yenching Institute Working Paper Series. Ho Chi Minh: Vietnam National University, 2009. http://www.harvard-yenching.org/working-paper-series.

Nhat Hanh, Thich. "New Heart Sutra Translation by Thich Nhat Hanh." Plum Village. 2014. http://plumvillage.org/news/thich-nhat-hanh-new-heart-sutra-translation.

Nienhauser, William H. *The Indiana Companion to Traditional Chinese Literature.* Bloomington, IN: Indiana University Press, 1986.

Oldstone-Moore, Jennifer. *Understanding Taoism: Origins, Beliefs, Practices, Holy Texts, Sacred Places.* London: Watkins, 2011.

Paris, Carrie. "Tarot and Psychometry." Presentation at San Francisco Bay Area Tarot Symposium, San Jose, CA. August 15, 2015.

Pas, Julian F. *Historical Dictionary of Taoism.* Lanham, MD: Scarecrow Press, 1998.

Payne-Towler, Christine, and Michael Dowers. *Tarot of the Holy Light: A Continental Esoteric Tarot.* San Bernardino, CA: Noreah/Brownfield Press, 2015.

Pickover, Clifford. *Archimedes to Hawking: Laws of Science and the Great Minds behind Them.* New York: Oxford University Press, 2008.

Pietre-Stones Review of Freemasonry. "The Regius Poem: The Halliwell Manuscript." 2012. http://www.freemasons-freemasonry.com/regius.html.

Powerhouse Museum. "Chinese Dress in the Qing Dynasty." https://www.powerhousemuseum.com/hsc/evrev/chinese_dress.htm.

Prasad, Rameshwar. *The Magic of Feng Shui: Golden Tips of Feng Shui with Causes and Cures of Problems.* New Delhi: Diamond Pocket Books, 2004.

Pregadio, Fabrizio. "Early Daoist Meditation." In *Daoism in History: Essays in Honour of Liu Ts'un-yan,* edited by Benjamin Penny. London: Routledge, 2006.

———, editor. *Encyclopedia of Taoism.* New York: Routledge, 2008.

———. *Great Clarity: Daoism and Alchemy in Early Medieval China.* Stanford, CA: Stanford University Press, 2005.

Pu, Jiang Qing. "八仙考" [Ba Xian Kao, Studies of the Eight Immortals]. *Tsing Hua Journal of Chinese Studies* 11:1 (1936).

Rawski, Evelyn S. *The Last Emperors: A Social History of Qing Imperial Institutions.* Oakland, CA: University of California Press, 1998.

Reader, Ian, and George J. Tanabe Jr. *Practically Religious: Worldly Benefits and the Common Religion of Japan.* Honolulu: University of Hawaii Press, 2004.

Reiter, Florian C. *Basic Conditions of Taoist Thunder Magic* [道教雷法]. Wiesbaden, Germany: Otto Harrassowitz Verlag, 2007.

Reynolds, Donald E. "Chinese Five Elements." Northern Shaolin Academy, 2005. http://www.northernshaolinacademy.com/new/docs/FiveElementsChart.xls.

Robinet, Isabelle. "Shang Qing—Highest Clarity." In *Taoism Handbook,* edited by Livia Kohn. Boston: Brill, 2000.

———. *Taoist Meditation: The Mao-shan Tradition of Great Purity,* translated by Julian F. Pas and Norman J. Girardot. Albany, NY: State University of New York Press, 1993.

Robinson, Clayton D. "The Laying on of Hands, with Special Reference to the Reception of the Holy Spirit in the New Testament." Doctoral dissertation, Fuller Theological Seminary, Pasadena, CA, 2008.

Rogers, Mark. *The Esoteric Codex: Hermeticism I.* self-published, 2011.

Routledge, Clay. "5 Scientifically-Supported Benefits of Prayer." *Psychology Today.* June 23, 2014. https://www.psychologytoday.com/blog/more-mortal/201406/5-scientifically-supported-benefits-prayer.

Sangren, P. *History and Magical Power in a Chinese Community.* Stanford, CA: Stanford University Press, 1987.

Sasaki, Chris. *The Constellations: Stars and Stories.* Edison, NJ: Sterling, 2003.

Saso, Michael. "Asian Art and Religion." http://www.michaelsaso.org.

———. "Orthodoxy and Heterodoxy in Taoist Ritual." In *Religion and Ritual in Chinese Society,* edited by Arthur P. Wolf and Robert J. Smith. Stanford, CA: Stanford University Press, 1974.

———. "Taiwan: Old Gods and Modern Society." In *Religions and Societies, Asia and the Middle East,* edited by Carlo Caldarola. Berlin: Walter de Gruyter/Mouton, 1982.

Savedow, Steve. *The Magician's Workbook: A Modern Grimoire.* Newbury Port, MA: Weiser Books, 1996.

Scafidi, Susan. *Who Owns Culture?: Appropriation and Authenticity in American Law.* New Brunswick, NJ: Rutgers University Press, 2005.

Se, Ang Tian. "Five Phases (Wuxing)." In *Encyclopaedia of the History of Science, Technology, and Medicine in Non-Western Cultures,* edited by Helaine Selin. New York: Springer Science & Business Media, 2008.

Sears, Richard [Uncle Hanzi (汉字叔叔)]. "Chinese Etymology." 2013. http://www.chineseetymology.org.

Shah, Sayed Idries. *Oriental Magic.* London: The Octagon Press, 1992. First published 1956.

Shaw, Miranda Eberle. *Buddhist Goddesses of India.* Princeton, NJ: Princeton University Press, 2006.

Shek, Richard. "Daoism and Orthodoxy." In *Heterodoxy in Late Imperial China,* edited by Kwang-Ching Liu and Richard Hon-Chun Shek. Honolulu: University of Hawaii Press, 2004.

Simoons, Frederick J. *Food in China: A Cultural and Historical Inquiry.* Boca Raton, FL: CRC Press, 1990.

Smith, Robert W. *The Expanding Universe: Astronomy's "Great Debate."* Cambridge, UK: Cambridge University Press, 1982.

Sosnoski, Daniel. *Introduction to Japanese Culture.* North Clarendon, VT: Tuttle/Periplus, 2013.

Spilka, Bernard, and Kevin L. Ladd. *The Psychology of Prayer: A Scientific Approach.* New York: The Guilford Press, 2012.

Steavu-Balint, Dominic Emanuel. "The Three Sovereigns Tradition: Talismans, Elixirs, and Meditation in Early Medieval China." Doctoral dissertation, Stanford University, 2010. http://searchworks.stanford.edu/view/8572529.

Steed, Robert Patterson. Robert Patterson Steed, "To Extend Love to All Creeping Things: Ethics in Ge Hong's 'Baopuzi.'" Doctoral dissertation, University of Iowa, 2008.

Strickmann, Michel. *Chinese Poetry and Prophecy: The Written Oracle in East Asia,* edited by Bernard Faure. Stanford, CA: Stanford University Press, 2005.

Tamura, Eileen. *China: Understanding Its Past,* Volume 1. Honolulu: University of Hawaii Press, 1997.

Tinsley, Howard E. A., and Steven D. Brown. *Handbook of Applied Multivariate Statistics and Mathematical Modeling.* Waltham, MA: Academic Press, 2000.

Townsend, Charles M. "Swastika." In *Encyclopedia of Asian American Folklore and Folklife,* edited by Jonathan H. X. Lee and Kathleen M. Nadeau. Goleta, CA: ABC-CLIO, 2010.

Tseng, Wen-Shing, and David Y. H. Wu. *Chinese Culture and Mental Health.* Waltham, MA: Academic Press, 1985.

Tsubaki Grand Shrine of America. "Omamori." http://www.tsubakishrine.org /omamori/omamori.html.

Tzu, Min. *Chinese Taoist Sorcery: The Art of Getting Even.* San Francisco: Vision Press Films, 2000.

Wang, Jun. *Cultivating Qi: An Introduction to Chinese Body-Mind Energetics.* Berkeley, CA: North Atlantic Books, 2011.

Wang, Ming. "The Apocryphal *Jia* Section in *Taipingjing Chao.*" In *Taoism,* edited by Zhongjian Mou, translated by Pan Junliang and Simone Normand. Leiden, Netherlands: Brill, 2012.

Wang, Zongyu. "The Taoist Concept of the 'Six Heavens.'" In *Taoism,* edited by Zhongjian Mou, translated by Pan Junliang and Simone Normand. Leiden, Netherlands: Brill, 2012.

Ware, James R. *Alchemy, Medicine and Religion in the China of AD 320: The Nei Pien of Ko Hung.* Mineola, NY: Dover, 1981.

Wen, Benebell. *Holistic Tarot: An Integrative Approach to Using Tarot for Personal Growth.* Berkeley, CA: North Atlantic Books, 2015.

West, Stephen H., and Wilt L. Idema. *Monks, Bandits, Lovers, and Immortals.* Indianapolis: Hackett, 2010.

Williams, Charles Alfred Speed. *Chinese Symbolism and Art Motifs: An Alphabetical Compendium of Antique Legends and Beliefs, as Reflected in the Manners and Customs of the Chinese.* North Clarendon, VT: Tuttle, 1941.

Wong, Eva. *Taoism: An Essential Guide.* Boston: Shambhala, 2011.

Wu, Zhongxian. *Chinese Shamanic Cosmic Orbit Qigong: Esoteric Talismans, Mantras, and Mudras in Healing and Inner Cultivation.* London: Singing Dragon, 2011.

———. *Seeking the Spirit of the Book of Change: 8 Days to Mastering a Shamanic Yijing (I Ching) Prediction System.* Philadelphia: Singing Dragon, 2009.

Xiang, Ah. "Chinese Pre-History." ImperialChina.org. Undated. http://www .imperialchina.org/Pre-history.html.

Yang, Ching Kun. *Religion in Chinese Society: A Study of Contemporary Social Func-*

*tions of Religion and Some of Their Historical Factors*. Long Grove, IL: Waveland Press, 1991.

Young, John K., and Barb Karg. *The Everything Freemasons Book: Unlock the Secrets of This Ancient and Mysterious Society*. Avon, MA: Adams Media, 2006.

Young, Robert J. C. *Postcolonialism: A Very Short Introduction*. Oxford, UK: Oxford University Press, 2003.

Yü, Chün-fang. *Kuan-yin: The Chinese Transformation of Avalokiteśvara*. New York: Columbia University Press, 2001.

Zhang, Tina Chunna. *Earth Qi Gong for Women: Awaken Your Inner Healing Power*. Berkeley, CA: Blue Snake Books, 2008.

三洞珠囊 [Sān Dòng Zhū Náng, *Three Caverns of the Pearl Theca*]. http://baike.baidu.com/view/343215.htm.

上清大洞真经 [Shàng Qīng Dà Dòng Zhēn Jīng or *Perfect Scripture of Great Profundity*]. http://vdisk.weibo.com/s/dEhRrv4RfUF2U.

中國哲學書電子化計劃 [The Chinese Texts Project]. Chapter 2, 論仙, in 內篇 [Inner Chapters] of 抱朴子 [*Bao Puzi*, or Book of the Master of Simplicity]. Undated. http://ctext.org/baopuzi/lun-xian/zh.

中國哲學書電子化計劃 [The Chinese Texts Project]. 三洞神符纪 [*Three Caverns of the Supernatural Fu Talismanic Records*]. Undated. http://ctext.org/library.pl?if=gb&file=98630&page=1&remap=gb.

中國哲學書電子化計劃 [The Chinese Texts Project]. 天道 [*The Way of Heaven from Zhuang Zi*]. Undated. http://ctext.org/zhuangzi/tian-dao.

中國哲學書電子化計劃 [The Chinese Texts Project]. 抱朴子 [*Bao Puzi*, or Book of the Master of Simplicity]. Undated. http://ctext.org/baopuzi/zh.

中國哲學書電子化計劃 [The Chinese Texts Project]. 神符類 [Shen Fu Lei, Types of Supernatural Talismans]. Undated. http://ctext.org/wiki.pl?if=gb&chapter=465546#口神符類.

中國哲學書電子化計劃 [The Chinese Texts Project]. 道法會元 [*Tao Fa Hui Yuan*]. Undated. http://ctext.org/wiki.pl?if=gb&res=54910.

中國哲學書電子化計劃 [The Chinese Texts Project]. 黃帝陰符經 [*Yellow Emperor's Classics of the Esoteric Talisman*]. Undated. http://ctext.org/yinfujing/zh.

二〇一五(乙未)年通书编委会 [The Editorial Board of the 2015 (Yi Wei) Annual Almanac]. 二〇一五(乙未)年通书 平装 [*The 2015 Yi Wei Almanac*], 第1版 [1st edition]. 广西人民出版社 [The Guangxi People's Publishing House], 2014.

張天師符 [*Talismans of the Celestial Master Zhang*]. Author unknown. Undated.

正統道藏電子文字資料庫 [Electronic Database of Traditional Taoist Texts]. 靈寶無量度人上經大法卷之三十六 [*The Ling Bao Scripture of Spells for Infinite Human Transformation*, Volume 36]. (CH010801-36). Undated. http://www.ctcwri.idv.tw/.

清微藏書閣 [Qīng Wēi Cáng Shū Gé]. 太上靈寶五符序 [Tài Shàng Líng Bǎo Wü Fú Xù, *The Ling Bao Order of the Five Talismans*]. In 洞玄部神符類 [Dòng Xuán Bù Shén Fú Lèi], 1997. http://www.ctcwri.idv.tw/godking.htm.

漳和國中 [Zhāng Hé Guó Zhōng]. 五路財神[Wǔ Lù Cái Shén, The Five Celestials of Wealth], 2010. http://mail.chjh.ntpc.edu.tw/chjh99/e06.htm.

謝世維 [Hsieh, Shu-Wei]. 古靈寶經中的大乘之道: 論中古時期道教經典型態之轉變 ["The Way of Great Vehicle in Early Lingbao Scriptures: The Transformation of Daoist Scriptures in Medieval China"]. 成大中文學報 [*The Chinese Journal of the National Cheng Kung University*], 1–36. 第三十六期 [volume 36]: March 2012. http://bec001.web.ncku.edu.tw/ezfiles/335/1335/img/1450/3601.pdf.

# INDEX

# ABOUT THE AUTHOR

**BENEBELL WEN** is a practitioner of various metaphysical arts. She studies tarot, feng shui, the I Ching, numerology, and both Chinese and Hellenisic astrology. Wen is the author of *Holistic Tarot: An Integrative Approach to Using Tarot for Personal Growth*. When not lecturing, teaching, or writing on metaphysics, Wen practices law in California and New York. She is of Taiwanese descent and currently lives in Northern California with her husband, James, and the spirit of their beloved cat.